Global Economic Synergy of Belt and Road Initiative

The core idea of the series is built on the theoretical framework the double circulation of global value chain which is possibly a way of explanation of current world economic structure. This book series is devoted to provide a comprehensive analysis of Belt and Road Initiative (BRI) on global economic development from the perspective of industrial cooperation, spatial synergy, global value chains and detailed area studies. In terms of the methodology, the series combine multiple research methods. On quantitative-wise, it quantifies the role of the world's major economies in the international division from the perspective of global value chains, and clarifies the value cycle system between China and developed and developing economies. On the qualitative-wise, it provides a volume on case studies and special topics. By doing so, the series may answer the initial question that is why BRI can be the bridge linking the diversified development.

The key words in GESBRI include but are not limited to:

- Global Synergic Development
- Double Circulation of Global Value Chain
- Belt and Road Initiative
- Industrial Cooperation
- Spatial Synergy

Hui Zhang · Yuxuan Tang · Tian Yi

Comparative Studies on Regional and National Economic Development

北京大学出版社
PEKING UNIVERSITY PRESS

Springer

Hui Zhang
School of Economics
Peking University
Beijing, China

Tian Yi
School of Economics
Peking University
Beijing, China

Yuxuan Tang
School of Economics
Peking University
Beijing, China

International Development Cooperation Academy
Shanghai University of International Business and Economics
Shanghai, China

Translated by
Ruoxi Li
China Institute of Water Resources and Hydropower Research
Beijing, China

ISSN 2661-9105 ISSN 2661-9113 (electronic)
Global Economic Synergy of Belt and Road Initiative
ISBN 978-981-16-2104-8 ISBN 978-981-16-2105-5 (eBook)
https://doi.org/10.1007/978-981-16-2105-5

Jointly published with Peking University Press
The edition is not for sale in the Mainland of China. Customers from the Mainland of China please order the print book from: Peking University Press.
ISBN of the Co-Publisher's edition: 978-7-301-28931-0

This Springer imprint is published by the registered company Springer Nature Singapore Pte Ltd.
The registered company address is: 152 Beach Road, #21-01/04 Gateway East, Singapore 189721, Singapore

Preface

In 2013, President Xi Jinping, during his visits to Kazakhstan and Indonesia, proposed to jointly build the Silk Road Economic Belt and the 21st-century Maritime Silk Road, namely the Belt and Road Initiative. According to President Xi, "we should take an innovative approach and jointly build and economic belt along the Silk Road. To turn this vision into reality, we may start in specific areas and connect them over time to cover the whole region" (Jinping 2013a). Southeast Asia has since ancient times been an important hub along the ancient Maritime Silk Road. "China will strengthen maritime cooperation with the ASEAN countries, and in a joint effort to build the Maritime Silk Road of the 21st century, so as to meet each other's needs and complement each other's strengths. This will enable us to jointly seize opportunities and meet challenges in the interest of common development and prosperity" (Jinping 2013b). On May 14, 2017, in his speech at the opening ceremony of Belt and Road Forum for International Cooperation, President Xi farsightedly pointed out, "spanning thousands of miles and years, the ancient Silk Road embodies the spirit of peace and cooperation, openness and inclusiveness, mutual learning and mutual benefit. The Silk Road spirit has become a great heritage of human civilization" (Jinping 2017).

In a brief retrospect of the history, we know that the concept of Silk Road (Seidenstrassen) was first put forward by the German geographer Ferdinand von Richthofen in the 1870s. As described by him, the Silk Road was some routes in the west of and to China which connected China, transoxiana and India for the trade of silk from 114 BC to AD 127 (Richthofen 1877). In 1903, Edouard Chavannes, a French sinologist, further categorized the concept into the land Silk Road and the maritime one: "the Silk Road in the north was on land and led to Qiangqu (Sogdiana), while the one in the south was maritime and connected ports in India, and Broach was the key port along this route. Rome sought to detour around Persia and trade with Indian ports; in AD 531, it sent an envoy to Yemen and struck a deal with the Himyarites who agreed to purchase silk from India and resell it to the Romans. This was because there were often ships traveling between Yemen and India" (Chavannes 1958).

Trade and mutual benefit have always been the two themes of human civilization and history. According to the chapter on *Dui hexagram of I Ching*, "as to relations between two countries, peace and harmony are the most precious". It is said in the *Analects*, "is it not a joy to have friends come from afar?" Five hundred years ago, the great geographical discovery made by the westerners brought them to Seres in the East; five hundred years later, the time-honored eastern civilization out forward the Belt and Road Initiative and voiced the common quest for peace, friendship, exchanges and prosperity. From Zhang Qian trekking through the Western Regions, to Zheng He exploring the Indian Ocean and to China spreading its successful experience around the world today, the journey along the Belt and Road has lasted a millennium. Today, the Belt and Road Initiative is not only engraved with the lines of history, but it emanates the fragrance of a new era.

If a common goal is shared, mountains and seas could not keep two friends apart. Since China and other countries along the Belt and Road share similar goals and missions of development with complementary development interests, the Initiative, as a bond, could connect countries and regions more closely. Under this framework, each takes what it needs, thereby achieving mutual benefit. This is indeed the original intention of President Xi Jinping in making such a proposal. As Mencius puts it, "it is only natural for things to differ". Each country has its own conditions and visions. President Xi has repeatedly stressed that the Belt and Road Initiative aims at integrating development plans of relevant countries by enhancing international cooperation, so as to utilize complementary advantages and promote common progress.

Four years have passed since the Initiative was first brought up. During the past four years, China has translated the Silk Road spirit of peace and cooperation, openness and inclusiveness, mutual learning and mutual benefit into actions of building the Belt and Road, accumulated abundant achievements and attracted active responses and participation from more than one hundred countries and international organizations. On November 17, 2016, with unanimous approval from its 193 member countries, the General Assembly of the United Nations for the first time included the Belt and Road Initiative into its resolution, which shows the Initiative is a significant action that conforms to the demand of global economic development and receives universal support from the international community.

Today, four years later, China could proudly tell the world: "put forward at the key point of a new era, the Belt and Road Initiative is a theory and paradigm of action that guides the shaping of the new landscape of globalization". In the past three decades of globalization, major economies in the world mainly followed the double-loop economic model, and China has been the core node within this circulatory system: generally speaking, developed countries import intermediate products and export final ones; the situation is the opposite in China and other developing countries—they import final products and export intermediate ones, and similar features could be seen in trade of light-industry and heavy-industry products. Among the 188 countries and regions with trade statistics, 123 countries see China as one of their top five import sources of final products, and 73 countries see China as one of their top five import sources of intermediate products. While China is among the top five importers of final products for 60 countries, and for 74 countries, China is among the top five importers of intermediate products. By now, 1/3 to 2/3 countries around the globe have close ties with China through trade of final and intermediate products, positioning China at the hub of the overall circulatory system. Meanwhile, along the global value chains, developing economies are troubled by low added value of export, while developed countries enjoy higher added value. China lies in the middle, connecting the developed and developing countries for economic cooperation, thereby forming a double-loop system of global value division.

In the last round of globalization, many less-developed countries were gradually marginalized, which manifested as economic backwardness and slowdown. According to World Bank's statistics of per capita GDP at PPP, per capita GDP in high-income economies grew by 26,780 international dollars from 1990 to 2014, while the growth in low-income economies was as small as 896 international dollars. In 1990, per capita GDP in high-income economies was 24.5 times that of low-income ones, and by 2014, the gap was widened to 27.4 times. Besides, in the past three decades, incomes in developed countries have been increasingly polarized, pushing up Gini coefficient on the whole. According to the statistics of WIID, among the G7 countries, the United States had the highest Gini coefficient in the last 30 years—it rose from 0.34 in 1983 to 0.38 in 2010, while the figure in Canada rose from 0.30 to 0.32 during the same period. In the book *Income Inequality*, OECD points out that the level of income disparity in OECD countries has reached a half-century high—the income of the richest 10% is 9 times that of the poorest 10%, and the gap was 7 times 25 years ago.

The existing international system of trade and investment rules, to some extent, disregards the interests of developing economies. Standards and thresholds under this framework mirror the interests of developed countries, making it hard for developing countries to profit; in addition, as developed countries are swamped by various social contradictions and conflicts caused by income polarization, it is increasingly difficult to maintain the existing international system. To cure the ills of the traditional international system of trade and investment rules, the world should commit itself to building a trade engine that could propel growth and formulating multilateral trade rules, thereby promoting liberalization and facilitation of trade and investment and reducing imbalances of global development. The 2010s is an age of rapid changes and a new starting point in history. Against such a backdrop, only allowing China to reach its full potential as a core hub could unite the two independent and inseparable economic circles of developing and developed economies. As President Xi said: "China wishes to provide neighboring countries with both opportunities and space for common development. All countries are welcome to get on board the express train of China's development". In the recent years, more and more countries and regions are benefiting from the concept and practice of the Belt and Road Initiative and gaining opportunities of leapfrog development. It is the win–win cooperation that has vivified the international stage and tied together the visions and actions of all countries.

Four years later, we could responsibly tell the world, China, by putting forward the Belt and Road Initiative, is undertaking its responsibility as a superpower and playing its role as a core hub of the global value cycle. The creation of the Belt and Road Initiative, as a response to the ills of the world economy, aims at constructing a fair, reasonable and inclusive international system of trade and investment rules, forming a larger platform of economic and social exchanges and cooperation, reshaping the economic and trade landscape dominated by developed countries and removing the barriers for cooperation among developing countries, thereby providing them with fair and sustainable opportunities of development. China should fully play its role as a connecting link in global economic development and expand global economic cooperation, so as to improve the efficiency of resource allocation, to secure more space for the development of developing countries and to alleviate the income polarization among countries.

Main features of the Belt and Road Initiative as the great construct of China serving as the core link in the world economic cycle include: first, among the more than 60 countries along the Belt and Road, China lies in the middle in terms of economic development level—almost half of the countries are ahead of China, while the other half falls behind. As to the level of economic development, China is like the hinge that connects the two cycle systems of developing and developed countries which take the shape of "8". The Belt and Road Initiative has apparently added a small 8-shaped double-loop cycle to the existing model of large double-loop cycle in the world. Second, trade and investment are the two approaches through which a country participates in the world economy, and trade is accompanied by increases of investment. As the Belt and Road Initiative unfolds, China has been scaling up its direct investment in countries along the Belt and Road, boosting its shares in the FDI of those countries. According to the Ministry of Commerce, in the past four years (i.e., 2013–2016), China's investment in countries along the Belt and Road exceeded 50 billion USD, and the figure in 2016 totaled 14 billion USD, and 8.5% of China's total outbound investment. From 2005 to 2015, China's direct investment in those countries surged 21.5 times from 910 million USD to 19.56 billion USD. Third, from the perspective of international division of labor, the Belt and Road Initiative aims at bringing into the new round of labor division the economies that were marginalized in the previous round of globalization, extending the space for resource allocation, enlarging the footing of the tower and increasing its height. As President Xi Jinping once said, the Belt and Road should be a road of opening up. China hopes that the global trade and investment environment is inclusive and open—this is a reflection of Chinese economy, also a suggestion, a voice and a proposal concerning future rules of global trade and investment. Fourth, the Belt and Road Initiative is building a platform for Chinese enterprises to go global based on industrial clusters. By means of this platform, China is building trade cooperation zones in countries along the Belt and Road, transboundary economic cooperation zones and border cooperation zones in China, thereby raising the going global strategy to a new level. As pointed out by President Xi, "Chinese companies have set up 56 economic and trade cooperation zones in over 20 countries, generating some 1.1 billion USD in tax revenue and 180,000 jobs". Fifth, impressive results have been delivered in the field of infrastructure connectivity. According to the analysis of the relations between infrastructure construction and economic development level, developed countries like the United States, Japan and Germany are "relatively lagging" in terms of infrastructure, and this conclusion also applies to developing countries like India and Brazil. In addition, during the period sampled by the analysis (2005–2013), the situation in both developed and developing countries did not improve much. Meanwhile, in 1995, infrastructure construction in China was "coordinated" with its economic development, and in 2005 and 2013, the former was "slightly ahead" of the latter. The Belt and Road Initiative has given full play to the strengths of Chinese companies in the field of infrastructure construction; as a result, they are taking on more and more infrastructure projects of transportation, energy and public services in countries along the Belt and Road which have become their important market for project contracting. In 2016, the value of contracts secured by Chinese companies in these countries totaled 304.9 billion USD. The investment projects of the Belt and Road Initiative, especially those infrastructure ones, are featured by large investment, long construction cycle and slow cost recovery; however, in the long run, they are of great and long-lasting significance in terms of enhancing regional infrastructure connectivity and improving the livelihood of people in these countries.

The construction of the six major economic corridors is the key approach of implementing the Belt and Road Initiative. On the one hand, economic corridors are important carriers of cooperation between China and neighboring countries under the Initiative; on the other hand, they are the priority areas and pivots of China's participation in regional and sub-regional economic cooperation. In his speech at the opening ceremony of the Belt and Road Forum for international cooperation, President Xi states China has set the goal of building six major economic corridors, which fully shows China has linked work at selected spots with that in the entire region when planning investment under the Belt and Road Initiative, set different priorities in different countries according to their specific conditions and integrated its plan of development with the demand for economic growth by local countries.

Four years after the creation of the Belt and Road Initiative, China could confidently tell the world: the Belt and Road Initiative is an open system that aims at spreading China's experience and achieving win–win cooperation and common development. Any country with the same aspirations is welcome to join the Belt and Road Initiative to build new orders for global governance and development. The size of the area covered by the Initiative means the social and economic development of these countries has a great impact on the economic landscape of the world. Among them, China is of great importance. Currently, the economy of the countries along the Belt and Road takes up more than 1/4 of the world economy, and within this 1/4 China alone contributes 40%. If China is taken out, per capita GDP in these countries is only 1/4 of the global level. This shows countries and regions along the Belt and Road face great demand for transformation of development patterns.

China's development has gone through a long and difficult journey. According to Maddison Historical Statistics, in 1950, per capita GDP in China ranked 133 among 142 countries in the world, only slightly higher than that of 8 countries of sub-Saharan Africa and other regions.[1] After reform and opening up, China was still a developing

[1] The eight countries are Tanzania, Ethiopia, Eritrea, Burundi, Lesotho, Botswana, Malawi, Guinea, Mongolia and Myanmar.

economy with low-income level. According to the United Nations (1978), among all 188 countries and regions, China ranked top 10 in terms of gross GDP but fell to No. 175 as to per capita income, making it an economy that lagged behind. However, 30 years after the reform, rapid growth has boosted China's per capita GDP from 7.8% of the world average in 1978 to 79.3% in 2015. Take India as an example. At the constant price of 2005, India's per capita GDP was 228.3 USD in 1960, similar to that in China in 1981 (229.81 USD). In 2014, the figure in India rose to 1233.95 USD, approximately what China achieved in 2001 (1212.47 USD), and only less than 1/3 of the Chinese level during the same period (3862.92 USD). It took India 54 years to raise per capita GDP from 220 USD to 1230 USD, while China delivered the same result in only 20 years.

The World Bank divides countries and regions into different categories according to their income. In 1987, 49 countries and regions were labeled as low income, among which 26 were still low income in 2015, 19 rose to the lower mid-income category, and only China, Equatorial Guinea, Guyana and Maldives evolved into the upper mid-income team.

According to the global report of manufacturing industry growth published by UNIDO, China has contributed greatly to the growth of global manufacturing industry. At the constant price of 2000, the share of the value added of Chinese manufacturing industry within the global total rose from 5.1% in 1995 to 20.8% in 2014, which means China has overtaken the United States (19.30%) and emerged as the largest manufacturer in the world. As to the products and output of manufacturing industry, in 2014, China ranked No. 1 for 7 out of the 22 categories of products (based on ISIC): 49.8% for tobacco, 29.2% for textiles, 24.7% for garments and furs, 33.4% for leatherware and shoes, 23.8% for alkalinous metal, 28.2% for power equipment and 34.1% for other vehicles. For another 15 categories, China ranked top 3; China ranks top 6 in 21 out of the 22 categories; and the only exception is the category of motor vehicle, trailer and semitrailer. Actually around half the following products are made in China: cement, sheet glass and ceramics for the construction industry, mobile phone, PC, color TV, display, PBX and digital camera. Apart from industries intensive in labor, capital and technology, China is also competitive in the knowledge-intensive internet industry—with internet giants like Alibaba, Tencent, Baidu and JD.com that rank top 10 in the world, China is the second largest player in this industry, only after the United States. It is reasonable to conclude that China has a complete industrial system covering diversified areas, laying a solid foundation for division of labor under the Belt and Road Initiative.

Besides, China has scored remarkable achievements in terms of urbanization. Quantitatively, from 1978 to 2015, the number of Chinese cities grew from 193 to 656, the number of officially established townships surged from 2173 to 20,515, urban population rose from 171 million to 763 million, and the rate of urbanization went from 17.9% up to 55.6%, exceeding the world average in 2013 with an increase much larger than the world level over the same period (38.5%–53.9%). Structurally, population of megalopolises (cities with population larger than 1 million) expanded from 76.2 million in 1978 to 337 million in 2015, much faster than the average growth rate in the world (16.3%–22.9%), and its share within the total population climbed from 8.0% to 24.6%.

According to the statistics of the World Bank, the changing share of trade within GDP since 1960 shows that world economic growth has gone through four stages: rapid growth before 1975 (average growth rate: 2.0%), slow growth in 1975–1989 (average growth rate: 1.1%), explosive growth in 1990–2007 (average growth rate: 2.2%) and stagnation since 2008 (average growth rate: –0.2%). During the first stage, Japan, benefiting from the wave of rapid globalization between WWII and 1975, achieved more than two decades of fast growth (including three rounds of long-lasting booms: Jinmu Boom from December 1954 to June 1957, Iwato Boom from July 1958 to December 1961 and Izanagi Boom from November 1965 to July 1970; and two short-run booms: "Olympics Boom" from October 1962 to October 1964 and the "Reconstructing the Japanese Islands" under the Tanaka government between December 1971 and November 1973), successfully passed the mid-income transition and emerged as one of the most developed economies. The second stage saw the downturn of globalization during which President Reagan adopted neoliberal policies, the United States returned to the center economically, the burst of property bubble dragged Japan into a crisis and the Fall of Communism resulted in the collapse of the Soviet Union. During the third stage, China, by successfully seizing the opportunity of globalization, maintained the rapid growth brought by the reform and opening up and ushered in two five-year booms with double-digit growth rates (1992–1996 and 2003–2007). The fourth stage is even tougher than the gloomy stage two. Standing at the turning point of the world economy, China, as the founding country of the Belt and Road Initiative, aims at promoting international economic exchanges and cooperation by building a large platform for international exchange, thereby fulfilling the following goals: breaking the bottleneck for areas such as labor force allocation, sustainable development and income polarization; breathing new life into world economic growth; and bringing about new opportunities for global development.

In January 2017, President Xi Jinping said at the opening ceremony of the World Economic Forum in Davos, "the Belt and Road Initiative originated in China, but it has benefited countries well beyond its borders". This means one should not overemphasize the Chinese elements when talking about the Belt and Road Initiative, but rather acknowledge the shared visions and values it carries. More than 2000 years ago, Mencius asked the famous question, "which is the more pleasant—to enjoy music by yourself alone, or to enjoy it with others?" During the process of implementing the Initiative, China constantly shows the world it does not want to become one of the few rich countries in the world; instead, it aspires to a world where all countries grow together. To achieve that goal, China offers actions of sincere help and will always honor its commitments. As the old saying goes, the jingling camel bells along the Silk Road have shortened the distance between the East and the West, so that people around the globe could together enjoy prosperity despite geological barriers of mountains and seas.

Beijing, China — Hui Zhang
Beijing/Shanghai, China — Yuxuan Tang
Beijing, China — Tian Yi

Contents

Part I
Theoretical Study

The jingling camel bells along the Silk Road have shortened the distance between the East and the West, so that people around the globe could together enjoy prosperity despite geological barriers of mountains and seas.

Chapter 1
"The Belt and Road": A Study of the Double-Loop Model of World Economy

The hoof prints along the Belt and Road are carriers of the harmony that flows out of diversity.

Globalization has walked through the four stages of rapid expansion, slow growth, explosive rise and sluggish development. As the world economy slows down, new trends are emerging. On the one hand, trade volumes generated by developed economies are taking ever smaller shares of the world trade, while developing countries are playing bigger parts. On the other hand, typical mid-income countries like Argentina, Brazil and Chile fell into the trap of comparative advantage; meantime emerging countries, within the current international industrial and trade system, are disadvantaged and face a series of problems—they are caught in the low end of the industrial chain and held back by the glass ceiling for further development. World economic structure is gradually shifting from the single cycle model (core-periphery) with developed countries as the core to the more complex double-loop model. Within the double-loop system, developed countries differ from developing ones in terms of their roles and degree of involvement along the global value chain. As to intermediate and final products, production in developed countries is generally of higher added value, while developing economies suffer underparticipation and depend too much on resource-intensive production. Based on the double-loop feature of global value chain, the Belt and Road Initiative could boost interaction and complementarity among countries with different industrial structure, thus coordinating industrial development along the double loop of value chain.

Part of this chapter is published by Zhang Hui, Yi Tian, and Tang Yuxuan on *Economic Science* (Issue 3, 2017) under the title "'The Belt and Road': A Study of the Double Loop of World Economy".

H. Zhang et al., *Comparative Studies on Regional and National Economic Development*, Global Economic Synergy of Belt and Road Initiative,
https://doi.org/10.1007/978-981-16-2105-5_1

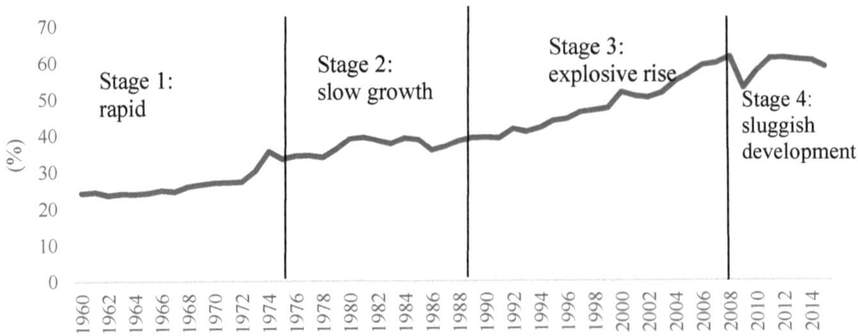

Fig. 1.1 Proportions of world trade within GDP. *Source of data* World Bank database

1.1 Development History of World Economic Cooperation

(I) Industry, trade and the course of globalization

Neither economic development nor globalization follows a one-way street. China bucking the downward trend and Europe and America suffering downward shock are the two huge waves in the changing world. Such waves are generated and strengthened by globalization. As a distinctive feature of today's world economy, globalization has experienced multiple setbacks since its early days. Figure 1.1 shows the changing proportions of world trade within GDP since 1960, unveiling the four stages of globalization: rapid expansion, slow growth, explosive rise and sluggish development. In the aftermath of the financial crisis, the stagnation of globalization is closely related to economic and social development around the world.

A detailed analysis of trade development in all countries would come to the conclusion that the share of developed countries within world trade is declining, while that of developing economies is rising. Figure 1.2 presents the shifting proportions contributed to world trade by developed and developing countries: the contribution made by developed countries has been stagnating since the 1970s–1980s; in recent years, especially after the financial crisis, the proportion plummeted. Meanwhile, the developing countries told a completely different story—their export trade has been booming since 2000, making an ever greater contribution to world trade.

What are the trade performances of different groups of developed countries? How do they differ from those of developing economies? Figure 1.3 is a comparison between major developed countries and the BRICS economies in terms of proportions within world export. The trend for developed countries is downward and especially so after the financial crisis. Although every country rebounded slowly after the financial crisis, its proportion within world export continued its decline, except America. Take Japan as an example: in 1990, its export took up 8.23% of the world's total; by 2015, the figure had dropped to 3.78%. At the same time, the proportions of the BRICS countries surged from 3.86% in 1990 to 19.06% in 2015.

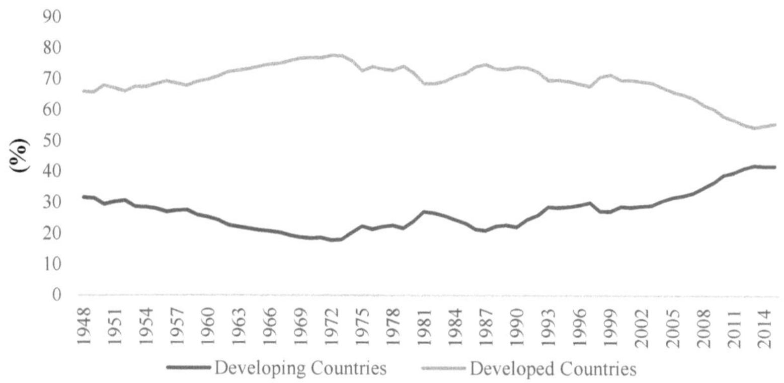

Fig. 1.2 Trends of trade development in developed and developing countries. *Source of data* UNCTAD database

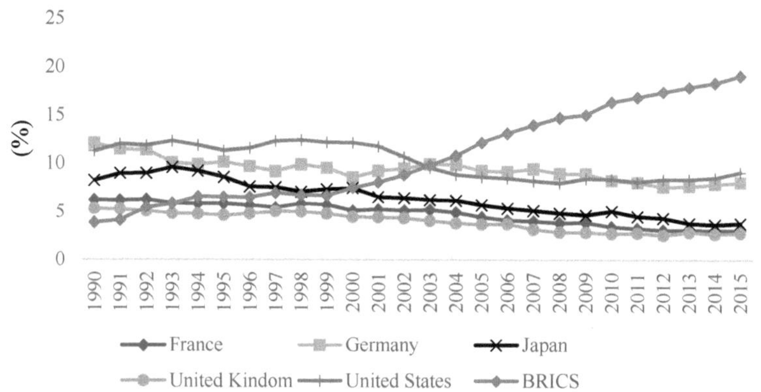

Fig. 1.3 A comparison between major developed countries and the BRICS economies in terms of proportions within world export. *Source of data* UNCTAD database

Figure 1.4 is a detailed description of trade development in the BRICS countries. All of them, with the exception of Brazil, have seen expanding shares within world export. China, with its share soaring from 1.78% in the 1990s to 13.74% in 2015, has generated the most notable rise.

Different from countries in Europe and America, emerging economies such as the BRICS countries enjoy good economic development and growing trade volume.

(II) Global economic landscape at critical stages of globalization

1. Stage of the flying-geese paradigm (1970s–1990s)

The flying-geese paradigm describes the process of industrial transfer made by Japan to other East Asian countries in the 1970s–1990s. During this period, the United States, with its huge demand, absorbed large quantities of goods made in East Asian

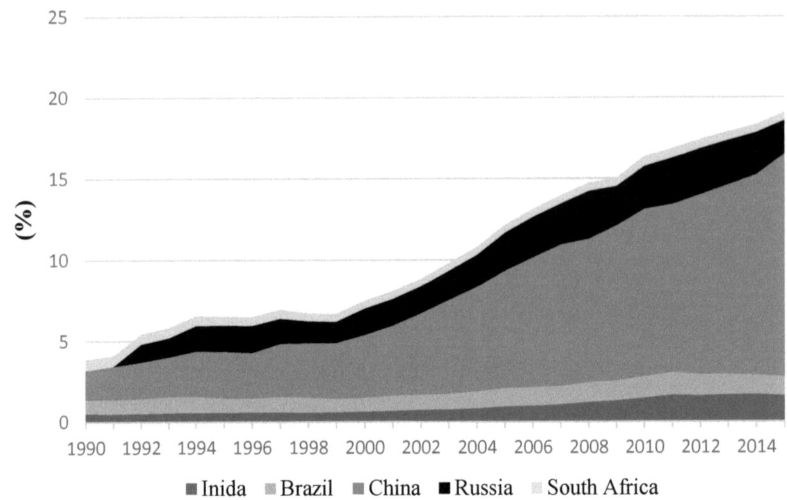

Fig. 1.4 Trend of trade development in the BRICS countries. *Source of data* UNCTAD database

countries, thus boosting their exports; at the same time, Japan, as the largest supplier of capital goods and intermediate products, supported the industrialization of other East Asian countries. In this way, the United States, Japan and other East Asian countries formed an integrated whole within which Japan, by exporting intermediate products and investment, provided other East Asian countries with the capacity to participate in vertical specialization, East Asian countries (Japan excluded) made profits and fixed its deficit with Japan by exporting final products to the United States, and Japan, by purchasing United States treasuries, returned its trade surplus to the United States and expanded its direct investment and official aid in other East Asian countries. As the leading goose, Japan played the central role in guiding the economic development of East Asia and Southeast Asia. The newly industrializing Asian economies in the 1970s, mainly South Korea, Singapore, Taiwan (China) and Hong Kong (China), were the close followers of the leading goose, while China and ASEAN countries like Myanmar, Cambodia, Laos and Vietnam flew at the tail of the group.

(1) Economic landscape

Table 1.1 shows Japan, as the leading goose, enjoyed absolute advantage in terms of GDP. In 1979, Japan's share of the world's GDP, at 10.6%, was 10 times the total share of South Korea, Singapore and Hong Kong, China. The fact that the shares of South Korea, Singapore and Hong Kong, China had been rising means Japan's growth, to some extent, served as a driving force for these economies.

However, representative economies of the flying-geese paradigm (including Japan, South Korea, Singapore and Hong Kong, China[1]) contributed a much lower

[1] Economic data of Taiwan, China is not found in the World Bank database.

Table 1.1 GDPs of different economies and their shares within the world total (Unit: 100 million USD at current price)

Year	Japan		South Korea		Singapore		Hong Kong, China		The mainland of China		The United States	
	GDP	Share (%)	GDP	Share (%)	GDP	Share (%)	GDP	Share (%)	GDP	Share (%)	GDP	Share (%)
1965	910	4.7	30	0.15	10	0.05	24	0.13	704	3.6	7437	38.2
1966	1056	5.0	38	0.18	11	0.05	25	0.12	767	3.6	8150	38.6
1967	1238	5.5	47	0.21	12	0.05	27	0.12	729	3.2	8617	38.2
1968	1466	6.0	60	0.25	14	0.06	27	0.11	708	2.9	9425	38.8
1969	1722	6.4	75	0.28	17	0.06	32	0.12	797	3.0	10,199	38.2
1970	2091	7.1	94	0.32	19	0.07	38	0.13	926	3.2	10,759	36.6
1971	2362	7.3	104	0.32	23	0.07	45	0.14	998	3.1	11,678	36.0
1972	3127	8.3	114	0.30	27	0.07	57	0.15	1137	3.0	12,824	34.2
1973	4249	9.3	145	0.32	37	0.08	80	0.18	1385	3.0	14,285	31.3
1974	4716	9.0	204	0.39	52	0.10	94	0.18	1442	2.7	15,488	29.5
1975	5129	8.8	228	0.39	56	0.10	100	0.17	1634	2.8	16,889	28.9
1976	5764	9.1	314	0.49	63	0.10	129	0.20	1539	2.4	18,776	29.6
1977	7094	9.9	403	0.56	66	0.09	157	0.22	1749	2.4	20,860	29.1

(continued)

Table 1.1 (continued)

Year	Japan		South Korea		Singapore		Hong Kong, China		The mainland of China		The United States	
	GDP	Share (%)	GDP	Share (%)	GDP	Share (%)	GDP	Share (%)	GDP	Share (%)	GDP	Share (%)
1978	9967	11.8	543	0.64	75	0.09	183	0.22	1495	1.8	23,566	27.9
1979	10,375	10.6	697	0.71	93	0.09	225	0.23	1783	1.8	26,321	26.8
1980	10,870	9.8	678	0.61	119	0.11	289	0.26	1912	1.7	28,625	25.9
1981	12,015	10.6	762	0.67	142	0.12	311	0.27	1959	1.7	32,110	28.3
1982	11,168	10.0	816	0.73	161	0.14	323	0.29	2051	1.8	33,450	29.8
1983	12,181	10.5	905	0.78	178	0.15	299	0.26	2307	2.0	36,381	31.4
1984	12,946	10.8	1000	0.83	197	0.16	335	0.28	2599	2.2	40,407	33.6

Source of data World Bank database

combined share of world's total GDP than the United States. In 1984, the combined share of the four economies was 12.07%, while that of the United States was 33.6%. Therefore, at the stage of the flying-geese paradigm, Asia made up a relatively small part of the world economy.

(2) Structure of trade

According to Table 1.2, from 1965 to 1984, the share of Japan, South Korea, Singapore, Hong Kong (China) and the mainland of China within world export was on the rise, up from 6.78 to 13.97%. During the same period, the share of the United States dropped from 16.5 to 13.5%. At the stage of the flying-geese paradigm, Asia's economic growth was mainly driven by export. Japan, as the leading goose, enjoyed absolute advantage in terms of export volume. In 1965, the mainland of China exported 2.56 billion USD of goods, higher than that of Hong Kong (China), Singapore and South Korea. By 1984, the situation had been reversed (the export volume of the mainland of China reached 24.77 billion USD), which means Hong Kong (China), Singapore and South Korea had achieved fast growth by following the leading goose closely.

Table 1.3 tells that from 1965 to 1984, import of Japan, South Korea, Singapore, Hong Kong (China) and the mainland of China were slowly gaining larger share of the world total (from 6.25 to 11.97%), while that of the United States kept rising from 13.98 to 17.53%. The conclusion is that Asia's import, at the stage of flying-geese paradigm, was of a much smaller share than its United States counterpart.

In addition, there was sufficient market demand for the export capacity of all members of the flying-geese paradigm. Japan, as the leader, should sharpen its edge by upgrading its industries, cooperating with the Four Tigers and the ASEAN countries, and providing them with machinery equipment and technologies. At that time, Japan, the Four Tigers and the ASEAN countries were at different stages of development. To be more specific, Japan and other East Asian countries in the 1970s–1990s adopted the flying-geese paradigm for the following reasons.

First, countries and regions that adopted the flying-geese paradigm were of small sizes and populations, which means they were not equipped to establish complete industrial systems; therefore, the option for industrial transfer at home did not exist. Without industrial advantage, outbound industrial transfer was the only option. During this process, destination economies seized the chance for growth. These adjacent countries and regions, usually granted with convenient geographic locations, are ready destinations for gradient transfer through direct investment, international trade and technology transfer; meanwhile, they act as supplement to each other since they differ in development level, which will facilitate the establishment of vertical specialization and gradient industrial transfer.

Second, though the industrial transfer and economic growth in East Asia was led by Japan, the United States also played a part. It was the support and aid from the United States that had turned Japan into the leader goose. The flying-geese paradigm of East Asia was realized in a peaceful environment controlled by the United States. In addition, the technologies and knowledge transferred from Japan to other East

Table 1.2 Export volumes of different economies and their shares within the world total (Unit: 100 million USD at current price)

Year	Japan	The mainland of China	Hong Kong, China	Singapore	South Korea	Total		The Unite States	
						Export volume	Share (%)	Export volume	Share (%)
1965	95.7	25.6	16.8	12.0	2.5	152.6	6.78	371.0	16.5
1966	111.7	26.8	18.9	13.5	3.8	174.8	7.07	409.0	16.5
1967	119.5	23.9	21.7	14.2	5.2	184.4	7.03	435.0	16.6
1969	181.8	24.3	30.3	21.9	9.7	268.0	8.16	519.0	15.8
1970	221.5	23.1	35.4	24.2	12.1	316.3	8.33	597.1	15.7
1971	271.1	27.8	40.0	27.0	14.7	380.8	8.95	629.6	14.8
1972	324.5	36.9	48.2	29.0	20.8	459.5	9.10	708.4	14.0
1973	418.0	58.8	68.6	43.7	39.3	628.4	9.10	952.7	13.8
1974	628.8	71.1	81.3	78.0	51.4	910.7	9.48	1266.5	13.2
1975	643.4	76.9	83.8	77.2	57.7	939.0	9.21	1387.1	13.6
1976	766.0	69.4	115.2	94.6	88.7	1133.9	9.96	1495.2	13.1
1977	910.7	75.2	131.0	107.7	115.2	1339.8	10.39	1593.5	12.4
1978	1086.5	68.1	156.7	124.4	145.3	1581.0	10.55	1868.9	12.5

(continued)

Table 1.2 (continued)

Year	Japan	The mainland of China	Hong Kong, China	Singapore	South Korea	Total		The Unite States	
						Export volume	Share (%)	Export volume	Share (%)
1979	1176.4	92.0	201.9	171.7	174.3	1816.4	9.62	2301.3	12.2
1980	1459.0	113.0	256.7	240.3	204.7	2273.7	9.95	2807.7	12.3
1981	1730.0	145.9	282.8	280.9	244.9	2684.5	11.77	3052.4	13.4
1982	1586.1	227.0	277.4	298.1	253.2	2641.9	12.26	2832.1	13.1
1983	1660.6	222.8	286.8	296.8	278.7	2745.6	12.93	2770.0	13.0
1984	1905.7	247.7	357.1	309.0	311.0	3130.6	13.97	3023.8	13.5

Source of data World Bank database

Table 1.3 Import volumes of different economies and their shares within the world total (Unit: 100 million USD at current price)

Year	Japan	The mainland of China	Hong Kong, China	South Korea	Singapore	Total of representative economies of the flying-geese paradigm		The United States	
						Import	Share (%)	Import	Share (%)
1965	83.1	22.5	17.6	4.8	13.1	141.1	2.57	315.0	13.98
1966	95.4	24.8	19.8	7.7	14.3	162.0	2.67	371.0	14.88
1967	117.0	21.7	20.5	10.3	15.1	184.5	2.52	399.0	14.92
1968	132.1	20.7	23.0	15.1	18.7	209.6	2.63	466.0	15.83
1969	154.6	19.2	27.5	18.8	23.5	243.5	2.68	505.0	15.21
1970	196.2	22.8	32.5	21.2	27.9	300.5	2.74	557.6	14.66
1971	209.1	21.3	38.1	25.2	31.7	325.4	2.76	623.4	14.78
1972	254.9	28.5	43.7	26.0	33.3	386.3	2.64	742.2	14.90
1973	419.0	52.1	63.5	43.6	47.1	625.3	3.06	911.6	13.50
1974	666.6	77.9	76.8	72.9	85.9	980.1	3.26	1274.7	13.26
1975	644.5	79.3	78.2	76.0	82.5	960.4	3.10	1227.3	12.06
1976	724.4	66.6	101.4	94.6	99.0	1086	3.15	1511.5	13.15
1977	800.8	71.5	120.8	118.4	108.7	1220.1	3.18	1824.4	13.85

(continued)

Table 1.3 (continued)

Year	Japan	The mainland of China	Hong Kong, China	South Korea	Singapore	Total of representative economies of the flying-geese paradigm		The United States	
						Import	Share (%)	Import	Share (%)
1978	921.2	76.2	154.9	164.4	127.2	1443.8	3.44	2122.5	13.98
1979	1274.7	105.6	199.0	220.6	177.0	1976.9	3.65	2526.8	13.15
1980	1562.2	124.5	258.2	255.1	248.5	2448.5	3.80	2938.3	12.61
1981	1647.0	145.9	287.5	283.5	285.8	2649.7	4.28	3177.6	13.56
1982	1515.7	177.9	275.6	272.5	301.1	2542.7	4.60	3031.8	13.57
1983	1458.3	193.9	281.4	288.0	295.7	2517.2	4.83	3286.4	15.00
1984	1569.2	247.1	330.3	313.6	309.4	2769.6	5.19	4051.1	17.53

Source of data World Bank database

Asian countries were first given to Japan by the United States. Besides, the United States provided a huge market for them, so that this growth model could achieve sustainability.

Third, it was necessary for Japan, the leader goose, to promote industrial transfer. First of all, Japan was facing the pressure of rising labor cost and worsening pollution. Then, labor-intensive industries such as fiber and electric appliance assembly started to move to other Asian countries for their cheap labor. Oil, chemical, steel and non-ferrous metal industries, causing serious pollution, triggered the outbreaks of minamata disease, itai-itai disease and photochemical smog. Second, the United States adopted anti-dumping measures against products made in Japan. To circumvent the barrier, the latter began to set up factories in surrounding developing countries. In this way, Japanese products could enjoy the preferential tariffs of the United States for developing countries, and Japan expanded its presence in the United States' market. Lastly, a stronger yen pushed up the production cost of domestic producers of Japan. After the signing of the Plaza Accord, yen rose so sharply that many Japanese enterprises moved their factories abroad. For instance, factories producing high-end consumer goods like automobiles were relocated to developed countries in Europe and America, while producers of electronics and industrial components and parts moved to ANIEs and ASEAN countries.

Fourth, late-developing countries and regions that made up the rest of the formation were capable of hosting the relocated industries. From the end of WWII to the 1960s–1970s, South East Asian countries and regions (excluding Hong Kong, China) had all adopted import substitution or similar development strategies. Such strategies could provide the basis for less-developed countries to build their own manufacturing industry, and to host factories moved from developed countries. As the marginal efficiency of import substitution began to fall, developing regions and countries of East Asia turned to export-oriented development. By adopting measures such as trade liberalization, they attracted foreign investment and industrial transfer from developing countries. With the motivations of developed countries (regions) and the appeal of backward ones, a virtuous cycle of capital and products, through dynamic and gradient industrial transfer (including technology transfer) centered around FDI, was formed among East Asian countries and regions. This led to upgraded industrial structure and higher level of industrialization, which had laid the foundation for economic takeoff and fast growth.

(3) The end of the flying-geese paradigm

Since the 1990s, with the bursting of the "bubbles", the Japanese economy fell into a long period of stagnation featuring deflation and periodic recession. Japan experienced three consecutive years of negative growth in 1996, 1997 and 1998. Even after the resumption of normal economic growth in 1999, GDP at that time still fell short of previous levels. Along with the lasting economic stagnation, the growth of Japan's foreign trade has also slowed down. Due to the sluggish performance of Japan, the leader goose, its trade volume with East Asian countries, especially the import volume, witnessed slowing growth. Imports from Hong Kong and Taiwan regions of China had even declined to different degrees.

The flying-geese paradigm was founded upon the gap of industrial gradient among different countries, driven by the sustained economic growth of the leader goose, i.e., Japan. Due to the growth of East Asian countries and the economic downturn of Japan, this gap was narrowing, which had directly led to the end of the flying-geese paradigm. Japan's status as the leader goose had taken a beating after more than ten years of recession in the 1990s. In addition, due to the rapid industrialization of other East Asian countries, the industrial gradient, the basic conditions for the formation of the flying-geese paradigm, had been flattening, and thus disabling industrial transfer, which ushered in the post-Flying-Geese-Paradigm era.

2. Stage of the neoliberal globalization

Neoliberalism is against any form of state intervention since it believes that Keynesianism, while easing the capitalist crisis of overproduction with state intervention, limits the free development of capitalism. The globalization pursued by neoliberalism, characterized by capitalist dominance and a clear ideological bent, will further enhance the domination of capital over labor and the rule of big powers over the weak countries—it is in fact removing obstacles for the global expansion of capitalism. The global expansion of capitalism requires neoliberalism to stretch from the West to the whole world and to become the implicit logic of globalization. Therefore, at this stage, a "center-periphery" pattern was formed—as the rich grew richer, and the poor became poorer, globalization had caused serious polarization of wealth.

(1) The economic pattern

After the end of the flying-geese paradigm, the world economy was swept by the wave of neoliberal globalization in 1985–2008. Within the composition of global GDP, the United States maintained its leading position, but its share declined from 34.38 to 23.32%. Japan's economy went through upheavals, and its share, starting from 10.95% in 1985, first rose to 17.36% in 1995 and fell to 7.68% in 2008. China's share of global GDP expanded further with the deepening of the reform and opening up, rising from 2.45% in 1985 to 7.28% in 2008, displaying the potential of overtaking Japan (Table 1.4).

During the period of neoliberal globalization, the per capita GDP growth of middle-income countries was significantly higher than that of lower-middle-income countries, and the per capita GDP of lower-middle-income countries was faster than that of low-income countries. In 1985, the per capita GDP of the United States amounted to 18,269 USD, and by 2008, it was close to 50,000 USD. At the same time, the deepening reform and opening up and other factors have also greatly boosted China's per capita GDP which rose from 294 USD in 1985 to 3471 USD in 2008. In contrast, per capita GDP of low-income countries had not seen significant growth in the 20 years after 1985; instead, it even experienced a large decline in the early 1990s. Before the financial crisis in 2008, the per capita GDP of low-income countries was only 483 USD (Table 1.5).

(2) Foreign trade structure

Table 1.4 The structure of global GDP at the stage of neoliberalism (Unit: million USD at current prices)

Year	China		The United States		Japan		EU	
	GDP	Share (%)	GDP	Share (%)	GDP	Share (%)	GDP	Share (%)
1985	309,486	2.45	4,346,734	34.38	1,384,532	10.95	3,162,057	25.01
1986	300,759	2.01	4,590,155	30.67	2,051,061	13.70	4,336,364	28.97
1987	272,973	1.60	4,870,217	28.60	2,485,236	14.59	5,365,622	31.50
1988	312,354	1.64	5,252,629	27.55	3,015,394	15.82	5,984,972	31.39
1989	347,767	1.74	5,657,693	28.27	3,017,052	15.08	6,110,947	30.54
1990	360,859	1.60	5,979,589	26.56	3,103,698	13.78	7,578,343	33.66
1991	383,373	1.61	6,174,043	25.88	3,536,801	14.83	7,864,846	32.97
1992	426,915	1.68	6,539,299	25.80	3,852,794	15.20	8,570,210	33.82
1993	444,731	1.72	6,878,718	26.68	4,414,963	17.12	7,814,538	30.31
1994	564,325	2.04	7,308,755	26.39	4,850,348	17.51	8,298,364	29.97
1995	734,548	2.39	7,664,060	24.94	5,333,926	17.36	9,610,436	31.27
1996	863,746	2.75	8,100,201	25.80	4,706,187	14.99	9,824,634	31.29
1997	961,603	3.07	8,608,515	27.48	4,324,278	13.81	9,273,327	29.61

(continued)

Table 1.4 (continued)

Year	China		The United States		Japan		EU	
	GDP	Share (%)	GDP	Share (%)	GDP	Share (%)	GDP	Share (%)
1998	1,029,043	3.30	9,089,168	29.13	3,914,575	12.55	9589D851	30.74
1999	1,093,998	3.38	9,660,624	29.86	4,432,599	13.70	9,576,747	29.60
2000	1,211,346	3.63	10,284,779	30.80	4,731,199	14.17	8,899,099	26.65
2001	1,339,395	4.03	10,624,824	31.99	4,159,860	12.53	9,000,493	27.11
2002	1,470,550	4.26	10,977,514	31.83	3,980,820	11.54	9,810,781	28.45
2003	1,660,288	4.29	11,510,670	29.72	4,302,939	11.11	11,945,411	30.84
2004	1,955,347	4.48	12,274,928	28.14	4,655,803	10.67	13,795,083	31.63
2005	2,285,966	4.84	13,093,726	27.74	4,571,867	9.68	14,426,313	30.56
2006	2,752,132	5.38	13,855,888	27.10	4,356,750	8.52	15,388,308	30.09
2007	3,552,183	6.17	14,477,635	25.14	4,356,348	7.56	17,780,816	30.87
2008	4,598,205	7.28	14,718,582	23.31	4,849,185	7.68	19,116,323	30.27

Source of data World Bank database

Table 1.5 Per capita GDP of different countries (Unit: USD at current prices)

Year	China		The United States		Upper-middle-income countries		Lower-middle-income countries		Low-income countries	
	Per capita GDP	GR (%)	Per capita GDP	GR (%)	Per capita GDP	GR (%)	Per capita GDP	GR (%)	Per capita GDP	GR (%)
1985	294		18,269		982		408			
1986	282	−4.25	19,115	4.63	1011	2.93	414	1.71		
1987	252	−10.68	20,101	5.16	993	−1.74	446	7.58		
1988	284	12.60	21,483	6.88	1074	8.14	450	0.93	294	
1989	311	9.64	22,922	6.70	1149	7.02	441	−1.90	282	−4.08
1990	318	2.25	23,954	4.50	1296	12.74	467	5.72	293	3.86
1991	333	4.80	24,405	1.88	1412	9.00	439	−6.03	292	−0.07
1992	366	10.00	25,493	4.46	1358	−3.85	458	4.35	251	−14.31
1993	377	2.98	26,465	3.81	1457	7.30	455	−0.53	233	−6.88
1994	473	25.47	27,777	4.96	1569	7.67	486	6.80	203	−13.10
1995	610	28.76	28,782	3.62	1731	10.32	536	10.15	227	12.13
1996	709	16.36	30,068	4.47	1861	7.54	576	7.59	247	8.48
1997	782	10.20	31,573	5.00	1962	5.40	584	1.39	248	0.64

(continued)

Table 1.5 (continued)

Year	China		The United States		Upper-middle-income countries		Lower-middle-income countries		Low-income countries	
	Per capita GDP	GR (%)	Per capita GDP	GR (%)	Per capita GDP	GR (%)	Per capita GDP	GR (%)	Per capita GDP	GR (%)
1998	829	5.99	32,949	4.36	1913	−2.47	519	−11.19	244	−1.56
1999	873	5.40	34,621	5.07	1793	−6.29	554	6.76	238	−2.54
2000	959	9.86	36,450	5.28	1956	9.12	575	3.77	268	12.37
2001	1053	9.77	37,274	2.26	1963	0.31	570	−0.77	235	−12.13
2002	1149	9.06	38,166	2.39	1952	−0.52	601	5.38	247	5.08
2003	1289	12.20	39,677	3.96	2180	11.64	678	12.82	264	6.73
2004	1509	17.07	41,922	5.66	2597	19.17	761	12.29	293	11.01
2005	1753	16.22	44,308	5.69	3105	19.56	861	13.02	329	12.38
2006	2099	19.72	46,437	4.81	3669	18.16	1003	16.57	355	7.95
2007	2695	28.40	48,062	3.50	4534	23.57	1199	19.50	412	16.05
2008	3471	28.79	48,401	0.71	5511	21.54	1320	10.08	483	17.21

Source of data World Bank database

Statistics show that during the two decades from 1985 to 2008, the imports and exports of developed countries accounted for 60–70% of the world's total, especially in the early 1990s, when the percentage was higher than 70% for many years in a row. In contrast, despite some increase, the proportion of foreign trade of developing countries stayed around 30% (Table 1.6).

(3) FDI inflow

Statistics suggests that the proportion of inbound FDI stock in developing countries within the world's total declined during 1985–2009, but the proportion of inbound FDI flow increased, which demonstrates the shortage of FDI supply in developing countries and the oversupply of FDI flows and stocks in developed countries (Table 1.7).

3. The global economic landscape went through drastic changes after the 2008 financial Crisis

The United States, the source of the crisis, was hit hard, and the crisis rapidly spread to its real economy after 2008. Table 1.8 shows the per capita GDP of the United States witnessed negative growth in 2008–2009 and struggled through a difficult adjustment period in the following five years. Dragged down by the United States' economy, the per capita GDP of upper-middle-income countries, mainly developed countries, had seen a slowdown of growth. The Chinese economy, less affected by the United States financial crisis, maintained high-speed growth in 2008–2011. Affected by the economic structure, the growth of China's per capita GDP gradually slowed down, the Chinese economy gradually entered the development stage of "new normal", and the supply-side reform was launched for economic restructuring. The economic growth of lower-middle-income countries was relatively steady, but slower compared to emerging economies such as China, which means a lack of vitality. In low-income countries, the growth rate of per capita GDP had been shrinking year by year.

In general, since 2008, the gap between middle- and high-income countries and low-income countries in terms of per capita GDP has widened, leading to increasingly serious problem of wealth gap. The economic downturn of developed countries has spread to the whole world through trade, investment and multinational corporations, and their driving force to the developing economies has weakened greatly. On the one hand, the overall market demand of developed countries has shrunk, and on the other hand, the products produced by the backward industrial systems of most developing countries cannot meet the needs of advanced economies. This has transformed the global economic structure into a double-loop system of global value division. The lower-level products produced by countries within the lower loop flow to emerging economies such as China; after further processing by the sound industrial system of the emerging economies, these products, having obtained better quality, then flow to the upper loop of developed countries. In this way, a full and closed cycle of economic operation is formed. In the double-loop structure, the role of emerging economies is more important: they have to constantly improve their industrial system and structure through complementarity with other countries, so as to better serve as the connecting link between the two loops and the engine of the global economy.

Table 1.6 Foreign trade structures of developed and developing countries (Unit: million USD at current prices)

Year	Developing countries				Developed countries			
	Import volume	Proportion of import within the world's total (%)	Export volume	Proportion of export within the world's total (%)	Import volume	Proportion of import within the world's total (%)	Export volume	Proportion of export within the world's total (%)
1985	574,786	25	579,483	25	1,691,248	73	1,666,175	72
1986	560,792	22	537,582	21	1,918,609	75	1,930,267	76
1987	644,113	21	667,269	22	2,281,538	76	2,266,160	75
1988	756,628	22	767,937	22	2,586,364	75	2,581,088	75
1989	844,082	23	860,705	23	2,787,075	75	2,758,706	74
1990	951,617	22	988,655	23	3,189,561	75	3,158,981	74
1991	1,074,589	24	1,041,483	24	3,216,584	73	3,233,853	74
1992	1,205,391	25	1,156,507	24	3,425,689	72	3,484,161	73
1993	1,317,377	28	1,246,512	26	3,276,531	70	3,394,040	72
1994	1,468,973	28	1,421,979	27	3,671,931	70	3,786,940	71
1995	1,771,977	28	1,712,274	27	4,348,726	70	4,492,073	71
1996	1,915,926	29	1,878,154	28	4,550,618	69	4,669,504	70
1997	2,028,655	30	2,009,313	29	4,660,571	68	4,800,698	69

(continued)

Table 1.6 (continued)

Year	Developing countries				Developed countries			
	Import volume	Proportion of import within the world's total (%)	Export volume	Proportion of export within the world's total (%)	Import volume	Proportion of import within the world's total (%)	Export volume	Proportion of export within the world's total (%)
1998	1,842,614	27	1,869,172	27	4,796,611	71	4,854,561	71
1999	1,919,665	27	2,011,087	28	5,073,871	71	4,984,942	70
2000	2,285,911	29	2,440,573	31	5,540,883	70	5,328,325	67
2001	2,185,449	28	2,307,284	30	5,391,863	70	5,202,239	68
2002	2,302,138	29	2,475,211	31	5,534,490	69	5,357,054	67
2003	2,672,840	29	2,918,893	31	6,408,728	69	6,201,410	66
2004	3,387,438	30	3,687,547	32	7,626,506	68	7,362,283	65
2005	3,989,778	31	4,475,022	35	8,487,896	66	8,047,179	62
2006	4,656,113	32	5,316,981	36	9,574,456	66	9,057,739	61
2007	5,531,336	33	6,259,703	36	10,878,032	64	10,462,188	60
2008	6,676,603	34	7,381,516	37	12,151,070	62	11,637,225	59

Source of data UNCTAD database

Table 1.7 Inward FDI in developing and developed countries (Unit: 10,000 USD at current prices)

Year	Developing countries				Developed countries			
	Stock of inbound FDI	Proportion within the world's total (%)	Flow of inbound FDI	Proportion within the world's total (%)	Stock of inbound FDI	Proportion within the world's total (%)	Flow of inbound FDI	Proportion within the world's total (%)
1985	370,369	37.54	14,070	25.20	616,241	62.46	41,744	74.77
1986	386,715	34.09	15,832	18.26	747,693	65.91	70,897	81.78
1987	414,046	31.03	21,763	15.90	920,469	68.97	115,108	84.10
1988	437,166	28.67	30,558	18.61	1,086,151	71.23	133,641	81.38
1989	467,400	25.51	30,388	15.43	1,363,181	74.40	166,543	84.57
1990	509,470	23.19	34,657	16.91	1,685,876	76.74	170,195	83.06
1991	547,372	22.14	39,318	25.53	1,922,379	77.77	114,480	74.35
1992	604,753	24.24	53,458	32.81	1,889,391	75.74	107,868	66.21
1993	681,577	25.25	75,691	34.39	2,015,828	74.67	141,404	64.24
1994	757,251	25.54	102,383	40.16	2,200,912	74.24	150,599	59.08
1995	843,341	23.65	117,761	34.48	2,711,006	76.04	219,764	64.35
1996	982,029	23.75	147,078	37.83	3,136,646	75.86	236,343	60.79
1997	1,089,641	23.07	185,401	38.50	3,605,801	76.36	286,294	59.46

(continued)

Table 1.7 (continued)

Year	Developing countries				Developed countries			
	Stock of inbound FDI	Proportion within the world's total (%)	Flow of inbound FDI	Proportion within the world's total (%)	Stock of inbound FDI	Proportion within the world's total (%)	Flow of inbound FDI	Proportion within the world's total (%)
1998	1,197,495	20.23	176,632	25.51	4,690,698	79.25	508,532	73.45
1999	1,540,158	21.72	216,290	20.09	5,509,553	77.71	852,939	79.24
2000	1,644,215	21.96	232,390	17.10	5,791,254	77.34	1,120,508	82.46
2001	1,735,815	23.79	215,794	31.56	5,481,062	75.12	459,715	67.23
2002	1,672,700	22.72	166,739	28.27	5,583,664	78.85	413,025	70.03
2003	1,929,613	21.05	195,584	35.52	7,097,819	77.41	337,172	61.24
2004	2,252,606	21.29	263,718	38.32	8,145,333	76.99	395,518	57.47
2005	2,635,508	23.00	331,752	34.92	8,565,673	74.76	587,710	61.86
2006	3,267,898	23.10	402,983	28.74	10,513,463	74.32	940,318	67.06
2007	4,353,591	24.33	525,525	27.63	12,915,495	72.17	1,289,494	67.79
2008	4,006,097	26.14	578,482	38.62	10,929,902	71.32	801,909	53.54

Source of data UNCTAD database

Table 1.8 Per capita GDP and its growth rate (measured in PPP) in some countries (Unit: international dollar)

Year		2008	2009	2010	2011	2012	2013	2014	2015
China	Per capita GDP	7635.07	8374.43	9333.12	10,384.37	11,351.06	12,367.97	13,439.91	14,450.17
	Growth rate of per capita GDP (%)	9.09	8.86	10.10	9.01	7.33	7.23	6.76	6.37
The United States	Per capita GDP	48,401.43	47,001.56	48,374.09	49,781.80	51,433.05	52,749.91	54,539.67	56,115.72
	Growth rate of per capita GDP (%)	−1.23	−3.62	1.68	0.83	1.45	0.93	1.57	1.79
Upper-middle-income countries	Per capita GDP	10,749.72	11,052.39	11,971.41	13,035.11	13,827.81	14,489.36	15,321.66	15,883.88
	Growth rate of per capita GDP (%)	5.17	0.83	6.78	5.34	3.98	3.91	3.09	2.42
Lower-middle-income countries	Per capita GDP	4370.44	4563.77	4890.44	5182.18	5468.97	5785.05	6130.18	6441.46
	Growth rate of per capita GDP (%)	3.18	3.41	5.79	3.82	3.63	4.06	4.02	3.79
Low-income countries	Per capita GDP	1230.97	1273.43	1336.88	1404.59	1446.16	1514.23	1591.41	1635.94
	Growth rate of per capita GDP (%)	4.32	1.04	6.14	4.60	3.51	3.58	2.95	2.38

Source of data World Bank database

Table 1.9 illustrates the proportion of foreign trade of developed countries within the world's total had been declining year by year after the 2008 financial crisis. In contrast, the proportion of the developing countries had seen slight increase. In general, developed countries, enjoying larger proportion, are net importers, while developing countries are net exporters.

Table 1.10 shows for both developing and developed countries, the proportion of trade within their own loop was higher than that with countries of the other loop, and the gap between the proportions was wider in developed countries, which shows that developed countries were more inclined to trade within their own loop. Since 2008, the proportion of intra-loop trade in developing countries had been rising—developing countries had increasingly targeted each other as trading partners since the financial crisis.

Table 1.11 illustrates that inbound FDI in developing countries had been taking up increasingly larger share within the world's total in terms of both stocks and flows since 2008, which shows developing countries with cheaper resource and labor cost were still the favored destination of global capital. As to OFDI, both stocks and flows had been dwindling in developed countries, which reflects the structural problem of FDI flows: in 2008–2014 when the developed economies were restructuring, their recession was spread to the developing economies through the movement of FDI, resulting in negative impact on the economic development of developing countries. In the previous global system of labor division, the global economy was mainly driven by developed countries which were at the top of the industrial value chain. However, from the perspective of FDI movement, the role of developed countries had been gradually eroded.

(III) Polarization of the global wealth gap and protectionism

The analysis above demonstrates that globalization will follow different paths in different types of countries. Developed countries such as the United States, feeling sensitive and disturbed, have stopped advocating free trade and refocused on domestic development, shifting from a neoliberal paradigm that emphasizes unleashing market power to social protection. For instance, the United States has continuously made protectionist remarks such as "abolishing the United States Trade Agreement" and "abolishing the Trans-Pacific Partnership Agreement (TPP)", reflecting its mixed attitude toward globalization as the largest economy in the world. Brexit, exposing the EU's combined plight of slow growth, weak recovery, sluggish employment and refugee crisis, has brought huge uncertainty to the global economy.

Such phenomena have deep roots. First, the global wealth gap is widening. In the process of economic globalization, the distribution of benefits has been uneven among different countries, leading to enormous wealth disparity: the general public and the vulnerable groups receive less, while large enterprises and elites gain more. Meanwhile, there is a growing income gap between developed and developing countries.

Table 1.9 Comparison between developing and developed countries in terms of foreign trade (Unit: 100 million USD)

Year		2008	2009	2010	2011	2012	2013	2014	2015
Developing countries	Import volume	57,520.33	46,477.97	60,201.23	73,423.41	76,802.64	79,629.36	79,780.79	69,717.29
	Proportion within the world's total	34.93	36.63	39.04	39.87	41.24	42.11	42.00	41.98
	Export volume	63,026.58	50,061.61	64,384.34	78,994.70	82,289.92	84,240.55	84,762.12	74,110.99
	Proportion within the world's total	39.03	39.87	42.08	43.07	44.49	44.48	44.62	44.78
Developed countries	Import volume	101,631.37	76,717.19	89,469.24	104,862.15	103,302.21	103,296.99	104,667.32	92,539.15
	Proportion within the world's total	61.72	60.46	58.02	56.94	55.46	54.63	55.10	55.72
	Export volume	91,217.10	70,828.19	82,545.60	96,288.60	94,458.39	97,072.59	97,548.73	86,145.41
	Proportion within the world's total	56.49	56.41	53.94	52.50	51.07	51.25	51.35	52.05

Source of data UNCTAD database

Table 1.10 Trade structures of developing and developed countries (Unit: %)

Year			2008	2009	2010	2011	2012	2013	2014	2015
Developing countries	Proportion of intra-loop trade	Export	50.62	53.39	54.75	55.55	56.83	58.41	58.21	57.95
		Import	56.30	55.90	57.24	58.04	58.73	58.71	59.38	59.13
	Proportion of trade outside the loop	Export	49.38	46.61	45.25	44.45	43.17	41.59	41.79	42.05
		Import	43.70	44.10	42.76	41.96	41.27	41.29	40.62	40.87
Developed countries	Proportion of intra-loop trade	Export	72.14	70.98	68.57	68.12	66.54	66.02	67.18	67.29
		Import	62.47	63.03	60.40	59.63	58.46	59.64	59.93	60.24
	Proportion of trade outside the loop	Export	27.86	29.02	31.43	31.88	33.46	33.98	32.82	32.71
		Import	37.53	36.97	39.60	40.37	41.54	40.36	40.07	39.76

Source of data UNCTAD database

Table 1.11 A comparison between FDI outflows from the developed countries and FDI inflows into the developing countries (Unit: 100 million USD)

Year		2008	2009	2010	2011	2012	2013	2014	2015
Developing countries	Stocks of inbound FDI	40,060.97	48,578.78	60,425.38	63,549.96	72,078.07	76,573.42	81,720.34	83,744.28
	Proportion within the world's total (%)	26.14	26.69	29.93	30.41	31.84	31.21	32.54	33.52
	Flows of inbound FDI	5784.82	4653.07	6253.30	6701.49	6587.74	6624.06	6984.94	7646.70
	Proportion within the world's total (%)	38.62	39.39	45.03	42.77	43.60	46.41	54.70	43.39
Developed countries	Stocks of OFDI	134,736.67	161,363.16	174,244.9	174,930.13	183,583.6	198,171.73	194,364.79	194,408.05
	Proportion within the world's total (%)	84.74	84.93	83.76	82.27	80.87	80.35	78.34	77.62
	Flows of OFDI	13,694.63	8203.81	9834.05	11,280.47	9177.83	8259.48	8007.27	10,651.92
	Proportion within the world's total (%)	80.38	74.66	70.65	72.42	70.12	63.02	60.73	72.25

Source of data UNCTAD database

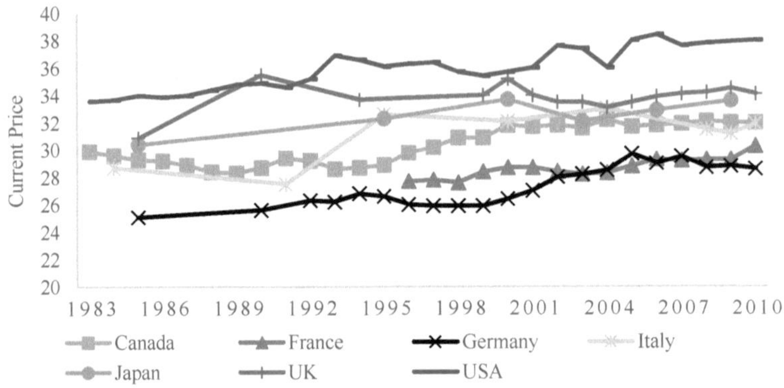

Fig. 1.5 Gini coefficients of G7 countries. *Source of data* WIID

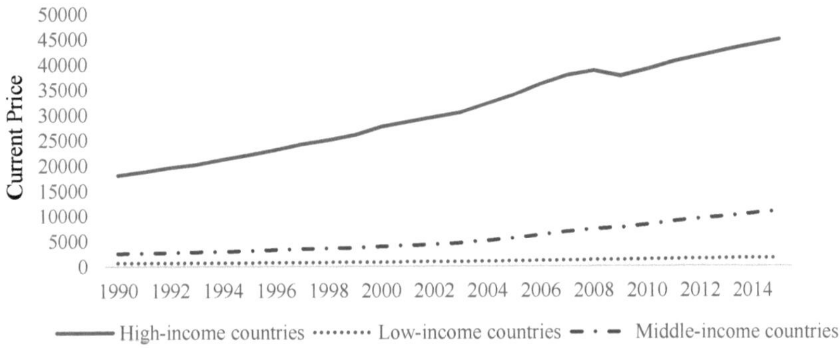

Fig. 1.6 Per capita GDP (measured in PPP). *Source of data* World Bank database

Figure 1.5[2] reflects the worsening income polarization within developed countries (represented by G7)—the trend is quantified by their rising Gini coefficient in the past 30 years. According to WIID statistics, among the G7 countries, the United States suffered the highest Gini coefficient in the past 30 years, rising from 33.6 in 1983 to 38 in 2010; in Canada, the figure grew from 29.9 in 1983 to 32 in 2010 (Gini coefficient reaches 100 when the income distribution is absolutely unfair).

Figure 1.6 reflects the intensifying polarization between high-income and low- and middle-income countries. According to the World Bank's per capita GDP statistics (measured in PPP), per capita GDP in high-income countries increased by 26,780 international dollars from 1990 to 2014, while the increase in low-income countries was only 896 international dollars. In 1990, per capita GDP of high-income countries was 24.5 times that of low-income ones. By 2015, this gap had expanded to 27.4 times.

Second, the unemployment problem is grave. Due to the division of labor in the global value chain, labor-intensive manufacturing industries are mainly distributed in

[2] https://www.wider.unu.edu/project/wiidGworldGincomeGinequalityGdatabase.

developing countries, leading to rising unemployment in the manufacturing sectors of developed countries.

Third, nationalism is resurging. The relationship between countries is fundamentally and essentially built upon interests. Globalization, as the cession of sovereignty, weakens the power of the state. As a result, the dissatisfied national government will turn conservative and the national economy will grow more domestically oriented.

(IV) The changes of global economic landscape

The Industrial Revolution was accompanied by several shifts of the global economic center, and thus, the drastic changes of global economic landscape appeared. In the first half of the nineteenth century, Britain first completed the Industrial Revolution and became the center of the world economy. In 1830, Britain contributed 21.5% of world trade; the percentage rose to 25% in 1870, but then fell to 19% in 1900; in 1938, it declined further to 14%. In the above-mentioned years, the United States generated 5.4%, 7.5%, 10.4% and 10.7% of the global trade, respectively, far below Britain. However, during the Second Industrial Revolution, the United States, by seizing the development opportunities of leading production sectors such as electric engineering, came out on top in 1894 in terms of industrial output value. After more than half a century of development since then, its share within the world trade grew to 16% in 1953, while that of Britain was only 10%—the United States had surpassed Britain in the area of global trade. From the 1950s to the 1970s, Japan vigorously promoted export. At that time, Japan, with abundant young labor force (in 1953, Japan had 87.5 million people, South Korea had 21 million, Thailand had 21.2 million, and Taiwan had 8.8 million), was one of the main sources of import to the United States. The considerable size of the United States' market had helped improve the labor productivity in Japan. In 1948, Japan's export was 0.44% of the world's total; by 1993, the percentage had hiked to 9.9%. But in the mid-1990s, as the size of its young labor force shrank, Japan's economic growth slowed down. Meanwhile, China, with the largest population and labor force in the world, had absorbed ceaseless flows of FDI. The proportion of Chinese exports within the world's total soared from 0.91% in 1980 to 13.72% in 2015. Table 1.12 lists trade, GDP and investment statistics of China and Japan. It can be summarized that China had surpassed Japan in all areas since the beginning of the twenty-first century; in 2005, its import of goods and services was 1.08 times that of Japan, and the gap further grew to 1.1 times in 2010; also in 2010, its inbound FDI was dozens of times that of Japan. As Table 1.13 shows, China's industrial added value grew much faster than that of Japan over the same period. With closer ties to the global economy, China had overtaken Japan as the engine of Asian economy. Driven by domestic reforms, foreign investment and exports, China has achieved long-term rapid growth.

Figure 1.7 shows the proportions of different continents within the global GDP from 1700 to 2012. Britain, the world economic center in the first half of the nineteenth century, led the European economy to grow from about 30% of the world's total to 47% in 1913. After that, the United States helped expand the proportion of the American economy from about 20% to around 40% in 1950. The proportion of

Table 1.12 A comparison between Chinese and Japanese economic data (Unit: 100 million USD)

Year	China	Japan	China/Japan (%)
Import of goods and services (BoP)			
1996	1541.27	4421.39	34.86
2005	6487.12	6030.31	107.58
2010	13,809.20	7917.93	174.40
2015	20,446.52	8035.74	254.44
Year	China	Japan	China/Japan
GDP			
1982	2035.50	11,168.41	18.23
1996	8608.44	47,061.87	18.29
2005	22,685.99	45,718.67	49.62
2010	60,396.59	54,987.18	109.84
2015	108,664.44	41,232.58	263.54
Net inbound FDI (BoP)			
1982	4.30	4.40	0.98
1996	401.80	2.08	193.51
2005	1041.09	54.60	19.07
2010	2437.03	74.41	32.75
2015	2498.59	−0.42	−5965.23

Source of data World Bank database

Table 1.13 A comparison between Chinese and Japanese annual industrial added rates (1982–2014) (Unit: %)

Year	China	Japan
1982	5.51	0.54
1996	12.11	2.75
2005	12.07	1.80
2008	9.80	−0.46
2014	7.30	1.49

Source of data World Bank database

the Asian economy, driven by Japan, rose from about 20% to about 30% in 1990, and it later climbed further to 40% thanks to China's rapid growth.

Table 1.14 lists the per capita GDP statistics of countries that have led the global industrial transfers. The percentage of British per capita GDP compared to that of the United States continued to rise from 1850 to 1900, and then began to decline, which indicates that the per capita GDP of the Britain grew fast and boosted European economy during this period. Compared with Japan, the United States witnessed decline in per capita GDP after 1960, which means it grew slower than Japan. Japan's

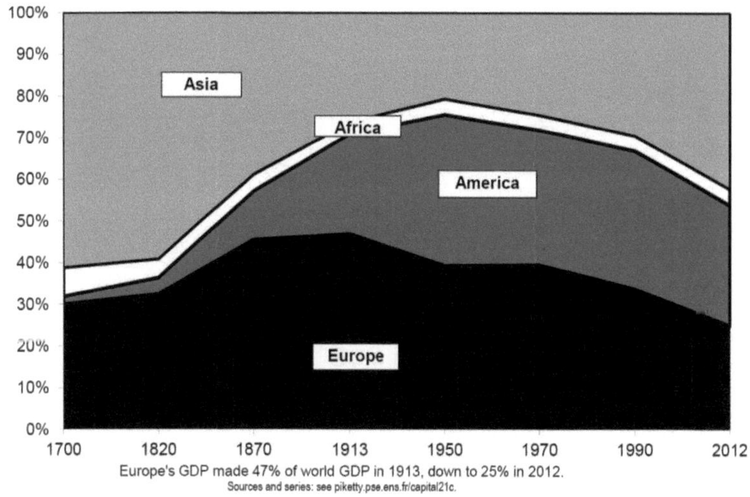

Fig. 1.7 The proportions of different continents within the global GDP (1700–2012). *Source of data* Capital in the Twenty-First Century[3]

per capita GDP fell after 2000 relative to that of China, which, again, verifies the historical facts of the shifts of the global economic center.

Since the 1950s, Europe and America have witnessed declining share within the world economy, while Asian economy has been growing rapidly, which has followed the same trend as the population growth across the world. Figure 1.8 illustrates the global population distribution from 1700 to 2012. The proportion of European and American population had fallen to 10% in 2012. The support of labor force is essential to economic development. Although most of the European and American countries are developed economies, their long-term development faces uncertainty due to the sluggish growth of population and thus the lack of labor force. Asia has always been the most populous continent, and its share of the world's population is still rising slowly. Despite its decreasing demographic dividends, China, with the largest population, still enjoys relatively abundant labor resources. Compared with India, the second most populous country, China has a better educated workforce. In 2015, adult literacy rate was only 72.22% in India, while it reached 96.36% in China. At the same time, the huge potential of domestic market demand and the growth dividends brought about by continuous reforms will provide China with a sustained impetus for boosting the Asian economy.

Since the reform and opening up in 1978, China has received a large number of outsourcing orders relying on the policy of opening up and cheap labor. By playing the role of the workshop of the world, China has achieved fast trade and economic growth, and grown from a country with a complete industrial system into a major manufacturing power. According to the Industrial Development Report of UNIDO (see Table 1.15), the growth rate of manufacturing added value was expected to be 1% in 2015, and China, with its growth rate expected to reach 7.4% despite some

Table 1.14 Historical GDP data of major countries (Unit: international dollar at 1990 constant prices)

Year	Britain		The United States		Japan		China
	Per capita GDP	Percentage within the United States per capita GDP (%)	Per capita GDP	Percentage within the Japanese per capita GDP (%)	Per capita GDP	Percentage within the Chinese per capita GDP (%)	Per capita GDP
1850	2330	1.29	1806	2.66	679	1.13	600
1870	3190	1.31	2445	3.32	737	1.39	530
1900	4492	1.10	4091	3.47	1180	2.16	545
1913	4921	0.93	5301	3.82	1387	2.51	552
1930	5441	0.88	6213	3.36	1850	3.26	568
1938	6266	1.02	6126	2.50	2449	4.36	562
1950	6939	0.73	9561	4.98	1921	4.29	448
1960	8645	0.76	11,328	2.84	3986	6.02	662
1970	10,767	0.72	15,030	1.55	9714	12.48	778
1980	12,931	0.70	18,577	1.38	13,428	12.66	1061
1990	16,430	0.71	23,201	1.23	18,789	10.04	1871
2000	20,353	0.71	28,467	1.37	20,738	6.06	3421
2008	23,742	0.76	31,178	1.37	22,816	3.39	6725

Source of data Maddison database

[3] Piketty, T. Capital in the Twenty-First Century [M]. The Belknap Press, 2014. Due to different sources, the data cited here are different from the statistics of the World Bank.

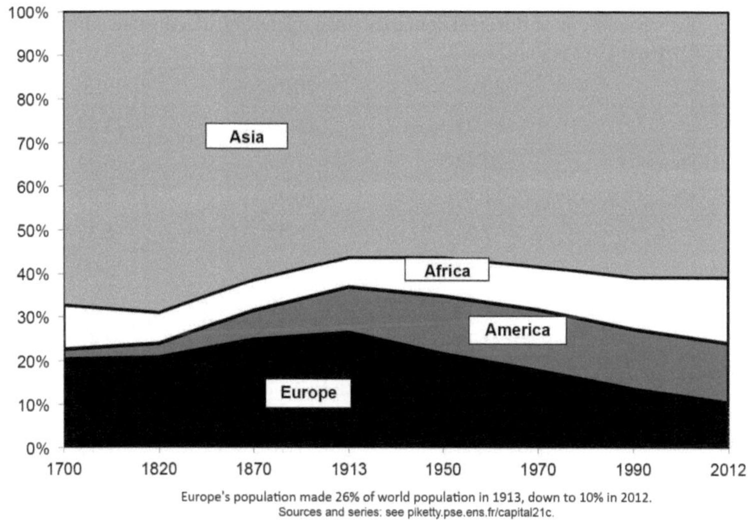

Fig. 1.8 Global population distribution (1700–2012). *Source of data* Capital in the Twenty-First Century

loss of speed, would still be the main engine of the growth of global manufacturing industry. Meanwhile, the proportion of China's manufacturing added value (at 2010 constant prices) had risen from 11.75% in 2005 to 23.84% in 2015, ranking first in the world.

Table 1.16 lists the changes in manufacturing-related indicators of China, upper-middle-income countries and the world average. It shows the growth rate of China's manufacturing added value has stabilized, and its per capita manufacturing added value has approached the world average and reached the level of upper-middle-income countries.

1.2 The Theoretical Progress of International Division of Labor and Trade of Developing Countries

The current international division of labor and trade system is built upon the contemporary theory of international division of labor based on Ricardo's principle of comparative advantage. Although the theory of international trade and division of labor has undergone a series of modern developments, its core is still the comparative advantage of the Ricardo model and the factor endowments of the Heckscher-Ohlin model (H–O model).

Ricardo explained in his *On the Principles of Political Economy and Taxation* the increase in the net benefits of "exchange income" and "trade income" through international division of labor and exchanges and concluded that all countries can gain more

Table 1.15 The proportions of different countries' manufacturing added value within the world's total (2005, 2010 and 2015) (Unit: %)

Country	2005	2010	2015
China	11.75	18.69	23.84
The United States	20.43	17.77	16.54
Japan	11.14	10.43	8.93
Germany	7.29	6.55	6.37
South Korea	2.54	2.95	3.09
India	1.74	2.36	2.45
Italy	3.70	2.94	2.42
France	3.13	2.61	2.34
Brazil	3.08	2.89	2.26
Indonesia	1.65	1.70	1.93
Britain	2.66	2.15	1.93
Russia	2.15	1.90	1.77
Mexico	1.91	1.69	1.70
Canada	2.20	1.57	1.45
Spain	2.18	1.69	1.44

Source of data The Industrial Development Report of UNIDO

Table 1.16 A comparison between China, upper-middle-income countries and the world average in terms of manufacturing industry

Indicator	Period	China	Upper-middle-income countries	The world average
Average annual growth rate of manufacturing added value (%)	2005–2010	11.10	5.85	2.03
	2010–2014	7.89	4.43	2.24
Manufacturing added value per capita (USD)	2005	914.36	884.80	1201.63
	2014	1218.99	1066.46	1276.66

benefit from international division of labor and trade. In the H–O model, the idea that countries can gain benefits from division of labor and trade through their comparative advantages, with its universality and ease of use, has become the starting point for many countries, especially developing countries, to formulate foreign trade strategies and policies. The H–O model has made outstanding contributions to China's economic development since the reform and opening up.

However, the current international trade process indicates there are obvious problems in the current international division of labor and trading system. In fact, the setting of international prices determines the ultimate allocation of the welfare increase resulting from the division of labor and trade. Due to the large number of developing countries and their similarity in factor endowments, coupled with their decentralized and weak power, they have weak bargaining power in the international market and face poor terms of trade. As the benefits of participating in international trade have been compressed, these developing economies are in a disadvantaged position and the situation is difficult to change. Some of the late-starting countries with weak competitiveness, marginalized by the current international trade system, have been deeply trapped in poverty. Therefore, while the current system has promoted economic development and increased welfare in some countries, it has also widened the gap of development between countries and posed a negative impact on many developing economies.

In addition, the principle of comparative advantage and the H–O model fail to discuss changes in productivity and factor endowments. In fact, from a dynamic point of view, there is an internal contradiction between the development of developing countries and the international trade division of labor: the outstanding advantages of developing countries in the early stages of development are generally ample cheap labor or a certain natural resource, and factors such as capital and technology are relatively scarce. However, economic development is the process of rising per capita income and GDP, improved capital accumulation and technological progress, or, the process of continuously consuming and weakening one's own endowment advantages. Therefore, developing the international division of labor and trade simply according to one's factor endowments would position the late-starting countries in the middle and low places of labor division, and the subsequent international division of labor would also hinder technological progress and even industrial development within the countries.

More than twenty years after Ricardo established the theory of international division of labor and trade, the German historical school represented by List put forward a series of trade protectionist theories. The reason to mention the protectionism of the historical school is that under the historical conditions at that time, Germany was also a late-starter compared to Britain, and the establishment of its industrial system was severely impacted by British cheap industrial products. The historical school's argument that backward countries should adopt protective policies such as high tariffs to support domestic industrial development also explains why some countries and their people oppose free trade today. Temporary sacrifices in welfare are tolerable in order to foster domestic industrial development, while focusing on the immediate benefits of participating in the international division of labor poses an adverse impact on a country's long-term development and the improvement of living standards. The protectionism and isolationism established upon this theory have tended to rise after many previous crises. However, the separation of the international industry from the trade system will undoubtedly worsen the post-crisis economic development. Therefore, it is worth pondering how to address the existing problems within the international order with fairer rules, so that each country can obtain tangible benefits from the international division of labor and trade and the centrifugal force of isolationism can be reduced.

These theoretical issues have caused a series of problems in the operation of the current international division of labor and trade system, putting the system in an increasingly difficult situation after the 2008 financial crisis, and also pushing many developing countries, especially those marginalized in the system, to fight for a change.

Different from those marginalized countries, a group of developing countries in Latin America and Southeast Asia seized the opportunity and achieved high-speed growth by joining the system, with their per capita income exceeding 3000–4000 USD; however, many of them are currently plagued by long-term stagnation, or the middle-income trap. For example, countries including Malaysia, Thailand, and the Philippines have fallen into long-term stagnation after the Asian financial crisis. In fact, both the rapid development in the early stage and the stagnation in the later stage are related to the current international division of labor and trade system. The rapid growth is a bonus brought by the difference between a country's endowments and the world market, and the stagnation is the result of being ensnared by "the trap of comparative advantage" in the process of international labor division and trade.

First, in the early stages of economic development in developing countries, the endowments of natural resources and labor have advantages over capital. However, economic growth based on this condition is a process of continuously converting resources and labor into capital at the factor level. Therefore, the density of the three factors will gradually change as economy grows: the growth of GDP is accompanied by the decrease of resources, and the rise of per capita GDP also means better wages brought by increasing capital and the relative scarcity of labor. Therefore, the increase in the total welfare obtained by the late-starting countries through participating in international trade with their comparative advantages is inherently contradictory and unsustainable, and these countries may eventually fall into irreversible economic stagnation. This is why the expansion of production may worsen the terms of trade and poverty, as described in the definition of the "comparative advantage trap of primary products".

Second, when a country actively develops and exploits its comparative advantage to participate in international trade, it will lead to a reduction in the cost of the industry that intensively uses that factor and thus an expansion of production, which will then squeeze other factors and industries by pushing up their prices relatively. A typical example of such is "Dutch disease", one of the cases of resource curse. This also applies to other factors. For instance, the rapid development of labor-intensive industries and the economies of scale may hinder industrial upgrade and scientific innovation, etc. This is the reason behind the lack of scientific research and innovation capacities described in the definition of the "comparative advantage trap of manufactured goods".

Due to the weak position of the emerging countries in terms of economic theory and international status, there are few international trade theories and paths suitable for their development. In development economics, there are also few successful examples of catching up. Therefore, developing countries usually adopt comparative advantage strategies to participate in international division of labor and trade, and how to prevent comparative advantages turning into traps is a common problem that lacks good solutions.

Regarding how to measure whether a country has fallen into the comparative advantage trap and which countries have fallen, we have not found specific conclusions from the existing research literature. In theory, once a country falls into the trap of comparative advantage, its industrial restructuring and upgrading will slow down. According to the theories of product life cycle and contemporary international industrial replacement, a country should go through industrial replacement at least every 20 years due to changes of advantage factors and the rise and fall of industries. Since a country's export products and industries often represent its current comparative advantages, industrial replacement usually manifests itself as the changes in the types and proportions of industries in the export sector. Therefore, if the types and proportions of the export-oriented industries in one country remain fixed for a long time, the country is likely to have fallen into the comparative advantage trap.

At the same time, when participating in international trade with their comparative advantages, developing countries may face shrinking advantages, narrowing profits and diminishing driving force for the economy due to the inherent contradictions mentioned above. For a country that is highly open and dependent on export, the dynamic changes in comparative advantage will weaken its development momentum, and as it falls into the comparative advantage trap, its economy will go through fluctuations or even stagnation.

In the current international industrial and trading system, the emerging countries face many problems. Overall, the late-starting countries are disadvantaged in the international market, always at the relative low end in the industrial chain, and restricted by the "industrial ceiling". For different countries, those lacking development have fallen into poverty due to their inability to join the international division of labor and the trading system, which further widens the gap with developed countries; those with certain development face the risk of long-term stagnation brought by the halt of industrial upgrades and the worsening terms of trade. From the perspective of industrial transfer, this situation is the opposite of East Asia's flying-geese paradigm led by Japan. Due to the financial crisis and economic downturn, the industrial upgrading and replacement of developed countries slowed down, thus forming an industrial ceiling for the late-starters. The late-starters, relatively inferior in terms of capital and science and technology, are in a low-end position in the industrial structure and cannot easily catch up. As they easily fall into stagnation, the subsequent industrial upgrade is often further obstructed. This means that for the current international division of labor and trade system to drive the growth of late-starting countries, the steady growth of the developed countries has to be maintained; when the developed economies are in recession or even crisis, the late-starters would be even more disadvantaged in the system.

Due to the gap of capital and technology and the current political and economic structure, it is difficult to reverse the disadvantages of the late-starters through market means within the existing international system. Therefore, many countries have adopted a series of non-market measures such as industrial policy support to achieve industrial upgrade and economic development. At the same time, regional trade agreements such as preferential trade arrangements can also assist regional industrial development. Therefore, on the basis of each pursuing their own development, all countries will also benefit from the establishment of regional trade agreements for the development of their domestic industries.

The rapid development of "North–North Trade" after Second World War and intra-industry trade indicate that in addition to the simple factor endowments, more complex factors are profoundly affecting international trade. From the perspective of production, the product life cycle theory is a far-reaching explanation: a product is produced in different countries at the different stages of R&D, maturity and standardization based on the cost of R&D, transportation and labor. Generally, the production is transferred from a country with advanced technology to a country with a large market and then to those with low labor costs. Thanks to its low labor cost, China has become a "world factory" in recent decades. With economic development, China's huge market has also contributed its status as the "world factory". The existing data and development shows that China, moving further toward developed countries in terms of income and technology for a long time to come, will become a significant link in the production cycle with its large market. Therefore, in the process of industrial transfer, China will connect countries with advanced technology and those with the cheap labor. From the perspective of demand, the preference similarity theory points out that income level affects consumer preferences. It is believed that consumers with similar income levels have similar quality preferences for a certain kind of product. The existing trade data demonstrate the price and quality of products made in China are more welcome by consumers of late-starting economies. In addition, the production and consumption levels of Southeastern China have gradually approached those of developed countries. Therefore, the manufacturing industry of China has emerged as the main hinge that links the developed and emerging countries and satisfies their demand.

1.3 The Participation of Developing Countries in the Global Value Chain

Economic globalization is still the general trend. Without economic exchanges and cooperation between countries, the world economy could not recover from recession. One of the highlights of economic globalization in the past 30 years has been the change in production mode: the production activities have become increasingly concentrated. 70% of intra-Asian trade is supply-chain trade. Japan, South Korea and Taiwan of China provide high-end parts, the Chinese mainland assembles the parts into finished products, and then, the final products are sold on the market. Supply-chain trade has been the fastest growing part of the international trade in the past three decades, which is closely related to the theory of global value chain.

The theory of global value chain (GVC) is rooted in the value chain theory proposed and developed by international business researchers in the 1980s. It mainly includes three aspects: the driving force of global value chain, governance and industrial cluster and upgrade within the global value chain. Specifically, the driving force of the global value chain generally has two sources: producers and buyers. When the driving force comes from producers, the market demand is boosted by investment made by producers, and the vertical labor division of the global chain of supply and production is formed. Investors could be multinational companies with technological edges aiming at market expansion, or governments striving to promote local economic growth and establish independent industrial systems. The driving force generated by buyers refers to the strong market demand formed by economic entities with great advantages of brand and domestic distribution channels through international network of commodity circulation composed of global procurement and original equipment manufacturers (OEM), and this demand could accelerate the industrialization of developing economies adopting export-oriented strategies. There are mainly five models of governance—market, modular value chains, relational value chains, captive value chains and hierarchy. Among the five models, market and hierarchy are at the lowest and highest ends of the coordination ability between the actors along the value chain. In the governance of global value chain in the real world, the choice among the five models is often made by dynamically balancing the benefits and risks of external procurement and vertical integration. Therefore, the five models are not only intertwined, but also dynamically interconvertible. Although the various links of the global value chain constitute a continuous process in form, they are in fact separated and fragmented in the process of globalization. Geographically, they are dispersed among different regions, characterized by "dispersion over the large area and agglomeration within the small area". The industrial upgrade within the global value chain mainly includes the upgrade of technological process, the upgrade of product, the upgrade of industrial function and the upgrade of value chain. The upgrade of technological process is outperforming one's competitors by improving the efficiency of the technological process of a link in the value chain. Product upgrade is to outstrip one's competitors by launching new products or improving the efficiency of existing products. The upgrade of industrial function is to gain competitive edges by rearranging the links of the value chain. To upgrade the value chain is to transform an industrial chain into another.

Since the 1980s, the progress of economic globalization has brought significant changes to the international division of labor. The traditional division based on product, after reaching a certain level of development, has evolved into the specialization of a link or a procedure within the production of one certain product, or, the labor division within the global value chain. The global value chain covers the entire process from product concept to consumer use, including all activities of manufacturing and marketing participated by domestic and foreign companies (UNCTAD 2013). The global value chain is sometimes referred to as the global supply chain, which includes the constant flow of investment, technology, professionals, assembled goods and business services. Within the framework of global manufacturing, a product is no longer "Made in Germany", "Made in the United States" or even "Made in China", but actually "Made globally". In today's world, 50% of imports of manufactured goods and 70% of service imports are intermediate goods. The vast majority of products and services are actually "made globally" (UNCTAD 2013).

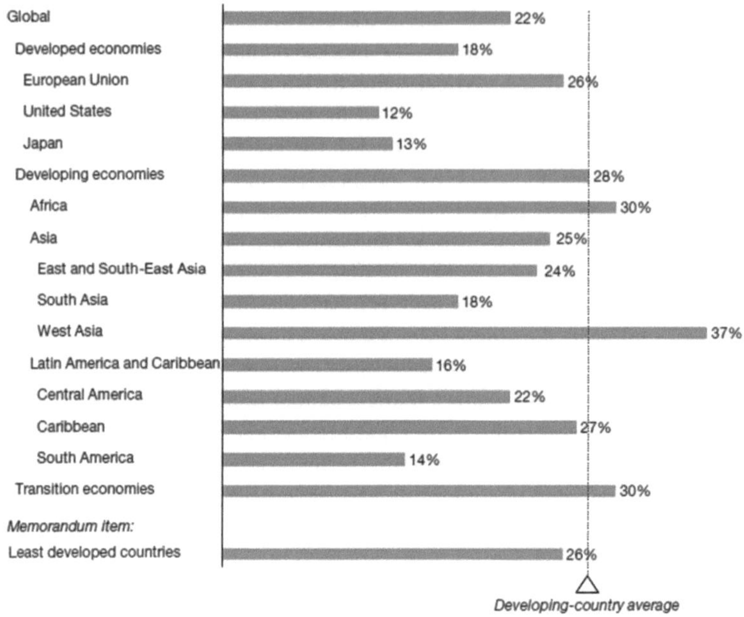

Fig. 1.9 TiVA's contribution rate to the GDPs of developing economies. *Source of data* UNCTAD-Eora GVC database

At present, from a global perspective, most developing countries have increasingly participated in global value chain. The share of developing countries in global trade in value-added (TiVA) rose from 20% in 1990 to 30% in 2000, and the percentage exceeded 40% in 2012. The benefits of a country, especially a developing country, by entering the global value chain are enormous. As Fig. 1.9 illustrates: as of 2013, the trade in value-added contributed 30% of GDP on average in developing countries; for developed countries, this proportion was 18%. Participation in the global value chain is positively correlated with the growth rate of per capita GDP. Per capita GDP growth in the economies with the fastest growing presence in the global value chain is about two percentage points higher than the world average. In addition, participation in the global value chain often helps developing countries create more jobs and achieve faster-growing employment.

Since the twenty-first century, especially after the global financial crisis, the United States' economy has remained sluggish due to industrial hollowing out and long-term over-borrowing and excessive consumption. The high cost and the welfare system have long weighed on the European economy, plunging the EU into debt crisis. Japan has been stuck in an economic stagnation that has lasted for more than a decade. Meanwhile, emerging powers such as China have risen rapidly.

The UNCTAD's *World Investment Report: Investment and Trade Development* shows that Asian countries are highly involved in the global value chain. The average participation rate worldwide is 57%, with an average annual growth rate of 4.5%.

For developed economies, the percentage is 59%, with an average annual growth rate of 3.7%; for the United States and Japan, the figures are 45% and 51%, up by 4.0% and 1.9% annually. For developing countries quickly integrated into the global value chain, the participation rate is 52% and the average annual growth rate is 6.1%. East Asia and Southeast Asia enjoy the highest participation rate at 56%, up by 5.1% annually. The least-developed countries and South Asia have the highest average annual growth rates of 9.6% and 9.5%, respectively, but their starting points of participation are relatively low at 45 and 37%. Participation rate in transition economies is 52%, with an average annual increase of 8.0%. Major developing countries such as India, Brazil, Argentina and Turkey are relatively less involved. China's participation rate is 59%, ranking 11th among the world's top 25 exporters. With EU members and entrepot countries excluded, China ranks third in the world after Malaysia and South Korea in terms of participation in the global value chain.

1.4 The Double-Loop System of Global Value Based on the Global Value Chain Theory

According to the previous conclusion, despite the stagnation of trade development in developed economies, the participation of developing countries in the overall global division of labor is yet to improve, which means that the global value chain has manifested itself in a new form. The global economic structure has gradually shifted from the "center-periphery" single-loop model with developed countries as the core to a more complex double-loop system. On the one hand, emerging countries of Asia such as China have maintained traditional economic ties with developed countries in Europe and America, forming the upper loop of circulation within the value chain; on the other hand, with rapid economic growth, China and other countries have emerged as new industrialized powers and the global manufacturing centers—by cooperating with and investing directly in developing countries of Asia, Africa and Latin America, they have managed to boost local industrialization and foster local market through trade, which has helped establish the lower loop within the value chain. The "Belt and Road" Initiative, based on this new feature of the global value chain, puts more emphasis on the openness and inclusiveness of the development-oriented economic and social cooperation among countries.

From the perspective of the three major economies of the European Union, North America and East Asia, China's trade with the EU in 2002 totaled 118.5473 billion USD, exceeding that of Japan (110.7711 billion USD). After that, the gap between China and Japan in terms of trade with the EU widened further. As of 2014, China's trade with the EU was 4.3 times that of Japan. In 1991, China's total trade with North America (the United States and Canada) was only 18.7% of that of Japan, but in 2003, the figure reached 208.3917 billion USD, exceeding that of Japan (189.0308 billion USD) for the first time. After that, the difference between China and Japan in terms of trade with North America grew larger. As of 2015, China's trade with North America was 3.2 times that of Japan. In 2000, China's trade with seven Southeast Asian countries (Vietnam, Cambodia, Philippines, Thailand, Malaysia, Singapore and Indonesia) was only 27.9% of Japan's. In 2007, China registered 172.1821 billion USD of trade with the seven countries, surpassing Japan (172.1179 billion USD) for the first time. After that, the gap between China and Japan further widened. As of 2014, China's trade with the seven countries was 1.6 times that of Japan.

In recent years, international trade has increasingly taken the form of trade within the global value chain. Therefore, an analysis of the roles played by various countries within the global value chain would reveal the double-loop system of value circulation. Next, an analysis is conducted on the structure of export and import of intermediary products by various countries by referring to the Eora Input–Output Tables. 188 countries and regions in the world are included as samples.

(I) Export and import of final consumer goods in various economies of the world

1. Export of final consumer goods in various economies of the world

Chinese mainland is the major destination for the export of final consumer goods of most economies. Figure 1.10 illustrates Chinese mainland's shares and rankings in terms of receiving other countries' export of final consumer goods. Among the 188 countries and regions, 178 export to Chinese mainland 0.00–15.00% of their final consumer goods. Although most economies export less than 15.00% of final consumer goods to Chinese mainland, the latter is still structurally significant to their export. For 121 economies, China ranks among the top 15 destinations of final consumer goods export. For most of the 178 countries and regions, China ranks among the top 20. This proves Chinese mainland's status as the major destination of final consumer goods export for most economies in the world.

Table 1.17 lists the economies for which Chinese mainland ranks among the top 5 destinations of final consumer goods export. For 9 economies, Chinese mainland is the largest destination; for 11 economies, it ranks No.2; for 13 economies, it stands at No.3; for 15 economies, it ranks No.4; and for 12 economies, it stands at No.5. This covers 60 economies, or 1/3 out of the 188 sampled economies, which demonstrates Chinese mainland is an important export destination of final consumer goods for most economies.

2. Import of final consumer goods in various economies of the world

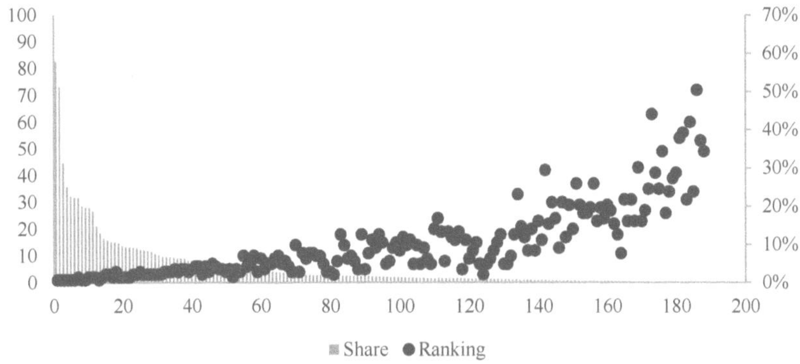

Fig. 1.10 China's shares and rankings in terms of receiving final consumer goods export from various economies

Table 1.17 Economies for which Chinese mainland ranks among the top five export destinations of final consumer goods (Chinese mainland as the importer)

Ranking	Quantity	Economies (share of export)
No.1	9	AGO (57.86%); MNG (51.15%); GAB (31.25%); MMR (25.01%); PRK (22.56%); CUB (22.26%); KOR (19.97%); HKG (19.65%); FIN (12.92%)
No.2	11	COG (22.15%); YEM (19.62%); OMN (18.66%); JPN (14.66%); LAO (11.46%); AUS (10.53%); KAZ (9.63%); CMR (9.29%); ISL (9.29%); NZL (9.19%); CAN (3.99%)
No.3	13	MYS (11.08%); MRT (10.66%); SGP (9.06%); CHE (8.50%); RUS (8.23%); VNM (8.15%); PAK (7.45%); SWE (7.20%); DEU (6.76%); THA (6.62%); URY (5.06%); LIE (1.76%); USR (0.79%)
No.4	15	IRQ (10.25%); IDN (8.46%); MAC (6.61%); PHL (6.54%); USA (6.33%); GRL (6.26%); PER (5.59%); TWN (4.70%); PNG (4.35%); ISR (3.29%); SDS (2.86%); MCO (2.11%); SMR (1.97%); ERI (1.85%); STP (1.84%)
No.5	12	IRN (6.31%); NOR (5.78%); ITA (5.71%); AUT (5.47%); LUX (4.62%); GBR (4.37%); LBR (4.31%); QAT (3.72%); RWA (2.74%); SRB (1.62%); DJI (1.59%); TJK (0.94%)

As to the import of final consumer goods, Chinese mainland is the largest source for most economies. Figure 1.11 depicts Chinese mainland's shares and rankings as the import source for various economies. Of the 188 economies covered, 168 import 0.00–15.00% of final consumer goods from Chinese mainland. For 182 economies, Chinese mainland ranks 0–15 as the import source. For all 188 economies, the rankings of Chinese mainland are no lower than No.25.

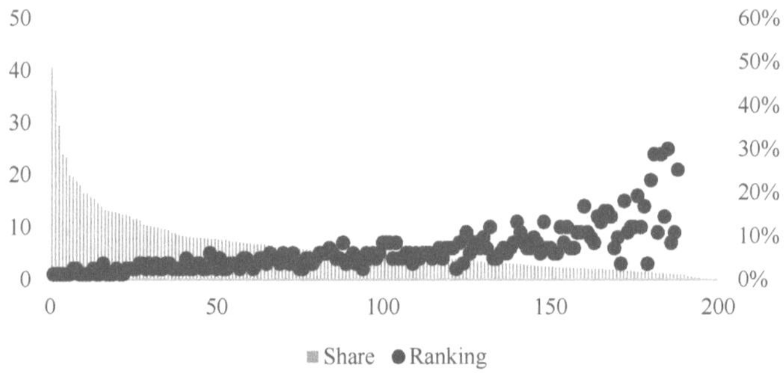

Fig. 1.11 Chinese mainland's shares and rankings as the import source of final consumer goods for various economies

Table 1.18 lists the economies for which Chinese mainland ranks among the top 5 import sources of final consumer goods. There are in total 123 economies (It ranks No.1 in 17 economies, No.2 in 29, No. 3 in 26, No.4 in 26 and No.5 in 25), nearly 2/3 of the 188 samples. For most economies, Chinese mainland is an essential import source of final consumer goods.

3. A comparison among various economies on the export to and import from chinese mainland (final consumer goods)

A comparison among different economies on their import from and export to Chinese mainland reveals that the Chinese mainland occupies a key position in the global export and import of final consumer goods—its role as the exporter is more prominent as all economies in the world take it as the main import source of final consumer goods. Tables 1.17 and 1.18 show 123 economies see Chinese mainland as one of their top five import sources of final consumer goods, while 60 considers Chinese mainland one of their top five export destinations. China's superiority as an exporter for other economies is consistent with the structural reality of its trade surplus.

(II) Export and import of intermediary products in various economies

1. Export of intermediary products in various economies

Chinese mainland is the main receiver of the export of intermediate products from various economies. Figure 1.12 shows the export of intermediate products from different economies. Among the 188 sample economies, there are 177 ones whose exports to Chinese mainland account for less than 15.00% of their total export of intermediate products. Angola registers the highest percentage—50.86% of its export of intermediate products flow to China, and the lowest proportion (0.01%) was achieved by Haiti. For 148 economies, Chinese mainland ranks among the top 15 destinations for their export of intermediate products. As globalization develops, each economy is facing more trade rivals and the diversification of trading partners. However, Chinese

Table 1.18 Economies for which Chinese mainland ranks among the top 5 import sources of final consumer goods (Chinese mainland as the exporter)

Ranking	Quantity	Economies (import share)
No.1	17	HKG (48.74%); MAC (43.37%); PRK (35.34%); MNG (28.72%); JPN (28.00%); PAK (23.93%); YEM (21.65%); KOR (19.82%); KHM (19.80%); NPL (18.99%); USA (17.49%); LSO (16.64%); JOR (15.81%); THA (15.51%); SYR (15.41%); NGA (14.91%); EGY (14.88%)
No.2	29	MDG (23.52%); BGD (22.58%); DJI (18.40%); IRQ (15.11%); AUS (14.63%); CUB (13.94%); GHA (13.91%); ARE (13.55%); PER (12.15%); SGP (11.96%); LBN (11.50%); IDN (11.34%); CAN (10.22%); IND (9.97%); LAO (9.86%); CIV (9.82%); SLE (9.53%); ZAF (9.49%); TTO (9.33%); COL (9.32%); SEN (9.03%); BEN (8.66%); NER (8.61%); CMR (8.31%); DEU (8.08%); MEX (6.67%); JAM (6.66%); ZWE (5.43%); MMR (4.15%)
No.3	26	PSE (15.86%); PRY (12.48%); ETH (12.40%); SUR (12.05%); VNM (11.71%); CHL (10.69%); SAU (10.60%); ARG (9.49%); NZL (9.40%); PYF (8.54%); MLI (8.37%); GIN (8.32%); RUS (8.13%); GMB (7.78%); IRN (7.30%); POL (7.21%); NLD (6.97%); URY (6.70%); ROU (6.48%); PNG (5.62%); KAZ (5.52%); CRI (5.45%); HTI (4.85%); AUT (4.00%); AM (1.56%); BWA (1.03%)
No.4	26	DZA (9.62%); MYS (9.03%); TZA (8.97%); MUS (8.16%); MAR (8.14%); KGZ (7.73%); GBR (7.41%); PHL (7.26%); AZE (7.22%); TUR (7.06%); ESP (6.56%); TGO (6.52%); SLV (6.29%); COD (5.75%); FIN (5.68%); CZE (5.58%); FJI (5.33%); BRB (5.26%); HUN (5.07%); SVK (5.00%); DOM (4.96%); VUT (4.81%); ERI (4.66%); MWI (4.63%); MOZ (3.53%); LBR (3.42%)
No.5	25	BOL (9.15%); QAT (7.29%); KWT (7.07%); CYP (6.90%); UKR (6.27%); BRA (6.26%); ECU (6.18%); ITA (5.75%); LTU (5.52%); NOR (5.42%); GUY (5.33%); BGR (5.23%); TUN (4.95%); GRC (4.95%); KEN (4.84%); MLT (4.77%); BDI (4.73%); TWN (4.70%); ALB (4.64%); ABW (3.89%); ZMB (3.37%); BLZ (3.14%); MDA (2.66%); USR (2.56%); LIE (2.51%)

mainland is still an important destination for intermediate product export from various economies.

Table 1.19 lists the economies where Chinese mainland ranks among the top 5 destinations for their export of intermediate products. There are in total 74 of them. For 9 economies, Chinese mainland ranks No.1; for 19, it stands at No.2; for 13, it is No.3; for 19, it stays at No.4; and for 15, the ranking is No.5.

2. Import of intermediate products in various economies

Figure 1.13 presents the proportions of different economies' intermediate product import that comes from Chinese mainland. In addition, it lists the rankings of Chinese mainland as the source of intermediate product import for various economies. For 183 economies, less than 15.00% of the intermediate product import comes from China. For 179 economies, China ranks among the top 15 sources of intermediate product import. For all economies, China is an essential source of such import.

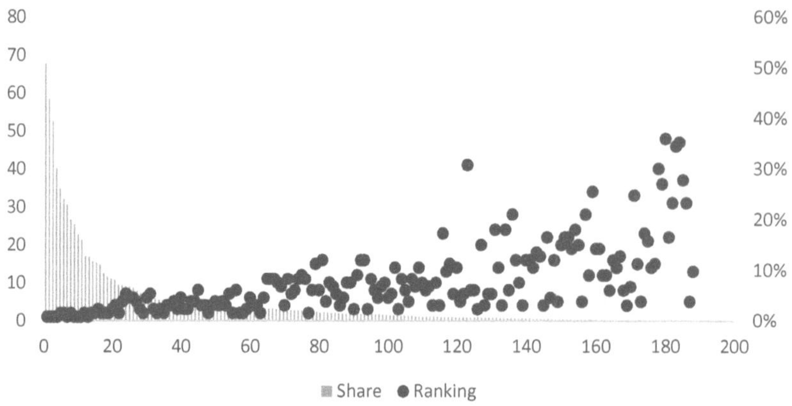

Fig. 1.12 The proportions of intermediate product export consumed by Chinese mainland and their rankings in various economies

Table 1.19 Economies where Chinese mainland ranks among the top 5 destinations for their export of intermediate products (Chinese mainland as the importer)

Ranking	Quantity	Economies (export share)
No.1	9	AGO (50.86%); COG (43.90%); YEM (39.46%); VNM (30.07%); ZMB (22.90%); SGP (19.04%); KHM (17.07%); RWA (15.98%); RUS (12.61%)
No.2	19	GAB (26.15%); HUN (24.09%); AUS (19.96%); BRA (12.75%); PAN (11.67%); MAR (11.44%); ZAF (9.28%); SDS (8.68%); OMN (8.18%); BOL (6.95%); CAN (4.77%); JOR (3.93%); TTO (3.51%); IRQ (2.91%); GHA (2.50%); CYP (2.39%); PNG (2.39%); POL (2.33%); MDG (1.61%)
No.3	13	CHL (11.06%); MDV (8.05%); AUT (4.90%); SMR (4.04%); FJI (3.89%); KEN (3.28%); STP (3.25%); LVA (3.22%); NER (2.38%); NPL (1.23%); IDN (1.16%); MKD (0.84%); THA (0.49%)
No.4	19	CMR (7.02%); SYR (3.43%); IRN (3.30%); SRB (3.14%); CPV (3.10%); SOM (2.78%); LAO (2.66%); CHE (2.55%); PER (2.35%); MDA (2.33%); BLR (1.95%); BTN (1.35%); USA (0.67%); URY (0.65%); COD (0.45%); NAM (0.41%); SLV (0.27%); MOZ (0.21%); LTU (0.08%)
No.5	14	EST (6.82%); PRT (5.36%); GMB (3.29%); ARG (3.21%); BRN (3.18%); MRT (2.72%); WSM (2.61%); JAM (1.43%); GRC (0.76%); MCO (0.58%); ANT (0.19%); MNE (0.14%); GEO (0.07%); SUR (0.01%)

Table 1.20 lists the economies where Chinese mainland ranks among their top five sources of intermediate product import. It shows 73 economies, more than 1/3 of the total, see Chinese mainland as their top five sources of import. Chinese mainland tops the list in two economies; stands at No.2 in 19 economies, No.3 in 17 economies, No.4 in 17 economies and No.5 in 18 economies. There is no doubt that Chinese mainland is a critical source of intermediate product import globally.

(III) A comparison of Chinese Mainland's dual status as the source and destination of the trade of final consumer goods and intermediate products

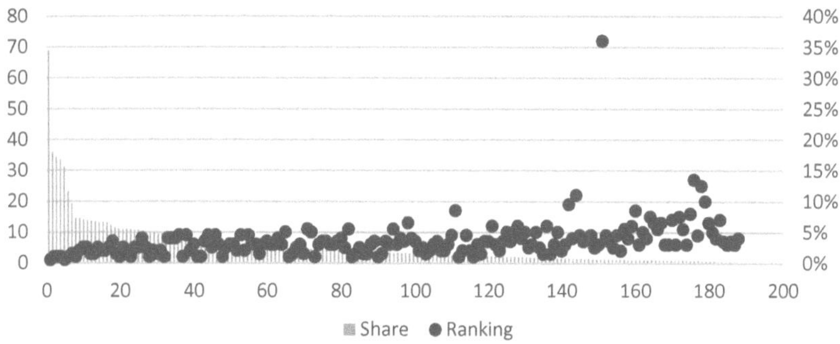

Fig. 1.13 The proportions of intermediate product import coming from China and their rankings in various economies

Table 1.20 Economies where Chinese mainland ranks among their top five sources of intermediate product import (Chinese mainland as the exporter)

Ranking	Quantity	Economy (import share)
No.1	2	HKG (34.48%); YEM (15.63%)
No.2	19	BGD (17.99%); VNM (17.23%); KHM (16.76%); AUS (11.56%); CAN (7.27%); BEN (5.53%); MAC (5.38%); MNG (4.82%); LSO (4.58%); ZWE (3.93%); THA (3.70%); KOR (3.68%); BDI (3.24%); NPL (2.32%); JPN (2.13%); PRK (1.79%); IRQ (1.65%); IND (1.15%); PAK (1.03%)
No.3	17	SGP (9.59%); SAU (6.82%); COL (6.74%); GMB (5.53%); SEN (5.43%); SLE (4.66%); MDG (2.55%); MEX (2.26%); JOR (2.19%); IDN (1.78%); DJI (1.72%); CUB (1.72%); ARE (1.64%); GHA (1.31%); USA (1.00%); CIV (0.74%); LAO (0.74%)
No.4	17	ZAF (7.26%); ARG (6.60%); BRA (6.57%); MUS (4.69%); MYS (4.64%); BTN (3.75%); PSE (2.89%); NGA (2.83%); SUR (1.34%); POL (1.30%); EGY (1.27%); SYR (1.24%); NZL (1.13%); IRN (1.03%); PRY (0.94%); MLI (0.65%); KAZ (0.46%)
No.5	18	ETH (7.04%); DZA (6.86%); BOL (6.64%); CHL (6.15%); RUS (5.52%); CMR (5.36%); PYF (5.11%); ROU (4.91%); CRI (3.31%); HUN (3.14%); LBN (2.25%); KGZ (1.84%); DEU (1.75%); GIN (1.33%); URY (0.80%); FJI (0.76%); MWI (0.54%); PNG (0.48%)

Overall, Chinese mainland occupies a key position in global trade both as the source and destination of intermediate products and final consumer goods. As a big trading power, China stands at the center of the double-loop system, which is solidly founded on the enormous size and expansive networks of its trade (Table 1.21).

(IV) The empirical data verification of the "double-loop model of global value chain"

In this part, the sources of data are the database of the World Bank and the multi region input–output table (MRIO) of the EORA global supply-chain database. The goods of global trade activities are categorized into intermediate goods and final

Table 1.21 Summary of Chinese mainland's rankings as the sources and destinations of the trade of intermediate products and final consumer goods

Ranking	Chinese mainland as			
	The importer of intermediate products	The exporter of intermediate products	The source of final consumer goods	The destination of final consumer goods
No.1	9	2	9	17
No.2	19	19	11	29
No.3	13	17	13	26
No.4	19	17	15	26
No.5	14	18	12	25
Total	74	73	60	123

consumer goods according to their uses. Intermediate goods refer to products for resale or used in the production of other goods, including raw materials, fuel, etc. Final consumer goods stand for products made during a certain period which are ultimately consumed and used rather than used in the production of another good.

From the Chinese perspective, the indicators could be divided into China's import/export of intermediate products, China's import/export of final consumer goods, export/import of intermediate goods to/from China, and export/import of final consumer goods to/from China.

1. Verification methods

Compared with the past, the manifestation of the global value chain has shown new characteristics. The world economic structure has gradually changed from the "central-peripheral" single-loop model centered around developed countries to a more complex double-loop model. On the one hand, emerging countries of Asia such as China have maintained traditional economic relations with developed countries in Europe and America, forming the upper loop in the value chain. On the other hand, with the rapid economic growth, China and other countries have emerged as newly industrialized regions and global manufacturing centers, and their economic cooperation with developing countries of Asia, Africa and Latin America, which are rich in resources and relatively low in industrialization, drives the industrialization of various countries through direct investment, extends local markets through trade and forms the lower loop in the value chain.

Two perspectives are adopted to verify the double-loop model with data. Explanations could be made from two different perspectives, complementing and verifying each other.

(1) Double-loop model I

From the Chinese perspective, world trade flows in the following direction: China imports intermediate goods from developing countries and then sells them final consumer goods. The trade between China and developed countries follows a similar

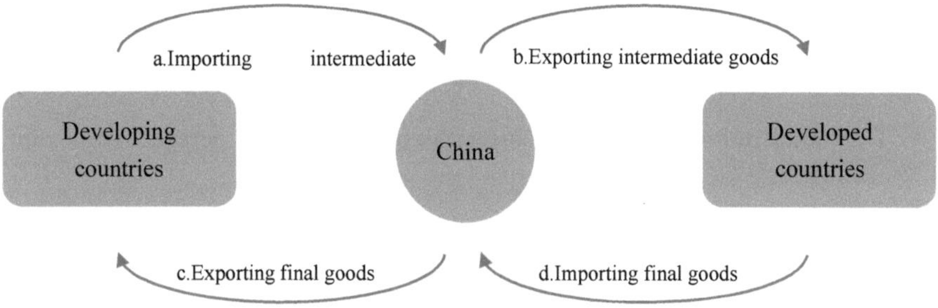

Fig. 1.14 The double-loop model diagram from the Chinese perspective

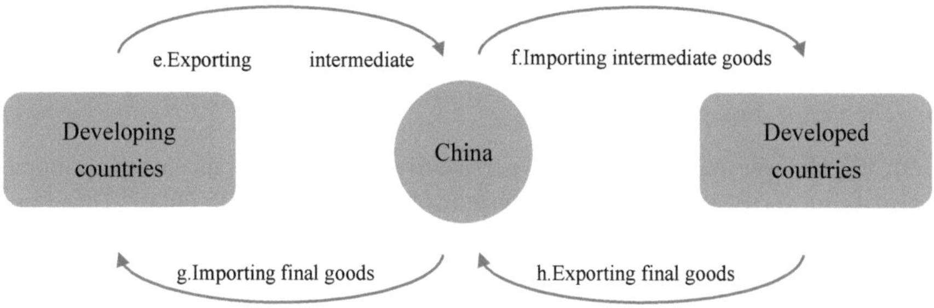

Fig. 1.15 The double-loop model diagram from the perspective of other countries

but reverse pattern. As Fig. 1.14 illustrates, China serves as the pivot of global trade flows during this process.

(2) Double-loop model II

From the global perspective (of other countries), trade flows have the following features: developing economies are net exporters of intermediate goods for China and net importers of its final consumer goods. A similar loop exists between China and developed countries, as shown by Fig. 1.15. Likewise, China is still the pivot of trade flows.

In the following section, data analysis and verification will be conducted for every resource flow direction (a–h) within the double-loop models based on different perspectives.

2. Definitions of the ratios

This chapter builds four indicators to verify the double-loop model at the data level. The four indicators are listed below.

(1) Two ratios, C_1 and C_2, are established from the Chinese perspective

$$C_1 = \frac{\text{intermediate goods imported by China}}{\text{intermediate goods exported by China}};$$

$$C_2 = \frac{\text{final consumer goods imported by China}}{\text{final consumer goods exported by China}}$$

(2) Two other ratios, W_1 and W_2, are established from the perspective of other economies.

$$W_1 = \frac{\text{intermediate goods exported to China}}{\text{final consumer goods exported to China}};$$

$$W_2 = \frac{\text{intermediate goods imported from China}}{\text{final consumer goods imported from China}}$$

Following is the verification process based on the above ratios which derive from the empirical global trade data of 189 countries and regions.

3. The verification process

Both the Chinese and non-Chinese perspectives are adopted in gathering empirical data to verify the double-loop system of the global value chain. These two methods, similar in internal logic and different in the perspective of measuring, could corroborate each other.

(1) From the Chinese perspective

This section makes a statistical analysis of international trade data from a Chinese perspective. First, it analyzes China's "import and export of intermediate goods" relative to other economies. In order to better characterize the flow direction of China's "import and export of intermediate goods" from and to each country, this chapter constructs C_1 as a measuring indicator. If it is greater than 1, China is a net importer of that country's intermediate goods; if it is smaller than 1, China is then a net exporter. Figure 1.16 shows the calculation results of C_1. Along the horizontal axis, countries arc ranked in order of per capita GDP (the World Bank database, 2013), from high to low. Therefore, more developed countries are positioned on the left side of the axis, while the developing ones are mostly on the right. This also applies to the horizontal axes of Figs. 1.17, 1.18 and 1.19, and no more explanation will be given to avoid repetition.

Figure 1.16 has two visible features. First, countries at the right side of the horizontal axis are more likely to have a ratio larger than 1 ($y = 1$ as the baseline), which means for developing countries (at the right side of the horizontal axis), China is a net importer of their intermediate goods, proving correct arrow a—the trade of intermediate goods between developing countries and China is characterized by the net inflows to China.

Then it is apparent that countries at the left side of the horizontal axis are more likely to have a ratio smaller than 1, which means for developed countries (at the left side of the horizontal axis), China is a net exporter of intermediate goods, verifying arrow b in Fig. 1.14—the trade of intermediate goods between China and developed countries is dominated by inflows to developed countries.

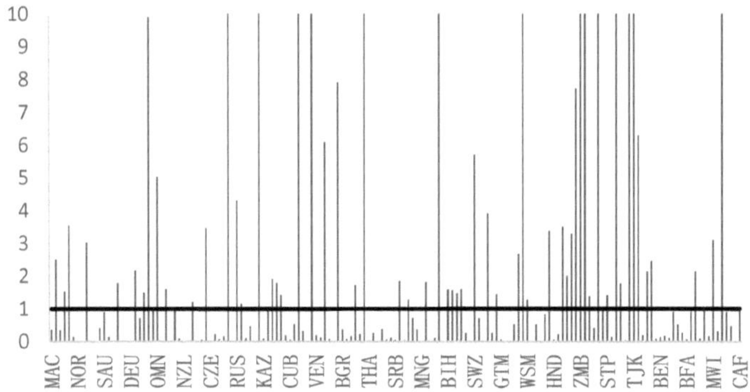

Fig. 1.16 The ratio of China's import to export of intermediate goods

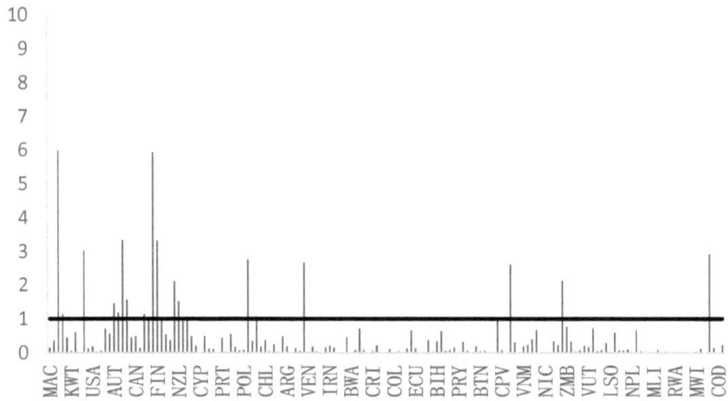

Fig. 1.17 The ratio of China's import to export of final consumer goods

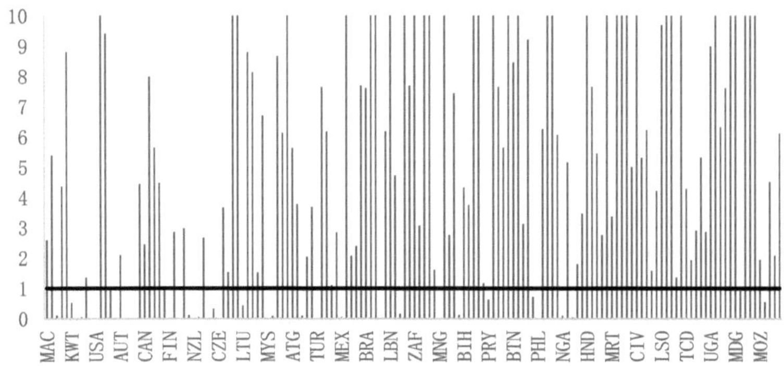

Fig. 1.18 The ratio of intermediate goods to final consumer goods exported to China

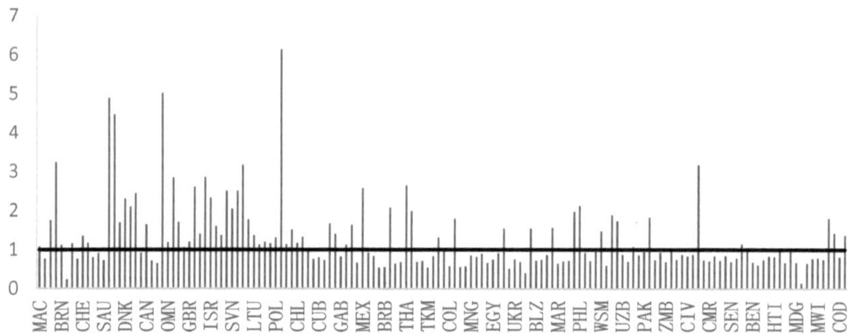

Fig. 1.19 The ratio of intermediate goods to final consumer goods imported from China

Next is the analysis of the trade of final consumer goods between China and other economies. Similarly, to visualize the direction of the trade flows, this chapter constructs the indicator C_2. If C_2 is larger than 1, then China is a net importer; if C_2 is smaller than 1, then China is a net exporter. Figure 1.17 shows the C_2 values of various economies.

Likewise, Fig. 1.17 has two visible features. First, countries at the left side of the horizontal axis are more likely to have a C_2 larger than 1 ($y = 1$ as the baseline), which means for developed countries (at the left end of the horizontal axis), China is a net importer of final consumer goods, proving correct arrow d in Fig. 1.14—the trade of final consumer goods between developed countries and China is characterized by net inflow to China.

It is also easy to find out that countries at the right end of horizontal axis are more likely to fall below the baseline $y = 1$. Therefore, for developing countries (at the right end of horizontal axis), China is a net exporter of final consumer goods, verifying arrow c in Fig. 1.14—the trade of final consumer goods between China and developing countries could be summarized as net inflow to the latter.

The analysis of the two bar charts from four angles proves correct arrow a to arrow d in Fig. 1.14, thus statistically verifying the "double-loop model of global value chain" based on the Chinese perspective.

(2) From the perspectives of other economies

Parallel to the previous section, this section collects statistics on international trade from the perspective of other economies in the world. First, the proportional relationship between "intermediate goods exported to China" and "final consumer goods exported to China" is analyzed. In order to better estimate the net flow direction and relationship of intermediate goods or final consumer goods, this chapter constructs the indicator W_1. If W_1 is greater than 1, that economy is a net exporter of intermediate goods for China; if it is smaller than 1, the economy is a net exporter of final consumer goods for China. Figure 1.18 is a statistical chart of W_1.

Two trends are visible in Fig. 1.18. First, countries at the right end of horizontal axis are more likely to have a ratio larger than 1 ($y = 1$ as the baseline), which means the majority of developing countries (at the right end of horizontal axis) are net exporters of intermediate goods for China, verifying arrow e in Fig. 1.15—the trade of intermediate goods between China and developing countries is dominated by net outflows from the latter.

Besides, countries at the left end of horizontal axis are more likely to have a ratio smaller than 1, which means the majority of developed countries (at the left end of horizontal axis) are net exporters of final consumer goods for China, proving correct arrow h in Fig. 1.15—the trade of final consumer goods between China and developed countries could be summarized as net outflows from the latter.

Then the proportional relation between "intermediate goods imported from China" and "final consumer goods imported from China" is discussed. To better estimate the net flow directions of and relation between intermediate goods and final consumer goods, this chapter establishes the indicator W_2. If W_2 is larger than 1, then that economy is a net importer of intermediate goods for China; if the ratio is smaller than 1, then the economy is a net importer of final consumer goods for China. Figure 1.19 shows the W_2 values of various economies.

Similarly, two patterns are visible in the above chart. First, countries at the left end of horizontal axis are more likely to have a ratio larger than 1 ($y = 1$ as the baseline), which means developed countries are probably net importers of intermediate goods made in China, verifying arrow f in Fig. 1.15—for these developed economies, trade with China is dominated by inflows of intermediate goods.

In addition, countries at the right end of horizontal axis are more likely to have a ratio smaller than 1, which means developing countries are probably net importers of final consumer goods for China, verifying arrow g in Fig. 1.15—for developing countries, trade with China could be summarized as net inflows of final consumer goods.

Therefore, similar to the previous section's discussion from the Chinese perspective, this section carries out the analysis from the perspectives of other economies in the world. The analysis of the two bar charts from four angles proves that arrow e to arrow h in Fig. 1.15 are reasonable, thus statistically verifying the "double-loop model of global value chain" from the perspectives of other economies.

(3) Summary

This chapter verifies the double-loop model of global value chain with empirical data. The discussion of the model's applicability of real data is broken down to two perspectives, four indicators and eight directions of trade flows. According to this model, China, on the one hand, has established with developed countries a loop of circulation based on international division of labor, trade, investment and indirect capital flows; on the other hand, it has formed another loop with developing countries of Asia, Africa and Latin America based on trade and direct investment. The empirical data also supports the model's conclusion that China is the pivot of the global trade system.

(V) Trade structure analysis of the double-loop model

Table 1.22 Categorization of the industries listed in the input–output table

Categorization of industries	Sub-industries included
The primary industry	Agriculture and fishery
The secondary industry_light industry	Food and beverage, textile, and lumbering and paper-making
The secondary industry_heavy industry	Other sectors of the secondary industry (steel and power sectors, etc.)
The tertiary industry	Retailing, hotels, tourism, etc

In the previous section, the double-loop theory is raised based on observations of the changes of global trade mode in recent years. In addition, the theory is verified with trade data (source of data: MRIO of EORA). According to the double-loop model, on the one hand, China and developed countries have formed a loop of merchandise trade in which China mainly exports intermediate products and imports final consumer goods; on the other hand, China has established with developing economies a loop in which China mainly sells final consumer goods and buys intermediate goods.

The double-loop theory is in fact the reflection of international labor division in trade data. Different economies, with diversified endowments, occupy different positions in the global value chain. Developed economies, with endowments such as core technologies and intellectual properties, stand on the top of the chain; developing ones, with cheap labor and abundant natural resources, settle for a place at the end of the chain. After 30 years of reform and opening up, Chinese economy, with its demographic dividend, complete industrial system and accumulating technological advantages, has gained a middle position along the global value chain—it imports from other developing countries primary products for further processing and then sell them to developed economies which turn them into high-end final consumer goods.

Further breaking down the trade data for further analysis could help reveal the global value chain hidden behind the double loop existing between China and developing/developed countries.

1. Method of the trade structure analysis

In our theory, the double-loop model reflects the reality that countries occupy different positions in the global value chain due to their different endowments. A look into the trade structure (categorizing trade data according to the degree of demand for natural resources, labor force, capital and technology) could validate this view.

The 26 industries listed in the Eora MRIO are divided into four sub-classes, as listed in Table 1.22.

This chapter chooses to focus on the features of the trade data of the primary and secondary industries since the products of the tertiary industry lack clear definition. From the top to bottom of Table 1.22, the reliance on capital and technology grows.

Following the method applied in the previous section, we break down trade into three categories: the primary industry and the secondary industry (light industry/heavy industry). Each category is analyzed for its trade status from the perspectives of China and other economies, thus validating the double-loop model.

$$C_1 = \frac{\text{intermediate goods imported by China}}{\text{intermediate goods exported by China}};$$

$$C_2 = \frac{\text{final consumer goods imported by China}}{\text{final consumer goods exported by China}}$$

C stands for the comparative advantage of China over a trade partner in terms of a certain commodity. If C is larger than 1, then China is a net importer of intermediate products; if it is smaller than 1, then China is a net exporter of intermediate products.

$$W_1 = \frac{\text{intermediate goods exported to China}}{\text{final consumer goods exported to China}};$$

$$W_2 = \frac{\text{intermediate goods imported from China}}{\text{final consumer goods imported from China}}$$

W implies the dominant commodity of a country's export to/import from China. If W is larger than 1, that country is a net exporter of intermediate goods to China; if it is smaller than 1, then the country is a net exporter of final consumer goods.

2. Trade structure analysis of the double-loop system

(1) The primary industry

The primary industry, also known as the first industry, is an industry involved in the extraction and collection of natural resources (e.g., local natural resources, and agricultural and fishery products which are labor intensive) and has lower demand for technology.

Following is the analysis of the trade status of the three industries based on the method employed in the previous section. Countries are ranked from left to right along the horizontal axis in order of per capita GDP from high to low (World Bank database, 2013), which means developed countries are at the left end, and developing ones are mostly at the right end. This also applies to the horizontal axes of rest figures in this chapter, and no more explanation will be given to avoid repetition.

A. From the Chinese perspective

A comparison is made between the intermediate goods and final consumer goods of the primary industry imported and exported by China. Figures 1.20 and 1.21 show two patterns. If the ratio is around 1 ($y = 1$ as the baseline), the country enjoys balanced trade with China in terms of that category of commodities. It is not difficult to find that countries on the right are more likely to have a ratio greater than 1 for both intermediate goods and final consumer goods, which means for developing countries (at the right end of the horizontal axis), China is a net importer of both categories of commodities. Or, other developing countries enjoy trade surplus with China in these

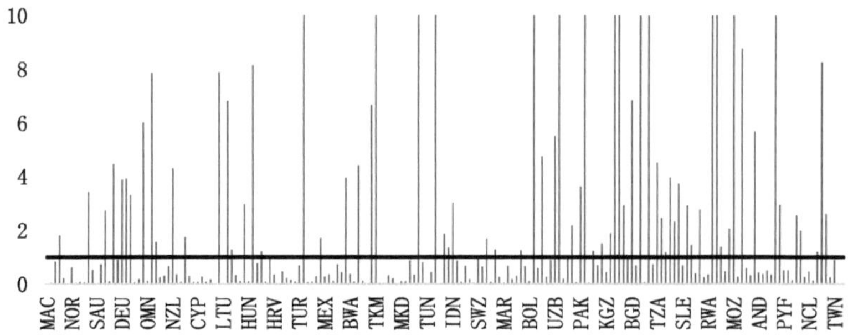

Fig. 1.20 The ratio of Chinese import to export of intermediate goods (the primary industry)

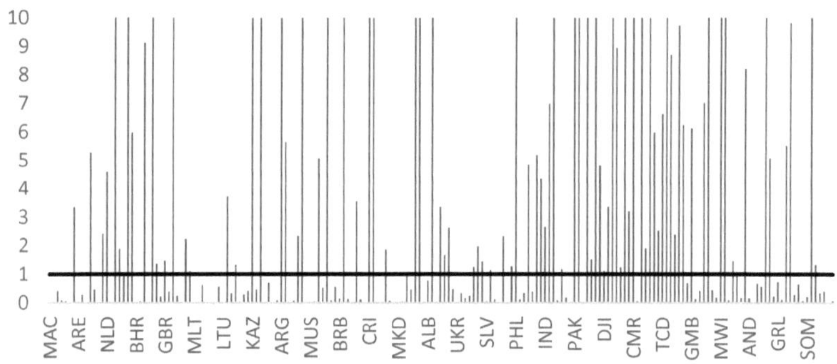

Fig. 1.21 The ratio of Chinese import to export of final consumer goods (the primary industry)

two categories. However, for the trade of the primary industry products between China and developed countries, China has advantage as the net exporter.

B. From the perspective of other economies

By analyzing the composition of the trade flow into China (the proportional relation between intermediate goods and final consumer goods), we have identified the dominant commodity (intermediate goods or final consumer goods) of the trade between China and other economies. Figures 1.22 and 1.23 show two patterns. If the ratio of one country is around 1 (y = 1 as the baseline), then intermediate goods and final consumer goods go fifty-fifty in its trade with China. According to Fig. 1.22, for export to China from both developing and developed economies, intermediate goods and final consumer goods take similar shares. However, in Fig. 1.23, countries at the right end of the horizontal axis are more likely to have a ratio larger than 1, which means developing countries (at the right end of the horizontal axis) are probably net importers of Chinese final consumer goods.

Therefore, in the trade of the primary industry, China widely imports primary products from other economies, and both developed and developing countries are

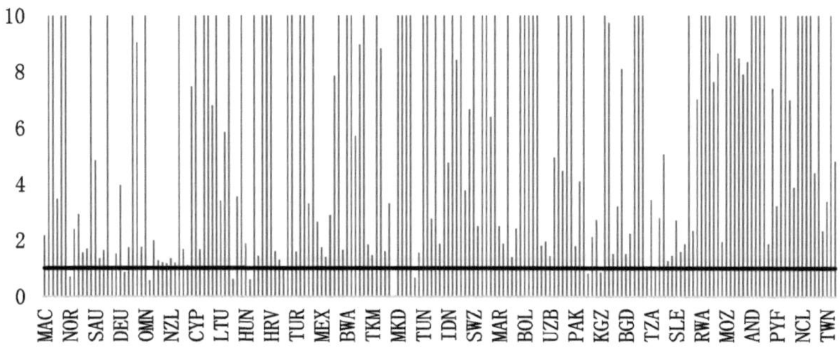

Fig. 1.22 The ratio of intermediate goods to final consumer goods exported to China (the primary industry)

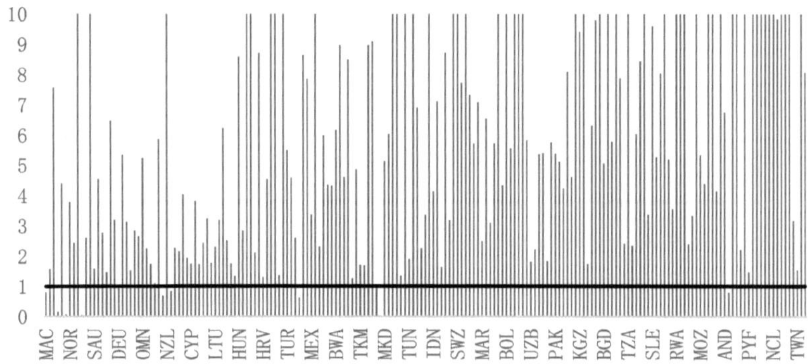

Fig. 1.23 The ratio of intermediate goods to final consumer goods imported from China (the primary industry)

China's sources of intermediate goods of the primary industry; meanwhile, developing economies are the major destination for China's final consumer goods of the primary industry.

(2) Light industry

A. From the Chinese perspective

Following is an analysis of the composition of China's trade of light industrial goods. Two trends are visible in Figs. 1.24 and 1.25. If the ratio of one country is around 1 (y = 1 as the baseline), then its trade with China in that specific category of commodities is balanced. It is not difficult to find that whether it is intermediate goods or final consumer goods and whether the other side is a developed or developing country, China always has the upper hand in the field of light industry. For intermediate goods of the light industry, only 21.2% of all countries enjoy a trade surplus with China; for final consumer goods, this proportion dropped to 8.4%. Therefore, it can be concluded that China is a true "world factory" in the field of light industry.

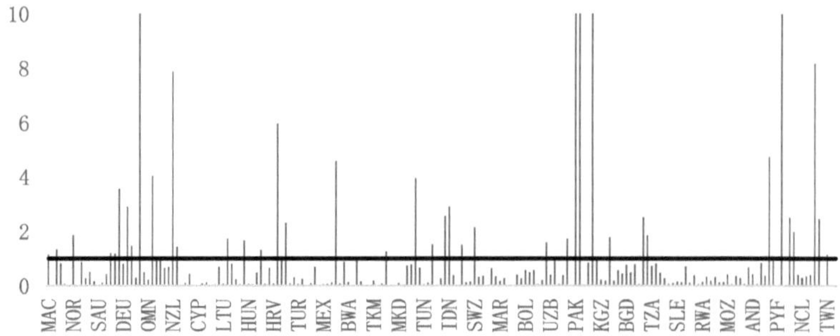

Fig. 1.24 The ratio of import to export of intermediate goods by China (light industry)

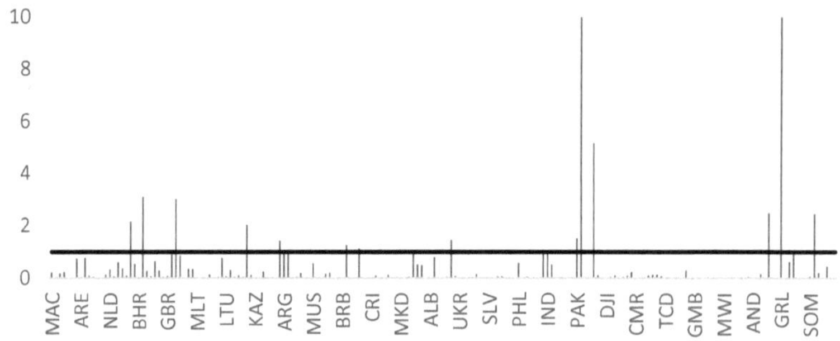

Fig. 1.25 The ratio of import to export of final consumer goods by China (light industry)

B. From the perspectives of other economies

By analyzing the composition of the trade flow into China (the proportional relation between intermediate goods and final consumer goods), we have identified the dominant commodity (intermediate goods or final consumer goods) of the trade between China and other economies. Figures 1.26 and 1.27 generally show two patterns. If the ratio of one country is around 1 (y = 1 as the baseline), then intermediate goods and final consumer goods go fifty-fifty in its trade with China. According to Fig. 1.26, other economies mainly exported intermediate goods of light industry to China. Generally, 88.4% of sample economies mainly export intermediate goods. In Fig. 1.26, countries on the right end of the horizontal axis are more likely to have a ratio larger than 1, which means more developing countries (at the right end of the horizontal axis), compared to developed ones, are net exporters of intermediate goods to China.

In Fig. 1.27, 72.5% of sample economies mainly import final consumer goods. Samples on the left end of the horizontal axis are more likely to have a ratio larger than 1. Therefore, developing countries are probably net importers of Chinese final consumer goods.

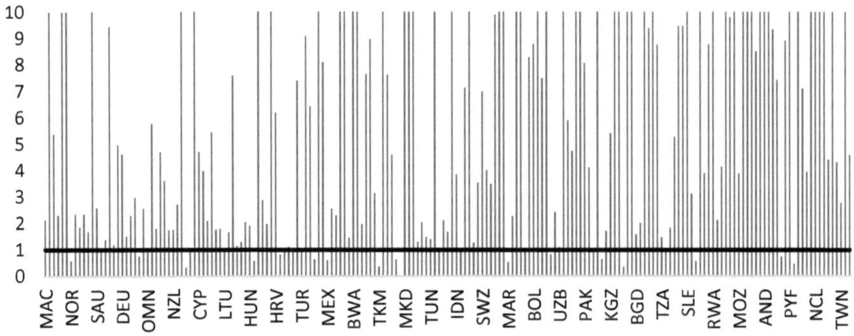

Fig. 1.26 The ratio of intermediate goods to final consumer goods exported to China (light industry)

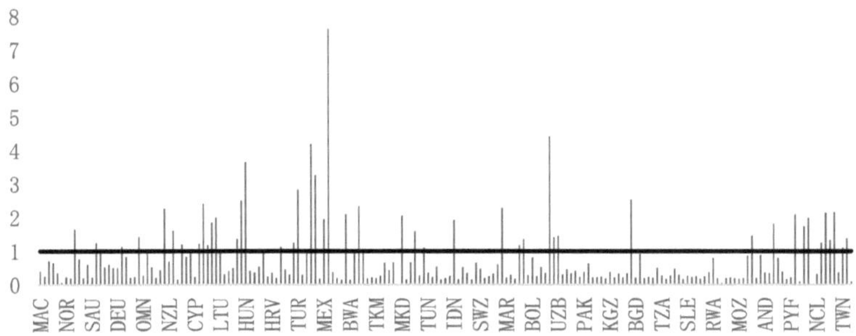

Fig. 1.27 The ratio of intermediate goods to final consumer goods imported from China (light industry)

To conclude, from the perspectives of other economies, developing countries mainly export to light industrial intermediate goods to China; and the final consumer goods of Chinese light industry are mostly exported to developing countries.

(3) Heavy industry

A. From the Chinese perspective

A comparison is made between the intermediate goods and final consumer goods of the heavy industry imported and exported by China. According to Figs. 1.28 and 1.29, China could also be characterized as the world factory in terms of the heavy industrial trade, just as for the light industrial trade. If the ratio of one country is around 1 ($y = 1$ as the baseline), the country enjoys balanced trade with China in terms of that category of commodities. It is not difficult to find that whether it is intermediate goods or final consumer goods and whether the other side is a developed or developing country, China has the upper hand in the field of heavy industry, too. For intermediate goods of the heavy industry, only 35.9% of all countries enjoy a trade surplus with China; for final consumer goods, this proportion dropped to 12.7%. Therefore, it can be concluded that China has huge competitive edge in the field of heavy industry.

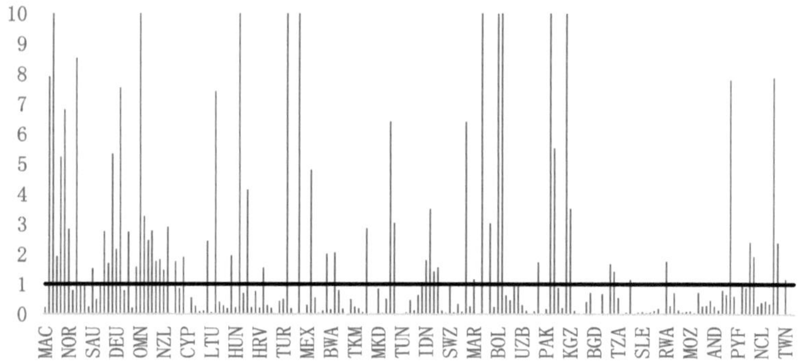

Fig. 1.28 The ratio of import to export of intermediate goods by China (heavy industry)

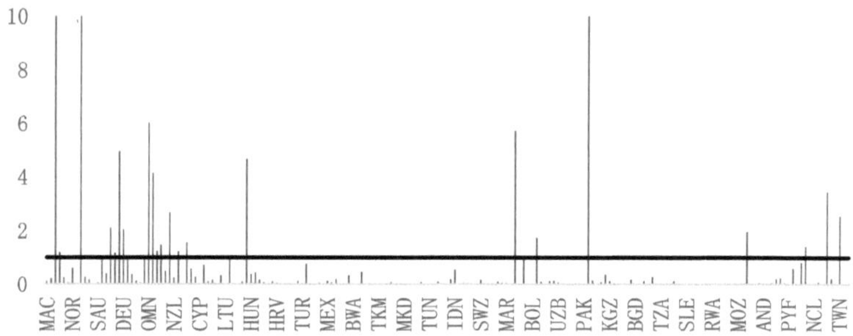

Fig. 1.29 The ratio of import to export of final consumer goods by China (heavy industry)

In Fig. 1.29, among the most developed countries (at the far left end of the horizontal axis), many are maintaining trade surplus with China in the field of heavy industry. As the heavy industrial trade is heavily reliant on technology and capital, more developed economies, compared to developing ones, are net exporters of final consumer goods to China, which also helps validate the double-loop model from the perspective of trade structure.

B. From the perspective of other economies

By analyzing the composition of the trade flow into China (the proportional relation between intermediate goods and final consumer goods), we have identified the dominant commodity (intermediate goods or final consumer goods) of the trade between China and other economies. Figures 1.30 and 1.31 generally show two patterns. If the ratio of one country is around 1 (y = 1 as the baseline), then intermediate goods and final consumer goods go fifty-fifty in its trade with China. According to Fig. 1.30, other economies mainly exported intermediate goods of heavy industry to China. Generally, 97.9% of the sample economies mainly export intermediate goods, which means China imports intermediate goods of heavy industry from all around the globe.

In Fig. 1.31, 64.6% of the sample economies mainly import final consumer goods. Countries at the left end of the horizontal axis are more likely to have a ratio larger

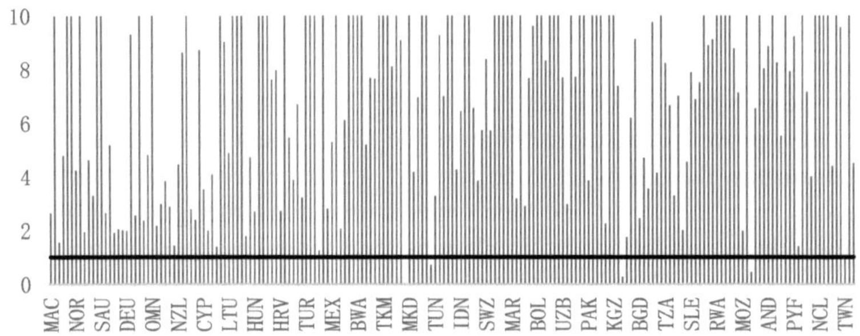

Fig. 1.30 The ratio of intermediate goods to final consumer goods imported by China (heavy industry)

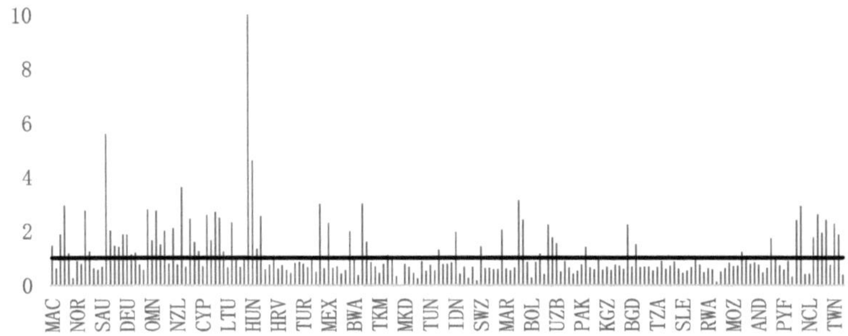

Fig. 1.31 The ratio of intermediate goods to final consumer goods imported from China (heavy industry)

than 1, which means developing countries (at the right end of the horizontal axis) are probably net importers of Chinese final consumer goods.

Therefore, in the trade of heavy industrial products, developing countries, compared to developed ones, are more likely to mainly import from China final consumer goods instead of intermediate goods.

3. Summary

According to the degree of dependence on capital and technology, this section divided the global trade data into three categories: the primary industry, and the light and heavy industries of the secondary industry. China enjoys comparative advantage in the trade of light industry with huge trade surplus. As to the intermediate goods of the light industry, only 21.2% of sample economies record trade surplus with China; for final consumer goods, this percentage falls to 8.4%. China's extensive export of intermediate goods and final consumer goods highlights its enormous competitive edge in the trade of labor-intensive products. In addition, China also maintains advantage in the commodity trade of technology-and-capital-intensive heavy industry. As to the intermediate goods of heavy industry, only 35.9% of the sample economies enjoy trade surplus with China; for the final consumer goods, the figure is as low as 12.7%.

In the commodity trade of the primary industry, China displays no overwhelming predominance.

From the perspectives of other economies, China's trade data in the secondary industry fully prove the existence of the double-loop system. Both the light and heavy industries display the following trade patterns—China extensively imports intermediate goods from the world and then exports final consumer goods to developing economies, thus completing the circulations represented by arrow e and arrow g in the previous section. Compared to developing countries, developed ones are more likely to buy intermediate goods from China and then sell it final consumer goods, which fulfills the circulations of arrow f and arrow h. China displays no such trade pattern in the less technologically demanding primary industry.

(VI) The double-loop system of the global value chain and "the Belt and Road"

Under the original global governance system, according to the theory of global value chain, many developing countries participated in the global value chain through OEM, which is regarded as an effective strategy for them to realize industrialization. However, this path of development, based on the OEM system of the global value chain, could only help them achieve entry-level industrialization. Many developing countries are "captured" when promoting further industrialization (Schmitz 2004). After participating in the global value chain, developing countries could upgrade their technological processes and products, but the upgrading and development of industrial functions and value chains would be severely hindered by buyers from developed countries or suppliers of large multinational companies, which would make further upgrade and growth impossible. As a result, developing countries would be stuck in the low end of the value chain—the low value-added manufacturing sector.

According to UNCTAD's *World Investment Report: Investment and Trade for Development*, developed economies, compared with developing countries, benefit more from the global value chain. According to UNCTAD statistics, in terms of the relative proportion of trade in value-added (the ratio of a country's global share of trade in value-added to its share of global export), countries such as Russia (1.25), India (1.23), United States (1.22), Australia (1.20), Brazil (1.20), Saudi Arabia (1.18), Japan (1.13) and Italy (1.00) have a ratio greater than 1, while China's ratio is 0.98. At the same time, in terms of the domestic value-added ratio (domestic value-added/GDP, measuring the contribution of a country's trade to its economic growth), the global domestic value-added ratio is 72% after the foreign value-added part of exports is deducted, and developed economies enjoy higher ratios—89% for the United States and 82% for Japan. Generally speaking, major economies have longer domestic value chains, less dependence on foreign investment and thus higher domestic value-added ratio, with the exception of China, Germany and the United Kingdom. China has both an ever-expanding domestic supply chain and a large amount of processing trade. Its domestic value-added ratio is only 70%.

In developing economies, a large portion of the value-added of the global value chains is created by subsidiaries of multinational companies, which may lead to relatively low "value capture". In the long run, global value chains may provide an important way for developing countries to build productive capacity, including creating opportunities for industrial upgrading through technology transfer and skill development. However, the potential long-term development benefits of the global value chain are not automatically obtained. To a certain extent, within the current system of international labor division, developing countries participating in the global value chain tend to rely excessively on a narrow technological foundation and to join the value chain coordinated by multinational companies (of developed economies). Therefore, they can only obtain limited added value and it has been difficult for them to achieve industrial upgrade.

In short, within the current labor division system, most developing economies are stuck in the middle and lower reaches of the global value chain, and many poorer developing countries, exporting natural resources, are trapped in the bottom of the chain. Developing countries have joined globalization mainly by exporting resources, raw materials and intermediate goods. Most developing countries lack a sound industrial foundation due to historical reasons or different resource endowments, which means it is difficult for them to achieve industrial upgrade within the existing international system of labor division, enter the upstream of the global value chain, and accelerate their domestic economic growth. Therefore, how to establish a fairer system of labor division that could benefit countries at all stages of development fairly and reasonably and promote balanced and coordinated development of all economies has become a burning issue of the international community.

During the bottleneck period of the globalization process, emerging developing countries represented by China has stood out, and the world economic cycle have evolved from the traditional "center-periphery" single-loop system to a double-loop system with China as the pivot. As Fig. 1.32 presents, one loop is between China and developed countries or regions, and the other is between China and other developing economies or regions in Asia, Africa and Latin America. On the one hand, China has formed with developed countries a loop of circulation with industrial division of labor, trade, investment, and indirect capital flow as carriers. On the other hand, China has formed with developing countries of Asia, Africa and Latin America another loop based on trade and direct investment.

Along the global value chain, as analyzed above, developing economies are at the low end, and their intermediate goods could not reach the technical standards to meet the demand of fragmented production due to the rapid technological progress in developed countries, leading to lower direct participation in the value chain curve C, shrinking space for industrial upgrade, stagnating value-added created by exports and a decline in the overall social welfare. Within the double-loop system, the two parts of the world economic circulation may form their internal systems of labor division, respectively, namely value chain curve A of the upper loop and curve B of the lower loop. Developing countries, especially the least-developed ones at the bottom, could participate in the fragmented production to a certain degree through the internal labor division within the lower loop and gradually obtain greater benefits and added value in the process of globalization through industrial upgrade at curve B. As the largest developing country in East Asia and the world, China has an industrial structure that is an integral part of the international system of labor division despite its relative independence and integrity. The conditions of natural and human resources

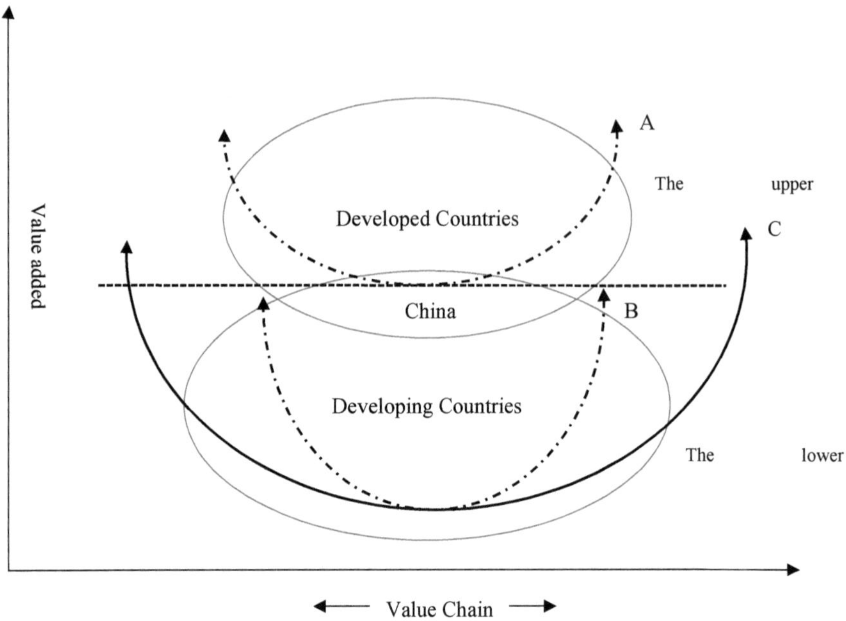

Fig. 1.32 The double-loop system of the global value chain and the value chain curves

vary greatly around China, leading to the regional imbalance in the development of productivity and thus diversified industrial structure. At the same time, while participating in the international division of labor, China has fully absorbed technology and capital from all over the world and comprehensively improved its own industrial structure, which has granted it with the most complete industrial structure in East Asia. Under this complete industrial structure, China not only has labor-and-capital-intensive industries under the vertical system of labor division, but also has modern technology industries under the horizontal system. Therefore, China could develop both the vertical and horizontal labor division relations. Therefore, China has high participation in both the loops, that is, it is deeply involved in the production links on curve A and curve B at the same time. Within the upper loop, as its industrial production has reached the level to participate in the labor division of the technology-and-knowledge-intensive industries, China, on curve A, provides high value-added industries in developed countries with intermediate products and services of relatively high added value. Countries of the lower loop (on curve B) are indirectly involved in the production of the upper loop (curve A) through China, thus returning to the international labor division system of curve C (the global value chain).

From the perspective of economic cooperation, within the upper loop, developed countries transfer most of their manufacturing, production services, etc., to emerging developing countries represented by China through the export of production factors such as capital and technology. Emerging developed countries, by exporting high-end intermediate products and production services, boost their own economic growths

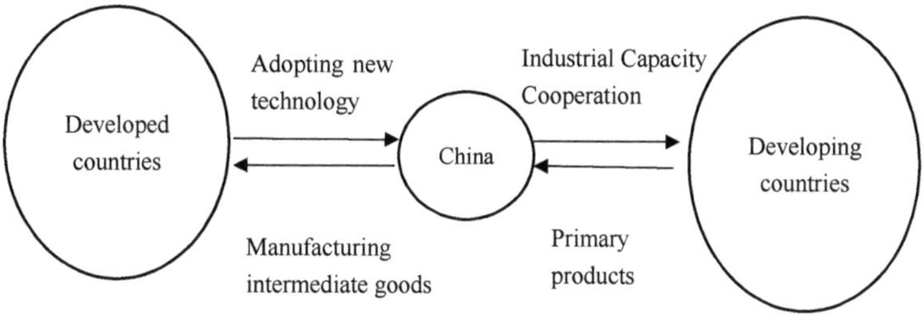

Fig. 1.33 Mode of economic cooperation within the double-loop system of the global value chain

and transfer their foreign reserves (brought by trade surplus and capital inflows) back to developed countries in the form of debt and indirect investment. The lower loop is the economic circulation among developing countries. Richer developing countries such as China, through direct investment in other resource-rich developing economies, develop and import the required resources and primary products, and export manufactured products, forming trade flows of resources and manufactured goods. Meanwhile, they transfer some industries to other developing countries in Asia, Africa and Latin America, fostering the mobility of production factors and industrial transfer (see Fig. 1.33). On one hand, emerging countries such as China have driven the industrialization and economic growth of other developing economies through import of resources, export of products and capital, and industrial transfer. On the other hand, they have also solved their own problems to some extent.

The two poles of the world, ensnared in economic stagnation, has been once again brought into a global industrial gradient of which China is the pivot. Since the global financial crisis, the role of developed countries as growth engines has been greatly reduced. Trade protectionism and anti-globalization trends have gradually emerged. Emerging developing economies, especially the "BRICS" represented by China, have increasingly become an important driving force for global economic cooperation and development. The previous single-engine (developed economies) growth model has been replaced by the double engines of developed and developing countries.

Within the double-loop system of the global value chain, China needs to fully tap its economic complementarity with countries along the "Belt and Road" which differ greatly in terms of industrial gradient, so as to establish a mutually beneficial and reasonable international system of labor division and create regional economic integration of Europe and Asia, thereby fulfilling the target of the Belt and Road Initiative.

The process of industrialization is actually the process of modernization. Industry plays the central role in modernization. It is the constant transformation of the industrial structure (from labor/resource-intensive to capital/technology/knowledge-intensive industries) that has stimulated economic development.

After the disintegration of the flying-geese paradigm, all countries are thinking about how to integrate regional resources of and build a new system of labor through bilateral or multilateral regional cooperation. With China's reform and opening up, a large developing country of 1.4 billion people suddenly squeezed into the flying-geese paradigm with its strong growth momentum. The Asian economy, feeling lost for its broken flying-geese paradigm, is at an important turning point. Relying on its unique position in the international division of labor, China has become the world's most important production base of the manufacturing industry. Fully and directly integrated into the globalization process, China's development has broken free from the original flying-geese paradigm of Asia's, or even the world's labor division system. China's growth in export could be attributed to the upgrade of its export structure—the export of electromechanical products, especially computer, telecommunication and auxiliary products have increased substantially. In the first half of 2001, monitors and mobile phones, replacing toys and shoes, emerged as China's top export commodities. By improving quality and cutting prices amid the fierce competition, Chinese appliance manufacturers brought down their Japanese rivals which assembled products in Southeast Asia. After 1998, they began to export products in large volumes. As the largest destination of foreign investment, the growing China is a large competitor for foreign investment to other East Asian countries. All the new changes have brought huge shocks to the existing flying-geese paradigm.

The core of the "Belt and Road" Initiative is to form an integrated economic production network, which requires industrial integration according to the development stage of each country. Countries along the "Belt and Road" are at different stages of industrialization, with varied levels of economic development and competitiveness in diversified industries. These industries have also formed three different gradients, namely technology-intensive and high value-added industries (countries at later stage of industrialization), capital-intensive industries (countries at the middle stage of industrialization), and labor-intensive industries (countries at the early stage of industrialization).

With the end of the cheap labor era in China, labor-intensive industries (such as textiles and toys) are expected to move to countries at early stage of industrialization (e.g., some Southeast Asian countries). Resource-intensive industries (such as energy products, chemical products and metal products) could move to countries rich in oil and gas (e.g., some Central and Eastern European countries) or mineral resources (e.g., some Central Asian countries). China could expand its export of capital, technology and high value-added products to these countries. Some technology-intensive and high value-added industries (such as electromechanical products and some equipment products) could be transferred from China to countries at the late stage of industrialization (e.g., some Central and Eastern European countries) to complement each other technologically.

In this way, the industrial upgrading of countries at the late stage of industrialization will stimulate the upgrade of countries at the middle stage of industrialization which will then inevitably boost the upgrade of countries at the early stage of industrialization. Then, the Belt and Road countries could achieve industrial transfer and set up production networks with clear division of labor to form the loops of labor division and cooperation.

1.5 A Comparative Analysis of the Levels of Economic Development Within the Double-Loop System

The inner consistency between China and the Belt and Road countries in their development decides they could complement and push forward each other's development. By helping these countries tap their geographic advantages, China could also realize its own industrial upgrading and adjustment. While providing products to countries of the upper loop, China could promote its own urbanization and industrialization by stimulating export from late-starters through trade. An analysis of the industrialization degree of different countries shows the Belt and Road Initiative could help tap the complementarity between countries with different industrial structures and achieve industrial synergy within the double-loop system of the global value chain.

By referring to the categorization of economic development stages made by Chenery et al. (1977, 1986), we could standardize per capita GDP with the following equation.

$$\mathrm{GDP}pc_t^n = \frac{\mathrm{GDP}pc_t - \mathrm{GDP}pc_{\mathrm{begin}}}{\mathrm{GDP}pc_{\mathrm{finished}} - \mathrm{GDP}pc_{\mathrm{begin}}}$$

$\mathrm{GDP}pc_t^n$ is the index of the change of economy N's per capita GDP over the standard period of t. $\mathrm{GDP}pc_{\mathrm{begin}}$ is the per capita GDP at the starting point of industrialization. $\mathrm{GDP}pc_{\mathrm{finished}}$ is the per capita GDP upon the completion of the industrialization. $\mathrm{GDP}pc_t$ is the directly calculated raw GDP per capita of economy N (in constant 2005 prices of USD).[4] When $H = 0$, economy N enters the early stage of industrialization. The bigger H is, the closer N is to the completion of industrialization.

(I) Levels of economic development in different countries

As a leading power, the People's Republic of China has established a relatively complete industrial system at the beginning of its foundation. According to our research, many countries along the "Belt and Road", still in the process of industrialization, are less industrialized. Therefore, on the one hand, China could cooperate with less industrialized countries to fully tap its advantages of complete industrial system and high-level manufacturing industry, and thereby narrowing its gap with countries with better industrial structures within the international system of labor division, and exporting manufactured goods with higher added value. On the other hand, it could export technologies and knowledge within the lower loop and obtain the resources and energy required for rapid development.

---

[4] Statistics used here are in constant 2005 prices. Based on standard structure model of Chenery (1986), 1141–2822 USD is considered the starting point of industrialization, 5645–10,584 USD is considered the completing point of industrialization (Statistics in Chenery's paper are in constant 1970 prices of USD. In this chapter, they are in constant 2005 prices. All the other USD statistics in this chapter are in constant 2005 prices.) beyond which an economy enters the developed stage (in 2005, the World Bank used the per capita income of 10,725 USD to divide developed and developing economies, its difference from this chapter's standard 10,584 USD is negligible).

A category-wise research into the characteristics of the industrialization levels of the countries along the "Belt and Road" (as shown in Tables 1.23 and 1.24) shows that South Asian countries are at the end of the early stage of industrialization, while resource-intensive countries in West Asia and some European countries are at the late stage of industrialization. Most countries in Southeast Asia and South Asia are at the early stage of industrialization. Most countries in Central and Eastern Europe, West Asia and the Middle East are at the late stage of industrialization.

(II) An analysis of the complementarity between China and other countries along the Belt and Road in terms of economic development

China's industrial structure has undergone tremendous changes since the 1990s. By directly obtaining investment and technology from developed countries, China has quickly passed the phase of industrial gradient transfer of the flying-geese paradigm—from labor-intensive to capital-intensive and then to technology-intensive industries. While maintaining its advantage in labor-intensive industries, China has accumulated some experience in technology-intensive industries in a short time.

With varied resource endowments, different regions in China have imbalanced growths of productivity and diversified industrial structures. On the one hand, the industry in China has large size and rapid growth, with the situation that overcapacity and capacity shortage coexist. On the other hand, China's industrial structure is an integral part of the international system of labor division while maintaining a certain degree of independence and integrity. Within its complete industrial structure, China not only has labor-and-capital-intensive industries under the vertical system of labor division, but also has modern technology industries under the horizontal system. Therefore, China serves as the connecting link of the double-loop system of the global value chain.

According to Table 1.25, from 2010 to 2015, China was at the stage of accelerated industrialization. The overall industrial structure improved by nearly 30% points. Among the Belt and Road countries, China performs better than average in terms of industrial development. Within the double-loop system of the global value chain, China plays a pivotal role in connecting the Belt and Road countries for economic development. Therefore, on the one hand, China could fully tap its strengths in manufacturing industry, narrow its gap with countries with better industrial structures within the international system of labor division, and increase the added value of its manufactured goods; on the other hand, it could export technologies and knowledge to less industrialized countries and obtain the resources needed for economic growth.

According to the theory of comparative advantage in international trade, by transferring its labor-intensive and capital-intensive industries to neighboring countries with relatively low levels of industrialization, China could reduce the overcapacity in some of its industries and boost the industrial upgrading of its neighbors. At the same time, China could absorb the technology-intensive industries of developed countries, and optimize and upgrade its own industrial structure. Moreover, in the post-crisis era, many developing countries turn to China to sell their raw materials and primary products as the market in developed countries shrinks. Therefore, China has gradually become the pivot connecting developed and developing countries.

Table 1.23 Levels of industrial development in different countries (based on income) (Ranked according to the calculated values in 2014)

Income level	Country	2010	2015	Income level	Country	2010	2015
High-income countries	Kuwait	8.671	6.568	Lower-middle-income countries	Albania	0.648	0.617
	Qatar	16.628	17.549		Egypt	0.311	0.546
	Singapore	10.837	12.379		Sri Lanka	0.348	0.623
	UAE	7.847	9.313		Georgia	0.380	0.586
	Bahrain	4.535	5.263		Ukraine	0.381	0.172
	The Czech Republic	4.404	3.789		The Philippines	0.182	0.368
	Saudi Arab	4.159	4.579		Uzbekistan	0.000	0.190
	Slovakia	3.632	3.489		Moldova	0.060	0.112
	Poland	2.689	2.664		Laos	−0.056	0.111
	Estonia	3.174	3.820		Pakistan	−0.083	0.011
	Hungary	2.775	2.594		Kyrgyzstan	−0.122	−0.067
	Omen	4.447	3.408		Syria	−0.333	−0.333
	Croatia	2.900	2.422		Tajikistan	−0.154	−0.109
	Bulgaria	1.290	1.306	Low-income countries	Cambodia	−0.145	−0.053
Upper-middle-income countries	Russia	2.239	1.842		Bangladesh	−0.151	−0.040
	Kazakhstan	1.861	2.218		Afghanistan	−0.196	−0.191
	Lithuania	2.541	3.074		Nepal	−0.190	−0.156
	Romania	1.661	1.827				
	Belarus	1.067	1.047				
	China	0.761	1.624				
	Latvia	2.380	2.953				

(continued)

Table 1.23 (continued)

Income level	Country	2010	2015	Income level	Country	2010	2015
	Turkey	2.089	1.851				
	Montenegro	1.274	1.208				
	Lebanon	1.771	1.597				
	Turkmenistan	0.752	1.375				
	Serbia	0.965	0.899				
	Maldives	1.189	1.521				
	Malaysia	1.844	2.014				
	Iran	1.185	−0.333				
	Armenia	0.419	0.511				
	Mongolia	0.309	0.643				
	Jordan	0.641	0.858				
	Bosnia and Herzegovina	0.740	0.672				
	Thailand	0.896	1.068				

Source of data Calculated based on the World Bank database

Table 1.24 Levels of industrial development of different countries (on a regional basis) (Ranked according to the calculated values in 2014)

Region	Country	2010	2015	Region	Country	2010	2015
	China	0.761	1.624	The Caucasus	Armenia	0.419	0.511
Southeast Asia	Singapore	10.837	12.379		Georgia	0.380	0.586
	Malaysia	1.844	2.014	Central and Eastern Europe	The Czech Republic	4.404	3.789
	Thailand	0.896	1.068		Slovakia	3.632	3.489
	The Philippines	0.182	0.368		Poland	2.689	2.664
	Laos	−0.056	0.111		Estonia	3.174	3.820
	Cambodia	−0.145	−0.053		Hungary	2.775	2.594
	Maldives	1.189	1.521		Lithuania	2.541	3.0 74
South Asia	Sri Lanka	0.348	0.623		Romania	1.661	1.827
	Pakistan	−0.083	0.011		Poland	2.689	2.664
	Bangladesh	−0.151	−0.040		Latvia	2.380	2.953
	Afghanistan	−0.196	−0.191		Russia	2.239	1.842
	Nepal	−0.19	−0.156		Belarus	1.067	1.047
	India	–	–		Moldova	0.060	0.112
Central Asia	Kazakhstan	1.861	2.218	Southern Europe	Croatia	2.900	2.422
	Turkmenistan	0.752	1.375		Bulgaria	1.290	1.306
	Uzbekistan	0.000	0.19		Montenegro	1.274	1.208
	Kyrgyzstan	−0.122	−0.067		Serbia	0.965	0.899
	Tajikistan	−0.154	−0.109		Bosnia and Herzegovina	0.740	0.672

(continued)

Table 1.24 (continued)

Region	Country	2010	2015	Region	Country	2010	2015
West Asia and North Africa	Kuwait	8.671	6.568		Albania	0.648	0.617
	Qatar	16.628	17.549		Cyprus	–	–
	UAE	7.847	9.313		Greece	–	–
	Bahrain	4.535	5.263				
	Saudi Arab	4.159	4.579				
	Oman	4.447	3.408				
	Turkey	2.089	1.851				
	Lebanon	1.771	1.597				
	Iran	1.185	−0.333				
	Jordan	0.641	0.858				
	Egypt	0.311	0.546				

Source of data Calculated based on the World Bank database

Table 1.25 A comparison between Chinese provinces and countries along the Belt and Road in terms of stage of development (according to per capita GDP) (Ranked according to calculated values in 2015)

Income level	Country	2010	2015	Province	2010	2015
High-income countries	Qatar	16.628	17.549	Tianjin	1.838	3.557
	Singapore	10.837	12.379	Shanghai	2.173	3.258
	UAE	7.847	9.313	Beijing	1.894	2.871
	Kuwait	8.671	6.568	Jiangsu	1.001	1.774
	Bahrain	4.535	5.263	Zhejiang	1.063	1.733
	Saudi Arab	4.159	4.579	Guangdong	0.924	1.557
	Estonia	3.174	3.820	Inner Mongolia	0.715	1.358
	The Czech Republic	4.404	3.789	Fujian	0.682	1.355
	Slovakia	3.632	3.489	Shandong	0.737	1.344
	Oman	4.447	3.408	Liaoning	0.716	1.193
	Poland	2.689	2.664			
	Hungary	2.775	2.594			
	Croatia	2.900	2.422			
	Bulgaria	1.290	1.306			
Upper-middle-income countries	Lithuania	2.541	3.074	Jilin	0.437	0.871
	Latvia	2.380	2.953	Chongqing	0.301	0.826
	Kazakhstan	1.861	2.218	Hebei	0.406	0.777
	Malaysia	1.844	2.014	Heilongjiang	0.399	0.758
	Turkey	2.089	1.851	Hubei	0.292	0.709
	Russia	2.239	1.842	Xinjiang	0.291	0.707
	Romania	1.661	1.827	Shaanxi	0.231	0.620

(continued)

Table 1.25 (continued)

Income level	Country	2010	2015	Province	2010	2015
	China	0.761	1.624	Henan	0.265	0.614
	Lebanon	1.771	1.597	Hunan	0.242	0.611
	Maldives	1.189	1.521	Hainan	0.250	0.583
	Turkmenistan	0.752	1.375	Shanxi	0.275	0.557
	Montenegro	1.274	1.208	Qinghai	0.198	0.553
	Thailand	0.896	1.068	Ningxia	0.202	0.523
	Belarus	1.067	1.047			
	Serbia	0.965	0.899			
	Jordan	0.641	0.858			
	Bosnia and Herzegovina	0.740	0.672			
	Mongolia	0.309	0.643			
	Armenia	0.419	0.511			
	Iran	1.185	−0.333			
Lower-middle-income countries	Sri Lanka	0.348	0.623	Jiangxi	0.172	0.497
	Albania	0.648	0.617	Sichuan	0.162	0.493
	Georgia	0.380	0.586	Tibet	0.139	0.487
	Egypt	0.311	0.546	Guangxi	0.152	0.451

(continued)

Table 1.25 (continued)

Income level	Country	2010	2015	Province	2010	2015
	The Philippines	0.182	0.368	Anhui	0.137	0.450
	Uzbekistan	0.000	0.190	Yunnan	0.062	0.335
	Ukraine	0.381	0.172	Gansu	0.033	0.272
	Moldova	0.060	0.112	Guizhou	-0.073	0.137
	Laos	−0.056	0.111			
	Pakistan	−0.083	0.011			
	Kyrgyzstan	−0.122	−0.067			
	Tajikistan	−0.154	−0.109			
	Syria	−0.333	−0.333			
Low-income countries	Bangladesh	−0.151	−0.040			
	Cambodia	−0.145	−0.053			
	Nepal	−0.190	−0.156			
	Afghanistan	−0.196	−0.191			

Source of data Calculated based on the World Bank database

Countries along the "Belt and Road" are at different stages of industrialization, with varied levels of economic development and competitiveness in diversified industries. These industries have also formed three different gradients, namely technology-intensive and high value-added industries (countries at later stage of industrialization), capital-intensive industries (countries at the middle stage of industrialization) and labor-intensive industries (countries at the early stage of industrialization). With different industrial structures and levels, these countries and Chinese provinces could complement each other for development. Chinese provinces, with different industrial structures, could match with the Belt and Road countries at the corresponding stages of development. These countries could establish connection with provinces of slightly better industrial structures and learn in advance how to deal with future development problems. Meanwhile, Chinese provinces could start targeted investment and cooperation in matching countries—their similarity and complementarity would make the cooperation smoother, helping them break through the bottleneck to progress and driving their economic growth and industrial upgrading.

1.6 Summary

The "Belt and Road" Initiative is a visionary plan for the future proposed at the critical point of development. Amid the waves of neoliberal globalization in the 1970s and 1980s, the polarization of global economic development grew increasingly serious. Developing economies were marginalized, and developed economies faced intensified polarization domestically. At this critical moment, China proposes to construct a more inclusive, just, peaceful, mutually beneficial and win–win version of globalization under the guidance of the Silk Road spirit (on the basis of solidarity, mutual trust, equality, inclusiveness, mutual learning and win–win cooperation, countries of different races, beliefs and cultural backgrounds are fully capable of sharing peace and development) and based on the five-pronged approach (policy coordination, connectivity of infrastructure and facilities, unimpeded trade, financial integration and closer people-to-people ties) and three communities (community of a shared future, community of shared interests and community of shared responsibilities).

The review and analysis of the historical data show the world economy is currently at a critical point of significant transformation after several major changes and transfers. Since the Age of Exploration, especially the Industrial Revolution, Asia had drifted away from the center of global economy. After the Second World War, the rapid rise of Japan, especially its rapid growth from the 1950s to the 1970s, brought Asia back to the center. Asia accounted for 16.53% of global GDP in 1970 (in 2005 constant prices). With the continuous deepening of China's reform and opening up, especially since its accession to the WTO in 2001, China's economy has achieved rapid growth for more than 30 years. The improving status of China has helped push Asia back to the top of the global economy. As of 2013, Asia contributed 30.69% of the global GDP, replacing Europe as the world's largest continent economically. In addition, with growing polarization within developed economies and globally, former advocates of free trade have shifted their focus back home, changing from a neoliberal paradigm that emphasizes the release of market forces to social protection. Brexit has exposed multiple difficulties faced by the EU, including slow growth, sluggish recovery, downturn in the job market, and refugee crisis. The United States has continuously made protectionist comments such as "rescinding the US trade agreements" and "canceling TPP", reflecting the largest economy's mixed attitude toward globalization and bringing huge uncertainty to the global economy.

From the perspective of trade of the three major economies (the EU, North America and East Asia), in 2002, China's total trade with the EU exceeded that between Japan and the EU for the first time. After that, the gap widened further. As of 2014, China's total trade with the EU was 4.3 times that of Japan. In 2003, China's total trade with North America (the United States and Canada) exceeded that of Japan for the first time. After that, the gap grew larger. As of 2014, China's total with North America was 3.2 times that of Japan. In 2007, China overtook Japan as the largest trading partner of the seven Southeast Asian countries (Vietnam, Cambodia, Philippines, Thailand, Malaysia, Singapore and Indonesia). Later, China extended the lead further. As of 2014, China's total trade with the seven countries was 1.6 times that of Japan. From 2002 to 2007, China gradually replaced Japan as the largest receiver of industrial transfer from North America, the EU and East Asia. In 2010, China surpassed Japan as the world's second largest economy. It is currently the only economy except the United States that is larger than 10 trillion USD. With the gradual improvement of its comprehensive national strength, China and the transformation of its macroeconomic development will have more impact over the Asian or even the global economy.

According to the World Bank's classification of national income, in 1987, there were 49 low-income countries, of which 26 remained as such in 2015, while China, Equatorial Guinea, Guyana and Maldives became upper-middle-income countries, and 19 countries were relabeled lower-middle-income countries in 2015. Most of the countries making progress are neighbors of China or located at the border of Asia and Africa. In 2015, low-income countries were mainly located in Africa and South Asia. As a major power, China is a good source of development experience in industrialization, urbanization, internationalization and informatization, which could serve as a reference for other countries. According to the existing labor division in the international industrial and trade systems, late-starting countries as a whole are disadvantaged in the international market, stuck in the low end of the value chain and confronted with industrial ceilings. Countries which are yet to achieve development, in particular, have fallen into poverty due to their inability to join the international system of labor division and trade, further widening their gap with developed countries. Countries which have made some progress are facing economic stagnation caused by slow industrial upgrading and worsening trade conditions. Inferior in terms of capital, science and technology, the late-starting countries are at the bottom of the industrial structure. Therefore, it is hard for them to catch up and easy to fall into stagnation, which will further hinder their industrial upgrading. Hence, one can see that for the current international system of labor division and trade to boost the development of late-starting countries, developed countries have to be growing steadily. When developed countries are in economic recession or even fall into crisis, the late-starting countries will be even more disadvantaged.

From the perspective of the global value chain, a double-loop system is displayed in the global economy. Developed countries are active in the trade of both intermediate and final consumer goods of all industries, while developing countries only see large trade volumes in some industries. However, trade exchanges between China and other developing countries along the value chain is frequent. In general, within the upper loop, developed countries transfer most of their manufacturing, production services, etc., to emerging developing countries represented by China through the export of production factors such as capital and technology. Emerging developed countries, by exporting high-end intermediate products and production services, boost their own economic growths and transfer their foreign reserves (brought by trade surplus and capital inflows) back to developed countries in the form of debt and indirect investment. The lower loop is the economic circulation among developing countries. Richer developing countries such as China, through direct investment in other resource-rich developing economies, develop and import the required resources and primary products, and export manufactured products, forming trade flows of resources and manufactured goods. Meanwhile, they transfer some industries to other developing countries in Asia, Africa and Latin America, fostering the mobility of production factors and industrial transfer. On the one hand, emerging countries such as China have driven the industrialization and economic growth of other developing economies through import of resources, export of products and capital, and industrial transfer. On the other hand, they have also solved their own problems to some extent.

As globalization is facing its bottleneck, developed countries are hesitant about globalization. China, despite the doubts and indecision of the developed economies, has timely proposed the "Belt and Road" Initiative, hoping to build upon the double-loop system of the value chain a more open and inclusive global governance mechanism under which fruits of development could be shared. At present, as to both economic development stage and industrial structure, China is located between the developed and developing countries, which determines its role as a connecting link between the two groups—it receives new technologies and industries from North America and Western Europe, and at the same time carries out capacity cooperation with developing countries in Asia, Africa and Latin America, thereby realizing the double-loop system of the global value chain. Within the "Belt and Road" system, China, on the one hand, has established with developed countries a loop of circulation based on international division of labor, trade, investment, and indirect capital flows; on the other hand, it has formed another loop with developing countries of Asia, Africa and Latin America based on trade and direct investment. The current development stages and division of labor of the 67 countries or regions along the

"Belt and Road" indicate there is a small double-loop system, or an 8-shaped circulation system among them. The construction of the "Belt and Road" could speed up the circulation between the upper and lower loops of the global economy (the double 8-shaped circulation model of the global value chain), which will help include more countries in the labor division system of the global value chain, and achieve mutually beneficial and coordinated economic cooperation and shared prosperity on a larger scale.

Chapter 2
Research on the Impact on Trade Made by China Through Direct Investment in Countries and Regions Along the Belt and Road

Keqi Guo, Hui Zhang, and Tian Yi

For thousands of years, the Belt and Road has attracted a great many explorers and traders.

The implementation of the Belt and Road Initiative requires not only visionary design and deliberation, but also down-to-earth analysis and actions. Most countries along the Belt and Road are developing economies with long history. On the one hand, China has only limited knowledge of the economic conditions of these countries; on the other hand, it has a high stake in their economic development. Therefore, fully understanding their economic conditions is key to the implementation of the Belt and Road Initiative. This chapter, taking direct investment as the starting point of the research on the trade development between China and the Belt and Road countries, aims at studying the impact of the Initiative on trade between China and its neighboring countries.

International trade and outward direct investment have always been the major approaches through which a country participates in the world economy. In the history of globalization, outward direct investment appeared late and was dominated at its early stage by a few developed countries (e.g., Britain and the United States), while most countries did not have that capacity; international trade has long been the main tool of cross-border economic exchanges.

From the 1990s to 2008 before the breakout of the financial crisis, international trade, as a major driving force of global economic growth, grew at an average annual rate of 6.9%. However, according to the World Trade Report published by WTO,

K. Guo (✉) · H. Zhang · T. Yi
School of Economics, Peking University, Beijing, China
e-mail: tang_yuxuan@hotmail.com

H. Zhang
e-mail: nk94zhang@126.com

T. Yi
e-mail: skutian@163.com

H. Zhang et al., *Comparative Studies on Regional and National Economic Development*, Global Economic Synergy of Belt and Road Initiative,
https://doi.org/10.1007/978-981-16-2105-5_2

the average annual growth rate dropped to 3.1% and stayed low after this watershed crisis (2008–2015).

Different from international trade, the late starter outward direct investment has displayed strong momentum of growth. In the end of the twentieth century, with the development of regional economic integration and financial liberalization, FDI witnessed rapid growth. According to the World Investment Report published by UNCTAD, from 1996 to 1999, the inflow of FDI grew at an average annual rate of 40.8%, while the outflow rose by 37% a year. Though the 2008 crisis, to some extent, reduced the vitality of international direct investment, it staged strong recovery after the crisis: in 2015, the inflow of FDI generated a growth rate of 38%, while the figure for the outflow was 12%, and this trend is likely to last.

At the same time, more and more countries began to join the team of ODI, and China's achievements are outstanding. China officially established a statistical system for ODI in 2002, and in 2008, it, for the first time, became one of the top three destinations for foreign investment; four years later, China emerged as one of the top three sources of ODI, and its outward investment would soon exceed the inflow, completing the strategic transition from "bring in" to "go global".

However, China's foreign trade is facing great downward pressure due to the new normal domestically and the trade environment globally, which has a serious impact on China's economic growth. Under the new situation, China is badly in need of new sources of economic growth, and Chinese government responded by putting forward the Belt and Road Initiative. By undertaking projects of construction under the Initiative, China is enhancing its trade with and investment in surrounding countries. Against such a backdrop, whether ODI could promote multilateral trade and whether investment and trade could interact benignly have a direct impact on the effectiveness of the Initiative.

ODI made by enterprises are often of multiple motives, causing uncertainty to the impact on trade; therefore, case-by-case analysis is needed. However, though individual enterprises may have multiple motives for ODI, some systematic patterns could still be noticed at the country level. From China's perspective, its direct investment in developed economies is motivated by market and innovative asset seeking; by investing in countries with rich oil and mineral resources, it is targeting at the resources; and it invests in emerging and developing economies to conquer the market and pursue efficiency. These patterns are the potential breakthrough points for the research on the diversified impacts of ODI made by China under the Belt and Road Initiative on different countries and regions.

2.1 Geographical Conditions, Economic Landscapes, Direct Investment and Trade of Countries Along the Belt and Road

(I) Geographical conditions and economic landscapes

Taking China as the center, the Belt and Road Initiative radiates its influence in a wide range of countries and regions across the western Pacific, the Indian Ocean, and Eurasia, generating great potential for development.

According to the 2015 statistics of World Bank, the 66 countries along the Belt and Road (China excluded) have a population of 3.208 billion, 43.66% of the world total; and a GDP of 11.67 trillion USD, 15.7% of the global economy. According to the classification standards of World Bank based on income, among these countries 20 are high-income, 22 are upper and lower mid-income, and Afghanistan and Nepal are labeled as low-income. See Table 2.1 for detailed classification.

However, despite their high per capita income, petroleum exporting countries are often not classified as developed economies considering their comprehensive national strengths. According to the World Investment Report published by the United Nations in 2015, among the countries along the Belt and Road, 14 are developed economies, 17 are transitioning from developing to developed economies, and 35 are developing economies. See Table 2.2 for detailed classification. Most of these countries are in transition, which means they enjoy great late-mover advantage.

Overall, the Belt and Road Initiative covers an extensive range of regions and diversified types of countries, providing great opportunities for China's outward investment and international trade.

(II) China's direct investment in countries along the Belt and Road

From 2003 to 2015, China's direct investment in countries along the Belt and Road has the following features:

1. Sustained rapid growth and great potential for further growth

In the twenty-first century, Chinese government has been deepening its mutually beneficial cooperation with surrounding countries, improving the system of "going global", and stepping up facilitating outward investment. Within this context, China's direct investment in countries along the Belt and Road has been expanding rapidly.

Table 2.1 Classification of countries along the Belt and Road based on their per capita income

Income level	Country
High-income countries (20)	Bahrain, Brunei, Cyprus, Israel, Kuwait, Oman, Qatar, Saudi Arabia, Singapore, UAE, Greece, Hungary, Poland, Estonia, Latvia, Croatia, Czech, Slovakia, Lithuania, Slovenia
Upper mid-income countries (22)	Iran, Iraq, Jordan, Lebanon, Malaysia, Mongolia, Thailand, Turkey, Kazakhstan, Turkmenistan, Albania, Bulgaria, Romania, Georgia, Azerbaijan, Bosnia and Herzegovina, Serbia, Montenegro, Belarus, Russia, Maldives, Macedonia
Lower mid-income countries (2)	Bangladesh, Myanmar, Cambodia, India, Indonesia, Laos, Pakistan, the Philippines, Yemen, Vietnam, Kyrgyzstan, Tajikistan, Uzbekistan, Egypt, Armenia, Ukraine, Bhutan, Palestine, East Timor, Sri Lanka, Syria, Moldova
Low-income countries (2)	Afghanistan, Nepal

Table 2.2 Classification of countries along the Belt and Road based on the level of economic development

Level of economic development	Countries
Developed economies (14)	Israel, Latvia, Lithuania, Estonia, Bulgaria, Romania, Croatia, Slovenia, Hungary, Slovakia, Czech, Poland, Cyprus, Greece
Economies in transition (17)	Serbia, Macedonia, Montenegro, Albania, Bosnia and Herzegovina, Moldova, Belarus, Georgia, Armenia, Russia, Azerbaijan, Ukraine, Turkmenistan, Uzbekistan, Tajikistan, Kyrgyzstan, Kazakhstan
Developing economies (35)	Sri Lanka, Bhutan, Nepal, Afghanistan, Bangladesh, Pakistan, India, East Timor, Myanmar, the Philippines, Brunei, Indonesia, Singapore, Malaysia, Egypt, Mongolia, Maldives, Thailand, Cambodia, Laos, Vietnam, Palestine, Jordan, Yemen, Oman, Lebanon, Kuwait, UAE, Iraq, Syria, Iran, Turkey, Bahrain, Qatar, Saudi Arabia

Figure 2.1 shows China's direct investment in these countries from 2003 to 2015. The bar graph reveals the changes of investment flow and stock; the line chart shows the share of China's direct investment stock (or flow) within the total stock (or flow) of direct investment around the world.

The bar graph above shows China has been enhancing its direct investment in the Belt and Road region. In 2003, the flow of direct investment was only 200 million USD, while in 2015 the figure had inflated to 20 billion USD, generating an average annual growth rate of 46%; similarly, the stock of direct investment surged from 1.3

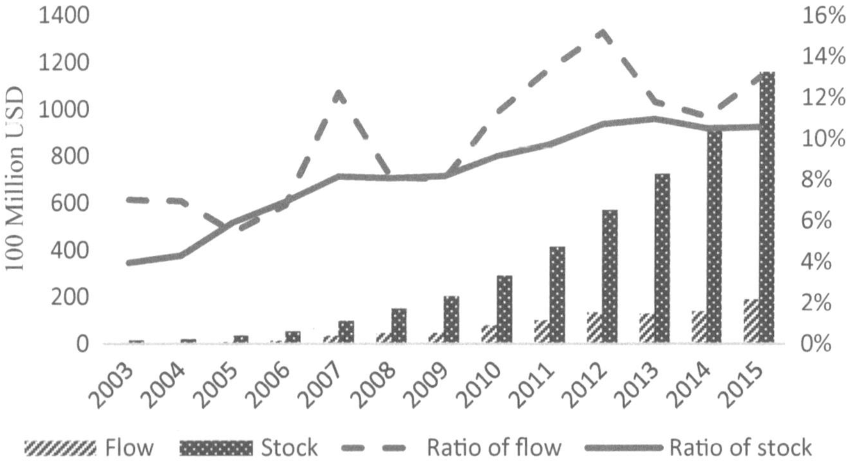

Fig. 2.1 Trend of China's direct investment in countries along the Belt and Road from 2003 to 2015. *Source of data 2008 Statistical Bulletin of China's Outward Foreign Direct Investment* and *2015 Statistical Bulletin of China's Outward Foreign Direct Investment* jointly published by Ministry of Commerce and National Bureau of Statistics

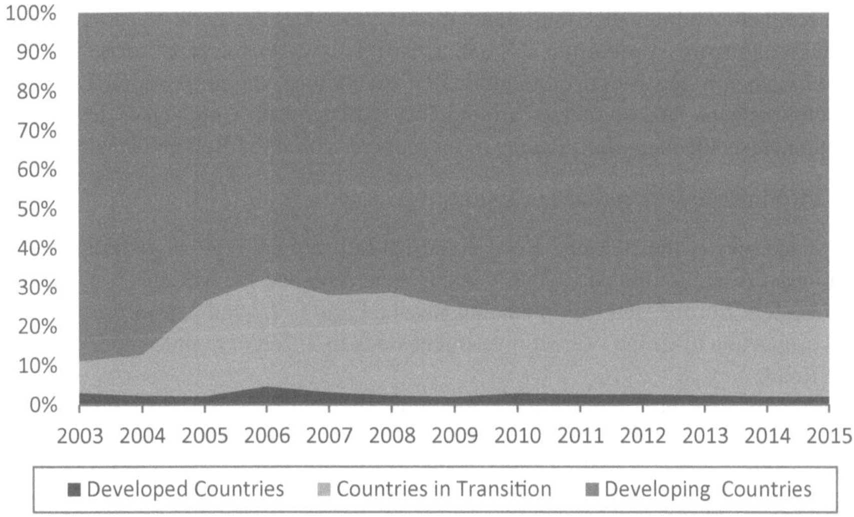

Fig. 2.2 Shares of China's direct investment stock in different economies along the Belt and Road. *Source of data 2008 Statistical Bulletin of China's Outward Foreign Direct Investment* and *2015 Statistical Bulletin of China's Outward Foreign Direct Investment* jointly published by Ministry of Commerce and National Bureau of Statistics

billion USD at the end of 2003 to 115.9 billion USD at the end of 2015, growing dramatically at an average annual rate of 45%.

According to the above line chart, China's direct investment flow in the Belt and Road region was only 7.02% of its total flow in the world. Since then the figure had been on the rise, but in a volatile way: in 2012, it reached an all-time high of 15.18% and then fell to 12.97% in 2015. As to the stock of direct investment, the Belt and Road region only took up 3.96% of China's total around the world in 2003, and then, it steadily rose to 10.56% in 2015.

It's noteworthy that despite the rapid growth, China's investment flow and stock are only less than 5% of the total foreign investment absorbed by this region,[1] which indicates China's investment level is still low there and large space exists for further growth.

2. Developing economies as the main destinations of investment

China's investment stock varies greatly in different countries of the Belt and Road region. Based on the classification of economies made by UNCTAD in its World Investment Report (Table 2.2), Fig. 2.2 reveals the shares of China's investment stock in different economies (developed economies, economies in transition, and developing economies) within its total investment stock in this region.

According to Fig. 2.2, from 2003 to 2015, the share of China's direct investment stock in developed economies within this region stayed around a low level of 3%

[1] Wang (2016).

and had been sliding since the financial crisis; in 2003, the stock in economies in transition took up a proportion as small as 8.07%, in 2006, the proportion surged to 27.49%, then it began to decline gradually; by contrast, the proportion of stock in developing economies stabilized around 76%, which means China takes developing economies as the main destinations of investment within the Belt and Road region.

3. Investment is concentrated in Southeast Asia and soaring in Mongolia and Russia

As stated above, the Belt and Road countries fall into six regions geographically: Southeast Asia, South Asia, Central Asia, West Asia and the Middle East, Central and Eastern Europe, and Mongolia and Russia. Figures 2.3 and 2.4 reflect the trend and proportion of China's direct investment stock in different regions along the Belt and Road.

As to the distribution of China's direct investment stock across different regions, Southeast Asia topped the rankings in 2003–2015, with its stock rising at an annual rate of 48% from 600 million USD at the end of 2003 to 62.7 billion USD at the end of 2015. In recent years, China's stock in Southeast Asia accounted for more than half of its total in the Belt and Road region. In 2015, the top three destinations for China's direct investment in Southeast Asia were Singapore (32 billion USD), Indonesia (8.1 billion USD) and Laos (4.8 billion USD).

In 2003, China's stock of direct investment in West Asia and the Middle East ranked No. 2 at 500 million USD, but its average annual growth rate was only 32.3%, the lowest among the six regions. By the end of 2015, the stock in this region had soared to 15 billion USD, 13% of the total stock within the Belt and Road region and third only to that in Mongolia and Russia.

Mongolia and Russia saw the most rapid growth in terms of investment stock. From 2003 to 2015, the figure rose from less than 100 million USD to 17.8 billion USD, up by 57.7% per year.

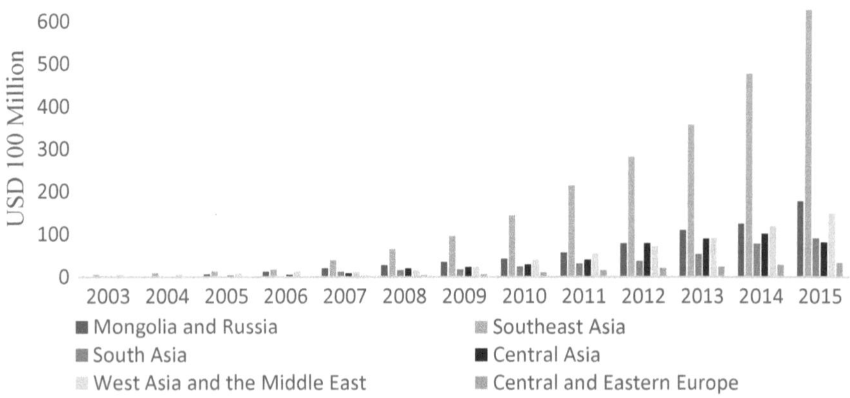

Fig. 2.3 China's direct investment stock in different regions along the Belt and Road. *Source of data* 2008 Statistical Bulletin of China's Outward Foreign Direct Investment and 2015 Statistical Bulletin of China's Outward Foreign Direct Investment jointly published by Ministry of Commerce and National Bureau of Statistics

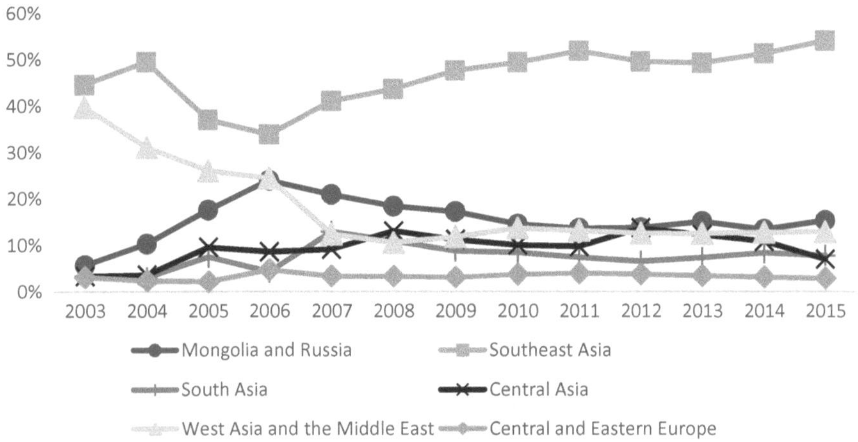

Fig. 2.4 Proportions of China's direct investment stock in different regions along the Belt and Road. *Source of data 2008 Statistical Bulletin of China's Outward Foreign Direct Investment* and *2015 Statistical Bulletin of China's Outward Foreign Direct Investment* jointly published by Ministry of Commerce and National Bureau of Statistics

Growth in South Asia and Central Asia were also strong. From 2003 to 2015, China's stock of direct investment in South Asia jumped from 45 million USD to 9.06 billion USD, up by 55.5% per year; the stock in Central Asia shot up from 44 million USD at the end of 2003 to 8.09 billion USD at the end of 2015, with an average annual growth rate of 54.4%. These two regions enjoyed similar stocks and growth rates.

China has been less active in investing in Central and Eastern Europe. At the end of 2003, China's stock of investment in this region was only 40 million USD, 3.1% of the total stock within the Belt and Road region; the figure rose to 3.3 billion USD at the end of 2015 but its proportion dropped to 2.8%.

In general, China's investment along the Belt and Road is concentrated in Southeast Asia, but investment in Mongolia and Russia is picking up rapidly. According to the statistics of 2015, the rankings of investment stock are as follows: Southeast Asia, Mongolia and Russia, West Asia and the Middle East, South Asia, Central Asia, and Central and Eastern Europe.

(III) China's import and export trade with Belt and Road countries

From 2003 to 2015, China's import and export trade with Belt and Road countries has the following features:

1. Belt and Road countries growing increasingly important while China facing difficulty in foreign trade

Figure 2.5 depicts China's trade with the Belt and Road countries in 2003–2015. The bar graph displays volumes of import and export, and the line chart suggests

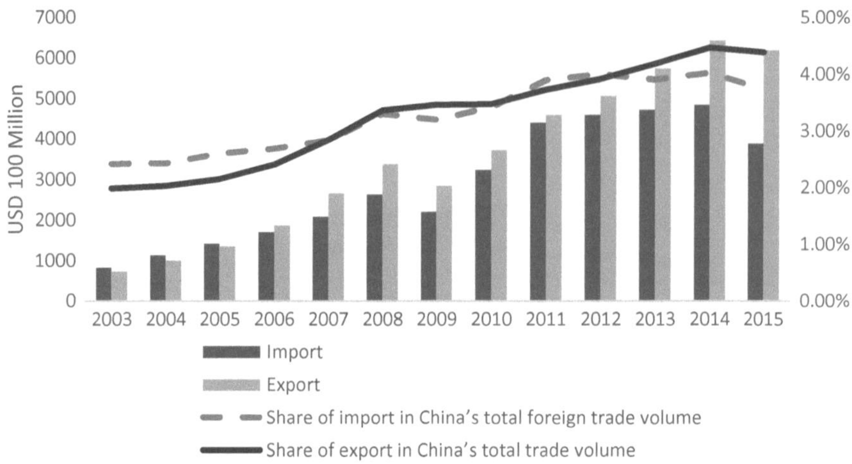

Fig. 2.5 China's import and export trade with Belt and Road countries in 2003–2015. *Source of data* National Bureau of Statistics

the share of trade with Belt and Road countries within China's total foreign trade volume.

According to the bar graph above, China's import and export trade with the Belt and Road countries in 2003–2008 grew at high speeds of 26% and 36%, respectively; due to the negative impact of the 2008 financial crisis on the environment of foreign trade, China's import and export trades with the Belt and Road region dived; in the six years since then, the figures rebounded and reached the historical highs in 2014: the volumes of import and export were 483.85 billion USD and 642.04 billion USD, up by 17.1% and 17.7% per year, respectively. It is worth mentioning that as world trade continued to be sluggish, the growth of China's trade with the Belt and Road countries had been slowing down too—in 2015, it saw negative growth, reflecting China's difficulty in foreign trade.

The above line chart shows the proportion of China's trade with the Belt and Road region within its total foreign trade volume had been rising, growing from 2.41 and 1.98% in 2003 to 4.02 and 4.46% in 2014. The Belt and Road countries are growing increasingly important to China as trade partners. However, the proportions dropped slightly in 2015.

2. Southeast Asia sees frequent trade with China, followed by West Asia and the Middle East

Data of China's import and export trade with different regions along the Belt and Road could be found in Figs. 2.6 and 2.7.

Among all the regions, Southeast Asia has been China's closest trade partner in terms of import—China's import from this region expanded from 47.3 billion USD at the end of 2003 to 194.5 billion USD at the end of 2015, up by 36% per year on average, much faster than that in other regions. According to the 2015 statistics,

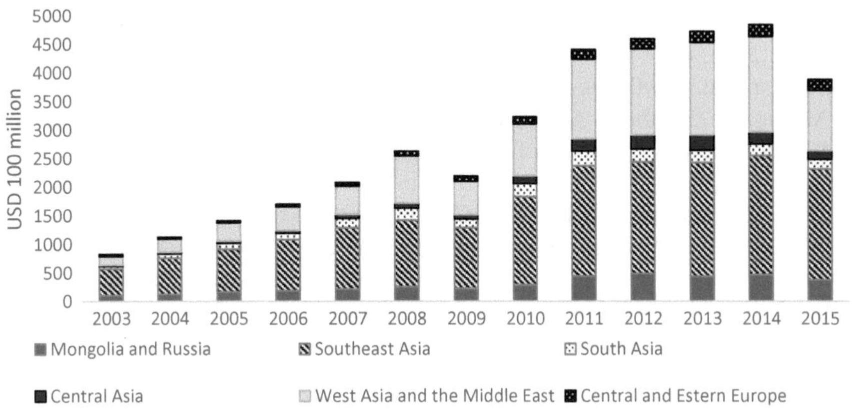

Fig. 2.6 Volumes of China's import from different Belt and Road regions. *Source of data* National Statistics Bureau

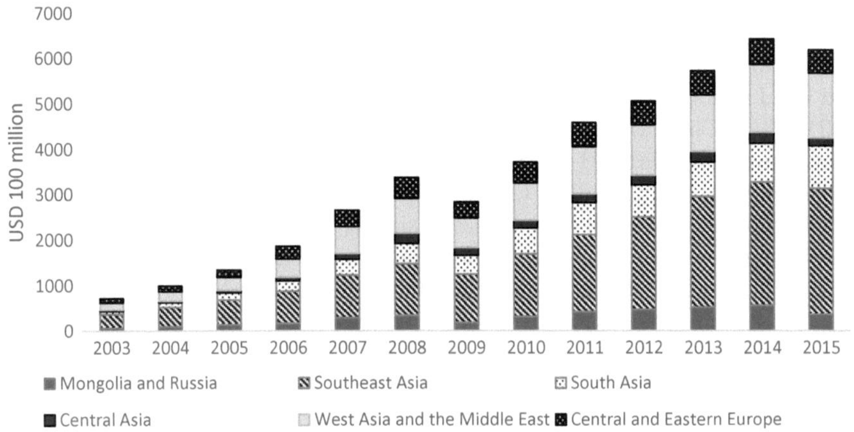

Fig. 2.7 Volumes of China's export to different Belt and Road regions. *Source of data* National Bureau of Statistics

China's import from Southeast Asia makes up half of its total from the Belt and Road countries.

Following Southeast Asia is West Asia and the Middle East. From 2003 to 2015, China's import from this region rose from 15.2 billion USD to 105.9 billion USD at an average annual growth rate of 17.6%. In 2015, within China's import from the Belt and Road region, 27% was from West Asia and the Middle East.

The region of Mongolia and Russia ranks No.3. China's import from this region grew at an annual rate of 11.5% from 10 billion USD at the end of 2003 to 37.1 billion USD at the end of 2015. In 2015, China's import from Mongolia and Russia was 9.5% of its total from the Belt and Road countries.

Central and Eastern Europe, South Asia, and Central Asia enjoy similar proportions. In 2015, their proportions were 5%, 4.4%, and 3.9%, respectively, and the average annual growth rates were 16%, 11% and 18%, respectively.

Meanwhile, Southeast Asia is also China's largest export destination in the Belt and Road region. The volume of export, at an average annual rate of 20%, shot up from 30.9 billion USD at the end of 2003 to 277.4 billion USD at the end of 2015. In 2015, Southeast Asia took 45% of China's export to the Belt and Road countries.

West Asia and the Middle East is the second largest destination. At the end of 2003, the volume of export was 16.5 billion USD, and the figure soared to 142.2 billion USD at the end of 2015, up by 20% per year. In 2015, 23% of China's export to the Belt and Road countries went to West Asia and the Middle East.

Ranking third is South Asia. From 2003 to 2015, China's export to South Asia inflated from 7.2 billion USD to 94.1 billion USD at an annual growth rate of 24%. In 2015, China's export to South Asia made up 15% of its total to the Belt and Road countries.

The situation in Central and Eastern Europe is similar to that in Mongolia and Russia. In 2015, the two regions took 8 and 6% of China's export to the Belt and Road countries, growing at annual growth rates of 15% and 16%, respectively.

Central Asia is the smallest destination of China's export among different Belt and Road regions. At the end of 2015, the volume of export was only 17.6 billion USD, 3% of China's total export to the Belt and Road countries, and the average annual growth rate in 2003–2015 was 20%.

Generally speaking, half of China's import and export trade with the Belt and Road countries is realized by Southeast Asia, and China's import from this region grows rapidly; West Asia and the Middle East contribute about 1/4 of China's trade with the Belt and Road countries; Central Asia ranks last as to both import and export volumes; however, considering it has only five countries, its import from China grows at a satisfactory rate.

2.2 Empirical Analysis

(I) Setting up a model and selecting variables

The model built in this Chapter is based on the traditional gravity model and takes the form of:

$$T_{ij} = AY_i^{\alpha} Y_j^{\beta} D_{ij}^{\gamma} \tag{2.1}$$

Here, T_{ij} stands for the mutual effect between object$_i$ and object$_j$; A represents gravity coefficient; Y_i and Y_j represent the mass of i and j; D_{ij} denotes friction, or factors, apart from mass, that have an impact on the mutual effect of two objects; α, β, and γ are all parameters.

The empirical analysis of this chapter is divided into two parts: first, an overall regression test is carried out for all the samples to examine the overall impact on trade made by China through direct investment in the Belt and Road countries; second, a variable parameter model is set up to measure the difference among the impacts in different regions and countries.

1. Regression analysis model for all the samples

This part examines the impact on overall trade made by China through direct investment in the Belt and Road countries. The model is expressed as:

$$\ln \text{EX} = \alpha_1 + \beta_1 \ln \text{ OFDIS } + \gamma_1 \text{lnGDP} + e_1 \tag{2.2}$$

$$\ln \text{IM} = \alpha_2 + \beta_2 \ln \text{OFDIS} + \gamma_2 \text{lnGDP} + e_2 \tag{2.3}$$

$$\ln \text{EX} = \alpha_3 + \beta_3 \ln \text{OFDIF} + \gamma_3 \text{lnGDP} + e_3 \tag{2.4}$$

$$\ln \text{IM} = \alpha_4 + \beta_4 \text{lnOFDIF} + \gamma_4 \text{lnGDP} + e_4 \tag{2.5}$$

where EX and IM represent China's export to and import from the Belt and Road countries, OFDIS and OFDIF stand for the stock and flow of China's direct investment in these countries, GDP is the total GDP generated by all these countries, α_i, β_i, γ_i ($i = 1, 2, 3, 4$) are all parameters to be estimated, and e_i ($i = 1, 2, 3, 4$) is random error. Logarithmic forms are applied for all variables in this model so as to enhance the comparability and stability of variables.

The focus is laid on β_i ($i = 1, 2, 3, 4$), the parameter to be estimated, especially its magnitude and whether it is a minus: if β_1 (or β_3) is a positive number, then the stock (or flow) of outward direct investment could stimulate export, while a negative β_1 (or β_3) denotes the effect of substituting export. If β_2 (or β_4) is positive, it means the stock (or flow) of ODI has the effect of creating import; a negative β_2 (or β_4) implies effect of substituting import. Larger β_i ($i = 1, 2, 3, 4$) means greater impact on trade.

The purposes of setting up four equations include: by comparing the values of β_1, β_2, β_3, and β_4, analyzing the difference between the impacts of ODI on import and export, and the difference between the impacts on trade made by ODI stock and ODI flow. As the difference between ODI stocks, ODI flow is closely correlated with ODI stock; therefore, the two items are placed in different models for regression analysis.

2. Analysis model for difference among countries

The sample data are from a limited period of time. Therefore, to guarantee the estimability of the model, this part, taking EX and IM as explained variables, and OFDIS and OFDIF as explanatory variables, sets up the regression model on the basis of the basic expression of the trade gravity model, so as to fully depicts the elasticity of the impact of China's direct investment in countries along the Belt and

Road. Logarithmic forms are also applied for all variables here, and the model is expressed as:

$$\ln \mathrm{EX} = \alpha_5 + \beta_5 \ln \mathrm{OFDIS} + e_5 \quad (2.6)$$

$$\ln \mathrm{IM} = \alpha_6 + \beta_6 \ln \mathrm{OFDIS} + e_6 \quad (2.7)$$

$$\ln \mathrm{EX} = \alpha_7 + \beta_7 \ln \mathrm{OFDIF} + e_7 \quad (2.8)$$

$$\ln \mathrm{IM} = \alpha_8 + \beta_8 \ln \mathrm{OFDIF} + e_8 \quad (2.9)$$

Similarly, α_i $(i = 5, 6, 7, 8)$ is the intmercept, e_i $(i = 5, 6, 7, 8)$ is the random error, β_5 and β_6, respectively, represent the elasticities of ODI stock's impacts on export and import, β_7 and β_8 stand for the elasticities of ODI flow's impacts on export and import. Larger value of β_i $(i = 5, 6, 7, 8)$ denotes greater impact on trade.

(II) Source and processing of data

The scope of this research includes countries along the Belt and Road. By the end of 2016, the Belt and Road Initiative had covered 66 countries (China excluded). See Table 2.1 for a detailed list.

Data of China's ODI stock and flow in the Belt and Road countries are from Statistical Bulletins of China's Outward Foreign Direct Investment jointly published by Ministry of Commerce and National Bureau of Statistics over the years; volumes of China's import from and export to these countries are from China Statistical Yearbooks published by National Bureau of Statistics; GDP statistics of these countries are from the official website of World Bank. Data of eight countries (Maldives, Bhutan, Palestine, Macedonia, Bosnia and Herzegovina, Serbia, East Timor, Montenegro) are missing; therefore, only 58 countries are sampled to build the database.

Since China was late to the stage of ODI, this chapter selects the panel data over the 13 years between 2003 and 2015 for analysis.

(III) Research method

Establishing a model of panel data could solve the problem of small sample size and make a comprehensive analysis of the impact of direct investment on trade from the dimensions of time series and cross section. Based on the standard procedures of panel data analysis, this chapter adopts the following research method.

The analysis of the whole sample should start with a stationary test of the data to prevent spurious regression caused by non-stationary data. Here, ADF test and LLC.

In the analysis of the difference among countries, the first step is the stationary test of the data, followed by test of the panel data model. There are three kinds of panel data model: constant coefficient model, variable intercept model and variable parameter model. Here, sample data should be tested to see whether they suit the variable parameter model for the purpose of studying the difference among countries in terms of ODI's impact on trade.

The constant coefficient model is expressed as:

$$\ln \mathrm{EX}_{it} = \alpha_5 + \beta_5 \ln \mathrm{OFDIS}_{\mathrm{it}} + e_{5it} \tag{2.10}$$

$$\ln \mathrm{IM}_{it} = \alpha_6 + \beta_6 \ln \mathrm{OFDIS}_{\mathrm{it}} + e_{6it} \tag{2.11}$$

$$\ln \mathrm{EX}_{it} = \alpha_7 + \beta_7 \ln \mathrm{OFDIF}_{\mathrm{it}} + e_{7it} \tag{2.12}$$

$$\ln \mathrm{IM}_{it} = \alpha_8 + \beta_8 \ln \mathrm{OFDIF}_{\mathrm{it}} + e_{8it} \tag{2.13}$$

The variable intercept model is expressed as:

$$\ln \mathrm{EX}_{it} = \alpha_{5it} + \beta_5 \ln \mathrm{OFDIS}_{\mathrm{it}} + e_{5it} \tag{2.14}$$

$$\ln \mathrm{IM}_{it} = \alpha_{6it} + \beta_6 \ln \mathrm{OFDIS}_{\mathrm{it}} + e_{6it} \tag{2.15}$$

$$\ln \mathrm{EX}_{it} = \alpha_{7it} + \beta_7 \ln \mathrm{OFDIF}_{\mathrm{it}} + e_{7it} \tag{2.16}$$

$$\ln \mathrm{IM}_{it} = \alpha_{8it} + \beta_8 \ln \mathrm{OFDIF}_{\mathrm{it}} + e_{8it} \tag{2.17}$$

The variable parameter model is expressed as:

$$\ln \mathrm{EX}_{it} = \alpha_{5it} + \beta_{5it} \ln \mathrm{OFDIS}_{it} + e_{5it} \tag{2.18}$$

$$\ln \mathrm{IM}_{it} = \alpha_{6it} + \beta_{6it} \ln \mathrm{OFDIS}_{it} + e_{6it} \tag{2.19}$$

$$\ln \mathrm{EX}_{it} = \alpha_{7it} + \beta_{7it} \ln \mathrm{OFDIS}_{it} + e_{7it} \tag{2.20}$$

$$\ln \mathrm{IM}_{it} = \alpha_{8it} + \beta_{8it} \ln \mathrm{OFDIS}_{it} + e_{8it} \tag{2.21}$$

Here, I (=1, 2, …, N) represents sample countries at the cross section, and t ($t = 1$, 2, …, T) stands for the year.

Specifically, expression (2.10)–(2.13) are of constant coefficient model, meaning intercept α and slope parameter β are the same for every sample country and there are no structural changes or difference among countries at the cross section; expression (2.14)–(2.17) are of variable intercept model, where slope parameter β is the same for every sample country but α_i differs, meaning difference among countries is embodied by intercept α; expression (2.18)–(2.21) are of variable parameter model, where both

α and β differ for every sample country, meaning individual differences at the cross section are embodied by both α and β, and the variation of β_i could be interpreted as the structural differences among economies.

(IV) Model estimation and analysis of the empirical results

This chapter tests and processes data using EViews 7.2.

1. Analysis of the whole sample

The results of F test and Hausman test are both above the significance level of 1%, rejecting the null hypothesis; therefore, this part adopts the fixed-effects model, and the results are shown below:

$$\ln \text{EX} = \underset{(-13.0315)}{-8.5157} + \underset{(11.2540)}{0.0.1248 \ln\ \text{OFDIS}} + \underset{(27.1530)}{1.2560 \ln \text{GDP}} \tag{2.22}$$

$$\ln \text{IM} = \underset{(-6.4782)}{-8.0317} + \underset{(7.6469)}{0.1608 \ln\ \text{OFDIS}} + \underset{(12.8495)}{1.1276 \ln \text{GDP}} \tag{2.23}$$

$$\ln \text{EX} = \underset{(-25.0512)}{-12.8508} + \underset{(3.1981)}{0.0118 \ln\ \text{OFDIF}} + \underset{(48.3400)}{1.5974 \ln\ \text{lnDP}} \tag{2.24}$$

$$\ln \text{IM} = \underset{(-6.4782)}{-13.4716} + \underset{(7.6469)}{0.0142 \ln\ \text{OFDIF}} + \underset{(12.8495)}{5597 \ln\ \text{GDP}} \tag{2.25}$$

The adjusted values of R^2 of the regression results of expression (2.22)–(2.25) are, respectively, 0.96, 0.94, 0.95, and 0.94, proving high degrees of fitting of the four models; all the p values of the F test are 0.00, meaning the model is statistically significant on the whole.

According to the regression results, within the countries along the Belt and Road, every 1% of growth of the ODI stock made by China will bring about 0.1248% of growth in China's export value to this region and 0.1608% of increase for the import value; every 1% of the growth generated by China's ODI flow in this region will push up the volumes of export and import by 0.0118% and 0.0142%, respectively.

Generally speaking, on the one hand, China's ODI in the countries along the Belt and Road displays the effect of creating trade, and the impact on import is often larger than that on export; on the other hand, the fact that the trade elasticity caused by ODI flow is only 1/10 of that by ODI stock suggests the impact of flow on trade is significantly smaller than that of stock, showing that the impact of China's ODI on trade is mostly long-term, or lagging. A likely explanation is that it takes time for direct investment to turn into productivity.

2. Analysis of the difference among countries and regions

Tables 2.3, 2.4, 2.5 and 2.6 show the regression results of the difference among countries in terms of ODI's impact on trade. To make the observation and analysis easier, all Tables are sorted by the size of β value, and non-significant results where p value is larger than 0.1 are listed at the end.

Table 2.3 Regression results of ODI stock and export volume

Country	β_5	*t* value	*p* value	Country	β_5	*t* value	*p* value
Tajikistan	0.92	11.93	0.00	Bahrain	0.61	5.89	0.00
Georgia	0.85	9.19	0.00	Uzbekistan	0.58	8.06	0.00
Vietnam	0.73	7.99	0.00	Romania	0.58	3.47	0.00
Bangladesh	0.70	5.67	0.00	Brunei	0.57	10.85	0.00
Kyrgyzstan	0.64	7.50	0.00	Egypt	0.57	6.30	0.00
Malaysia	0.62	5.29	0.00	Qatar	0.56	8.90	0.00
Thailand	0.62	5.79	0.00	Nepal	0.56	7.08	0.00
Lithuania	0.62	2.46	0.01	Mongolia	0.54	7.59	0.00
Jordan	0.61	4.46	0.00	Cambodia	0.52	6.64	0.00
Yemen	0.49	4.42	0.00	Czech	0.30	5.44	0.00
Laos	0.48	8.23	0.00	Slovenia	0.30	4.80	0.00
Albania	0.48	4.29	0.00	Oman	0.30	6.11	0.00
Poland	0.45	6.10	0.00	Ukraine	0.29	4.65	0.00
Indonesia	0.44	5.78	0.00	Turkmenistan	0.29	8.29	0.00
Moldova	0.43	2.19	0.03	Singapore	0.28	4.13	0.00
UAE	0.43	5.23	0.00	Belarus	0.27	5.52	0.00
Russia	0.39	5.19	0.00	Turkey	0.26	5.30	0.00
Iran	0.39	5.72	0.00	Saudi Arabia	0.25	5.80	0.00
The Philippines	0.38	5.41	0.00	Afghanistan	0.23	6.16	0.00
Myanmar	0.38	6.78	0.00	Croatia	0.22	1.66	0.10
Sri Lanka	0.36	5.12	0.00	Kuwait	0.21	4.44	0.00
Slovakia	0.36	8.46	0.00	Bulgaria	0.20	3.44	0.00
Pakistan	0.35	4.93	0.00	Syria	0.20	1.69	0.09
India	0.35	7.44	0.00	Hungary	0.18	2.91	0.00
Lebanon	0.35	4.33	0.00	Greece	0.12	2.37	0.02
Armenia	0.33	2.05	0.04	Latvia	−1.11	−5.06	0.00
Azerbaijan	0.32	3.73	0.00	Estonia	0.26	1.46	0.15
Kazakhstan	0.32	5.22	0.00	Iraq	0.08	0.87	0.38
Israel	0.32	5.00	0.00	Cyprus	0.07	1.19	0.23
Adjusted $R^2 = 0.94$				*p* value of the F test = 0.00			

(1) Export and ODI stock

According to Table 2.3, the adjusted R^2 is 0.94, suggesting the model enjoys high degree of fitting (goodness of fit); the *p* value of the F test is 0.00, meaning the model is statistically significant on the whole. As to the regression results, only Latvia ends up with a negative β_5, while other countries present positive results and Tajikistan, Georgia, and Vietnam rank top three.

Table 2.4 Regression results of ODI flow and export volume

Country	β_7	t value	p value	Country	β_7	t value	p value
Vietnam	0.75	5.23	0.00	Laos	0.42	4.93	0.00
Tajikistan	0.54	4.61	0.00	Cambodia	0.42	3.76	0.00
Russia	0.51	3.13	0.00	Indonesia	0.42	3.61	0.00
Egypt	0.51	3.62	0.00	UAE	0.39	3.29	0.00
Kyrgyzstan	0.50	4.07	0.00	Myanmar	0.39	3.52	0.00
Bangladesh	0.39	3.30	0.00	Moldova	0.10	0.95	0.34
Thailand	0.35	3.11	0.00	Lithuania	0.09	1.02	0.31
Georgia	0.34	2.65	0.01	Mongolia	0.09	1.41	0.16
Saudi Arabia	0.32	3.61	0.00	Afghanistan	0.07	1.26	0.21
Iraq	0.30	5.81	0.00	The Philippines	0.06	1.04	0.30
Poland	0.28	3.09	0.00	Kuwait	0.06	1.17	0.24
Nepal	0.25	3.10	0.00	Greece	0.06	0.62	0.53
Qatar	0.21	3.58	0.00	Bulgaria	0.05	0.98	0.33
Turkey	0.21	2.76	0.01	Armenia	0.05	0.47	0.64
India	0.19	3.39	0.00	Jordan	0.05	0.56	0.58
Romania	0.19	1.57	0.12	Czech	0.05	0.54	0.59
Slovakia	0.18	2.81	0.01	Yemen	0.05	0.81	0.42
Belarus	0.17	2.65	0.01	Lebanon	0.04	0.38	0.70
Bahrain	0.17	1.92	0.05	Azerbaijan	0.03	0.45	0.65
Ukraine	0.15	1.69	0.09	Iran	0.03	0.60	0.55
Sri Lanka	0.14	2.62	0.01	Kazakhstan	0.03	0.59	0.56
Hungary	0.14	1.66	0.10	Albania	0.03	0.27	0.79
Israel	0.14	2.10	0.04	Syria	0.02	0.30	0.76
Singapore	0.14	2.59	0.01	Cyprus	0.01	0.14	0.89
Malaysia	0.13	2.12	0.03	Croatia	−0.01	−0.05	0.96
Brunei	0.13	1.92	0.06	Slovenia	−0.01	−0.19	0.85
Uzbekistan	0.12	2.27	0.02	Oman	−0.03	−0.41	0.68
Pakistan	0.12	2.11	0.04	Estonia	−0.13	−1.20	0.23
Turkmenistan	0.10	2.44	0.01	Latvia	−0.18	−1.83	0.07
Adjusted $R^2 = 0.84$				p value of the F test = 0.00			

(2) Export and ODI flow

In Table 2.4, almost half of the countries tested have a p value larger than 10%, which means ODI flow has weak impact over the export volume of the same year. As a result of the contrast with Table 2.3, the regression results of ODI stock will be used for further analysis.

(3) Import and ODI stock

Table 2.5 Regression results of ODI stock and import volume

Country	β_6	*t* value	*p* value	Country	β_6	*t* value	*p* value
Moldova	1.71	5.13	0.00	Kuwait	0.36	4.39	0.00
Lithuania	1.41	3.30	0.00	Kazakhstan	0.33	3.20	0.00
Armenia	1.31	4.73	0.00	Iran	0.33	2.88	0.00
Bangladesh	1.00	4.77	0.00	Indonesia	0.33	2.55	0.01
Laos	0.85	8.66	0.00	Uzbekistan	0.32	2.63	0.01
Romania	0.71	2.52	0.01	Bahrain	0.31	1.77	0.08
Albania	0.71	3.76	0.00	Pakistan	0.31	2.55	0.01
Turkmenistan	0.70	11.78	0.00	Afghanistan	0.31	4.78	0.00
Cambodia	0.69	5.26	0.00	Turkey	0.30	3.53	0.00
Vietnam	0.68	4.40	0.00	Russia	0.29	2.21	0.03
Qatar	0.61	5.71	0.00	Lebanon	0.27	2.00	0.05
Egypt	0.60	3.91	0.00	Slovenia	0.25	2.40	0.02
UAE	0.60	4.32	0.00	Saudi Arabia	0.25	3.33	0.00
Myanmar	0.53	5.57	0.00	Israel	0.24	2.19	0.03
Azerbaijan	0.53	3.62	0.00	Greece	0.22	2.57	0.01
Mongolia	0.52	4.32	0.00	Estonia	0.22	0.71	0.48
Bulgaria	0.49	4.91	0.00	Croatia	0.21	0.94	0.35
Sri Lanka	0.49	4.10	0.00	Ukraine	0.20	1.91	0.06
Malaysia	0.47	2.34	0.02	Singapore	0.17	1.50	0.14
Cyprus	0.4.6	4.70	0.00	Oman	0.16	1.97	0.05
Jordan	0.45	1.92	0.06	India	0.15	1.90	0.06
Nepal	0.43	3.19	0.00	The Philippines	0.14	1.18	0.24
Slovakia	0.42	5.94	0.00	Yemen	0.11	0.57	0.57
Hungary	0.41	3.88	0.00	Belarus	0.06	0.76	0.45
Thailand	0.41	2.25	0.03	Iraq	0.04	0.26	0.79
Georgia	0.40	2.52	0.01	Brunei	−0.01	−0.10	0.92
Poland	0.38	3.10	0.00	Kyrgyzstan	−0.10	−0.72	0.47
Tajikistan	0.37	2.85	0.00	Syria	−0.12	−0.60	0.55
Czech	0.36	3.81	0.00	Latvia	−0.95	−2.56	0.01
Adjusted $R^2 = 0.92$				*p* value of the F test = 0.00			

According to Table 2.5, the adjusted R^2 is 0.92, suggesting high degree of fitting (goodness of fit); *p* value of the F test runs at 0.00, a proof of statistical significance. As to significant regression results, only Latvia and Brunei have negative β_6 values, while the rest countries enjoy positive regression results with Moldova, Lithuania and Armenia as the top three.

(4) Import and ODI flow

Table 2.6 Regression results of ODI flow and import volume

Country	β_8	t value	p value	Country	β_8	t value	p value
Laos	0.78	7.35	0.00	Malaysia	0.11	1.36	0.18
Vietnam	0.68	3.81	0.00	Pakistan	0.10	1.43	0.15
Bangladesh	0.55	3.78	0.00	Israel	0.10	1.26	0.21
Egypt	0.54	3.09	0.00	India	0.09	1.30	0.20
Cambodia	0.54	3.88	0.00	Singapore	0.08	1.22	0.22
UAE	0.53	3.59	0.00	Armenia	0.07	0.55	0.58
Myanmar	0.50	3.66	0.00	Bahrain	0.07	0.65	0.51
Iraq	0.37	5.78	0.00	Kuwait	0.07	1.06	0.29
Russia	0.37	1.79	0.07	Yemen	0.06	0.92	0.36
Indonesia	0.32	2.25	0.02	Kazakhstan	0.06	1.06	0.29
Saudi Arabia	0.30	2.77	0.01	Mongolia	0.05	0.66	0.51
Hungary	0.30	2.90	0.00	Afghanistan	0.05	0.73	0.47
Moldova	0.27	2.09	0.04	Turkmenistan	0.05	0.92	0.36
Qatar	0.27	3.60	0.00	The Philippines	0.05	0.62	0.53
Nepal	0.26	2.60	0.01	Iran	0.04	0.73	0.47
Tajikistan	0.26	1.74	0.08	Albania	0.04	0.33	0.74
Slovakia	0.25	3.16	0.00	Belarus	0.04	0.47	0.64
Turkey	0.25	2.66	0.01	Brunei	0.03	0.40	0.69
Thailand	0.24	1.71	0.09	Czech	0.03	0.25	0.80
Azerbaijan	0.23	2.72	0.01	Uzbekistan	0.03	0.38	0.71
Poland	0.23	2.04	0.04	Syria	0.02	0.28	0.78
Georgia	0.21	1.35	0.18	Croatia	0.01	0.11	0.91
Bulgaria	0.20	2.92	0.00	Lebanon	0.01	0.05	0.96
Sri Lanka	0.19	2.84	0.00	Oman	0.00	−0.01	0.99
Greece	0.18	1.67	0.10	Slovenia	0.00	−0.04	0.97
Cyprus	0.15	2.14	0.03	Latvia	−0.04	−0.35	0.72
Lithuania	0.15	1.27	0.21	Ukraine	−0.07	−0.65	0.52
Jordan	0.12	1.10	0.27	Kyrgyzstan	−0.11	−0.73	0.47
Romania	0.11	0.71	0.48	Estonia	−0.12	−0.89	0.37
Adjusted $R^2 = 0.89$				p value of the F test = 0.00			

Table 2.6 shows almost half of the countries have a p value larger than 10%, meaning ODI flow has a weak impact over the export volume of the same year.

Based on the analysis above, further analysis could be carried out using the regression results of ODI stock (Tables 2.3 and 2.5). A spatial description of the impact on export and import made by China's ODI stock in the Road and Belt countries will be conducted according to the sorting of β_5 and β_6 values so as to produce an overall picture. The host countries could be categorized according to the two indicators of β_5

(impact of ODI stock on export) and β_6 (impact of ODI stock on import), with arithmetic means of significant β_5 and β_6 values as the cutoff points for differentiating between high and low impacts on export and import, respectively. Therefore, these countries could be divided into the following categories: countries where China's ODI stock has a high impact on both export and import, countries where China's ODI stock has high impact on export but low impact on import, countries where China's ODI stock has low impact on both export and import, and countries where China's ODI stock has a low impact on export and import.

The positions of the four types of countries could be displayed in the four quadrants of a coordinate system where the x axis represents the size of impact on export and the y axis stands for the size of the impact on import. In this way, a visual comparison could be carried out for the impact on trade in different countries and regions. It should be noted that countries with high impact on export and low impact on import are marked on the x axis, and countries with the opposite situation are marked on the y axis.

See Fig. 2.8 for details:

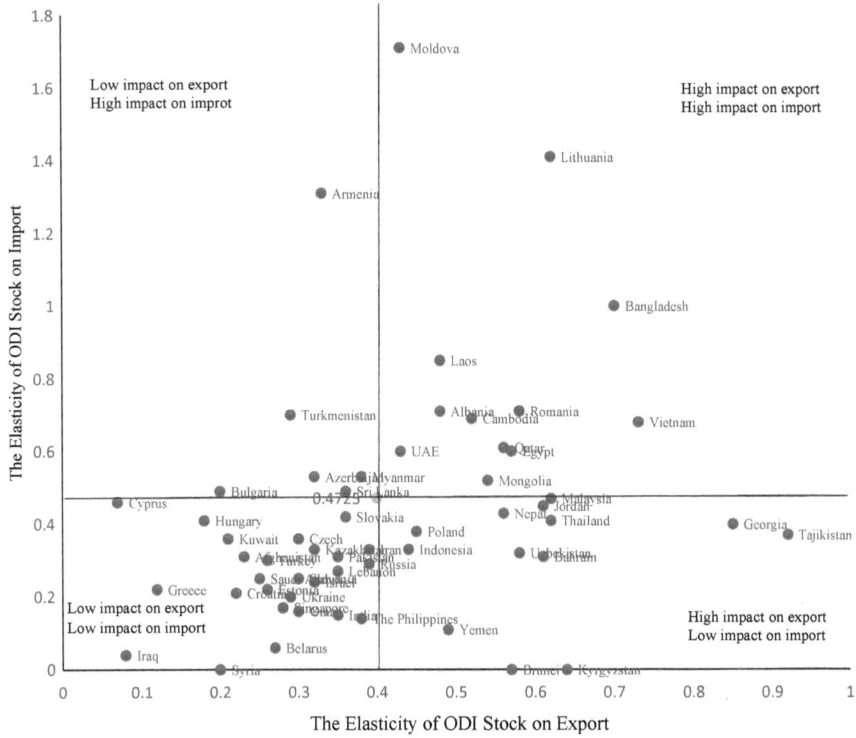

Fig. 2.8 Scatter plot of impacts on trade made by China's ODI in the Belt and Road countries. *Note* Given the limited space available, Latvia where both the impacts on export and import are negative is not shown in the plot

Table 2.7 Impacts on trade made by China's ODI in different regions along the Belt and Road

	Southeast Asia	Mongolia and Russia	West Asia and the Middle East	Central Asia	South Asia	Central and Eastern Europe
Impact on export	0.5159	0.4660	0.4159	0.5503	0.4261	0.2705
Impact on import	0.5670	0.4015	0.4674	0.4316	0.4470	0.4645

3. Analysis of regional differences

The scatter plot roughly shows that differences exist among countries and regions along the Belt and Road in terms of the impact on trade made by China's ODI. The following is a detailed analysis of the situations in the six regions along the Belt and Road.

Table 2.7 is based on the sorting of the significant results listed in Tables 2.3 and 2.5 and the arithmetic means of the impacts on export and import made by ODI stock in the six regions along the Belt and Road.

Table 2.7 proves regional differences exist in terms of ODI's impact on trade. On the aspect of export, China's ODI in Central Asia and Southeast Asia has strong effects of creating export, and the effects are weaker in Mongolia and Russia, South Asia, and West Asia and the Middle East, and the weakest in Central and Eastern Europe; for import, the import-creating effects of China's ODI are the strongest in Southeast Asia, followed by that in West Asia and the Middle East, Central and Eastern Europe, South Asia, and Central Asia, and Mongolia and Russia see low effects of creating import.

2.3 Conclusion

The following conclusions could be drawn based on the data of China's ODI in and trade with the six regions along the Belt and Road:

As the region that has attracted more than half of China's ODI along the Belt and Road, Southeast Asia sees the greatest impact of ODI on import and export. Southeast Asia, neighboring China, enjoys great geographical advantages—among the six regions along the Belt and Road, it is the closest to the coastal regions of China where ODI and trade are prosperous. Meanwhile, since Southeast Asia is mainly composed of developing countries, China's direct investment in infrastructure and construction projects there will greatly stimulate export of mechanic equipment; the fact that Southeast Asia is endowed with cheap labor and land and rich resources of rubber and energy has stimulated ODI that seeks efficiency and resources, and driven up export of manufacture equipment and semifinished products and import of natural resources.

Mongolia and Russia are the second largest host region of China's ODI stock with fast annual growth rate, but the export-creating effects of ODI are only modest there, and ODI's positive impact on import is the weakest in this region. And this is especially true in Russia. Possible causes for the weak effects in Russia include: 70% of China's import from Russia are energy products,[2] and Russia started to set limit on equity controlled by foreign capital in the field of resource development.

The trade-creating effects of China's ODI stock in West Asia and the Middle East (the third largest host region) get a middling ranking. With rich reserves of oil and natural gas, this region mainly attracts resource-seeking ODI. Central Asia is also rich in oil and gas, but its light industry is less sophisticated; therefore, China's ODI in this region is concentrated in areas such as oil exploration and drilling and light industry. Meanwhile, China mainly exports textiles, garments and mechanic equipment to Central Asia and imports energy products. With a structure similar to that of trade, ODI could deliver impact on trade more easily.

South Asia is close to China and densely populated. China's ODI in this region has moderate trade-creating effects. With rich labor resources and a huge market, South Asia is a good choice for China to relocate its labor-intensive industry. Investment flowing in this direction is often market and efficiency oriented.

Among the six regions along the Belt and Road, Central and Eastern Europe are the farthest from China. Most countries in this region are developed economies. China has been less active in investing in this region—its ODI stock and the impact of ODI on export are the lowest here compared to that in other regions. However, the import-creating effects of China's ODI are at a medium position. This is probably because Chinese enterprises target their investment at innovative assets, which could stimulate China's import of technology-intensive products.

[2] Source of data: www.haiguan.info.

Chapter 3
A Study of the Synergistic Trade Development of the Belt and Road Economic Corridors

Fan Wenqi and Hui Zhang

Through trade, Chinese businessmen have established contact with all countries along the Belt and Road.

"Corridor" is a phenomenon of regional economic agglomeration. In regional economics and regional cooperation practices, it is usually defined as a mechanism of economic cooperation by which the production, investment, trade and infrastructure construction are organically integrated within a specific transnational region.[1] Economic corridors are important carriers for China to implement the cooperation of Belt and Road construction with neighbouring countries or regions. They are also the priority and basis for China's participation and integration into regional and subregional economic cooperation. The Belt and Road Initiative is entering the stage of implementation, for which the construction of the six economic corridors is bound to be a key direction. While pushing forward the construction of the economic corridors, one could choose simultaneous development, or prioritize and accelerate the construction of one or two corridors as pilot projects.[2]

As Table 3.1 presents, the six economic corridors cover 38 countries or regions, of which Russia and Kazakhstan both belong to two economic corridors.

[1] Zhi and Guangsheng (2017).

[2] Maochun and Bin (2016).

F. Wenqi (✉) · H. Zhang
School of Economics, Peking University, Beijing, China

H. Zhang et al., *Comparative Studies on Regional and National Economic Development*, Global Economic Synergy of Belt and Road Initiative,
https://doi.org/10.1007/978-981-16-2105-5_3

Table 3.1 Countries/regions covered by the belt and road economic corridors

Economic corridor	Countries/regions
China–Pakistan economic corridor	Pakistan
Bangladesh–China–India–Myanmar economic corridor	Bangladesh, India, Myanmar
China–Mongolia–Russia economic corridor	Mongolia, Russia
China–Indochina Peninsula economic corridor	Vietnam, Laos, Cambodia, Thailand, Malaysia, Singapore
China–Central Asia–West Asia economic corridor	Kazakhstan, Kyrgyzstan, Tajikistan, Turkmenistan, Uzbekistan, Turkey, Israel, Saudi Arabia, Iraq, Iran, Afghanistan, Cyprus, Lebanon, Syria, Jordan, Palestine, Oman, Yemen, Kuwait, Bahrain, Qatar, UAE
New Eurasian land bridge	Kazakhstan, Russia, Belarus, Poland, Germany, the Netherlands

3.1 An Analysis of the Competitiveness and Complementarity Using Indexes

This section will use the trade indexes to analyze the trade status of the six economic corridors of the "Belt and Road". The data are from the International Trade Statistics Database of UN (UN Comtrade), and the selection of commodity types is based on the Standard International Trade Classification (SITC). According to SITC standards, international trade commodities can be divided into ten categories: SITC 0–9, as listed by Table 3.2.

In the UN Comtrade database, most of the data of Laos, Uzbekistan, Myanmar, Tajikistan, Turkmenistan, Afghanistan and Syria are missing. Therefore, unless

Table 3.2 Standard international trade classification (SITC)

Classification	Code	Commodities included
Resource-intensive primary products	SITC 0	Food and live animals
	SITC1	Beverages and tobacco
	SITC3	Crude materials, inedible, except fuels
	SITC 4	Animal and vegetable oils, fats and waxes
Capital-and-technology-intensive manufactured goods	SITC 5	Chemicals and related products
	SITC 7	Machinery and transport equipment
Labor-intensive manufactured goods	SITC 6	Manufactured goods classified chiefly by material
	SITC 8	Miscellaneous manufactured articles
	SITC 9	Commodities and transactions not classified elsewhere in the SITC

otherwise specified, Laos, Uzbekistan, Myanmar, Tajikistan and Turkmenistan, Afghanistan and Syria are not included in the calculation in this section.[3]

(I) Export similarity index

The calculation formula of the export similarity index (ESI) of country/region i and countries/regions j in the world market is as follows:

$$\mathrm{ESI}_{ij} = \left[\sum\nolimits_k \mathrm{Min}\left\{\frac{X_i^k}{X_i}, \frac{X_j^k}{X_j}\right\}\right] \times 100 \tag{3.1}$$

x_i^k and x_j^k represent the total export volumes of product k from country i and country j to the world. X_i and X_j represent the total export volumes from country i and country j to the world. If the export structures of country i and country j are exactly the same, then the ESI is 100, indicating fierce export competition between them. If their export structures are completely different, then the index is 0. The index varies between 0 and 100. If it declines, the competition between the two countries is gradually reduced, and the degree of specialized division of labor is rising.[4]

Table 3.3 lists the ESIs of China and other countries covered by the six economic corridors in the world market. First, horizontally, as Table 3.3 shows, China, Mongolia and Russia have the largest difference in the structure of commodities exported to the world market, which means there are little competition between them and large potential for bilateral trade. China and Central Asia–West Asia also have small trade competition and strong complementarity. China and Indochina countries have the highest ESI (77.40 in 2015), so they are the most severe export competition. Following the countries along the New Eurasian Land Bridge which also compete fiercely with China. Second, vertically, from 1996 to 2015, the export structures of China and Indochina countries gradually converged, and their competition in the world market grew fiercer. The ESIs of China, Mongolia–Russia and Central Asia–West Asia first decreased to hit the bottom in 2011 and then began to rise slightly, indicating that the trade competition between China and these two groups of countries first weakened and then intensified. China, Pakistan and Bangladesh–India–Myanmar witnessed weakening competition, improving degree of specialized division of labor and growing difference in export structures.

[3] Trade data dearth of other countries: for Bangladesh, data of 1999 and 2012–2015 are missing; for Mongolia, data of 2008–2012 are missing; for Cambodia, only data of 2000–2015 are available; for Vietnam, data of 1996 are missing; for Belarus, data of 1996 and 1997 are missing; for Kyrgyzstan, data of 1997 and 2014 are missing; for Lebanon, data of 1996 and 2015 are missing; for Iran, data of 1996, 2007–2009, and 2012–2015 are missing; for Saudi Arabia, data of 1997 are missing; for Jordan, data of 1996 are missing; for Palestine, data of 1996–1999 are missing; for Bahrain, data of 1997–1999 are missing; for Iraq, only export data of 2000–2002 and 2004–2015 and import data of 2000–2002, 2007, 2008 and 2014 are available; for Kuwait, export data of 2012 and import data of 2005, 2009 and 2012 are missing; for Qatar, export data of 1997 and import data of 1997, 2009 and 2011 are missing; for the UAE, data of 1996–1998 are missing; for Yemen, data of 1996–2000 are missing.

[4] Yanfang and Bo (2014).

Table 3.3 ESI of China and other countries covered by the six economic corridors

Year	China–Pakistan	Bangladesh–China–India–Myanmar	China–Mongolia–Russia	China–Indochina Peninsula	New Eurasian Land Bridge	China–Central Asia–West Asia
1996	56.80	67.47	41.23	59.76	68.18	46.83
1998	56.24	68.09	39.06	61.64	69.76	51.53
2000	57.90	66.37	36.42	65.62	70.18	32.22
2002	57.24	62.06	35.66	71.21	75.09	36.89
2004	56.18	61.70	33.26	74.83	71.96	34.32
2006	52.61	59.40	27.71	74.79	68.72	29.68
2008	53.43	59.38	25.48	70.00	64.84	30.80
2010	51.22	57.76	22.82	73.65	64.26	31.48
2011	51.98	59.59	21.27	69.94	65.20	28.41
2012	52.47	55.46	24.95	69.65	62.75	31.34
2013	51.30	51.99	24.46	71.61	62.89	30.95
2014	53.21	56.42	25.33	72.70	64.67	33.42
2015	52.87	58.91	29.83	77.40	67.87	35.55

Table 3.4 RCA index of China

SITC	0	1	2	3	4	5	6	7	8	9
1996	0.96	0.77	0.72	0.54	0.53	0.63	1.21	0.59	2.93	0.04
1998	0.89	0.49	0.58	0.51	0.32	0.57	1.16	0.65	2.91	0.00
2000	0.94	0.34	0.59	0.32	0.15	0.54	1.25	0.80	2.81	0.05
2002	0.80	0.32	0.46	0.29	0.08	0.46	0.68	0.96	2.48	0.05
2004	0.60	0.24	0.32	0.24	0.06	0.42	1.21	1.15	2.23	0.04
2006	0.55	0.16	0.24	0.13	0.10	0.45	1.28	1.25	2.22	0.06
2008	0.45	0.15	0.24	0.14	0.08	0.56	1.39	1.43	2.36	0.03
2010	0.46	0.16	0.21	0.11	0.05	0.50	1.23	1.45	2.19	0.02
2011	0.47	0.16	0.18	0.10	0.05	0.56	1.30	1.47	2.28	0.02
2012	0.44	0.16	0.17	0.09	0.05	0.53	1.32	1.44	2.39	0.01
2013	0.43	0.15	0.17	0.09	0.05	0.52	1.35	1.44	2.37	0.01
2014	0.41	0.15	0.18	0.10	0.06	0.54	1.38	1.35	2.26	0.02
2015	0.41	0.17	0.18	0.12	0.06	0.51	1.37	1.28	2.04	0.02

(II) Revealed Comparative Advantage Index

The calculation formula of the revealed comparative advantage index (RCA) is as follows:

$$\text{RCA} = \frac{X_a^i / X_a}{X_w^i / X_w} \tag{3.2}$$

In Formula (3.2), X represents the total export volume of region a, X_a^i is the export volume of commodity i in region a, X_w^i stands for the export volume of commodity i worldwide and X_w refers to the total export volume of the world.[5]

Generally speaking, if RCA > 2.5, region a is extremely competitive as an exporter; if 1.25 < RCA < 2.5, region a has good competitiveness globally; if 0.8 < RCA < 1.25, then region a exhibits moderate competitiveness in the export of a certain commodity; if RCA < 0.8, region a has little competitiveness.[6]

As Formula (3.2) gives the RCA indexes of China and the six economic corridors (from which China is excluded), the following conclusions could be drawn from Tables 3.4, 3.5, 3.6, 3.7, 3.8, 3.9 and 3.10.

As Table 3.4 shows, China's SITC 8 commodities, the RCA of which was always greater than 2 in 1996–2015, enjoy the strongest comparative advantage. For SITC 6 commodities, the RCA is often around 1.25 (except in 2002), indicating strong international competitiveness. This also confirms that in 1996–2015, China's most competitive products were labor-intensive manufactured goods (SITC 6 and 8 commodities). However, the comparative advantage of SITC 8 commodities has been

[5] Yonghui et al. (2015).

[6] Yunxia (2008).

Table 3.5 RCA index of Pakistan

SITC	0	1	2	3	4	5	6	7	8	9
1996	1.25	0.02	1.74	0.10	0.00	0.08	3.61	0.01	2.06	0.05
1998	2.03	0.07	0.67	0.06	0.20	0.07	3.52	0.02	2.18	0.05
2000	1.93	0.08	1.07	0.14	0.82	0.18	3.84	0.03	2.43	0.04
2002	1.84	0.09	0.61	0.21	0.46	0.20	2.19	0.03	2.39	0.01
2004	1.73	0.19	0.76	0.26	1.02	0.20	3.53	0.10	2.49	0.01
2006	2.25	0.25	0.55	0.36	1.60	0.25	3.45	0.05	2.57	0.02
2008	3.32	0.13	0.79	0.38	1.56	0.34	3.20	0.09	2.54	0.00
2010	2.81	0.20	0.94	0.37	0.76	0.34	3.34	0.08	2.33	0.00
2011	3.22	0.31	0.92	0.30	1.25	0.39	3.23	0.05	2.26	0.00
2012	2.76	0.24	1.28	0.08	1.51	0.36	3.42	0.05	2.57	0.22
2013	3.19	0.17	1.13	0.13	1.18	0.42	3.61	0.05	2.18	0.00
2014	2.95	0.13	1.04	0.17	0.91	0.40	3.51	0.05	2.15	0.00
2015	3.05	0.07	0.89	0.12	0.55	0.36	3.41	0.04	2.21	0.00

Table 3.6 RCA index of Bangladesh, India and Myanmar

SITC	0	1	2	3	4	5	6	7	8	9
1996	2.28	0.53	1.52	0.19	1.12	0.90	2.24	0.19	1.84	0.54
1998	2.25	0.49	1.13	0.07	0.87	0.84	2.23	0.15	2.27	0.77
2000	2.07	0.47	1.15	0.31	1.64	1.03	2.68	0.16	2.24	0.42
2002	1.98	0.44	1.40	0.47	0.80	0.98	1.46	0.19	1.95	0.57
2004	1.66	0.44	1.82	0.71	1.01	1.00	2.31	0.23	2.04	0.25
2006	1.54	0.42	1.95	0.98	0.69	1.04	2.07	0.27	1.89	0.25
2008	1.67	0.58	1.88	1.06	0.61	1.05	1.97	0.38	1.74	0.34
2010	1.20	0.59	1.89	1.07	0.63	0.90	2.09	0.39	1.62	0.37
2011	1.30	0.44	1.21	1.02	0.60	0.90	1.85	0.40	1.73	0.87
2012	1.62	0.50	1.62	1.11	0.61	1.13	1.88	0.42	1.37	0.17
2013	1.69	0.50	1.22	1.24	0.63	1.11	2.03	0.42	1.05	0.39
2014	1.65	0.47	1.08	1.29	0.62	1.09	1.95	0.45	1.14	0.22
2015	1.58	0.52	1.02	1.17	0.77	1.22	2.06	0.45	1.19	0.50

declining, reflecting the weakening competitiveness of Chinese textiles in the international market. The overall RCA index of China's SITC 7 commodities is on the rise, indicating that China's international competitiveness in capital-intensive manufactured products is increasing, and its machinery and transport equipment manufacturing are improving. The RCA index of SITC 5 commodities stays unchanged at lower than 0.8, indicating the lack of competitiveness for China's chemical products. The steady decline of the RCA index of SITC 0–4 commodities in 1996–2015

Table 3.7 RCA index of Mongolia and Russia

SITC	0	1	2	3	4	5	6	7	8	9
1996	0.14	0.19	1.58	5.89	0.09	0.63	1.27	0.18	0.12	5.23
1998	0.18	0.07	2.41	7.04	0.08	0.56	1.67	0.18	0.16	4.01
2000	0.18	0.09	1.59	5.06	0.25	0.67	1.30	0.15	0.17	2.76
2002	0.32	0.17	1.57	5.82	0.12	0.42	0.66	0.19	0.15	2.80
2004	0.21	0.17	1.59	5.30	0.14	0.41	1.21	0.15	0.10	2.51
2006	0.26	0.23	1.24	4.51	0.38	0.37	1.07	0.10	0.06	2.19
2008	0.28	0.26	1.06	4.17	0.32	0.48	0.91	0.10	0.06	1.92
2010	0.28	0.20	0.89	4.38	0.28	0.37	0.87	0.08	0.05	2.08
2011	0.32	0.19	0.77	3.92	0.31	0.39	0.76	0.07	0.04	2.14
2012	0.43	0.29	0.79	4.16	0.67	0.44	0.88	0.11	0.08	0.62
2013	0.40	0.30	0.88	4.21	0.72	0.42	0.84	0.12	0.10	0.63
2014	0.49	0.32	1.04	4.55	0.81	0.44	0.84	0.12	0.11	0.61
2015	0.58	0.40	1.27	6.12	0.95	0.51	0.99	0.15	0.13	0.63

Table 3.8 RCA index of countries of Indochina Peninsula

SITC	0	1	2	3	4	5	6	7	8	9
1996	0.82	0.77	0.93	1.02	4.20	0.47	0.52	1.43	0.80	0.37
1998	0.99	0.76	0.71	1.11	4.55	0.51	0.47	1.34	0.84	0.86
2000	1.00	0.57	0.70	0.80	3.86	0.61	0.48	1.40	0.87	0.58
2002	1.01	0.55	0.73	0.84	4.34	0.65	0.28	1.34	0.94	0.69
2004	0.93	0.51	0.76	0.95	4.09	0.78	0.50	1.33	0.94	0.53
2006	0.93	0.52	0.79	0.88	3.59	0.82	0.52	1.33	0.92	0.81
2008	1.10	0.63	0.74	1.00	4.44	0.76	0.60	1.24	1.01	1.64
2010	1.01	0.68	0.78	0.86	4.15	0.79	0.60	1.28	1.04	0.88
2011	1.08	0.74	0.80	0.88	4.32	0.89	0.61	1.22	1.07	0.85
2012	1.05	0.82	0.66	0.89	3.75	0.92	0.63	1.23	1.03	0.83
2013	0.98	0.85	0.67	0.87	3.45	0.88	0.66	1.27	1.07	0.70
2014	1.03	0.86	0.59	0.91	3.40	0.89	0.65	1.22	1.08	0.76
2015	1.03	0.93	0.67	0.95	2.94	0.83	0.66	1.23	1.10	0.50

indicates the weakening competitiveness of China as a primary product exporter. In fact, its primary products have little comparative advantage.

As Table 3.5 shows, the RCA of Pakistan's SITC 6 commodities has been around 3.5—SITC 6 commodities are the most competitive export products of the country. The RCA of its SITC 8 commodities has always been between 2.0–2.5, indicating good international competitiveness, which also confirms that labor-intensive manufactured products (SITC 6, 8) were the most competitive export products of Pakistan

Table 3.9 RCA index of countries along the New Eurasian land bridge

SITC	0	1	2	3	4	5	6	7	8	9
1996	0.92	0.94	0.76	1.05	0.75	1.35	0.99	0.96	0.72	2.03
1998	0.91	0.86	0.85	1.07	0.78	1.30	1.05	1.00	0.73	1.31
2000	0.91	0.98	0.80	0.94	0.79	1.27	0.97	0.94	0.70	2.34
2002	0.91	1.09	0.83	0.96	0.78	1.15	0.56	0.99	0.73	1.94
2004	0.92	1.00	0.84	1.00	0.63	1.14	0.95	0.99	0.71	1.99
2006	0.96	1.10	0.81	1.05	0.68	1.17	0.98	0.97	0.74	1.71
2008	0.99	1.09	0.79	1.09	0.71	1.20	0.98	1.01	0.75	1.97
2010	0.97	1.13	0.77	1.08	0.60	1.12	0.94	0.97	0.74	1.69
2011	1.00	1.19	0.70	1.11	0.65	1.15	0.97	1.03	0.77	0.99
2012	1.03	1.12	0.70	1.21	0.76	1.18	0.98	0.99	0.72	0.89
2013	1.07	1.11	0.68	1.26	0.86	1.20	0.97	1.00	0.75	0.59
2014	1.07	1.09	0.71	1.27	0.75	1.21	0.95	0.99	0.74	0.68
2015	1.06	1.08	0.73	1.44	0.75	1.23	0.95	0.99	0.74	0.64

Table 3.10 RCA index of Central Asia and West Asia

SITC	0	1	2	3	4	5	6	7	8	9
1996	0.64	1.02	0.43	7.67	0.50	0.73	0.90	0.21	0.58	0.03
1998	0.81	0.95	0.62	8.67	0.58	0.82	1.01	0.26	0.69	0.13
2000	0.43	0.64	0.31	6.60	0.32	0.46	0.70	0.16	0.40	1.19
2002	0.46	0.60	0.41	6.23	0.34	0.48	0.49	0.20	0.45	2.26
2004	0.43	0.37	0.36	5.67	0.31	0.44	0.77	0.20	0.42	2.21
2006	0.44	0.32	0.34	4.67	0.35	0.43	0.64	0.19	0.34	1.86
2008	0.40	0.28	0.36	4.07	0.23	0.48	0.74	0.23	0.34	1.58
2010	0.50	0.31	0.39	4.00	0.19	0.59	0.74	0.22	0.33	1.63
2011	0.39	0.25	0.32	3.78	0.24	0.56	0.65	0.19	0.29	1.59
2012	0.37	0.47	0.33	3.44	0.25	0.61	0.70	0.26	0.37	1.84
2013	0.36	0.50	0.31	3.58	0.28	0.57	0.66	0.28	0.35	1.63
2014	0.38	0.58	0.31	3.71	0.28	0.58	0.68	0.30	0.38	2.12
2015	0.48	0.40	0.37	4.10	0.33	0.63	0.80	0.27	0.43	3.68

in 1996–2015. However, in 2008–2015, SITC 0 overtook SITC 8 in terms of comparative advantage, and the overall RCA of SITC 0 has exhibited an upward trend since 1996, which means Pakistan's international competitiveness in food and live animals has gradually increased, making SITC 0 its second most competitive export products. With their RCA indexes always smaller than 0.8, SITC 1, 3, 5, 7, and 9 commodities of Pakistan basically have no comparative advantage, indicating Pakistan's weakness in capital-intensive manufactured goods (SITC 5, 7).

As Table 3.6 shows, for Bangladesh, India and Myanmar, SITC 6 commodities have the strongest comparative advantage. Since 1996, the RCA indexes of SITC 0, 2 and 8 have also been relatively large, indicating strong international competitiveness. It also shows that Bangladesh, India and Myanmar were the most competitive as exporters of labor-intensive manufactured products (SITC 6 and 8 products) and primary products in 1996–2015. However, the comparative advantages of SITC 0 and 8 exhibit a downward trend. SITC 3 and 7 are growing more competitive. The comparative advantage indexes of SITC 1 and 9 have stabilized at less than 0.8, which means these commodities have little comparative advantage.

As Table 3.7 shows, the most internationally competitive products of Mongolia and Russia are SITC 3 (fossil fuels, lubricating oil and crude oil)—their RCA indexes have always been greater than 4.0. The following SITC 3 are SITC 2 products (crude materials, inedible, except fuels)—this has something to do with Russia's rich oil and gas resources. The comparative advantage of SITC 9 products has weakened significantly. The RCA indexes of SITC 0 and 4 products have been growing, but they have stayed lower than 1.0. Commodities of SITC 1, 5, 7 and 8 have always lacked comparative advantages in the international market. To conclude, Mongolia and Russia, with imbalanced structures of export, are more competitive as exporters of primary products such as raw materials (SITC 3 and 2).

As Table 3.8 shows, the most internationally competitive products of Indochina countries are SITC 4 commodities (animal and vegetable oils, fats and waxes). The following SITC 4 are SITC 7 products (machinery and transport equipment). Since 1996, the comparative advantage of SITC 4 has been strong, as its RCA always stays above 2.5, leading to its great international competitiveness. However, since 2008, the comparative advantage of SITC 4 has been declining. Since 1996, the RCA of SITC 7 has stayed around 1.25, indicating strong international competitiveness. The comparative advantage indexes of SITC 0 and 8 have always been between 0.8 and 1.25, showing Indochina countries are relatively competitive in the export of food, live animals and miscellaneous products. The comparative advantage indexes of SITC 1, 2, 6 and 9 have basically stayed unchanged at below 1.0, which means these products have not comparative advantage and are uncompetitive in the global market.

As Table 3.9 shows, countries along the New Eurasian Land Bridge have strong international competitiveness in SITC 3 and 5. Following them are SITC 0 and 1. Since 1996, the comparative advantage index of SITC 9 has been shrinking, while that of other commodities has generally stabilized at 0.8–1.25 (moderate international competitiveness). This shows countries along this economic corridor enjoy balanced industrial structures and evenly high levels of development for primary products, labor-intensive products and capital-intensive products.

As Table 3.10 shows, SITC 3 products (fossil fuels, lubricants and related raw materials) of Central Asia and West Asia are extremely competitive globally. The RCA of SITC 3 has always been greater than 3.5, similar to that of Mongolia and Russia, placing natural resources such as oil as the most competitive products of Central Asia and West Asia during 1996–2015. Since 1996, the RCA of SITC 9 (commodities and transactions not classified elsewhere in the SITC) has been on the rise (always greater than 1.25 since 2002), indicating strong international competitiveness. Except for their SITC 3 and 9 products, Central Asia and West Asia have little comparative advantage in the international market. Suffering from extremely unbalanced trade structure, this region depends on oil export for trading income.

(III) Trade complementarity index

The trade complementarity index (TCI), displaying both the import and export advantages of one commodity, is a supplement to the RCA index. It can examine the compatibility and trade complementarity of two economies. The calculation formula of TCI for a single commodity (or industry) is as follows:

$$\mathrm{TCI}_{ij}^{k} = \mathrm{RCA}_{xi}^{k} \times \mathrm{RCA}_{mj}^{k} \tag{3.3}$$

TCI_{ij}^{k} represents the trade complementarity index of country i and country j in terms of product (or industry) k. RCA_{xi}^{k} represents the comparative advantage of country i in product k measured by export. RCA_{mj}^{k} represents the comparative disadvantage of country j in product k measured by import.[7] The formula can be decomposed into two parts: one part is RCA_{xi}^{k}, or the revealed comparative advantage index of commodity/industry k of country i. Its calculation, similar to formula (2), is as follows:

$$\mathrm{RCA}_{xi}^{k} = \frac{X_i^k / X_j}{X_w^k / X_w} \tag{3.4}$$

The other part is RCA_{mj}^{k}, calculated as follows:

$$\mathrm{RCA}_{mj}^{k} = \frac{M_j^k / M_j}{M_w^k / M_w} \tag{3.5}$$

M_j^k and M_w^k represent the import volumes of product k in country j and the world, and M_j and M_w represent the total import volumes of country j and the world.[8] The greater the value of RCA_{xi}^{k}, the greater the advantage of country i in product k; the greater the value of RCA_{mj}^{k}, the greater the disadvantage of country j in product k. Therefore, the larger the product of RCA_{xi}^{k} 和 RCA_{mj}^{k}, that is, the greater the value of TCI_{ij}^{k}, the stronger the trade complementarity of product k between i and j.[9]

The calculation formula of the comprehensive trade complementarity index is as follows:

$$\mathrm{TCI}_{ij} = \sum_{k} \left(\mathrm{RCA}_{xi}^{k} \times \mathrm{RCA}_{mj}^{k}\right) \times \frac{X_w^k}{X_w} \tag{3.6}$$

[7] Jinping (2003).

[8] Yanfang and Bo (2014).

[9] Jinping (2003).

Table 3.11 TCI of China and Pakistan (export by China, import by Pakistan)

SITC	0	1	2	3	4	5	6	7	8	9	Overall
1996	1.14	0.05	0.87	1.26	7.04	1.17	0.81	0.41	0.59	0.04	0.73
1998	1.29	0.00	0.90	1.26	6.82	1.18	0.44	0.37	0.57	0.00	0.69
2000	1.45	0.01	0.95	1.01	2.14	1.05	0.71	0.37	0.57	0.03	0.64
2002	0.67	0.01	1.11	0.83	1.09	0.77	0.49	0.57	0.56	0.01	0.60
2004	0.49	0.01	0.76	0.46	0.68	0.71	0.91	0.82	0.45	0.03	0.68
2006	0.66	0.01	0.43	0.23	0.85	0.56	1.06	1.02	0.53	0.03	0.72
2008	0.56	0.01	0.45	0.27	0.65	0.73	0.92	0.94	0.65	0.00	0.68
2010	0.53	0.01	0.39	0.22	0.45	0.68	1.03	0.87	0.61	0.00	0.65
2011	0.37	0.01	0.30	0.19	0.49	0.81	1.08	0.79	0.62	0.00	0.62
2012	0.36	0.01	0.27	0.18	0.45	0.72	1.11	0.81	0.64	0.00	0.61
2013	0.34	0.01	0.27	0.18	0.48	0.68	1.21	0.80	1.00	0.00	0.65
2014	0.39	0.01	0.33	0.19	0.51	0.73	1.32	0.79	0.81	0.00	0.67
2015	0.40	0.01	0.39	0.24	0.02	0.74	1.53	0.82	0.63	0.00	0.7

TCI_{ij} represents the comprehensive trade complementarity index of country i and country j. It takes the share of each type of commodity in global trade as the weight and calculates the average value of the trade complementarity indexes of all commodities. The larger the value of TCI_{ij}, the larger the import compatibility of country i and country j, and the stronger their trade complementarity.

It is generally believed that if the trade complementarity index is greater than 1, the trade complementarity of two countries is strong; if not, the trade complementarity is weak.[10]

An analysis of Tables 3.11 and 3.12 shows, the integrated TCI of China and Pakistan has always been smaller than 1, indicating low trade complementarity. However, China's TCI with Pakistan when the latter as the exporter of SITC 6 and 8 commodities (manufactured goods classified chiefly by material and miscellaneous manufactured articles) has always been greater than 1—in fact, the TCI of SICI 6 has always been greater than 2, which shows that the two countries are complementary in the trade of labor-intensive products. The TCI of SITC 0 products (food and live animals) has also been greater than 1 in the past three years, indicating good trade complementarity. When China is the exporter and Pakistan is the importer, the TCI of SITC 6 has been greater than 1 since 2010 and still rising, indicating high trade complementarity.

As Tables 3.13 and 3.14 show, whether China is the exporter or importer, the integrated TCI of China and Bangladesh–India–Myanmar is smaller than 1, indicating low trade complementarity. The integrated TCI with BIM as the exporter is higher than that with China as the exporter, indicating greater complementarity in this trade direction. When Bangladesh, India and Myanmar are the importers, the

[10] Ibid.

Table 3.12 TCI of China and Pakistan (import by China, export by Pakistan)

SITC	0	1	2	3	4	5	6	7	8	9	Overall
1996	0.71	0.01	3.10	0.06	0.00	0.11	5.42	0.02	0.97	0.01	1.15
1998	0.83	0.00	1.35	0.04	0.42	0.11	3.12	0.03	0.99	0.01	0.73
2000	0.76	0.01	2.73	0.13	1.15	0.25	5.24	0.03	1.10	0.01	1.02
2002	0.56	0.01	1.43	0.15	0.68	0.25	2.65	0.03	1.24	0.00	0.92
2004	0.52	0.02	2.09	0.20	1.87	0.22	3.40	0.12	1.84	0.00	0.89
2006	0.58	0.04	1.55	0.28	2.15	0.26	2.77	0.06	2.06	0.00	0.79
2008	0.78	0.03	2.78	0.33	2.75	0.33	2.26	0.10	2.12	0.00	0.77
2010	0.77	0.05	3.18	0.33	0.95	0.32	2.49	0.09	1.75	0.00	0.79
2011	0.93	0.09	3.10	0.27	1.38	0.36	2.21	0.06	1.62	0.00	0.76
2012	0.95	0.08	4.25	0.07	1.97	0.32	2.34	0.05	1.88	0.18	0.80
2013	1.18	0.05	3.79	0.12	1.29	0.37	2.35	0.05	1.50	0.00	0.75
2014	1.17	0.04	3.36	0.17	0.87	0.35	2.56	0.06	1.42	0.00	0.77
2015	1.47	0.03	2.82	0.12	0.51	0.31	2.26	0.05	1.49	0.00	0.73

TCI of SITC 6 products (manufactured goods chiefly classified by material) has long been greater than 1, indicating good trade complementarity. When the three countries are exporters, the TCI of SITC 2 and 6 (crude materials, inedible, except fuels and manufactured goods chiefly classified by material) has long been greater than 1—in fact, the TCI of SITC 2 has been greater than 2, indicating that very strong trade complementarity is very.

Table 3.13 TCI of China and Bangladesh–India–Myanmar (export by China, import by BIM)

SITC	0	1	2	3	4	5	6	7	8	9	Overall
1996	0.44	0.05	1.04	1.65	3.37	0.79	1.68	0.29	0.73	0.09	0.77
1998	0.56	0.01	0.89	1.38	2.93	0.69	0.98	0.26	0.85	0.01	0.71
2000	0.41	0.04	1.01	1.02	1.63	0.53	1.77	0.30	0.90	0.09	0.69
2002	0.41	0.03	0.80	0.85	0.77	0.41	0.92	0.44	0.93	0.12	0.60
2004	0.26	0.02	0.50	0.62	0.44	0.36	1.48	0.63	0.76	0.10	0.68
2006	0.23	0.01	0.42	0.30	0.50	0.39	1.21	0.80	0.72	0.14	0.66
2008	0.15	0.01	0.30	0.28	0.24	0.58	1.35	0.88	0.61	0.06	0.67
2010	0.18	0.01	0.24	0.22	0.21	0.44	1.60	0.78	0.63	0.05	0.65
2011	0.16	0.01	0.20	0.18	0.21	0.47	1.64	0.77	0.68	0.08	0.63
2012	0.10	0.02	0.20	0.19	0.20	0.43	1.24	0.71	0.87	0.04	0.57
2013	0.10	0.02	0.20	0.21	0.23	0.44	1.42	0.70	0.68	0.03	0.57
2014	0.11	0.02	0.23	0.23	0.27	0.50	1.48	0.64	0.68	0.05	0.58
2015	0.15	0.02	0.25	0.29	0.02	0.52	1.62	0.71	0.67	0.04	0.65

Table 3.14 TCI of China and Bangladesh–India–Myanmar (import by China, export by BIM)

SITC	0	1	2	3	4	5	6	7	8	9	Overall
1996	1.30	0.19	2.71	0.11	3.02	1.22	3.36	0.20	0.87	0.10	1.04
1998	0.92	0.01	2.27	0.05	1.85	1.22	1.97	0.15	1.03	0.14	0.77
2000	0.81	0.09	2.95	0.27	2.32	1.48	3.66	0.16	1.02	0.08	0.99
2002	0.60	0.06	3.26	0.33	1.19	1.21	1.77	0.23	1.01	0.08	0.94
2004	0.50	0.05	4.97	0.54	1.85	1.08	2.22	0.27	1.51	0.02	0.96
2006	0.39	0.07	5.53	0.76	0.93	1.08	1.66	0.33	1.52	0.02	0.95
2008	0.39	0.13	6.60	0.91	1.07	1.03	1.39	0.45	1.45	0.03	0.97
2010	0.33	0.13	6.41	0.95	0.78	0.84	1.56	0.45	1.22	0.12	0.98
2011	0.38	0.12	4.07	0.92	0.67	0.83	1.27	0.45	1.24	0.63	0.92
2012	0.56	0.16	5.39	1.05	0.79	1.01	1.29	0.46	1.00	0.14	0.96
2013	0.62	0.15	4.07	1.14	0.69	0.98	1.32	0.46	0.72	0.44	0.91
2014	0.66	0.14	3.48	1.29	0.58	0.95	1.42	0.49	0.75	0.24	0.91
2015	0.76	0.22	3.24	1.23	0.72	1.06	1.37	0.49	0.80	0.51	0.89

As Tables 3.15 and 3.16 show, the integrated TCI with Mongolia and Russia as the importers and China as the exporter has been greater than 1 since 2006. The integrated TCIs of the opposite trade direction have exceeded 1 since 2014 and 2015, indicating that China and Mongolia–Russia have been complementary in trade (especially in trade with China as the exporter) in recent years. The TCI of SITC 8 (miscellaneous manufactured articles) with China as the exporter has been greater than 1 since 1996 (even greater than 2 in 2008–2015); the TCI of SITC 6 (manufactured goods chiefly classified by material) has also been greater than 1 since 2004, revealing good trade complementarity of capital-intensive manufactured goods. The TCI of machinery and transport equipment (SITC 7 products) with China as the exporter has also exceeded 1 since 2004, revealing strong trade complementarity. The TCI of SITC 2 and 3 with China as the importer has always stayed above 1—the TCI of SITC 3 (fossil fuels, lubricating oil and related raw materials) has long been larger than 3, and the TCI of SITC 2 (raw materials, inedible, excluding fuel) has long been above 2, indicating extremely great complementary of trade. Overall, China mainly sells Mongolia and Russia capital-intensive manufactured products and machinery and transportation equipment and buys back fossil fuels and inedible raw materials.

As Tables 3.17 and 3.18 show, the integrated TCI with China as the importer and Indochina countries as the exporters has stayed around 0.95–1.05 despite slight fluctuations since 1996. The integrated TCI of the opposite trade direction also stayed around 1, the critical value, remaining in a tight range of 0.95–1 from 2004 to 2015. This indicates that the trade complementarity between China and Indochina countries has been in the critical state. The TCIs of SITC 6, 7 and 8 with China as the exporter have long been above 1, revealing good complementarity in the trade of labor-intensive manufactured goods and machinery and transport equipment. The TCIs of SITC 2, 4 and 7 with China as the importer have stayed above 1—the index

Table 3.15 TCI of China and Mongolia–Russia (export by China, import by Mongolia–Russia)

SITC	0	1	2	3	4	5	6	7	8	9	Overall
1996	1.98	1.93	0.63	0.18	0.72	0.47	0.86	0.31	1.56	0.41	0.71
1998	2.37	0.29	0.68	0.28	0.65	0.56	0.54	0.46	1.67	0.00	0.82
2000	2.72	1.32	1.21	0.14	0.57	0.68	1.28	0.49	1.63	0.13	0.86
2002	2.22	0.99	0.62	0.08	0.29	0.51	0.62	0.75	1.62	0.12	0.82
2004	1.47	0.69	0.37	0.05	0.12	0.45	1.19	1.07	1.40	0.11	0.90
2006	1.32	0.37	0.20	0.02	0.16	0.51	1.18	1.44	1.53	0.11	1.00
2008	0.83	0.29	0.17	0.01	0.11	0.52	1.22	2.05	2.05	0.03	1.17
2010	0.96	0.31	0.10	0.01	0.06	0.56	1.16	1.65	2.24	0.04	1.08
2011	0.83	0.28	0.08	0.01	0.05	0.58	1.20	1.90	2.24	0.06	1.12
2012	0.81	0.30	0.11	0.01	0.05	0.58	1.45	2.05	2.75	0.00	1.24
2013	0.80	0.29	0.11	0.01	0.05	0.59	1.48	1.94	2.77	0.00	1.22
2014	0.75	0.30	0.13	0.01	0.05	0.62	1.45	1.74	2.57	0.00	1.17
2015	0.71	0.34	0.17	0.02	0.00	0.65	1.40	1.43	2.04	0.00	1.07

Table 3.16 TCI of China and Mongolia–Russia (import by China, export by Mongolia–Russia)

SITC	0	1	2	3	4	5	6	7	8	9	Overall
1996	0.08	0.07	2.82	3.40	0.25	0.86	1.91	0.18	0.06	0.94	0.85
1998	0.08	0.00	4.82	5.29	0.17	0.81	1.48	0.18	0.07	0.75	0.87
2000	0.07	0.02	4.06	4.55	0.35	0.96	1.77	0.15	0.08	0.51	1.00
2002	0.10	0.02	3.67	4.04	0.18	0.52	0.80	0.22	0.08	0.42	0.84
2004	0.07	0.02	4.36	4.05	0.26	0.44	1.16	0.18	0.07	0.19	0.85
2006	0.07	0.04	3.53	3.47	0.51	0.39	0.86	0.12	0.05	0.16	0.82
2008	0.07	0.06	3.73	3.58	0.57	0.47	0.65	0.12	0.05	0.18	0.88
2010	0.08	0.05	3.02	3.88	0.35	0.34	0.65	0.09	0.04	0.67	0.89
2011	0.09	0.05	2.60	3.53	0.34	0.36	0.52	0.08	0.03	1.54	0.94
2012	0.15	0.09	2.61	3.92	0.87	0.40	0.60	0.12	0.06	0.52	0.97
2013	0.15	0.09	2.94	3.89	0.79	0.37	0.54	0.14	0.07	0.71	0.98
2014	0.19	0.10	3.35	4.52	0.77	0.38	0.62	0.13	0.07	0.67	1.03
2015	0.28	0.17	4.03	6.43	0.89	0.45	0.66	0.16	0.09	0.65	1.06

for SITC 4 (animal and vegetable oils, fats and wax) had long been larger than 3 before 2014 (it was as high as 11.37 in 1996), indicating extremely strong trade complementarity. However, the TCI of SITC exhibits a downward trend. Based on Tables 3.17 and 3.18, China mainly exports to Indochina Peninsula SITC commodities and labor-intensive manufactured goods and imports primary products such as animal and vegetable oils, fats and wax, inedible raw materials (fuels excluded), and machinery and transport equipment.

Table 3.17 TCI of China and countries of Indochina Peninsula (export by China, import by IP countries)

SITC	0	1	2	3	4	5	6	7	8	9	Overall
1996	0.47	0.60	0.39	0.46	0.23	0.47	1.03	0.86	1.75	0.03	0.85
1998	0.50	0.05	0.31	0.53	0.20	0.47	0.55	0.90	1.77	0.00	0.87
2000	0.52	0.23	0.35	0.32	0.09	0.45	1.01	1.12	1.67	0.02	0.91
2002	0.47	0.20	0.30	0.31	0.06	0.35	0.60	1.32	1.35	0.03	0.88
2004	0.36	0.14	0.20	0.26	0.05	0.33	1.10	1.55	1.27	0.02	0.99
2006	0.33	0.09	0.13	0.15	0.07	0.34	1.20	1.64	1.28	0.05	0.99
2008	0.30	0.10	0.14	0.17	0.06	0.42	1.41	1.70	1.35	0.03	1.00
2010	0.33	0.11	0.12	0.14	0.05	0.40	1.27	1.78	1.31	0.01	1.01
2011	0.33	0.12	0.11	0.13	0.06	0.46	1.34	1.72	1.41	0.02	0.97
2012	0.32	0.12	0.10	0.11	0.05	0.42	1.40	1.73	1.50	0.01	0.98
2013	0.31	0.12	0.10	0.12	0.04	0.41	1.48	1.70	1.48	0.01	0.98
2014	0.31	0.12	0.11	0.13	0.05	0.44	1.53	1.54	1.40	0.01	0.96
2015	0.33	0.14	0.11	0.16	0.00	0.42	1.60	1.48	1.30	0.01	0.99

Table 3.18 TCI of China and countries of Indochina Peninsula (import by China, export by IP countries)

SITC	0	1	2	3	4	5	6	7	8	9	Overall
1996	0.47	0.28	1.66	0.59	11.37	0.64	0.78	1.48	0.38	0.07	1.01
1998	0.40	0.01	1.43	0.83	9.74	0.73	0.42	1.34	0.38	0.16	0.93
2000	0.39	0.11	1.79	0.72	5.45	0.88	0.65	1.42	0.40	0.11	0.97
2002	0.31	0.07	1.71	0.59	6.44	0.80	0.34	1.59	0.49	0.10	1.02
2004	0.28	0.06	2.07	0.73	7.49	0.84	0.48	1.56	0.69	0.04	1.04
2006	0.24	0.09	2.24	0.68	4.84	0.85	0.42	1.64	0.73	0.06	1.05
2008	0.26	0.15	2.59	0.86	7.84	0.74	0.42	1.45	0.84	0.16	0.98
2010	0.28	0.15	2.64	0.76	5.17	0.73	0.44	1.47	0.78	0.28	0.99
2011	0.31	0.21	2.68	0.79	4.79	0.81	0.42	1.35	0.76	0.61	0.99
2012	0.37	0.26	2.19	0.84	4.86	0.82	0.43	1.34	0.75	0.69	0.98
2013	0.36	0.25	2.23	0.81	3.78	0.78	0.43	1.39	0.74	0.79	0.98
2014	0.41	0.26	1.90	0.90	3.23	0.77	0.47	1.32	0.71	0.83	0.96
2015	0.50	0.39	2.12	1.00	2.76	0.72	0.44	1.35	0.74	0.51	0.98

As Tables 3.19 and 3.20 show, the integrated TCI with China as the importer and other countries along the New Eurasian Land Bridge as the exporters has remained between 0.9 and 1.0 since 1996, and the integrated TCI of the opposite trade direction has stay around the critical value 1 within the range 0.9–1.05. The TCIs of SITC 6, 7 and 8 with China as the exporter has been greater than 1 since 2004, and that of SITC 8 (miscellaneous manufactured articles), in particular, has been greater than

3, indicating good trade complementarity in labor-intensive products and machinery and transport equipment. The TCIs of the SITC 2, 5 and 7 with China as the importer has always remained above 1, revealing the high trade complementarity in capital-intensive manufactured products and inedible raw materials (fuels excluded). In addition, the TCI of SITC 3 exhibits an upward trend, rising from 0.61 in 1996 to 1.51 in 2015, indicating improved trade complementarity in fossil fuels, lubricants and related raw materials.

As Tables 3.21 and 3.22 show, whether China is the exporter or importer, the integrated TCI of China and Central Asia–West Asia is less than 1. However, the integrated TCI with Central Asia–West Asia as the exporter has been rising since 2002, indicating improved complementarity with China as the importer. The TCIs of SITC 6, 7 and 8 with China as the exporter has stayed above 1 since 2004, revealing the strong complementarity in labor-intensive manufactured goods and machinery and transport equipment. When China is the importer, the TCI of SITC 3 (fossil fuels, lubricants and related raw materials) has remained above 3, indicating extremely high complementarity. The TCI of SITC 2 (raw materials, inedible, except fuels) has stayed above 1 since 2008; the TCI of SITC 9 rose substantially from 0.01 in 1996 to 3.78 in 2015, suggesting great improvement of complementarity.

Table 3.23 lists all the commodity types of the six economic corridors with a TCI larger than 1. It shows when China is the exporter, the commodities with good trade complementarity are mainly labor-intensive manufactured goods (SITC 6 and 8) and capital-intensive machinery and transport equipment (SITC 7). Along the opposite trade direction, resource–intensive primary products (SITC 0–4), especially inedible raw materials (fuels excluded), enjoy good trade complementarity.

Table 3.19 TCI of China and countries along the New Eurasia Land Bridge (export by China, import by NELB countries)

SITC	0	1	2	3	4	5	6	7	8	9	Overall
1996	1.24	0.90	0.69	0.48	0.52	0.63	1.20	0.50	3.07	0.10	1.00
1998	1.08	0.08	0.60	0.48	0.33	0.60	0.70	0.59	2.86	0.00	0.98
2000	1.05	0.38	0.60	0.28	0.16	0.55	1.15	0.70	2.53	0.14	0.92
2002	0.96	0.38	0.47	0.27	0.10	0.48	0.65	0.89	2.28	0.09	0.89
2004	0.71	0.27	0.29	0.20	0.06	0.43	1.11	1.09	1.92	0.11	0.93
2006	0.68	0.18	0.23	0.11	0.13	0.49	1.27	1.24	1.94	0.10	0.96
2008	0.54	0.16	0.19	0.10	0.08	0.59	1.37	1.42	2.16	0.06	1.00
2010	0.57	0.18	0.16	0.09	0.05	0.54	1.18	1.40	2.15	0.04	0.98
2011	0.58	0.19	0.15	0.08	0.05	0.62	1.36	1.49	2.40	0.03	1.03
2012	0.58	0.19	0.14	0.07	0.05	0.59	1.41	1.46	2.52	0.01	1.02
2013	0.57	0.18	0.13	0.08	0.07	0.59	1.45	1.44	2.57	0.01	1.03
2014	0.53	0.18	0.15	0.08	0.06	0.61	1.44	1.34	2.48	0.02	1.02
2015	0.51	0.20	0.15	0.11	0.00	0.58	1.42	1.21	2.19	0.01	1.00

Table 3.20 TCI of China and countries along the New Eurasia Land Bridge (import by China, export by NELB countries)

SITC	0	1	2	3	4	5	6	7	8	9	Overall
1996	0.53	0.34	1.36	0.61	2.03	1.83	1.49	1.00	0.34	0.37	1.00
1998	0.37	0.01	1.70	0.80	1.67	1.88	0.93	1.00	0.33	0.24	0.93
2000	0.36	0.19	2.03	0.84	1.12	1.82	1.33	0.96	0.32	0.43	0.97
2002	0.28	0.15	1.94	0.67	1.15	1.43	0.67	1.17	0.38	0.29	0.98
2004	0.28	0.11	2.29	0.76	1.16	1.23	0.91	1.16	0.53	0.15	0.95
2006	0.25	0.19	2.30	0.81	0.91	1.21	0.79	1.19	0.59	0.12	0.96
2008	0.23	0.25	2.79	0.93	1.25	1.18	0.69	1.18	0.63	0.19	0.93
2010	0.27	0.26	2.59	0.96	0.75	1.04	0.70	1.12	0.56	0.54	0.93
2011	0.29	0.33	2.37	1.00	0.73	1.05	0.66	1.14	0.55	0.72	0.96
2012	0.36	0.36	2.34	1.14	0.98	1.05	0.67	1.08	0.53	0.74	0.96
2013	0.40	0.33	2.28	1.17	0.94	1.05	0.63	1.09	0.51	0.67	0.95
2014	0.43	0.33	2.30	1.26	0.71	1.05	0.69	1.07	0.48	0.74	0.97
2015	0.51	0.45	2.33	1.51	0.70	1.06	0.63	1.09	0.50	0.66	0.97

Table 3.21 TCI of China and Central Asia–West Asia (export by China, import by CW countries)

SITC	0	1	2	3	4	5	6	7	8	9	Overall
1996	1.15	1.05	0.73	0.46	0.86	0.67	1.71	0.55	1.98	0.03	0.95
1998	1.14	0.08	0.60	0.44	0.76	0.64	0.93	0.61	1.97	0.00	0.94
2000	1.46	0.47	0.58	0.22	0.34	0.58	1.73	0.69	1.93	0.08	0.94
2002	1.05	0.35	0.45	0.23	0.13	0.42	0.92	0.82	1.61	0.14	0.81
2004	0.71	0.23	0.33	0.17	0.10	0.38	1.66	1.00	1.38	0.13	0.89
2006	0.62	0.13	0.21	0.09	0.14	0.37	1.77	1.07	1.44	0.26	0.90
2008	0.58	0.11	0.21	0.06	0.09	0.46	2.18	1.39	1.69	0.07	1.03
2010	0.63	0.13	0.18	0.05	0.06	0.43	1.78	1.30	1.55	0.06	0.94
2011	0.62	0.13	0.16	0.04	0.06	0.48	1.88	1.31	1.66	0.09	0.94
2012	0.54	0.16	0.15	0.04	0.05	0.44	1.88	1.40	1.94	0.04	0.98
2013	0.53	0.15	0.13	0.04	0.05	0.43	1.89	1.41	1.95	0.04	0.98
2014	0.53	0.17	0.15	0.04	0.06	0.47	1.85	1.34	1.95	0.06	0.99
2015	0.49	0.15	0.14	0.05	0.00	0.40	1.71	1.09	1.52	0.06	0.88

(IV) Trade integration index

The calculation formula of the trade integration index of country a and country b is as follows:

$$\mathrm{TCD} = \frac{X_{ab}/X_a}{M_b/M_w} \tag{3.7}$$

Table 3.22 TCI of China and Central Asia–West Asia (import by China, export by CW countries)

SITC	0	1	2	3	4	5	6	7	8	9	Overall
1996	0.37	0.37	0.77	4.43	1.36	0.99	1.35	0.22	0.28	0.01	0.81
1998	0.33	0.02	1.24	6.51	1.23	1.19	0.90	0.26	0.31	0.02	0.83
2000	0.17	0.12	0.80	5.94	0.46	0.66	0.96	0.17	0.18	0.22	0.92
2002	0.14	0.08	0.96	4.33	0.51	0.59	0.59	0.23	0.23	0.33	0.77
2004	0.13	0.04	0.98	4.33	0.57	0.47	0.74	0.24	0.31	0.16	0.78
2006	0.11	0.05	0.98	3.60	0.48	0.45	0.51	0.24	0.27	0.13	0.78
2008	0.09	0.06	1.26	3.50	0.41	0.47	0.52	0.27	0.29	0.15	0.84
2010	0.14	0.07	1.31	3.54	0.24	0.55	0.55	0.25	0.25	0.52	0.86
2011	0.11	0.07	1.09	3.40	0.27	0.51	0.45	0.21	0.20	1.15	0.90
2012	0.13	0.15	1.10	3.25	0.33	0.55	0.48	0.29	0.27	1.53	0.93
2013	0.13	0.15	1.03	3.31	0.31	0.50	0.43	0.31	0.24	1.84	0.94
2014	0.15	0.18	1.01	3.69	0.26	0.51	0.50	0.32	0.25	2.30	0.98
2015	0.23	0.16	1.17	4.31	0.31	0.55	0.53	0.29	0.29	3.78	0.99

Table 3.23 Comparison of the TCIs of China and other countries covered by the six economic corridors

	China as the exporter	China as the importer
China–Pakistan		SITC6, 8
Bangladesh–China–India–Myanmar	SITC6	SITC2, 6
China–Mongolia–Russia	SITC6, 7, 8	SITC2, 3
China–Indochina Peninsula	SITC6, 7, 8	SITC2, 4, 7
New Eurasia Land Bridge	SITC6, 7, 8	SITC2, 5, 7
China–Central Asia–West Asia	SITC6, 7, 8	SITC2, 3

X_{ab} represents the total export of country a to country *b*. X_a is the total export of country *a*. M_b refers to the total import of country *b*. M_w stands for the total import globally. TCD > 1 means that the two countries have close trade ties. TCD < 1 indicates that the two countries have loose trade ties. TCD = 1 suggests that the bilateral trade is of average intensity.[11]

Table 3.24 lists the trade integration indexes with China as the exporter:

Table 3.25 lists the trade integration indexes with China as the importer:

Tables 3.24 and 3.25 show that when China is the exporter, all corridors except the China–Indochina Peninsula Economic Corridor have a trade integration index larger than 1. When China is the importer, only the index of China–Indochina Peninsula Economic Corridor is greater than 1, and the indexes of the rest are all smaller than 1.

[11] Sisi (2015).

Table 3.24 Trade integration indexes of China and other countries covered by the six economic corridors (China as the exporter)

Year	China–Pakistan	Bangladesh–China–India–Myanmar	China–Mongolia–Russia	China–Indochina Peninsula	New Eurasia Land Bridge	China–Central Asia–West Asia
1996	1.77	1.02	1.00	0.56	0.90	1.00
1998	1.64	0.99	1.26	0.61	1.09	1.00
2000	1.58	1.06	1.77	0.65	1.09	1.00
2002	2.24	1.12	1.59	0.64	1.24	0.99
2004	2.15	1.11	1.91	0.72	1.21	0.98
2006	1.78	1.14	1.46	0.75	1.25	1.11
2008	1.61	1.20	1.43	0.79	1.31	1.39
2010	1.77	1.20	1.30	0.81	1.29	1.19
2011	1.84	1.10	1.29	0.79	1.28	1.23
2012	1.87	1.00	1.30	0.77	1.36	1.20
2013	2.10	1.04	1.35	0.74	1.53	1.15
2014	2.19	1.13	1.51	0.75	1.63	1.23
2015	2.64	1.30	1.37	0.56	1.71	1.15

Table 3.25 Trade integration indexes of China and other countries covered by the six economic corridors (China as the importer)

Year	China–Pakistan	Bangladesh–China–India–Myanmar	China–Mongolia–Russia	China–Indochina Peninsula	New Eurasia Land Bridge	China–Central Asia–West Asia
1996	0.48	0.65	1.70	1.04	0.56	0.25
1998	0.70	0.48	1.79	1.23	0.51	0.41
2000	0.77	0.45	1.54	1.15	0.50	0.52
2002	0.53	0.62	1.46	1.24	0.52	0.27
2004	0.37	0.82	0.95	1.24	0.46	0.39
2006	0.46	0.99	0.85	1.34	0.45	0.35
2008	0.51	0.73	0.64	1.29	0.45	0.42
2010	0.73	0.80	0.54	1.19	0.50	0.42
2011	0.68	0.54	0.69	1.19	0.56	0.44
2012	1.06	0.51	0.68	1.13	0.53	0.34
2013	1.00	0.46	0.70	1.13	0.50	0.31
2014	0.86	0.40	0.79	1.10	0.52	0.44
2015	0.84	0.35	0.88	1.17	0.50	0.41

This shows that China has close export relations with Pakistan, Bangladesh–India–Myanmar, Mongolia–Russia, other countries of the New Eurasian Land Bridge and Central Asia–West Asia, and close import ties with Indochina countries.

(V) Index of intra-industry trade

The G-L index takes the following form:

The calculation formula of the intra-industry trade index for product group i is follows:

$$\mathrm{IIT}_i = \left(1 - \frac{|X_i - M_i|}{X_i + M_i}\right) \times 100\% \tag{3.8}$$

X_i and M_i, respectively, represent the export and import volumes of product group i.

The calculation formula of a country's overall intra-industry trade level is as follows:

$$\mathrm{IIT} = \frac{\sum_{i=1}^{n} \mathrm{IIT}_i (X_i + M_i)}{\sum_{i=1}^{n} (X_i + M_i)} \times 100\% = \left[1 - \frac{\sum_{i=1}^{n} |X_i - M_i|}{\sum_{i=1}^{n} (X_i + M_i)}\right] \times 100\% \tag{3.9}$$

However, Formula (3.9) does not take into account the problem of overall imbalance. When the trade is imbalanced, the G-L index may skew downward. In response to this problem, Grubel and Lloyd (1971) proposed a fix:

$$\mathrm{IIT}_{\mathrm{adj}} = \frac{\sum_{i=1}^{n} (X_i + M_i) - \sum_{i=1}^{n} |X_i - M_i|}{\sum_{i=1}^{n} (X_i + M_i) - \left|\sum_{i=1}^{n} (X_i - M_i)\right|} \times 100\% \tag{10}$$

As the G-L index varies between 0 and 1, the greater its value, the larger the proportion of intra-industry trade. When the index exceeds 0.5, intra-industry trade is dominant, and when it is below 0.5, intra-industry trade takes the lead.[12]

The intra-industry trade indexes of specific product groups calculated with formula (3.8) are listed in Tables 3.26, 3.27, 3.28, 3.29, 3.30 and 3.31.

Table 3.26 shows that China and Pakistan have a relatively high level of intra-industry trade for SITC 0, 2 and 6, and the G-L indexes of SITC 0 and 2 have been increasing year by year. The two countries are expected to maintain for a long time the dominance of intra-industry trade for food and live animals and inedible raw materials (fuels excluded). For SITC 1, 3, 4, 5, 7, 8 and 9, the bilateral trade is dominated by inter-industry trade.

Table 3.27 shows that China and Bangladesh–India–Myanmar have higher levels of intra-industry trade for SITC 0, 6, 8 and 9, with the G-L indexes of SITC 6 and 8 first rising and then falling. For labor-intensive manufactured goods (SITC 6 and 8), the dominance of intra-industry trade is expected to be replaced by the dominance of inter-industry trade. The G-L indexes of SITC 1 and 2 commodities were once very low in 2000–2012, but then rose substantially in 2013–2015.

[12] Kuangda (2013).

Table 3.26 G-L index of China and Pakistan (Unit: %)

SITC	0	1	2	3	4	5	6	7	8	9
1996	25.39	0.00	5.84	35.38	0.00	1.49	56.11	0.03	1.80	0.00
1998	63.33	0.00	17.97	79.95	0.00	0.55	37.27	0.18	0.11	–
2000	30.11	0.00	24.61	0.00	0.00	33.67	43.39	0.06	6.09	0.00
2002	28.40	0.00	67.18	86.03	0.00	29.44	55.84	1.41	8.15	0.00
2004	33.22	0.00	39.48	0.05	0.00	8.10	99.94	0.11	1.98	0.02
2006	38.06	0.00	55.47	0.00	0.51	10.82	81.87	0.12	0.67	0.00
2008	50.93	36.82	53.71	0.00	21.28	5.97	56.67	0.06	0.96	0.24
2010	52.82	0.00	74.16	11.16	16.83	6.45	67.09	1.11	3.32	1.15
2011	51.41	61.02	86.37	58.07	0.02	9.31	69.15	0.29	3.80	26.36
2012	69.49	0.00	71.36	0.02	0.00	6.83	81.60	0.03	5.88	0.00
2013	77.34	51.36	66.55	0.02	0.00	5.46	72.84	0.02	7.07	79.03
2014	79.03	0.42	89.70	75.46	0.00	3.88	56.29	0.01	7.94	0.00
2015	98.85	9.65	99.71	0.62	0.00	13.14	44.55	0.01	6.23	0.00

Table 3.27 G-L index of China and Bangladesh–India–Myanmar (Unit: %)

SITC	0	1	2	3	4	5	6	7	8	9
1996	15.05	5.78	52.45	24.53	1.95	23.21	61.89	3.85	25.56	0.50
1998	10.49	0.00	56.94	27.86	17.63	34.89	49.95	5.19	35.29	89.46
2000	72.85	0.01	5.73	12.07	23.05	68.69	62.55	22.85	42.78	0.00
2002	41.02	0.03	2.67	7.13	1.58	74.58	80.72	32.97	52.91	19.75
2004	57.28	0.11	0.46	5.24	5.22	51.79	87.46	46.29	57.90	94.09
2006	95.17	0.06	0.61	4.44	3.25	30.34	66.11	55.25	61.09	31.69
2008	96.82	0.09	0.99	7.37	3.81	13.50	50.96	38.82	56.77	94.65
2010	89.42	0.09	0.93	9.00	6.01	12.53	61.76	37.68	60.75	95.16
2011	86.19	0.07	1.38	3.03	6.24	15.29	74.36	38.48	77.08	0.02
2012	91.26	0.40	3.03	9.26	8.77	17.68	70.29	35.36	72.30	47.61
2013	44.64	21.75	36.09	10.72	36.12	42.41	27.47	34.21	50.07	77.93
2014	77.93	47.03	43.66	30.03	22.37	19.99	41.76	92.80	68.86	89.33
2015	89.33	35.11	52.83	68.86	0.89	24.24	16.06	33.07	51.17	14.87

Table 3.28 shows that the level of intra-industry trade is high between China and Mongolia–Russia for SITC 0, 5 and 6—the intra-industry trade plays a dominant role. The G-L indexes of SITC 1 and 5 exhibit upward trends, indicating that in recent years, intra-industry trade ha3.s replaced inter-industry trade as the dominant force in the trade of beverages and tobaccos and chemicals and related goods. For SITC 2, 3, 4, 7, 8 and 9 commodities, the intra-industry trade is small in scale, and the inter-industry trade takes the lead.

Table 3.28 G-L index of China and Mongolia–Russia (Unit: %)

SITC	0	1	2	3	4	5	6	7	8	9
1996	63.02	0.94	17.01	18.78	37.76	6.08	14.70	20.65	29.37	0.00
1998	96.86	0.19	11.18	65.64	0.00	10.02	30.58	19.55	26.60	–
2000	53.60	1.78	6.44	13.82	18.78	14.86	20.25	84.14	12.19	0.00
2002	73.48	1.66	5.84	7.34	1.53	15.15	40.98	49.40	6.05	1.40
2004	76.62	4.31	5.87	3.97	0.00	26.53	73.92	54.11	1.82	1.48
2006	77.65	7.94	3.62	3.21	0.00	58.50	60.36	8.36	0.85	12.53
2008	98.99	21.87	4.23	5.07	0.69	79.98	43.37	5.89	0.96	50.08
2010	98.33	14.17	4.30	3.38	0.00	72.67	70.36	5.80	1.36	64.63
2011	95.95	11.84	4.78	3.12	11.21	81.58	62.92	2.72	1.34	51.75
2012	90.16	12.63	4.94	2.00	61.11	86.27	47.04	2.39	1.73	23.15
2013	86.02	68.86	4.52	3.24	68.71	93.45	41.46	2.04	1.35	15.24
2014	80.70	88.29	4.58	2.21	84.69	78.23	37.53	3.81	1.21	4.63
2015	92.96	94.39	3.99	3.03	9.18	88.69	73.84	8.69	2.16	0.00

Table 3.29 G-L index of China and countries of Indochina Peninsula (Unit: %)

SITC	0	1	2	3	4	5	6	7	8	9
1996	88.45	3.93	34.31	18.96	14.02	87.87	70.89	91.88	31.12	16.43
1998	70.23	4.75	37.38	41.27	12.06	63.34	78.08	89.85	41.79	0.01
2000	77.97	28.00	26.72	59.59	3.46	56.58	82.48	89.26	44.08	13.06
2002	73.36	11.72	22.60	59.90	1.57	46.98	74.55	87.79	50.07	31.60
2004	99.62	10.34	15.52	42.45	2.76	56.03	58.28	78.87	63.06	44.89
2006	98.46	36.74	15.95	61.47	3.08	58.40	42.77	89.82	57.01	75.51
2008	84.80	56.23	20.18	48.50	4.99	82.25	37.30	98.36	46.50	56.61
2010	90.56	68.53	19.76	61.56	3.15	72.82	49.28	85.66	48.31	55.68
2011	85.91	58.49	17.03	42.98	2.75	73.50	46.54	85.89	49.90	53.10
2012	98.17	53.41	21.63	46.55	3.53	75.06	40.11	91.72	42.67	29.49
2013	92.15	59.92	20.99	63.25	3.55	74.69	33.74	98.00	35.10	61.15
2014	92.10	59.62	26.01	70.0 7	4.64	80.32	31.33	96.48	37.61	67.11
2015	89.58	70.22	26.21	73.85	5.77	90.21	27.12	94.55	41.62	0.00

Table 3.29 shows that China and Indochina countries enjoy high levels of intra-industry trade for SITC 0, 1, 3, 5 and 7 commodities. In other words, for primary and manufactured products which are resource-intensive, the two sides focus on intra-industry trade. The low level of intra-industry trade for SITC 2 and 4 commodities indicates the dominance of inter-industry trade for commodities like inedible raw materials (fuels excluded) and animal and vegetable oils, fats and waxes.

Table 3.30 G-L index of China and countries along the New Eurasian Land Bridge (Unit: %)

SITC	0	1	2	3	4	5	6	7	8	9
1996	44.81	47.09	91.94	62.18	27.83	62.34	76.98	58.70	20.83	1.49
1998	61.56	62.58	83.87	98.00	14.54	86.23	93.48	86.51	18.58	16.87
2000	88.22	72.13	43.76	33.83	39.90	64.38	84.76	99.33	26.38	0.17
2002	84.00	95.47	38.53	23.79	34.47	56.87	76.04	91.43	34.75	1.54
2004	83.25	61.00	37.76	20.55	80.86	58.03	95.63	90.64	30.39	24.59
2006	80.36	52.49	39.84	9.92	9.35	71.87	76.42	71.23	22.65	72.20
2008	68.07	75.29	35.54	14.43	74.99	84.21	63.89	69.30	19.87	78.32
2010	67.65	68.87	25.93	7.27	31.61	73.03	76.17	77.77	23.92	78.76
2011	72.33	90.04	22.82	7.14	31.66	75.05	71.36	83.06	26.48	50.64
2012	79.46	73.94	22.76	6.11	74.87	71.17	67.47	81.07	27.37	53.36
2013	83.59	61.17	22.17	6.02	23.93	72.04	66.07	82.24	26.10	23.32
2014	84.70	41.29	26.90	5.23	91.63	74.94	63.50	85.75	25.89	5.35
2015	98.53	35.18	25.92	6.04	60.74	70.45	69.12	82.11	28.18	0.00

Table 3.31 G-L index of China and Central Asia–West Asia (Unit: %)

SITC	0	1	2	3	4	5	6	7	8	9
1996	3.92	0.00	17.31	2.88	14.63	62.67	47.06	25.14	2.49	0.06
1998	4.34	28.99	25.33	3.66	0.00	84.85	37.24	15.78	2.45	–
2000	17.90	57.17	17.94	2.61	0.01	67.63	48.94	17.12	3.52	0.03
2002	13.99	44.16	29.45	4.02	14.93	56.21	60.10	10.89	5.68	38.00
2004	18.52	16.97	16.86	4.01	12.49	54.14	49.19	13.07	5.82	22.73
2006	14.96	0.03	16.83	2.96	1.94	65.58	29.61	7.86	4.34	14.94
2008	12.89	1.74	13.09	2.26	19.91	78.99	19.46	6.04	2.47	35.51
2010	24.44	2.48	12.76	2.30	34.91	50.30	27.56	7.37	3.41	16.92
2011	13.86	12.34	16.25	1.29	38.26	48.07	25.06	5.17	3.83	9.92
2012	20.32	6.20	16.11	1.44	13.83	49.81	24.03	5.78	3.14	24.49
2013	17.02	12.66	15.42	1.56	11.16	51.43	21.44	6.47	3.32	26.27
2014	23.71	17.51	23.22	2.21	19.75	55.81	16.15	5.55	3.25	5.78
2015	24.45	16.51	34.96	2.89	26.55	55.62	16.29	5.62	3.97	0.00

Note statistics of Uzbekistan considered

Table 3.30 shows that China and the countries along the New Eurasian Land Bridge have higher level of intra-industry trade for SITC 0, 1, 5, 6 and 7 commodities, indicating the dominance of intra-industry trade for commodities like food and live animals, beverages and tobaccos and manufactured goods. In trade of SITC 2, 3 and 8 commodities, inter-industry trade takes the lead.

Table 3.31 shows that the inter-industry trade dominates the trade between China and Central Asia–West Asia. The level of intra-trade industry is relatively high for SITC 5 commodities alone.

Table 3.32 shows the intra-industry trade mainly dominates the trade of SITC 0, 5 and 6 commodities (food and live animals, chemicals and related goods and manufactured goods chiefly classified by material) within the six economic corridors. The economic corridors of China–Indochina Peninsula and the New Eurasian Land Bridge have the largest number of commodity types dominated by intra-industry trade. The China–Central Asia–West Asia Corridor has the largest number of commodity types dominated by inter-industry trade.

The overall regional G-L indexes are calculated according to Formula (3.9) and listed in Table 3.33.

The revised overall regional G-L indexes are calculated according to Formula (3.10) and listed in Table 3.34.

As Tables 3.33 and 3.34 show, the economic corridors of China–Indochina Peninsula and the New Eurasian Land Bridge have high G-L indexes (both the original and the revised), indicating trade balance and high level of intra-industry trade. The China–Pakistan Economic Corridor has low G-L index but high revised G-L index, revealing serious trade imbalance and relatively high level of intra-industry trade in reality. Both the G-L indexes and the revised G-L indexes are low for the corridors of China–Central Asia–West Asia and China–Mongolia–Russia, indicating the dominance of inter-industry trade in these regions.

(VI) Summary

The comprehensive analysis made in this section from the three aspects of trade competitiveness, trade complementarity and intra-industry trade level leads to the following conclusions.

1. The competitiveness of trade

In terms of trade competitiveness, China, Mongolia and Russia, with the largest difference in export structures, face little competition from each other in the world market and have good potential for bilateral trade growth. China faces fierce export competition from Indochina countries and countries along the New Eurasian Land

Table 3.32 Comparison of the intra-industry trade indexes of China and other countries covered by the six economic corridors

	Dominated by intra-industry trade
China–Pakistan	SITC 0, 2, 6
Bangladesh–China–India–Myanmar	SITC 6, 8
China–Mongolia–Russia	SITC 0, 5, 6
China–Indochina Peninsula	SITC 0, 1, 3, 5, 7
New Eurasia Land Bridge	SITC 0, 1, 5, 6, 7
China–Central Asia–West Asia	SITC 5

Table 3.33 Comparison of the G-L indexes of China and other countries covered by the six economic corridors(Unit: %)

Year	China–Pakistan	Bangladesh–China–India–Myanmar	China–Mongolia–Russia	China–Indochina Peninsula	New Eurasia Land Bridge	China–Central Asia–West Asia
1996	23.44	35.15	20.86	65.18	55.12	21.26
1998	21.13	32.94	30.75	70.04	71.10	19.50
2000	28.28	40.34	19.72	73.32	71.60	16.15
2002	28.27	43.75	26.26	71.71	70.18	22.67
2004	36.95	33.44	25.81	66.54	71.79	18.79
2006	37.01	25.40	18.86	72.86	57.76	13.84
2008	23.84	15.26	19.38	74.90	55.13	10.95
2010	36.83	19.99	23.41	70.67	60.18	12.55
2011	38.36	24.49	20.02	67.66	60.72	10.90
2012	44.90	28.85	15.97	69.87	58.22	10.54
2013	42.33	33.30	15.55	70.51	58.16	10.55
2014	32.10	47.69	13.42	70.53	60.76	10.58
2015	26.06	32.09	22.31	70.67	61.70	12.46

Note statistics of Uzbekistan considered

Table 3.34 Comparison of the revised G-L indexes of China and other countries covered by the six economic corridors (Unit: %)

Year	China–Pakistan	Bangladesh–China–India–Myanmar	China–Mongolia–Russia	China–Indochina Peninsula	New Eurasia Land Bridge	China–Central Asia–West Asia
1996	33.05	54.76	41.62	68.63	60.02	21.59
1998	24.78	52.94	46.27	77.30	80.98	22.99
2000	33.39	60.41	35.03	84.20	73.83	19.38
2002	45.63	61.66	44.08	83.65	73.24	22.80
2004	95.08	35.27	30.31	82.43	77.06	20.01
2006	96.40	35.32	20.27	77.58	72.34	14.27
2008	83.55	21.48	22.68	76.41	73.47	11.04
2010	92.22	33.16	24.48	75.98	71.96	13.56
2011	95.60	42.58	20.61	73.29	67.61	13.07
2012	88.76	56.67	16.20	70.75	64.39	12.56
2013	88.35	70.64	17.14	77.87	65.45	12.22
2014	93.20	80.16	14.74	83.02	69.73	11.21
2015	99.73	83.23	22.50	85.89	72.30	14.23

Note statistics of Uzbekistan considered

Bridge due to their very similar export structures (the similarity with Indochina Peninsula is higher). From 1996 to 2015, China's competition with Indochina countries for the world market became increasingly fierce. Its competition with Pakistan and Bangladesh–India–Myanmar gradually weakened.

From the perspective of commodity subdivisions, in 1996–2015, the most competitive products of China, Pakistan, Bangladesh, India and Myanmar had always been labor-intensive manufactured products (SITC 6 and 8). For Mongolia, Russia, Central Asia and West Asia, SITC 3 (fossil fuels, lubricants and crude oil) goods are the most competitive export commodities since all of them are rich in oil and natural gas. The star export products of Indochina countries are SITC 4 commodities (animal and vegetable oils, fats and waxes), followed by SITC 7 products (machinery and transport equipment). The overall export competitiveness of various products produced by countries along the New Eurasian Land Bridge is relatively high. The comparative advantage of China's SITC 8 commodities has been shrinking. With weakening competitiveness, primary products of China have long been disadvantaged in the global market. Pakistan's SITC 0 commodities (primary products such as food and live animals) are highly competitive.

2. The complementarity of trade

As to trade complementarity, China is highly complementary with Mongolia and Russia, especially in the area of merchandise trade. China is less complementary with Pakistan and Bangladesh–India–Myanmar. For Indochina Peninsula and countries along the New Eurasian Land Bridge, China is a medium-complementary trading partner. In the trade of SITC 3 commodities (fossil fuels, lubricants and related raw materials), China and Central Asia–West Asia are highly complementary as buyer and seller. For SITC 2 commodities (raw materials, inedible, except fuels), they are also complementary. For SITC 9 goods (commodities and transactions not classified elsewhere in the SITC), their complementarity has been growing.

From the perspective of the trade integration index, China has close export relations with other countries of the five out of six economic corridors (excluding the China–Indochina Peninsula Economic Corridor), and close import ties with Indochina countries. When China is the exporter, it enjoys strong trade complementarity for labor-intensive manufactured products (SITC 6 and 8) and capital-intensive machinery and transport equipment (SITC 7). As an importer, China is complementary in resource-intensive primary products (SITC 0–4), especially inedible raw materials (except fuels) (SITC 2).

3. The intra-industry trade level

In general, intra-industry trade is dominant between China and Pakistan, Indochina countries and other countries along the New Eurasian Land Bridge. Inter-industry trade is the mainstream between China and Central Asia–West Asia and Mongolia–Russia. Food and live animals, chemical products and related products and manufactured goods chiefly classified by material are mainly traded through intra-industry trade between China and other countries of the six corridors. The economic corridors of China–Indochina Peninsula and the New Eurasian Land Bridge have the largest number of commodity types dominated by intra-industry trade. The China–Central Asia–West Asia Corridor has the largest number of commodity types dominated by inter-industry trade.

From the perspectives of different commodity groups, intra-industry trade dominates the trade of food and live animals and inedible raw materials (except fuels) between China and Pakistan. For the trade of labor-intensive manufactured goods between China and Bangladesh–India–Myanmar, the dominance of intra-industry trade is expected to be replaced by the dominance of inter-industry trade. China and Mongolia–Russia focus on intra-industry trade for food and live animals, chemical products and related products and manufactured goods chiefly classified by material. Between China and Indochina countries, the trade of resource-intensive primary and manufactured goods is dominated by intra-industry trade, while that of inedible raw materials (except fuels) and animal and vegetable oils, fats and waxes is dominated by inter-industry trade. Intra-industry trade takes the lead for the trade of food and live animals, beverages and tobaccos and manufactured goods between China and other countries along the New Eurasian Land Bridge. Between China and Central Asia–West Asia, chemicals and related raw materials are the only areas where intra-industry trade is dominant.

3.2 Empirical Research on the Trade Potential Based on the Gravity Model

(I) The extended gravity model of trade

According to the law of gravity, any particle of matter in the universe attracts any other with a force varying directly as the product of the masses and inversely as the square of the distance between them.[13] The formula for the gravitational force is as follows:

$$F_{ij} = \frac{m_i m_j}{d_{ij}^2} \tag{3.11}$$

The gravity model of trade is developed from Formula (3.11). Its basic form is as follows:

$$T_{ij} = A(Y_i Y_j)/D_{ij} \tag{3.12}$$

T_{ij} represents the total trade flows between the two countries. A stands for the constant term. Y_i and Y_j are the GDPs of the two countries. D_{ij} refers to the geographic distance between the two countries. The natural logarithm of the two sides of the formula could be taken:

[13] Newton (2006).

$$\ln T_{ij} = c + \beta_1 \ln Y_i + \beta_2 \ln Y_j + \beta_3 \ln D_{ij} + u_{ij} \quad (3.13)$$

$\ln T_{ij}$, $\ln Y_i$, $\ln Y_j$ and $\ln D_{ij}$ are, respectively, the logarithmic forms of T_{ij}, Y_i, Y_j and D_{ij}. C is the constant term. β_1, β_2 and β_3 are regression coefficients. u_{ij} is the random error term.

On the basis of the previous researches, dummy variables such as population, shared borders, and memberships of the same economic organizations are added. The indexes measuring trade competitiveness and complementarity (calculated in the previous section) are taken as explanatory variables. In this way, the extended gravity model of trade is obtained, as follows:

$$\begin{aligned} \ln T_{it} = c &+ \beta_1 \ln \mathrm{GDP}_t + \beta_2 \ln \mathrm{GDP}_{it} + \beta_3 \ln \mathrm{POP}_t + \beta_4 \ln \mathrm{POP}_{it} \\ &+ \beta_5 \ln D_i + \beta_6 \mathrm{ADJ}_i + \beta_7 \mathrm{APEC}_i + \beta_8 \mathrm{WTO}_i \\ &+ \beta_9 \ln \mathrm{ESI}_{it} + \beta_{10} \ln(\mathrm{TCDEX}_{it} \times \mathrm{TCDIM}_{it}) + \beta_{11} \ln \mathrm{GL}_{it} + u_{ij} \end{aligned} \quad (3.14)$$

T_{it}, the dependent variable, refers to the total trade volume between China and country i in year t. Data here come from the International Trade Statistics Database of the UN (UN Comtrade). See Table 3.35 for detailed explanations and sources of explanatory variables.

In this section, the trade data between China and other countries along the six economic corridors of the Belt and Road from 1996 to 2015 are selected as samples. Since some data are missing for Syria, Palestine, Afghanistan, Qatar and Myanmar, the samples of this section do not cover these five countries. As a result, there are 33 countries apart from China covered by the samples. China officially joined the World Trade Organization on December 11, 2001 and the Asia–Pacific Economic Cooperation (APEC) in November 1991. This chapter aims to examine if these two dummy variables have had significant impact on the trade flows between China and other countries of the six Belt and Road economic corridors.

Using EViews 8.0, a multiple linear regression analysis is performed on the trade flows between China and other countries along the six Belt and Road economic corridors in 1996–2015.

First, whether the explanatory variables suffer, serious multi-collinearity is examined. See Table 3.36 for the correlation matrix. All correlation coefficients are below 0.6 except for those of $\ln D$ and ADJ, ln GL and ln ESI and $\ln \mathrm{GDP}_t$ and $\ln \mathrm{POP}_t$. Moreover, later in this article, population variables ($\ln \mathrm{GDP}_t$ and $\ln \mathrm{POP}_t$), G-L index and ADJ are eventually excluded when variables are filtered. Therefore, the problem of high correlation coefficients caused by these variables has been solved. As a result, this model does not have the problem of multi-collinearity.

The author performed regression analysis on the panel data of this section using the random-effects model, the mixture regression model and the fixed-effects model before determining which of the three estimation methods is more suitable here. The regression results are demonstrated in Table 3.37.

Table 3.35 Detailed descriptions of the explanatory variables

Explanatory variable	Meaning	Expected symbol	Theoretical analysis	Source of data
GDP_t	The real gross GDP of China in year t (in constant 2010 prices)	+	There is a positive correlation between GDP and potential trade capacity; therefore, GDP is positively correlated with bilateral trade flows	World Bank
GDP_{it}	The real gross GDP of country i in year t (in constant 2010 prices)	+		
POP_{it}	The total population of China in year t	+ (−)	Larger population implies greater production capacity; however, large population also implies large domestic market, and thus smaller demand for international trade. The two factors have opposite impacts on trade flows	World Bank
POP_{it}	The total population of country i in year t	+ (−)		
D_i	The geographical distance between China and country i	−	The larger the distance, the higher the cost of transport, which hinders trade development	CEPII database[14]
ADJ_i	Dummy variable, if China shares border with country i, its value is 1; if not, its value is 0	+	If two countries share border, the transport cost would be lower, which could boost trade flows	The map of the People's Republic of China
$APEC_i$	Dummy variable, if China and country i are both APEC members in year t, its value is 1; if not, its value is 0	+	If the two are both APEC members, there would be fewer trade barriers, which could boost trade flows	The official Website of APEC
WTO_i	Dummy variable, if China and country i are both WTO members in year t, its value is 1; if not, its value is 0	+	If the two are both WTO members, there would be fewer trade barriers, which could boost trade flows	The official Website of WTO

(continued)

[14] The official Website: http://www.cepii.fr/CEPII/en/bdd_modele/bdd.asp.

Table 3.35 (continued)

Explanatory variable	Meaning	Expected symbol	Theoretical analysis	Source of data
ESI_{it}	ESI	–	The larger the index, the fiercer the trade competition between two countries, and the smaller the bilateral trade	Calculated above
$TCDEX_{it} \times TCDIM_{it}$	The product of the TI indexes with China as the exporter and the importer	+	The larger the index, the closer the trade ties between two countries, and the larger the bilateral trade flows	Calculated above
GL_{it}	Revised G-L index, measuring the level of intra-industry trade	+ (−)	Intra-industry and inter-industry trade have uncertain impact on trade flows	Calculated above

According to the results of the regression analysis listed in Table 3.37, the Durbin-Watson statistic[15] is small (DW statistics are 1.003005, 0.449004 and 1.121772, respectively), indicating first-order autocorrelation. Therefore, the variable $\ln T_{it}$ (-1) is added to the model, and the formula of the extended gravity model of trade becomes:

$$\begin{aligned}\ln T_{it} = {} & c + \beta_1 \ln \mathrm{GDP}_t + \beta_2 \ln \mathrm{GDP}_{it} + \beta_3 \ln \mathrm{POP}_t + \beta_4 \ln \mathrm{POP}_{it} + \beta_5 \ln D_i \\ & + \beta_6 \mathrm{ADJ}_i + \beta_7 \mathrm{APEC}_i + \beta_8 \mathrm{WTO}_i + \beta_9 \ln \mathrm{ESI}_{it} \\ & + \beta_{10} \ln(\mathrm{TCDEX}_{it} \times \mathrm{TCDIM}_{it}) + \beta_{11} \ln \mathrm{GL}_{it} + \beta_{12} \ln T_{it}(-1) + u_{ij}\end{aligned} \tag{3.15}$$

The regression results are listed in Table 3.38. After the variable $\ln T_{it}$ (-1) is added, the DW statistic increases significantly and approximates 2 (DW statistics are 1.724861, 1.724861 and 1.491162, respectively), basically solving the problem of first-order autocorrelation.

Then, an F test is run on the mixture regression model and the fixed-effects model of the panel data (using EViews 8.0). The test results are presented by Table 3.39. As the p value is 0, the null hypothesis is rejected. Therefore, the fixed-effects model is considered better than the mixture regression model.

As for the choice between the fixed-effects model and the random-effects model, it is necessary to perform the Hausman test. As Table 3.40 demonstrates, the p value of the Hausman test equals 1, which is significantly greater than 0, indicating that the

[15] The DW statistic could examine the autocorrelation of residual series. The DW statistic will always have a value between 0 and 4. A value of 2.0 means that there is no autocorrelation detected in the sample. Values from 0 to less than 2 indicate positive autocorrelation (the closer the value is to 0, the stronger the positive autocorrelation), and values from 2 to 4 indicate negative autocorrelation (the closer the value is to 4, the stronger the negative autocorrelation).

Table 3.36 Correlation matrix

Correlation	ADJ_i	$APEC_i$	In D_i	In ESI_{it}	In GDP_t	In GDP_{it}	In GL_{it}	In POP_t	In POP_{it}	In ($TCDEX_{it} \times TCDIM_{it}$)	WTO_i
ADJ_i	1										
$APEC_i$	0.252	1									
	***										
In D_i	−0.630	−0.218	1								
	***	***									
In ESI_{it}	0.132	0.392	−0.113	1							
	***	***	***								
In GDP_t	0.000	0.026	0.000	−0.226	1						
				***							
In GDP_{it}	−0.147	0.251	0.364	0.137	0.427	1					
	***	***	***	***	***						
In GL_{it}	0.262	0.471	−0.280	0.832	−0.160	0.182	1				
	***	***	***	***	***	***					
In POP_t	0.000	0.031	0.000	−0.235	0.989	0.423	−0.148	1			
				***	***	***	***				
In POP_{it}	0.254	0.189	−0.091	0.268	0.092	0.594	0.345	0.091	1		
	***	***	**	***	***	***	***	**			
In ($TCDEX_{it} \times TCDIM_{it}$)	0.456	0.620	−0.590	0.394	0.116	−0.007	0.438	0.111	0.185	1	
	***	***	***	***	***		***	***	***		
WTO_i	−0.024	0.087	−0.018	0.003	0.554	0.368	0.027	0.569	0.036	0.161	1
		**			***	***		***		***	

Note *** indicates $P < 1\%$; ** indicates $P < 5\%$; * indicates $P < 10\%$

Table 3.37 Regression results of the gravity model (without lagged variables)

Explanatory variable	Random-effects model	Mixture regression model	Fixed-effects model[16]
c	−146.0718	51.70166	−158.3765
	(−1.836308)*	(0.391350)	(−1.961093)*
ln GDP_t	−0.336460	0.935451	−1.302017
	(−1.222533)	(2.239428)**	(−3.773654)***
ln GDP_{it}	1.363592	0.913930	1.971350
	(15.71809)***	(27.43158)***	(11.95174)***
ln POP_t	8.021017	−2.652211	7.917129
	(2.027192)**	(−0.402483)	(1.973282)**
ln POP_{it}	−0.358031	−0.151753	−0.353437
	(−4.117008)***	(−4.898241)***	(−1.910152)*
ln D_i	−1.629897	−0.802919	
	(−4.093296)***	(−6.017926)***	
ADJ_i	0.442316	0.293239	
	(1.318450)**	(3.148590)***	
$APEC_i$	−0.057897	0.885654	−0.334739
	(−0.269739)	(6.718713)***	(−1.319102)
WTO_i	0.014137	0.464693	0.043455
	(0.220767)	(5.604059)***	(0.659340)
ln ESI_{it}	−0.973337	−0.413521	−1.123726
	(−5.695995)***	(−2.197922)**	(−6.294307)***
ln ($TCDEX_{it}$ × $TCDIM_{it}$)	0.503681	0.127890	0.509223
	(6.458829)***	(1.479961)	(6.305255)***
ln GL_{it}	−0.186960	0.230134	−0.254682
	(−2.229142)**	(2.425725)**	(−2.882213)***
R^2	0.890580	0.866427	0.958541
Adjusted R^2	0.888723	0.864160	0.955790
F statistic	479.4678	382.1179	348.4948
Probability (*F* statistic)	0.000000	0.000000	0.000000
Durbin-Watson statistic	1.003005	0.449004	1.121772

Note within the parentheses are the *t* statistic; *** indicates $P < 1\%$; **: $P < 5\%$; *: $P < 10\%$

Table 3.38 Regression results of the gravity model (with lagged variables)

Explanatory variable	Random-effects model	Mixture regression model	Fixed-effects model[17]
c	−53.16672	−53.16672	−134.7929
	(−0.664104)	(−0.575432)	(−1.558625)
In GDP_t	−0.137351	−0.137351	−1.164171
	(−0.561240)	(−0.486302)	(−3.627863)***
In GDP_{it}	0.168180	0.168180	1.170797
	(7.457913)***	(6.462117)***	(8.116463)***
In POP_t	2.727011	2.727011	6.909018
	(0.684050)	(0.592714)	(1.608590)
In POP_{it}	−0.018185	−0.018185	−0.219876
	(0.2158)	(−1.073707)	(−1.433844)
In D	−0.095640	−0.095640	
	(−1.506478)	(−1.305330)	
ADJ_i	0.039974	0.039974	
	(0.920365)	(0.797476)	
$APEC_i$	0.111864	0.111864	−0.195370
	(1.722710)*	(1.492690)	(−0.714597)
WTO_i	0.139799	0.139799	0.122167
	(3.586569)***	(3.107683)***	(2.231805)**
In ESI_{it}	−0.185129	−0.185129	−0.803865
	(−2.137067)**	(−1.851721)*	(−5.340995)***
In ($TCDEX_{it}$ × $TCDIM_{it}$)	0.102659	0.102659	0.454721
	(2.479426)**	(2.148368)**	(6.474890)***
In GL_{it}	0.052511	0.052511	−0.108457
	(1.194178)	(1.034729)	(−1.516503)
In T_{it} (−1)	0.800356	0.800356	0.462704
	(44.47357)***	(38.53536)***	(14.84300)***
R^2	0.961744	0.961744	0.972681
Adjusted R^2	0.960996	0.960996	0.970716
F statistic	1286.297	1286.297	495.0732
Probability (F statistic)	0.000000	0.000000	0.000000
Durbin-Watson statistic	1.724861	1.724861	1.491162

Note within the parentheses are the t statistic; *** indicates $P < 1\%$; **: $P < 5\%$; *: $P < 10\%$

Table 3.39 *F*-test results

Redundant fixed-effects test Cross-section fixed-effects test			
Effect test	Statistic	Degree of freedom	Probability
Cross-section *F*	7.444833	32,584	0.0000
Cross-section Chi-square	214.512272	32	0.0000

Table 3.40 Hausman test result

Hausman random-effects test Cross-section random-effects test			
Summary of the test	Statistic of Chi-Sq	Degree of freedom of Chi-Sq	Probability
Cross-section random effects	0.000000	10	1.0000

random-effects model will be a better choice.[18] Moreover, the fixed-effects model cannot contain time invariant variables, since the fixed-effects model considers by default time invariant, independent variables have no impact on dependent variables. However, the time invariant variable in this chapter, geographic distance, is of theoretical significance in gravity model of trade, so it is clear that the fixed-effects model is not suitable for adoption in this chapter.[19] To conclude, the random-effects model is adopted for the regression analysis in this chapter.

According to the regression results of the random-effects model in the first column of Table 3.38, GDP_{it}, D_i, $APEC_i$ (dummy variable), WTO_i (dummy variable), ESI_{it} (export similarity index), $TCDEX_{it} \times TCDIM_{it}$ (trade integration index) and first-order lagged variable T_{it} (-1) have all passed the significance test, but China's GDP, the population of China, the population of China's trading partner and the dummy variables of ADJ (shared border) and the G-L index have failed the test. As a result, GDP_t, POP_t, POP_{it}, GL_{it} and ADJ_i are eliminated from the extended regression equation, and a more reasonable extended regression model is obtained, as follows:

$$\ln T_{it} = c + \beta_1 \ln \text{GDP}_{it} + \beta_2 \ln D_i + \beta_3 \text{APEC}_i + \beta_4 \text{WTO}_i + \beta_5 \ln \text{ESI}_{it} + \beta_6 \ln(\text{TCDEX}_{it} \times \text{TCDIM}_{it}) + \beta_7 \ln T_{it}(-1) + u_{ij} \tag{3.16}$$

[16] When the regression is carried out with the fixed-effects model, the adding of ln D or ADJ will lead to singular matrix; therefore, these two variables are removed from the regression based on the fixed-effects model.

[17] When the regression is carried out with the fixed-effects model, the adding of ln *D* or ADJ will lead to singular matrix; therefore, these two variables are removed from the regression based on the fixed-effects model.

[18] IF p value of Hausman test equals 1, the null hypothesis adopting the random-effects model is not rejected.

[19] Haiying (2013).

The regression results of the modified random-effects gravity model of trade are demonstrated in Table 3.41.

According to the results listed in Table 3.41, the following model is obtained:

$$\begin{aligned}\ln T_{it} = {} & 1.635895 + 0.151711 \ln \mathrm{GDP}_{it} - 0.115975 \ln D_i + 0.139127\mathrm{APEC_i} \\ & + 0.158212\ \mathrm{WTO}_i - 0.124719 \ln \mathrm{ESI}_{it} \\ & + 0.090359 \ln(\mathrm{TCDEX}_{it} \times \mathrm{TCDIM}_{it}) + 0.810527 \ln T_{it}(-1) + u_{ij}\end{aligned} \tag{3.17}$$

Table 3.41 Regression results of random-effects gravity model of trade

Method: GLS estimation of panel data Swamy and Arora estimation of variance				
Variable	Coefficient	Standard error	t statistic	Probability
C	1.635895	0.417318	3.920024	0.0001
LNGDPI	0.151711	0.017623	8.608874	0.0000
LND	−0.115975	0.051837	−2.237285	0.0256
APEC	0.139127	0.060848	2.286453	0.0226
WTO	0.158212	0.035594	4.444899	0.0000
LNESI	−0.124719	0.048816	−2.554891	0.0109
LOG (TCDEX × TCDIM)	0.090359	0.040041	2.256674	0.0244
LNT (−1)	0.810527	0.016061	50.46520	0.0000
Effect analysis				
			Standard deviation	Overall correlation coefficient
Cross-section random effects			0.000000	0.0000
Hedonic random-effects			0.370011	1.0000
R^2	0.961524	Mean of dependent variables		21.59217
Adjusted R^2	0.961089	Standard deviation of dependent variables		2.132907
Standard error of the regression	0.420735	RSS		109.5739
F statistic	2209.856	Durbin-Watson statistic		1.734270
Probability (F statistic)	0.000000			

According to the regression results, the adjusted R^2 is 0.961089, the model is in general significant and of satisfying goodness of fit, and the regression coefficients of all variables are significant at 5% and consistent with the expected symbols. All of the following factors have significant impact on the trade flows between China and other countries of the six Belt and Road economic corridors: the GDP of the trading partner, the geographic distance to China, the ESI with China, the trade integration indexes of both export and import and the memberships of the same organizations such as APEC and WTO. For every 1% increase in GDP of the countries of the corridors, their trade flows with China grow by 0.15%. For every 1% increase in the geographic distance, the trade flows between China and these countries decreases by 0.12%, which is in line with the theoretical expectations. The coefficients of the dummy variables of APEC and WTO are both positive: for countries with APEC or WTO membership in the same year as China, their trade flows with China increase by 0.14% and 0.16%, respectively. It is particularly worth noting that for every 1% increase in the export similarity index that measures trade competitiveness, the trade flows between China and other countries of the six corridors decrease by 0.12%; for every 1% increase in the product of the import integration index and export integration index (both measuring trade complementarity), the trade flows between China and other countries of the six corridors rise by 0.09%.

In the process of model modification, the regression coefficients of China's GDP, China's population, the population of the trading partner, shared borders and intra-industry trade index are not significant. This model discusses the trade flows between China and other countries along the Belt and Road, which means all trading partners, over the year, face the same Chinese GDP and population; as a result, Chinese GDP and population have insignificant impact on the trade flows, leading to insignificant regression coefficients. The insignificant impact of the population of the trading partner may be due to the fact that population has both positive and negative impacts on trade flows—in the end, they balance each out. The fact that the regression coefficient of the shared borders is insignificant may be because the variable is to some extent positively correlated with the geographic distance, and the latter could better express the difference of impacts. The G-L index, which measures the level of intra-industry trade, has an insignificant coefficient because intra-industry trade and inter-industry trade mainly affect the types and profits of trade—their influence on trade flows is uncertain.

(II) Measuring the potential of trade

In this section, the method of Qingfeng and Shuzhu (2002) is used to calculate trade potential, that is, to calculate the ratio between the real bilateral trade volume (T) and the fitted volume (T^*). There are three kinds of bilateral trade potentials based on the size of the ratio: large potential ($T/T^* \leq 0.8$), which means there is very large room for improvement in trade flows; potential in need of further development ($0.8 < T/T^* < 1.2$), which means there is big room for improvement in trade flows, and

Table 3.42 Trade potential between China and other countries covered by the six economic corridors of the belt and road

Country/region	Actual value/fitted value				Country/region	Actual value/fitted value			
	2000	2005	2010	2015		2000	2005	2010	2015
Vietnam	1.42	1.14	1.20	1.01	Malaysia	1.20	1.04	1.14	0.86
Jordan	0.91	1.09	0.87	0.95	Lebanon	0.82	0.88	1.09	0.85
India	0.96	1.12	1.16	0.84	Laos	0.97	0.76	1.06	0.55
Israel	1.05	0.87	1.12	0.92	Kuwait	1.34	0.68	0.69	0.77
Iran	0.78	1.08	1.66	0.73	Cambodia	1.46	0.95	1.22	1.04
Iraq	1.30	1.53	1.52	0.96	Kyrgyzstan	1.08	1.57	1.00	0.97
Yemen	1.03	1.73	1.04	0.45	The Netherlands	1.32	1.40	1.38	1.04
Singapore	1.35	1.28	1.20	0.99	Kazakhstan	1.17	1.56	1.58	0.60
Uzbekistan	0.74	0.90	0.65	0.72	Russia	0.97	1.04	1.13	0.52
Turkmenistan	0.74	0.71	0.50	0.67	Germany	1.17	1.16	1.37	0.92
Turkey	1.08	0.99	1.03	0.74	Poland	0.91	1.00	1.02	0.89
Thailand	1.18	1.00	1.11	0.85	Belarus	0.87	1.21	2.14	0.84
Tajikistan	1.31	1.92	1.25	0.72	Bahrain	1.36	0.93	1.19	0.58
Saudi Arabia	0.94	1.16	0.95	0.83	Pakistan	0.89	1.04	0.96	0.92
Cyprus	1.18	1.12	0.97	0.47	Oman	3.90	1.20	1.67	0.75
Bangladesh	1.11	0.91	1.17	1.03	UAE	1.18	1.10	1.05	0.94
Mongolia	1.08	0.92	1.07	0.67					

new forms of trade could also be developed; potential in need of recreation ($T/T^* \geq 1.2$), which means new economic factors need to be created to boost trade flows.[20]

Trade potentials between China and other countries along the six Belt and Road economic corridors in 2000, 2005, 2010 and 2015 are calculated based on the estimate parameters of the regression results.

As Table 3.42 shows, from a horizontal perspective, in 2015, China's trade flows with Iran, Yemen, Uzbekistan, Turkmenistan, Turkey, Tajikistan, Cyprus, Mongolia, Laos, Kuwait, Russia, Bahrain, Oman and Kazakhstan were of huge potential for future growths. Its trade flows with Vietnam, Jordan, India, Israel, Iraq, Singapore, Thailand, Saudi Arabia, Bangladesh, Malaysia, Lebanon, Cambodia, Kyrgyzstan, Netherlands, Germany, Poland, Belarus, Pakistan and the UAE are of big potential for further improvement.

Vertically, compared with 2000–2010, 2005 witnessed increasing trade potentials in most countries along the corridors, which shows that China has gradually created new forms of trade and thus boosted trade flows with these countries.

According to the corridors they belong to, the 33 countries listed in Table 3.42 fall into three categories in terms of trade potential. In 2015, the corridors of China–Mongolia–Russia and China–Central Asia–West Asia generally had huge trade

[20] Ying (2012).

potentials. The corridors of China–Pakistan, the New Eurasian Land Bridge and the China–Indochina Peninsula were generally of big trade potential, but further development was needed. The trade between China and the countries along the New Eurasian Land Bridge Corridor showed a potential in need of recreation in 2010, and in 2015, it evolved to show a potential in need of further development, indicating the creation of new economic factors and thus the improvement of trade flows between China and this region in recent years. Since the implementation of the Belt and Road Initiative, the trade potential between China and the countries along the six economic corridors has expanded, indicating that the Initiative has played a positive role in promoting trade development.

According to the above analysis, from the perspective of trade potential, China could give priority to the development of the China–Mongolia–Russia Economic Corridor and the China–Central Asia–West Asia Economic Corridor since there is still much room for improvement in trade flows between China and the two regions.

3.3 Conclusions and Suggestion

In summary, the following conclusions could be reached. First, in terms of trade competitiveness, China differs greatly from Mongolia–Russia and Central Asia–West Asia in the structure of export commodities and thus faces low competition from the latter two in the global market. With great similarity in the structure of export commodities, China, Indochina Peninsula and countries along the New Eurasian Land Bridge encounter intensive rivalry from each other in the world market. From the perspective of timeline, in 1996–2015, China's competition with Indochina countries in the global market had grown fiercer, while its competition with Pakistan, Bangladesh, India and Myanmar had subsided. From the angle of commodity categories, in 1996–2015, the most competitive products of China, Pakistan, Bangladesh, India and Myanmar had been labor-intensive manufactured goods. Mongolia, Russia and countries of Central and West Asia, rich in oil and natural gas, have been competitive in areas of fossil fuels, lubricants and crude oil. For Indochina countries, animal and vegetable oils, fats and waxes and machinery and transport equipment have been the star export commodities. The countries along the New Eurasian Land Bridge, with balanced industrial structure, enjoy evenly high development levels in the areas of primary products, labor-intensive goods and capital-intensive goods. Suffering from extreme imbalance of trade structure, Central and West Asian countries have mainly depended on crude oil export for trade income.

Second, in terms of trade complementarity, China and Mongolia–Russia are highly complementary—this is especially the case when China exports and Mongolia–Russia imports. China has relatively low complementarity with Pakistan and Bangladesh–India–Myanmar. Medium trade complementarity exists between China and Indochina countries and the New Eurasian Land Bridge countries. China and Central and West Asian countries are extremely complementary in the trade in fossil fuels, lubricating oils and related raw materials (China as the importer). Overall, China has close export relations with Pakistan, Bangladesh–India–Myanmar, Mongolia–Russia, other countries of the New Eurasian Land Bridge and Central Asia–West Asia. As to different commodity categories, when China is the exporter, the commodities with good trade complementarity are mainly labor-intensive manufactured goods and capital-intensive machinery and transport equipment. Along the opposite trade direction, resource–intensive primary products, especially inedible raw materials (fuels excluded), enjoy good trade complementarity.

Third, in general, intra-industry trade is dominant between China and Pakistan, Indochina countries and other countries along the New Eurasian Land Bridge. Inter-industry trade is the mainstream between China and Central Asia–West Asia and Mongolia–Russia. Food and live animals, chemical products and related products and manufactured goods chiefly classified by material are mainly traded through intra-industry trade between China and other countries of the six corridors. The economic corridors of China–Indochina Peninsula and the New Eurasian Land Bridge have the largest number of commodity types dominated by intra-industry trade. The China–Central Asia–West Asia Corridor has the largest number of commodity types dominated by inter-industry trade.

Fourth, all of the following factors have significant impact on the trade flows between China and other countries of the six Belt and Road economic corridors: the GDP of the trading partner, the geographic distance to China, the ESI with China, the trade integration indexes of both export and import and the memberships of the same organizations such as APEC and WTO. These factors, except for distance and ESI, all generate positive impact. For every 1% increase in the export similarity index that measures trade competitiveness, the trade flows between China and other countries of the six corridors decrease by 0.12%. For every 1% increase in the product of the import integration index and export integration index (both measuring trade complementarity), the trade flows between China and other countries of the six corridors rise by 0.09%.

Fifth, as to trade potential, in 2015, the corridors of China–Mongolia–Russia and China–Central Asia–West Asia generally had huge trade potentials. The corridors of China–Pakistan, Bangladesh–China–India–Myanmar, the New Eurasian Land Bridge, and the China–Indochina Peninsula were generally of big trade potential, but further development was needed. Since the implementation of the Belt and Road Initiative, the trade potential between China and the countries along the six economic corridors has expanded, indicating that the Initiative has played a positive role in promoting trade development.

The analysis of this chapter has produced the following findings and suggestions.

First, the trade competitiveness and complementarity calculated through index analysis are consistent in essence with the trade potential estimated by the gravity model. According to the extended gravity model of trade, the weaker the trade competitiveness, the larger the trade flows; the stronger the trade complementarity, the larger the trade flows. Therefore, countries with weak trade competitiveness and strong trade complementarity between them tend to enjoy greater trade potential.

Second, based on the analysis of trade data in this chapter, it is suggested that China could give priority to the development of the China–Mongolia–Russia Economic

Corridor and the China–Central Asia–West Asia Economic Corridor. China and the two corridors, with low competitiveness and great complementarity between them, are granted with huge trade potential, which means there is still much room for improvement in trade flows. However, this is only a suggestion from the trade perspective. As to national policies, the early start and rapid progress of China–Pakistan Economic Corridor is mainly the result of national strategies instead of market-oriented decisions. Therefore, the construction of the economic corridors should take into consideration both factors of national strategies and market conditions.

Third, China should guarantee and promote the coordinated and synergistic development of trade relations through institutional arrangements. For example, the trade between China and the countries along the New Eurasian Land Bridge Corridor showed a potential in need of recreation in 2010, and in 2015, it evolved to show a potential in need of further development, illustrating the positive impact of policy stimuluses such as the Belt and Road Initiative, the establishment of free trade zones and the formulation of regional trade agreements.

Chapter 4
An Analysis of China's Investment in Countries or Regions Along the Belt and Road

Zhibin Zhu and Yuxuan Tang

Along the Belt and Road, trade has brought businessmen shovel loads of cash, and the spreading of the papermaking technique has fostered exchanges among different countries.

With the advancement of the Belt and Road Initiative and the "Going Global" strategy, China's direct investment in countries along the Belt and Road has continued to increase, expanding from neighboring countries to Central Asia and West Asia, and its proportion within local FDI has been growing year by year. In terms of its geographical distribution, China's direct investment along the Belt and Road mainly flows to emerging economies and countries with greater potential for capacity cooperation: Southeast Asia has the largest stock. In terms of its distribution among different industries, most of the investments go to the fields of capacity cooperation and infrastructure construction, and the structure is increasingly diversified. Large and medium-sized state-owned enterprises are still the main source of investment, and the role of private capital is also increasing. In addition, buying minority stake has become the main approach of investing overseas by Chinese companies. With the overall situation improving, China's investment along the Belt and Road still has unresolved issues such as the host country's political environment risks, corporate-level obstacles, and unclear domestic coordination mechanisms.

Z. Zhu (✉)
School of Software and Microelectronics, Peking University, Beijing, China

Y. Tang
School of Economics, Peking University, Beijing, Beijing, China

H. Zhang et al., *Comparative Studies on Regional and National Economic Development*, Global Economic Synergy of Belt and Road Initiative,
https://doi.org/10.1007/978-981-16-2105-5_4

4.1 The Overall Conditions of China's Investment in Countries Along the Belt and Road

(I) The scale and growth rate of China's investment in countries along the Belt and Road

Figure 4.1 shows China's direct investment in countries along the Belt and Road has continued to grow—the stock has increased 34 times from 3.39 billion USD at the end of 2005 to 115.91 billion USD at the end of 2015, maintaining a growth rate of over 20%.

As Fig. 4.2 shows, China's direct investment flows in countries along the Belt and Road has expanded 21.5 times from 910 million USD at the end of 2005 to 19.56 billion USD at the end of 2015. The growth rate of the flows fluctuated greatly: –12.46% in 2013, 5.27% in 2014 and 10.22% in 2015, which also indicates that the Belt and Road Initiative formally put forward at the end of 2013 effectively fueled the growth of China's OFDI.

Despite its rapid growth, China's direct investment along the Belt and Road is still small in size compared to the total amount of foreign investment absorbed by local countries. As of the end of 2015, the stock of China's direct investment accounted for 2.61% of the total FDI absorbed, and the flows took up 6.62% of the FDI received that year. There is still great room for future growth.

As Tables 4.1 and 4.2 show, for both flows and stock, the proportion of China's direct investment in the total FDI attracted by countries along the Belt and Road has been growing. In 2005–2015, the proportion of the flows grew faster than that of the stock; in addition, the proportion of the flows was always larger than that of the stock, indicating great growth potential.

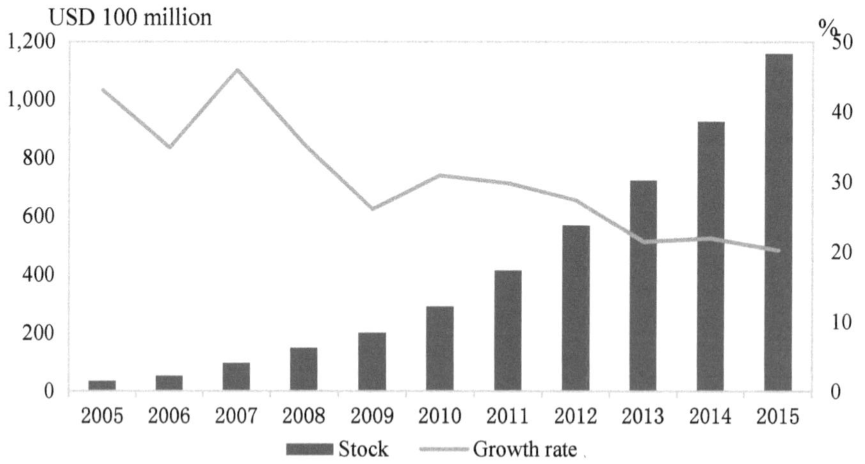

Fig. 4.1 China's direct investment stock in countries along the Belt and Road and its growth rate

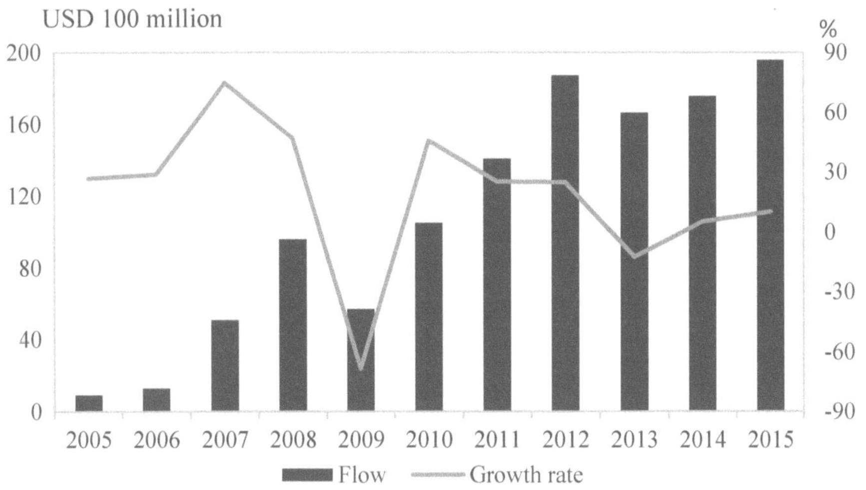

Fig. 4.2 China's direct investment flows in countries along the Belt and Road and the growth rate

Table 4.1 FDI stock in countries along the Belt and Road (2005–2015) (Unit: 100 million USD)

Year	FDI stock in countries along the Belt and Road	The stock of China's direct investment in countries along the Belt and Road	The proportion of Chinese investment in FDI absorbed by countries along the Belt and Road (%)
2005	13,794.69	33.92	0.25
2006	18,709.85	51.99	0.28
2007	26,766.73	96.10	0.36
2008	26,361.77	148.47	0.56
2009	31,903.89	200.71	0.63
2010	37,493.52	290.32	0.77
2011	37,936.25	413.30	1.09
2012	43,018.43	568.57	1.32
2013	45,400.77	723.05	1.59
2014	44,671.44	925.16	2.07
2015	44,338.07	1159.05	2.61

Source of data The statistics of FDI in countries along the Belt and Road are from UNCTADstat; the statistics of China's direct investment in countries along the Belt and Road are from WIND

As Figs. 4.3 and 4.4 show, in 2013–2015, Nepal, Saudi Arabia, East Timor, Kuwait, Macedonia, Bosnia and Herzegovina, Turkey, Israel and the Czech Republic, all countries along the Belt and Road, witnessed fast growth in the proportion of Chinese OFDI flows within the total FDI absorbed annually. In 2014, Nepal was the country with the fastest increase, and in 2015, Saudi Arabia and East Timor saw most

Table 4.2 FDI flows in countries along the Belt and Road (2005–2015) (Unit: 100 million USD)

Year	FDI flows in countries along the Belt and Road	Flows of China's direct investment in countries along the Belt and Road	The proportion of Chinese investment in the FDI flows absorbed by countries along the Belt and Road (%)
2005	1900.50	9.12	0.48
2006	3060.47	12.78	0.42
2007	3746.31	50.71	1.35
2008	4028.58	95.84	2.38
2009	2672.95	56.88	2.13
2010	3582.10	104.97	2.93
2011	3051.09	140.50	4.60
2012	3370.80	187.12	5.55
2013	3216.15	166.38	5.17
2014	3155.57	175.64	5.57
2015	2952.87	195.63	6.62

Source of data the statistics of FDI in countries along the Belt and Road are from UNCTADstat; the statistics of China's direct investment in countries along the Belt and Road are from WIND

rapid growth. The Czech Republic, located at the heart of Europe, is the terminus or crossed by many Asian-European railways; such geographical advantage determines that it occupies a strategic position along the Eurasian Continental Bridge Multiple economic, and geographical factors decide the Czech Republic which could play a pivotal role in promoting economic and trade cooperation between China and Central and Eastern Europe under the Belt and Road Initiative. In contrast, as Fig. 4.5 shows, in 2012–2015, Laos, Myanmar and Cambodia witnessed decline in this proportion, and the decline in Laos was the worst.

As Figs. 4.6 and 4.7 show, in 2013–2015, Yemen, Nepal, East Timor, Uzbekistan, Sri Lanka, UAE, Kuwait and Belarus, all countries along the Belt and Road, witnessed fast growth in the proportion of Chinese OFDI flows within the total FDI absorbed annually. Among them, Nepal, East Timor and Kuwait are countries with the most rapid growth. By contrast, China's direct investment stock in Iraq as a percentage of the total local FDI stock had been shrinking year by year, dropping from 6.15% in 2011 to 1.46% in 2015.

To sum up, China's OFDI used to concentrate in neighboring countries. Since the implementation of the Belt and Road Initiative, the focus of investment has gradually shifted to West Asia, Central and Eastern Europe and other regions.

(II) Top 10 destinations of Chinese investment along the Belt and Road and their characteristics

In 2015, there were 24 countries with more than 100 million USD of direct investment flows from China, accounting for 36.3% of the 66 countries along the Belt and Road; 44 out of the 66 countries (66.7%) had stocks of over 100 million USD.

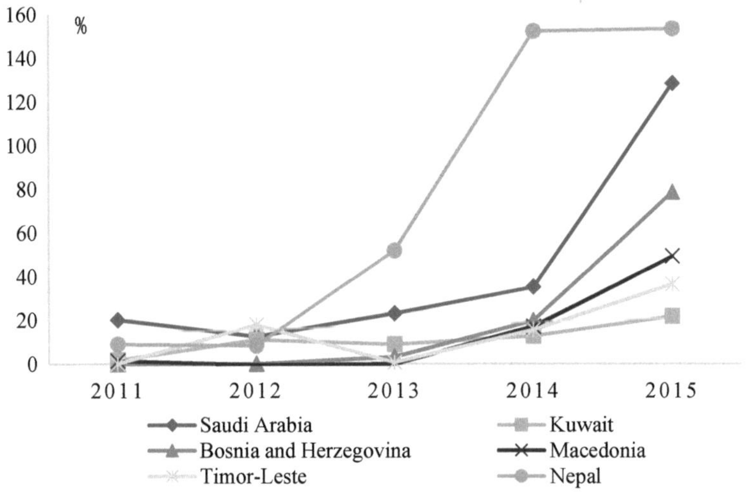

Fig. 4.3 Countries witnessing fast growth in the proportion of Chinese OFDI flows within the annual total FDI absorbed (2011–2015)—group 1

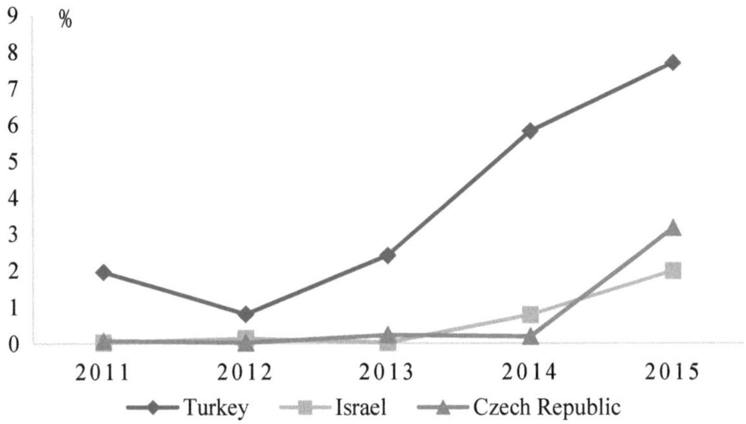

Fig. 4.4 Countries witnessing fast growth in the proportion of Chinese OFDI flows within the annual total FDI absorbed (2011–2015)—group 2. *Source of data* UNCTADstat

As Fig. 4.8 shows, in 2015, the top 10 countries along the Belt and Road with the largest stock of Chinese direct investment were Singapore, Russia, Indonesia, Kazakhstan, Laos, UAE, Myanmar, Pakistan, India and Mongolia (ranked from largest to smallest). Among them, Russia, Kazakhstan, Laos, Myanmar, Pakistan, India and Mongolia are all China's land neighbors. Indonesia is a maritime neighbor of China. Only Singapore and the UAE do not share borders with China. With a large Chinese population (more than 50% of the total), Singapore enjoys convenient land and sea transportation and a high level of economic development. Therefore, it has become

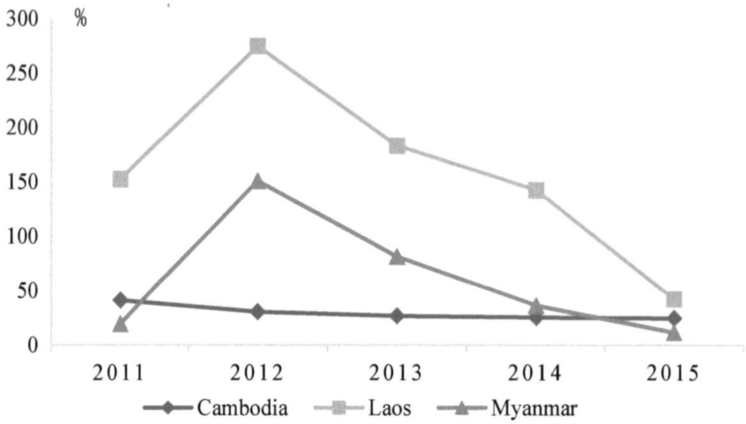

Fig. 4.5 Countries witnessing continuous decline in the proportion of Chinese OFDI flows within the annual total FDI absorbed (2012–2015)

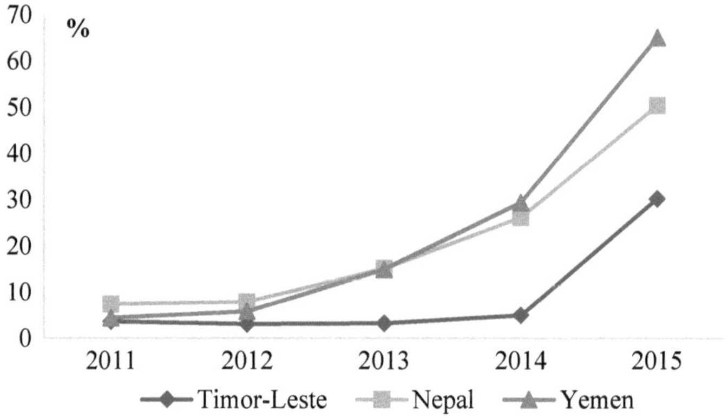

Fig. 4.6 Countries witnessing fast growth in the proportion of Chinese OFDI stock within the annual total FDI absorbed (2011–2015)—group 1

the country with the largest stock of Chinese OFDI. In addition, all ten countries are in Asia except Russia which spans the two continents of Europe and Asia, and 4 out of 10 are in Southeast Asia. In summary, China's OFDI along the Belt and Road used to concentrate in its neighboring countries.

As Fig. 4.9 shows, in 2015, the top 10 countries along the Belt and Road with the largest flows of Chinese direct investment were Saudi Arabia, Yemen, Russia, Indonesia, Turkey, India, Turkmenistan, Uzbekistan, Laos and Malaysia. Among them, Saudi Arabia, Turkey and Yemen are in West Asia; Turkmenistan and Uzbekistan are in Central Asia; and Indonesia, Laos and Malaysia are in Southeast Asia. This shows that China's investment in Central Asia and West Asia has been expanding with the advancement of the Belt and Road Initiative.

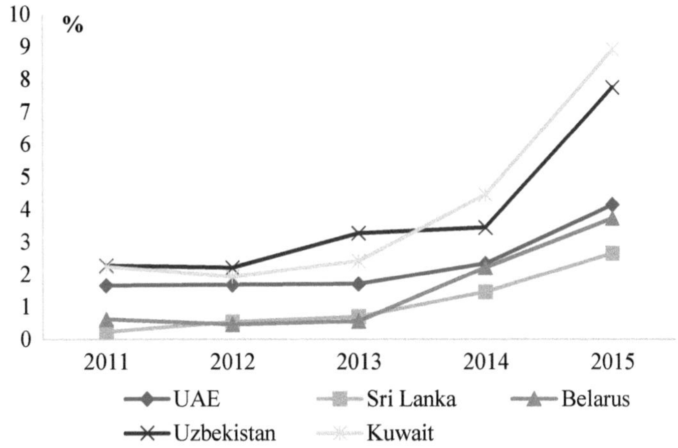

Fig. 4.7 Countries witnessing fast growth in the proportion of Chinese OFDI stock within the annual total FDI absorbed (2011–2015)—group 2

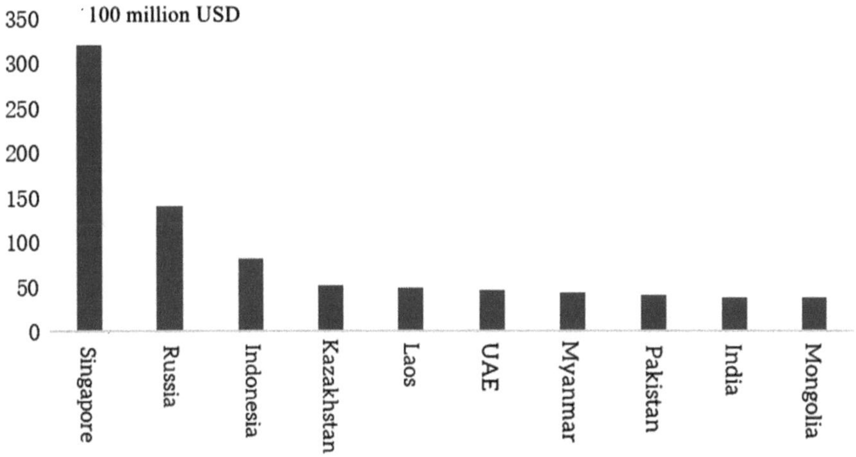

Fig. 4.8 Top 10 countries along the Belt and Road with the largest stock of Chinese direct investment 2015

The China–Central Asia–West Asia Economic Corridor starts from Xinjiang and reaches the Persian Gulf, the Mediterranean coast and the Arabian Peninsula, crossing the five Central Asian countries (Kazakhstan, Kyrgyzstan, Tajikistan, Uzbekistan, Turkmenistan) and West Asian countries such as Iran and Turkey. Although Central Asia and West Asia are rich in natural resources, their economic and social development is restricted by many factors, among which the problem of poor infrastructure and the lack of capital and technology stand out. The construction of the Economic Corridor could open new channels for trade and economic cooperation and cash

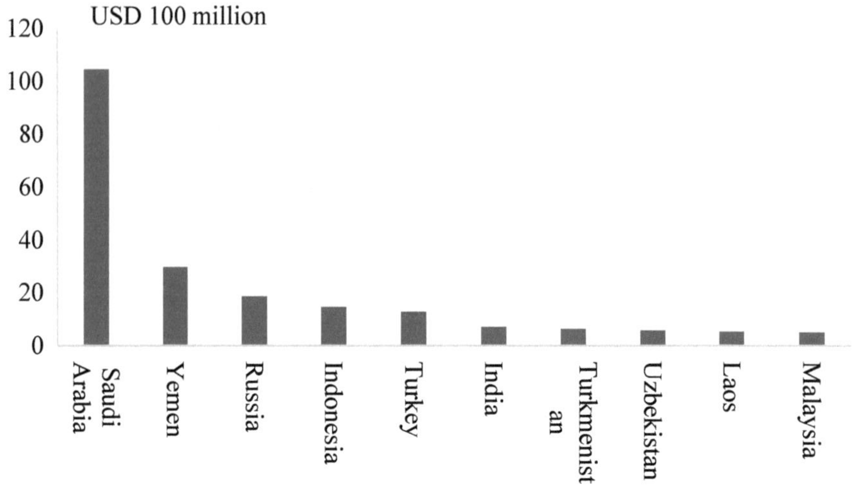

Fig. 4.9 Top 10 countries along the Belt and Road with the largest flows of Chinese direct investment 2015. *Source of data* WIND

flows, which will undoubtedly boost the economic and social development of relevant countries.

As Table 4.3 shows, Laos, Nepal, Tajikistan, East Timor, Kyrgyzstan, Cambodia, Pakistan, Uzbekistan and Russia took the lead in the proportions of Chinese OFDI within both their total FDI stocks and flows. All of them are Asian countries, with the exception of Russia: three are in Southeast Asia, three in Central Asia and two in South Asia. In addition, three countries in West Asia (Yemen, Afghanistan and Iran), one in South Asia (Sri Lanka) and two neighbors of China (Mongolia and Myanmar) have large proportions of Chinese OFDI in their FDI stocks. As to the proportions of Chinese OFDI within their total FDI flows, the top 15 include three West Asian countries (Saudi Arabia, Kuwait and Qatar) and three Central and Eastern European countries (Macedonia, Bosnia and Herzegovina, Estonia), which means China's investment in these regions is likely to rise substantially.

In the Eurasian Economic Belt, Central and Eastern Europe links the EU, the most developed integrated market, and the major energy producing regions. With such significant geographical advantages, it is an important entry point to the EU market. Compared with the Western European market, it is cheaper in cost and faster in growth; compared with Russia and Central Asia, it has more mature market, more developed economy and stronger product competitiveness. As an important part of the Eurasian Economic Belt, Central and Eastern Europe, with its industrial and geographical advantages, could serve as a regional pivot for the Belt and Road Initiative.

(III) A comparison between China's investment in countries along the Belt and Road and its overall overseas investment

Table 4.3 Top 15 countries along the Belt and Road with the highest proportions of Chinese direct investment within the total FDI absorbed 2015 (Unit: %)

Rankings	The proportion within stock		The proportion within flows	
1	Laos	99.82	Nepal	153.35
2	Yemen	65.08	Saudi Arabia	128.39
3	Nepal	50.39	Tajikistan	117.76
4	Tajikistan	43.04	East Timor	78.64
5	East Timor	30.18	Uzbekistan	52.43
6	Kyrgyzstan	27.54	Kuwait	49.21
7	Cambodia	24.94	Laos	42.40
8	Afghanistan	24.00	Qatar	37.80
9	Mongolia	22.44	Kyrgyzstan	37.47
10	Myanmar	20.80	Pakistan	37.09
11	Pakistan	12.77	Macedonia	36.36
12	Uzbekistan	8.92	Cambodia	4.67
13	Sri Lanka	7.75	Bosnia and Herzegovina	21.73
14	Iran	6.54	Estonia	21.17
15	Russia	5.43	Russia	18.81

Source of data The statistics of FDI in countries along the Belt and Road are from UNCTADstat. The statistics of China's direct investment in countries along the Belt and Road are from WIND. The proportions are calculated according to these statistics

In 2006–2015, China's OFDI continued to grow. In 2006–2013, the gap between the FDI flows and the OFDI flows kept narrowing. In 2014, the amount of OFDI flows exceeded that of FDI flows for the first time. In 2015, the OFDI flows reached a record high of 145.67 billion USD, up by 18.3% on a year-on-year basis, accounting for 9.9% of the global flows, ranking second in the world for the first time (the United States ranked the first at 299.96 billion USD and Japan ranked the third at 128.65 billion USD). In addition, it exceeded the FDI absorbed by China during the same period (135.6 billion USD), realizing the net export of capital. See Fig. 4.10 for details.[1]

As Fig. 4.11 shows, in 2011–2013 and 2015, the growth rates of China's direct investment stock in countries along the Belt and Road were higher than in other regions. The growth rate in 2015 was 20.18%.

As Fig. 4.12 shows, in 2012–2015, the growth rates of China's direct investment flows in countries along the Belt and Road were lower than in other regions. This was because China's recorded negative investment in some of the countries, which means China had a net inflow of capital from them. The inflow offset part of the net outflow leading to the low growth rate mentioned above. Outside the Belt and Road region are Latin American and African countries. Most of the African countries had

[1] Source of data: 2015 Statistical Bulletin of China's Outward Foreign Direct Investment.

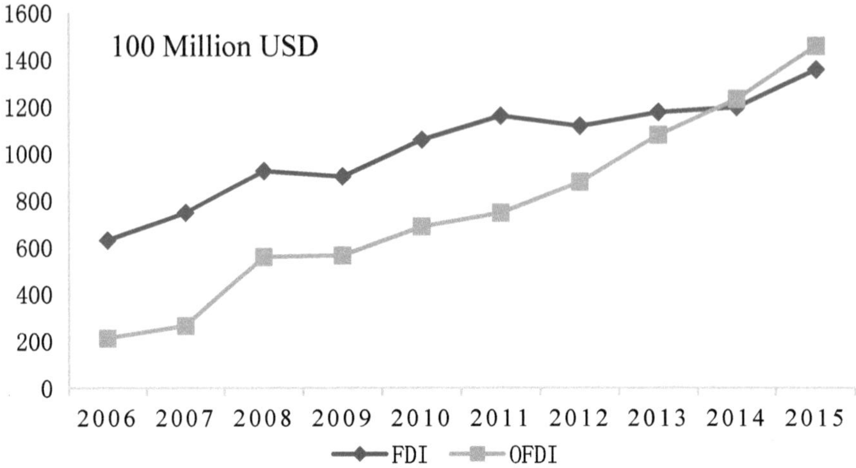

Fig. 4.10 FDI in China and China's OFDI. *Source of data* WIND

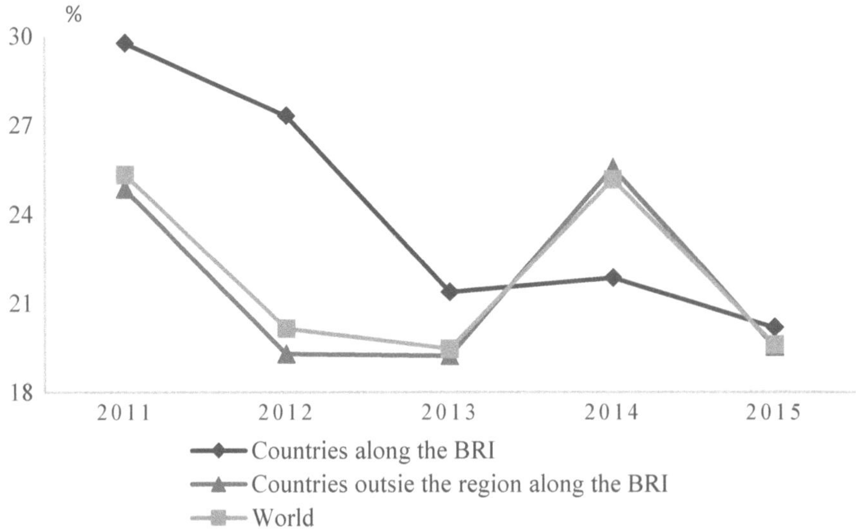

Fig. 4.11 Growth rate of China's OFDI stock

a net inflow of capital from China, which means China had positive direct investment in Africa.

The proportion of China's direct investment stock along the Belt and Road within its total OFDI stock rose from 5.93% at the end of 2005 to 10.56% at the end of 2015. From 2012 to 2015, the proportion generally stayed around 10.5%. See Table 4 for details.

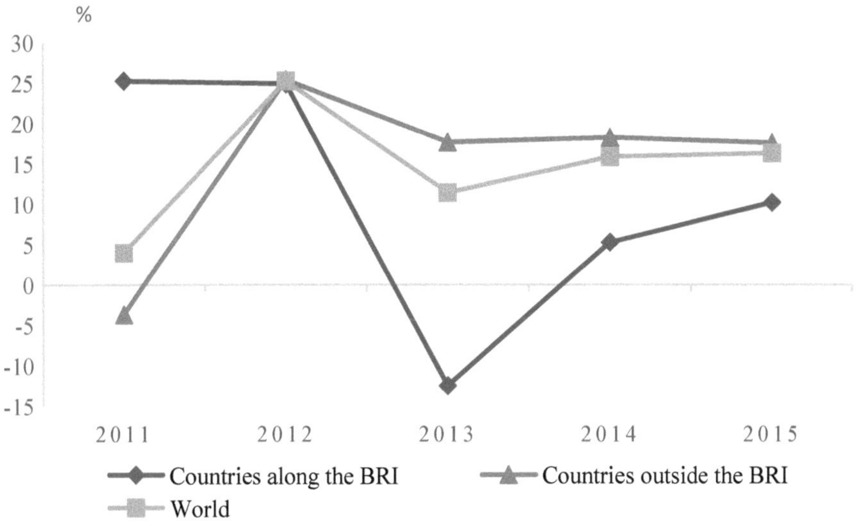

Fig. 4.12 Growth rate of China's OFDI flows

Table 4.4 Stock and flows of China's direct investment in countries along the Belt and Road 2005–2015 (Unit: 100 million USD)

Year	Stock			Flows		
	Countries along the Belt and Road	World	Proportion (%)	Countries along the Belt and Road	World	Proportion (%)
2005	33.92	572.06	5.93	9.12	47.59	19.16
2006	51.99	750.26	6.93	12.78	78.91	16.20
2007	96.10	1179.11	8.15	50.71	177.83	28.52
2008	148.47	1839.71	8.07	95.84	440.56	21.75
2009	200.71	2457.55	8.17	56.88	436.03	13.04
2010	290.32	3172.11	9.15	104.97	510.40	20.57
2011	413.30	4247.81	9.73	140.50	531.70	26.43
2012	568.57	5319.41	10.69	187.12	711.51	26.30
2013	723.05	6604.78	10.95	166.38	803.21	20.71
2014	925.16	8826.42	10.48	175.64	954.41	18.40
2015	1159.05	10,978.65	10.56	195.63	1140.65	17.15

Note Statistics of Maldives and Bhutan are missing (Bhutan is the only neighboring country of China that has not established diplomatic relations with it)
Source of data WIND

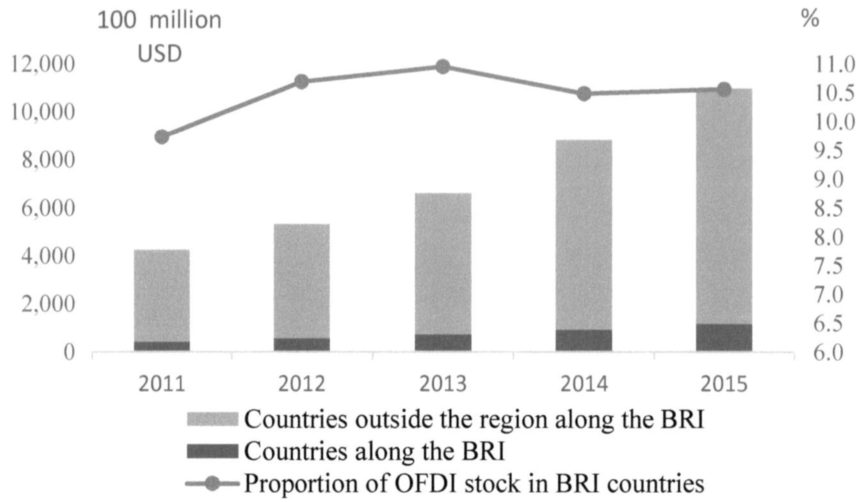

Fig. 4.13 China's OFDI stock in countries along the Belt and Road and its proportion within the total OFDI

As Fig. 4.13 shows, in 2011–2015, China's total OFDI stock increased year by year, and the share taken by countries along the Belt and Road was always higher than 9.5%. In 2015, the percentage was 10.56%. Meanwhile, the total amount of China's direct investment stock along the Belt and Road witnessed steady growth.

As Fig. 4.14 shows, in 2005–2015, the proportion of China's direct investment flows along the Belt and Road within its total OFDI flows, despite a slight drop, stayed relatively high. In 2015, the figure was 17.15%.

4.2 Structural Characteristics of China's Direct Investment in Countries Along the Belt and Road

China's direct investment in countries along the Belt and Road exhibits an overall upward trend and evident structural characteristics. As of 2014, the stock reached 89.838 billion USD.

(I) The geographic distribution of investment along the Belt and Road

As to the geographic distribution, Southeast Asia takes the largest share of China's direct investment stock along the Belt and Road (53.0% at 47.653 billion US dollars). Among Southeast Asian countries, Singapore ranks first at 20.64 billion USD (22.3% of the total). According to the Eclectic Paradigm of International Production (Dunning, 1977), when a host country enjoys geographic advantages, there would be sufficient condition for an enterprise to make direct investment, and making OFDI in that country would be the best choice for the enterprise. Singapore enjoys political

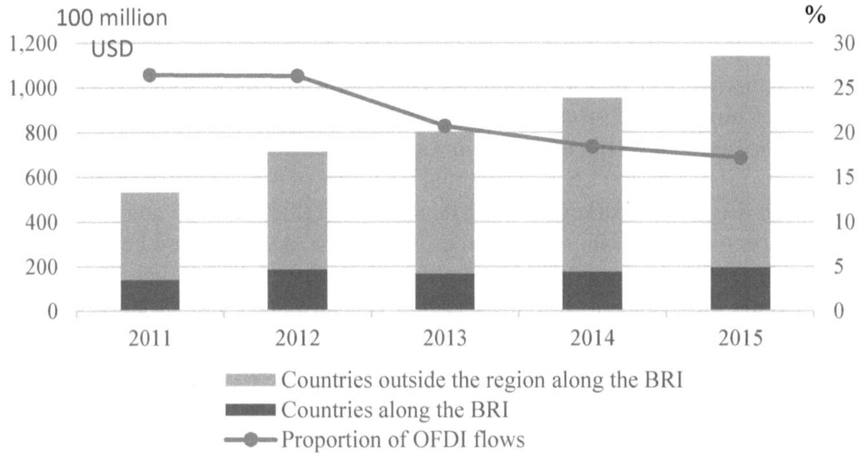

Fig. 4.14 China's OFDI flows in countries along the Belt and Road and the proportion within the total ODFI flows. *Source of data* WIND

stability, social harmony, a culture similar to China's, and fast-growing economy. In 2015, its per capita GDP exceeded 60,000 USD. In addition, it has loose policies for foreign capital inflows and provides foreign companies with national treatment: the free flow of foreign exchange, supervision without discrimination and supportive policies. In addition, China and Singapore signed China-Singapore Free Trade Agreement in 2009, which has contributed to the substantial progress of bilateral economic and trade cooperation.

China's direct investment stock in West Asia and North Africa is 11.413 billion USD, accounting for 12.7% of the total stock. Iran, the UAE and Saudi Arabia are the largest destinations of China's direct investment, receiving 3.484 billion, 2.333 billion and 1.987 billion USD, respectively. Iran ranks first in the world in natural gas reserves and fourth in oil reserves. Since President Rowhani, a pragmatic reformist, took office in 2013, Iran has been actively building a "resilient economy". Within such a framework, foreign investment is encouraged, and the restriction on the inflow of foreign capital is relaxed. Since the signing of the Iran nuclear deal, Iran has become increasingly attractive to foreign capital. The UAE is located at the traffic hub of the Gulf region. As one of the richest countries in the world, it is politically stable and economically developed. Its fast-growing segments such as renewable energy, aerospace, nuclear power, infrastructure construction, communications, finance and education, favored by Chinese investors, play a key role in promoting China's industrial transformation. China and Saudi Arabia have close economic and trade relations. The two countries have signed a number of bilateral economic and trade cooperation agreements, such as the "Investment Promotion and Protection Agreement" and the "Protocol on Cooperation in the Field of Oil, Gas and Minerals". In addition, with political stability and fast economic growth, Saudi Arabia is a great destination for investment. Overall, countries in West Asia and North Africa have rich oil and mineral resources and thus great potential for investment and cooperation. Chinese investment in the region is concentrated in oil exploration and development and infrastructure construction. However, the political instability in some countries has restricted China's direct investment to some degree.

China's direct investment stock in Central and Eastern European countries amounts to 10.925 billion USD, accounting for 12.2% of the total stock along the Belt and Road. Russia and Turkey have the largest stocks (8.695 billion and 882 million USD, respectively). Russia shares border with China. As the largest country in the world, it is rich in energy, minerals and forest resources. Russia has a high level of economic development, low fiscal deficit and advanced and strong aerospace, nuclear energy and military industries. The two countries have close diplomatic ties. Chinese investment in Russia is mainly concentrated in the fields of energy, mineral exploration and development, forestry, construction and building material production, textiles and communication services.

At present, China's direct investment in Turkey is in communications, energy, mining, transportation and textile industries. Investors include companies such as Huawei, ZTE, China General Technology, Sinosteel Group Corporation Limited, China Machinery Engineering Corporation, China National Aero-Technology International Engineering Corporation, China Railway Construction Corporation Limited, China Electric Equipment Group, CRRC, Air China, and ICBC. Turkey's tertiary industry is the focus of foreign investment. In 2013, Turkey's manufacturing industry absorbed only 2 billion USD of foreign investment, its financial industry received 3.7 billion USD, an increase of 79%, and the real estate sector attracted 3 billion USD, an increase of 16%. Turkey is the largest investee of the European Bank for Reconstruction and Development, with an investment amount of more than 1 billion euros. China's investment in Turkey's tertiary industry accounts for a small proportion and has huge growth potential. Overall, China has been restricted from investing in EU countries, but in recent years (after the financial crisis and the European sovereign debt crisis), Central and Eastern European countries have encouraged investment from non-EU countries. In 2003–2013, the stock of Chinese direct investment in Central and Eastern Europe increased 28 times.[2]

The stock of Chinese direct investment in Central Asia totals 10.094 billion USD (11.2% of the total) of which Kazakhstan takes the largest share. Kazakhstan is the third largest destination of China's OFDI, with a stock of 7.541 billion USD, and enjoys good economic and trade relations with China. In 2014, the two countries signed the "Bilateral Agreement on Settlement and Payment in Local Currencies" and renewed the "Bilateral Agreement on Currency Swap". At present, 2945 Chinese-funded enterprises have been registered in Kazakhstan, making the country the third largest host of Chinese-funded enterprises overseas. Kazakhstan is rich in oil and natural gas and has great potential for exploitation. At present, the proven oil reserves total 8 billion tons, and the natural gas reserves exceed 1 trillion cubic meters. Therefore, oil exploration and processing and oil and gas project construction

---

[2] Lei and Zhigao (2015).

are fields favored by Chinese investors. Major bilateral economic and trade cooperation projects, usually of oil and gas exploration, exploitation and processing, are undertaken by companies such as CNPC, SINOPEC, CITIC Group and Zhen Hua Oil.

China's direct investment stock in South Asia is 5.364 billion USD, accounting for 6.0% of its total along the Belt and Road. China–Pakistan Economic Corridor and Bangladesh–China–India–Myanmar Economic Corridor have been established. Pakistan has 3.737 billion USD of direct investment from China, the largest amount in this region (69.7% of the regional total). Pakistan suffers from poor infrastructure. Therefore, China's investment mainly concentrates in fields of communications, electricity, water projects, transportation facilities construction, real estate and resource development. In addition, China has established a special economic zone in Pakistan—one of the first Chinese special economic zones overseas. South Asia is close to China and densely populated. However, due to its backward economy and susceptibility to political fluctuations, the region receives limited Chinese investment which mainly flows to hydropower, mining, energy, processing and manufacturing and construction industries.

China's direct investment in the eight southern European countries is relatively small in scale, with stocks of 627 million USD, accounting for 0.7% of the total. Mongolia, with stocks of 3.762 billion USD (4.2% of the total), is the seventh largest destination of direct investment from China. In 2013, Mongolia abolished the "Law on the Coordination of Foreign Investment in Strategic Areas" and implemented the "New Investment Law", providing foreign-funded enterprises with equal treatment, simplifying registration procedures and lifting restrictions on the areas accessible for foreign investors.

Table 4.5 shows the geographic distribution of China's direct investment in countries along the Belt and Road. In general, it is concentrated in emerging economies and countries with greater potential for capacity cooperation.[3]

ASEAN has close economic and trade relations with China and is the region most favored by Chinese direct investment along the Belt and Road. Many ASEAN countries have abundant labor resources, low labor costs and large mineral reserves; however, they suffer from weak power infrastructure and electricity shortage; therefore, Chinese investors focus themselves on power, mining and manufacturing industries.

As Fig. 4.15 shows, in 2015, the flows of China's direct investment in ASEAN countries exceeded 10 billion USD for the first time and hit the record high of 14.604 billion USD, generating a year-on-year increase of 87%.

In West Asia and Central Asia, direct investment from China is large in scale. West Asia, rich in energy resources, is one of the major energy suppliers of China. Chinese investment in West Asia is concentrated in energy, infrastructure and manufacturing industries of Iran, Saudi Arabia, Yemen, the UAE and Turkey. Central Asia has abundant oil and gas resources, but its light industry is less developed. As a

[3] The raw data are from Country (Region) Guidelines for Outward Investment and International Cooperation.

Table 4.5 Geographic distribution of China's direct investment in countries along the Belt and Road (Unit: 100 million USD)

	Volume of direct investment	Proportion (%)
Southeast Asia (Malaysia, Indonesia, Thailand, the Philippines, Singapore, Brunei, East Timor, Vietnam, Laos, Myanmar and Cambodia)	4,765,330	53.04
South Asia (India, Pakistan, Bangladesh, Sri Lanka, Nepal, Bhutan, Maldives, Afghanistan)	536,381	5.97
Central Asia (Turkmenistan, Kyrgyzstan, Uzbekistan, Tajikistan, Kazakhstan)	1,009,400	11.24
West Asia and North Africa (Iran, Iraq, Turkey, Syria, Jordan, Lebanon, Israel, Palestine, Saudi Arabia, Yemen, Oman, UAE, Qatar, Kuwait, Bahrain, Egypt, Libya)	1,141,272	12.70
Central and Eastern Europe (Poland, Lithuania, Estonia, Latvia, the Czech Republic, Slovakia, Hungary, Slovenia, Croatia, Bosnia and Herzegovina, Russia, Ukraine, Belarus, Georgia, Azerbaijan, Armenia, Moldova)	1,092,452	12.16
Southern Europe (Montenegro, Macedonia, Bulgaria, Albania, Romania, Serbia, Greece, Cyprus)	62,785	0.70
Mongolia	376,200	4.19

Note The raw data are from *Country (Region) Guidelines for Outward Investment and International Cooperation*

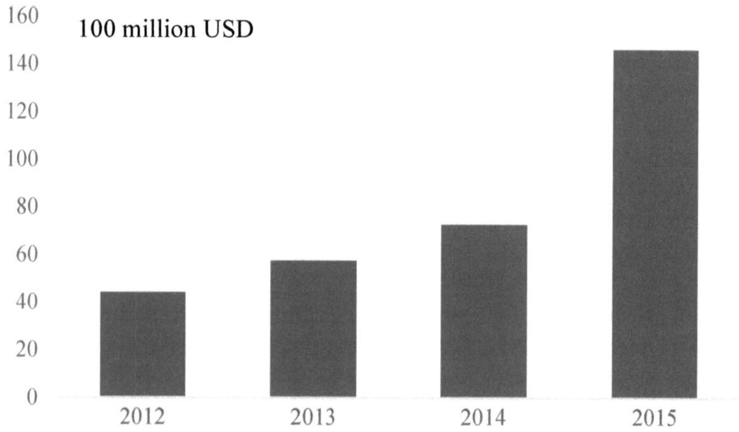

Fig. 4.15 China's investment in ASEAN countries. *Source of data* 2015 Statistical Bulletin of China's Outward Foreign Direct Investment

result, Chinese investment mainly flows to the fields of petroleum exploration and exploitation, construction of transportation and communication facilities, chemical production and agricultural and sideline product processing.

As a neighbor of China, Mongolia, rich in mineral resources, is an important destination for China's OFDI. In 2013, China's investment stock in Mongolia was 2.83 billion USD, accounting for .8% of its total investment along the Belt and Road. Chinese investment in the CIS and South Asia is relatively small in scale. In 2013, China's investment stock in the CIS was 5.48 billion USD (9.4% of the total stock) which was mainly distributed in Russia, with a focus on forestry, energy extraction and processing and manufacturing industries. Due to geopolitical reasons, China's direct investment in South Asia lags behind. In 2013, the investment stock in this region was only 3.72 billion USD, 6.4% of the investment made along the Belt and Road. In South Asia, India and Pakistan are the largest destinations of Chinese investment, and machine manufacturing, textiles, energy extraction and infrastructure are areas favored by Chinese investors. The scale of Chinese investment is the smallest in Central and Eastern Europe—in 2013, the stock was only 950 million USD, 1.6% of China's investment along the Belt and Road.

(II) The distribution of investment along the Belt and Road among different industries

As to the distribution among industries, according to non-financial industry statistics, by 2015, leasing and business service had taken the largest chunk of China's OFDI (29.9%), followed by manufacturing (16.5%), wholesale and retailing (15.8%), mining (9.3%) and real estate (6.4%). China's direct investment in countries along the Belt and Road covers areas such as energy, transportation, mining, technology, finance and real estate. The Middle East, rich in oil, gas and mineral resources, lacks communication facilities and infrastructure. Therefore, China has invested more in the fields of energy, mining, communication and infrastructure construction. Chinese investment in Southeast Asia mainly flows to areas of energy, mining and infrastructure construction. Southeast Asia, rich in oil and natural gas, could help ensure China's energy security, but at the same time, about 20% of the local population suffers from power shortage. China has advanced technologies in the fields of hydropower and thermal power. As of 2013, 17 and 15% of Chinese investment in Southeast Asia had flown to the industries of power and heat generation and mining.[4] In the more developed economies of Central and Eastern Europe and the ASEAN region, the growth of China's direct investment happened in the context of the financial crisis and the European sovereign debt crisis, and the major receivers of investment have been real estate, technology and financial industries. At present, China's direct investment in countries along the Belt and Road still focuses on capacity cooperation and infrastructure construction, but the portfolio is growing more diversified.

Since 2005, the structure of China's investment in large-scale projects in countries along the Belt and Road has been growing more diversified, with its coverage

[4] Lei and Zhigao (2015).

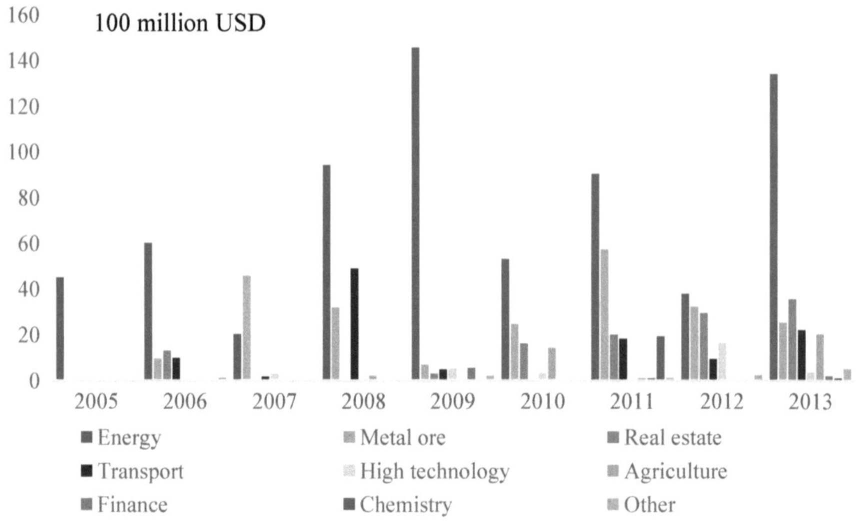

Fig. 4.16 Distribution of China's large investment projects along the Belt and Road among different industries

expanding from the energy industry to areas such as mining and metals, real estate, transportation, high technology, agriculture, finance and chemical production. As Fig. 4.16 shows, in 2005, Chinese investment in large-scale projects along the Belt and Road was limited to energy industry (mainly oil, but also natural gas and coal). In 2006–2008, Chinese investors began to touch upon large projects of mining and metals, real estate and transportation. The investment in mining and metals was at first focused on aluminum and copper, and then iron was included. Transportation includes aircraft, shipbuilding, automobile and train building industries; the focus was first on shipbuilding, and then, the automobile industry has caught up. Real estate is mainly property and construction. In 2009–2013, the investment map further expanded to include high-tech, agricultural, financial and chemical industries, which reflects the steady improvement of the investment capacity of Chinese enterprises in countries along the Belt and Road.

(III) Characteristics of Chinese enterprises investing overseas

In recent years, in response to the call to go global, more and more Chinese enterprises have been investing overseas. As of 2015, there were more than 30,000 Chinese enterprises abroad, covering 188 countries (regions), or 80.3% of the world. The area of investment has been expanding, mainly covering wholesaling and retailing, manufacturing, leasing and business service, construction, and mining industries, etc. The number of large investment projects is also rising.[5] In countries along the Belt and Road, the number of Chinese-funded enterprises has grown rapidly. For example, in

[5] Source of data: WIND.

Uzbekistan, there are about 482 registered Chinese-funded enterprises, and 71 representative offices. There are about 260 companies registered in Kyrgyzstan, and 216 companies registered with the Chinese Embassy in Russia. The scope of investment has expanded from project contracting at the beginning to trade, communication services, mineral resources exploration and development, manufacturing, agriculture, animal farming, transportation, real estate development, construction, catering, tourism, entertainment, etc. Most of the enterprises making investment are large and medium-sized SOEs, but there are also private enterprises and individuals (mainly wholly-owned or joint venture companies). The investment is carried out in various ways. For large project contracting and cooperative exploitation of resources, equity investment is adopted to boost profitability. For some projects, BOT or PSC is applied. In general, Chinese investment along the Belt and Road exhibits the characteristics of rapid growth in scale, expanding scope and diversified methods.

From the perspective of investment scale, state-owned enterprises under the central government are the main investors along the Belt and Road, while local enterprises serve as a complementary force. As Fig. 4.17 shows, as of the first half of 2014, the investment stock of central-level enterprises in large-scale projects along the Belt and Road totaled 86.45 billion USD, accounting for 67.4% of China's total investment in large-scale projects along the Belt and Road. Among these central-level enterprises, those directly under the SASAC invested 78.22 billion USD, contributing 90.5% of the investment made by all central-level enterprises; CIC invested 5.91 billion USD (4.6% of the total); central-level financial enterprises, represented by the four major state-owned banks, had a relatively small stock of 2.32 billion USD, only 1.8% of the total.

The investment stock of China's local enterprises in large-scale projects along the Belt and Road was 41.9 billion USD, accounting for 32.6% of China's total

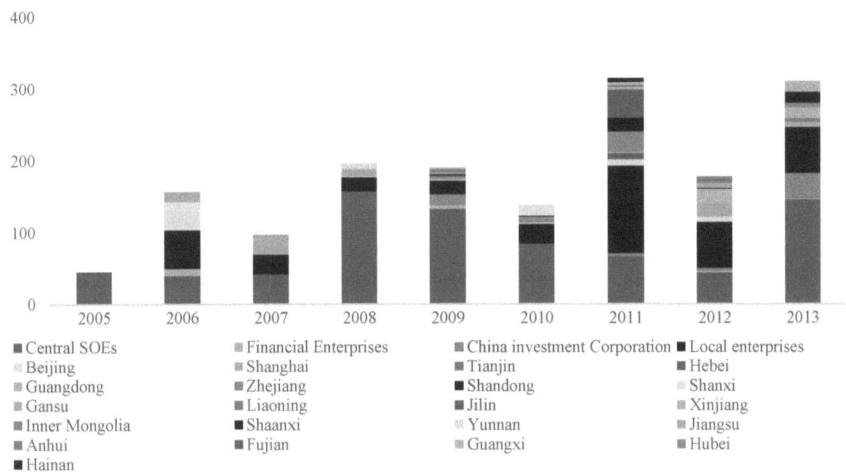

Fig. 4.17 Structure and geographic distribution of Chinese enterprises investing on large scales in countries along the Belt and Road

investment stock. Most of these local enterprises were from the more developed eastern regions. Among them, Shanghai enterprises had the largest investment stock of 9.9 billion USD (23.6%); Beijing enterprises ranked second, at 5.81 billion USD (13.9%); it was a close race for enterprises from Zhejiang, Guangdong, Jilin and Shandong which invested .21 billion USD (10.0%), 3.96 billion USD (9.5%), 3.92 billion USD (9.4%) and 3.75 billion USD (8.9%), respectively.

With the further advancement of the Belt and Road Initiative, large SOEs are no longer fighting alone in the process of going global; private capital, which has been a major force in the domestic market, will gradually take the center stage of Chinese investment overseas.

(IV) Investment patterns

1. An analysis of China's investment activities of M&A in countries along the Belt and Road

Cross-border mergers and acquisitions are one of the important means for enterprises to make direct investment abroad. The active allocation of production factors in broader areas is the more advanced stage of Chinese enterprises going global and also the true aim of the capacity cooperation along the Belt and Road. Mergers and acquisitions are not only a dynamic game between individual companies but also an important driving force for industrial transfer and capacity cooperation. In the context of global competition today, the frequent mergers and acquisitions of a large number of companies over a certain period reflect to some extent the rules of international industrial restructuring. By analyzing the statistics of 5623 cross-border transactions since 1997 (source of data: the global M&A database of Zephyr) in which China participated as the acquirer, this chapter studies the characteristics of China's investment in countries along the Belt and Road.

According to the Zephyr statistics with complete record of the amount of M&A and completion time, the scale of overseas mergers and acquisitions made by Chinese enterprises has been spiraling up since it was first recorded in 1997, as Fig. 4.18 shows.

Looking at the development trend of China's cross-border mergers and acquisitions, one could find that the financial crisis in 2008 is a turning point—before the crisis, the scale of cross-border mergers and acquisitions made by Chinese companies was in the stage of steady growth; after the crisis, the growth slowed down. It was not until 2013, when RMB was expected to depreciate, that cross-border mergers and acquisitions had resumed rapid growth. According to statistics from the Ministry of Commerce of China, the rapid growth of overseas investment and mergers and acquisitions by Chinese companies continued into 2015. In the first eight months of 2015, there were 486 overseas M&A projects by Chinese companies, involving a total of 16 major industries in 67 countries and regions and achieving 61.7 billion USD of actual transaction amount, larger than the total in 2014.[6]

As the host of M&A activities, different regions along the Belt and Road enjoy varied popularity among Chinese acquirers, as Fig. 4.19 shows.

[6] Source of data: http://www.mofcom.gov.cn/article/i/dxfw/nbgz/201609/20160901399593.shtml.

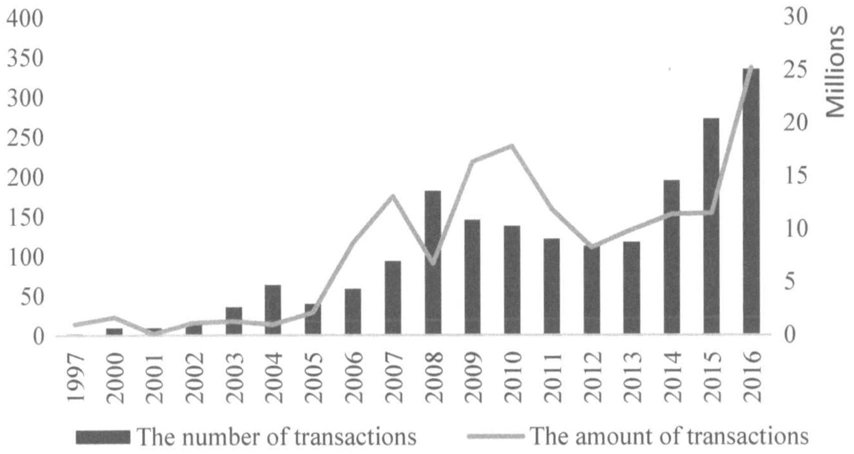

Fig. 4.18 Scale of overseas M&A deals made by China

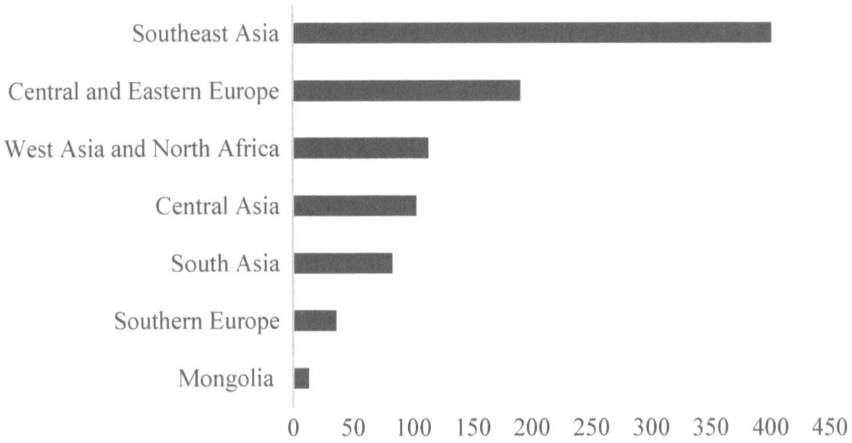

Fig. 4.19 Numbers of M&A deals in different regions along the Belt and Road

Southeast Asia is the most popular host of M&A activities among Chinese acquirers—it has witnessed 401 deals since 1997, followed by 191 transactions in Central and Eastern Europe and 113 in West Asia and North Africa. Other regions have seen relatively few transactions.

Since each region enjoys its unique resource endowments and technological environment, China has different takeover targets in different regions. The takeover targets in Southeast Asia are involved in a broad span of industries, but most of them are in other services, equipment manufacturing and wholesaling and retailing—actually, the three industries together take 53% of the total number of investment transactions. Other services mainly include information technology, Internet services and

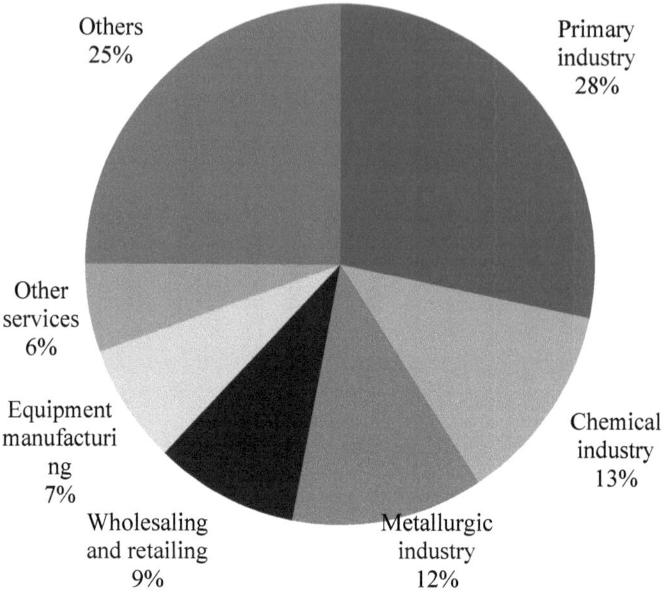

Fig. 4.20 Distribution of investment in Southeast Asia

financial services, accounting for 28% of the total number of transactions, as Fig. 4.20 shows.

In Central and Eastern Europe, the M&A targets of Chinese companies are concentrated in equipment manufacturing, primary industry,[7] chemical industry and other services. Among them, the equipment manufacturing industry contributes 22.2% of the investment transactions, the primary industry accounts for 16.9%, other service (mainly financial services) account for 15.3% and the petrochemical industry accounts for 9%. The Central and Eastern European countries are mainly the former Soviet states, such as Ukraine, Belarus, Lithuania, Latvia and Estonia. These countries have a relatively solid foundation of traditional manufacturing industries and good R&D and manufacturing capacity in areas such as space development, electrical engineering, vehicle engineering, aviation industry, agriculture and optics and laser technology.

In West Asia and North Africa, the M&A targets of Chinese companies are concentrated in other services (mainly information technology and Internet services), equipment manufacturing, chemical industry and primary industry which account for 32.7, 17.7, 10.6 and 6.2% of the total transactions, respectively. In terms of the transaction amount, the petrochemical industry ranks above other industries.

In South Asia, the takeover targets are concentrated in equipment manufacturing and other services. The equipment manufacturing industry, or more specifically, the power equipment industry, accounts for 39.3% of the total transactions and other

[7] Primary industry includes agriculture and mining, etc.

services (mainly communication and information technology industries), contributes 18.1% of the total.

In Central Asia, most of the M&A targets are in primary industry (34.9%), equipment manufacturing (19.8%), metallurgical industry (14%) and other manufacturing industries (12.8%). In southern Europe, the targets are mostly in the energy industry (electricity, natural gas, etc., 22.5%), equipment manufacturing (20%), other services (15%) and metallurgical industry (12.5%).

According to their functions, cross-border takeovers could be divided into the horizontal type, the vertical type and the mixed/conglomerate type. The horizontal type occurs between competing companies of the same industry. For example, a merger of two steel plants is a horizontal merger. Through horizontal M&A, companies could integrate resources and obtain synergy. The synergistic effect refers to the fact that the combined whole is greater than the sum of individual parts, that is, $1 + 1 > 2$. In addition to synergies, horizontal M&A could also bring enterprises more power in the market. This type of cross-border M&A is the most popular in the pharmaceutical, petrochemical, automobile and some service industries.

The vertical cross-border M&A takes place between customers and suppliers and between buyers and sellers. By linking the downstream and upstream of the production chain, this kind of takeover could reduce uncertainty and transaction costs. In addition, the enterprises, growing larger after the mergers, can also benefit from economies of scale. Mergers and acquisitions between parts suppliers and their customers (such as electronics manufacturers and automobile manufacturers) are typical examples of vertical cross-border M&A.

The mixed type refers to mergers and acquisitions which occur between companies of unrelated industries. The main purpose of this type of cross-border M&A is to spread risks and further exploit economies of scale. For example, in financial investment acquisitions, the acquirers are not the industrial capital; instead, they purely aim at obtaining returns on their financial investment.

Following is an analysis of Southeast Asia, the most popular region along the Belt and Road among Chinese acquirers. Most of the 401 mergers and acquisitions made by Chinese companies in Southeast Asia happened in Singapore, Vietnam, Indonesia and Malaysia—all countries with large population and economy.

China's mergers and acquisitions in Southeast Asia, as Fig. 4.21 shows, are mostly horizontal ones (75%), while the global average proportion of cross-border horizontal takeovers is 50–60%.[8] This shows that most of China's cross-border M&A activities are aimed at expanding market and increasing capacity. As China's foreign exchange reserves continue to rise, cross-border M&A of the financial investment type has increased significantly, contributing 16% of all investment transactions. Most of these acquisitions are concentrated in the Internet, media and communication industries, and the majority of investors are large private equity funds and national sovereign wealth funds.

In cross-border mergers and acquisitions, the proportion of mergers is very small, and most are acquisitions. The possible reason is: if the legal entity of the acquired

[8] Huang et al. (2016).

Fig. 4.21 Structure of China's M&A deals in Southeast Asia

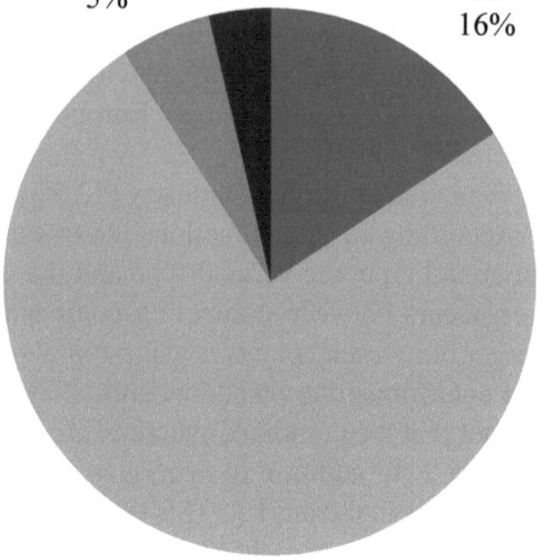

company stays unchanged, that company still belongs to and pay tax in the host country; from the perspective of national feelings, this is more acceptable for the host country; and the risk could be reduced for the acquirers.

Therefore, as the analysis of the acquisition methods adopted by Chinese companies in Southeast Asia indicates, the buyers have no special preference for acquisition method. If the acquirer purchases more than 50% of the shares, then it is a majority stake acquisition. If less than 50% of the shares are purchased, it is called a minority stake acquisition. Sometimes, less than 51% of the shares could also ensure one's control over a company. Sometimes, even buying more than 10% of the shares of a foreign company could be called a cross-border acquisition. In most acquisitions, the buyer could gain control over the seller. Most acquisitions in the world are buy-outs. However, Chinese companies are more interested in joint venture and minority stake investment when investing abroad, which reflects their cautious attitude toward the still unfamiliar cross-border M&A. In addition, minority stake acquisition could escape from public attention more easily and is subject to simpler procedures. Some companies tend to start with minority stake acquisition and gradually make the acquisition complete by increasing capital. For example, according to the foreign investment law of Germany, only when a non-EU investor (or an investor from a country which is not a member of the EU Free Trade Agreement) acquires a German company in a certain industry (including the military, aerospace and certain other industries), and the proportion of vote acquired exceeds 25%, an approval has to be secured from the German Ministry of Economy. According to the research done by Zhang Yuhan, a special contributor to the Financial Times, more than 1800 cases of overseas mergers and acquisitions of the manufacturing industry from 2003 to 2013 show that Chinese companies began to seek minority stake investment in the

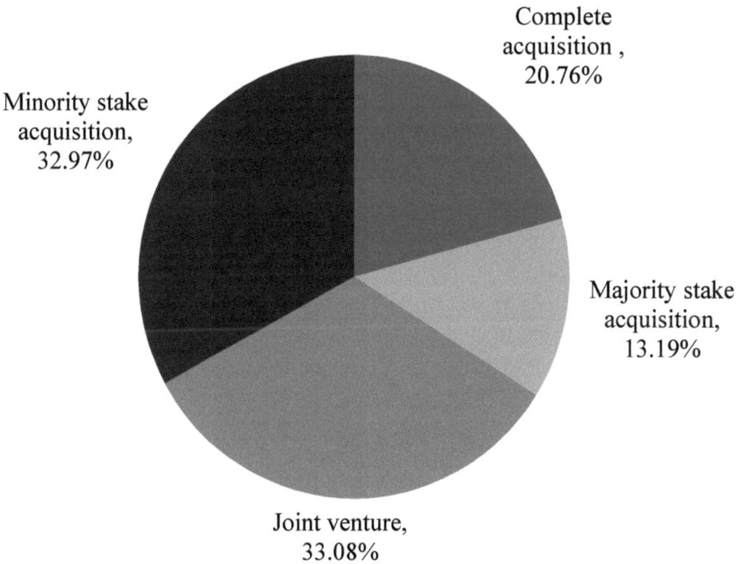

Fig. 4.22 Structure of acquisitions carried out by China along the Belt and Road

three years up to 2013. Ten years before 2013, 90% of overseas mergers and acquisitions done by Chinese manufacturers were buy-outs or majority stake acquisition. But in 2012, the proportion fell to around 67%. In the energy sector, the vast majority of overseas takeovers by Chinese oil, and clean energy companies are minority stake investment.[9] This trend shows that Chinese companies have learned from the past experience—they are aware of their lack of reputation, credibility and managerial experience in other countries and choose minority stake acquisition to prevent failure caused by regulator intervention or poor management.

As Fig. 4.22 and Table 4.6 show, statistics of China's acquisition types along the Belt and Road generally confirms the preference of Chinese companies for joint venture and minority stake acquisition.

2. An analysis of the greenfield investment activities carried out by China along the Belt and Road.

China is changing from the net receiver to the net exporter of FDI. In 2015, it ranked first in the Asia–Pacific region with a total OFDI of 59 billion USD.[10] From January to April 2016, China surpassed the United States for the first time and became the world's largest source of greenfield investment. According to the Xinhua News Agency, from January to April 2016, Chinese companies had 126 greenfield investment projects abroad, with a total investment of 29.48 billion USD. American

[9] Advice for Chinese enterprises on cross-border mergers and acquisitions, http://www.ftchinese.com/story/001048581?full=y.

[10] Source of data: fDi Markets.

Table 4.6 Types of acquisitions made by China along the Belt and Road (Unit: %)

	Southeast Asia	South Asia	Central Asia	West Asia and North Africa	Central and Eastern Europe	Southern Europe
Complete acquisition	25.44	9.71	14.46	18.02	20.42	25.00
Majority stake acquisition	9.73	14.56	18.07	10.81	17.28	22.22
Joint venture	28.68	48.54	57.83	24.32	30.37	22.22
Minority stake acquisition	36.16	27.18	9.64	46.85	31.94	30.56

companies launched 661 greenfield investment projects over the same period, but the total investment was only 22.81 billion USD. As to the investment amount, China ranked first in the world. According to the statistics from fDi Markets, a monitoring agency of greenfield investment, in the one and a half years up to June 2016, Chinese investors announced 315 greenfield investment projects in countries along the Belt and Road with a total value of 75.9 billion USD, doubling the figure compared to 18 months ago.

As Fig. 4.23 shows, developing countries have always been the favored hosts for China's greenfield investment projects overseas.

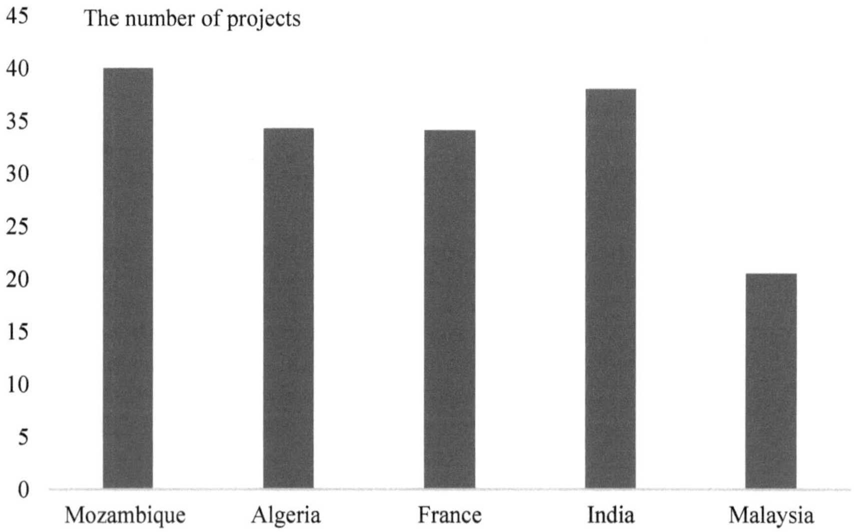

Fig. 4.23 Top destinations of greenfield investment made by Chinese enterprises (the first four months of 2014)

The proportion of greenfield investment in China's outward investment has been declining, and its scale is now smaller than that of cross-border M&A investment. According to the statistics from the Chinese Ministry of Commerce, in the first seven months of 2016, Chinese companies implemented a total of 459 M&A projects overseas, involving 63 countries and regions, covering 15 industries (including information transmission, software and information services and manufacturing) and generating a transaction amount of 54.3 billion USD (52.8% of the total outward investment over the same period). Among the 2858 cases of Chinese companies investing overseas in 2000–the first half of 2016 (recorded by CCG), 2515, or 88% of the total, are cross-border takeovers, which reflects that this approach has become the mainstream of China's OFDI.[11]

Chinese companies investing abroad choose cross-border takeover because it helps them enter the local market fast. If they choose to build new factories, it would be hard for them to break into the local market at the beginning. However, with the development of enterprises, the performance of the newly built factories will continue to improve, narrowing the gap between the two entry modes, and each mode will eventually form its own advantages. Wang and Sunny (2009) studied statistics of 84 countries and regions and found that greenfield investment could substantially boost growth of the host country. From Indonesia to the Middle East, thermal power plants built by China have sprung up all over Eurasia. In Pakistan alone, Chinese investors have announced new power plants worth approximately 8.5 billion USD, which may add 5260 megawatts of installed capacity to Pakistan's power grid. E-commerce group Alibaba and home appliance brand Haier are also becoming big investors overseas—they have moved their production operations overseas to prepare to serve large consumer markets like India.[12]

Geographically, in the first four months of 2016, the largest destinations for Chinese greenfield investment along the Belt and Road were India (3.8 billion USD) and Malaysia (2.05 billion USD). In terms of the number of greenfield investment projects, India ranked first among all countries in the Belt and Road region (20 projects).[13] Compared with cross-border takeovers, China's greenfield investment overseas is concentrated in the labor-intensive and resource-intensive industries of emerging countries (rich in raw materials and labor). Within the framework of the Belt and Road Initiative, most Chinese companies investing in Africa have chosen greenfield investment. In addition, to upgrade the manufacturing industry of China, Chinese companies have turned to Germany.

Which approach of direct investment is more favored by Chinese enterprises, greenfield investment or M&A? To answer this question, Sha et al. (2012) conducted a questionnaire survey of 223 Chinese companies and reached two conclusions. First, for Chinese companies, cross-border takeovers are more complicated, riskier

---

[11] Blue Book of Chinese Enterprise Globalization—Report on Chinese Enterprises Globalization (2016), http://www.ccg.org.cn/dianzizazhi/qiye2016.pdf.

[12] The Belt and Road: could a good story end well? http://m.ftchinese.com/story/001068864.

[13] China Becomes the Largest Greenfield Investor in the World, http://paper.people.com.cn/rmrbhwb/html/2016-06/28/content_1690828.htm.

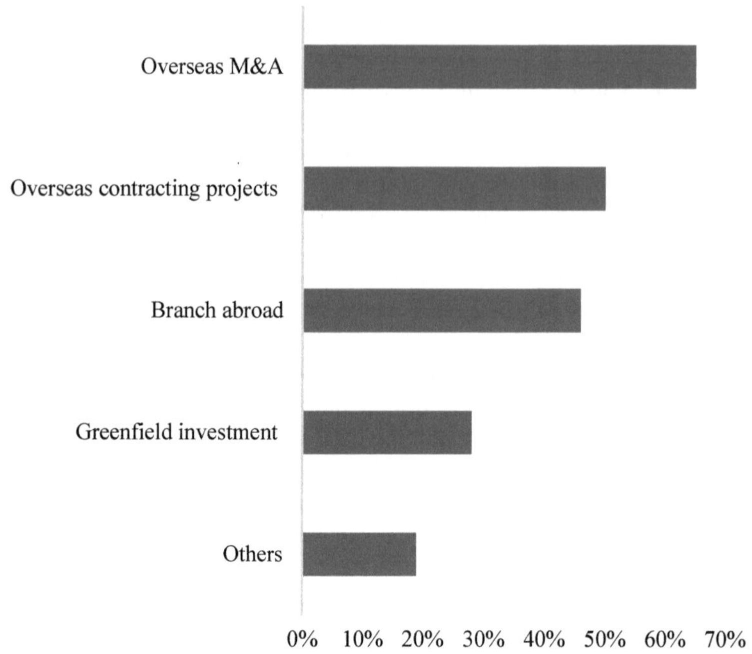

Fig. 4.24 Approaches of internationalization of SOEs. *Source of data* Deloitte China

and more challenging. Therefore, only those with rich investment experience in overseas markets tend to choose this approach. Second, Chinese companies seeking to expand their market shares are more inclined to choose the approach of greenfield investment, because as start-ups, they usually target at new products and markets. Therefore, Chinese companies which prefer cross-border takeovers to greenfield investment often have highly differentiated products, larger market shares and also larger scale and higher capital intensity.

As Fig. 4.24 shows, Deloitte China conducted a questionnaire survey of 54 Chinese SOEs seeking internationalization in 2015 and found their approaches to internationalization which are diversified, and the number of greenfield investment projects will increase with the launch of the Belt and Road Initiative.[14]

For the surveyed SOEs, overseas takeover is the most commonly used approach to internationalization, followed by contracting projects overseas and setting up branch offices abroad to reach out for business. For overseas takeovers, the vast majority prefers buy-outs, and only a minority prefers minority stake acquisition. In addition, some SOEs choose to go global through trade overseas or cooperation with foreign organizations. Many of the Belt and Road projects will adopt PPP (Public Private

[14] Ushering in the new era of SOE internationalization by seizing the opportunity of the Belt and Road development,
https://www2.deloitte.com/content/dam/Deloitte/cn/Documents/process-and-operations/deloitte-cn-soe-transformationseries-issue3-zh-151020.pdf.

Partnership, or the cooperation between the host government and Chinese enterprises). SOEs will invest to set up factories abroad or make investment and contract projects simultaneously, which means the number of greenfield investment projects will surge.

4.3 Main Obstacles to Investment Along the Belt and Road

(I) Risks of host countries

According to the risk analysis report of the countries along the "Belt and Road" issued by China Export & Credit Insurance Corporation, compared with the 2014 ratings, in 2015, 14 countries, 7.3% of the total, had lower risk levels and higher ratings. For 159 countries (82.8%), the risk level and rating remained the same. 19 countries (9.9%) had rising risk levels and downgraded ratings.

The countries with improved ratings are India, Indonesia, Mexico, Tanzania, etc., where smooth structural reforms brought good development prospects. The countries with downgraded ratings are Ukraine, Yemen, etc., which were greatly affected by geopolitical tensions. The findings of this survey could be summarized as follows: the geopolitical conflicts in hot spots would intensify; and the world economy exhibited the "new normal" of imbalance and moderate recovery.

1. Political risks of host countries

It is generally believed that political risks refer to possibilities of harms to the investing enterprises caused by their own acts and other factors such as political instability, policy inconsistency, geopolitical conflicts, nationalist and religious conflicts, regional wars, bureaucracy and terrorist attacks in host countries. In general, the political risks of host countries mainly include political instability, riots, terrorist attacks or armed conflicts.[15]

According to the *Report on Chinese Enterprises Globalization (2014)*, the first Blue Book of Chinese Enterprise Globalization, 25% of the 120 "going out" failures in 2005–2014 are due to political reasons, 17% of which are results of political instability and leadership changes in host countries.

Tables 4.7, 4.8, 4.9, 4.10, 4.11, 4.12 and 4.13 are the rankings of political stability indexes of various regions in 2015 based on the Worldwide Governance Indicators (WGI) of the World Bank.

With the full implementation of the Belt and Road construction in future, it will be inevitable for the international economic cooperation and investment to collide with regional factors of instability. Therefore, the cost of infrastructure construction and development may far exceed the pure economic cost. Many problems may rise in this link of economic cooperation, which will soon become a key challenge facing the Belt and Road Initiative.

[15] Litai (2008).

Table 4.7 Political stability indexes of Southeast Asian countries

Country	2013	2015
Singapore	1.34	1.24
Brunei	1.08	1.21
Laos	0.06	0.48
Malaysia	0.05	0.19
Vietnam	0.22	0.01
Cambodia	−0.17	−0.10
East Timor	−0.39	−0.22
Indonesia	−0.50	−0.60
The Philippines	−1.06	−0.84
Thailand	−1.31	−0.96
Myanmar	−1.15	−1.17

Table 4.8 Political stability indexes of South Asian countries

Country	2013	2015
Bhutan	0.80	1.10
Maldives	0.22	0.48
Sri Lanka	−0.59	−0.03
India	−1.18	−0.92
Nepal	−1.11	−0.93
Bangladesh	−1.63	−1.15
Afghanistan	−2.50	−2.50
Pakistan	−2.60	−2.54

Table 4.9 Political stability indexes of countries in West Asia and North Africa

Country	2013	2015
UAE	0.89	0.76
Oman	0.45	0.69
Kuwait	0.14	−0.11
Saudi Arabia	−0.41	−0.54
Jordan	−0.62	−0.58
Iran	−1.26	−0.91
Bahrain	−1.35	−1.08
Israel	−1.09	−1.12
Turkey	−1.20	−1.28
Egypt	−1.65	−1.34
Lebanon	−1.69	−1.72
Iraq	−2.02	−2.29
Yemen	−2.35	−2.63
Syria	−2.68	−2.94

Table 4.10 Political stability indexes of countries in the Caucasus

Country	2013	2015
Armenia	0.07	−0.29
Georgia	−0.43	−0.40
Azerbaijan	−0.41	−0.69

Table 4.11 Political stability indexes in Central Asia

Country	2013	2015
Tajikistan	−1.13	−0.87
Kazakhstan	−0.38	−0.10
Kyrgyzstan	−0.91	−0.87
Turkmenistan	0.17	−0.11
Uzbekistan	−0.55	−0.42

Table 4.12 Political stability indexes of Central and European countries

Country	2013	2015
The Czech Republic	1.05	0.96
Slovakia	1.10	0.96
Poland	0.96	0.87
Hungary	0.78	0.73
Lithuania	0.94	0.70
Estonia	0.73	0.62
Latvia	0.59	0.45
Romania	0.16	0.20
Belarus	−0.04	0.00
Moldova	−0.02	−0.39
Russia	−0.74	−1.05
Ukraine	−0.76	−1.93

Table 4.13 Political stability indexes of Southern European countries

Country	2013	2015
Slovenia	0.87	0.92
Croatia	0.61	0.58
Cyprus	0.55	0.54
Serbia	−0.08	0.23
Montenegro	0.46	0.13
Bulgaria	0.15	0.02
Macedonia	−0.37	−0.20
Greece	−0.17	−0.23
Bosnia and Herzegovina	−0.38	−0.45

2. Obstacles posed by government management of the host countries

The Country Risk Indexes released by the World Bank contain the government management indexes. The data of countries along the Belt and Road are listed in Table 14. The indexes cover four areas: government efficiency, regulatory quality, corruption control and laws and regulations. Government efficiency is the performance of public management, which refers to the level and ability of the government to achieve the optimal output with lower costs and fewer resources in the process of public management. The regulatory quality index reflects whether the government has the ability to formulate and implement sound policies and regulations to allow and promote the development of the private sector. The smaller the index, the lower the efficiency of government management.

3. Environment risks of host countries

The investment in infrastructure construction is a precursor to the actual operation of the Belt and Road. If the infrastructure is well built, the regions along the route can fully play the latecomer advantage to achieve great economic growth. If the infrastructure is poorly constructed, waste will be inevitable, and regional economic development will be dragged down.

The construction and investment in infrastructure are mainly the responsibilities of the government. Infrastructure, requiring large investment, takes long to build and suffers from low returns. Therefore, although infrastructure may bring great social benefits, regular enterprises do not have the capacity or the motivation to build and manage it. Even if private capital is to be introduced, the government has to provide adequate subsidies.

4. Government intervention of host countries
(1) Intervention in the name of national security

Including escape clauses in bilateral investment agreements is a "safety valve" which balances and coordinates investors and protects the national security and public interests of the host country. Security exception clauses have been accepted by the WTO Agreement and many bilateral investment agreements.

In the context of economic globalization today, national security includes not only traditional military security but also national economic security. National security clauses are in nature national self-judging clauses. Although international customary law requires countries to enforce treaties in good faith, national security clauses are often abused in the absence of clear standards.[16]

(2) Policy intervention

The host country, concerned about the impact of foreign companies on its own industries, may adopt some policy interventions to protect the development and survival of its own industries, such as setting up a quota system to guarantee the use of locally produced raw materials and parts, formulating the policy of capital

[16] Jinsong (2011).

Table 4.14 Government management indexes of different countries

Region	Country	2013	2015	Region	Country	2013	2015
South Asia	Afghanistan	−1.40	−1.34	The Caucasus	Armenia	0.09	−0.14
	Bangladesh	−0.80	−0.73		Azerbaijan	−0.46	−0.23
	India	−0.17	0.10		Georgia	0.58	0.40
	Bhutan	0.40	0.41	Central and Eastern Europe	Belarus	−0.93	−0.48
	Maldives	−0.31	−0.38		Moldova	−0.39	−0.63
	Sri Lanka	−0.16	0.01		Poland	0.72	0.80
	Nepal	−0.93	−1.04		Romania	−0.06	−0.04
	Pakistan	−0.79	−0.66		Russia	−0.35	−0.18
	Brunei	0.87	1.05		The Czech Republic	0.89	1.05
Southeast Asia	Cambodia	−0.91	−0.69		Estonia	1.00	1.09
	Indonesia	−0.19	−0.22		Hungary	0.66	0.49
	Laos	−0.73	−0.50		Ukraine	−0.64	−0.51
	Malaysia	1.01	0.96		Slovakia	0.79	0.84
	The Philippines	0.12	0.11		Latvia	0.89	1.10
	Singapore	2.09	2.25		Lithuania	0.84	1.20
	Vietnam	−0.27	0.08	Southern Europe	Slovenia	1.01	0.97
	Thailand	0.24	0.36		Montenegro	0.17	0.16
	Myanmar	−1.51	−1.24		Bulgaria	0.16	0.22
	East Timor	−1.21	−1.05		Bosnia and Herzegovina	−0.43	−0.54
Central Asia	Turkmenistan	−1.31	−0.87		Greece	0.46	0.25
	Tajikistan	−1.07	−0.82		Croatia	0.70	0.51
	Uzbekistan	−0.94	−0.68		Cyprus	1.36	1.04
	Kazakhstan	−0.53	−0.05		Serbia	−0.09	0.11
	Kyrgyzstan	−0.64	−0.90		Macedonia	−0.05	0.13
West Asia and North Africa	Bahrain	0.60	0.57		Mongolia	−0.54	−0.40
	Iran	−0.69	−0.20				
	Iraq	−1.12	−1.27				
	Israel	1.23	1.38				
	Jordan	−0.04	0.14				
	Kuwait	−0.06	−0.02				
	Saudi Arabia	0.07	0.21				
	UAE	1.18	1.54				
	Egypt	−0.89	−0.76				
	Oman	0.22	0.09				

(continued)

Table 4.14 (continued)

Region	Country	2013	2015	Region	Country	2013	2015
	Syria	−1.43	−1.63				
	Turkey	0.39	0.23				
	Yemen	−1.21	−1.64				
	Lebanon	−0.40	−0.47				

return and implementing special pollution laws. These interventions may bring risks to the investment activities of foreign companies. At the same time, in the countries along the Silk Road, the high tariffs on cross-border trade and the low efficiency, inaction and even corruption of the border management agencies have all obstructed the revival of the Silk Road.[17]

(II) Obstacles to investment posed by enterprises themselves

1. Operation obstacles

(1) Human resource obstacle

Enterprises investing overseas face the lack of international management capacities and international talents. Most of the middle-and-high-level managerial personnel working in the host countries are sent by the parent companies, so they are unfamiliar with the local working environment, related business laws, market conditions and culture and customs, which can easily lead to conflicts and mistakes in operation and decision making. In addition, there is a risk of changing labor costs, such as the cost of work visas and the extra cost of re-applying for visas due to project extension. In addition, hiring local workers has to meet the requirement of local labor law on work time and insurance, which will further push up the labor costs. Besides, there is the uncertainty in the local prices of equipment and raw materials.

(2) Supply-chain obstacles

Supply-chain obstacles are seen in both the supply and demand chains of production. Risks along the supply chain include the restriction on resources required for production set by upstream suppliers of the host country and thus the instability of production cost. Risks along the demand chain are brought by the wrong prediction of local consumer behaviors, and the substitute products produced by local competitors.[18]

(3) Risk management obstacles

On one hand, due to lack of the early risk warning mechanism of risk information or such mechanism needs to be improved, and enterprises don't have management professionals with international experience, they fail to be fully aware of the information on emergencies, thus being slow in taking actions.[19]

[17] Maochun (2015).

[18] Shiguang (2014).

[19] Ji (2015).

On the other hand, the risk warning capacity is limited. Although some companies attempt to establish an early warning mechanism of risk information, their warning capacity is limited due to the lack of strategic arrangement for risk management mechanisms, the lack of connections in the host countries, limited access to information and low efficiency of data collection.[20] Countries along the Belt and Road have very different legal requirements for business operation and investment. If no precautions are taken, companies will get into trouble.

2. Market risks

Having just entered the local markets, the companies are disadvantaged compared to local rivals in terms of brand, popularity, customer sources and business relationships. Confronted with the aggression from local market leaders, the enterprises will have to bear the double losses of competition costs and market shares once their countermeasures fail. The bargaining power of upstream raw material suppliers will bring cost risks. The supply–demand relations will cause demand price risks. The financing, channels and asset structure will cause capital price risks.

4.4 Summary

China has grown into one of the major sources of OFDI in the world. Over the past decade, China's OFDI has continued to grow, narrowing its gap with FDI inflows. In 2014, FDI outflows outweighed inflows for the first time, turning China into a net exporter of foreign investment. In 2015, China's OFDI flows hit a record high of 145.67 billion USD, accounting for 9.9% of the global flows, second only to that of the United States.

Countries along the Belt and Road are important destinations for Chinese capital. As to both flows and stock, the proportion of China's direct investment along the "Belt and Road" within the total FDI absorbed by the region has been growing. Although China's direct investment in this region has grown so fast that China has become the main source of FDI stock for some countries, there is still a lot of room for growth considering the total amount of foreign capital absorbed in the region. As of the end of 2015, China's direct investment stock in the region accounted for 2.70% of the total FDI absorbed, and the flows accounted for 6.72% of FDI absorbed annually, indicating great potential for future growth.

In terms of geographic distribution, industries involved and investment methods, China's OFDI in countries along the Belt and Road is becoming increasingly diversified. From a geographic point of view, China's OFDI in the region used to concentrate in its neighboring countries. The Southeast Asia has the largest stock of Chinese direct investment at 47.653 billion USD, accounting for 53.0% of China's total direct investment stock along the Belt and Road. Other regions along the Belt and Road

[20] Guodong (2015).

also attract Chinese investment with different industries such as energy, transportation, mining, technology, finance and real estate. As to investment methods, China's direct investment in the region still focuses on capacity cooperation and infrastructure construction, but the portfolio is growing increasingly diversified. In addition to overseas greenfield investment, Chinese enterprise has also launched cross-border takeovers. The proportion of greenfield investment in outward investment has shrunk to a level lower than that of mergers and acquisitions. In areas such as large-scale project contracting and cooperative development of resources, equity investment has appeared; for some investment projects, BOT and PSC have been applied.

To achieve mutual benefit and shared prosperity through investment along the Belt and Road, China still has a series of obstacles to tackle, including host country risks, market risks and industry risks. At present, China is also facing the challenge of vague coordination mechanisms among government departments and between government and non-government sectors.

Part II
Country-Specific Study

A ship flying the flag of tea is kissed by the gentle waves of Southeast Asia; the music of Huqin is accompanied by the bright moonlight and the silver sand along the Silk Road.

Chapter 5
Southeast Asia Region

The Southeast Asia region is composed of 11 countries: Vietnam, Laos, Cambodia, Thailand, Malaysia, Singapore, Myanmar, Indonesia, Brunei, the Philippines and Timor-Leste.

Most Southeast Asian countries are located in coastal areas. The tropical climate and natural environment make the region's overall economic development distinctive. With abundant water resources and fertile soil, most countries in this region are traditional agricultural countries. Myanmar is known as the Asian granary, and Thailand is the only net food exporter in Asia. Southeast Asia is rich in forest and mineral resources, and energy also plays an important role in its economic development: Brunei is the third largest oil producer in Southeast Asia and the fourth largest natural gas producer in the world. Indonesia also has abundant oil, natural gas, coal, gold and silver resources. The Philippines, located on the seismic belt of the Pacific Rim, is unique in its geographical environment and geological structure, which is conducive to the formation of mineral deposits.

Most Southeast Asian countries are traditional agricultural countries with weak industrial bases, especially Cambodia, Laos, Myanmar, Timor-Leste and Vietnam. Myanmar's industrial development is slow, and its industrial output accounts for 34.6% of its GDP. Laos is one of the least developed countries in the world: the development of its heavy industry is lagging behind, a complete industrial system has not yet been formed, and the industrial output makes up a small proportion of GDP at about 30–35% in the past five years. For most countries in Southeast Asia, the energy industry is still the pillar of economic development, and the economic structure is in urgent need of transformation and improvement. The production and export of oil and natural gas have become the mainstay of Brunei's national economy, and with the development of the oil industry, the disadvantages of the under-diversified economic structure have become increasingly apparent.

Economic development in Southeast Asian countries is severely polarized. In some countries, the economy is backward with large population in poverty and low urbanization rate. Cambodia, which has a weak industrial base, has been rated by

H. Zhang et al., *Comparative Studies on Regional and National Economic Development*, Global Economic Synergy of Belt and Road Initiative,
https://doi.org/10.1007/978-981-16-2105-5_5

the World Bank as one of the least developed countries in the world, and its poverty rate is 26%. According to World Bank data, Timor-Leste's total GDP in 2015 was 1.41 billion USD, ranking 167th out of more than 220 countries and regions in the world, with a per capita GDP of 1130 USD. In 2011, 37% of its population lived below the poverty line. The per capita income of the Philippines was 3,112 USD in 2015, which is defined by the World Bank as a lower-middle-income country. By 2015, Cambodia's urbanization rate was only 20.72%, and Myanmar's was only 34.1%, seeing little change in the past 20 years. Meanwhile, China's rate exceeded 50% in 2015.

In contrast, Singapore, Malaysia, Thailand and Brunei have more prominent economic developments. Singapore is a successfully transformed economy with sustained economic growth. According to World Bank data, Singapore's GDP in 2015 was 287.02 billion USD, an increase of 2.1% over the previous year, and per capita GDP increased by 0.81% to 51,855 USD. Malaysia is a developing country, and its economic development is at the forefront of ASEAN countries. Services and industries account for a relatively high share of its national economy. Malaysia is also one of the most urbanized countries in East Asia, with an urbanization rate close to 75%. Thailand is an ASEAN member and was one of the "Four Tigers" in Asia. It is an emerging industrial country in the world, the world's largest exporter of natural rubber, and one of the world's five largest agricultural exporters. Local per capita GDP is 5814.77 USD, ranking after ASEAN countries like Singapore, Brunei and Malaysia and among the upper-middle-income countries. In 2015, Brunei's GDP reached 15.492 billion USD and per capita GDP was 36,607.9 USD, which is classified as a high-income country. Its urbanization rate was 77.2%.

It can also be seen from Table 5.1 that the polarization of economic development in Southeast Asian countries is very serious. According to the standards published by the World Bank in 2010: 1005 USD or less for low-income economies; 1006–3975 USD for lower-middle-income economies; 3976–12,275 USD for upper-middle-income economies; 12,276 USD or more for high-income economies. Of the 11 countries along the Belt and Road in Southeast Asia, there are two high-income countries (Singapore and Brunei), and two upper-middle-income countries (Malaysia and Thailand), while Indonesia, the Philippines, Vietnam, Laos, Myanmar, Cambodia and Timor-Leste belong to lower-middle-income countries. Countries with higher per capita GDP also have higher urbanization rates. These facts further explain that the economic gap among different countries is wide.

5.1 Cambodia

I. **Geographical and historical backgrounds**

Connecting the inland and the sea, Cambodia is a country with a long history. Located between the two major civilizations of India and China, it has significant geographical advantages. It has become an important transportation route between East and West

Table 5.1 Economic development of Southeast Asian countries

Country	Gross GDP (100 million USD)	Per capita GDP (USD)	Urbanization rate (%)
Singapore	2870.20	51,855.00	
Brunei	154.92	36,607.90	77.2
Malaysia	3299.00	10,877.00	Almost 75
Thailand	3952.00	5814.77	Higher than 50
Indonesia	8619.34	3346.49	Higher than 50
The Philippines	2919.70	3112.00	44.37
Vietnam	1936.00	2111.14	33.6
Laos	123.27	1812.33	Almost 40
Myanmar	649.00	1204.00	34.1
Cambodia	180.00	1158.00	20.72
Timor-Leste	14.10	1130.00	

since the dawn of history (Wang 1999). With an area of 181,035 km^2, Cambodia ranks 8th among Southeast Asian countries. The topographic features are obvious. There are high mountains in the territory: the Phnom Aural in the Kezo Mountains between Pursat Province and Kampong Speu, 1813 m above sea level, is the highest peak in Cambodia. There are plains: the central area was originally a large bay and then turned into the largest plain in the country due to sedimentation of the Mekong River. The Cardamom Mountains and the Dâmrei Mountains run across the country. There are also lakes: and Tonle Sap Lake (also known as the Phnom Penh Lake), is the largest freshwater lake in Southeast Asia. There are rivers—its central region is centered around the Mekong River. In short, Cambodia, with fertile land and abundant water resources, has good conditions for crop farming.

With precipitation and a network of rivers and lakes formed by the Tonle Sap and Mekong river systems, Cambodia has abundant water resources. There are 75 billion m^3 (excluding accumulated rainwater) of surface water and 17.6 billion m^3 of groundwater. The average annual rainfall is 1400–3500 mm, the annual flow of the Mekong River is about 475 billion m^3.[1] The country has about 6.7 million ha of arable land, but currently the actual cultivated area is only about 2.6 million ha.[2] Due to constant wars, mergers, imbalances in possession, disputes and other issues, there is a lot of room for improvement in land resource utilization. The agricultural resources are abundant. The main agricultural products are rice, corn, potatoes, peanuts, beans, etc. The cash crops are rubber, pepper, cotton, tobacco, brown sugar, sugar cane, coffee, sesame and so on. There are abundant fishery resources. For instance, Tonle

[1] Status, Problems and Solutions of Water Resource Development in Cambodia [N], International Business Daily/China-ASEAN Business Weekly, 2015-12-21.

[2] Source of data: Economic and Commercial Counsellor's Office of the Embassy of the People's Republic of China in the Kingdom of Cambodia.

Sap Lake is the world's famous natural freshwater fishing ground and the largest fishing ground in Southeast Asia. Mineral resources, with huge potential, are important to Cambodia's socio-economic development. Currently, there are more than 20 proven mineral deposits, mainly gold, iron, phosphate rock, limestone and petroleum. In addition, the country is rich in teak, ironwood, rosewood, black sandalwood, white linden and many kinds of bamboo. The national forest coverage rate is 61.4%, and the wood reserves are more than 1.1 billion m^3.[3]

There are more than 20 nationalities and tribes in Cambodia, including overseas Chinese. Chinese people settled in Cambodia as early as in the Song Dynasty, and more moved there after the Qing Dynasty. Buddhism is the state religion of Cambodia. Other religions include Islam, Catholicism and Brahmanism.

II. **Economic development**

As a traditional agricultural country with a relatively weak industrial base, Cambodia has been rated by the World Bank as one of the least developed countries in the world. Its poverty rate is 26%. Therefore, the Cambodian government takes economic development and poverty reduction as its top priorities. Economically, Cambodia adopts a free and open market. All economic activities are highly liberalized. The degree of economic privatization and trade liberalization is relatively high. Cambodia has been granted GSP treatment in 28 countries, including the United States, the European Union and Japan.

In recent years, with political stability and thus policy continuity, Cambodia has been growing steadily, leading to increasing investment in fixed assets and improving infrastructure. According to the World Bank report, Cambodia's economy has grown at an average annual rate of 7.7% over the past 20 years, ranking the sixth fastest in the world.[4]

In 1993, after the election, the People's Party and FUNCINPEC Party jointly came to power and formally established the "market economy" model and the development goals of "developing the economy and eliminating poverty". The new government elected in 2008 announced to further deepen reforms, strengthen financial and fiscal supervision, improve management of fiscal, taxation and administrative systems and continue to implement the "Four Corners Strategy".

(I) Domestic economy

In 2015, Cambodia maintained a relatively stable political environment. The government implemented the "Four Corners Strategy", which focuses on optimizing administrative management and aims at accelerating agricultural development, infrastructure construction, private economy and employment improvement, and human resource development. Agriculture, processing industry, tourism, infrastructure construction and personnel training are the priority development areas. Now

[3] Country Profile: Cambodia, by Ministry of Foreign Affairs, China. http://www.fmprc.gov.cn/web/gjhdq_676201/gj_676203/yz_676205/1206_676572/1206x0_676574/.

[4] Source of data: Economic and Commercial Counsellor's Office of the Embassy of the People's Republic of China in the Kingdom of Cambodia.

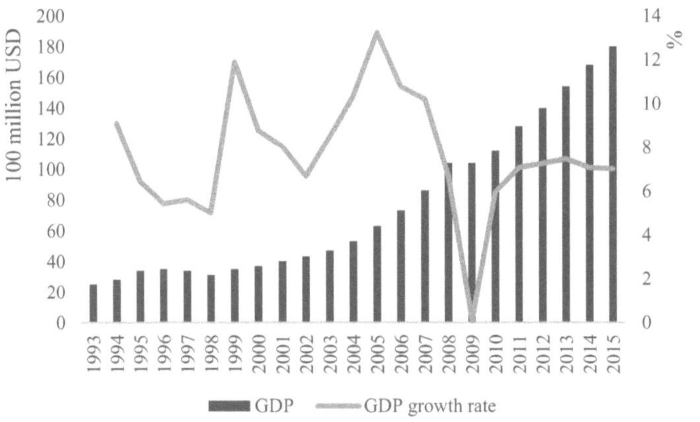

Fig. 5.1 Economic development of Cambodia. *Source of data* World Bank database

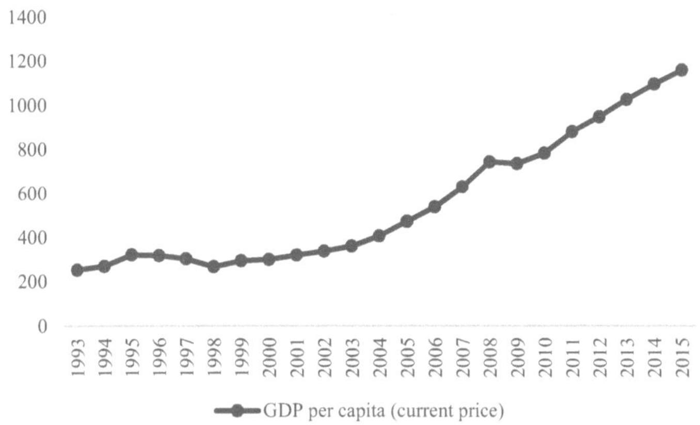

Fig. 5.2 Per capita GDP of Cambodia. *Source of data* World Bank database

Cambodia has entered the third stage of implementing the "Four Corners Strategy". The government is deepening reforms, strengthening foreign exchanges, and actively engaged in regional and ASEAN integration. Its four economic pillars—agriculture, industry led by garment and footwear manufacturing and construction sector, the service sector led by tourism and foreign direct investment—have continued to steadily driven the macroeconomy forward.

In 2015, Cambodia's macroeconomy grew steadily, with a GDP of 18 billion USD, a real increase of 6.9%, a per capita GDP of 1158 USD, a year-on-year increase of 9.4% and an inflation rate of 3%.[5] Domestic economic indicators and developments are shown in Figs. 5.1 and 5.2.

[5] Ibid.

Since Cambodia resumed peace in 1993, the government has focused its attention on economic development and social transformation. By adopting a free and open economic policy, it has witnessed greater development in terms of economy and other aspects, and due to its rich nature resources, cheap labor, and other uniquely favorable factors, investment, foreign trade and official development aid have become important sources and pillars of its economic growth. It enjoys great potential for economic development.

1. Industrial structure

In recent years, Cambodia's industrial structure has continued to improve, and the share of agricultural output in GDP has continued to decline. In 2015, the added value of agriculture, industry and service industries were 4.798 billion, 4.996 billion and 7.19 billion USD, accounting for 28.25%, 29.42% and 42.33% respectively, as shown in Fig. 5.3.

(1) The primary industry

Agriculture is the economic foundation of Cambodian economy. It has been a pillar industry of the whole country for a long time, and it is also the top priority of the national economic development strategy. After its independence, Cambodia's agriculture has made great progress as its output value grows gradually and the output expands.

Cambodia has plenty of sunshine, abundant rainfall and fertile land. The average annual temperature is between 29 and 30 °C, which is suitable for the cultivation of a variety of crops, especially rice. In 1994, Cambodia promulgated the *Investment Law*, listing agricultural product processing as a priority area for government support. In 1996–2000, the Cambodian government formulated the first five-year plan specifically for agriculture. After 2008, the Cambodian government has given

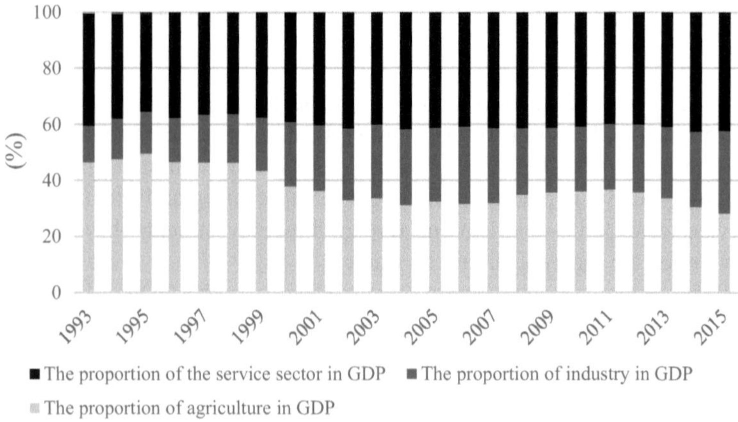

Fig. 5.3 Changes of Cambodian industrial structure in recent years. *Source of data* World Bank database

special support to rice cultivation and export. In 2010, the Cambodian government's investment in irrigation systems increased to 59.2 million USD.

After 2000, the proportion of the primary industry's output value within Cambodian GDP had stayed at about 30%, and by 2015 it had fallen to 28.25%, falling below 30% for the first time. Within the total output value of the primary industry, agriculture contributed 60%, forestry 7%, fishery 22% and animal husbandry 11%. The total rice planting area was 3.051 million ha, a year-on-year decrease of 0.13%, and the rice yield per hectare was 3.085 tons, a year-on-year increase of 0.22%. The annual rice output reached 9.335 million tons, a year-on-year increase of 0.12%, and rice exports reached 2.9 million tons. The annual export value of agricultural products was 4.157 million tons.[6] At present, the main problems facing Cambodian agriculture include: inadequate "Land Law", weak infrastructure and backward technology, lack of funds, reduced soil fertility and the lack of crop diversity (Bi et al. 2014). These deficiencies also provide space for cooperation with other countries.

(2) The secondary industry

The prolonged war has severely affected Cambodia's industrialization process. In general, Cambodia has a weak industrial base and few industrial categories—mainly light industry and food processing industry. After its independence in 1953, Cambodia began to build its industry with the assistance from the United States and the Soviet Union. By 1970, its industrial output accounted for about 19% of the total GDP. After that, the war broke out, and it was not until 1993 that peace was resumed and economic reforms were introduced. Since then, private capital has been allowed to enter industry. By 2000, its industrial output value reached 800 million USD, about 23% of the GDP.

After 2000, Cambodia's industry began to grow rapidly. In 2005, the share of industrial output value within GDP reached 26.4%. The fastest growing sector was the garment industry, contributing 15.4% of the GDP. In 2008, Cambodia's GDP exceeded 10 billion USD, and the proportion of industrial output value reached 27%. Within it the garment industry's made up 11.2%, a significant decrease compared to 2005. The reason behind is the shrinking international demand brought about by the financial crisis. In 2009, Cambodia's industrial growth was almost zero. In 2010, Cambodia opened 50 new shoe and garment factories, of which more than 40% were relocated from China. In 2011, Cambodia's garment industry clearly performed better—it, together with the construction industry, was the pillar of Cambodian industry.

In 2015, a total of 160 new industrial enterprises were registered in Cambodia and 859,500 jobs were created. Its industrial output value reached 8.873 billion USD, 29.42% of the GDP, the highest level since the founding of New China. A large number of new enterprises in clothing and footwear were established, and more than 750,000 jobs were created, the export value reached 7.17 billion USD, an increase of 18%. The main export destinations for clothes and footwear were the European Union

[6] Source of data: Economic and Commercial Counsellor's Office of the Embassy of the People's Republic of China in the Republic of Philippines.

and the United States, accounting for 45.6% and 30% respectively.[7] In the next few years, Cambodia will continue to receive manufacturing capacity transferred from China and other countries.

In addition, in order to solve the problem of energy shortage, Cambodia formulated the National Development Plan 2008–2021, which plans to increase the power capacity to 1539 MW, and build 29 hydropower stations (7 of which require more than 1.1 billion USD to build). By 2014, China had participated in six hydropower projects in the form of BOT, with a total investment of 2.821 billion USD.

(3) The tertiary industry

On the whole, Cambodian economic development lags behind, but its service sector, especially tourism, performed better than the other two major industries. After 2000, the output value of the tertiary industry surpassed that of agriculture to take up the largest part of the GDP. By 2015, the GDP of the entire service industry reached 42.33%. The tourism industry was the largest engine of the service industry, and tourism-related hotels and catering industries have also developed rapidly over the years. After Cambodia's market-oriented reforms in 1993, abundant tourism resources and sufficient labor force laid the foundation for the development of tourism. By 2012, tourism revenue was 2.21 billion USD, an increase of more than 10%. In 2015, the number of Cambodian foreign tourists was 4,775,200, an increase of 6.1% year-on-year. Although the growth rate slowed, the number of tourists from China reached 695,000, up by 24%. The entire tourism industry generated 3.01 billion USD in revenue for Cambodia and created 620,000 jobs. In the same year, Cambodia's top five source countries for tourists were Vietnam, China, Laos, South Korea and Thailand.

In terms of transportation, due to poor infrastructure and slow development, Cambodia still needs a lot of investment and improvement. From 2007 to 2013, with the help of ADB, Cambodia carried out a nationwide repair of the railway network. And healthcare and education are the two challenges for the Cambodian government to take on.

2. Population and cities

By 2015, Cambodia's urbanization rate was only 20.72%, while China's was over 50%. In April 1975, when the Cambodian "Khmer Rouge" seized power, it forced city residents to move to the countryside every time it conquered a city. This led to a dramatic drop of the urban population, while the proportion of the rural population rose sharply. After 1982, the urbanization rate in Cambodia has slowly recovered and this trend has continued to this day, as shown in Fig. 5.4. The low level of urbanization is a silhouette of Cambodia's underdeveloped economy, but it also means huge space for investment and development.

Cambodia has only two cities with a population of over 500,000, one of which is the capital Phnom Penh. Here is a brief introduction to the main cities of Cambodia.

---

[7] Source of data: Philippine Statistical Authority.

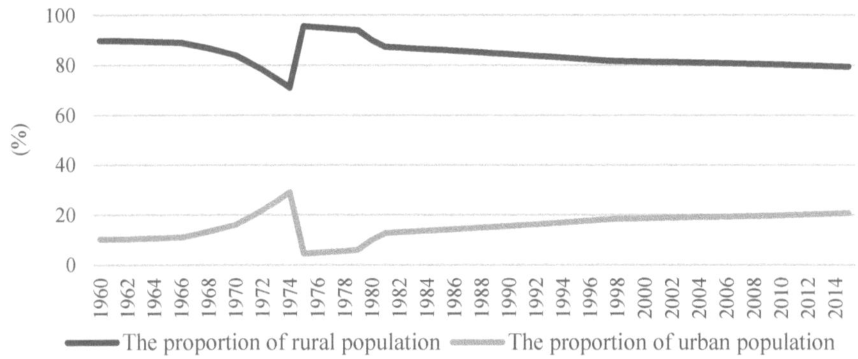

Fig. 5.4 Urbanization rate of Cambodia. *Source of data* World Bank database

Phnom Penh is the capital and largest city of Cambodia. It is also the political, economic, cultural, transportation, trade and religious center of the country. Phnom Penh is located in the delta between the Mekong River and the Tonle Sap River. The city covers an area of about 375 km^2. In 2015, the population was about 2.2 million, over 90% of which were Khmer. More than 90% of the people believe in Buddhism. Phnom Penh is home to major companies and is the center of financial institutions such as banks. Phnom Penh has relatively developed land and air transportation capabilities. It is an important transportation hub in Indochina. As an important inland port, Phnom Penh sees ships flow down the Mekong River to southern Vietnam and enter the South China Sea. As the center of education, Phnom Penh has 38 universities. In addition, it is a beautiful historic city, with famous tourist destinations such as the Royal Palace, Ta Tsai Mountain, Silver Hall, Independence Monument, National Museum and so on.

Sihanoukville is located on the southeast coast of Kampong Som Bay, 232 km from Phnom Penh. It is a special economic zone in Cambodia and one of the four municipalities. The total area of Sihanoukville is approximately 868 km^2 and the port area is 10 km^2. The city was formerly known as Kampong Som City. The Kampong Som port was built in 1960 with French assistance and was renamed in 1993 under the name of then King Sihanouk. The seaport has excellent natural conditions and is the country's most important trade entrance. Sihanoukville is the only seaport city in Cambodia. It is also the three major tourist attractions in Cambodia along with Phnom Penh and Angkor Wat. The northern part of Sihanoukville is an important industrial area of Cambodia. Sihanoukville and China's Nanning are sister cities.

3. Government finances

Since its independence, Cambodia's fiscal performance has been poor. Starting in the early 1970s, half of Cambodia's finances were aid from the United States, the Soviet Union and some Eastern European countries. With the establishment of the coalition government in 1993, the financial situation has improved. As the economic and social structure continues to change, its economic development has reached a new

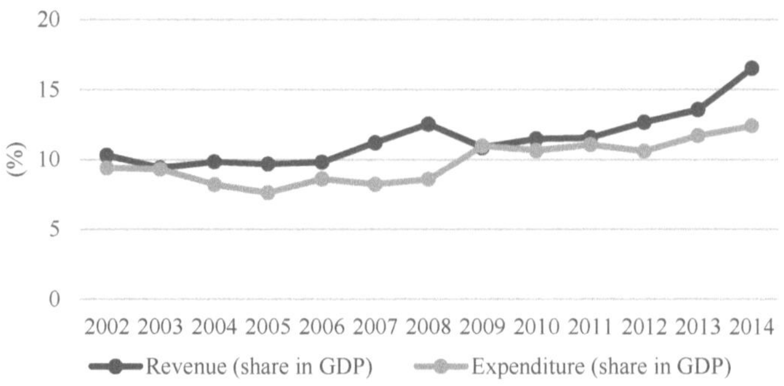

Fig. 5.5 Fiscal situation of Cambodia over the years. *Source of data* World Bank database

stage. Since 2003, the Cambodian government has begun to register fiscal surplus. In 2014, the General Department of Taxation Cambodia received 1.06 billion USD of tax revenue, an increase of 17.7% compared to 2013. At the same time, the General Department of Customs and Excise of Cambodia reported that a total of 1.34 billion USD of import and export duties were levied in 2012, an increase of 1 billion USD compared with 2013.

Cambodia's foreign exchange reserves in 2015 were 4.926 billion USD, which can meet the 4.5-month import demand for products and services. The country's annual budget balance was 462 million USD. The real revenue was approximately 2.916 billion USD, an increase of 12.1% year-on-year, accounting for 15.76% of GDP, and the real expenditure was 3.876 billion USD, an increase of 10.8%; and the fiscal deficit is 3.886999 trillion riel, about 960 million USD, accounting for 5.19% of GDP.[8]

According to Cambodia's National Budget in 2016, the Ministry of Economy and Finance planned to increase the budget to 4.35 billion USD, an increase of 11.1% compared to 2015. It was intended to support the government's development policy to ensure the economic growth rate (7%). Figure 5.5 presents Cambodia's financial situation from 2002 to 2014.

4. National income

As a traditional agricultural country, Cambodia's per capita income has been at a relatively low level for a long time, almost synchronizing with the growth of per capita GDP. By 2015, Cambodia's per capita GNI was 1070 USD, which was classified by the World Bank as a low- and middle-income country. See Fig. 5.6 for details. In terms of wealth distribution, the Gini coefficient reached 0.41 in 2007. After that it began to decline and fell to about 0.31, a relatively proper level, by 2012, as shown in Table 5.2.

As shown in Fig. 5.7, Cambodia's national savings reached its highest point in 2008 to 1.1 billion USD. However, probably affected by the global financial crisis, it

[8] Source of data: Economic and Commercial Counsellor's Office of the Embassy of the People's Republic of China in the Kingdom of Cambodia.

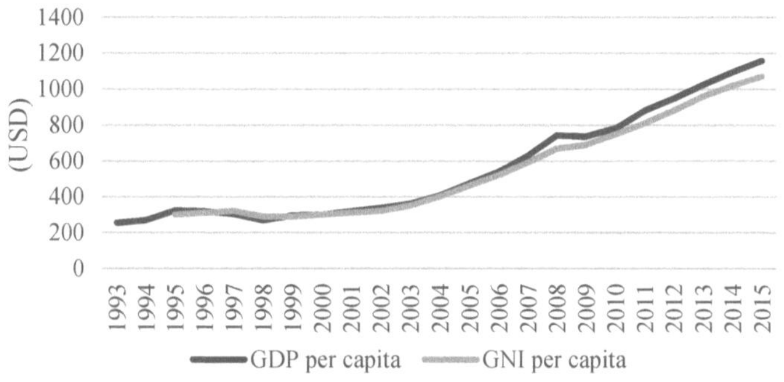

Fig. 5.6 Per capita income in Cambodia. *Source of data* World Bank database

Table 5.2 Wealth gap in Cambodia in recent years (Unit: %)

Year	1994	2004	2007	2008	2009	2010	2011	2012
The Gini coefficient	38.15	35.46	41.14	35.1	34.65	33.44	31.7	30.76

Source of data National Institute of Statistics of Cambodia

fell sharply in 2009 and the downturn continued for several years. It was until 2014 that the figure began to rebound, but still it could not return to its peak.

5. Population structure

Protracted war and poverty have resulted in a sparse population in Cambodia at the beginning of its independence. In 1953, Cambodia's population was less than 4 million. After the independence, as the government adopted pronatalist policies, the population began to grow rapidly. During the "Khmer Rouge" period in 1975,

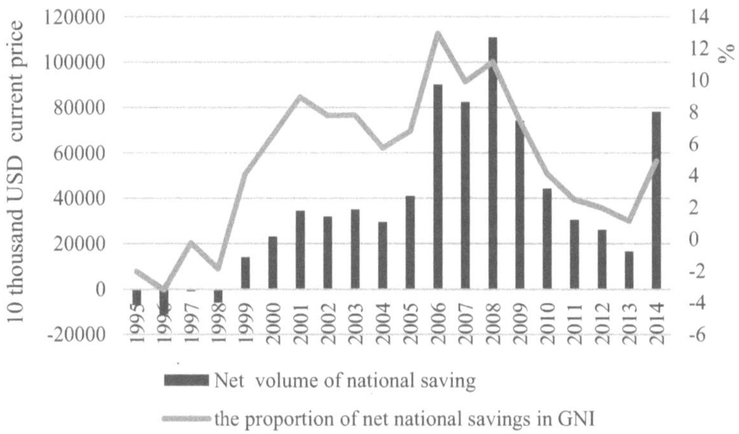

Fig. 5.7 National savings of Cambodia. *Source of data* World Bank database

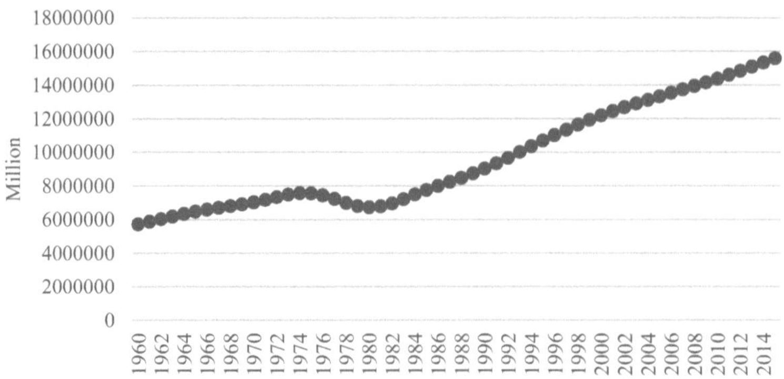

Fig. 5.8 Population growth in Cambodia. *Source of data* World Bank database

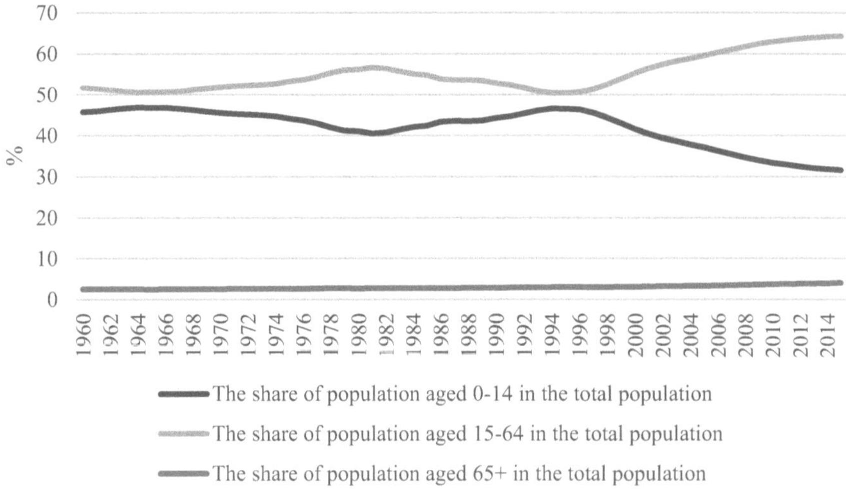

Fig. 5.9 Population distribution in Cambodia. *Source of data* World Bank database

the massive killing caused the unnatural deaths of about 2 million people, and the population dropped sharply. Life expectancy in Cambodia has been low due to backward medical equipment and the spread of diseases. Low life expectancy and high fertility and birth rates mean Cambodia's population is dominated by young adults. As shown in Fig. 5.8, by 2015, Cambodia's population was 15.58 million, 48.8% of which were males and 51.2% females. In terms of age structure, as shown in Fig. 5.9, the population aged 15–64 began to rise after the low point in 1996, and by 2015, the proportion of the population in this age group reached 64.28%.[9]

(II) Foreign trade and investment

[9] Source of data: National Institute of Statistics of Cambodia.

1. Foreign trade

Cambodia has long been an exporter of primary products and an importer of manufactured goods. Prior to the market-oriented reforms, Cambodia's main trading partners were the Soviet Union, Vietnam, Eastern Europe, Japan and India (Bi et al. 2014). In 1992, the United States lifted its trade embargo against Cambodia. After the reform in 1993, the domestic market gradually opened to the outside world, and the degree of trade liberalization gradually increased. Based on abundant natural and human resources, foreign trade, investment and international aid have gradually developed into an important driving force for Cambodian economy. With Cambodia's entry into the ASEAN in 1999 and its formal accession to the WTO in 2007, tariffs have gradually decreased and trade further liberalized. To date, Cambodia is a member of the Greater Mekong Subregional Cooperation (GMS), the ASEAN Free Trade Area (AFTA) and the China–ASEAN Free Trade Area (CAFTA).

From 2001 to 2005, Cambodia's total foreign trade maintained a growth rate of up to 16% per year. In 2007, Cambodia imported 6 billion USD and exported 4.48 billion USD, generating a deficit of 1.52 billion USD. In 2008, when the international financial crisis broke out, Cambodia's trade deficit further expanded to 2.47 billion USD, but the total import and export volume exceeded 10 billion USD. In 2010, the total trade volume reached 11 billion USD, an increase of 26.67%.

In 2015, Cambodia's total foreign trade exceeded 20 billion USD and reached 20.534 billion USD, an increase of 12.6%. Of this total, 8.99 billion USD was exported, 11.544 billion USD was imported, and the trade deficit was 2.543 billion USD. Clothing, footwear, rice, rubber and cassava were Cambodia's main export commodities. The most important of these were clothing and footwear, accounting for nearly 80%. In addition, 544,800 tons of rice were exported, an increase of 48.1% over the previous year. Cambodia's main imports include raw materials for garment processing, building materials, automobiles, oil, machinery, food, beverages, medicines and cosmetics. Its main trading partners included the United States, China, the European Union, Japan, South Korea, Thailand, Vietnam and Malaysia.[10]

In 2015, the total bilateral trade between China and Cambodia reached 4.43 billion USD, an increase of 18%. Cambodia's total exports to China grew the fastest, reaching 670 million USD, an increase of 38.1%.

2. International investment

Prior to the market-oriented reforms of 1989, due to tensions caused by the Cold War, Cambodia received almost no FDI. In 1993, Cambodia passed a new investment bill (amended in 2003) to promote and protect foreign investment. In 2008, the number of FDI projects in Cambodia reached a new high, including the hydropower development projects with China, the coast development projects with Hong Kong, China, and the international financial development projects with South Korea. In 2009, Cambodia obtained close to 1500 FDI projects with a total value of 25 billion USD.

[10] Source of data: Economic and Commercial Counsellor's Office of the Embassy of the People's Republic of China in the Kingdom of Cambodia.

By 2015, the total investment in Cambodia was 4.64 billion USD, an increase of 18%. Within it foreign investment, at 1.473 billion USD, accounted for 30.7%. The amount of investment from China reached 865 million USD, ranking first, larger than the total investment from all other countries. Specifically, China's non-financial direct investment in Cambodia was 390 million USD, the value of newly signed contracted projects was 1.42 billion USD, the cumulative value of contracted projects was 12.11 billion USD, and the turnover was 7.66 billion USD.[11] The total domestic investment was 3.217 billion USD, 69.3% of the total. Within the total investment, 3.13 billion USD flew into infrastructure construction, 920 million USD into industry, 483 million USD into agriculture and 110 million USD into the tourism industry.

At present, the major investors of Cambodia are China, Japan, South Korea, the United States, the European Union, Singapore and Hong Kong, China. In general, Cambodia's advantages in attracting foreign investment are: a good political environment and gradual improvement of the investment system; huge potential and rapid development of various industries; abundant human and natural resources; and a high degree of market development. In addition, the World Bank, IMF and other international agencies have also provided continuous assistance to Cambodia.

5.2 Indonesia

I. Geographical and historical backgrounds

Indonesia, located in Southeast Asia, is an ASEAN member country and was one of the "four tigers" in Asia. Indonesia's strategic position is very important as it holds the Straits of Malacca. Geographically, Indonesia is composed of about 17,508 islands, known as the "Country of Thousand Islands". The main islands are Java Island (having about 60% of the population), Sumatra, Kalimantan (shared with Brunei and Malaysia), New Guinea Island (shared with Papua New Guinea), etc. The Sunda Strait, Malacca Strait, Lombok Strait, etc. are important passages connecting the Pacific Ocean and the Indian Ocean. The land area of Indonesia is 1,904,443 km^2, the ocean area (excluding the exclusive economic zone) is 3,166,163 km^2, and the coastline is 54,716 km long. In terms of natural conditions, Indonesia is located in the tropics and is warm and humid throughout the year; it is located in the earthquake zone of the Pacific Rim, and earthquakes are frequent.

As of 2015, Indonesia had a population of 255.5 million, ranking fourth in the world, next to China, India and the United States. It has more than one hundred ethnic groups, including the Javanese, the Sunda, the Madura and the Malay. The official language is Indonesian. About 87% of Indonesia's population believes in Islam, making it the most populated Muslim country in the world. In terms of politics and judicature, Indonesia is a single republic with separate administrative, legislative and judicial powers and a multiparty system and a presidential system. The president is

[11] Source of data: Economic and Commercial Counsellor's Office of the Embassy of the People's Republic of China in the Kingdom of Cambodia.

directly elected by the people. The president sets up a cabinet every five years, and the cabinet is accountable to the president.

Indonesia is rich in mineral resources such as petroleum, natural gas, coal, tin, bauxite, nickel, copper, gold and silver. Mining occupies an important position in the Indonesian economy, with output value accounting for about 10% of GDP. Indonesia's oil reserves are 9.7 billion barrels (1.31 billion tons). In 2013, the daily output of crude oil was 857,000 barrels. Natural gas reserves were 4.8 trillion–5.1 trillion m^3. Proved reserves of coal were 19.3 billion tons, and potential reserves could reach more than 90 billion tons. Granted with rich natural resources, the country is known as the "Tropical Treasure Island". Its palm oil and natural rubber outputs rank first and second in the world.

II. **Economic development**

(I) Domestic economy

As one of the ASEAN's largest economies and one of the "Four Tigers" in Asia, Indonesia witnessed economic boom in the 1990s, with an average annual GDP growth of 6%, making it a middle-income country. However, in 1997, it was hit hard by the Asian financial crisis, the economy was in a severe recession, and the currency depreciated sharply. The slow recovery began at the end of 1999. In 2004, President Susilo Yudhoyono took power and actively took measures to attract foreign investment, develop infrastructure, rectify the financial system and support the development of small- and medium-sized enterprises. As a result, the economy maintained a growth rate of higher than 5%. In the global financial crisis of 2008, the Indonesian government responded properly and the economy maintained rapid growth. However, since 2014, due to the global economic downturn and FED's adjustment of monetary policy, the Indonesian rupiah had rapidly depreciated. In the first quarter of 2015, Indonesia's growth rate was below 5% for the first time, and pressures on economic growth increased. In 2015, Indonesia's GDP was 861.934 billion USD, with an inflation rate of 6.36%, and a per capita GDP of 3346.49 USD. It is a lower-middle-income country. For more information on GDP, see Figs. 5.10, 5.11 and 5.12.

1. Industrial structure

As shown in Fig. 5.13, Indonesia's structure of three industries has been relatively stable over the past 20 years. Service industry and industry are the two most important industrial sectors in Indonesia. The industry was slightly heavier than the service industry till 2014. In 2015, the service sector overtook industry as the largest contributor to Indonesian GDP. Compared to other Southeast Asian countries, Indonesia's agricultural share is relatively high, but it has been slowly decreasing over the past 20 years.

(1) The primary industry

Indonesia's agriculture is relatively developed, accounting for a higher proportion than other Southeast Asian countries. Indonesia is a large producer of cash crops—its palm oil, rubber, coffee and cocoa outputs are among the highest in the world.

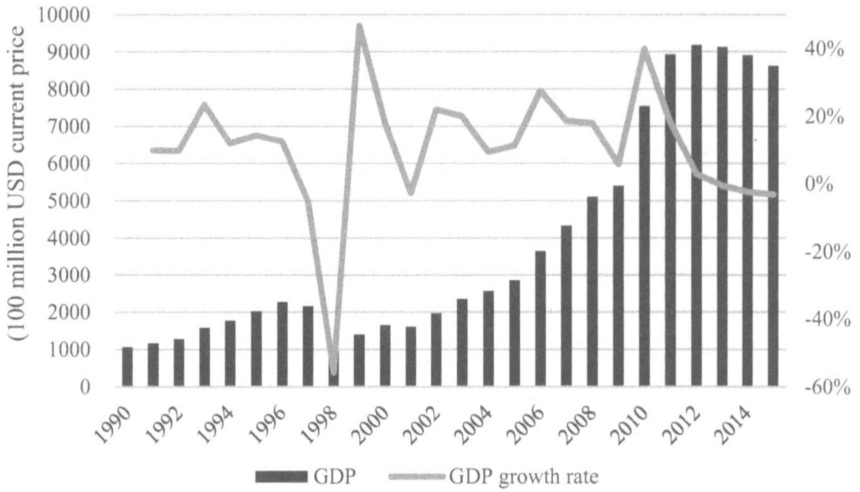

Fig. 5.10 GDP growth of Indonesia. *Source of data* World Bank database

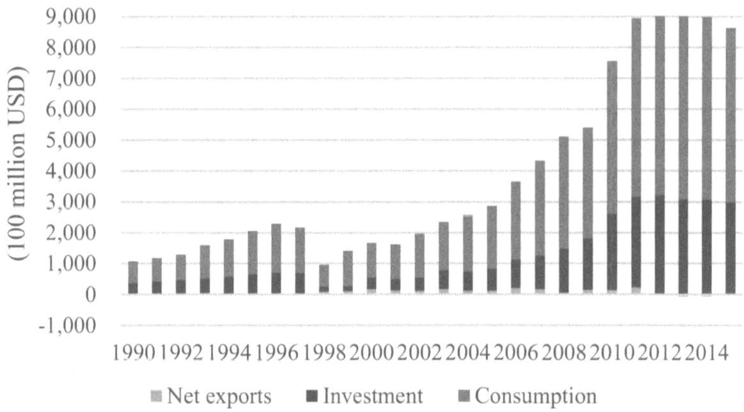

Fig. 5.11 Composition of Indonesian GDP. *Source of data* World Bank database

Fishery resources are abundant, and the government estimates that the potential catch is more than 8 million tons per year. The forest coverage rate exceeds 60%, and the timber export of has been banned since 2002.

(2) The secondary industry

Industry is one of the pillar industries in Indonesia. The main sectors are mining, textiles, light industry, etc. The output of tin, coal, nickel, gold, silver and other minerals ranks among the highest in the world. Since 2012, the growth rate of industrial added value has exceeded the growth rate of GDP, as shown in Fig. 5.14.

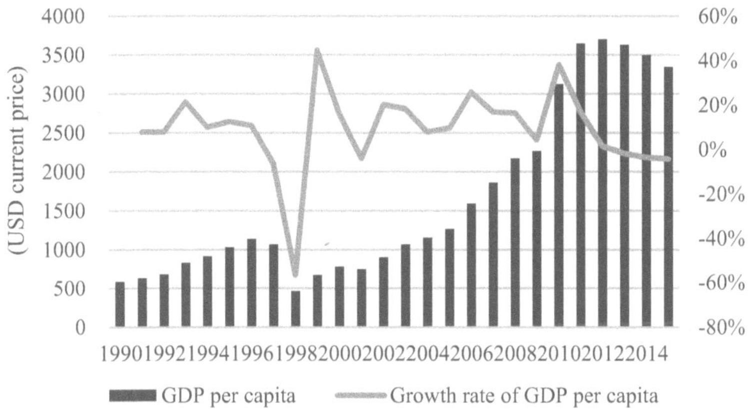

Fig. 5.12 Per capita GDP in Indonesia. *Source of data* World Bank database

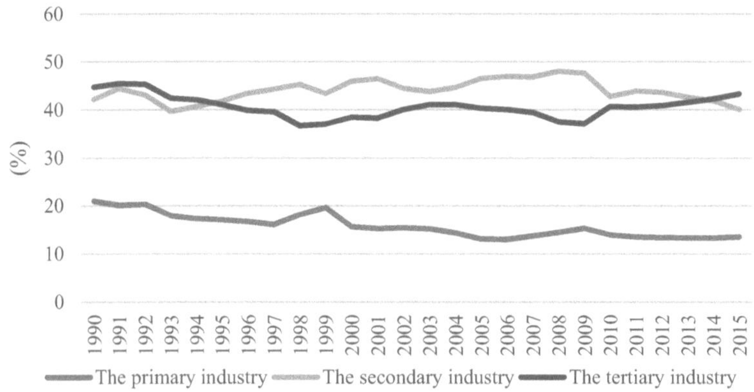

Fig. 5.13 Indonesian structure of three industries. *Source of data* World Bank database

Indonesia's more developed industrial sub-sectors include food, household goods, and textiles and clothing, and the relatively weak industrial sub-sectors include machinery and equipment, molds, motors, electronics, and metals and plastics processing. Indonesia's light industry is relatively developed. Most of the daily necessities are produced locally in Indonesia. The food, household goods, and textile and garment industries have always been the pillars of Indonesia's manufacturing industry, important to solving employment problems and earning foreign exchange. The Indonesian government has continued to increase support for these industries by streamlining investment procedures and offering tax incentives and financial subsidies.

Indonesia has a weak industrial foundation. The mold, motor, electronics, metal and plastic processing industries are relatively backward. The production equipment is outdated. Most of the raw materials, components and molds are imported.

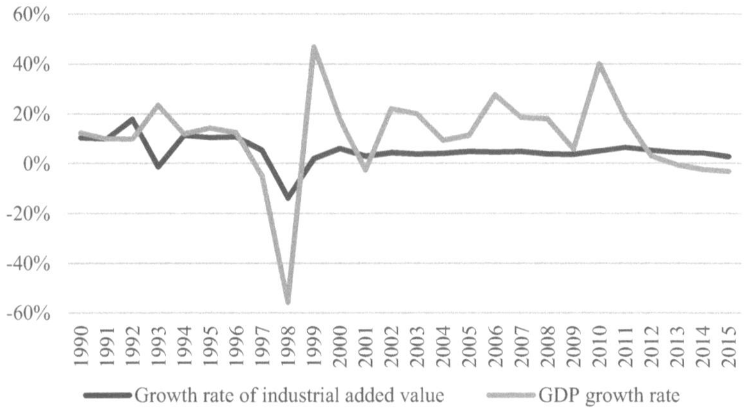

Fig. 5.14 Growth rate of the secondary industry versus the growth rate of GDP. *Source of data* World Bank database

Indonesia's main sources of manufactured goods are Japan, Taiwan of China, South Korea, Chinese Mainland and Europe. Take textile and garment machinery as an example. Garment processing is the largest export industry in Indonesia. However, Indonesia's textile and garment machinery are mainly imported from Japan, Chinese Mainland, Germany, Taiwan of China, Korea, India, Switzerland and Italy. Japanese machinery manufacturers provide the most favorable payment terms, while machinery of Chinese Mainland is cheaper; as a result, China and Japan together have a market share of more than 40%; European machinery, especially the Italian one, is most respected by Indonesia for its quality, but it is less competitive due to high price and poor channel. In recent years, the Chinese textile machinery industry is working hard to expand its presence in the Indonesian market. Every April, Jakarta holds an international textile and clothing machinery exhibition. The scale and influence of the exhibition is growing. It is a good platform for companies from all countries to showcase their products and obtain customer resources. Chinese enterprises arc also taking advantage of this platform to expand their market share.

In the future, Indonesia's industry will develop in the direction of improving technology, innovation and human resources. The Indonesian government will continue to promote industrial optimization strategies. For agriculture and forestry (oil palm, cocoa, rubber, rattan, etc.), mineral resource (iron, aluminum, nickel, copper, etc.) and oil and gas industry, more efforts will be made to develop the downstream industries to increase domestic added value. At the same time, the focus will be shifted to developing human resources and technology based industries through research and development capacity building, in-depth development of resources, technological innovation, implementation of Indonesian national standards, product certification and training of human resources. In addition, the Indonesian government will vigorously develop supporting infrastructure for industrial construction, ensuring the supply of raw materials such as electricity, water and natural gas, and the construction of roads, ports and railways. Besides, it will promote industrial development by utilizing platforms and carriers such as industrial parks. In addition, the Indonesian government will introduce a series of supporting measures such as tax reductions and simplification of investment approval procedures.

(3) The tertiary industry

In the past 15 years, Indonesia's tertiary industry has developed rapidly, becoming the largest job creator and contributor to GDP in three industries. Such development has boosted Indonesia's overall economic growth and helped maintain fast economic growth despite economic crisis. How to develop the modern service industry and improve its internal structure are the main problems facing Indonesia's development of the tertiary industry.

Tourism is the second largest foreign exchange earner in Indonesia's non-oil-and-gas industry after electronics exports. The government has long attached importance to the development of tourism, not only working to strengthen supporting infrastructure, but also vigorously promoting and cooperating with neighboring countries. Indonesia's main attractions are Bali, Jakarta Miniature Park, Borobudur Stupa of Yogyakarta, South Temple of Prabang, Sultan Palace, Lake Toba of North Sumatra, etc.

Roads and waterways are important means of transportation in Indonesia—roads carry nearly 90% of domestic passenger traffic and 50% of freight. Railway facilities are relatively backward—only Java and Sumatra have railways. Air transportation has developed rapidly in recent years—many large airports have been built, including Jakarta International Airport and Bandung International Airport. According to the government's 2015–2019 Medium-Term Development Plan, Indonesia would strengthen the construction of large-scale infrastructure projects in 12 areas, including the construction of 3650 km of highways, 15 airports, 24 large ports, 3258 km of railway, 60 docks, etc.

Indonesia's urbanization process is advancing steadily. In 2015, the urbanization rate exceeded 50%. Large cities include Jakarta, Surabaya and Bandung. For more information, see Fig. 5.15 and Table 5.3.

In terms of education, Indonesia has introduced nine-year compulsory education. Famous universities include Indonesian University, Gadjha Mada University, University of Erlangen and Bandung Institute of Technology. The quality of labor force needs to be further improved. The proportion of labor force with higher education is only 8.5%.

(II) Foreign trade and investment

1. Foreign trade

Foreign trade plays an important role in Indonesia's national economy. The government has adopted a series of measures to encourage and promote the export of non-oil-and-gas products, simplify export procedures and reduce tariffs. As shown in Fig. 5.16, since 1990, Indonesia's foreign trade performed generally well, but since 2012, due to the global trade downturn, both imports and exports had declined. In 2014, exports were 176.29 billion USD, a year-on-year decrease of 3.4%, and

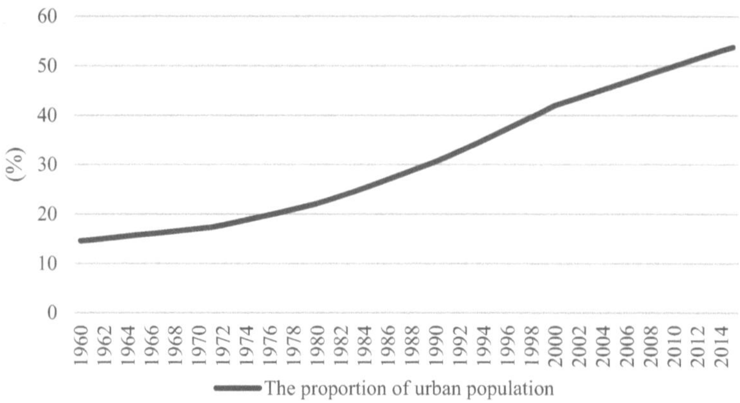

Fig. 5.15 Proportion of urban population. *Source of data* World Bank database

Table 5.3 Top 10 cities in Indonesia

City	City profile
Jakarta	The capital, ranking 17th among the top 200 cities in the world. Finance, industry and business are its pillar sectors. Its population density is above 14,400 people/km^2
Surabaya	The most important port of export and import in Indonesia
Bandung	Known as Paris in Java, the famous tourist city has Tangkuban Perahu (volcano) and Bandung Hot Spring and is equipped with Bandung International Airport
Medan	The largest city in Sumatra
Bekasi	A city near Jakarta with developed manufacturing industry
Semarang	The fifth largest city and an important port
Tangerang	With more than 1000 factories, it is one of the manufacturing centers in Java
Depok	A satellite city of Jarkarta where the University of Indonesia stands
Palembang	An important river port with convenient sea transportation; a trade hub
South Tangerang	A satellite city of Jarkarta

Source of data Based on public data

imports were 178.18 billion USD, a year-on-year decrease of 4.5%, positioning the trade deficit at 1.89 billion USD.

Indonesia's main export products are oil, natural gas, textiles and garments, wood, rattan products, handicrafts, shoes, copper, coal, pulp and paper products, electrical appliances, palm oil, rubber, etc.; the main imported products are mechanical transport equipment, chemical products, automobiles and spare parts, power generation equipment, steel, plastics and plastic products, cotton, etc. The main trading partners

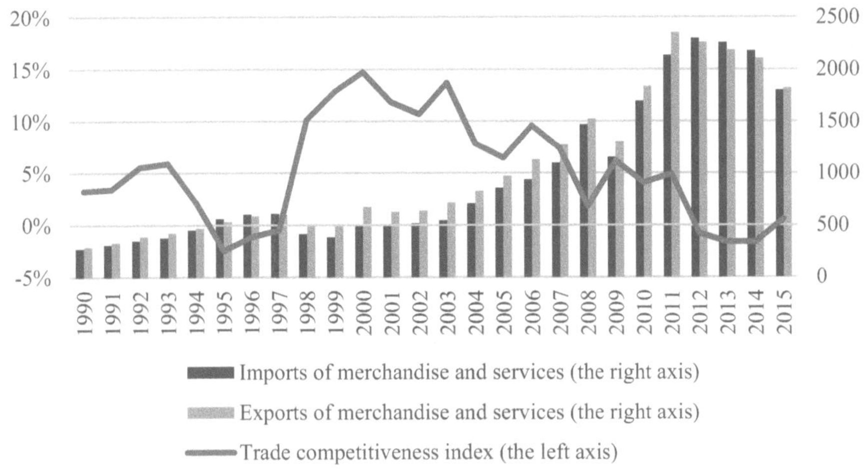

Fig. 5.16 Foreign trade development in Indonesia. *Source of data* Statistics Indonesia

are China, ASEAN countries, the United States, European countries and Japan, as shown in Figs. 5.17 and 5.18.

From the perspective of the trade competitiveness of various industries, the figure for agricultural products has always been above 0.3, indicating strong competitiveness. The figure for fuel and mineral products has always been above 0, but the trend is downward. The figure for manufactured goods has always been below 0 (covering products such as steel, chemicals, pharmaceuticals, machinery and transportation equipment), suggesting the lack of competitiveness. However, office and

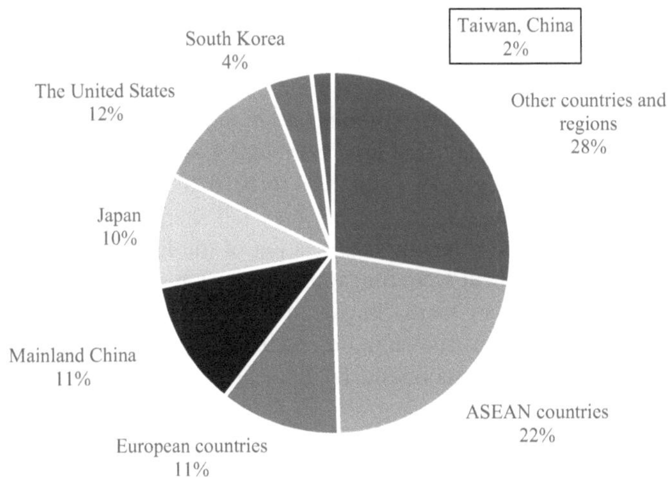

Fig. 5.17 Major markets of Indonesian exports. *Source of data* Statistics Indonesia

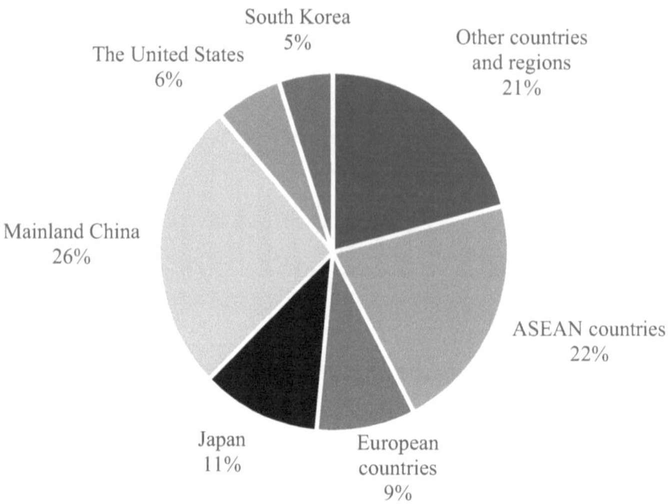

Fig. 5.18 Major sources of Indonesian imports. *Source of data* Statistics Indonesia

telecommunications equipment, electronic data processing and office equipment, telecommunications equipment and electronic components had a certain international competitiveness before 2008. Garment is the only finished product that maintains a positive trade competitiveness (Zhang 2017).

2. International trade

Foreign capital plays an important role in promoting Indonesia's economic development. The Indonesian government attaches importance to improving the investment environment and attracting foreign investment. The Indonesian Investment Law of 2007 stipulated that foreign investors are free to invest in any sector except those restricted and prohibited by laws and regulations. In the following years, investment in film services, information and communication, mining and coal industries, and infrastructure projects were less and less restricted. A series of tax incentives were introduced. As shown in Fig. 5.19, from 2004 to 2016, the scale of Indonesia's FDI generally increased, but in 2009 and 2015, they fell sharply due to the impact of the financial crisis and the dramatic depreciation of the Rupiah. Indonesia's main sources of foreign investment were Singapore, Japan, China, the United States and the United Kingdom. Among them, Singapore's investment was the largest and the amount is growing rapidly, as shown in Fig. 5.20. Chinese companies are gradually increasing their investment in Indonesia, but the scale is still small and there is plenty of room for growth.

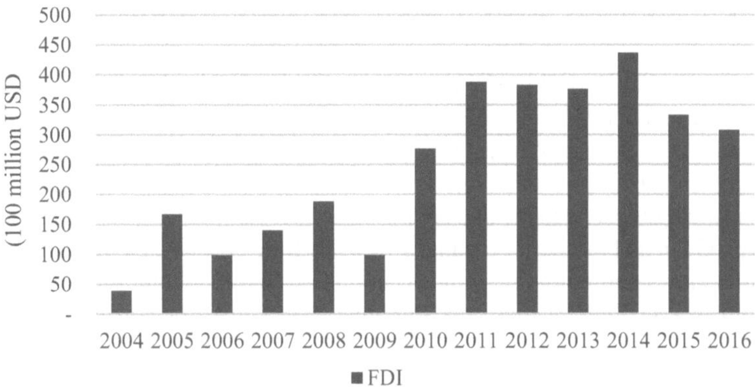

Fig. 5.19 FDI in Indonesia. *Source of data* Bank Indonesia

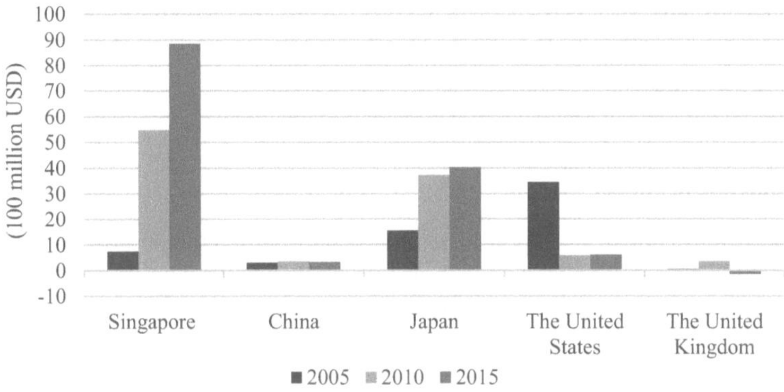

Fig. 5.20 Changes of investment volumes of major investors in Indonesia. *Source of data* Bank Indonesia

5.3 Laos

I. Geographical and historical backgrounds

Laos is located in the northern part of the Indo-China Peninsula and is the only landlocked country in the region. It borders China's Yunnan Province, Vietnam, Cambodia, Thailand and Myanmar, with a land area of 236,800 km^2. Its terrain is mainly mountains and plateaus.

Laos is rich in natural resources. The unique Mesozoic fold terrain of Laos makes it rich in metal and non-metallic ores. Among them, non-ferrous metal ore and jade ore are not only rich in species but also huge in storage. Laos also has abundant water resources. Due to its abundant water reserves, stable riverbed, concentrated water energy and excellent coastal vegetation, the development conditions are superior.

Due to the warm climate, abundant rainfall and extensive vegetation coverage, it has extremely rich animal and plant resources and is known as a "natural zoo".

Laos is connected to China by mountains and rivers, and since ancient times the two countries have maintained close and harmonious relations. As early as the AD third century, the State of Wu sent envoys to Funan, a great power on the Indo-China Peninsula. In AD 227, an ambassador from Funan visited China, marking the official start of exchanges between the two countries. By the beginning of the eighth century, the Viang Chan had frequent exchanges with the Tang Dynasty, paying tribute to the latter four times and enjoying grand receptions in return. From 1403 to 1613, the Kingdom of Lan Xang at that time sent envoys to China for 34 times, and China sent envoys in return for 9 times. The frequency of exchanges was unprecedented. From 1729 to 1893, the Kingdom of Luang Prabang at that time sent ambassadors to the Qing Dynasty 20 times and Qing sent ambassadors to Luang Prabang once (Hao et al. 2012). After 1893, Laos became a French colony, and its patriarchal relationship with the Qing Dynasty ended. After the Second World War, relations between the two countries have seen ups and downs. After 1989, the bilateral relations began to fully recover and improve. As both are socialist countries, Laos and China have close relations and support each other.

II. **Economic development**

(I) Domestic economy

Laos has been an underdeveloped agricultural country for a long time. Due to its long history of being plundered and exploited by feudalism and colonialism, its economic development is slow and its people's living standards are low. Since 1893, Laos' economy has roughly gone through several major stages (Li and Li 2012):

① From1893 to 1975, colonial economy: the proportion of agricultural output value stayed above 90%;
② From 1976 to 1985, the socialist planned economy: the proportion of agricultural output value stayed above 80%;
③ From 1986 to 1995, the socialist market economy: the proportion of agricultural output value gradually decreased;
④ From 1996 to present, the stage of deepening reform and opening up.

As a typical agricultural country, Laos' rural population accounts for about 61.4% of the total (end of 2015), and agricultural output value makes up a relatively large part of GDP (27.2%). The secondary industry suffers from weak foundation, unbalanced development, a backward heavy industry and an incomplete system. The Lao People's Revolutionary Party held its fourth congress in 1986, marking that Laos has entered the stage of "reform and opening up". Since then, Laos' economy has developed rapidly and has maintained a steady growth rate so far. From 1991 to the Asian financial crisis, Laos' GDP grew at an average annual rate of 7%. In 1997, the Laos economy was severely impacted. Subsequently, the Lao government strengthened macroeconomic regulation, rectified financial markets and promoted agricultural development, which basically restored economic and social stability. In the twenty-first century, Laos' GDP grew at an average annual rate of 6.8% in the first five years; from 2006 to 2010, Laos' GDP grew at an average annual rate of 7.9%.[12]

In 2015, the total GDP of Laos reached 12.327 billion USD, while per capita GDP hit 1812.33 USD. For more information, see Fig. 5.21. Although the economy has developed rapidly for more than a decade, Laos' economic development is still at a relatively low level because of a weak foundation and a late start of reform and opening up. 2015 is the last year of Laos' "Seventh Five-Year Plan" (2011–2015), and its overall economic performance was mixed. On the positive side, the economic growth rate was still as high as 7.5%, and the proportion of poor families were reduced to 6.59%. On the negative side, the financial situation was still worrying—the taxation target was not accomplished, and the budget deficit, external debt and trade deficit all expanded, bringing about more challenges and difficulties (Chen 2016).

1. Industrial structure

(1) The primary industry

Laos is a typical agricultural country. In 2010, people working in agricultural accounted for 71.3% of the total employment. In 2013, the cultivated land area accounted for 6.5% of the total, and the land was fertile.[13] Laos has a tropical monsoon climate, long sunshine hours and heavy rainfall. It can be said that Laos has unique geographical conditions for developing agriculture. Its forest coverage rate is 52%. Laos' agriculture as a whole is still a self-sufficient traditional one with a low degree of mechanization. Its main crops include food crops, cash crops, fruit crops and medicinal crops, such as corn, rice, coffee, rubber and various precious medicinal herbs. In recent years, despite declines due to the development of the secondary and tertiary industries, the proportion of agriculture in GDP has remained high, as shown in Fig. 5.22.

(2) The secondary industry

Laos is one of the least developed countries. The industrial output value accounts for a small part of GDP and the foundation is weak. The proportion within GDP has remained at 30–35% in the past five years despite high growth rate (above 10%), as shown in Fig. 5.23. Its industry mainly focuses on the processing of farming, forestry and animal husbandry products and garment manufacturing. Although Laos' industry has developed rapidly in recent years, the production capacity of most industrial products is weak and import dependence is strong, resulting in negative current account balances in the past five years. In the future, Laos' industrial development will focus on energy and mineral development which is expected to become its economic pillar.

[12] Country Profile—Laos, website of Ministry of Foreign Affairs, China.

[13] Source of data: World Bank database.

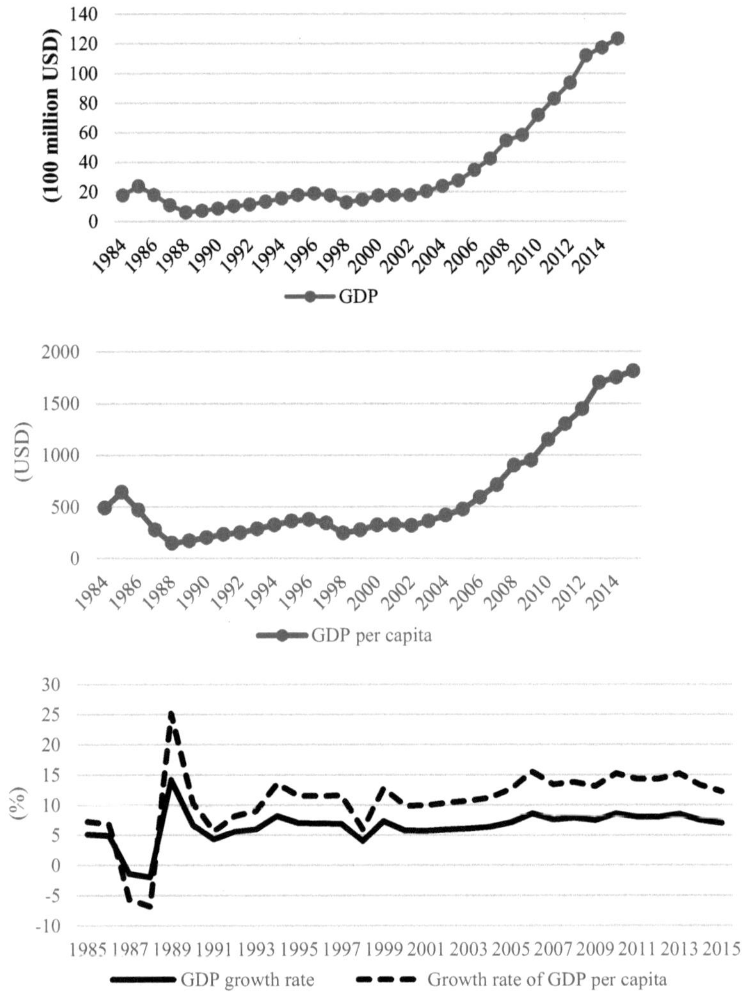

Fig. 5.21 Economic development of Laos. *Source of data* World Bank database

(3) The tertiary industry

The service industry in Laos started late and its overall level of development was insufficient, accounting for only 36% of the GDP at best, as shown in Fig. 5.24. However, Laos has a large number of natural landscapes and historical relics such as the Mekong River, Pakse, Plain of Jars, Luang Prabang and the ancient capital of Champasak Temple. In addition, some regional organizations such as ASEAN attach great importance to the development of tourism in the region. These have created good environment for the development of the tourism industry in Laos. It is expected that the tourism industry will boost the overall development of the tertiary industry (Hao et al. 2012).

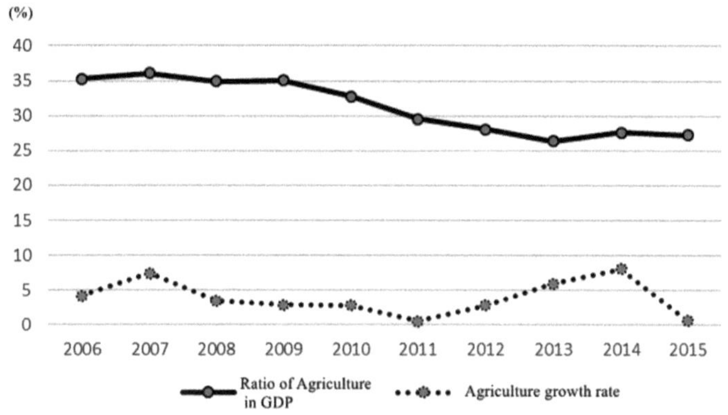

Fig. 5.22 Growth rate of agriculture and the proportion of agricultural added value in GDP. *Source of data* World Bank database

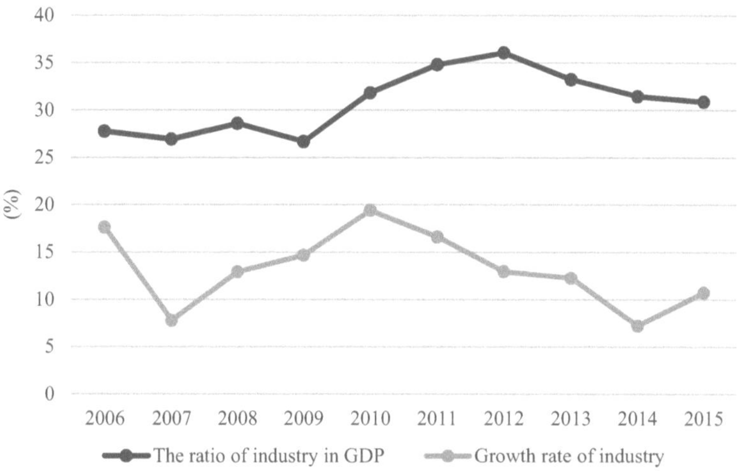

Fig. 5.23 Growth rate of industry and the proportion of industrial added value in GDP. *Source of data* World Bank database

In general, since its implementation of socialist market economy in 1986, Laos has maintained rapid economic growth. The proportion of agriculture has gradually decreased, while the industrial and service industries have gained weight (Fig. 5.25). The overall speed of development ranks among the best in Southeast Asia. 2015 is the last year of the "Seventh Five-Year Plan" of Laos. As Fig. 5.25 shows, the effect of the five-year plan to improve the industrial structure is very significant.

2. Population and cities

Laos is a traditional agricultural country. As can be seen from Fig. 5.26, the highest urbanization rate in Laos was lower than 44%. As far as ASEAN is concerned, Laos

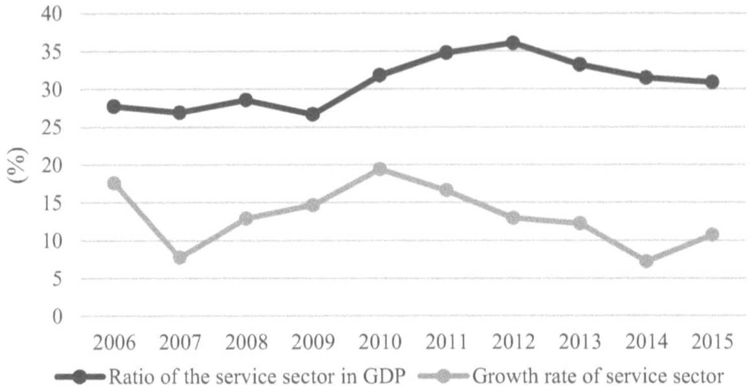

Fig. 5.24 Growth rate of the service sector and the proportion of the service sector added value in GDP. *Source of data* World Bank database

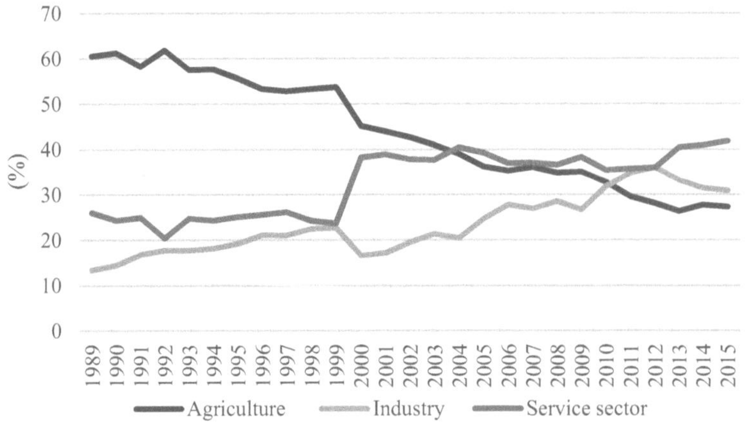

Fig. 5.25 Changes of Laotian structure in three industries. *Source of data* World Bank database

remains one of the countries with the lowest levels of urbanization. In contrast, in the same period, China's urbanization rate (also an agricultural power) reached 57.1%, and that of the United States reached 82.4%. However, thanks to Laos' "innovation and opening up" policy, a feasible five-year plan, and assistance from other countries, its urbanization has gradually accelerated. Especially in recent years, with rapid economic growth, urbanization is also expanding fast. By 2015, Laos' urbanization rate was close to 40%, and there is still much room for improvement.

The ratio of Laos' investment to consumer spending has remained basically 1:2 in the past 10 years. In 2013, investment accounted for 29% of GDP and consumer spending accounted for 65%. In 2014, investment was 30% of GDP and consumption was 65%; in 2015, investment took up 32%, and consumption at 62%, as shown in Fig. 5.27. Compared with China's overcapacity problem caused by investment-driven

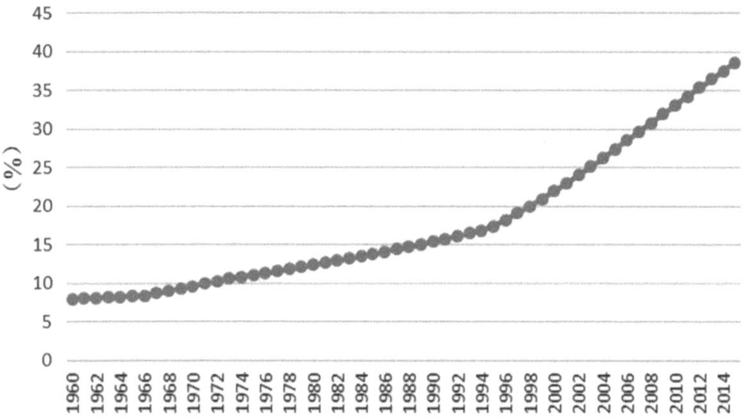

Fig. 5.26 Urbanization Development in Cambodia. *Source of data* World Bank database

GDP growth, Laos' economic structure seems more reasonable. The investment in Laos is mainly foreign investment. There are three types of investment according to the nature of the business license issued. The first is general business, and the license is issued by the Ministry of Industry and Commerce. The second is franchise, and the license is issued by the Ministry of Planning and Investment. The third is special economic zones and special economic zone development activities, and the license is issued by the special economic zone secretariat of the parliament. After the "reform and opening up" in 1980, economic aid has gradually transformed into investment in Laos. In recent years, the main fields of foreign investment are industry, service industry, transportation, hydropower station, telecommunications, forestry and animal husbandry, handicraft industry and tourism. The main investors are China, Japan, Australia and Vietnam.

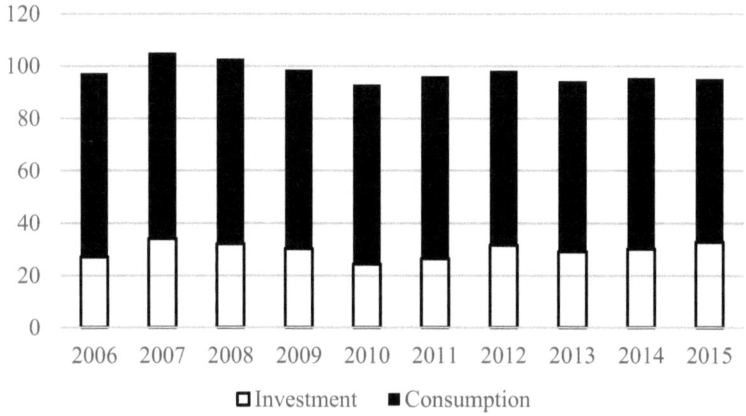

Fig. 5.27 Investment and consumer spending in Laos. *Source of data* World Bank database

In 2012, Laos suspended the approval of new franchise projects in the fields of mining, rubber and eucalyptus plantation, and foreign investment once declined. Later, it made some positive adjustments. In 2014, it obtained a total of 2073 investment projects, with a total value of 9.723 billion USD, an increase of 216.7%, of which 5169 were government-funded projects, totaling 780 million USD.[14]

In terms of government finance, with the rapid economic development after 2006, the revenue and expenditure of the Lao government have been steadily increasing, and the revenue has been slightly higher than expenditure. By 2013, as Laos began to increase investment in infrastructure, industry and other fields; consequently, expenditures increased significantly compared to 2012, but the increase in 2014 and 2015 were slight. In addition, fiscal liabilities rose to the later level of 3 billion USD. The total budget deficit of Laos in 2015 was 5184 billion kip, 5.07% of the GDP. The National Audit Office found that in 2014, a total of 118 national investment projects were implemented without the approval of the Congress, 58 approved projects and 43 unapproved projects did not go through the formal bidding process, 36 government investment projects were implemented in steps inconsistent with the initial plan and 382 national investment projects (involving more than 15.548 trillion kip) were approved without a feasibility assessment (Chen 2016). In addition, the non-performing ratio of bank loans in Laos increased from about 2.16% in 2014 to 3.11% in 2015, which is worrying.

3. National income

Since 2000, Laos' national income has grown rapidly. By 2012, Laos' per capita income reached about 1000 USD. In 2011, the per capita national income rose to 1130 USD, after which it grew at a rate of more than 10% for four consecutive years; in 2015, the growth rate slowed down, and per capita national income was 1730 USD. In 2015, Laos' gross national income was 11.090 billion USD, and total national savings were 1043 million USD, which remained at a relatively small scale. For more information, see Fig. 5.28.[15] Since 2002, as the economy started to grow rapidly, the wealth gap has been widening: in 2012, the Gini coefficient was an acceptable 0.38, lower than the warning level of 0.4 (some consider 0.5 as the alert line). See Fig. 5.29.

(II) Foreign trade and investment

International trade, especially merchandise exports, has promoted Laos' economic development. From 1995 to 2010, the average annual growth rate of its exports exceeded 30%. In 2014, Laos' total foreign trade was worth 8.135 billion USD, an increase of 5%; of which, imports were 4.553 billion USD, an increase of 11.4% year-on-year; exports were 3.582 billion USD, a decrease of 1.75%; and the trade deficit reached 971 million USD, an increase of 6%. The reason for the deficit was that

[14] Economic and Commercial Counsellor's Office of the Embassy of the People's Republic of China in the Laos People's Democratic Republic: Economic development in Laos 2014. http://la.mofcom.gov.cn/article/zt-dy/201506/20150601009466.shtml.

[15] Source of data: National Statistics Center, Laos.

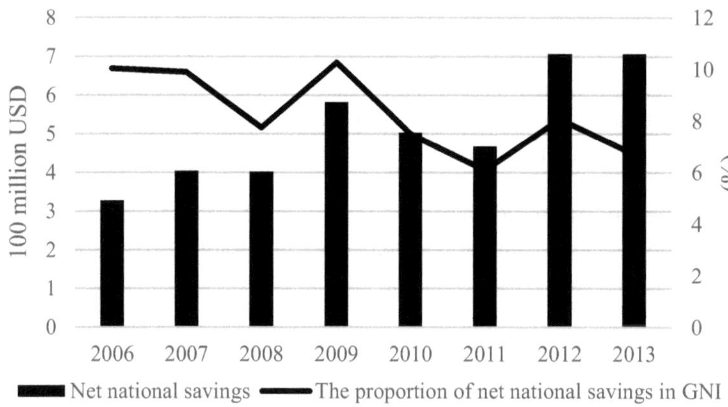

Fig. 5.28 National savings of Laos. *Source of data* World Bank database

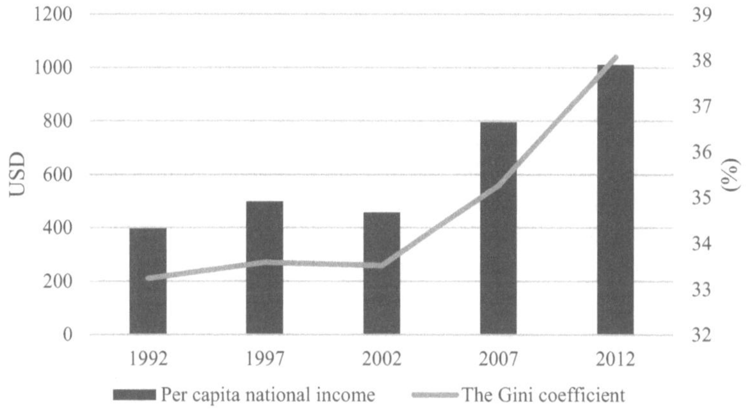

Fig. 5.29 National income and the wealth gap in Laos. *Source of data* World Bank database

exports were sluggish and downward. Laos mainly imports infrastructure construction materials and consumer goods, and mainly exports natural resources such as gold and copper. Such goods are greatly affected by price fluctuations in the international market.[16]

Laos' foreign trade is mainly oriented to neighboring countries. The top five trading partners include Thailand, China, Vietnam, Japan and Switzerland. Among them, Thailand ranks first because of its geographical advantage. Laos' foreign trade also includes export of labor services (mainly low-level labor services). The importing countries are mainly developed countries or regions around it, such as Thailand and Japan. At the same time, Laos actively introduces high-level talents,

[16] Source of data: Economic and Commercial Counsellor's Office of the Embassy of the People's Republic of China in the Laos People's Democratic Republic.

including talents of the emerging industries and special skills personnel, high-tech personnel and senior management personnel.

Due to its economic backwardness, Laos has been receiving aids from other countries for a long time. Its main sources of aids include China, Japan, the United States and once the Soviet Union. In 2014, Laos obtained a total of 784 official development aid projects with a total value of 795 million USD (of which more than half/644 are grant assistance projects, with a value of 471 million USD), 58 loan projects (totaling 242 million USD) and 82 human resources projects (totaling 81.91 million USD). Official development aids were 10.3% of the total aids it received.[17] Other main donors include Germany, Sweden, France and South Korea.

5.4 Malaysia

I. **Geographical and historical backgrounds**

The Federation of Malaysia consists of "West Malaysia" and "East Malaysia". The capital Kuala Lumpur is located in the central part of West Malaysia. Malaysia is a developing country, and its economic development level is among the highest in ASEAN countries. It was hailed as the "fifth dragon" in Asia before the financial crisis in 1997. Malaysia is located at the junction of the Asian continent and the Southeast Asian islands, and the confluence of Asia, Oceania and the Pacific Ocean and the Indian Ocean. It, at the center of Southeast Asia, covers an area of 332,400 km^2. West Malaysia is bordered by Thailand to the north, Johor Strait to the south (Singapore) and Malacca Strait to the west and southwest.

II. **Economic development**

(I) Domestic economy

The past 30 years have been an important period for Malaysia's economic development. In February 1991, Prime Minister Mahathir announced the Vision 2020, the main goal of which is to transform Malaysia into a fully developed country by 2020. The specific indicators are that by continuously increasing the proportion of the manufacturing industry in the GDP, the GDP doubles every 10 years, the average annual economic growth rate reaches 7%, and the per capita national income increases 4 times to 12,000 USD. In June 1991, the government promulgated the "1991–2000 Outline for Economic Development", also known as the "Second Vision Plan Outline", which includes two five-year plans (the "Sixth Five-Year" and "Seventh Five-Year Plan"). The outline stipulates that the "new economic policy" should be replaced by the "new development policy". The main goal is to double the national economy within the next 10 years and to push the average annual growth rate of GDP to 7%. "During the sixth five-year plan period, Malaysia's economy grew rapidly, with an average annual GDP growth rate of 8.6%. In 1990, the economic

[17] Ibid.

growth rate was 9.4%, and the per capita national income exceeded 2000 USD. In 1995, per capita national income had reached 5000 USD. Foreign trade increased from 195.3277 billion ringgits in 1991 to 379.331 billion ringgits in 1995. However, when Prime Minister Mahathir submitted to the Parliament the "Seventh Five-Year Plan" proposal to implement the "high-growth, low-inflation" economic policy, a sudden financial crisis swept Southeast Asia and hit Malaysia's economy. In 1998, the growth rate of Malaysia's GDP dropped from 7.7% in the previous year to − 6.7%, and the growth rate of the manufacturing industry decreased from 12.5% in 1997 to − 10.2%. At the same time, total imports and exports also fell by 25.9 and 6.9. In July 1998, the government promulgated the Economic Revitalization Program that adopted developmental macroeconomic policies and loose monetary policies. In 1999, Malaysia's economy gradually recovered, reaching 300.340 billion ringgits in terms of GDP, an increase of 6.1% over the previous year. In 2000, the economy maintained a steady growth momentum, and the GDP increased to 340.706 billion ringgits.

After 2000, the Malaysian economy entered the stage of the "Third Vision Plan Outline". The goals of listed by the outline include: Malaysia should develop a knowledge-based economy, maintain sustained economic growth and strengthen the vitality of the industry; promote domestic private investment, encourage foreign direct investment and implement prudent fiscal policies and monetary policy; enhance the banking industry; broaden and deepen the capital market; strengthen the supervision of corporate organizations. In 2001, the Eighth Five-Year Plan was launched. However, due to the slowdown of the US economy and the deterioration of the Japanese economy, the Malaysian economy was facing challenges again—the GDP grew by only 0.3%, and both the exports and the imports decreased by more than 10%. In order to accomplish the goals set in the Eighth Five-Year Plan, the government adopted a series of adjustment measures: stimulating domestic demand, adjusting foreign trade, attracting foreign investment and restructuring the financial industry. In 2002, Malaysia's economy began to pick up, with a GDP growth rate of 4.2%, of which agricultural grew by 0.3%, mining industry by 4.5%, manufacturing industry by 4.1%, construction industry by 2.3% and service industry by 4.5%. According to the statistics of the Central Bank of Malaysia, as of the end of 2002, the country's total foreign debt was 185.3 billion ringgits (about 48.763 billion USD), of which short-term foreign debt was 25.27 billion ringgits (about 6.65 billion USD). In March 2004, after Badawi won the election and formally came to power, he took various measures to improve economic competitiveness. The first is to maintain a healthy and rapid economic growth through policies such as stabilizing the exchange rate, restructuring bank and corporate debt, expanding exports, introducing foreign capital, and adjusting the scale of infrastructure. The second is to attach great importance to the problem of fiscal deficits, cancel a batch of costly image projects, shift the focus to the construction of basic industries such as agriculture and promote rural development, promote consumption and investment, and use the private economy as a new pillar of national economic growth. The third is to establish new development areas, especially education, telecommunications, tourism and other service areas and high value-added agriculture, attach importance to the development of the biotechnology industry, implement the "Bio Valley" plan and achieve economic diversification. The fourth is to adjust the scale of infrastructure construction and prevent economic overheating. Fifth, support the development of SMEs and improve technological innovation. Sixth, improve the investment environment and accelerate the introduction of foreign capital. Seventh, promote foreign economic cooperation and strive to create a win–win situation. The above policies have generated positive effects. Malaysia's economy has maintained rapid growth. At the end of the Eighth Five-Year Plan in 2005, its GDP grew by 5.6%. In 2006, the economy continued to maintain a strong momentum, and the current account surplus rose significantly. The public sector turned a profit, and both private investment and domestic consumption saw expansion. In January 2006, the ringgit rose by 0.67%, the largest monthly appreciation since August 2005. In the first half of 2006, the ringgit rose against the US dollar by 3.2%. Exports continued to boost economic growth, and trade activities in February 2006, increasing by 13.3% over the previous year, further supported the strengthening of ringgit. Increasing global demand for raw materials has made Malaysia's economy, highly dependent on raw material exports, grow faster. The appreciation of the ringgit reduced the cost of imports and the impact of rising oil prices. The government encouraged the development of processing industries based on domestic raw materials and focused on the electronics and electrical industries. Malaysia has become a major producer and distributor of semiconductor components, automotive assembly, steel, and petrochemicals in Southeast Asia. The economic structure has gradually changed, with shrinking proportion of agriculture and rising share of manufacturing.

In 2008, under the impact of the US financial crisis, the economies of ASEAN countries generally slowed down, and the turmoil in Malaysian financial markets worsened. In 2008, Malaysia's economic growth rate was only 4.6%, 0.4% point lower than the official forecast of 5.0%, and significantly lower than the 6.3% growth in 2007. Overall, the economic situation in the first half of 2008 was good, and economic growth slowed significantly since the third quarter. The economic growth rate from January to June was 6.7%, an increase of 1.1% over the same period last year, and the figure from July to December was only 2.4%. The government proposed to implement an expansionary fiscal policy, focusing on expanding domestic demand and private investment, and announced a number of measures to stabilize the economy, including an injection of 500 million ringgits to buy back undervalued shares of listed companies, opening up the service industry, and reviewing the foreign investment committee regulations. Later, the government announced a 700-million-ringgits economic revitalization plan, including the construction of low-cost housing, maintenance of schools and hospitals and other infrastructure, as well as the upgrading of public transport systems in major cities. It also announced the abolition of import taxes on cement and steel, allowing foreigners to purchase real estate worth 500,000 ringgits. On December 24, the Central Bank announced that it reduced the interest rate paid on statutory reserves for commercial banks from 4 to 3%, and also lowered the overnight policy rate by 25 basis points to 3.25%. This was the first time that the Central Bank of Malaysia cut interest rates since 2003. At the same time, to alleviate the impact of the economic crisis,

Malaysia actively broadened its economic cooperation with East Asia and Islamic countries, and strengthened economic cooperation with Vietnam and Indonesia. In August, Vu Huy Hoang, Vietnam's Minister of Industry and Trade, met with Tan Sri Muhyiddin Yassin, Minister of International Trade and Industry in Malaysia. The Vietnamese government agreed to revisit the Investment Guarantee Agreement signed by the two countries in 1992 to encourage Malaysia to invest in Vietnam to provide effective protection against economic crises. In October, the Indonesian and Malaysian governments also agreed to re-examine the Border Trade Agreement signed in 1970 to strengthen bilateral trade exchanges. On February 8, 2009, the People's Bank of China and the Central Bank of Malaysia signed a bilateral currency swap agreement of 8 billion yuan, which aims to promote bilateral trade and investment and thus economic growth. Malaysia has signed free trade agreements with India, Australia and New Zealand, which will greatly promote multilateral trade and economic development and inject vitality into the recessionary economy. Malaysia will also discuss the signing of a free trade agreement with members of the Gulf Cooperation Council. Malaysia is committed to actively building a global Islamic financial center. Currently, Malaysia's Islamic financial assets account for 17.8% of the total, and it has the largest Islamic bond market in Southeast Asia. As of June 2008, Malaysia, having issued a total of 66 billion USD in Islamic bonds, 62.6% of the world's total, has become an important Islamic financial market in the world. The development of the Islamic financial market has largely relieved the pressure on Malaysia's domestic financial market and laid the foundation for its recovery from the crisis.

In 2011, the Malaysian government began implementing the "10th Five-Year Plan" with the theme "Economic Prosperity and Social Justice". It planned to use the private economy and innovative industries as the main driving force for economic development, improve the efficiency and transparency of government services, further improve the social environment, strengthen human resource development, continue to train high-quality talents, improve productivity and national competitiveness and ensure the sustainable development of the society as a whole, so as to achieve the "2020 Vision" of transforming Malaysia into a high-income country by 2020. In 2015, Malaysia's GDP was 329.9 billion USD (calculated at constant prices in 2005), an increase of 4.95% year-on-year, and the per capita GDP reached 10,877 USD, an increase of 3.47% year-on-year, as Figs. 5.30, 5.31, and 5.32 show.

As shown in Fig. 5.33, Malaysia's economic structure is stable, with consumption as the dominant factor. The proportion of investment in GDP has gradually increased since 2012, and the net export surplus has remained stable throughout the year.

1. Industrial structure

As shown in Fig. 5.34, within the Malaysian GDP of 2015, 8.43% was from agriculture, 39.12% from the manufacturing and other industries and 44.3% from the service sector. Within the structure of three industries, the service sector and industry have always taken up a big share. Since 1996, the proportions of industrial added value and the service sector added value had been similar till 2007 when the former

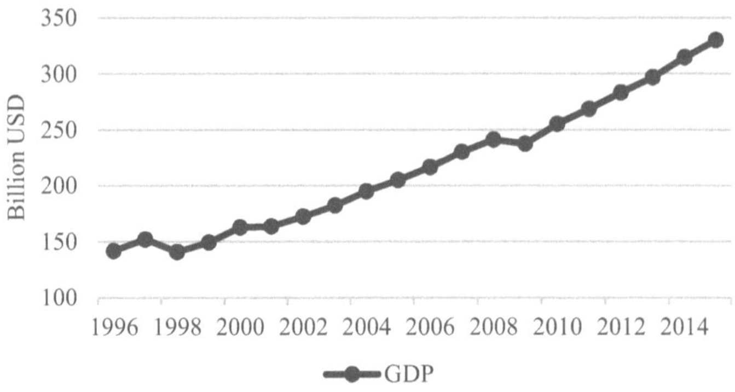

Fig. 5.30 GDP of Malaysia. *Source of data* World Bank database

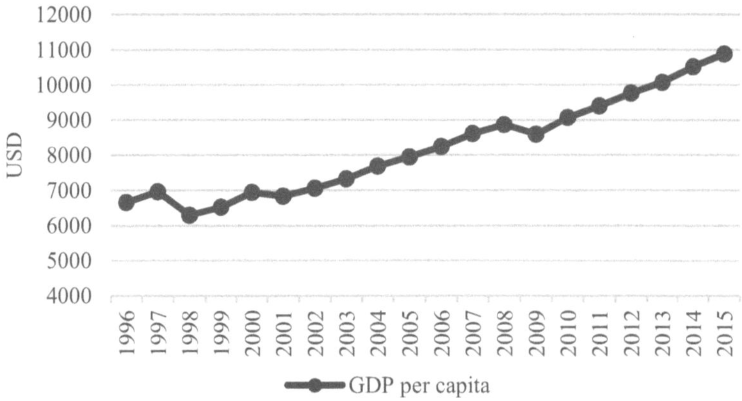

Fig. 5.31 Per capita GDP of Malaysia. *Source of data* World Bank database

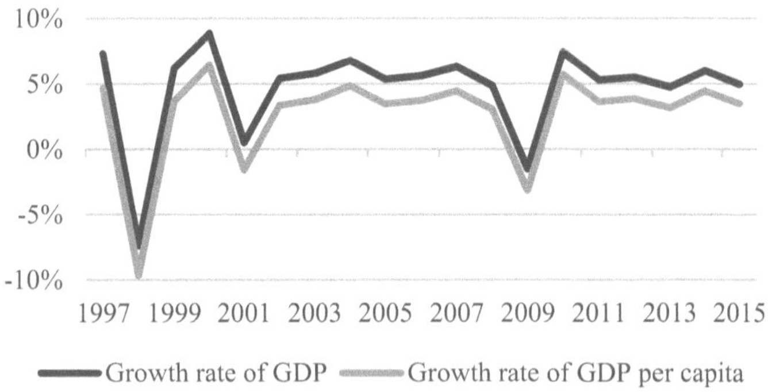

Fig. 5.32 Growth rates of GDP and per capita GDP in Malaysia. *Source of data* World Bank database

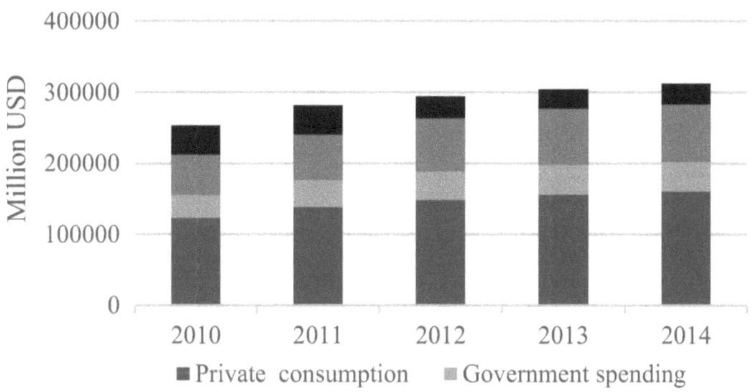

Fig. 5.33 Composition of Malaysian GDP (expenditure approach). *Source of data* Department of Statistics, Malaysia, Bloomberg

began to decline. The service sector is on average 10% higher than the industry in terms of proportion within GDP. The proportion of Malaysia's agricultural added value has been relatively stable at about 10%.

(1) The primary industry

In 2014, Malaysia's agricultural output was worth 57.528 billion ringgits, an increase of 2.6% year-on-year, accounting for 6.9% of GDP. The total agricultural exports were 69.2 billion ringgits, an increase of 0.6% year-on-year, accounting for 9.0% of the total export value. Malaysian agricultural products are mainly cash crops such as palm oil, rubber, cocoa, rice, pepper, tobacco, pineapple, tea, etc. According to the Malaysian Palm Oil Commission, in 2014, the cultivated area of oil palm was 5.39 million ha, an increase of 3.1% year-on-year; the crude palm oil production was 19.67 million tons, an increase of 2.3% year-on-year. By the end of 2014, a year-on-year increase of 1.3% was achieved for reserves of palm oil (2.01 million tons).

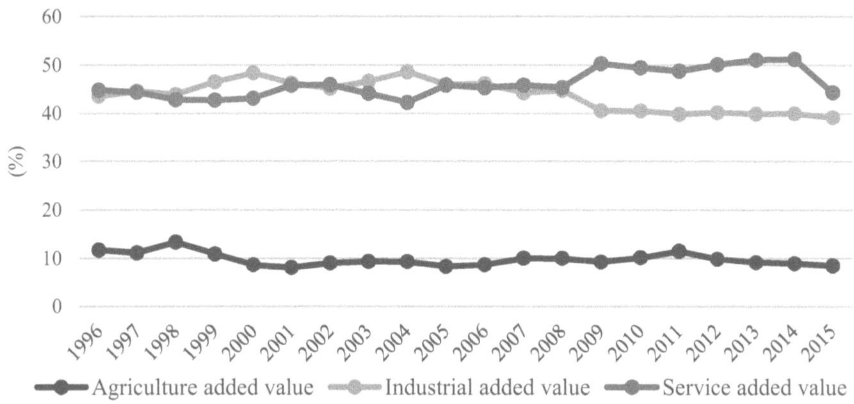

Fig. 5.34 Malaysian industrial structure. *Source of data* UN database

Malaysia is the world's second largest producer and exporter of palm oil, second only to Indonesia. According to the Malaysian Rubber Commission, Malaysia's natural rubber output was 669,000 tons in 2014, and the import volume was 905,000 tons, of which 48.7% came from Thailand; 722,000 tons were exported, 45.9% of which went to China.

(2) The secondary industry

In 2014, Malaysia's manufacturing output was worth 205.200 billion ringgits, a year-on-year increase of 6.2 and 24.6% of GDP. Manufacturing industry is one of the main driving forces for the Malaysian economy. The main industrial sectors include electronics, petroleum, machinery, steel, chemical and automobile.

(3) The tertiary industry

In 2014, the output of Malaysia's service industry was 462.027 billion ringgits, a year-on-year increase of 6.3 and 55.3% of GDP. The service industry is the largest economic sector in Malaysia, hiring 60.3% of the working population in Malaysia. The tourism industry is one of the key divisions of the service sector.

2. Urban structure

Malaysia is one of the most urbanized countries in Southeast Asia. As the urban population steadily increased over the past 20 years, its urbanization rate has reached a high level close to 75%, as shown in Fig. 5.35. However, the population density of urban areas in Malaysia is the smallest in East Asia. Kuala Lumpur City is the most densely populated area in the region. Table 5.4 lists Malaysia's major cities.

Kuala Lumpur is the capital and largest city of Malaysia, as well as a cultural and economic center in Southeast Asia.

Johor Bahru is the second largest city in the Federation. It is an important industrial, transportation and commercial city, with large companies involved in electronics, resources and petrochemical refining, as well as shipbuilding.

George Town is an important port in Penang, Malaysia, and the third largest city in the country after Kuala Lumpur (the capital) and Johor Bahru.

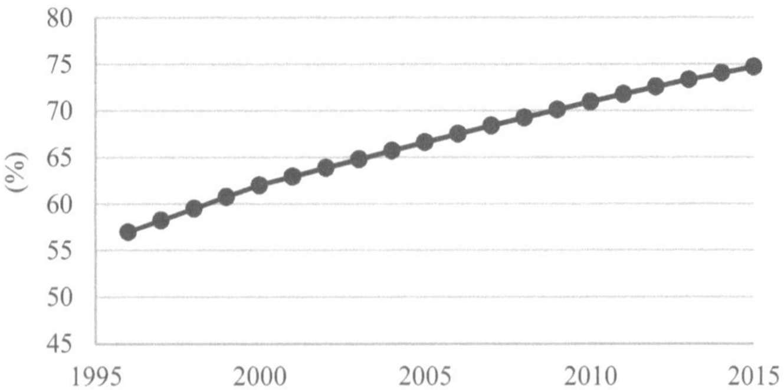

Fig. 5.35 Urbanization rate of Malaysia. *Source of data* World Bank database

Table 5.4 Major cities in Malaysia

City	Population (10,000)	City profile
Kuala Lumpur	158.90	The capital, and the economic, cultural and political center of Malaysia
Johor Bahru	49.71	A sea port in the south that neighbors Singapore
George Town	74.02	A tourist city, and the political, tourist and cultural center of the north
Ipoh	75.79	State capital, and the center of industry, business and transport
Shah Alam	17.44	State capital with developed road network
Petaling Jaya	19.79	A satellite of the capital Kuala Lumpur

Source of data UN database

3. Population structure

Malaysia is a less populated country in Southeast Asia. In terms of geographical distribution of the population, more than 80% of the country's population is concentrated in West Malaysia, and 3/4 of the population in West Malaysia is concentrated in the fertile and resource-rich West Coast. Within the labor force, the proportion of males is as high as 87.2%, and the number is still growing. The proportion of females has remained unchanged in recent years. In the early 1990s, Malaysia's population was still young, with 37% of the population being people under 14. In recent years, Malaysia's population has grown younger. In 2008, the population aged over 65 accounted for 4% of the total, as shown in Fig. 5.36.

(II) Foreign trade and investment

From Malaysia's independence to the 1970s, the economy was dominated by agriculture and relied on exports of primary products. In the 1970s, Malaysia, by using its relatively cheap labor resources to attract foreign capital and technology, vigorously developed labor-intensive industries and built an export-oriented economy,

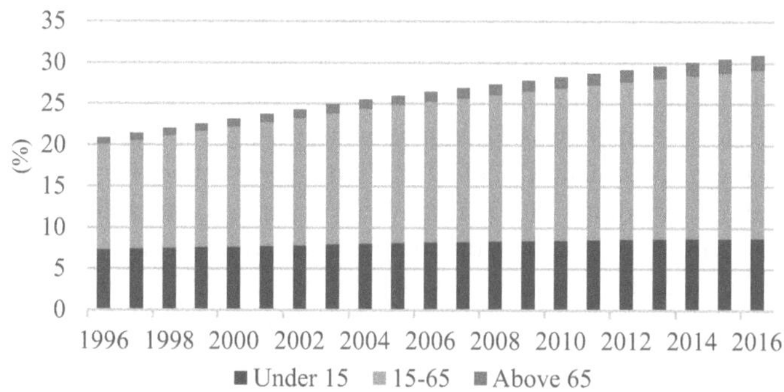

Fig. 5.36 Age structure of Malaysian population. *Source of data* United States Census Bureau

leading to the fast growth of industries such as electronics, manufacturing, construction and services. After the Southeast Asian financial crisis in 1997, Malaysia relied on exports of industrial and agricultural products to boost economic recovery. As a result, the industrial restructuring in the 1980s and 1990s, characterized by a decline in the proportion of agriculture and an increase in the proportion of industry, had stalled. Since the twenty-first century, the industrial structure has been stable.

Generally speaking, Malaysia's competitive products (according to their market shares) roughly fall into three categories: first, products that rely on local animal and plant resources; second, primary chemical products that rely on oil and gas resources; and third, a small amount of primary manufactured goods. Most of Malaysia's competitive export products are gaining market shares, which reflects the overall improvement of Malaysia's trade situation in recent years.

1. Foreign trade

In 2014, the trade competitiveness index of Malaysian crude wool and animal hair and waste thereof, fur (whole or chipped) and gaseous hydrocarbons all reached 1.00, and the figure for bird eggs and broken wood reached 0.99. Among the products exported in 2014, edible flour, fish meat and fish balls, fresh or frozen fish fillets and other fish products enjoyed higher competitiveness. According to the trade competitiveness index, Malaysia's competitive products are those relying on local animal, plant and mineral resources and having a low degree of processing. Malaysia's TV receiver is highly competitive, but such products are considered outdated by developed countries, and the market is shifting to less developed countries. In addition, semifinished iron and non-alloy steel are rated competitive due to the backwardness of heavy industry and infrastructure in Malaysia, which means that such products are not competitive in the international market. Storage batteries are competitive industrial products of Malaysia, but the main export products are batteries used for electric vehicles, which means lower technological level and limited added value.

2. International investment

In recent years, Malaysia's FDI has been generally stable at around 10 billion USD per year, as shown in Fig. 5.37. As of the end of 2014, Malaysia's stock of foreign investment was 133.77 billion USD. According to data released by the Malaysian Investment Development Authority (MIDA), the approved investment in manufacturing in 2014 totaled 71.853 billion ringgits (approximately 20.529 billion USD), of which domestic investment was 32.260 billion ringgits (approximately 9.217 billion USD) and foreign investment was 39.593 billion ringgits (about 11.312 billion USD). In 2015, Malaysia absorbed 11.30 billion USD in foreign capital flows.

As shown in Fig. 5.38, in 2008, the sources of direct investment in Malaysia were evenly distributed among different regions, but in the next 10 years, the sources of FDI in Malaysia changed significantly, shifting from Europe and the United States to neighboring Asian countries. Northeast Asia's direct investment in Malaysia has grown rapidly. By 2015, it had become Malaysia's most important source of FDI. Central and South America's investment in Malaysia has gradually decreased. At

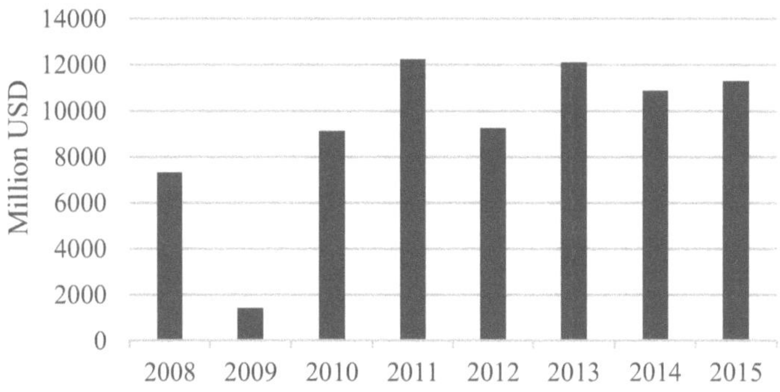

Fig. 5.37 FDI in Malaysia. *Source of data* Central Bank of Malaysia, Bloomberg

present, Southeast and Northeast Asian countries are Malaysia's largest investors, which to some extent reflects the economic integration of Asian countries.

Malaysia's main sources of investment are Japan and Singapore. The scale of Chinese direct investment in Malaysia is relatively small, and even negative in some years, as shown in Fig. 5.39 for details.

FDI in Malaysia has been concentrated in extractive, manufacturing and service industries in the past 10 years. Among them, the manufacturing and service industries have been the most favorable destinations of FDI. Direct investment in the extractive industry has increased rapidly in the past 10 years, exceeding that in the service sector in 2015. The manufacturing, as the largest recipient of FDI, has gained increasing popularity among foreign investors since 2008. For more information, see Fig. 5.40.

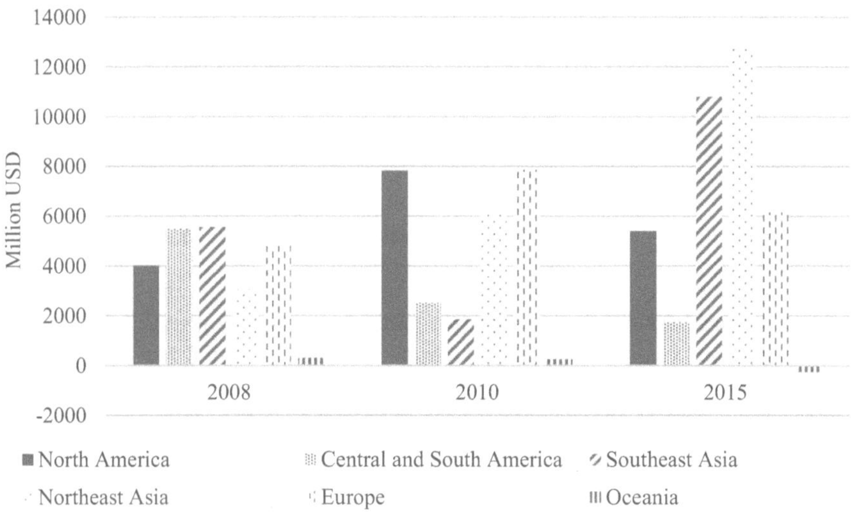

Fig. 5.38 Statistics on sources of FDI in Malaysia. *Source of data* Bloomberg

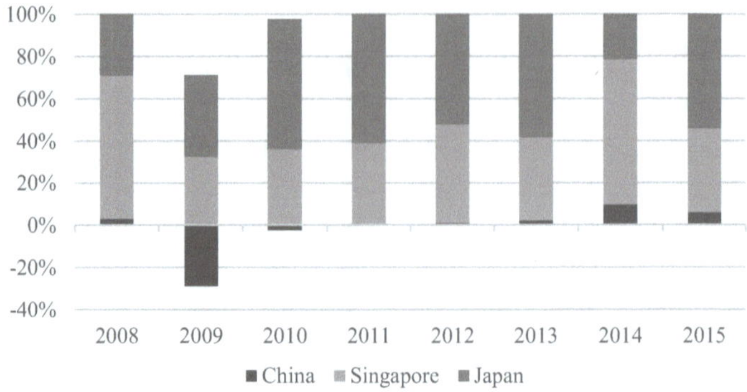

Fig. 5.39 Some countries' direct investment in Malaysia. *Source of data* Central Bank of Malaysia, Bloomberg

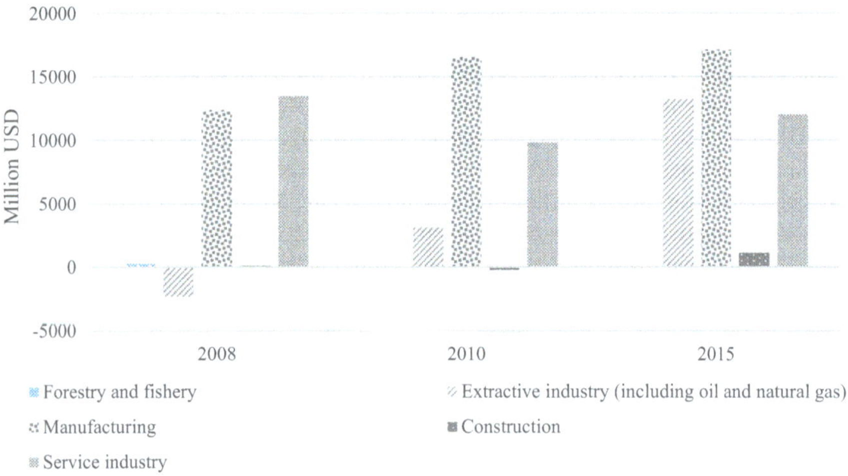

Fig. 5.40 Distribution of FDI in Malaysia. *Source of data* Bloomberg

III. **Future orientation of cooperation between China and Malaysia**

Malaysia is currently China's third largest trading partner in Asia and China's largest trading partner among ASEAN countries. China has been Malaysia's largest trading partner for many years. In 2000, the total import and export volume between Malaysia and China kept growing, and Malaysia has always maintained a trade surplus with China. According to the statistics of the IMF during 2000–2011, the proportion Malaysia's exports to China within its GDP from 2010 to 2011 increased by about 6 percentage points from the 2000–2007 average, reflecting the growing importance of the bilateral trade to the Malaysian economy. In 2013, Malaysia's imports to, exports from, and total trade with China reached 45.9 billion USD, 60.2 billion USD and 106.1 billion USD, respectively. According to the WTO statistics, China was Malaysia's largest import source (13.5%) and second largest export market (16.4%) in 2013. China mainly imports mechanical and electrical products, mineral products, plastics and rubber, animal and vegetable fats and oils, base metals and products, chemical products, optical instrument, clocks and watches, and medical equipment, food and beverages, and tobacco from Malaysia. Malaysia mainly imports from China integrated circuits, base metals and products, chemical products, plastics and rubber, optical instrument, clocks and watches, and medical equipment, transportation equipment, textiles and raw materials.

Zhou and Hao (2015) studies the trade complementarity between the two countries based on the trade statistics.

According to the bilateral trade statistics, the comprehensive complementarity index of Malaysian imports and Chinese exports is on the rise, exceeding 1 for the first time in 2004, which indicates growing complementarity. The complementarity index in the area of miscellaneous products has been greater than 1 since 1995, and the index in the area of transportation machinery has been increasing, indicating strong trade complementarities for such products.

The trade complementarity index of Malaysian exports and Chinese imports has always been greater than 1 from 1995 to 2009, indicating strong complementarities. In terms of animal and vegetable oils and waxes, the complementarity index exceeds 20, indicating strong complementarities and China's large demand for such commodities. The complementarity index for non-edible raw materials has also basically maintained above 2, and the index of machinery and transportation equipment has been greater than 1, indicating the two countries are highly complementary as to such products. In short, China and Malaysia are highly complementary in trade of both directions, and such complementarity are both intra-industry and inter-industry, especially for industries such as animal and vegetable oils and waxes, inedible raw materials, machinery and transportation equipment, and miscellaneous products.

5.5 Myanmar

I. Geographical and historical backgrounds

Myanmar, located in the southeast of Asia and the west of the Indo-China Peninsula, has a total area of about 676,600 km^2, ranking second in Southeast Asia after Indonesia. The country, with strategic importance, is long and narrow from north to south, connecting East Asia, South Asia and Southeast Asia, namely China in East Asia, India and Bangladesh in South Asia, and Thailand and Laos in Southeast Asia. The terrain of Myanmar is relatively complicated—dominated by mountains and plateaus, it slopes from north to low south, which means its mountains and rivers run from north to south. Myanmar is the most northerly country in Southeast Asia. The Tropic of Cancer passes through most of the country. Due to the high mountains and plateaus on the east, north and west, it is difficult for the cold air on the Asian continent to go south in winter. The whole region is of tropical monsoon climate or subtropical monsoon climate. The coastal areas are hot, humid and rainy throughout the year, while the climate in the inland areas varies greatly with different terrains.

Myanmar is an ancient civilization. After undergoing the feudal dynasties of Bagan, Toungoo and Konbaung, it was colonized by the British. In 1948, it won independence from the Commonwealth, and established the Union of Myanmar. It renamed Socialist Republic of the Union of Burma in January 1974. According to World Bank's statistics, Myanmar's total population was 53.9 million in 2015, with a growth rate of 0.9%, and a population density of 82.5 people/km^2. 27.5% of the population are people aged 0–14, 67.1% are those aged 15–64, and 5.3% are those aged 65 and above, making the population relatively young. Myanmar is a multiethnic country with a total of more than 50 ethnic groups and 135 branches. Among them, the Burmese ethnic group accounts for about 69% of the total population and ethnic minorities account for 31%. Myanmar is also a very religious country—Buddhism, primitive fetishism, worship of the gods, Islam, Hinduism and Christianity all have followers here. Among them, Theravada Buddhism is the most dominant and influential force. Buddhists make up 88% of the total population and 98% of the Burmese population, Christians and Muslims account for about 5 and 4% of the total population.

Myanmar is a country with extremely rich water resources. Of its many rivers, most of the major ones originate from China's Tibet Plateau or mountainous areas in northern Myanmar. The Irrawaddy and the Salween are the two largest river systems. The basin area of the top 10 rivers is about 737,800 km^2 (Liao et al. 2014). These rivers are traffic routes that connect the south and the north of the country, the source of irrigation water for millions of acres of good land, and also a bonanza of water resources. Myanmar, once known as a granary of Asia, enjoys abundant land resources and rainfall. There are 44.787 million acres of land suitable for agricultural production in the country, accounting for 37% of the country's land area. Triple-cropping of rice can be applied here. At the same time, with a wide variety of plants, it is the country with the richest biodiversity in the Indo-China Peninsula. As one of the countries with the richest natural resources in Southeast Asia, Myanmar has always depended on its natural gas and oil for foreign exchange revenue. According to the BP Statistical Review of World Energy, as of the end of 2014, Myanmar's proven natural gas reserves were 18.7 trillion cubic feet, accounting for 0.3% of the world's total; its oil reserves were 3.2 billion barrels, ranking 10th in the world. Proved mineral resources include tin, tungsten, copper, zinc, aluminum, antimony, gold, silver, manganese, iron, jade, gemstone, etc. Among them, the proven copper ore reserves in the Monywa deposit were about 133 million tons, with an average grade of 0.72%. The oil, natural gas, minerals, gems and wood produced in Myanmar have made huge contribution to the country's GDP.

II. **Economic development**

(I) Domestic economy

Myanmar was once a feudal and autocratic country, and had a self-sufficient small-scale peasant economy. After the British invasion, Myanmar's traditional economic model that had lasted for nearly a thousand years was completely dismantled, the colonial economy began to spread, and commodity production grew greatly. Post-independence Myanmar was governed by the U Nu administration and the Ne Win administration. The U Nu government encouraged private national capital, nationalized foreign capital, welcomed foreign capital and foreign aid, and adopted the policy of opening up; however, the economic development was slow during this period, the planned goals were not achieved, and foreign capital still occupied an important position in Myanmar. After General Ne Win took power, major changes took place to Myanmar's economic policy. Measures such as nationalizing national capital, establishing state-owned enterprises, restricting the private sector, launching land reform and setting up agricultural cooperatives were adopted to enable the government to grasp the lifeblood of the national economy, allocate domestic resources and labor and comprehensively control the economy.

Driven by the reform in 1988, the new government of Myanmar gradually turned to more flexible and pragmatic policies to transform the planned economy to market economy, and to open up the country to the world. After the Asian financial crisis broke out in 1997, the Myanmar government adopted some new policies and measures, attaching importance to agricultural and industrial development, strengthening economic and trade relations with neighboring countries, continuously adjusting the development structure, striving to attract foreign investment and expanding foreign trade. Myanmar's economy has been improving since then.

The 2015 general election was a success. Overall, the political stability was resumed, and large amount of foreign investment flooded in as the Western sanctions were lifted and offshore gas fields were discovered and exploited. The economic development enjoyed a good and fast growth was achieved despite slight fluctuation. In 2015, Myanmar's GDP was 64.9 billion USD, growing at a rate of 7.5%; and GDP per capita was 1204 USD, with a growth rate of 6.08%. For more details, please refer to Figs. 5.41, 5.42 and 5.43.

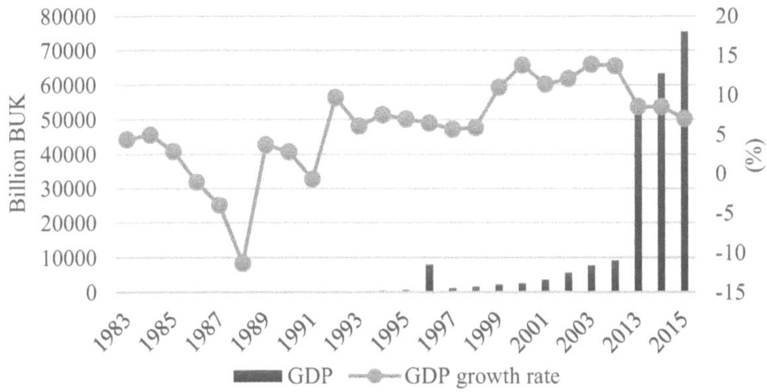

Fig. 5.41 Burmese GDP and its growth rate. *Note* April 2, 2016, 1 USD = 1911 BUK. *Source of data* World Bank database

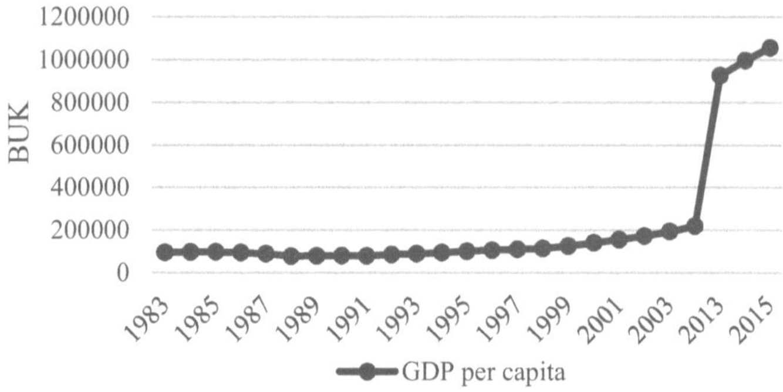

Fig. 5.42 Per capita GDP in Myanmar. *Source of data* World Bank database

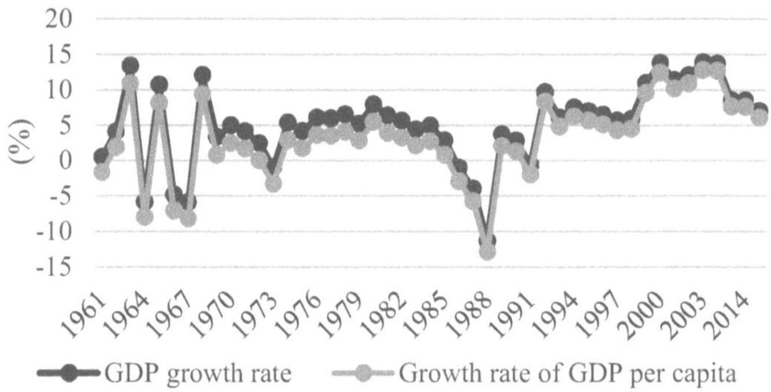

Fig. 5.43 GDP growth rate of Myanmar. *Source of data* World Bank database

1. Industrial structure

(1) The primary industry

Myanmar is a traditional agricultural country, with agriculture accounting for about 30.9% of GDP. The main crops are rice, wheat, corn, peanuts, sesame, cotton, beans, tobacco, coffee, etc. Among them, rice is dominant, covering 45% of the total planting area, followed by oilseed crops, vegetables and fruits, Beans and industrial raw materials. Agricultural mechanization is underdeveloped in Myanmar—almost only small-scale agricultural machinery is employed and the area of mechanized agriculture covers only 15%. Generally, extensive farming is practiced. Myanmar also has abundant forest resources. In 2015, the total forest area was 290,410 km^2, accounting for 44% of the land area. Timber exports are one of the main sources of foreign exchange. In addition to wood, there are abundant bamboo forests and rattan plants. Myanmar's animal husbandry is also relatively developed, with good foundations. The area of natural pastures is more than 400,000 hectares. The main breeds are chicken, duck, cattle, sheep and pig. In addition, Myanmar's 2832 km coastline and 228,700 km^2 of shallow coastal terraces provide an excellent environment for fishery. The vast inland waters and rivers also provide abundant resources. Fishery has become one of the major foreign exchange earning industries, with an export value of 503 million USD in 2015. As 65.9% of the total population lived in rural areas in 2015, agricultural production weighs a lot for the national economy.

(2) The secondary industry

Myanmar's industrial foundation is weak and its development is slow. The total industrial output value accounts for 34.6% of GDP. It mainly includes small machinery manufacturing, textiles, printing and dyeing, rice milling, wood processing, sugar making, etc., and its industrial categories are limited in number. In the energy industry, the commercial energy resources are mainly oil, natural gas, electricity and coal. Among them, oil and natural gas account for the vast majority of energy consumption. As of the end of 2014, Myanmar's proven natural gas reserves were 18.7 trillion cubic feet, accounting for 0.3% of the world total, and oil reserves reached 3.2 billion barrels. In 2014, expenditures on natural gas were 2.94% of GDP and the figure was 0.64% for oil. However, the per capita use of natural gas in Myanmar is still low and a large amount of natural gas is used for export. At present, natural gas is already one of Myanmar's major export products. As of the end of June 2016, there were 96 foreign-invested oil and gas projects with a total investment of 21 billion USD, making oil and gas the largest recipient sector of foreign investment.[18] Coal is less used in Myanmar, accounting for only 0.03% of the total domestic energy mix. As to electricity, the problem of power shortage has always existed. According to the Myanmar Times, power supply in Myanmar currently only covers one-third of the population, which brings a lot of inconvenience to production and life. In 2013, power generation by oil, natural gas and coal accounted for 25.3% of the total. Hydropower development has become a promising and hot destination for foreign investment in Myanmar. According to the National Investment Commission of Myanmar, the power industry is one of the main recipients of foreign investment, and the investors of hydropower stations are mainly neighboring countries such as China, Thailand, India and Bangladesh. For the raw material industry, Myanmar is rich in mineral resources. Mining is operated by state-owned enterprises, producing 6.1% of GDP. As of the end of 2015, FDI in mining was 2.868 billion USD. Besides, the building materials industry has also developed rapidly. In the manufacturing industry, due to lack of funds, talent, advanced technology and proper infrastructure, the industries of machinery, electronics and information products are relatively weak. As to consumer goods, Myanmar is known for jewelry and jade. The total transaction volume during the 53rd Jewelry Show 2016 was 533.49 million euros. The textile industry is dominated by garment manufacturing. Before 2003, garments made in Myanmar were mainly exported to the United States, and Japan replaced the United States in 2010. In 2015, Japan had the largest number of orders, totaling 580 million USD.

(3) The tertiary industry

[18] Source of data: Economic and Commercial Counsellor's Office of the Embassy of the People's Republic of China in the Republic of the Union of Myanmar.

The tertiary industry in Myanmar is divided into two major parts: transportation and logistics, and services. The development is relatively uneven among different sectors—the hotel industry, tourism, transportation and telecommunications are doing well, while education, culture, broadcasting and finance are sluggish. In 2015, the service industry accounted for 34.5% of GDP. Since the independence of Myanmar, after decades of development, the scale of transportation infrastructure has reached a certain level. IWT has played an important role in domestic transportation. Due to Myanmar's geographical advantage, the port industry has also developed rapidly, making it possible for the country to become a trade and transportation center in the ASEAN region. In contrast, the development of road transportation is lagging. Myanmar has abundant tourism resources. The main tourist attractions include the Shwedagon Pagoda in Yangon, the ancient capital Mandalay, Bagan, the city of a ten thousand pagodas, and Ngapali Beach. After years of hard work, the tourism industry has expanded to a certain level and made good profits. In 2013–2014, about 2 million international tourists visited Myanmar. From 2014 to 2015, the number of international tourist arrivals reached 3 million and the economic benefit hit 1.1 billion USD. For Myanmar, Thailand is the largest source of international tourists, followed by China, Japan and South Korea. Tourism has become a new hot destination for foreign investment, ranking 7th among all industries.

2. Population and cities

As Fig. 5.44 shows, Myanmar's urbanization rate is low—the figure was 34.1% in 2015, changing little in the past 20 years. The reasons may be as follows: although its proportion within the entire national economy has declined with the development of industry and services, agriculture is still a pillar of the national economy, agricultural exports are an important source of the fiscal revenue and foreign exchange, and the rural population is as large as 35.52 million; and due to various reasons such as economic backwardness and political instability, Myanmar's urban transport infrastructure is poor and outdated, and cities with more than 200,000 people are limited to Yangon, Mandalay, Naypyidaw and Bassein (see Table 5.5).

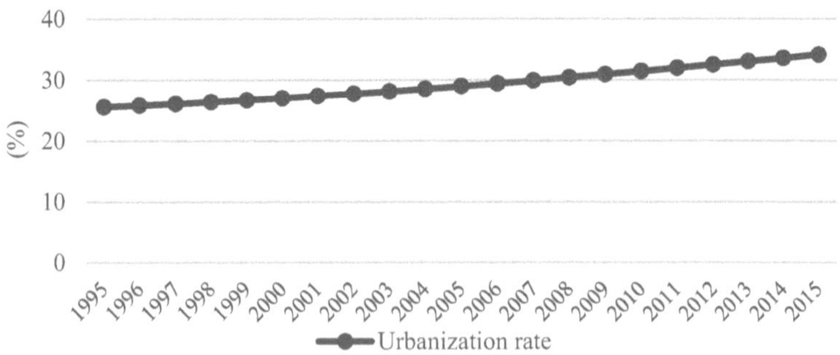

Fig. 5.44 Urbanization rate in Myanmar. *Source of data* World Bank database

Table 5.5 Capitals, areas and populations of the 14 provinces and states of Myanmar

Province/State	Capital	Area (km^2)	The proportion of population (%, 2014 census)	Profile
Yangon	Yangon	10,171	14.30	Myanmar's largest city, a transportation hub, a city where government agencies, universities, and industrial enterprises are concentrated
Ayeyarwady	Bassein	35,138	12.01	The fifth largest city; most of its residents are Burmese and Karen; a trade center of agricultural commodities; rice, timber and cement are exported here to other countries
Mandalay	Mandalay	37,024	11.95	The second largest city; 95% of the population are Burmese; an important city north of central Myanmar; a trade and industrial city
Shan	Taunggyi	155,801	11.31	The largest state in Myanmar, which accounts for about a quarter of the country's total area and has 11 counties, 55 towns, and numerous ethnic minorities
Sagaing	Sagaing	94,625	10.35	Located in the northwestern part of Myanmar, it is the largest province in Myanmar with 8 counties, 38 towns and 198 village groups. The main ethnic groups are the Burmese, Shan and Chin people
Pegu District	Pegu	39,404	9.46	It is located in the south-central part of Myanmar. As the fourth largest city in Myanmar, it has relatively developed trade and industry. It population are mainly Burmese, with a small number of Kayin and Mon people

(continued)

Table 5.5 (continued)

Province/State	Capital	Area (km^2)	The proportion of population (%, 2014 census)	Profile
Magwe	Magwe	44,820	9.46	Located in central Myanmar, it is a large town for trade. Most local people are Burmese
Rakhine State	Sittwe	36,778	6.20	It is located in the west, bordering the Bay of Bengal in the west and bordering Bangladesh in the northwest. It is a port city with an airport and the main ethnic groups are Rakhine and Burmese people
Mon State	Moulmein	12,297	3.99	Located in the southeast and bordering Thailand, it's Myanmar's third largest city. As a port city, it has developed industry and trade. Most local people are Burmese and Mon
Kachin State	Myitkyina	89,041	3.06	Located in the east of Myanmar, the state has 2 counties and 7 townships under its jurisdiction
Tanintharyi	Dawei	43,343	2.74	It is located in the southeast, borders Thailand in the east and south, and borders the Andaman Sea in the west. It is a trade center for rice, rubber, fruit, wood, tin, and tungsten produced in the surrounding area. The main ethnic groups are the Burmese and Kayin
Naypyidaw	Naypyidaw	7054	2.25	It is located in the mountainous area in the central part, with mountains to the north and plains to the south. It has an important strategic position. Agriculture and forestry are the pillar industries, with products such as rice, jute and teak

(continued)

Table 5.5 (continued)

Province/State	Capital	Area (km^2)	The proportion of population (%, 2014 census)	Profile
Chin State	Hahka	36,019	0.93	It is located in the west, bordering India in the north and northwest, and Bangladesh in the west. It has 2 counties, 9 towns, and 505 village groups. Most local people are Chin
Kayin State	Hpa-an	11,753	0.56	Located in the southeast, it borders Thailand to its east. Myawaddy is an important border town in the Thai–Myanmar trade. Most local people are Kayin

Source of data Liao Yahui, etc. Economic and Social Geography of Myanmar; http://www.renkou.org.cn

Naypyidaw is the new capital and the third largest city in Myanmar. It is located in the central region of Myanmar, sitting on the narrow strip of the Sittang River Valley between the Shan Yoma and the Bago Yoma. With mountains to its north and plains to its south, the city is of strategic importance. Covering a total area of 2725 square miles, it is home to 920,000 people, of which most are Burmese. The main crops are rice, jute, teak, vegetables and fruits. At present, local infrastructure is improving.

Covering about 598 km^2, Yangon is the largest city in Myanmar, the largest economic center, a major industrial city, and an economic, cultural and transportation center. It has a population of about 6 million, of which about 200,000 are overseas Chinese.[19] Located in the eastern part of the Ayeyarwady Delta and the downstream of the Yangon River, it enjoys fertile soil and good natural conditions and is the most developed and affluent region in Myanmar. Rice, teak and gems are the major export commodities of Yangon. With the Yangon River which is 34 km away from the estuary and a low and flat terrain, the city is the largest port in Myanmar and one of the largest ports in Southeast Asia.

Mandalay, located in the north-central inland of Myanmar, is the second largest city and the second largest industrial center in Myanmar. As the economic and cultural center of central Myanmar, it is home to about 800,000 people. Tea packaging, silk spinning, wine making, jade processing, copper casting and gold foil producing are the major industrial sectors. Other sectors include shipbuilding, food processing, woodcarving and silver and gold jewelry manufacturing. Mandalay is one of the holy cities of Burmese Buddhism and is listed as a World Cultural Heritage. Its

[19] Source of data: Economic and Commercial Counsellor's Office of the Embassy of the People's Republic of China in the Republic of the Union of Myanmar.

streets are laid out in a regular grid pattern and named with numbers. Mandalay is also the largest transport and trade hub in central Myanmar.

3. Government spending and consumption

In 2011, Myanmar's fiscal revenue was 5.5 trillion kyats, of which tax revenue was 1.68 trillion kyats, or less than a quarter of the total; in 2012, Myanmar's fiscal revenue surged to 13.2 trillion kyats, and the proportion of tax revenue did not change much; in 2013, the figures were 14 and 4.46 trillion kyats, and the share of the latter rose to 31.5%; in 2014, the figures grew to 16.9 and 5.94 trillion kyats, and the percentage continued to rise to 35.1%. In 2015, the estimated fiscal revenue was about 17 trillion kyats, and the tax revenue was estimated at 5.95 trillion kyats, accounting for about 35%.[20] In general, the fiscal revenue has increased significantly in recent years, and tax revenue is gaining weight.

The substantial increase in the tax revenue was the result of increasing foreign investment and expanding domestic tax base. According to the Myanmar Times, U Win Shine, Minister of Finance, publicly stated in April 2015 that Myanmar's tax revenue accounted for only 8% of GDP—despite increasing, it was still the lowest among ASEAN countries, and Myanmar will strive to enlarge the percentage to 10%. In addition, Myanmar was expected to receive 186 billion kyats (143 million USD) in international loans and 350 billion kyats (270 million USD) in international aid in the new fiscal year of 2016.

4. Population structure

According to the World Bank, Myanmar's total population was 53.89 million in 2015, and the labor force was about 2/3 of the total. The population growth rate was 0.86%. Its abundant labor force is dominated by people with secondary or higher education and English competence. However, due to the poor quality of university education, there are few high-caliber talents. More information can be found in Figs. 5.45 and 5.46.

(II) Foreign trade and investment

1. Foreign trade

90% of Myanmar's foreign trade is conducted with Asian countries from Southeast Asia, South Asia and East Asia. More than half is with ASEAN countries. For details, see Figs. 5.47 and 5.48. Since 1988, most foreign investment in Myanmar has come from Asia and some European and American countries. Among them, Asian investment comes from the Chinese mainland, Japan, South Korea, Hong Kong of China and ASEAN countries such as Singapore, Thailand, Malaysia, Indonesia and the Philippines; investment from Europe and America is mainly from the United States, the United Kingdom, the Netherlands and France.

According to the official website of the Ministry of Finance, from April 2015 to December 2015, Myanmar's foreign trade totaled 20.49 billion USD, of which

[20] Source of data: Ministry of Commerce of the People's Republic of China.

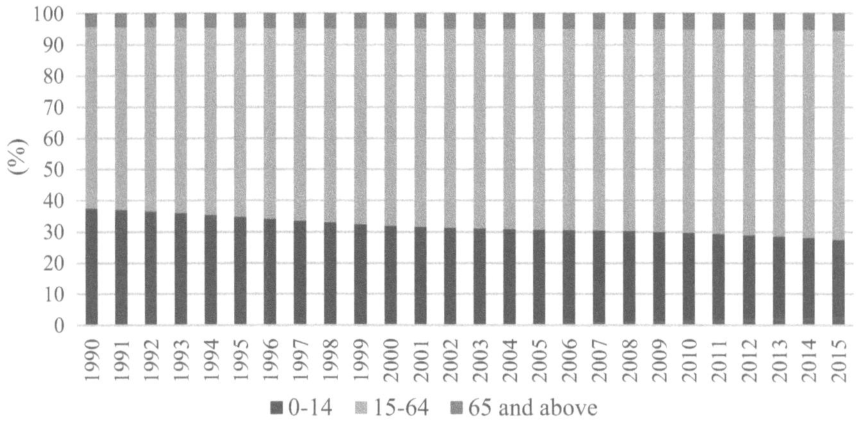

Fig. 5.45 Age structure of population of Myanmar. *Source of data* World Bank database

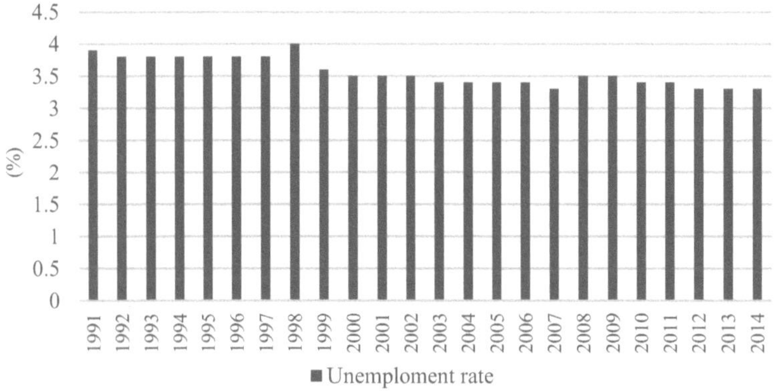

Fig. 5.46 Unemployment rate in Myanmar. *Source of data* World Bank database

8.06 billion USD were exports, and 12.43 billion USD were imports, positioning the deficit at 4.37 billion USD. Myanmar mainly exports agricultural products, animal products, mineral products, forest products and finished industrial products, such as natural gas, rice, corn, beans, aquatic products, rubber, leather, wood, pearls, gems, etc. According to official statistics, Myanmar's natural gas exports in 2011 accounted for 78% of the total output. In 2014, the value of natural gas exports reached 4.18 billion USD, an increase of 18.6% year-on-year, accounting for 37.9% of the total export value, and the percentage rose to 81% in 2015, making natural gas Myanmar's largest export product. Domestically, natural gas is mainly used for power generation—in 2013, 68% of the natural gas consumed domestically was used for power generation, and it rose to 78% in 2014. In 2014, Myanmar's jade exports totaled 1.07 billion USD, a year-on-year increase of 11.7%, accounting for 9.7% of Myanmar's total exports, making jade Myanmar's second largest export product.

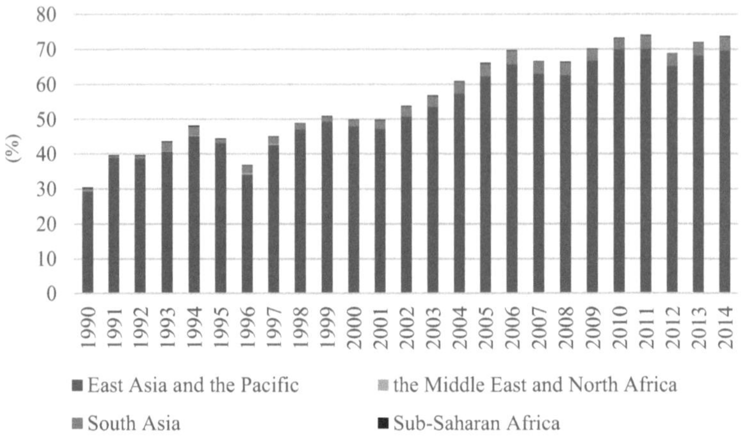

Fig. 5.47 Proportions of imports from different regions. *Source of data* World Bank database

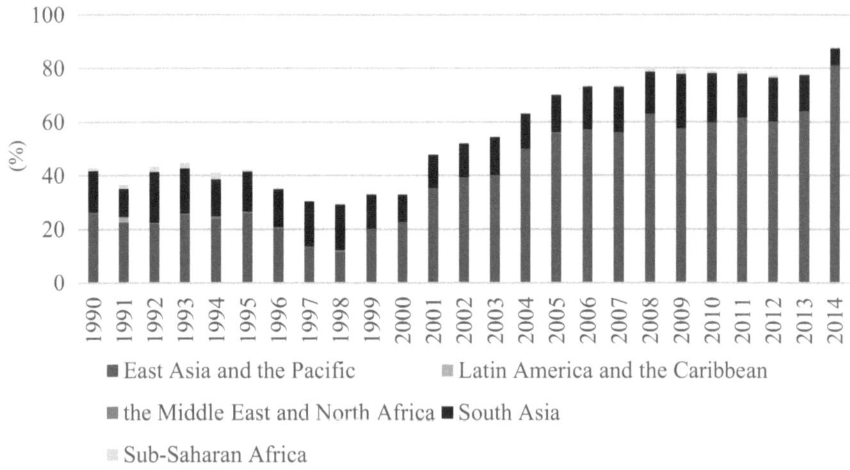

Fig. 5.48 Proportions of exports from different regions. *Source of data* World Bank database

In recent years, garment export, the second-fastest growing industry after natural gas, is absorbing more and more foreign investment.[21] Myanmar mainly imports daily goods, industrial raw materials, equipment for investment, etc., such as fuel oil, industrial raw materials, chemical products, machinery and equipment, spare parts, hardware products and consumer goods.

From April to December 2015, the total trade value between Myanmar and China was 8.44 billion USD, of which Myanmar exported 3.35 billion USD, and China

[21] Source of data: Economic and Commercial Counsellor's Office of the Embassy of the People's Republic of China in the Republic of the Union of Myanmar.

Table 5.6 Investment made by different countries

Country/Region	Number of investment projects	Total (100 million USD)	Ranking
China	108	179.28	No. 1
Singapore	173	126.46	No. 2
HK, China	107	72.54	No. 3
The Netherlands	11	7.55	No. 1 among EU countries
France	3	5.37	
Luxemburg	3	0.45	
Switzerland	3	0.28	
Germany	2	0.06	

Source of data Economic and Commercial Counsellor's Office of the Embassy of the People's Republic of China in the Republic of the Union of Myanmar

exported 5.09 billion USD, positioning the trade deficit at 1.74 billion USD. Trade between the two made up the largest part of Myanmar's total foreign trade at 41%. In the first nine months of 2015, foreign investment in Myanmar totaled 4.92 billion USD, of which Singapore contributed nearly 3 billion USD, or 61% of the total, making it the largest foreign investor in Myanmar. China invested 820 million USD (including 150 million USD from Hong Kong, China), or 16.7% of the total, ranking second. The Netherlands stands at the third place with 430 million USD, 8.7% of the total.[22]

2. International investment

According to the Myanmar Department of Investment and Corporate Guidance, as of the end of June 2016, investors from 41 countries had invested in the country, with a total of 53.348 billion USD distributed among 837 projects. China and Singapore were the largest investors, as shown in Table 5.6.

As to the sector-wise distribution of the foreign investment, as of the end of June 2016, there were 96 oil and gas projects with a total investment of 21 billion USD, making oil and gas the largest recipient sector; ranking second was energy of other kinds, with 9 projects and a total investment of 13 billion USD. The manufacturing was the third largest recipient, with 544 projects and a total investment of 5.271 billion USD.

[22] Source of data: website of Ministry of Planning, Finance and Industry, Myanmar.

5.6 The Philippines

I. Geographical and historical backgrounds

The Philippines, located in the western Pacific and Southeast Asia, has a coastline of about 18,500 km and a total land area of about 300,000 km^2. Sitting on the Pacific Rim seismic belt, it is subject to natural disasters such as earthquakes and typhoons all the year round, but its geographical environment and geological structural characteristics are conducive to the formation of mineral deposits, so it has considerable mineral resources. There are six main types of proven mineral reserves: mineral fertilizers, gems and decorative stones, industrial ores, iron ores, noble metal ores and base metal ores. Among them, the reserves of gold, copper, nickel and chromium rank third, fourth, fifth and sixth in the world, respectively. As of 2010, the total value of unearthed Philippine mineral deposits was about 840 billion USD. In addition, the country has 8.9 billion barrels of potential oil reserves, ranking high among Southeast Asian countries, but in reality it is still an oil importer. Besides, it enjoys geothermal resources equaling 2.09 billion barrels of crude oil and 3.48 trillion cubic feet of natural gas reserves.[23]

As a tropical country, the Philippines is granted with fertile soil, and abundant sunshine and rainfall, which is very conducive to the growth and reproduction of plants and animals. The national forest coverage rate reaches 53%, with a total area of nearly 16 million ha. There are nearly 10,000 kinds of flowers in the Philippines, and there are more than 900 kinds of orchids alone. Among them, the phalaenopsis, crane plant and spider orchid are larger in size and are typical representatives of tropical flowers. In addition, the Philippines produces a variety of fruits, represented by coconut (the world's largest producer), mango, durian, banana and papaya. Banana is quite popular on the international and especially the Asian markets. There are fewer species of animals than birds (more than 850). With its large number of islands and the surrounding sea, the Philippines is rich in aquatic resources—it has more than 2400 fish species.

There are many ethnic groups and cultures in the Philippines. The Negrito people may be the natives. With population movement, the spread of religions and trade development, the Indian culture, Chinese culture and Islamic culture have integrated. Since ancient times, the Philippines and China have had close trade relations. In 1417, the three kings of Sulu came to China for a friendly visit. In 1405, when Zheng He sailed to the west, he took the order from the Emperor of Yongle and appointed Xu Chailao, a Chinese immigrant, the Governor of Luzon (the Philippines). The rule of Xu Chailao lasted for more than 20 years. In 1726, the king of Sulu sent another emissary to pay tribute to the Qing court. Catholicism is currently the dominant religion in the Philippines, and its followers make up 83% of the population. Other major religions include Protestantism and Islam.

II. Economic development

[23] Source of data: Mines and Geosciences Bureau, Republic of the Philippines.

According to statistics from the World Bank, the Philippine economy grew at a rate of 5.8% in 2015, generating a total GDP of 291.97 billion USD (2875 USD per capita), ranking 40th in the world. This was slower than the 7–8% target set at the beginning of the year and the slowest since 2012. However, compared to other Asian countries, it was the fourth fastest growing economy in Asia, after India, China and Vietnam, and the second among ASEAN countries. The per capita income of the Philippines was 3112 USD in 2015, making it a low-and-middle-income country according to the World Bank definition. In addition, the Philippines ranked 47th in the 2015 Global Competitiveness Report.[24]

(I) Domestic economy

Enjoying abundant natural and human resources, and a geographical advantage, the Philippines is a natural transit hub for business and trade. It has undergone rapid growth since the 1960s by opening up to the world and absorbing foreign investment. By 1982, it was rated as a middle-income country by the World Bank. The Asian financial crisis that broke out in 1997 did not make much impact. Despite economic fluctuations in the past ten years, its growth rate stabilized at around 5%. In 2009, the Philippine economy was hit hard by the international financial crisis, and the growth rate dropped to 1.1%. By 2010, against the background of global economic recovery and the general election, its growth rate rebounded to 7.3%. From 2016 to 2017, the Philippines was expected to become the fastest growing economy among the 11 ASEAN countries.[25]

1. Industrial structure

The Philippine economy is mainly export-oriented. By 2010, more than 60% of its total exports were electronics (mainly semiconductor products). As Fig. 5.49 presents, by 2012, the proportions of the three industries were 11.89%, 31.05% and 57.06%, and the service industry was the dominant force. By 2015, the shares of agriculture, industry and service changed to 10.27%, 30.89% and 58.84% respectively—slight declines were seen by agriculture and industry, while service gained importance.

(1) The primary industry

Most parts of the country have ample rainfall. Since 2000, the area of farmland has been increasing year by year and in 2009 it exceeded 40% of the total land area. The export of agricultural products has boosted the input of land and promoted the demand for agricultural machinery and equipment, which provides good export opportunity for Chinese manufacturers and great potential for future cooperation. In 2015, the total agricultural output was worth 29.97 billion USD, up by only 0.2% (the average rate of other developing countries in Asia was 3%). Under the impact of weather events such as the El Niño and droughts, the grain yield, more than half of the total farm output, fell by 1.95%.

[24] Source of data: World Economic Forum.

[25] Reference: Regional Economic Outlook 2016: Asia and Pacific, by IMF.

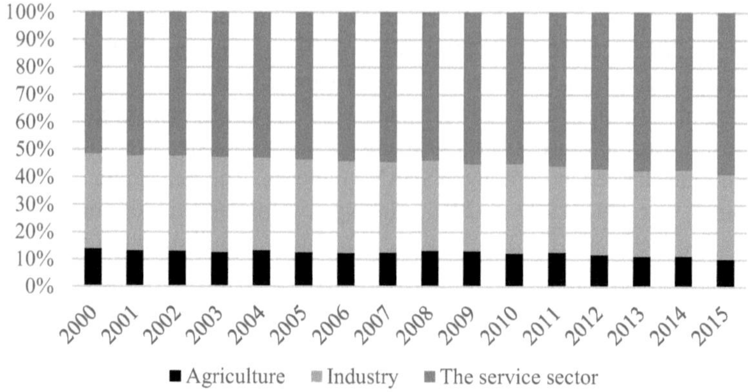

Fig. 5.49 Industrial structure of the Philippines. *Source of data* World Bank database

(2) The secondary industry

The total industrial output value of the Philippines in 2015 grew by 5.97% to 90.188 billion USD, within which the manufacturing contributed 65.05%, the construction 22.3%, energy 10.2% and mining 2.5%. Light industrial products such as electronics and food accounted for about 60% of the manufacturing output. The average production index of the Philippines in 2015 was − 4.42%, and the growth rate of the manufacturing industry was only 2.5%, much lower than the 10.5% in 2014. These were the results of sluggish global economy and weak demand. The construction sector stood out and continued its rapid growth at more than 10% (the fourth consecutive year).

(3) The tertiary industry

As the dominant force among the three industries, the service industry has a significant impact on the overall economic development of the Philippines. In 2015, its added value totaled 171.803 billion USD, a year-on-year increase of 6.7%. The total value of import and export of services was 55.44 billion USD, up by 17.5%, while the trade of goods decreased by 1.7%. Service outsourcing is the biggest feature of its service industry. More than 1000 housekeeping service outsourcing companies made about 22 billion USD in 2015, a year-on-year increase of 16.4%, and created more than 1.2 million jobs. In terms of tourism, the number of international tourist arrivals in the Philippines reached 5.36 million in 2015, an increase of 10.9%, and tourism revenue climbed by 5.9% to 5 billion USD, accounting for 8% of the GDP.

2. Urban structure

As Fig. 5.50 shows, by 2015, the Philippine urbanization rate was 44.37%, which had great potential for growth. One thing special about the urbanization rate is that it has been declining since it hit 48.95% in 1990. Investment in construction and fixed equipment, increasingly important to economic growth, both increased by more than

10% in 2015, pushing up the social capital by 4.8% to 60.9 billion USD, or 23.5% of the GDP. See Fig. 5.51 for more information. Foreign capital mainly flows to the manufacturing and energy sectors.

3. Government finances

Due to its continued strong economic growth in recent years and the gradual reduction of the fiscal deficit after the financial crisis, the Philippine sovereign credit rating was upgraded to BBB by the world's three major rating agencies. In terms of balance of payments, in 2014, the fiscal deficit was 2.858 billion USD, and in 2015 there was a balance of 2.616 billion USD. At the end of 2015, the foreign exchange reserve exceeded 80 billion USD, which was six times the short-term foreign debt, and could cover the total imports in the last 10 months. In 2015, the fiscal deficit soared to 121.7 billion pesos, an increase of 66.5%, and 1.6% of the GDP (which was basically

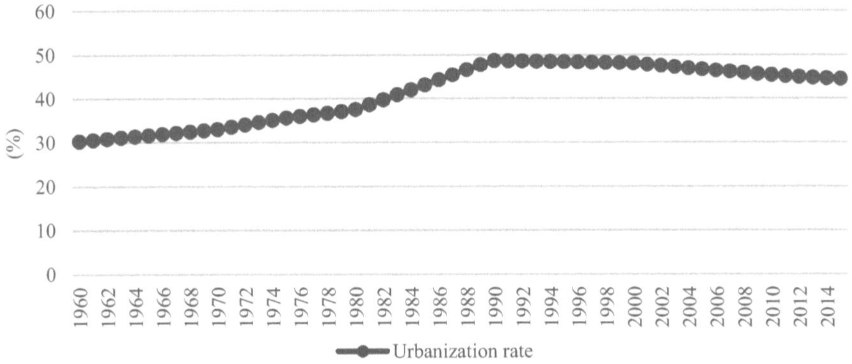

Fig. 5.50 Urbanization rate of the Philippines. *Source of data* World Bank database

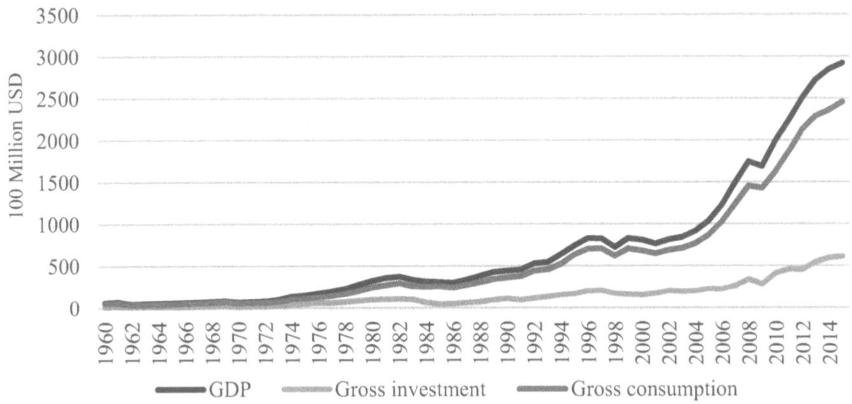

Fig. 5.51 Gross investment and consumption in the Philippines. *Source of data* World Bank database

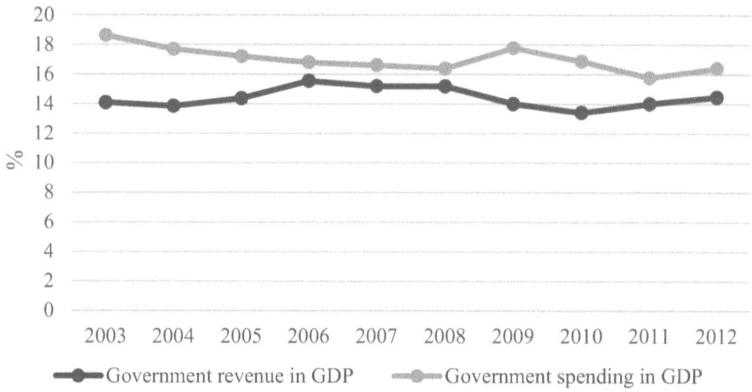

Fig. 5.52 Proportions of government revenue and spending in the Philippine GDP. *Source of data* World Bank database

controllable). For more details, see Fig. 5.52. The domestic debt balance accounted for 36.8% of GDP, a significant decrease compared to 2010; the total external debt reached 77.4 billion USD, or 26.5% of the GDP, continuing the downward trend after the financial crisis.[26]

4. Income level

Thanks to the rapid economic development, the per capita disposable income had increased significantly since 2003, reaching 3112 USD in 2014, higher than the per capita GDP over the same period (2873 USD). The Gini coefficient declined steadily after reaching a peak of 0.46 in 2000 and was 0.43 in 2012, still higher than the internationally recognized alert line of 0.4, as Fig. 5.53 presents. The national savings plunged in 2011 and then steadily recovered. During the same period, the national saving rate performed similarly, but still fell short of the level in 2000–2010. Figure 5.54 shows the national savings accounted for 29.3% of the GNI in 2014. In 2015, the Philippines was rated as a low-and-middle-income country by the World Bank.

5. Population structure

In 2015, the total population of the Philippines was 100.7 million, ranking 12th globally. In terms of age structure, as shown in Fig. 5.55, the large working population base provides the Philippines with sufficient human resources. However, with the rapid population growth, the burden of education, employment, social security, etc. had been growing, and the scale of poverty and social instability had expanded.

In terms of the education level of the labor force, 73.30% of the labor force has received secondary education and approximately 25% is of higher education. For more information, see Table 5.7. Due to long-term colonization by European and

[26] Source of data: Economic and Commercial Counsellor's Office of the Embassy of the People's Republic of China in the Republic of Philippines.

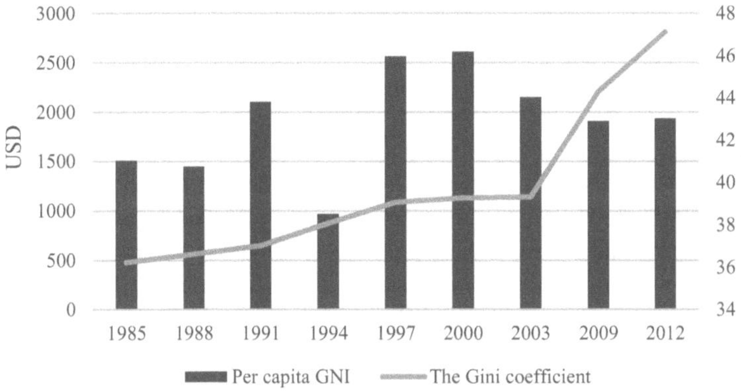

Fig. 5.53 Per capita GNI and the Gini coefficient in the Philippines. *Source of data* World Bank database

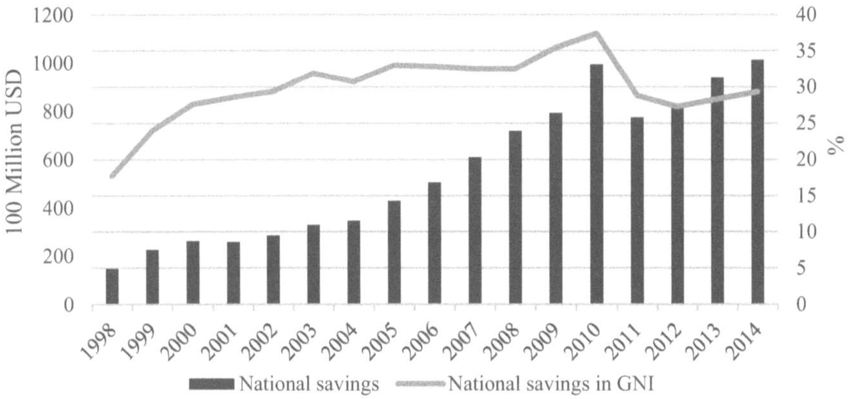

Fig. 5.54 National savings in the Philippines. *Source of data* World Bank database

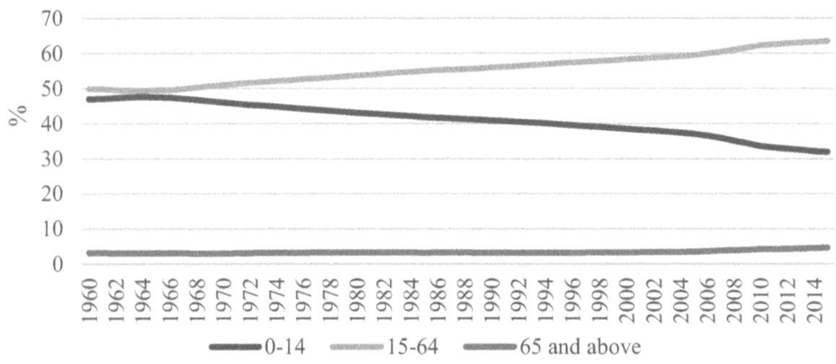

Fig. 5.55 Human resources of the Philippines. *Source of data* World Bank database

American countries, Filipinos are tolerant of different cultures, and more than 70% of them speak fluent English.

Table 5.8 lists the industrial features and functions of major cities in the Philippines.

Quezon is the largest metropolis and the former capital of the Philippines. It was founded in 1939 and is named after the former President of the Philippines, Manuel Quezon. In 1948, the Philippine Congress passed a resolution to make it the capital. Till 1976, Quezon had served as the capital and is still the seat of the Congress. After 1976, Manila was made the capital again. In 1975, Quezon, together with Manila and Pasig, formed the Greater Capital Region, of which Quezon takes up a quarter. Quezon has two prestigious universities: the University of the Philippines and the Ateneo De Manila University. The citizens are mainly Catholic, and the mayor is

Table 5.7 Human resources and education levels in the Philippines in 2015

Category of the labor force	Proportion/Amount
The proportion of females with middle school education within the total female labor force	66.60%
The proportion of males with middle school education within the total male labor force	77.60%
The proportion of people with middle school education within the total labor force	73.30%
The proportion of females with higher education within the total female labor force	31.80%
The proportion of males with higher education within the total male labor force	20.70%
The proportion of people with higher education within the total labor force	25%
The proportion of females within the total labor force	39.09%
Total labor force	42.0277 million
Total population	101 million

Source of data Philippine Statistical Authority

Table 5.8 Major cities of the Philippines in 2015

City	Population	City profile
Quezon	2,936,116	The satellite city of the capital Manila; the largest city
Manila	1,780,148	The capital; the center of economy, industry, culture and education; the largest port
Davao	1,632,991	A port; a hub of foreign trade; the processing center of Manila hemp
Cebu	922,611	The shipping center in the central Philippines; the second largest economic center
Zamboanga	861,799	An important port of transshipping in the south; a tourist resort

Source of data Philippine Statistical Authority

directly elected by the citizens. The Quezon City government is quite wealthy and the infrastructure is second to none in the Philippines.

As the capital of the Philippines, Manila is located on the eastern shore of Manila Bay in Luzon. Founded by Spanish colonists in 1571, it is the second largest city in the country. Due to its long history, Manila has a large number of landmark sights and buildings. It serves as the economic, cultural, educational and industrial center and the core of the development for the greater capital region. With small land area and large population, the megacity has a population density of 42,000/km^2,[27] ranking first in the world. Manila is a highly international city—located at the center of the maritime trade routes in the Western Pacific, it is called the "Pearl of the East".

Davao is the third largest city in the Philippines. It has been a municipality directly under the central government since 1936. Located at the southeast of Mindanao and the north of Davao Bay, it has an area of 2433 km^2. In addition, it is an important tourism and port city in the Philippines. With a large seaport and an airport, it is a transport hub that connects the Philippines to the outside world.

Cebu, also a municipality directly under the central government, is the capital of the Cebu province and the economic and cultural center of the Visayas. Built in 1565, Cebu was Magellan's first landing place in the Philippines. Many Spanish castles, churches and streets still remain in the city. Cebu Port, located on the northwest side of the city, is a natural harbor and the second largest port in the Philippines. Today Cebu has developed into a shipping and air transportation center in the south-central Philippines. The majority of Cebu citizens are Catholic.

Located in the southwest of Mindanao, Zamboanga is also a municipality under the central government. Founded in 1635, it is an important international transshipment port in the southern Philippines. The main industries include tourism, cocoa oil production and fishing. More than 64% of the citizens are Catholics and 24% are Muslims. Because of the concurrent influence of two major religions at the same time, Zamboanga, home to both Catholic churches and mosques, is an integration of European and Islamic cultures. Due to its proximity to Brunei, Indonesia and Malaysia, Zamboanga has close trade relations with them.

(II) Foreign trade and investment

Against the background of negative growth (over − 10%) of global trade, the total trade value of the Philippines in 2015 was 125.33 billion USD, down by 1.7%; of which total exports were 58.648 billion USD, a decrease of 5.6%, and total imports were 66.685 billion USD, up by 2%. Overall, the Philippines performed well. However, it is worrying that the Philippines continued to run deficits for many years. For instance, the deficit in 2015 soared to 8037 billion USD, up by 143.8%.

1. Foreign trade

In 2015, the total trade between the Philippines and its top ten trading partners was worth 101.928 billion USD, accounting for nearly 80% of its total foreign trade. The

[27] Source of data: 2015 Census of the Philippines.

three major import sources of the Philippines are the Chinese mainland, the United States and Japan, and its three major export destinations are Japan, the United States and Hong Kong, China.

If both import and export count, its largest trading partner in 2015 was Japan (total trade volume of 18.67 billion USD), contributing 14.4% of the total foreign trade. Its trade surplus with Japan was 5.93 billion USD (12.30 billion USD for exports and 6.37 billion USD for imports). Its main exports to Japan are electronic goods (30.2%), followed by woodcarvings and furniture. Electronics and transportation equipment are the main import commodities.

China was its second largest trading partner. The total bilateral trade was worth 17.65 billion USD, slightly smaller than that with Japan. In 2015, the Philippines exported 6.175 billion USD of goods to China and imported 11.471 billion USD in goods. Different from with Japan, the Philippines had a trade deficit with China (5.296 billion USD). Its exports to China mainly included electronics and minerals, and the main imports were electronics and steel.

The Philippines' third largest trading partner was the United States, with a bilateral trade volume of 16.49 billion USD and a surplus of 1.554 billion USD. The Philippines mainly exports electronics and clothing to the United States and imports electronics and animal feed. Following the United States, other large trading partners were Singapore (at 8.81 billion USD), Hong Kong of China (at 8.23 billion USD), Taiwan of China, Thailand, South Korea, Germany and Malaysia. If the mainland and Hong Kong of China are combined, their trade volume with the Philippines will be much larger than Japan's.

2. International investment

According to the Philippine Statistical Authority, the growth rate of foreign investment absorbed in 2015 reached 5.39 billion USD, up by 31.2%. The Netherlands, Japan, South Korea, the United States and Singapore were the top five investors, contributing 33.7%, 22.3%, 9.4%, 8.9% and 6.9%, respectively. Surprisingly, the total investment from China dropped by 87.3% in 2015, accounting for only 0.6%. The fluctuations of their diplomatic relations might be the reason. Sector-wise, the manufacturing, power, gas, steam and air-conditioning supply industries are favored by foreign investment. There is competition between the two countries in these areas, but opportunities of cooperation also exist.

In the field of foreign equity investment, the Philippines absorbed a total of 2.59 billion USD in 2015, an increase of 4.5%. 1.84 billion USD was newly added, an increase of 15.1%; the reinvestment amounted to 750 million USD, a decrease of 14.8%.[28] In 2015, 31.42 million USD of direct investment flew from China to the Philippines. As of the end of 2015, China's direct investment stock in the country was 432 million USD. The total turnover of Chinese companies in the Philippines was 857 million USD, an increase of 35.6% compared to 2014, and the value of newly signed contracts reached 1.316 billion USD. China sent 1255 workers of various

[28] Source of data: Bangko Sentral ng Pilipinas.

types throughout the year, and 1665 workers were in the Philippines at the end of the year, which was of a relatively small scale.[29]

5.7 Singapore

I. Geographical and historical backgrounds

Singapore is a city-state built on an island to the south of the Malay Peninsula. Guarding the southernmost exit of the Malacca Strait, it is separated from Indonesia by the Singapore Strait to the south, and from Malaysia by the Johor Strait to the north. Due to its special location, Singapore was the most important British strategic base in Southeast Asia until the Second World War. On August 9, 1965, Singapore became independent from the Malaysian Federation. On September 21, 1965, it joined the United Nations. In October of the same year, it joined the British Commonwealth. On August 8, 1967, it helped establish the ASEAN. Since independence in 1965, Singapore has grown fast under the leadership of Prime Minister Lee Kuan Yew. It has been transformed into a rich country, and one of the "Four Dragons" in Asia. As a country of immigrants, it is home to diverse races and cultures, and ranks among the most international countries in the world.

II. Economic development

(I) Domestic economy

Singapore has succeeded in its economic transformation. In the 1970s, although Singapore developed rapidly, it encountered many difficulties and challenges. For example, the economic stagnation of western countries, the shrinking of markets, and the rise of trade protectionism had all affected its exports and imports. Moreover, the fast economic development of neighboring countries and their efforts to build export-oriented economy and achieve industrialization gradually weakened Singapore's advantages. In such a context, Singapore had to evaluate the situation, meet the challenges and formulate proper economic development strategies. When Singapore began to study and formulate economic development plans for the 1980s in the late 1970s, it actively exchanged and cooperated with developed countries by studying their economic conditions and introducing them to Singaporean economy. High-ranking officials such Lee Kuan Yew himself made many special trips to Japan, South Korea, the United States and European countries. Later, the Singapore Economic Development Board set up 17 offices in Western European countries, the United States, Canada, Japan, etc. Outstanding talents were selected to work in those offices to promote the investment environment of Singapore, and to attract foreign investors. In addition, the country began to prioritize the development of high-tech products.

---

[29] Source of data: Ministry of Commerce of the People's Republic of China.

In July 1979, the government timely proposed a new economic development strategy, known as the "second industrial revolution", also known as the economic restructuring strategy. Regarding this policy, Lee Kuan Yew stated: "The old method is no longer applicable, and a new strategy is imperative. We must not fail on this". "In the past 15 years, we have achieved outstanding results in the process of industrialization. Our industrial output value has grown to 35% of GNP, reaching the standards of developed countries. Singapore's trade volume exceeds that of all other Southeast Asian countries combined. However, we need a second industrial revolution to move from labor-intensive industries to high-technology Industry, that is, to build precision industry through mechanization, automation, and computerization". To achieve the above goals, the government formulated a series of specific measures, such as revising the wage policy and shifting from low wages to high wages: in order to make the industrial structure more reasonable, a substantial increase in employee wages was a necessary choice because raising wages would force enterprises to carry out technological transformation and abandon labor-intensive products, which would relocate talents to technology- and capital-intensive industries; encouraging foreign investment in high-tech industries and providing preferential treatments to emerging industries: 11 products were prioritized for the next 10 years of development, mainly including components of automatic equipment, mechanical equipment, medical equipment, chemicals, computer software and hardware, optical instruments, electronic equipment and hydropower control products; encouraging scientific research and the R&D of new products: considering the government's proposal, the Parliament amended the Income Tax Act to provide double tax reductions for expenditures on scientific research and development projects, and other measures included building the National Science and Technology Industrial Park near the National University of Singapore to create a good environment for scientific research, and setting up the National Computer Committee to bring in advanced foreign experts and scholars for training and research; improving technical training and the quality of human resources: Singapore lacks natural resources but is rich in human resources, to take advantage of which it had to first improve the quality of talents, and measures for such purpose include reforming the education system, adjusting and expanding higher education institutions, improving the quality of teaching, providing training courses to generate professionals and jointly building training centers with multinational companies.

The Asian financial crisis that spread from Thailand in 1997 severely affected the development of Singapore. The shrinking demand for its electronics and its high labor costs forced many multinational companies to close their factories in Singapore and relocate to other countries. By 1998, as the crisis worsened, the growth rate of Singaporean economy slowed to 1.5% and even turned negative. The losses and even bankruptcy of some enterprises caused more than 30,000 employees to lose their jobs, pushing up the unemployment rate to 3.2%. The state revenue decreased by 7.8%, the transaction volume on the foreign exchange market fell by 16%, and total foreign trade plunged by 75%. At that time, many factories were vacant overnight in the famous Jurong Industrial Park. Seagate Technology, a large multinational company that produces disk drives, moved two factories to China at once, reducing the share of Singaporean output from 73 to 50% of the world's total. Facing the harsh financial environment and the challenge of low labor costs in emerging industrial countries, Singapore begun to adjust its economic structure and industrial structure: it reduced its dependence on the low-end electronics industry and began to attract and enhance high-end electronics industry; it kept introducing and cultivating emerging industries to upgrade its industrial structure; it developed life sciences and environmental protection industries to break the bottleneck of Singapore's heavy dependence on electronics, precision machinery, oil refining, petrochemicals and shipbuilding; it took advantage of its clean air and first-class ecological environment to promote development of life sciences and environmental protection industries; it expanded the water industry, making Singapore the center of sewage treatment technology and industry center, and thus turning water scarcity from a disadvantage into an advantage; it turned itself into a regional education center by developing its education industry; it continued to attract talents with high salaries, in the hope of attracting elites from all walks of life (including doctors, lawyers, accountants, university professors, entrepreneurs, bankers and other outstanding talents with capability and good moral characters) to work as government leaders. In 2002, Singapore began a new round of economic transformation to maintain its competitive edges with innovative, flexible and pragmatic measures: it carried out a comprehensive review of its development strategies; it introduced and developed life sciences and the environment protection industry to break the stereotype; it built two casinos and hosted the first F1 night event; it successfully bid for the 2010 Youth Olympic Games; it successfully operated a sovereign wealth fund; and it signed free trade agreements with the world's major economic powers. At the same time, with Singapore as the center and a 7-h flight distance as the radius, Singapore formulated the "7-hour Economic Circle Development Strategy". Based on the successful realization of the "Headquarters Economy" strategy, it continued to consolidate its status as the regional center for world trade, transshipment, aviation, conference, education, healthcare and medicine, as well as finance. (A 7-h flight radius covers all Southeast Asian countries, and Hong Kong, Taipei, Beijing, Shanghai, Tokyo, Seoul, New Delhi, Mumbai, Mauritius, Perth, Melbourne, Sydney and other cities.) Because the concept of a creative "bilateral free trade agreement" was first proposed, Singapore has been highly appreciated by the WTO and received positive response from various countries for putting forward the concept of "bilateral free trade agreement" for the first time. So far, it has signed free trade agreements with more than a dozen countries and regions including the United States, China, Japan, South Korea and the European Union. Visionary economic policies, flexible responses, efficient administrative measures and extensive world connections have laid a solid foundation for Singapore to continue to be a globally competitive economy. Since 2009, Singapore's economy has achieved sustained growth. According to World Bank data, Singapore's GDP in 2015 was 287.02 billion USD, an increase of 2.1% over the previous year, and per capita GDP increased by 0.81% to 51,855 USD.

Singapore is a developed country with relative rapid economic growth. Before the financial crisis, the economy had been growing at a rate of 5–10%. Affected by the sluggish global growth in 2010, Singapore's GDP growth slowed down and had fallen below 5% in the past three years. For more information, see Figs. 5.56, 5.57 and 5.58.

As shown in Fig. 5.59, thanks to its status as a trade center, Singapore is an obvious export-oriented country. Net exports account for an important part of the GDP, and the proportion has gradually increased. Its gross trade volume occupies a leading position in the world.

1. Industrial structure

As shown in Fig. 5.60, the service industry had always dominated Singapore's economy—it had slowly increased from 66.2% in 1996 to 70% in 2014. It can be said that the service industry is the absolute dominating force in Singapore. The industry also occupies a relatively important position in Singaporean economy, and its proportion had fallen from 33.6 to 25.9% in the past 20 years. Singapore has almost no agriculture.

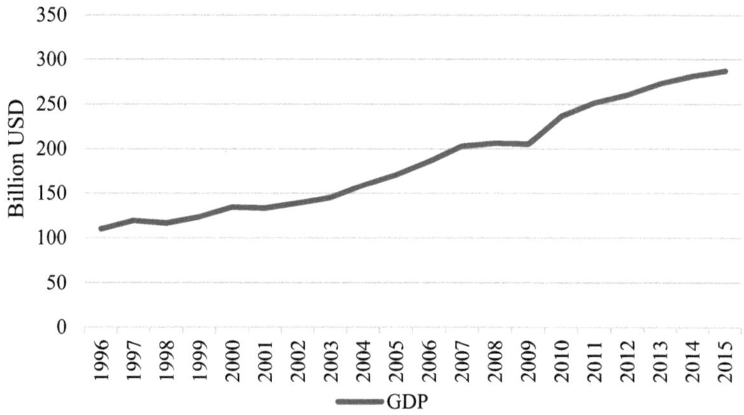

Fig. 5.56 GDP of Singapore. *Source of data* World Bank database

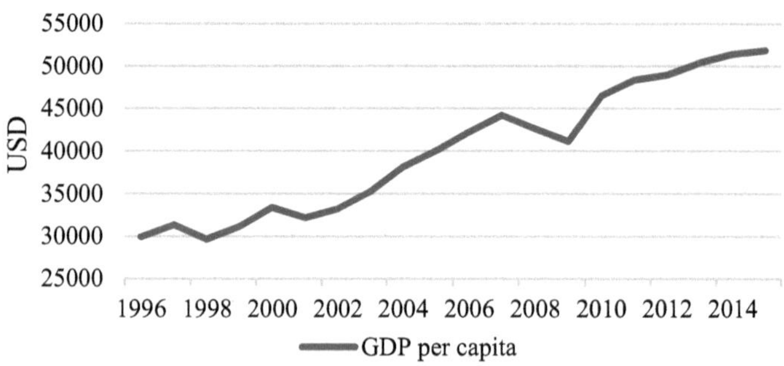

Fig. 5.57 Per capita GDP of Singapore. *Source of data* World Bank database

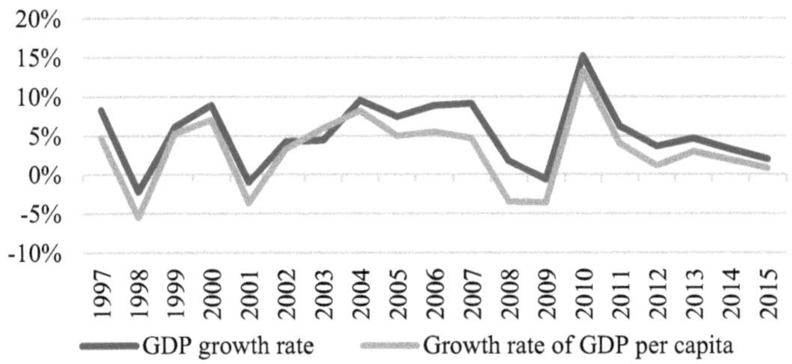

Fig. 5.58 Growth rates of GDP and per capita GDP of Singapore. *Source of data* World Bank database

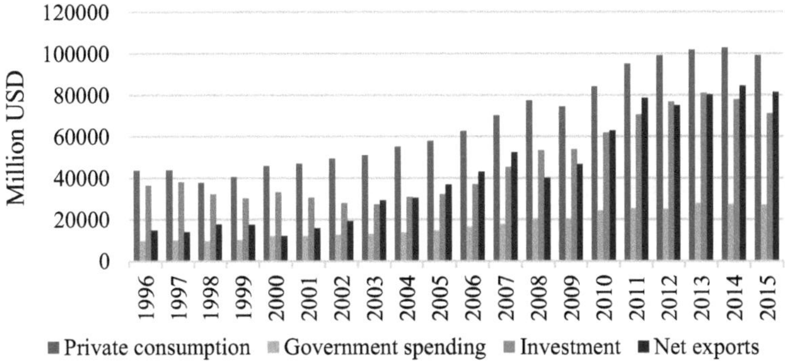

Fig. 5.59 GDP structure of Singapore. *Source of data* Ministry of Trade and Industry, Singapore; Bloomberg

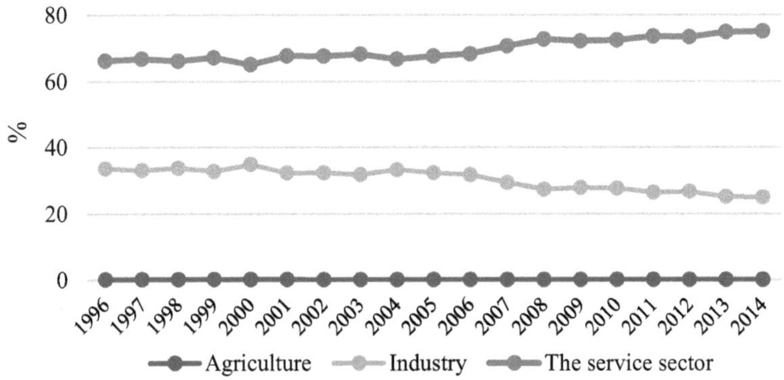

Fig. 5.60 Changes of industrial structure in Singapore. *Source of data* World Bank database

In Singapore's GDP in 2014, manufacturing accounted for 17.4%, wholesale and retail industry 16.5%, business services 14.9%, finance and insurance industry 11.8% and transportation and storage 6.5%.

(1) The secondary industry

As the world's third largest oil refining center and one of the oil trading hubs, Singapore is Asia's pricing center of petroleum products. Its daily crude oil processing capacity exceeds 1.3 million barrels. In 2014, Singapore's petrochemical industry generated 103.48 billion SGD, 34.1% of its total manufacturing output, and employed 26,200 people. As one of Singapore's traditional industries, the electronics industry in 2014 produced 82.69 billion SGD, 27.2% of the total manufacturing output. The precision engineering industry in 2014 registered 37.18 billion SGD of output, 12.2% of the total manufacturing output. As an emerging strategic industry given priority in recent years, the biopharmaceutical industry achieved an output of 21.47 billion SGD in 2014, 7.1% of the total manufacturing output. The internationally renowned pharmaceutical companies, including the top 10 giants, have built branches at Biopolis and the Tuas Biomedical Park.

(2) The tertiary industry

Singapore is the fourth largest financial center, the third largest foreign exchange trading center and the sixth largest wealth management center in the world. It is also the dollar market center in Asia and the second largest clearing center for offshore renminbi. The output value of the finance and insurance industry in 2014 was 46.03 billion SGD, accounting for 11.8% of GDP. The major commercial banks in Singapore are Development Bank of Singapore (DBS), United Overseas Bank (UOB) and OCBC Bank. In addition, the wholesale and retail sector and business services also take up an important part of GDP.

2. Population structure

Singapore's population experienced rapid growth after 2004 and has stabilized in recent years. As shown in Fig. 5.61, Singapore's total population in June 2014 was 5.4697 million, of which 3.871 million were local residents (including 3.343 million citizens and 528,000 permanent residents), and 1.599 million were non-residents. The growth rate of population was 1.3%, and the population density was 7615 people/km^2. Singapore has no rural population.

The Singapore government's white paper on population policy published in 2013 pointed out that the country's population was aging. Its fertility rate was as low as in other developed countries and regions such as Japan, and Hong Kong and Taiwan of China. For more information, see Fig. 5.62.

(II) Foreign trade and investment

According to the statistics of the International Enterprise Singapore (IES), in 2014, Singapore achieved 776.06 billion USD of foreign trade, a decrease of 0.9% from the previous year (the same below): the exports were 409.79 billion USD, down

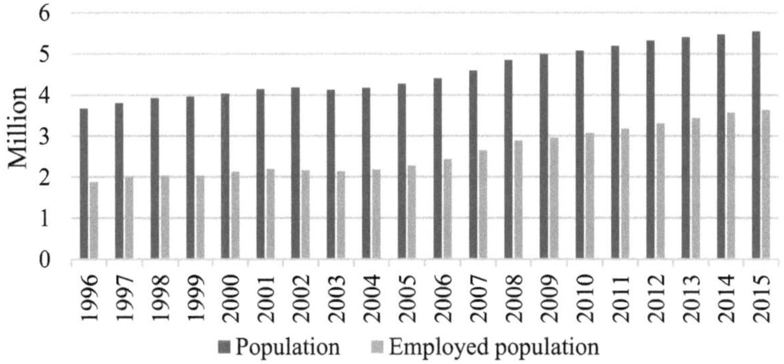

Fig. 5.61 Population and working population of Singapore. *Source of data* Department of Statistics, Singapore, Ministry of Manpower, Singapore; Bloomberg

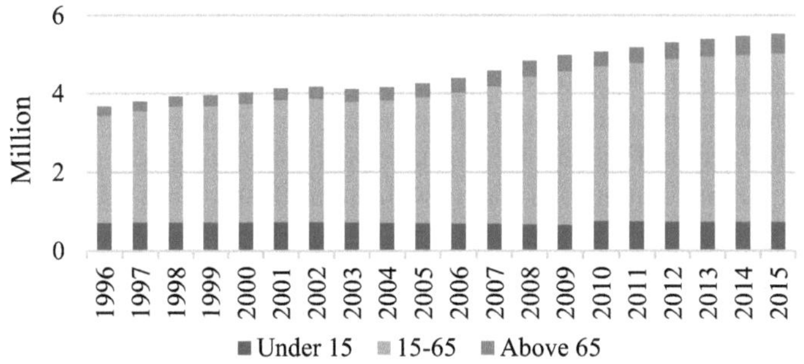

Fig. 5.62 Age structure of Singaporean population. *Source of data* United States Census Bureau

0.1%; the imports were 366.27 billion USD, down 1.8%; and trade surplus was 43.52 billion USD, up 16.8%. From 2005 to 2014, the growth rate of Singapore's exports decreased to around 2.3% except for 2008 (when it was less than 2.25% due to the financial crisis) and 2014 (when it grew to 2.58%).

Singapore mainly exports mechanical and electrical products, mineral products and chemical products. In 2014, the export values of these three types of goods were 178.75 billion USD, 68.94 billion USD and 38.05 billion USD, accounting for 43.6%, 16.8% and 9.3% of Singapore's total exports. The export values of mechanical and electrical products and mineral products fell by 3.6 and 2.7%, and for chemical products there was a 2.7% increase. At the same time, mechanical and electrical products and mineral products are the top two categories of goods imported by Singapore. In 2014, their import values, at 139.36 billion USD and 114.85 billion USD and down by 3.0% and 2.8% respectively, accounted for 38.1% and 31.4% of the country's total.

1. Foreign trade

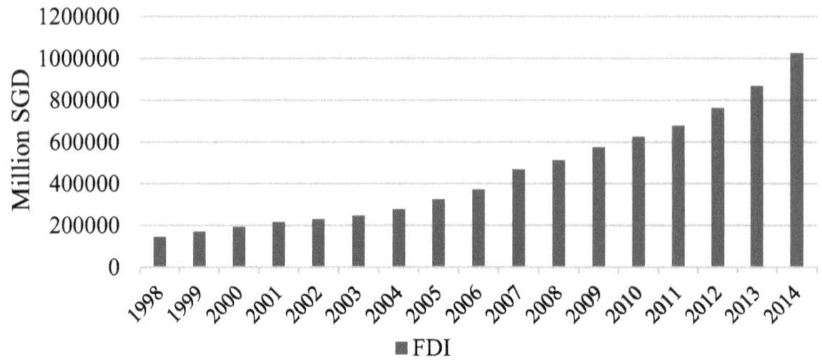

Fig. 5.63 FDI in Singapore. *Source of data* Department of Statistics, Singapore, Bloomberg

The trade competitiveness index is the ratio of the trade surplus against the total trade volume. From 2005 to 2014, the index of Singapore's mineral products was negative, indicating that the import value of such products was greater than the export value, and the trade deficit of resource-intensive products was expanding; in contrast, the index for chemical products and mechanical and electrical goods were positive and saw little fluctuation. For instance, for mechanical and electrical products, the gap between export and import was stable, with an index at around 0.1.

2. International investment

Encouraging foreign investment is the basic policy of Singapore. According to the World Investment Report 2015 released by UNCTAD, the foreign investment flow in Singapore reached 73.287 billion USD in 2014, as shown in Fig. 5.63. As of the end of 2014, Singapore's stock of foreign investment reached 912.36 billion USD. Foreign investment in Singapore mainly comes from the European Union (26.1%), the United States (13.4%), Japan (8.4%) and offshore financial centers such as the British Virgin Islands, Cayman Islands and Bermuda. China's direct investment in Singapore is of relatively small scale.

The distribution of FDI among different industries reflects the characteristics of Singapore's economic structure. FDI is concentrated in manufacturing, consumer services, finance, and technology and education services—47.85% for financial insurance, 17.67% for manufacturing, 17.14% for wholesale and retail, 6.05% for professional and administrative services, 4.32% for transportation and storage, and 3.47% for real estate industry. For more information, please see Fig. 5.64. The finance industry is a large recipient of foreign investment—the increase from 100 billion SGD in 2005 to more than 600 billion SGD in 2015 proves Singapore's status as Asia's financial center. The direct investment absorbed by manufacturing industry and consumer service industry has also been growing. It is worth noting that the scale of FDI in technology and education services reached 100 billion SGD in 2015.

The sources of FDI in Singapore are relatively stable. As Fig. 5.65 presents, Europe had been the dominant investor and its share was growing. ASEAN countries, China,

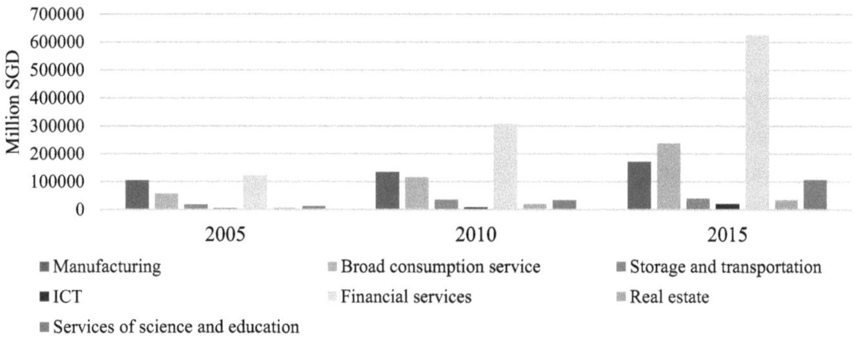

Fig. 5.64 Distribution of FDI in Singapore. *Source of data* Bloomberg

Japan and the United States had increased direct investment in Singapore over the years. In 2005, China was hardly involved, but this is no longer the case.

III. Future orientation of cooperation between China and Malaysia

Yang Xiaoyan (2015), in the *Blue Book of Industry: Annual Report on Industrial Competitiveness of China*, calculates the trade complementarity index of China and Singapore using the WTO data of the bilateral trade (Yang 2015). It is generally believed that the larger the index, the greater the proportion of intra-industry trade between the two countries, and thus the higher the trade complementarity.

The trade complementarity indexes of major trade commodities indicate that China and Singapore are complementary in some industries. Specifically, as Table 5.9 shows, for mechanical and electrical goods, China's exports are complementary with Singapore's imports of major commodities, and such relations exist for textiles and clothing, too, but the complementarity is waning. For mineral products, chemical products and especially mechanical and electrical products, China's imports are complementary with Singapore's exports.

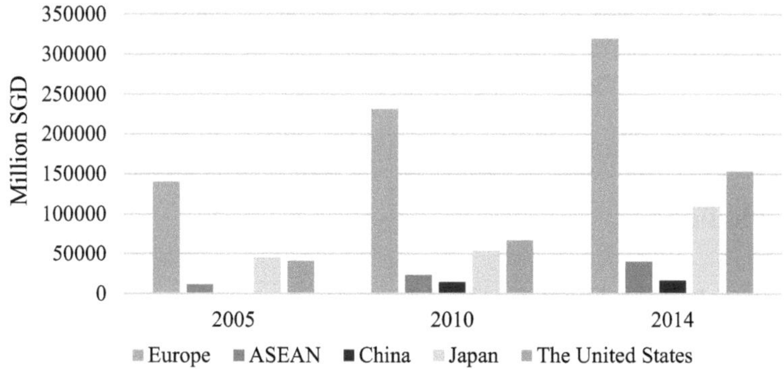

Fig. 5.65 Sources of FDI in Singapore. *Source of data* Bloomberg

Table 5.9 Trade complementarity index based on major Chinese exports and Singaporean imports

Category	2000	2005	2010	2014
Agricultural products	0.32	0.18	0.14	0.14
Mineral products	0.38	0.27	0.21	0.22
Steel and iron products	0.45	0.49	0.49	0.76
Chemical products	0.33	0.26	0.29	0.33
Mechanic and electric products	1.22	1.90	2.01	1.76
Transportation equipment	0.09	0.13	0.21	0.16
Textiles	1.05	0.73	0.58	0.47
Garment	2.19	1.52	0.94	0.80

In general, China and Singapore enjoy strong industrial complementarity, especially in the area of mechanical and electrical products. The complementarity index is above 1.5 for trades of both directions, indicating both countries have competitive products within a certain industrial sector. In future cooperation, China and Singapore should continue to import each other's competitive goods.

In addition, the sector-wise distribution of FDI in Singapore suggests China should focus its investment in the following sectors of Singapore.

① Biopharmaceutical industry. As an emerging industry with good prospects and great vitality, it has attracted the attention of many countries, including Singapore. Singapore has adopted a series of measures to attract foreign capital to invest in a variety of industries, including the biopharmaceutical industry.

② Information Technology and Communications. In 2006, the Singaporean government proposed the ten-year development blueprint of "Smart Country 2015", in which the IT and communication industry is listed as a key driver for the country's functional transition and the forging of a global city.

③ Logistics and storage. Since the eighteenth century, Singapore has been the main transit point for trade between China, India and Southeast Asia. Therefore, it has a developed logistics and storage industry, and great demand for such products.

④ Consumer services in a broader sense. It includes retailing, tourism and food processing. With its unique natural scenery and the status as a shipping center, Singapore has attracted a large number of foreign visitors, which means a big travel market.

5.8 Thailand

I. **Geographical and historical backgrounds**

Thailand, located in the central part of the Indo-China Peninsula, is an ASEAN member country and one of the "four tigers" in Asia. It is an emerging industrial power, the largest natural rubber exporter, the fifth largest exporter of agricultural products, the only net grain exporter in Asia, and a famous tourist resort. Geographically, it borders the Gulf of Thailand on the east, the Andaman Sea on the southwest, Myanmar on the west, Laos and Cambodia on the east and north, and Malaysia on the south. Its land area is 513,120 km^2, more than 50% of which are plains and lowlands. It has vast sea area with a coastline of 2705 km. In terms of natural conditions, it has a tropical monsoon climate with three seasons: the hot season, the rainy season and the dry season. The average annual temperature is 20–30 °C, and the average humidity is 66–82%.

As of 2016, there were 64.5 million people in Thailand, of which 40% were Thai and more than 90% were Buddhists. The official language is Thai. In terms of politics and judicature, Thailand adopts the constitutional monarchy and separates powers between the king, the government and the army.

Thailand is rich in mineral resources, such as potash, tin, lignite, oil shale, natural gas, zinc, lead, tungsten, iron, antimony, chromium, barite, gemstones and petroleum. Among them, potassium salt reserves are 400 billion tons, ranking first in the world; tin reserves are about 1.2 million tons, accounting for 12% of the world's total. The total forest area is 14.4 million ha, with a coverage rate of 25%. It enjoys abundant fishery resources, with marine fishing grounds such as the Gulf of Thailand and Andaman Bay, and more than 1100 km^2 of freshwater fish farms. It has the third largest marine fishery in Asia, after Japan and China.

II. **Economic development**

(I) Domestic economy

As an emerging industrial country, Thailand is the second largest economy in Southeast Asia after Indonesia. Adopting a laissez-faire approach, it has an export-oriented economy that depends on foreign markets such as the United States, Japan and China. In the 1990s, Thailand maintained a high growth rate before the Asian financial crisis in 1998, and was listed as one of the "four tigers" in Asia. It was hit hard by the financial crisis. In the twenty-first century, the Thai economy has performed well. In July 2003, the 17.2 billion USD loan provided by the International Monetary Fund during the financial crisis was paid off two years in advance. Later, the Thai economy saw fluctuations due to the impact of the global financial crisis in 2008 and recovered again after 2010. After 2013, Thailand saw economic downturn and even negative growth under the influence of political instability and weak global economic recovery. At present, Thailand has regained political stability. The Thai government will launch a 20-year national development strategy, "Thailand 4.0", to build high value-added industries.

Living standards in Thailand are relatively high. In 2015, Thailand's per capita GDP was 5814.77 USD, ranking No. 4 in ASEAN after Singapore, Brunei and Malaysia, making it an upper-middle-income country. For more information, see Figs. 5.66, 5.67 and 5.68.

1. Industrial structure

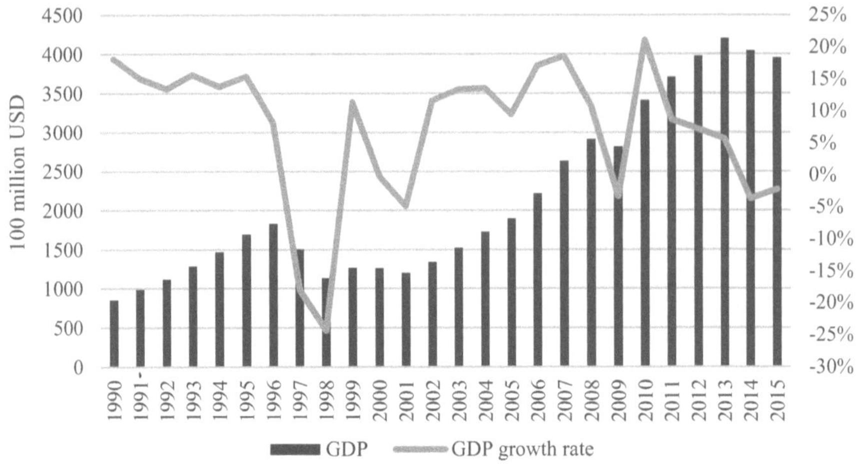

Fig. 5.66 GDP of Thailand. *Source of data* World Bank database

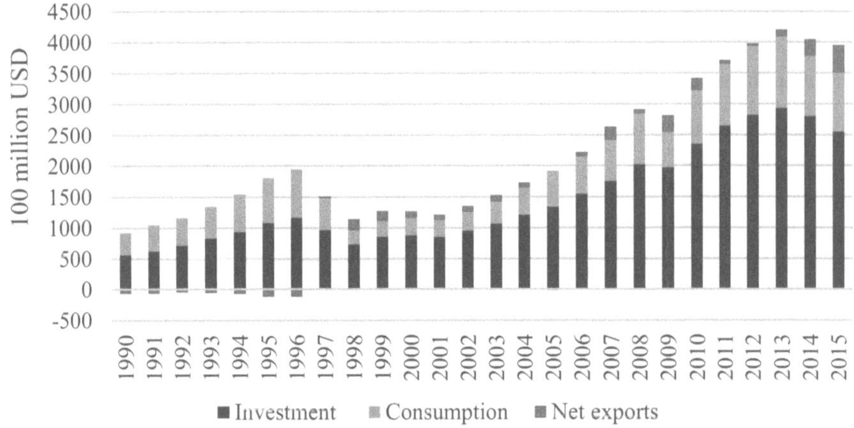

Fig. 5.67 GDP structure of Thailand. *Source of data* World Bank database

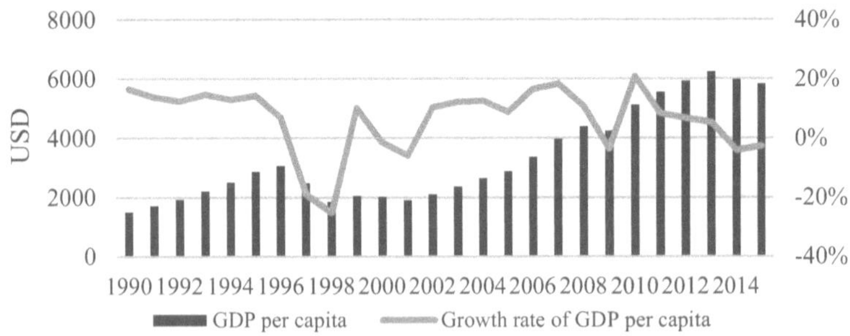

Fig. 5.68 Per capita GDP of Thailand. *Source of data* World Bank database

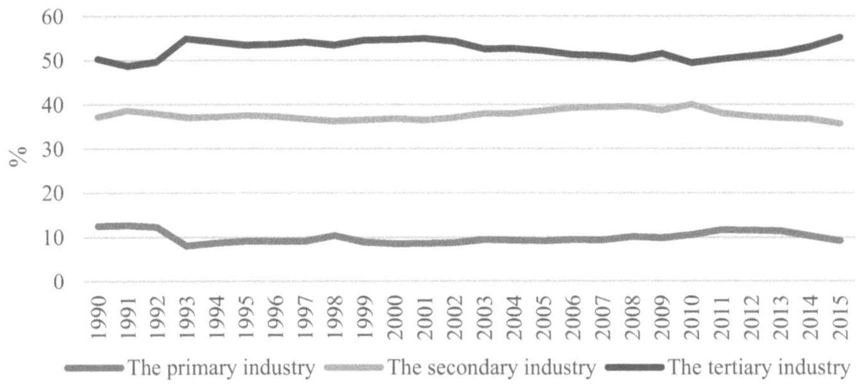

Fig. 5.69 Industrial structure of Thailand

As for the changes of the structure of three industries, Fig. 5.69 shows that Thailand's industrial structure has been relatively stable. The service industry is of the largest proportion (over 50%); following it is industry at about 40%; agriculture contributes about 10%.

(1) The primary industry

Thailand is a traditional agricultural country, and agricultural products are one of the main sources of foreign exchange. Major agricultural products include rice, natural rubber, cassava, corn, sugar cane, mung bean, hemp, tobacco, coffee beans, cotton, palm oil, coconut and so on. Thailand is one of the leading natural rubber exporters in the world.

Thailand has vast sea area and rich fishery resources. There are natural marine fishing grounds such as the Gulf of Thailand and Andaman Bay, and more than 1100 km^2 of freshwater fish farms. Bangkok, Songkhla, Phuket and other places are important fishery centers and fishery markets. Thailand is one of the major suppliers of fish products in the world and the third largest marine fishery country in Asia after Japan and China. There are about 500,000 people engaged in fishing in the country.

(2) The secondary industry

Thailand's industry is export-oriented and has a good foundation. The main categories are mining, textiles, electronics, plastics, food processing, toys, automobile assembly, building materials, petrochemicals, software, tires, furniture, etc.

The automobile industry in Thailand is relatively developed. In 2015, it produced 1.91 million vehicles, of which 330,000 were commercial vehicles. It is the largest automobile producer and exporter in ASEAN, larger than Malaysia, Vietnam and the Philippines combined. It is also the twelfth largest automobile producer and the sixth largest commercial vehicle producer in the world. In addition, Thailand is also the second largest hard disk exporter in the world and the fifth largest petrochemical center in Asia.

Under the "Thailand 4.0" strategy, ten industries have been identified as new engines for Thai economy. Among them, five enjoy competitive edges already, including next-generation automobile manufacturing, intelligent electronics, high-end tourism and medical tourism, agriculture and biotechnology and food processing. The other five are to be further developed, including industrial robotics, aviation and logistics, bioenergy and biochemical engineering, digital economy and medical centers.

(3) The tertiary industry

Tourism is the most important sector of Thailand's tertiary industry. Thailand is rich in tourism resources, and its tourism industry grows steadily, earning the country a lot of foreign exchange. There are more than 500 attractions in the country. Bangkok, Phuket, Pattaya, Chiang Mai, Chiang Rai, Hua Hin and Koh Samui are the most popular ones. Affected by the domestic political instability, the number of international visitors and international tourism revenue both declined in 2014, as shown in Fig. 5.70.

Road and air transportation are the major means of transportation in Thailand. All provinces and counties are connected by roads in all directions. There are 57 airports nationwide, 8 of which are international airports and 21 domestic cities are connected by flights. And the country has direct flights to more than 40 cities around the globe. Thailand's railway system is relatively underdeveloped—only 63% of districts are connected by railways. In terms of water transportation, the Mekong River and the Chao Phraya River are the two main waterway transportation routes in Thailand. There are also 47 ports in the country. Among them, most important ports are Laem Chabang Port, Bangkok Port, Chiang Saen Port, Chiang Khong Port and Ranong Port. In 2014, the Thailand's National Security Council approved the strategic planning of transportation infrastructure for 2015–2022, allocating 80 billion USD to update railways, highways and other infrastructure. Thailand has decided to cooperate with China to build high-speed railways and an intergovernmental cooperation framework agreement will be signed.

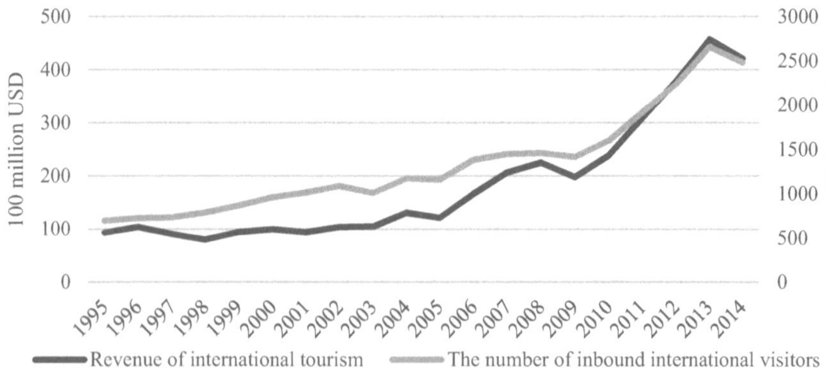

Fig. 5.70 Development of tourism in Thailand. *Source of data* World Bank database

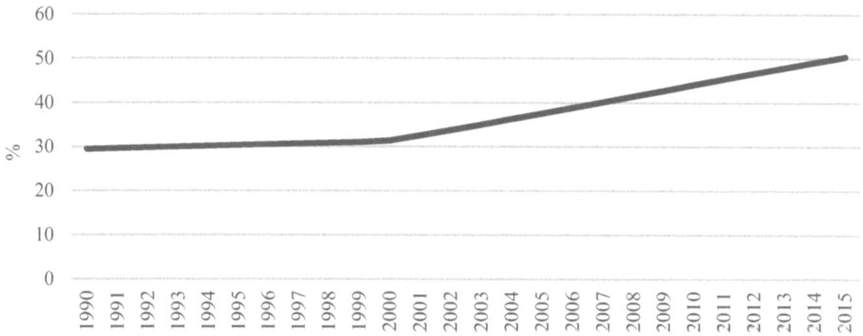

Fig. 5.71 Proportion of urban population. *Source of data* World Bank database

Table 5.10 Top five cities of Thailand

City	City profile
Bangkok	The capital and the economic center, producing 44% of Thailand's economy. It has well equipped ports on the Chao Phraya River and a well-developed tourism industry
Chiang Mai	The second largest city, and the capital of Chiang Mai Province. The political, economic and cultural center of northern Thailand. In 2006, the "Chiang Mai Initiative" was signed hire during the ASEAN "10 + 3" conference. It is also one of the host cities of Thailand's Ayutthaya World Expo in 2020
Kele	A border town and the northeast gate of Thailand. The main transportation hub and economic center of the northeast
Nonthaburi	Located on the left bank of Chao Phraya River; the satellite city of the capital; the capital of Nonthaburi Province and a trade center of agricultural product
Pattaya	A tourist city with beach resort

Source of data Based on public data

2. Population and cities

Urbanization is steadily making progress in Thailand. In 2015, the urbanization rate exceeded 50%, as shown in Fig. 5.71. The major cities are Bangkok (the capital), Chiang Mai, Kele, etc., as shown in Table 5.10. According to the World Bank report, Thailand's growth of urban population in the recent 10 years is mainly concentrated in Bangkok which has become the fifth largest city (area) and the ninth most densely populated city in Southeast Asia.[30]

Thailand's education has undergone three stages of recovery, rectification and development after the Second World War. It has implemented 12-year compulsory education. Famous universities include Chulalongkorn University, Thammasat University, Mahidol University, Kasetsart University, Chiang Mai University, etc. At present, the "Thailand 4.0" strategy is undermined by the lack of high-quality talents.

[30] East Asia's Changing Urban Landscape: Measuring a Decade of Spatial Growth.

In 2015, only 12.8% of the labor force have received higher education. According to the results of OECD's recent International Student Assessment Project (PISA), Thai students rank low in reading, math and science, and the percentage of students who are functionally illiterate (lack of common sense of life and work) grew 33% in 2012 to 50% in 2015. Against this background, the Thai government is not only looking for ways to improve the quality of the labor force, but also formulating various facilitation measures for the introduction of foreign talents.

(II) Foreign trade and investment

1. Foreign trade

Thailand is an export-oriented developing country. It has harmonious trade relations with major powers and thus large market coverage. The major trading partners of Thailand are China, Japan, South Korea, ASEAN, Europe and America, Australia and New Zealand, and India. Thailand is a full member of the WTO. It has bilateral preferential trade arrangements with Australia, New Zealand, Japan, India, Peru and other countries, and has signed free trade zone agreements with China, South Korea, Japan, India, Australia and New Zealand within the ASEAN framework. Since 1990, foreign trade of Thailand had performed well. But both imports and exports have declined since 2012 due to the impact of domestic political instability and global trade downturn. In 2014, exports were 272.90 billion USD, a year-on-year decrease of 2.58%, imports were 228.18 billion USD, a year-on-year decrease of 9.95%, and the trade surplus was 44.72 billion USD. For more information, see Fig. 5.72.

The Chinese mainland, Japan and the United States are Thailand's top three trading partners. Together, they absorb 31.7% of Thailand's total exports and contribute 42.5% of the total imports. Hong Kong of China is Thailand's largest source of trade surplus—the surplus in 2015 was 10.07 billion USD, a year-on-year decrease of 10.7%. In addition, the trade surplus with the United States was 9.86 billion USD, an

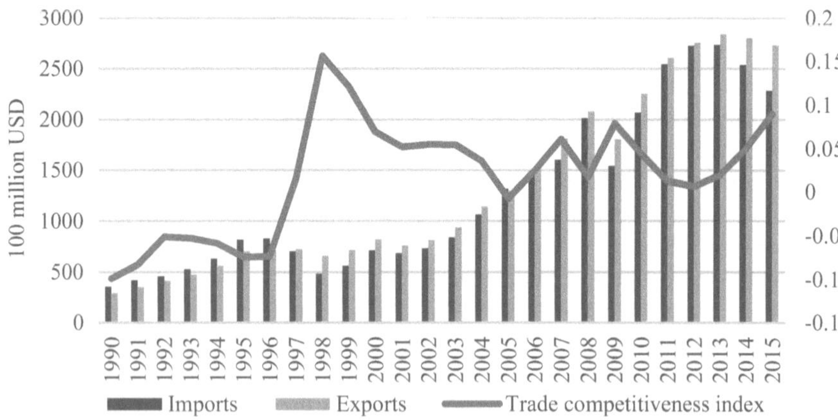

Fig. 5.72 Foreign trade of Thailand. *Source of data* World Bank database

increase of 9.1%. Thailand's trade deficit mainly comes from China and Japan—the figures in 2015 were 17.6 billion USD and 11.38 billion USD, respectively.

Thailand's main export commodities are industrial manufactured products, agricultural products, processed agricultural products and mineral products. In 2015, the proportions of the above items within total exports were 68.7%, 14.3%, 9.3% and 7.7%, respectively. Thailand mainly imports raw materials, semifinished products, capital goods and fuels, and their proportions in 2015 were 38.4%, 28.6% and 15.6%, respectively. See Figs. 5.73 and 5.74 for more information.

In the future, with the establishment of the ASEAN Community and the advancement of ASEAN "10 + 3", ASEAN "10 + 6" and various trade arrangements in the Asia-Pacific region, Thailand's market standing and economic development are expected to improve further.

2. International investment

Thailand has an excellent environment for FDI. It has established an "export-oriented economy that attracts foreign investment", and the volume of foreign investments has been growing. Thailand's main sources of investment are Japan, EU countries and Singapore. Among them, the investment of OECD member countries accounts for a large proportion and is mainly concentrated in the field of industrial manufacturing. Chinese companies are stepping up investment in Thailand, but the scale is still small, and there is big room for future growth. See Figs. 5.75, 5.76 and 5.77 for more information.

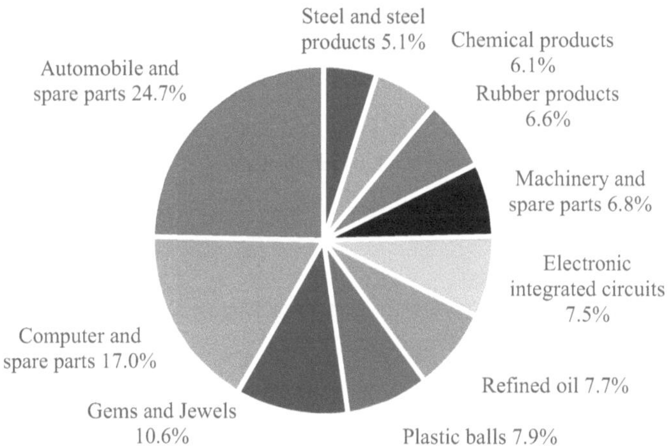

Fig. 5.73 Proportions of top 10 export products of Thailand in 2015. *Source of data* World Bank database

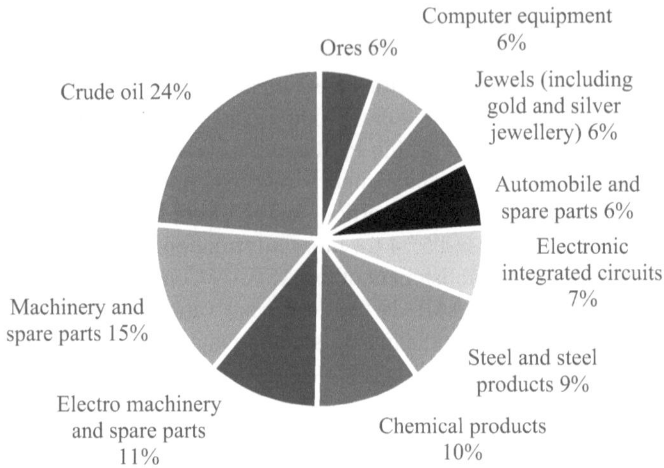

Fig. 5.74 Proportions of top 10 import products of Thailand in 2015. *Source of data* World Bank database

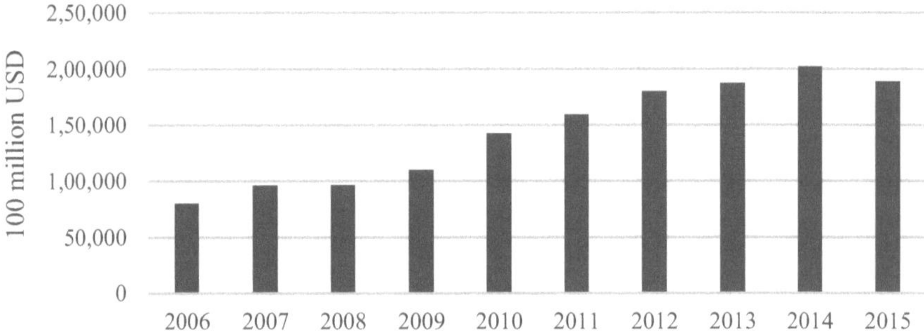

Fig. 5.75 FDI in Thailand. *Source of data* Bank of Thailand

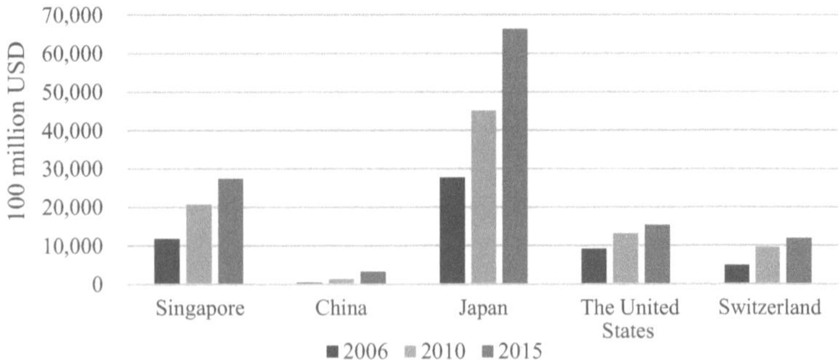

Fig. 5.76 Changes of investment made by major investors. *Source of data* Bank of Thailand

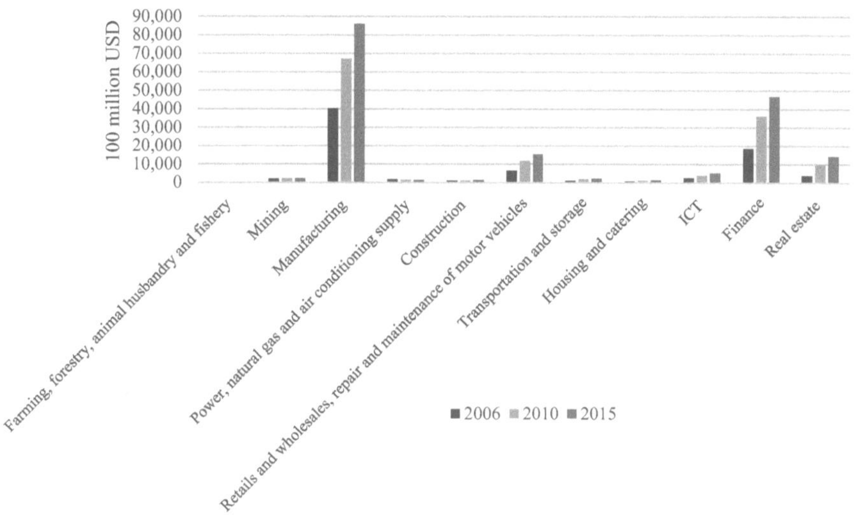

Fig. 5.77 Changes of the recipient sectors of FDI in Thailand. *Source of data* Bank of Thailand

5.9 Timor-Leste

I. **Geographical and historical backgrounds**

With a land area of 14,874 km^2, Timor-Leste is a country located on the eastern tip of Timor Island in Southeast Asia. Its capital Dili is the political, economic and cultural center of the country. About 80% of Timor-Leste's economic activities are carried out in Dili. Timor-Leste has a population of 1.167 million,[31] 78% of which are indigenous people (mixed race of Papua and Malay or Polynesian), 20% are Indonesians, and 2% are Chinese. Over 90% of the local population believes in Catholicism.[32]

Geographically, Timor-Leste faces Australia on the southeast, Indonesia on the north, and West Timor of Indonesia on the west. Historically, it was a Portuguese colony. It gained independence through referendum in 1999. In 2002, it officially set up its own government and joined the UN. Its independence process was turbulent—constant struggles and conflicts with Indonesia lasted for more than 20 years. With the hard-won independence and peace, Timor-Leste has always looked forward to working with the international community for peaceful development. As early as Zheng He's voyages to the west, Timor-Leste had already set up successful economic relations with China. Therefore, it fully supports China for the 21st Century Maritime Silk Road Initiative. At the Boao Forum in 2014, Timor-Leste Prime Minister said: "All countries along the maritime silk road should welcome this initiative".

II. **Economic development**

[31] Source of data: 2015 census of Timor-Leste.

[32] Source of data: Country profile: Timor-Leste, Ministry of Foreign Affairs, China.

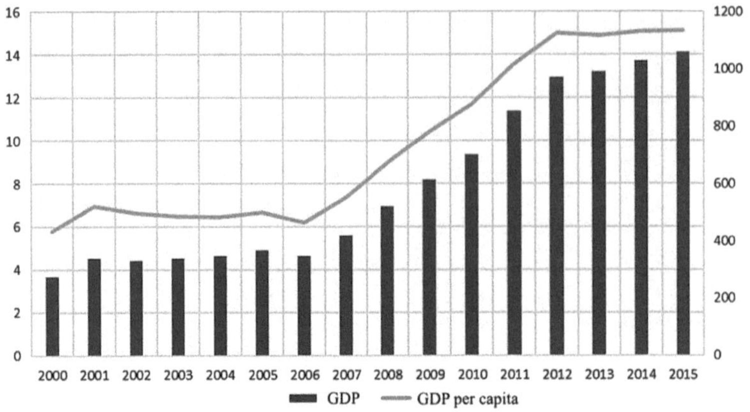

Fig. 5.78 Gross GDP and per capita GDP in Timor-Leste. *Source of data* World Bank database

Timor-Leste is relatively poor in Southeast Asia. According to World Bank data, as shown in Fig. 5.78, its gross GDP in 2015 was 1.41 billion USD, ranking 167 out of more than 220 countries and regions in the world; the per capita GDP is 1130 USD. In 2011, 37% of the population lived in poverty.[33] As a young country, it suffers from weak economic foundation. At present, the petroleum industry is the absolute pillar force of the national economy, and its national finance relies heavily on aids from Australia, the EU, the World Bank and other countries and organizations.

64% of the country's labor force is concentrated in agriculture, 10% works in the industrial sector, and the service industry has employed 26%. However, agriculture contributes only 5.9% of the gross GDP, industry produces 77.4% and the service industry generates 16.8%, as shown in Fig. 5.79. This is mainly due to the country's heavy dependence on the oil industry and the backwardness of agricultural production. It can be seen from Fig. 5.78 that after the oil price soared due to the Iraq war in 2004 and the hurricanes that hit Mexico's oil-producing areas in 2005, Timor-Leste witnessed fast growth of GDP in 2006–2011, with an annual growth rate of over 9%. As the largest employer of labor force, agriculture is underdeveloped and inefficient, causing waste of agricultural resources and leaving the country little food self-sufficiency.

In terms of infrastructure, the country has about 6000 km of roads, but only 8% are in relatively good condition. There are no highways or railways. The Presidente Nicolau Lobato International Airport of Dili is the only international airport in the country, and Dili Port is the only container terminal. The country established the National Petroleum Fund in 2005 as the main source of funding for infrastructure and social projects. As of June 2015, the balance of the National Petroleum Fund was 16.86 billion USD.[34]

[33] Source of data: CIA, The World Factbook 2015.

[34] Source of data: Timor-Leste channel of Maucaohub.

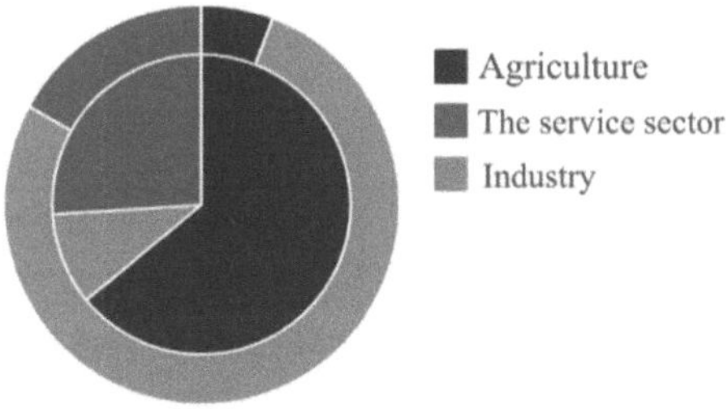

Fig. 5.79 Proportions of population employed in the three industries of Timor-Leste. *Note* The outer ring displays the proportions of the three industries within the gross GDP, while the inner pie presents the proportions of population working for the three industries within the total labor force. *Source of data* Based on the World Factbook 2015 by CIA

In terms of foreign trade and investment, due to the heavy dependence on imported food and machinery, and the plunge in oil prices, Timor-Leste's trade deficit has continued to expand in recent years. The country's main trading partners are Indonesia, Australia, China, Singapore, Malaysia and Portugal. The International Monetary Fund has pointed out that Timor-Leste's participation in CPLP (Comunidade dos Países de Língua Portuguesa) and improved relations with Australia and the European Union will help it benefit from global and regional integration.

According to the UN Conference on Trade and Development, in 2014, the cumulative FDI in Timor-Leste totaled 316 million USD, an increase of 11.3% over 2013. According to the Ministry of Commerce of the People's Republic of China, from 2010 to 2014, China's cumulative investment in Timor-Leste doubled from 7.5 to 15.8 million USD. The oil and gas sector is the most favored destination of FDI. The local government also encourages foreign investment in agriculture, infrastructure and tourism.[35]

Timor-Leste has stated its intention to join the WTO, and its application to join ASEAN is under review. At the same time, it imposes a 2.5% tariff and a 2.5% sales tax on most imported goods, and alcohol, tobacco and automobiles are subject to an additional consumption tax.

To sum up, its economy mainly faces two challenges: poor infrastructure and the lack of diversity in its economic structure. In order to turn the tide, the government formulated and adopted in 2011 the *National Strategic Development Plan 2011–2030* which prioritizes the development of infrastructure and agriculture, and the exploitation of oil and gas resources. In addition, the Plan aims at boosting the non-oil-and-gas sector by increasing public expenditure and encouraging foreign investment. Considering what is discussed above, China can start full economic and trade cooperation with Timor-Leste within the framework of the "Belt and Road" initiative. Table 5.11 lists the trade statistics of the two countries in recent years. Most of the imports from China are clothing, machinery and construction materials. Chinese companies are interested in Timor-Leste's infrastructure and utility markets.

[35] Source of data: Hong Kong Trade Development Council.

Table 5.11 Statistics of trade between China and Timor-Leste

Item	2010	2011	2012	2013	2014
Total trade volume	4308	7218	6316	4778.3	6044.8
China's exports	4283	7044	6247	4738.6	6034.8
China's imports	250	174	68	39.7	10

Source of data Country (region) specific guide for Outward Foreign Direct Investment Cooperation—Timor-Leste

In August 2002, PetroChina Company Limited and the government of Timor-Leste signed a memorandum of understanding on cooperation in oil and gas exploration and development in Timor-Leste, marking the first step in the cooperation between China and Timor-Leste. In July 2010, China decided to gradually implement zero-tariff treatment for Timor-Leste's exports to China. The two governments have signed trade agreements and various economic and technological cooperation agreements. China has supported Timor-Leste in the construction of multiple office building projects, donated agricultural machinery, fishing gear and other materials, provided training for local civil servants and sent medical teams. In 2014, China and Timor-Leste formally established a comprehensive partnership of good-neighborliness, mutual trust and mutual benefit.

China's investment in Timor-Leste is mainly from private enterprises and individuals, but large- and medium-sized state-owned enterprises are also involved. The main recipient areas are catering, hotels, department stores, building materials and service industries. Shandong Hi-speed Group is one of the state-owned enterprises investing in Timor-Leste. It has completed the construction of foreign aid projects such as the office buildings for the president, the Ministry of National Defense and the Army Command, and the Ministry of Foreign Affairs and Cooperation and its Learning Center. Thanks to its good reputation in East Timor, the group has won more projects, including a power plant, the office building of the Ministry of Justice, LOT1 road upgrade, and projects of Dili municipal government, with a total contract value of over RMB 1 billion.

Hunan Province stands out in helping its enterprises do business in Timor-Leste. According to its Strategic Action Plan for Synergizing with the Belt and Road Initiative (2015–2017), Hunan Province encourages enterprises to invest in less developed countries such as Timor-Leste in resource-intensive industries such as building materials, clothing, textiles, food, etc. At present, Hunan has established Timor-Leste & Hunan Agricultural High-tech Zone.

5.10 Vietnam

I. Geographical and historical backgrounds

Vietnam is located at the southeast end of the Indo-China Peninsula. It is an ASEAN member country and a socialist country. Geographically, Vietnam borders China on the north, and Laos and Cambodia on the west. Surrounded by sea on three sides, it has a narrow landform with a land area of 329,556 km^2, a coastline of more than 3260 km. Vietnam has interconnected waterways, including the Red River, Mekong (Kowloon) River, Tuojiang River (Heishui River), Lujiang River and Taiping River. In terms of natural conditions, Vietnam has a tropical monsoon climate, with high temperatures and abundant rainfall. Its average annual temperature is about 24 °C. There are four distinctive seasons in the north and two seasons of rain and drought in the south.

As of 2015, Vietnam has a population of 91.7 million, of which 86% are Kinh people. The official language is Vietnamese. The main religions are Buddhism, Catholicism, Hoahaoism and Caodaism. Politically and judicially, Vietnam is under the leadership of the Communist Party and follows the path of socialism.

Vietnam is rich in mineral resources, such as coal, iron, titanium, manganese, chromium, aluminum, tin and phosphorus. It enjoys abundant fishery resources—there are 6845 kinds of sea creatures, including 2000 kinds of fish, 300 kinds of crabs, 300 kinds of shellfish and 75 kinds of shrimps. The annual fish output in the central, eastern and southern coastal areas and the Gulf of Siam can reach hundreds of thousands tons.

II. Economic development

(I) Domestic economy

Since the introduction of "reform and opening up" in 1986, Vietnam's economy has maintained rapid growth, the industrial structure has become more coordinated, and the level of opening up has continued to increase. The Vietnamese economy is dominated by the state-owned sector, while multiple economic components coexist. In recent years, due to domestic economic instability and weak global economic recovery, Vietnam's GDP growth has slowed down to some extent but maintained proper speed. In 2015, Vietnam's per capita GDP was 2211.14 USD, making it a lower middle-income country, but its growth rate ranks second in the world, behind China. For more information, see Figs. 5.80, 5.81 and 5.82.

1. Industrial structure

As shown in Fig. 5.83, Vietnam is a traditional agricultural country. Despite its declining proportion, agriculture is self-sufficient, exporting a large amount of rice, tea, fish, coffee, cashews, etc.; the proportion of industry has been increasing rapidly since 1996; the service industry has always taken up a relatively big share of the national economy.

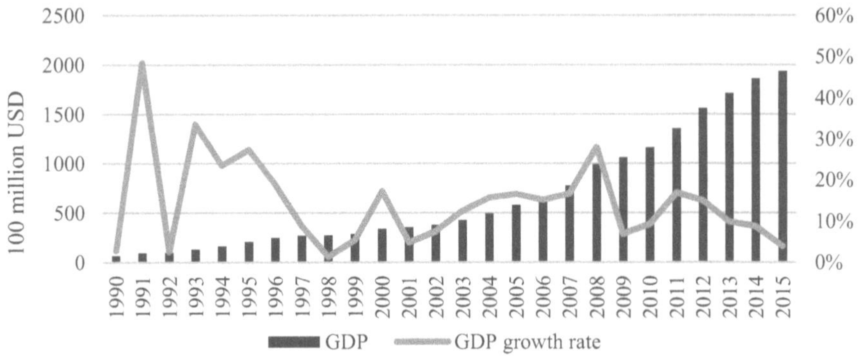

Fig. 5.80 Changes of gross GDP of Vietnam. *Source of data* World Bank database

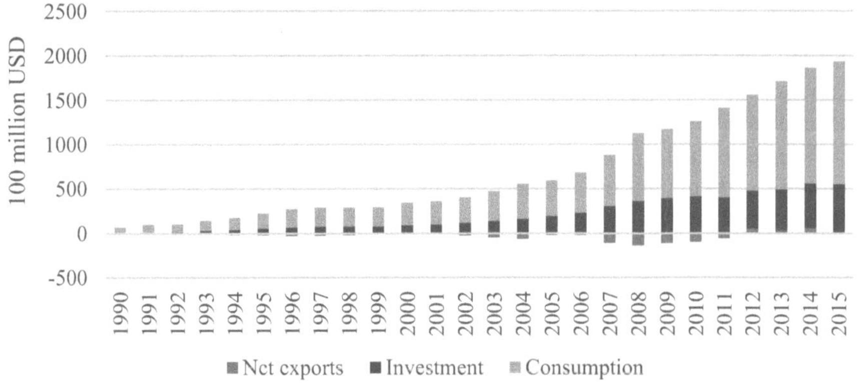

Fig. 5.81 GDP structure of Vietnam. *Source of data* World Bank database

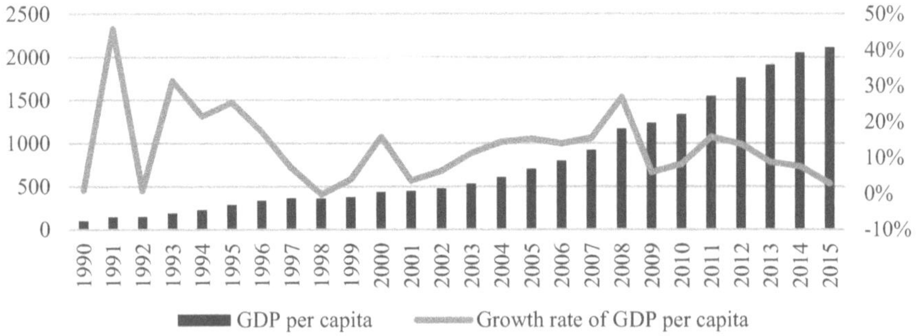

Fig. 5.82 Per capita GDP of Vietnam. *Source of data* World Bank database

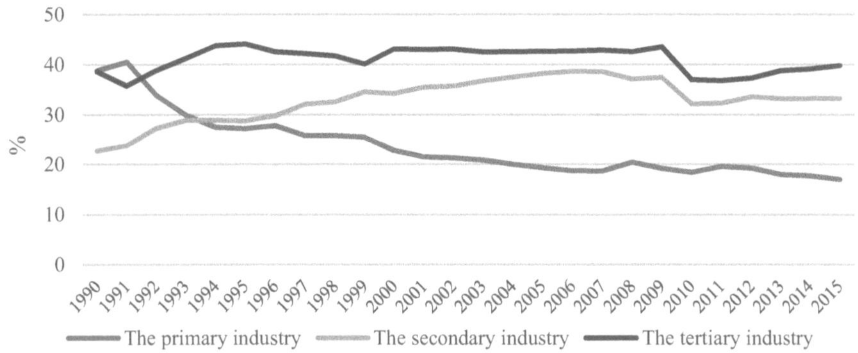

Fig. 5.83 Proportions of the three industries in Vietnam. *Source of data* World Bank database

(1) The primary industry

Vietnam is a traditional agricultural country. The agricultural population accounts for about 75% of the total population, and cultivated land and forest land make up 60% of the total land area. Food crops in Vietnam include rice, corn, potatoes, sweet potatoes and cassava; cash crops include coffee, rubber, pepper, tea, peanuts and sugar cane. The Vietnamese government offers a series of preferential treatment to attract foreign investment in the agricultural sector, including incentives of land, funds and tax.

(2) The secondary industry

Vietnam has a weak industrial foundation, but enjoys rapid industrial growth in recent years. In 2015, Vietnam's industrial index increased by 9.8%. At present, Vietnam is becoming a production base for labor-intensive industries such as clothing and footwear, and wood processing. Moreover, Vietnam is gaining popularity among manufacturers of electronic products. Samsung, Intel, Microsoft, Nokia and other multinational companies have expanded their production scale in Vietnam, and many overseas electronics companies have also invested in the country, which has jointly boosted the total output value of the Vietnamese electronics industry—its average annual compound growth rate from 2008 to 2013 reached 59%, doubling the growth rate of the manufacturing output (24%). Since 2013, electronics have become its largest export.[36] In addition, Vietnam is also the fifth largest cement producer in the world, following China, India, Iran and the United States. After the latest 6 cement production lines go into operation, its ranking may rise to third or fourth.

In 2016, Vietnam's industry and commerce authority set a goal of increasing the industrial production index by 9–10% year-on-year, and transforming Vietnam into a modern industrial country by 2020. Vietnam will increase inspection and supervision of key investment projects in the industrial sector, and study and formulate policies

[36] http:mt.sohu.com/20160914/n468399435.shtml.

for the development of industrial clusters, industrial zones, auxiliary industries, high-tech industries and industries that serve the development of agriculture and the rural economy. Vietnam will give priority to the development of the following industries: processing manufacturing and chemical industry, including machinery and metallurgy, chemical industry, farming, forestry and aquatic products processing industry, textile and footwear industry; electronic communication industry; new energy and renewable energy.

(3) The tertiary industry

In recent years, the Vietnamese service industry has maintained rapid growth. In 2015, the Vietnamese service industry grew by 5.82%, but it is not mature enough and lacks a systematic industrial chain. Vietnam, rich in tourism resources, has a rapid-growing tourism industry with considerable economic benefits. The main source countries (regions) of foreign visitors are Chinese Mainland, South Korea, Japan, the United States, Taiwan of China, Malaysia, Australia, Thailand and France.

In terms of transportation, roads and highways in Vietnam are well connected and are the main mode of transportation. The freight and passenger volume of inland water transportation is second only to road transportation, and each port handles 7 million tons of cargo annually. The development of maritime transportation is also relatively fast—its 49 seaports have an annual handling capacity of 400 million tons. The railway infrastructure is backward, and the speed is less than 90 km per hour, which is not competitive. Air transportation has developed rapidly, and passenger traffic increased by 96% from 2008 to 2013. In recent years, Vietnam has continued to increase infrastructure investment despite financial difficulties to improve the investment environment. The Vietnamese government plans to invest a total of 130 billion USD by 2020 to improve the status of infrastructure, or nearly 10.2 billion USD per year. By then, the capacity of Vietnam's railways, highways, aviation and ports will be significantly improved.

In terms of urban construction, although the level of urbanization in Vietnam is relatively low, it is developing rapidly, as shown in Fig. 5.84. The Ministry of Construction of Vietnam has proposed national urbanization development goals for 2012–2020, including achieving an urbanization rate of 38% by 2015 and 45% by 2020. The Vietnamese government will also invest 50 billion USD to upgrade infrastructure and livelihood projects to ensure the realization of urbanization goals. But in fact, in 2015, the goal of urbanization was not achieved, mainly due to the challenges brought by the excessive concentration of the population and its status as an agricultural country.

The basic information of several major cities in Vietnam is shown in Table 5.12.

In terms of education, Vietnam has nine-year compulsory education and has set up an education system including early childhood education, primary education, secondary education, higher education, teacher education, vocational education and adult education. Famous universities include the Vietnam National University, Hanoi, Viet Nam National University Ho Chi Minh City, Hue University, the University of Danang, etc.

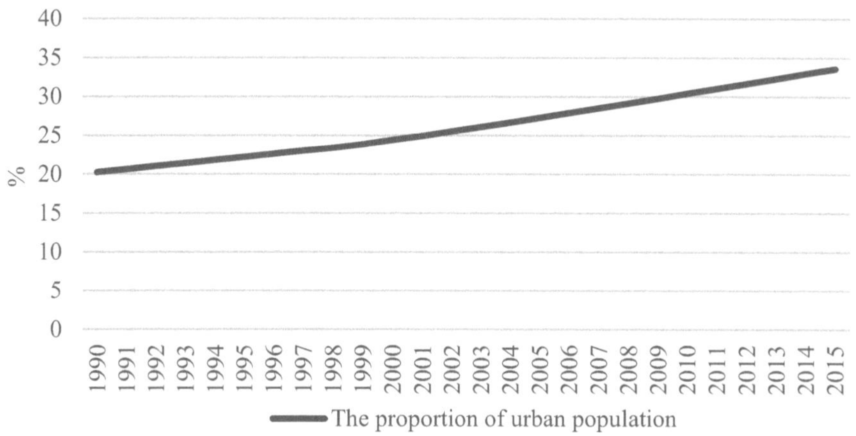

Fig. 5.84 Proportion of urban population in Vietnam. *Source of data* World Bank database

Table 5.12 Main cities in Vietnam

City	City profile
Hanoi	The capital. With a history of more than a thousand years, it has been the political, economic and cultural center of Vietnam since ancient times
Haiphong	A northern port city and a municipality directly under the central government. It is the third largest city in Vietnam and the second largest industrial center in northern Vietnam
Ho Chi Minh city	Vietnam's largest city, a municipality directly under the Central Government, and Vietnam's economic, trade, transportation and cultural center
Da Nang	A port city with the naval base and rich tourism resources
Ha Long city	Vietnam's coal capital, a tourist city, and a world natural heritage

Source of data Based on public data

(II) Foreign trade and investment

1. Foreign trade

Vietnam's foreign trade is growing at a high speed, with improving export structure, increasing technical content and added value of exported goods, and expanding proportion of exports of electronic products and general machinery and equipment. See Figs. 5.85, 5.86 and 5.87 for more information.

2. International investment

Thanks to constant reform and opening up, fast economic growth and great potential, and improving investment policies, the volume of foreign investment absorbed by Vietnam is increasing year by year, as shown in Fig. 5.88. The main investment sources are South Korea, Malaysia, the United States, Japan, etc., as Fig. 5.89 shows.

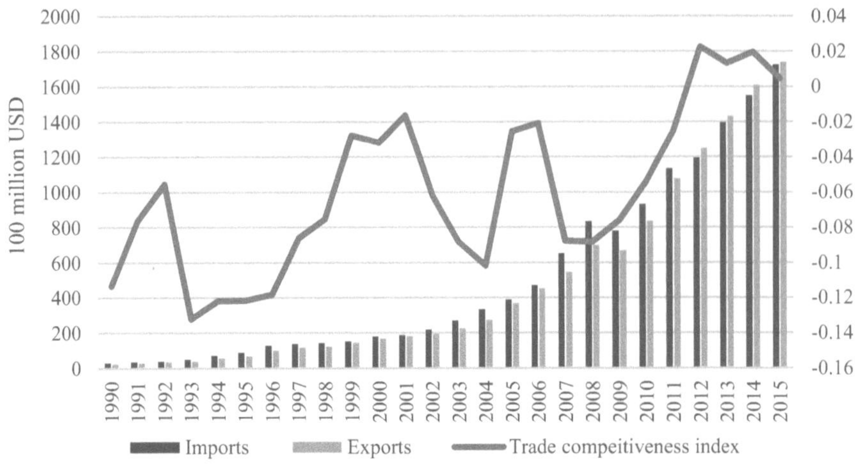

Fig. 5.85 Foreign trade of Vietnam. *Source of data* World Bank database

Fig. 5.86 Export structure of Vietnam in 2015. *Source of data* General Statistics Office of Vietnam

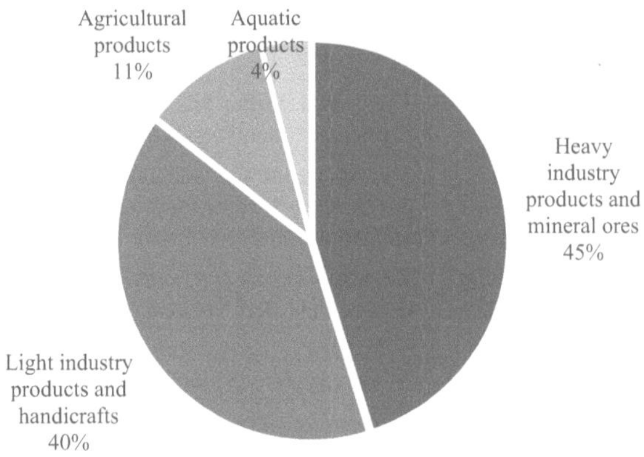

Fig. 5.87 Import structure of Vietnam in 2015. *Source of data* General Statistics Office of Vietnam

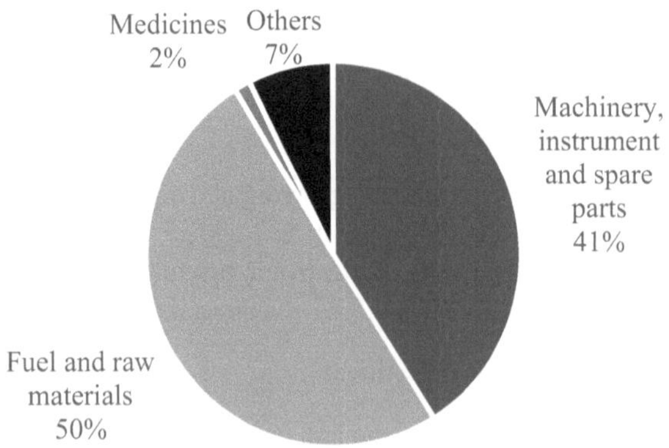

Chinese investment has been rising in recent years, but it is still small in scale and enjoys great potential for further growth.

The Vietnamese government attaches great importance to foreign investment. In 2015, it stepped up such efforts, giving priority to the simplification of procedures concerning taxation, customs and social security, and the reinforcement of inspections and supervision by relevant authorities. In addition, it urges the central and local governments to improve the foreign investment environment by establishing a modern market system. Besides, Vietnam is one of the founding countries of the Asian Infrastructure Investment Bank, the development of which will gradually fill the investment gaps in the area of infrastructure construction in Vietnam.

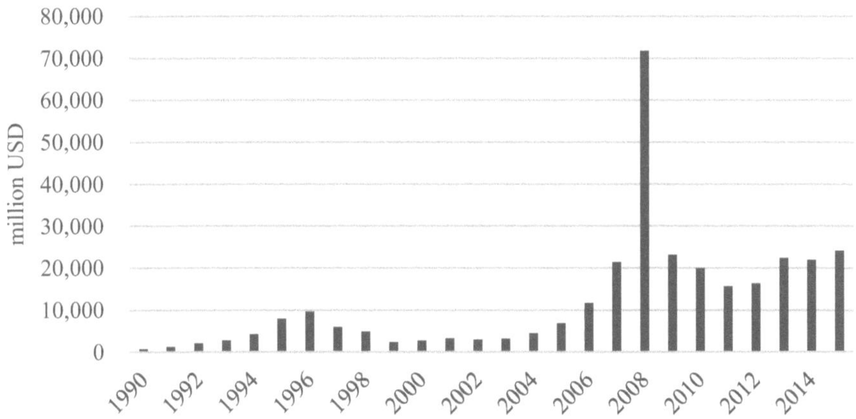

Fig. 5.88 FDI in Vietnam. *Source of data* General Statistics Office of Vietnam

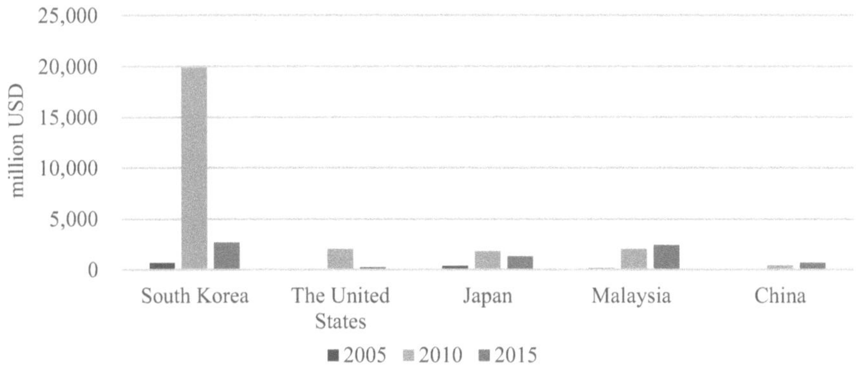

Fig. 5.89 Changes of investment made by major investors in Vietnam. *Source of data* The State Bank of Vietnam

Chapter 6
South Asia Region

South Asia refers to the vast region lying between the middle and western Himalayas and the Indian Ocean. It has given birth to one of the four great ancient civilizations. Meanwhile, it is where Buddhism and Hinduism originated. This sub-continent is rich in mineral sources such as iron, manganese and coal. Wheat and paddy are its major food crops. The South Asian countries that have embraced the Belt and Road Initiative include Afghanistan, Bangladesh, Bhutan, India, Maldives, Nepal, Sri Lanka and Pakistan. All of them, underdeveloped, are facing transformation of economic structures.

Home to more than 30 million people, Afghanistan is landlocked country in the middle and southern Asia. Agriculture and animal husbandry are the mainstays of local economy, employing 85% of the population. In contrast, its industrial output, mainly from light and handicraft industries, makes up only 20% of the GDP. Energy and mining industries are given strategic importance and priority by the local government. After the war, finance, telecommunication, logistics and service industries have seen rapid growth. In 2015, 26.7% of the country was urbanized. Afghanistan mainly trades with its neighbors—it imports from Iran and Pakistan and exports to Pakistan and India.

Located on the delta created by the Ganges and the Brahmaputra in the northeast of the sub-continent, Bangladesh is endowed with fertile plains and interconnected waterways, creating favorable conditions for the development of agriculture and fishery. As an underdeveloped export-oriented economy, Bangladesh mainly relies on textile industry and has a competitive leather industry. Its weak heavy industry and manufacturing industry hire only 8% of the population. It was not until the early twenty-first century that the proportion of urban residents had exceeded 20%.

Bhutan is a landlocked country lying in the south of Asia and also the south of the eastern Himalayas. Agriculture is the pillar of its economy. The proportion of industry within its economy had been rising slowly from 11.7% in 1980 to 42.9% in 2014. In the past three decades, urbanization rate grew significantly from 10% in 1980 to

H. Zhang et al., *Comparative Studies on Regional and National Economic Development*, Global Economic Synergy of Belt and Road Initiative,
https://doi.org/10.1007/978-981-16-2105-5_6

38.7% in 2015 (but still under 40%). It mainly trades with SAARC members—India, with a free trade agreement, is its largest trading partner.

Once one of the four great ancient civilizations, India has abundant resources, including almost 100 kinds of mineral reserves. Since the twenty-first century, Indian economy has been growing fast, achieving annual growth larger than 7% for many successive years. Traditionally an agricultural country, India is still threatened by food insecurity and dependent on import due to its large population and outdated farming techniques (mainly manual). In 2014, the total value industrial output in India contributed 30% of its national economy. The tertiary industry is major engine of Indian economy—in 2014, the share of the tertiary industry hit 72.4%.

Located in the Indian Ocean, Maldives is an island nation consisting of more than 1200 atolls. With 300 km^2 of land area (exclusive of territorial seas), it is the smallest country in Asia, but the largest country of atolls in the world. Tourism, shipping and fishery are the three pillars of its economy, while agriculture and industry lag far behind. Shipping is the major means of transportation, and aviation industry is underdeveloped. In 2015, its urbanization rate was 45.5%. Asia and Europe are the main destinations of its exports—the top importers of Maldivian products are Thailand, France, Sri Lanka, Italy and Britain.

As a mountainous landlocked country in South Asia, Nepal has the Himalayas in the north, the hilly areas in the middle which account for more than half of the national territorial area and plains in the south. This multi-ethnic country is rich in mineral and hydropower resources. Nepal is an agricultural country—80% of its population are employed in agriculture, and total agricultural output composes 40% of the GDP. The service sector has been growing. Tourism is Nepal's pillar industry, producing 29% of GNP. Tourists in Nepal mainly come from Asian countries. Its urbanization stayed lower than 20% despite rapid growth in the past two decades.

Pakistan and India used to be one country. Located in the sub-continent, it has a territory of more than 800,000 km^2, and a population of 150 million (most of which are Muslims). It has abundant mineral, animal and plant resources. Its agricultural output is 5% of the world's total. It is the fifth largest cotton producer in the world. Due to its weak industry, Pakistan mainly exports unprocessed or roughly-processed low-skilled agricultural products and textiles. As a result, it is only present in a small slice of the global market.

Located in the southwest of Asia, as a tropical island, Sri Lanka has a population of more than 20 million. Agriculture, mainly plantations, is its economic mainstay. Its industry is so weak that there is hardly any heavy industry. It suffers long-term international imbalances. Incomes from international labor services and tourism are its major source of foreign exchange. Attaching great importance to cooperation within South Asia, it is an active supporter and participant of SAARC.

6.1 Bangladesh

I. Geographical and historical backgrounds

Bangladesh, officially the People's Republic of Bangladesh and spanning 147,570 km^2, shares land borders with India to the west, north and the east and Myanmar to the southeast, whereas the Bay of Bengal lies to its south. Bengalis are one of the oldest nationalities living in the sub-continent of South Asia. In 1757, Bangladesh became a province of British India. At the time of Pakistan's partition from India in 1947, Bangladesh was named East Pakistan as part of the newly formed state of Pakistan. In 1971, Bangladesh emerged as an independent sovereign. With sub-tropical monsoon climate for the nation and monsoon-type tropical savanna climate for its coastal area, it is endowed with fertile land and interconnected waterways, enjoying good conditions for the development of agriculture and fishery. Meanwhile, flooding and tropical cyclones are frequent in the monsoon season. It has mining resources such as natural gas, coal, titanium and zirconium. Jute is its main source of income. Bangladesh is both the most densely populated country and the poorest country in the world.

II. **Economic development**

(I) Domestic economy

In 2015, the real GDP of Bangladesh was 173.82 billion USD. Textile industry is the pillar of this export-oriented economy. In the fiscal year of 2014, the volume of garment export reached 16.384 billion USD, 81% of its total exports. It has a competitive leather industry which produces 150 million square feet of leather every year on average, or 2–3% of the world's total. In the fiscal year of 2013, the value of leather and leather article exports hit 691 million USD, or 3.4% of the country's total exports. Overall, the country is still underdeveloped, suffering inadequate infrastructure, as well as land and energy shortages.

Despite its status as one of the least-developed countries, Bangladesh is achieving steady economic development, annually growing faster than 6% of GDP for recent 9 years in a row. Its government plans to accomplish 10% growth of GDP in 2017. In future, by insisting its export-oriented economy, fully playing its competitive edges such as abundant and cheap labor, improving its infrastructure, attracting more foreign investment and encouraging export, Bangladesh hopes to pull itself out of the ranks of the least-developed countries and emerge as a developing country in 2021 (Fig. 6.1).

1. Industrial structure

As one of the least-developed countries, Bangladesh, with a weak economic foundation, mainly depends on agriculture. In recent years, Bengalese government has been promoting privatization and improving investment environment, so as to draw foreign investment and set up export processing zones. In 2008, under the impact of global financial crisis, its GDP growth rate was only 6.21% due to declining export.

(1) The primary industry

Agriculture is the mainstay of Bengalese economy. Its major agricultural products include tea, rice, wheat, sugarcane, jute and articles thereof, white sugar, cotton

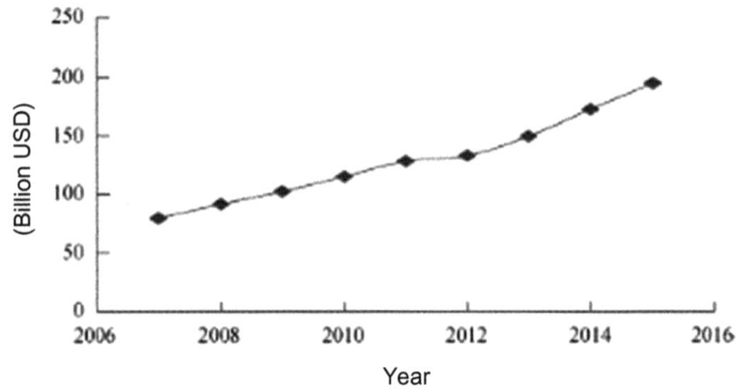

Fig. 6.1 GDP growths of Bangladesh in recent years. *Source of data* World Bank database

yarn and soybean oil. Jute growing dates back to 1971 when the country was newly independent. Since local climate conditions are good, jute in Bangladesh is of high yield and good quality (the fibers are long, pliable and tough and glossy). Jute fibers soaked in the clear water of the Brahmaputra River are of the best quality—they are called "golden fibers" for their color and gloss. Once the main source of foreign exchange for Bangladesh, jute production has been the lifeline of the economy. Its produces 1/3 of the world's total every year, and the export volume was once 80% of the country's export earnings. However, the prosperity of synthetic fibers and thus the decline of demand for jute fibers since the 1980s have sent jute industry in Bangladesh into a downward spiral—its output and export continue to drop. Today, only 5% of the country's export earnings are from jute products. Statistics show that Bangladesh is the largest jute fiber exporter and the second largest jute fiber producer (next only to India) in the world. In the fiscal year of 2006–2007, its output of raw jute fibers was around 1.186 million ton, 39% of the world's total; its export of raw jute fiber was 95% of the world's total; it exported 65% of the world's jute products. Raw jute fibers and articles thereof of Bangladesh have established a presence in the Middle East, European, Asian and American countries.

(2) The secondary industry

Bangladesh has a weak heavy industry and an underdeveloped manufacturing industry. Industry employs only 8% of its total labor force. Bengalese industry mainly produces raw materials and primary goods such as cement, fertilizer and paper.

(3) The tertiary industry

Bangladesh is rich in tourism resources. With the help of UNDP, UNWTO has formulated a strategic plan for the tourism industry in Bangladesh. As a comprehensive plan, it identifies the tourism products and facilities to be developed in the country. With the aid of foreign advanced technologies, Bengalese government has made revisions of and improvements upon this plan—it will set up tourism zones nationwide and provide foreign tourists with better services. Among these zones are Cox's Bazar,

Sandarbans and Kuakata. Consisting of three districts, the Chittagong Hill will also be transformed into a special tourism zone. The five-star Sonargaon Hotel in Dhaka is invested by the government. Besides, the government is also the major shareholder of the Sheraton Hotel in Dhaka. Major tourist sites in the country include Dhaka, Rangamati, Khagrachari District, Sylhet, Cox's Bazar, etc. Tourism facilities within these regions are invested and constructed by Bangladesh Parjatan Corporation, the National Tourism Organization of the country.

Bangladesh has set up trading relations with more than 130 countries and regions in the world. Among them, the major destinations for its exports include the United States, Germany, Britain, France, Netherlands, Italy, Belgium, Spain, Canada and Hong Kong SAR, China. Its major export products are jute and articles thereof, leather, tea, aquatic products and garment. It mainly imports from India, Chinese mainland, Singapore, Japan, Hong Kong SAR of China, South Korea, the United States, Britain, Australia and Thailand. Its major import products include means of production, textiles, oil and oil products, basic metals like steel, edible oil and cotton. Its major investors include the United States, Britain, Malaysia, Japan, China, Saudi Arab, Singapore, Norway, Germany and South Korea.

Generally speaking, all three industries of the country are on the rise, as shown in Fig. 6.2. Among them, the secondary industry takes the lead—after replacing agriculture as the economic mainstay in 2008, it has been growing rapidly and become the engine of Bengalese economy. Currently, the Bengalese government, prioritizing economic development, is promoting privatization, improving investment environment and pushing forward the secondary industries such as the textile and garment industries by fully tapping its labor resource. Bangladesh is transitioning from an agricultural economy into an industrial economy, and its demand for industrial developments has been growing. As a hub of transportation in South Asia, the country is equipped with good harbors. For some time, Bangladesh, highly dependent on India and thus land transportation, had neglected the development of sea transportation. But in recent years, it has been actively exploring sea transportation during its industrialization. As its overall strengths rise, Bangladesh, though poor now, has great growth potential with the help of the Belt and Road Initiative.

2. Urbanization

Figure 6.3 shows urbanization rate of Bangladesh which has increased markedly in 50 years. This urbanizing process officially started from its independence from Pakistan in 1971. Since then, masses of farming population have migrated to cities to work in the secondary and tertiary industries. In this way, more and more Bengalis have become urban residents, which has greatly boosted Bengalese economy. However, despite such rapid urbanization, the urbanization rate of the country did not reach 20% until early twenty-first century.

As the largest city and capital of Bangladesh (also the principal city of Dhaka Division), Dhaka is the country's center of politics, economy and culture. This historic city was first built in the fifteenth century. By the early twentieth century, it had emerged as the commercial and academic center of Bangladesh. In 1947, it was named the capital of East Bengal province. In 1956, it became the capital of East

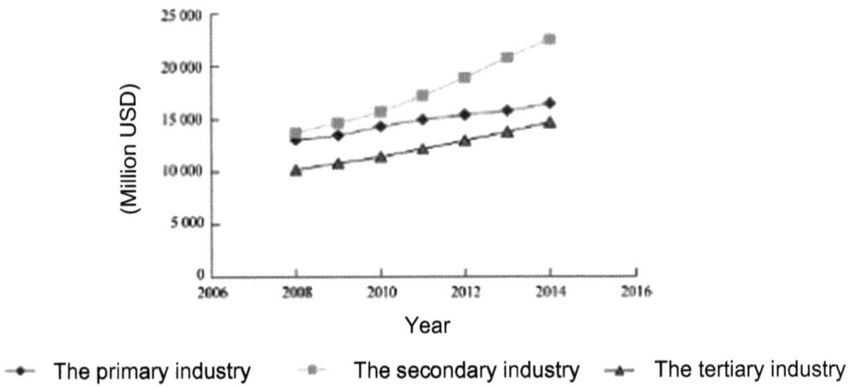

Fig. 6.2 Industrial structure of Bangladesh. *Source of data* UN database

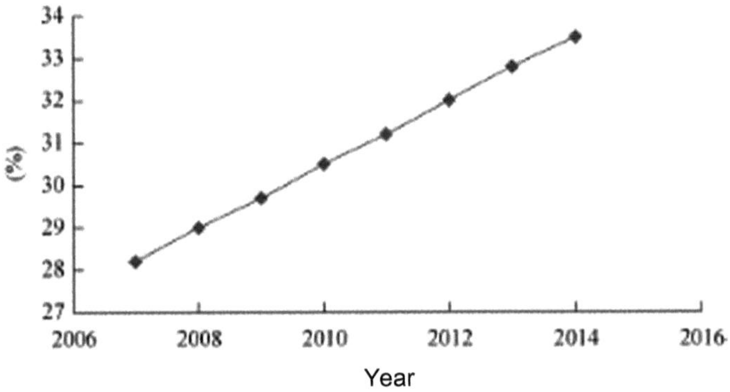

Fig. 6.3 Urbanization rate of Bangladesh. *Source of data* World Bank database

Pakistan. Dhaka suffered heavy damage during the war of independence in 1971 but emerged as the capital of Bangladesh after being reconstructed. Located on a level plain 6–7.5 m above the sea level, Dhaka is surrounded by fertile plain of the delta created by multiple rivers. Major local farm produces include jute, rice, sugarcane and rapeseeds. With Narayanganj 16 km to its south, Dhaka is the largest industrial center and trading hub of the country. It has cotton spinning industry, jute industry, food processing industry and paper making industry. Local specialties include embroidery, silk products and jewels.

With a developed transport system, Dhaka is the railway, highway and inland navigation hub of Bangladesh. It is also connected with Chittagong and foreign cities through air lines.

As the largest port city, Chittagong is the second most populous city in the country. Lying about 16 km north of the mouth of the Karnaphuli River, it is a fine natural harbor. First built in the sixteenth century, it has 28 wharfs with berths 6.4–8.5 m deep and modern freight-handling facilities. Seagoing vessels could reach the port through 198–274 m wide waterway of the Karnaphuli River. Chittagong is a developed industrial and commercial city with hydropower stations and factories of cotton spinning, bast fiber spinning, tea processing, oil refining, steel making, paper making, synthetic fiber, glass and fertilizer. In 1966, it set up University of Chittagong. In 1981, it built an export processing zone.

(II) Foreign trade

1. Foreign trade

Bangladesh joined the GATT one year after its independence in 1971. In 1995, it became a WTO member country automatically. Having adopted free trade policies since the 1980s, Bangladesh is the advocate of free trade by cutting tariffs and removing non-tariff barriers. It sets no direct limit to the volume of import, and the collection of tariffs is its main tool of regulating foreign trade. Apart from this, Bengalese government prefers economic measures (e.g., foreign exchange rate, interest rate, LC deposit rate, cash subsidy, development fund and additional tax) to administrative measures for the adjustment of foreign trade. Despite the pro-trade policies, trade barriers still exist in Bangladesh. According to the World Bank, its unweighted average import tax rate (including customs duties and other protective import taxes) was 26.5% in 2004, the highest of its kind in South Asia and one of the highest in the world.

Taxation is the main measure taken by the Bengalese government to encourage investment, redirect industrial development and adjust foreign trade and national income. To stimulate investment (including foreign investment) and export, the government, through industrial, trade and export processing zone policies, has formulated a series of complicated tax reduction and exemption policies. For instance, new investment in areas such as textile industry and garment industry with high added value enjoys 4–10 years of tax exemption. Companies preferring not to exercise the privileges could enjoy accelerated depreciation. For companies that have been exempt from taxation, they could enjoy discounts of 80% depreciation for the second year and 20% depreciation for the third year as long as they make more investment. Completely export-oriented enterprises could import its capital equipment and 10% of parts duty-free. At early stage of establishment and during the renovation, upgrading and expansion of existing projects, all enterprises could import the capital equipment and 10% of parts at the import tax rate of 7.5% and some refundable indemnity deposit. The import of capital equipment is exempt from value added tax. Export earnings of garment enterprises enjoy preferential tax rate of 10%. Earnings of jute and textile exports enjoy preferential tax rate of 15%. Interest on foreign loans is exempt from tax. Royalties, technology transfer fee and technical service fee are exempt from tax. Foreign technicians working in Bangladesh are exempt from income tax for three years. After paying tax to the Bengalese administration of foreign exchange, foreign shareholders could sell their shares to local shareholders or investors and the capital income tax-free; power projects are free from income tax for 15 years.

2. Trade with China

Economically complementary, Bangladesh and China enjoy great potential for economic cooperation. On one hand, as the growth of Bangladesh picks up speed, its ever larger market potential has attracted more and more Chinese players, and Chinese investment is gradually moving from low-end to high-end sectors. On the other hand, rising production cost, especially labor cost, in China has pushed up commodity prices, putting labor-intensive industry under great pressure. Therefore, more and more labor-intensive factories, such as garment factories, are relocating to Bangladesh; at the same time, many international customers choose to buy luxury materials from China and make shirts in Bangladesh, during which foreign exchange flows from Bengalese factories to Chinese fabric producers.

Trade between China and Bangladesh used to take two forms—clearing account trade and cash account trade. During the 7th Session of Sino-Bengalese Joint Trade Committee held in 1992, both sides agreed to adopt only the cash account trade starting from January 1, 1993. In December 1992, China and Bangladesh signed a new trade deal based on the new paying system. In recent years, trade between the two countries has been developing smoothly. According to China's customs agency, the bilateral trade volume was 687 million USD in 2008, down by 8.4% on a year-on-year basis—Chinese export was 661 million USD, down by 5.1%, while its import from Bangladesh dived to 26 million USD, down by 51.3%. In 2012, Sino-Bengalese trade reached 715 million USD, up by 4.1% compared to last year—China's export grew by 6.1% to 701 million USD, while its import plunged by 46% to 14 million USD.

Exports from China to Bangladesh mainly include cotton; boilers, mechanical appliances, parts there of; electric machinery, sound equipment and parts thereof; man-made staple fibers; man-made filaments; fertilizer; knitted or crocheted fabrics; vehicles and parts thereof, railway locomotives and rolling stock excluded; special woven fabrics; tufted textile fabrics; embroidery and articles of iron or steel. Imports by China from Bangladesh mainly include other vegetable fibers; paper yarn and woven fabrics of paper yarn; articles of apparel and clothing accessories, not knitted or crocheted; articles of apparel and clothing accessories, knitted or crocheted; other made up textile articles; ores, slag and ash; plastics and articles thereof; raw hides and skins (other than furskins) and leather; fish or other aquatic invertebrates; optical, photographic, precision medical instruments and parts thereof; cotton.[1]

In 2014, the bilateral trade volume soared 21.98% to 12.547 billion USD, with Chinese export and import reaching 11.785 billion USD and 762 million USD, respectively. In the first 11 months of 2015, trade between the two countries grew to 13.364 billion USD, up by 19.2% on a year-on-year basis. See Fig. 6.4 for more information. As one of the major recipients of Chinese aids, Bangladesh is one of the main contract markets of China in South Asia. By the end of November 2015, China had made 185 million USD of direct investment in Bangladesh and received 41.14 million USD of actual investment from Bangladesh.

[1] MOFCOM: Q&A on foreign trade of Bangladesh, http://www.mofcom.gov.cn/article/i/jshz/new/201609/20160901390273.shtml.

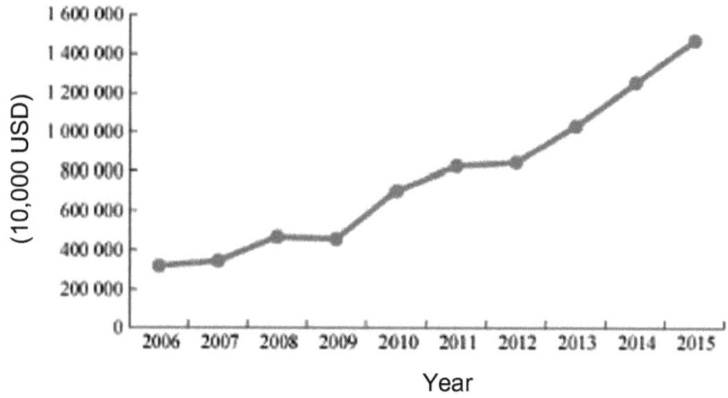

Fig. 6.4 Sino-Bengalese trade volume

6.2 India

I. Geographical and historical backgrounds

As the birthplace one of the four great ancient civilizations, India has a very long history. After the emergence of the Indus valley civilization in 2500–1500 BC, a group of Aryans, originally living in Central Asia, moved to the sub-continent of South Asia. They conquered the indigenous peoples and founded Brahmanism. In the fourth century BC, the rising Maurya dynasty unified India. One hundred years later, India reached its heyday under the rule of Ashoka, and Buddhism became the state religion. In June 1947, Britain adopted the Mountbatten Plan and partitioned India. On August 15, 1947, India declared independence. On January 26, 1950, the Republic of India was founded, and its Constitution came into force. India is still a member pf the British Commonwealth. With traditions of cultural pluralism, India is still a diverse country.

India has a territory of 2.98 million km^2 (excluding the Sino-Indian border area occupied by India and India-administered Kashmir), 20.6% of which is covered by forests. It borders China, Nepal, Bhutan, Myanmar and Pakistan. Its coastline is 5,560 km long. India is the 7th largest country in the world but ranks no.2 in terms of population (hitting 1.295 billion in 2014). As a multi-national country, it is home to more than 100 nationalities among which Hindustanis predominate.

II. Economic development

(I) Domestic economy

Since its official independence in 1947, India has gone through economic development featuring three models, namely the Nehru model (1947–late 1960s), the mixed development model (1970s–1980s) and the market economy model (1990s till now). In the early days of its independence, India was left with economic backwardness, stagnating industries and large-scale unemployment. After drawing on the economic development model of the Soviet Union, Nehru administration prioritized the development of public economy, especially the basic industry and heavy industry, and this approach to development is called the Nehru model. This model, while bringing about industrial development and improving the industrial system, was a fatal blow to light industry and agriculture. Eventually, this model came to a stop after Nehru died. After Gandhi took office, he adjusted Nehru's policies and carried out SOE reforms, advocating the development of both public and private economy, and the growth of both agriculture and industry. During his reign, Indian economy witnessed mixed development. In the late 1980s, Gandhi, by lifting price control and loosening restrictions on domestic investment, attempted to boost Indian economy. However, against the backdrop of the Soviet collapse and the Gulf War, Indian government was on the verge of bankruptcy. The IMF provided the Indian government with an emergency loan of 1.8 billion USD on the premise of economic reform, and the mixed development model was abandoned. In the early 1990s, India undertook economic reforms and set the targets of liberalization, privatization and globalization. SOEs were privatized, and controls of some SOEs were relaxed; market regulation replaced government intervention; and the economy was redirected—from export-oriented to import-oriented. These measures brought about significant economic growth: basic agricultural self-sufficiency was achieved; a comprehensive industrial system was built so that excessive reliance on import was alleviated; the service sector made great headway, with its share within the economy expanding every year.

Indian economy has been growing rapidly since the beginning of the twenty-first century. Its growth rate of GDP exceeded 7% many years in a row—in 2010, it even hit 10.26%. In 2014, its GDP was 2.2 trillion USD (at constant price of 2010), up by 7.24% compared to 2013. In 2015, the figure was 2.36 trillion USD (at constant price of 2010), 7.57% more on a year-on-year basis (see Fig. 6.5). The World Bank once estimated that India would maintain a growth rate higher than 7% in 2016 and replace China in 2016 or 2017 as the fastest growing major economy in the world.

1. Industrial structure

(1) The primary industry

Traditionally, India has been an agricultural country. With tropical monsoon climate, it is granted with abundant precipitation and weather conditions suitable for agricultural production all around the year. However, it is challenged by food shortage and excessive reliance on food import due to outdated agricultural technology (mainly manual) and big population. After its independence, India reformed its land ownership system but little effect was produced. After the food security crisis in 1965–1967, India adopted the "Green Revolution" strategy for its agricultural development—to cultivate high-yield crops and modernize agriculture with new technologies. The implementation of "Green Revolution" has greatly boosted the production efficiency of Indian agriculture, transforming the country from a net food importer into a net exporter. By 2013, its agricultural land had reached 1.8 million km^2, 60.64% of its total land area. In 2015, 67.3% of Indians, 880 million, lived in the rural area and 17.4% of the total employment held agricultural jobs. Major food crops in India

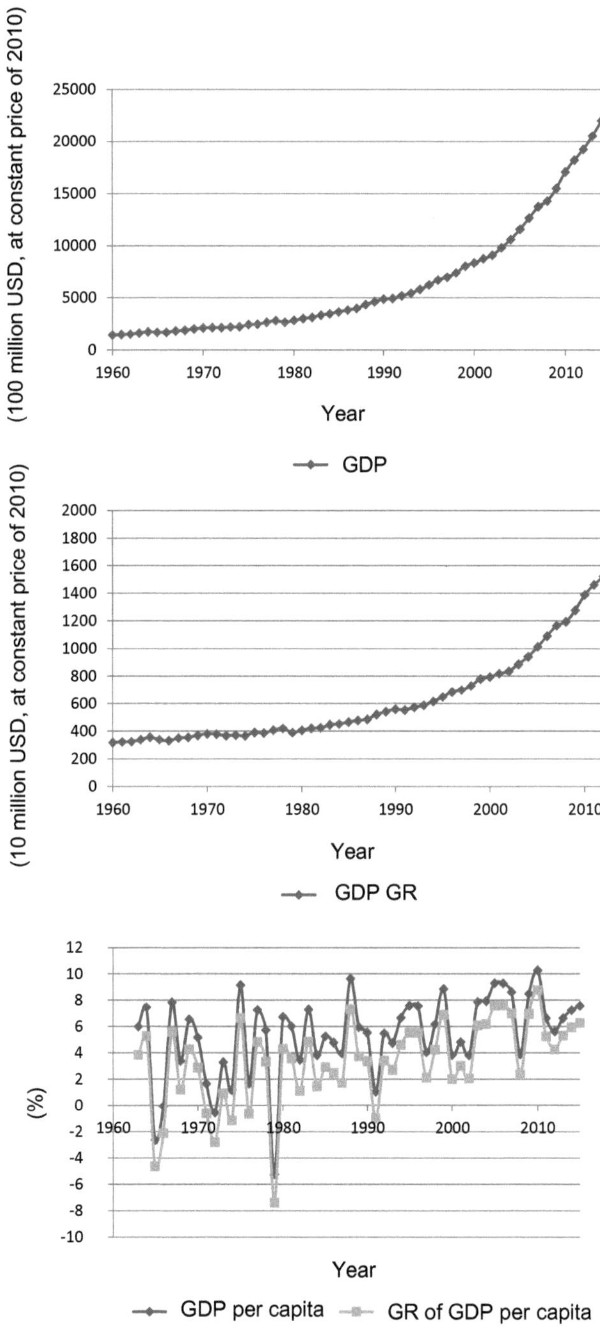

Fig. 6.5 Economic indicators of India

Table 6.1 Yields of major agricultural products 2012–2014 (Unit: million tons)

	2012	2013	2014
Total grain output	257.13	265.57	257.07
Rice	105.24	106.65	103.04
Legumes	18.34	19.78	18.43
Grains excluding wheat and rice	40.04	42.70	39.83
Oilseed crops	30.94	32.75	29.83
Sugarcane	341.22	348.00	354.95
Cotton	34.22	36.50	35.15

include rice, legumes, grains except wheat and rice and oilseeds. Sugarcane is the major cash crop—its annual output in 2014 is 3.5495 million ton. See Table 6.1 for more information.

(2) The secondary industry

India is rich in natural resources—it ranks no.1 for its mica output and no.3 for the yield of barite and coal. Currently, its exploitable reserves of natural gas, petroleum oil, gold, coal, zinc, chromite, lead, alumina, copper, iron ore, manganese ore and phosphate are 1075 billion m^3, 756 million ton, 68 ton, 253.301 billion ton, 9.7 million ton, 97 million ton, 2.381 million ton, 2.462 billion ton, 5.297 million ton, 13.46 billion ton, 167 million ton and 142 million ton, respectively. Traditional industrial sectors in India include textile, chemical, pharmaceutical, food processing, cement, steelmaking, mining, petroleum and machinery industries (Table 6.2). Meanwhile, emerging industries of automobile and aircraft are making great headway. In 2014, industrial output took up 30% of its national economy.

(3) The tertiary industry

As the most significant pillar of Indian economy, the tertiary industry contributed 72.4% of the economy in 2014. The service sector is the major job provider and target for foreign investment. In 2014, India's service sector grew by 6.8%, reaching 57% of the total GDP. Within it, the shares of hotel and trade service, financing service, social service and construction were 24%, 18.5%, 14.5 and 7.8%, up by 4.5%, 10.9%, 5.6% and 1.6%, respectively.

Table 6.2 Output of major industrial products 2011–2014 (Unit: 10,000 tons)

	2011	2012	2013	2014
Coal	42,040	58,310	60,982	61,000
Crude oil	3819	3810	3778	–
Steel	6957	8280	83,253	86,500
Iron ore	2080	1673	–	–
Power generation (million kWh)	1051.4	1108.5	1175.6	1256.0

Table 6.3 Number of visits paid by foreigners and the amount of foreign exchange earned

	2010	2011	2012	2013	2014	2015
The number of visits paid by foreigners (10,000)	577.5	630.9	657.7	696.7	770.3	800.0
Year-on-year growth rate	11.8	9.2	4.3	5.9	10.6	3.8
The amount of foreign exchange earned (million USD)	14,193	16,564	17,737	18,445	19,657	19,700
Year-on-year growth rate (%)	27.5	16.7	7.1	4.0	6.6	0.2

Tourist industry, playing an essential role in attracting foreign investment and creating jobs, is the priority of development for Indian government. In recent years, inbound tourist arrivals have been growing, hitting 7.67 million in 2014, 10.2% up on a year-on-year basis and much higher than the global average. What follows is the expansion of tourism revenue—in 2012, tourism generated 6.89% of GDP and 12.4% of jobs nationwide (see Table 6.3 for more information). Major tourist cities in India include Delhi, Agra, Chandigarh, Nalanda, Mysore, Goa, Hyderabad and Trivandrum.

Overall, India is yet to complete the transformation of its industrial structure. The change of its industrial structure follows Kuznets' theory of growth. As shown by Fig. 6.6, the share of agricultural output within Indian economy shrank from 42.6% in 1960 to 17.4% in 2014; however, the volume of agricultural output has not declined. In fact, as agricultural production grows more efficient, the released labor force moves to the secondary and tertiary industries, promoting the development of industry and service sector. In 1960, India's industrial output contributed 19.3% of its economy; in 2014, the figure shot up to 30%. In the second half of the twentieth century, the share of the tertiary industry within the Indian economy was around 40%. In 2014, the tertiary industry had emerged as its economic pillar, making up 52.6% of the economy.

2. Population and cities

Before its independence, India, oppressed by Britain, was of a weak economic foundation. Starting from the late nineteenth century, Britain had invested heavily in India, building ports and railways (mainly in mines) and promoting urbanization. When the Republic of India was founded in 1950, its rate of urbanization reached 17.3%, higher than the average level of developing countries (17.0%) and the Asian average (16.4%).[2] Urbanization is the result of industrialization. After its independence, India witnessed rapid industrial development, the improvement of industrial system and the acceleration of urbanization (see Fig. 6.7).

Table 6.4 lists the major cities in India and their populations.

Mumbai, the capital of Maharashtra, is the largest city and seaport of India and an important trade hub of Asia. Once the colony of Portugal and Britain, it is now

[2] MOFCOM: Q&A of foreign trade in Bangladesh, http://www.mofcom.gov.cn/article/i/jshz/new/201609/20160901390273.shtml.

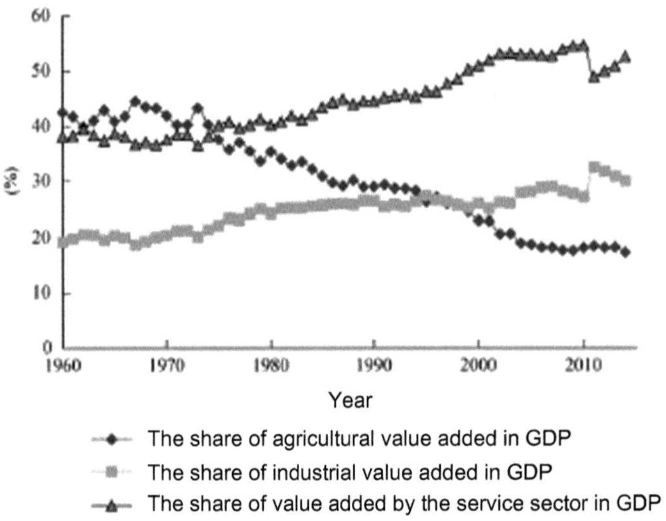

Fig. 6.6 Changes of industrial structure in India

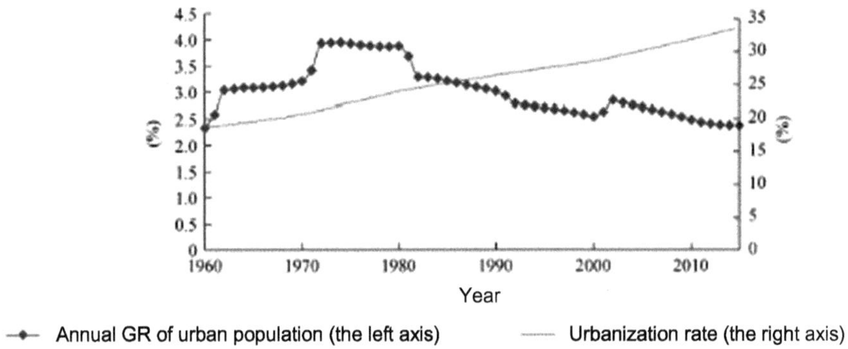

Fig. 6.7 Urbanization in India

Table 6.4 Top 5 cities in India

City	Population in 2016	City profile
Mumbai	12,691,836	The largest city and seaport in India
Delhi	10,927,986	The capital of India
Bangalore	5,104,047	The center of heavy industry; the "Silicon Valley" in Asia
Calcutta	4,631,392	A city located at the Ganges Delta in the east of India
Chennai	4,328,063	A city known for its world heritages

Source of data World Population Review

India's financial center—many financial institutions are headquartered in the city, including the Reserve Bank of India, the Bombay Stock Exchange and the National Stock Exchange of India. Many Indians prefer to live in Mumbai for its abundant employment opportunities and relatively high living standards.

Delhi, the capital of India, is composed of the old Delhi and the New Delhi. Old Delhi is home to many historic buildings, temples and monuments. New Delhi, located in the south of Delhi, is a modern city built in 1911.

Bangalore, the capital of Karnataka, is the third largest city in India. Located on the Deccan Plateau in the southern India, the city is 174.7 km^2 large and has a population of 5.1 million. Also called the Silicon Valley of Asia, it is the center of heavy industry and high technology. Combining Kannada, Telugus and Tamil cultures, the city is also the cultural center of India. It has many cultural and educational institutions, including Bangalore University, Indian National Science Academy, Indian Institute of Science, University of Agricultural Sciences and National Institute of Dynamics. It also has monuments such as the Bangalore Fort built in 1761 and many historic temples.

Calcutta, the capital of West Bengal that sits on the Ganges delta and the east bank of Hooghly River, is the 4th largest city in India. It also serves as the center of modern education, science and culture. When India was a British colony, Calcutta was its capital. After the country claimed independence in 1947, Calcutta fell into economic stagnation. Recovery did not arrive until the beginning of the twenty-first century.

Chennai, the capital of Tamil Nadu, stands in the southeast of India and on the shore of Bengal Bay. Covering an area of 130 km^2, it is the 5th largest city and also the commercial and industrial center of India. Tamil, English, Telugu and Malayalam are the most commonly used languages. The southwest of the city is where the affluent classes reside, while the north is the industrial zone.

3. Consumer spending

Consumer spending varies as India's level of economic development changes. As shown by Fig. 6.8, in the second half of the twentieth century, India's economic development was at a low level, so was its consumer spending; in the twenty-first century, its consumption level witnessed a rapid rise as its economy boomed. In addition, Indian population has been on the rise too—it shot up from the 450 million in 1990 to 1.311 billion in 2015, emerging as the second most populated country in the world. From the perspective of economic structure, India is a developing country at the early stage of industrialization. It has abundant supply of labor force—its working population makes up 40% of the population, and the proportion of population employed in agriculture is still large (49.7% of the total working population in 2013). The population employed in industry is increasing and its share within the total working population had risen from 15.7% in 1994 to 21.5% in 2013. The population employed in the service sector stays stable, and its share within the total working population was 22% in 1994 and 21.5% in 2013.

(II) Foreign trade and investment

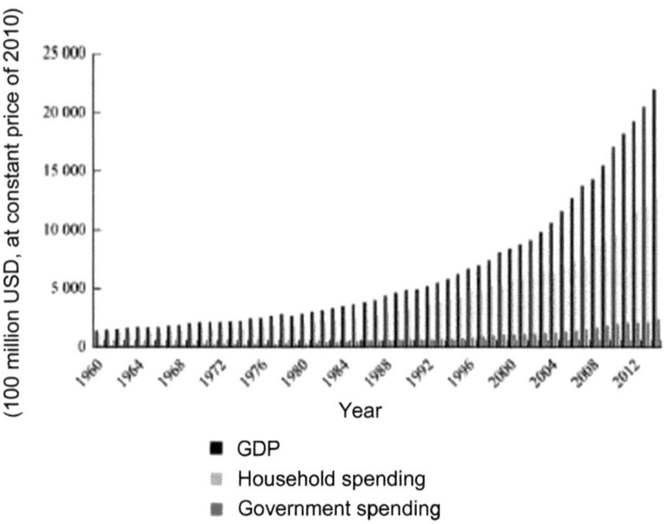

Fig. 6.8 Consumer spending in India

1. Foreign trade

According to its Ministry of Commerce, India's foreign trade volume reached 658.3 billion USD in 2015, 15.6% down compared to 2014. Within the overall volume, import generated 391.6 billion USD, 15.1% lower compared to 2014, and export contributed 266.7 billion USD, 17.1% lower than last year (see Table 6.5). In 2015, India's major trading partners include China, the United States, Switzerland, UAE, Britain, Singapore, Germany, Saudi Arab, Bangladesh, Sri Lanka and Vietnam. The United States is India's largest export destination (40.242 billion USD), followed by UAE (30.537 billion USD). Its main export products are precious metals, textiles and raw materials, chemical products, mineral products and transportation equipment. China is the largest source of imports for India (61.14 billion USD), followed by Switzerland (21.124 billion USD) and Saudi Arab (21.058 billion USD). It mainly imports mineral products, electro-mechanical products, precious metals and articles thereof, chemical products and base metals and articles thereof. See Tables 6.5, 6.6, 6.7, 6.8 and 6.9 for more information.

2. Foreign investment

In the past, India did not have special policies for attracting foreign investment. Instead, it treated foreign and domestic investors equally, and foreign investors also enjoyed preferential treatment in areas with government support. However, in recent years, facing economic slowdown and rising unemployment, India has relaxed restrictions on the areas where foreign investment is allowed. Cable TV network, satellite TV network, duty-free shops and limited liability companies are allowed to be wholly owned by foreign investors; foreign investors are allowed to own up to

Table 6.5 Annual trade profile of India (Unit: million USD)

Year	Total volume	Year-on-year (%)	Export	Year-on-year (%)	Import	Year-on-year (%)	Gap	Year-on-year (%)
2004	172,943	34.4	75,631	31.6	97,313	36.7	−21,682	58.0
2005	238,021	37.6	99,651	31.8	138,370	42.2	−38,719	78.6
2006	294,136	23.6	121,259	21.7	172,876	24.9	−51,617	33.3
2007	365,107	24.1	147,564	21.7	217,543	25.8	−69,978	35.6
2008	470,882	29.0	178,034	20.7	292,848	34.6	−114,814	64.1
2009	413,134	−20.0	163,167	−16.4	249,967	−22.2	−86,800	−31.3
2010	551,907	30.5	223,176	35.1	328,731	27.6	−105,555	14.2
2011	772,162	14.2	307,086	14.3	465,076	14.0	−157,990	49.7
2012	780,469	1.1	291,187	−5.1	489,282	5.2	−198,095	5.8
2013	780,028	0.1	312,470	5.1	467,558	−4.7	−155,088	−21.7
2014	779,660	−0.4	319,546	1.4	460,114	−1.7	−140,568	−8.1
2015	658,365	−15.6	266,711	−17.1	391,654	−15.1	124,943	−11.1

Table 6.6 Volume of export to major trading partners (Unit: million USD)

Countries and regions	Volume	Year-on-year (%)	Proportion (%)
Total volume	266,711	−17.1	100.0
The United States	40,242	−5.1	15.1
UAE	30,537	−7.9	11.5
Hong Kong, China	12,167	−11.0	4.6
Mainland, China	9694	−27.2	3.6
Britain	8893	−8.0	3
Singapore	7818	−24.1	2.9
Germany	7034	−9.2	2.6
Saudi Arab	6979	−44.8	2.6
Bangladesh	5761	−15.6	2.2
Sri Lanka	5534	−14.0	2.1
Vietnam	5336	−18.0	2.0
Belgium	5013	−15.4	1.9
Malaysia	4945	3.3	1.9
Netherlands	4935	−28.5	1.9
France	4775	−4.1	1.8

49% of the stakc of news TV stations and radio stations, and up to 74% of the stake of private local banks. In addition, foreign investors are allowed to have a 49% stake in defense companies and regional airlines without securing government approval.

Tables 6.10 and 6.11 list the major investors in India and their fields of investment. Till 2015, top investors in India included Singapore, Netherlands, Japan, the United States, Britain, Germany, France, Cyprus and UAE. For most of them, especially for Singapore, Netherlands, Japan and Germany, their investment in India has been rising. Investment from Britain, once India's largest foreign investor (2007), has been declining. As to the areas receiving foreign investment, the service sector has always been the most attractive area, and industries of telecommunication and automobile have exceeded the IT industry to be another major recipient of foreign investment.

In 1991, India started economic reform. It lowered the access threshold to draw in more foreign investment. In the fiscal year 2011/2012, direct foreign investment in India was 32.95 billion USD; the figure rose to 36.4 billion USD in the fiscal year 2013/2014. Mauritius, Singapore and Britain were the top 3 investors in India. Major recipients of foreign investment include the manufacturing industry, the construction industry and the service sector. From April to November 2014, 27.7 billion USD of foreign investment flew to India; the figure over the same period in 2015 was 34.8 billion USD, 60% of which was from small countries such as Singapore, Mauritius, Netherlands and the United States. Most of the money flew into IT industry,

Table 6.7 India's major export products in 2015 (Unit: million USD)

Customs classification	HS code	Commodity category	2015	Same period last year	Year-on-year (%)	Proportion (%)
		Total volume	266,711	321,740	−17.1	100.0
Class 14	71	Precious metals and articles thereof	38,824	42,119	−7.8	14.6
Class 11	50–63	Textiles and raw materials	37,201	38,664	−3.8	14.0
Class 6	28–38	Chemical products	38,229	37,113	3.0	14.3
Class 5	25–27	Mineral products	35,042	67,915	−48.4	13.1
Class 17	86–89	Transportation equipment	22,303	26,056	−14.4	8.4
Class 15	72–83	Base metals and articles thereof	21,414	25,553	−16.2	8.0
Class 16	84–85	Electro-mechanical products	21,263	22,683	−6.3	8.0
Class 2	06–14	Plant products	15,708	20,651	−23.9	5.9
Class 1	01–05	Live animals; animal products	9341	11,046	−15.4	3.5
Class 7	39–40	Plastics; rubber	7377	8167	−9.7	2.8
Class 4	16–24	Prepared foodstuffs; beverage; tobacco	5725	6525	−12.3	2.2
Class 8	41–43	Articles of leather; goods; cases	3526	3919	−10.0	1.3
Class 12	64–67	Light industrial products such as footwear and umbrellas	3106	3312	−6.2	1.2
Class 13	68–70	Ceramics and glass	2934	2882	1.8	1.1
Class 18	90–92	Optical instrument, clocks and watches, and medical equipment	2439	2444	−0.2	0.9
		Others	2281	2692	−15.3	0.8

the service sector and trade. As shown by Fig. 6.9, the proportion of FDI within gross GDP has been rising since 1980—FDI has become a key component of Indian economy. The proportion plunged after the financial crisis in 2008 and recovered in a volatile way after 2010. By 2015, the proportion had rebounded to 2%. Meanwhile, the share of OFDI had continued to tumble since 2008—it was smaller than 0.5% in 2015.

In recent years, trade relations between China and India have been growing stronger. According to Indian Bureau of Commercial Statistics as well as Ministry

Table 6.8 Volume of import from major trading partners in 2015 (Unit: million USD)

Countries and regions	Volume	Year-on-year (%)	Proportion (%)
Total volume	391,654	−15.1	100.0
China	61,140	4.9	15.6
Switzerland	21,124	−0.2	5.4
Saudi Arab	21,058	−35.4	5.4
The United States	20,676	−3.3	5.3
UAE	20,455	−24.9	5.2
Indonesia	13,997	−7.0	3.6
South Korea	13,116	−3.0	3.4
Germany	11,893	−7.7	3.0
Iraq	11,322	−29.7	2.9
Nigeria	10,220	−34.8	2.6
Qatar	9671	−41.3	2.5
Japan	9646	−3.4	2.5
Malaysia	9564	−12.9	2.4
Australia	9477	−5.4	2.4
Belgium	8362	−25.9	2.1

of Commerce and Industry, the volume of Sino-Indian trade in 2015 was 70.83 billion USD, 1.1% lower on a year-on-year basis. More specifically, export from India to China was 9.69 billion USD, 27.2% down compared to 2014 and 3.6% of India's total export; meanwhile, India imported 61.14 billion USD of goods from China, 4.9% higher compared to 2014 and 15.6% of its total import. Top 5 export products from India to China include cotton, copper and copper products, organic chemicals, building materials and fossil fuels to China; top 5 import products from China to India include electro-mechanical products, machinery, organic chemicals, fertilizer and steel. By the end of 2014, China was India's 4th largest trading partner and largest source of import. Among the top 10 import products of India, textiles, Chinese products such as electro-mechanical products, furniture, metal products, optical instrument and ceramics are of significant competitive edges among similar goods. However, products such as transportation equipment, chemicals, precious metal products and steel still face fierce competition from developed countries such as the United States, Japan and European countries.

Table 6.9 India's major import products in 2015 (Unit: million USD)

Customs classification	HS code	Commodity categories	2015	Same period last year	Year-on-year (%)	Proportion (%)
		Total volume	391,654	461,363	−15.1	100.0
Class 5	25–27	Mineral products	113,752	187,065	−39.2	29.0
Class 16	84–85	Electro-mechanical products	67,502	63,111	7.0	17.2
Class 14	71	Precious metals and products	59,705	60,195	−0.8	15.2
Class 6	28–38	Chemical products	41,973	42,125	−0.4	10.7
Class 15	72–83	Base metals and products	26,675	26,807	−0.5	6.8
Class 7	39–40	Plastics; rubber	14,275	15,181	−6.0	3.7
Class 17	86–89	Transportation equipment	13,575	14,018	−3.2	3.5
Class 22	98	Other special goods	10,882	10,646	2.2	2.8
Class 3	15	Animal and vegetable oils	10,488	10,657	−1.6	2.7
Class 2	06–14	Plant products	8248	6619	24.6	2.1
Class 18	90–92	Optical instrument, clocks and watches, and medical equipment	7528	7390	1.9	1.9
Class 11	50–63	Textiles and raw materials	5859	5884	−0.4	1.5
Class 10	47–49	Cellulose; paper	4465	4687	−4.8	1.1
Class 20	94–96	Furniture, toy, miscellaneous products	2457	2142	14.7	0.6
Class 9	44–46	Wood and wooden products	2442	2716	−10.1	0.6
		Other	1828	2119	−13.8	0.5

Table 6.10 Major foreign investors of India (Unit: million USD)

Year	Singapore	Netherlands	Japan	The United States	Britain	Germany	France	Cyprus	UAE
2015	6742	3436	2084	1824	1447	1125	635	598	367
2010	2379	899	1183	1943	657	626	303	1627	629
2007	578	644	85	856	1878	120	117	58	260

Table 6.11 Changes of fields receiving foreign investment in India (Unit: million USD)

Year	Service	Telecommunication	Vehicle	IT	Construction	Electricity
2015	4443	2895	2726	2296	769	707
2010	4176	2539	1236	872	2852	1272
2007	4664	478	276	2614	985	157

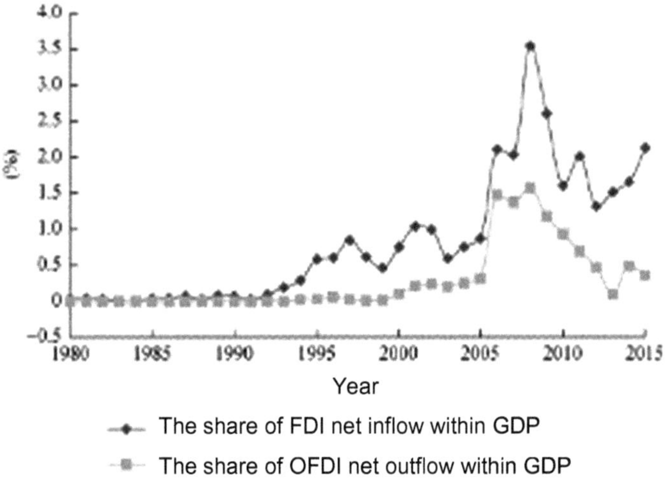

Fig. 6.9 International investment of India

6.3 Pakistan

I. Geographical and historical backgrounds

Pakistan and India, both located on the sub-continent of South Asia, belonged to the same country till their partition in 1947. Pakistan has a territory of more than 800,000 km^2 and a population of 150 million. Most Pakistanis are Muslims. Facing the Arabian Sea on the south, Pakistan has a coastline as long as 1046 km. The distance from the west end of its coastline to Muscat (the capital of Oman) as the crow flies is only 390 km. Therefore, Pakistan is of great significance in strategies concerning the Persian Gulf. The shape of the country is somewhat like a rectangle. Besides, it also owns 25,220 km^2 of territorial waters. To its east lies India, with 1610 km of shared border; to its northeast lies China, with a shared border of 595 km; to its northwest is Afghanistan, with a shared border of 2430 km, and the 16–19 km wide Wakhan Corridor of Afghanistan connects the country with Tajikistan of Central Asia; to its southwest lies Iran, with 805 km of shared border.

II. Economic development

(I) Domestic economy

According to the historic data from the World Bank, GNP of Pakistan has been growing steadily (except for the slight decline in 2009 after the financial crisis in 2008), which is especially outstanding in the context of weak recovery in developed countries and global economic slowdown. According to the IMF, GNP per capita of Pakistan was 1343 USD in 2014, ranking No.152 in the world and making it a lower mid-income country; however, during the same period, gross GDP of the country was 246.876 billion USD, ranking No.43 in the world and better than other similar developing countries. Steady growth and large economic aggregate have created unlimited potential for Pakistani economy. See Fig. 6.10 for more information.

In its latest report, the World Bank expresses optimism about the future of Pakistani economy. It believes energy shortage in Pakistan will be alleviated as the environment of doing business and security improve, and the development of China–Pakistan Economic Corridor makes progress. According to the report, in the mid and long term, Pakistani economy, with the help of three free rides, could achieve an annual growth rate of 5.5% in the fiscal year of 2016–2017: the first free ride is the growing Chinese investment as the result of China–Pakistan Economic Corridor; the second is the potential upgrade of Iranian–Pakistani energy cooperation following the lifting of sanctions on Iran; the third is the benefit of low oil price for investors and consumers.

1. Industrial structure

(1) The primary industry

Pakistan is a developing capitalist country and an agriculture-based economy. 25% of its GNP is contributed by agriculture. Pakistan has generally achieved food self-sufficiency. It exports rice and cotton. As the 5th largest cotton producer in the world, it produces 5% of cotton in the world. Located in the sub-tropical zone, the country also has abundant fruit resources.

(2) The secondary industry

Pakistan has a small industrial sector, and many categories are missing. Major mineral reserves include natural gas (492 billion m^3), oil (184 million barrel), coal (185 billion ton), iron (430 million ton) and alumina (74 million ton).

Since its independence in 1947, Pakistan has gone through three stages of economic development—the encouragement of private investment and light industry in 1947–1959, the nationalization of industrial enterprises in 1972–1976 and the liberalization after 1977. Today, Pakistani industry is still mainly light industry and non-durable goods manufacturing.

In Pakistan, 24% of GDP is industrial output. Textile industry is the mainstay of Pakistani economy. Energy sector, IT sector and small and medium-sized industry are expanding fast. Pakistan mainly imports oil and oil products, machinery and transportation equipment, steel products, fertilizer and electric appliance. Its major export products are cotton, textiles, rice, fruit, fishery products, leather products, sporting goods, medical equipment and carpet.

(3) The tertiary industry

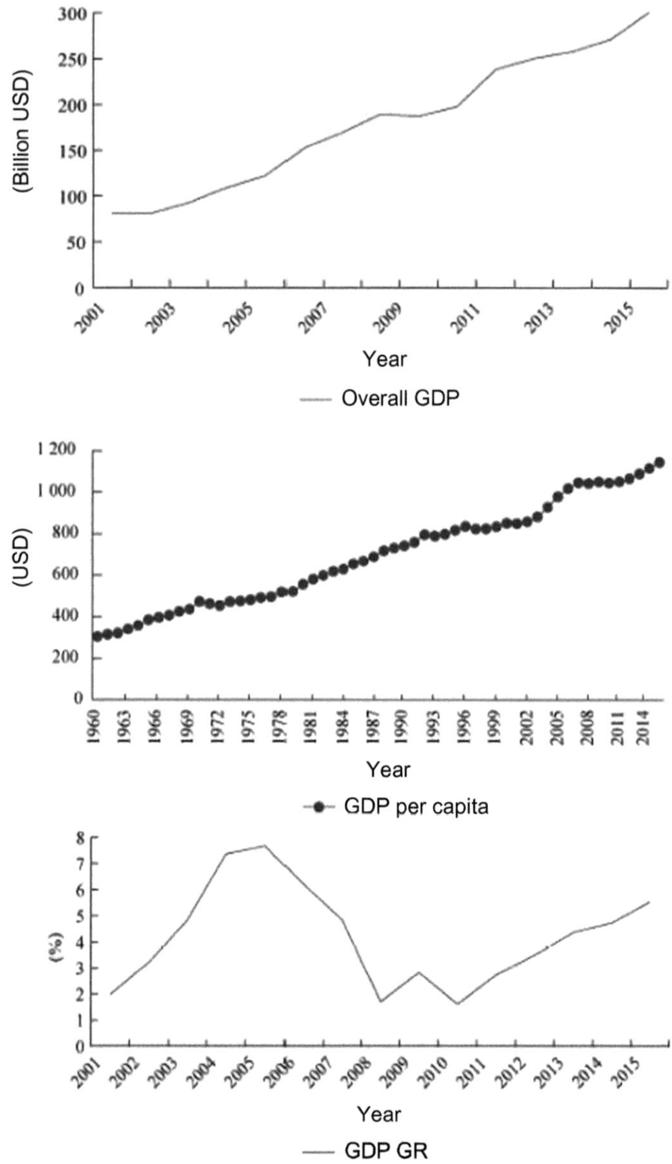

Fig. 6.10 Economic indicators of Pakistan

In recent years, IT industry in Pakistan is growing fast. Currently, there are more than 1500 IT companies; every year more than 10,000 computer science graduates enter the labor market. In 2015, the size of its programmer market is the 3rd largest in the world.

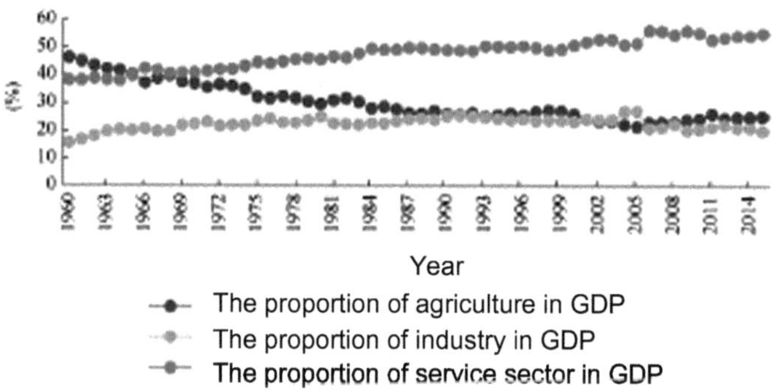

Fig. 6.11 Industrial restructuring in Pakistan

Pakistan started its economic transformation since the 1950s, and the process is still going on. As shown in Fig. 6.11, the weight of agriculture has been declining. In 2015, the proportion of agriculture in national economy was 25.1%. The proportion is still relatively large due to the low efficiency of agricultural production and the large labor force involved in this sector. As a weak link, industry takes up a smaller share within the national economy compared to agriculture and the service sector. Lacking growth momentum, the industrial sector lends little impetus to economic development. As the dominant force of Pakistani economy, the service sector for the first time exceeded agriculture in terms of output in 1968. Currently, the service sector, running far ahead of agriculture and industry, is the main engine of economic growth in Pakistan.

2. Population and cities

Due to its weak economic foundation, the lagging behind of industrial development and the impact of wars, urbanization in Pakistan has been slow and does not match its economic and industrial development. In recent years, as Pakistan begins to attract foreign investment and utilize foreign aids, its urbanization rate gradually grows. As shown by Fig. 6.12, the urbanization rate has risen from 22.1% in 1960 to 38.7% in 2015, one of the highest in South Asia.

Table 6.12 lists the major cities of Pakistan.

Karachi is the largest city in Pakistan and the capital of Sindh Province. Located on the southern coast of Pakistan and the northwest of the Indus delta (on the plain between the Malir River and the Layari River), the city faces the Arabian Sea to its south and covers an area of 3527 km^2 (of which 1821 km^2 belongs to the metropolitan area). With a population of 11.624 million, the city is the major port in the Indus basin, and also once the largest grain export port of British India. As WWI ended, Karachi began to develop the manufacturing and service industries. Its first airport, Jinnah International Airport, was completed in 1924 and later evolved into one of the major entrances to British India.

Lahore, the cultural and art center of Pakistan, has been known as the Garden City. With more than 2000 years' history, it was the capital of the Mughal Empire and

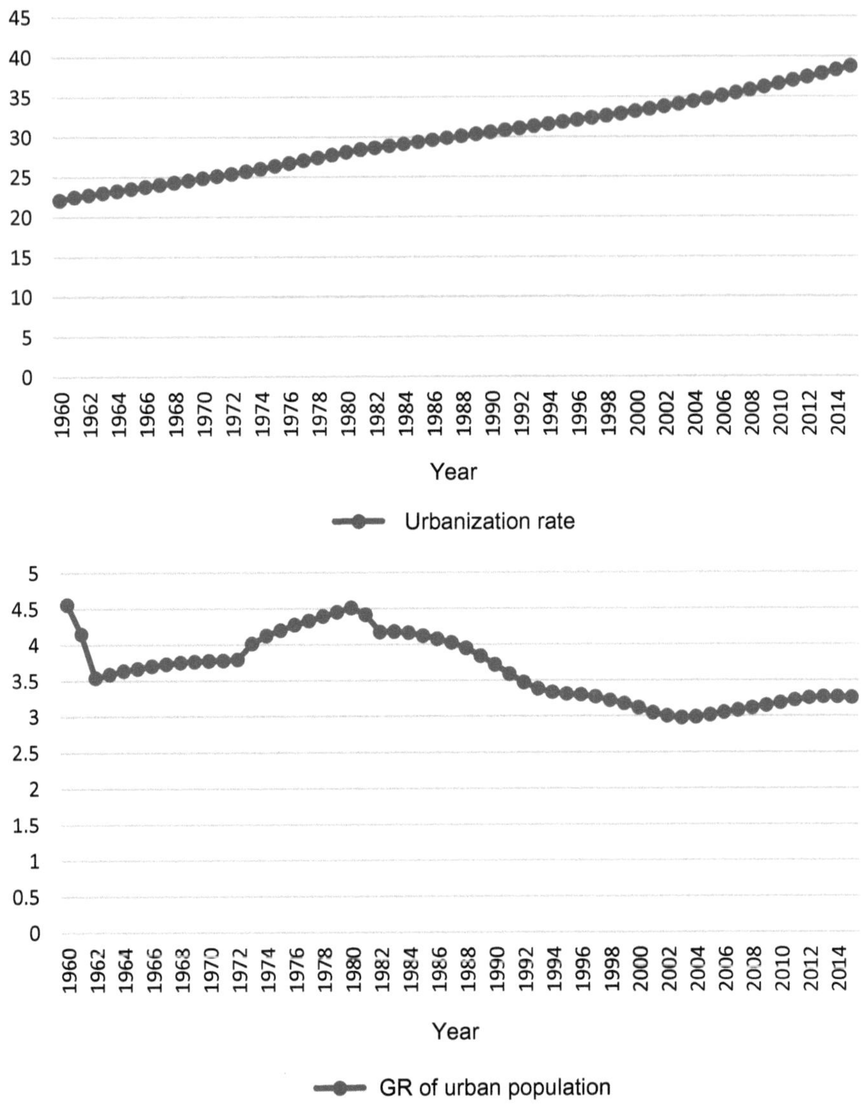

Fig. 6.12 Urbanization in Pakistan. *Source of data* World Bank database

visited by the Chinese Monk Xuanzang in AD 630. After Pakistan's independence in 1947, it became the capital of Punjab Province, the richest region in the country. With rapid economic growth and 10 million residents, it has turned into the second largest city and the key industrial center of Pakistan.

Faisalabad, once known as Lyallpur, is the third largest city of Pakistan. Located in the northeast of the country, it is the center of textile industry. Producing cotton and wheat, it is also the wholesale market of agricultural products. Meanwhile, it has

Table 6.12 Top 5 cities of Pakistan

City	Total population in 2016	Description
Karachi	11,624,219	The largest city in Pakistan
Lahore	6,310,888	A garden city; also the center of culture and art
Faisalabad	2,506,595	Center of textile industry
Rawalpindi	1,743,101	Once the temporary temple
Multan	1,437,230	A historic city

capacity of agricultural research thanks to its agricultural university, cotton research institute and institute of agricultural sciences. Its industrial capacity is concentrated on the textile and food processing industries. The city has textile mills of various levels and manufacturers of fertilizer and canned food. It is connected by road, rail and air with other key cities in Pakistan.

Rawalpindi is a city in Punjab Province. Lying on the Potwar Plateau, it is 14 km southwest of Islamabad. With a population of 1.74 million and 526 m above the sea level, the city occupies the site of an old village inhabited by the Rawals. Since its capture by the British army in 1849, it has been valued as a vital point of defense in Northwest India. During the construction of the new capital Islamabad in 1959–1967, it served as the provisional capital. After the completion of the new capital to its northeast, the two cities merged into the Islamabad–Rawalpindi metropolitan district. This region, left with traces of the colonial rule, is in sharp contrast with the oriental styled Rajabasa area. Rawalpindi has the Ayub National Park and 6 schools of the Punjab University. The city is divided into the old and new areas. The new area, once the military camp of the British army and now granted with prosperous markets and convenient transportation, is home to government officials and wealthy businessmen and their courtyard houses. The old area, cluttered and crowded, is where the ordinary people live. Apart from the wholesale markets of wood and livestock, Rawalpindi, as one of the industrial and commercial centers of Pakistan, also has textile, food, chemistry and metal industries. The city is the starting point of the road to Kashmir, it is crossed by the Lahore–Peshawar Railway and links with Afghanistan, Srinagar and Lahore by highway and it is also equipped with an airport, all of which have made it the transportation hub between the Himalayas and the Gangetic Plain.

Multan, located at the downstream of the Chenab River in the east of Pakistan, is a city of 1.43 million people and 2500 years' history. As the administrative center of Multan District and a center of textile industry, it has the second largest textile mill in Pakistan. Besides, it has the largest fertilizer factory in the country and also a gas-fired power station. Other industries are glassmaking, sugar refining and oil pressing. Famous local handicrafts include pottery, ivory products, leatherware and carpet. Major agricultural products are cotton, wheat, rice and sugarcane. The city is also a hub of transportation. Local landmarks include medieval mosques and castles.

As shown by Fig. 6.13, as Pakistani economy grows, consumer spending is increasing. However, its government spending has remained stable due to political instability. Affected by economic and security situations, the population of Pakistan

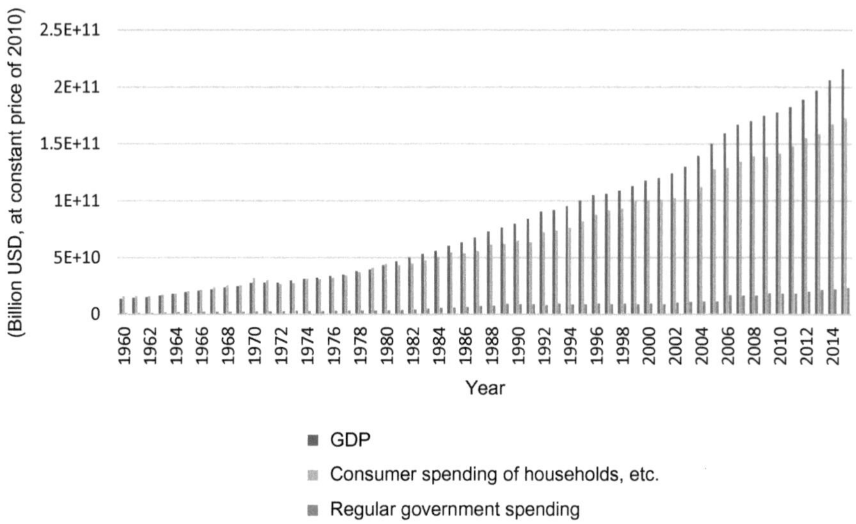

Fig. 6.13 Consumer spending in Pakistan

grows slowly: it grew from 107 million in 1990 to 189 million in 2015. The labor force takes a relatively small share of the population—35.3% in 2014. The proportion of labor force engaged in agriculture has been declining, but still, half of the country's working population is employed by the farming sector. Meanwhile, the industrial sector is absorbing fewer people than agriculture and the service sector. See Fig. 6.14 for more information.

(II) 国际贸易

As one of the founding members of GATT and also WTO, Pakistan has signed trade deals with many countries. To boost economic growth and promote restructuring, Pakistan has relaxed through legislation restrictions on foreign investment and offered preferential treatment to foreign companies, including exempting them from government approval procedure, allowing them to remit capital, profits and dividends back to their own countries, lifting the constraints on the proportion of foreign ownership and offering tax cuts. The preferential policies are usually targeted at companies investing in priority sectors or regions listed by the Pakistani government.

Export from Pakistan, mainly limited to unprocessed or primary agricultural and textile products due to low technical content and industrial level, has a small presence in the global market. In 2014, only eight categories of products achieved a market share higher than 10%: all of them are agricultural and textile products, and none of the rates exceeded 20%.

As to goods and services, Pakistan is highly dependent on import. Import takes up a bigger share within the national economy compared to export, as shown by Fig. 6.15.

2. International investment

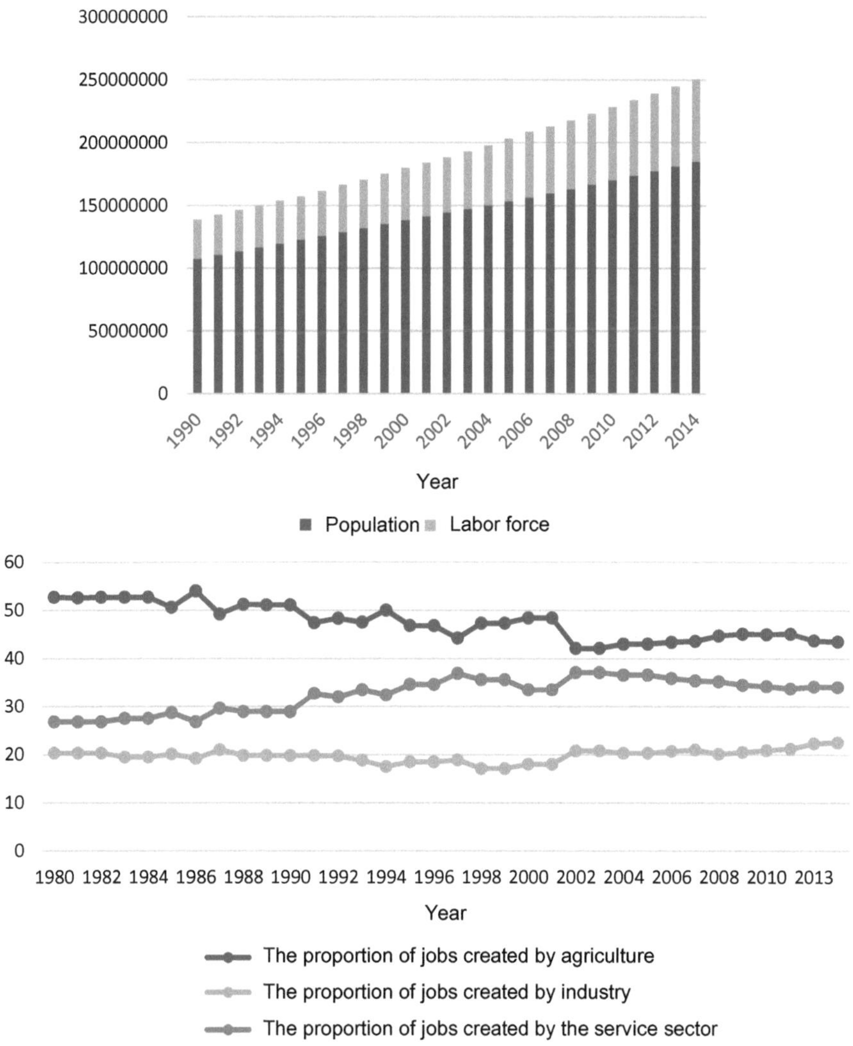

Fig. 6.14 Population and labor force in Pakistan

Pakistan makes little overseas investment—its outward investment takes up only 0.01% of the national economy. Instead, it is highly dependent on FDI, as shown by Table 6.13 and Fig. 6.16.

China has a developed good trade relations with Pakistan. In 2015, bilateral trade reached 18.93 billion USD, up by 18.2% on a YOY basis. Export from China to Pakistan was worth 16.45 billion USD, 24.17% up; import from Pakistan to China was down by 10.26% to 2.477 billion USD; the gap between export and import hit 13.973 billion USD, up by 104.9%. As to investment, Chinese direct non-financial investment in Pakistan was 210 million USD in 2015, down by 79.2% on a YOY

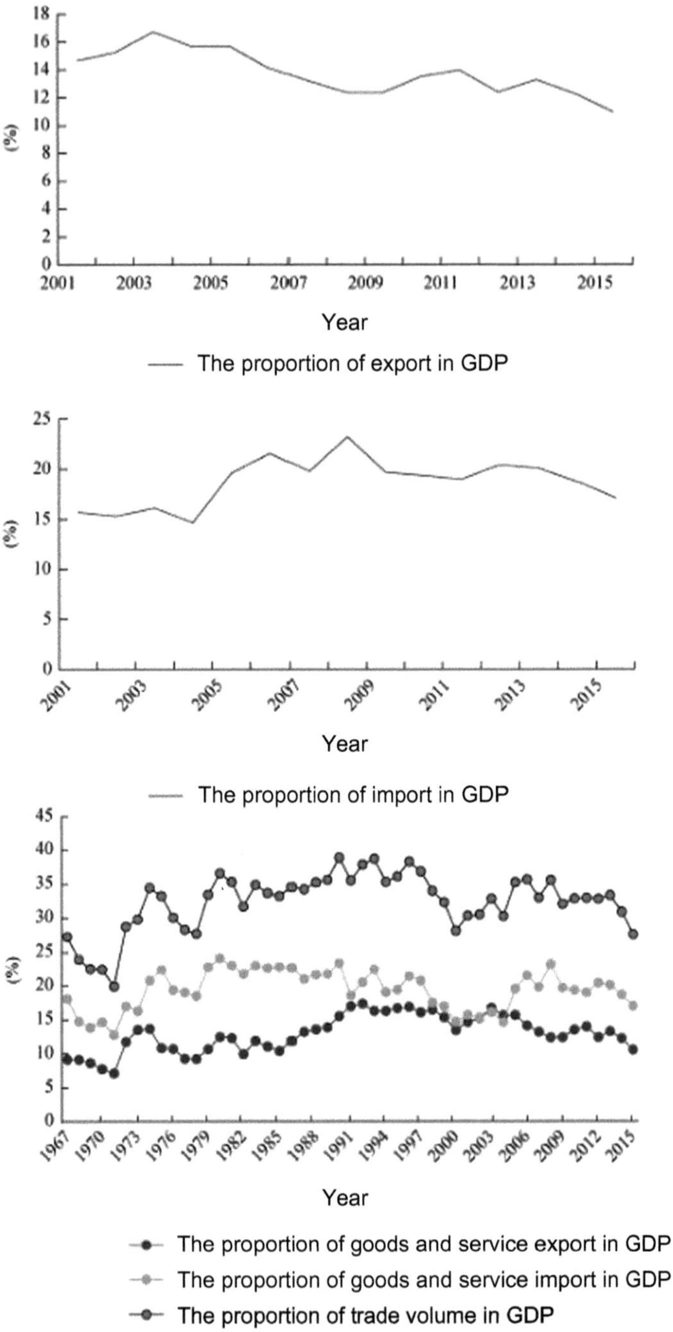

Fig. 6.15 Foreign trade of Pakistan

Table 6.13 FDI in Pakistan (Unit: million USD)

Year	FDI
2013	1456.5
2012	820.6
2011	1634.7
2010	2150.8
2009	3719.9
2008	3719.1
2007	5152.8

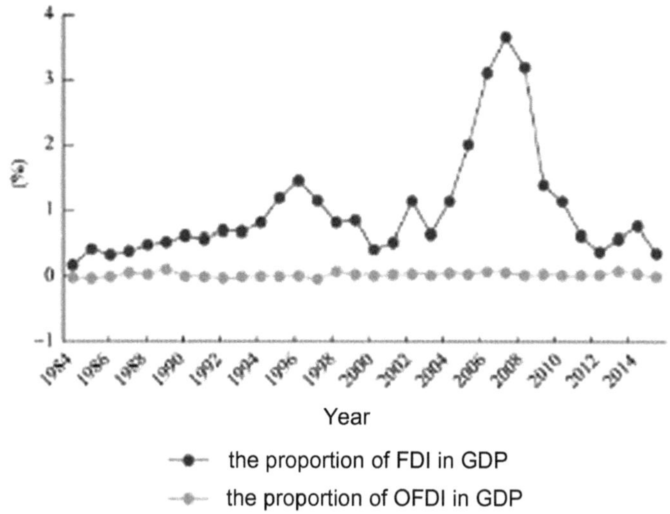

Fig. 6.16 International investment of Pakistan

basis; also in 2015, Pakistan has in total 66 investment projects in China, the same as in 2014; however, the actual volume of Pakistani investment in China was only 650,000 USD, down by 97.2% on a YOY basis. By the end of December 2015, China had 510 direct investment projects in Pakistan totaling 111 million USD, most of which are projects contracted to Chinese enterprises. In 2015, the value of newly signed contracts by Chinese enterprises reached 12.180 billion USD, 377.6% up on a YOY basis, and the turnover was hiked by 21.6% and hit 5.163 billion USD. By the end of December 2015, the cumulative value of project contracts signed by Chinese enterprises in Pakistan had reached 45.448 billion USD and the turnover 33.079 billion USD.

6.4 Sri Lanka

I. **Geographical and historical backgrounds**

Sri Lanka, short for the Democratic Socialist Republic of Sri Lanka, is a tropical island country on the Indian Ocean. It is a member of the British Commonwealth. Once known as Ceylon, the country was also called the country of lions and Sinhala in ancient China.

Agriculture is the economic mainstay of Sri Lanka. As one the three tea producers in the world, it is sensitive to tea production economically since Ceylon black tea is its most important export product. The country is endowed with rich mineral resources and good location. Ranking top five in terms of gem production, it is hailed as the "Gem Island". At the early stage of economic development, the mining industry had earned it many advantages of development. Every year, its volume of gem export could reach 500 million USD, and rubies, sapphires and opals are the most famous kinds.

Sri Lanka has a time-honored history of participation in global governance. It is the founding member of SAARC and a member of the United Nations; it also joined the British Commonwealth, G77 and the Non-Aligned Movement. Currently, it is the only South Asian country rated "high" in terms of the UN Human Development Index.

II. **Economic development**

(I) Domestic economy

As shown by Fig. 6.17, GDP and per capita GDP in Sri Lanka have been growing steadily. It has maintained prominent growth despite global economic slowdown. Statistics suggest its economic aggregate reached 82.3 billion USD and per capita GDP 3930 USD in 2015, making it one of the middle- and low-income countries. In the past 20 years, its economic growth rate stayed above 4% despite minor fluctuations.

1. Industrial structure

(1) The primary industry

As an agricultural country, Sri Lanka is granted with the good conditions for developing agriculture, including fertile land, suitable climate and diverse tropical cash crops. The country is mainly of plantation economy. Meanwhile, it is rich in forest resources and valuable timbers such as rosewood, ebony and teakwood. Tea, coconut and rubber are Sri Lanka's three major sources of revenue and export products.

(2) The secondary industry

Major industrial sectors in Sri Lanka are based in the Colombo district and include textile, garment, leatherware, food, beverage, tobacco, papermaking, timber, chemical engineering, oil processing, rubber, plastic, metal processing and machine

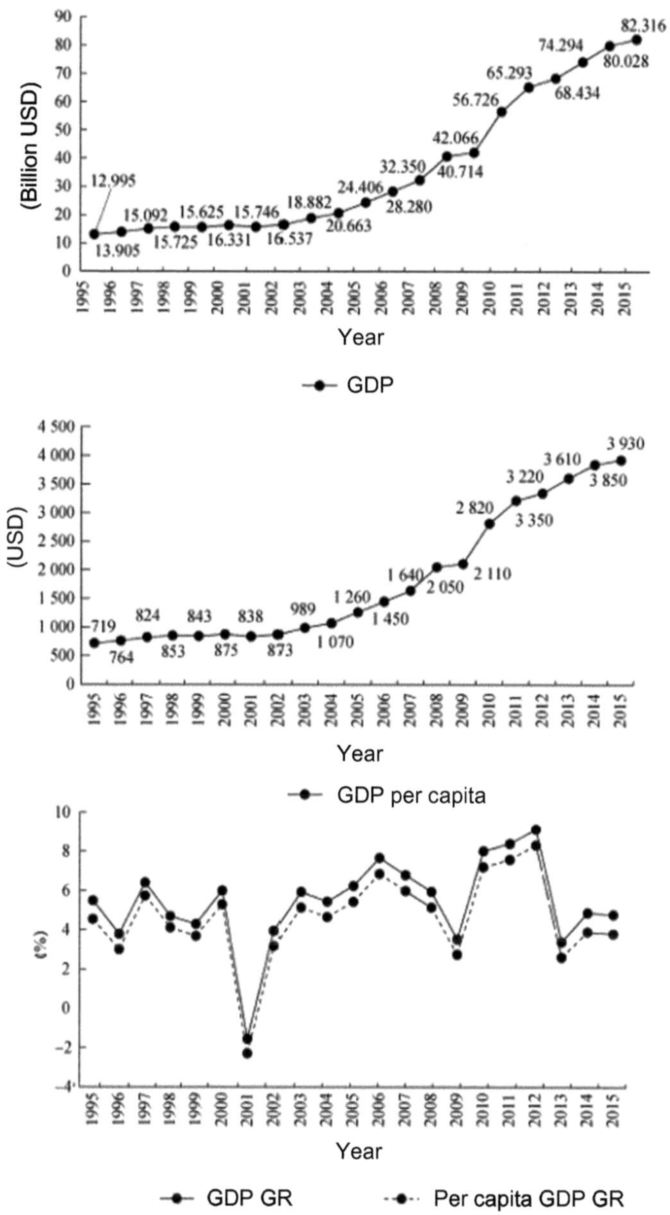

Fig. 6.17 Economic indicators of Sri Lanka. *Source of data* World Bank database

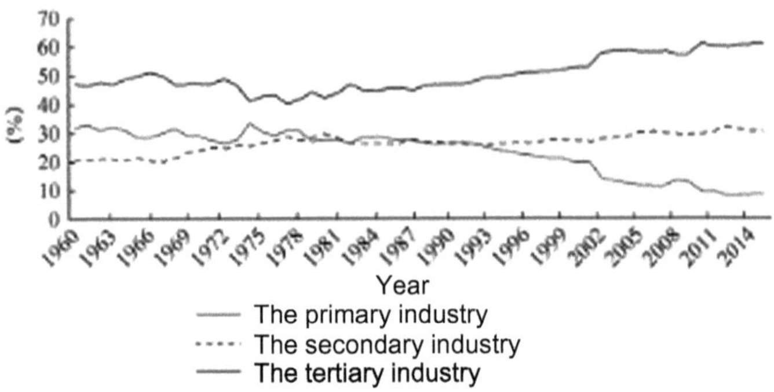

Fig. 6.18 Industrial structure of Sri Lanka. *Source of data* UN database

assembly. Due to the lack of industrial resources, industry in Sri Lanka is of a weak foundation. Most raw materials and oil and coal for industrial production are imported; capital-intensive and technology-intensive industries are yet to take shape, and the heavy industry barely exists. Sri Lanka government takes seriously the protection and conservation of environment and resources and sets strict limit to the exploitation of mineral resources.

(3) The tertiary industry

The service sector in Sri Lanka mainly covers wholesale and retail, hotel, catering, transportation, warehousing, telecommunication, tourism, financial services and real estate. In recent years, local government, by fully tapping the improving literacy rate and working skills, is trying to build a service-oriented economy. Now, the service sector has become the major driving force of the national economy. See Fig. 6.18 for more information.

2. Urbanization and cities

In 2009, Sri Lanka ended its internal armed conflict which had lasted for 26 years and embraced peace and development. Improved security situation has served as a boost to its economic growth. In recent years, local government has stepped up its investment in infrastructure and built a series of key projects, covering areas such as electricity, energy, aviation, transportation, water resources and telecommunication. A national highway network is coming into being, the transportation capacity of local roads has been growing, and the energy structure is improving as it has become the only country in South Asia that has got rid of power shortage.

As seen in Fig. 6.19, the overall urbanization rate in Sri Lanka has seen slight decline. From 1995 to 2015, the figure stayed between 18.35 and 18.60%. Sri Lanka is an agriculture-based country, and its infrastructure still lags behind, which has hindered urbanization on a larger scale.

Table 6.14 lists the major cities of Sri Lanka.

Situated on the west coast of the Sri Lanka Island, Colombo is a principal port of the Indian Ocean. It is one of the largest artificial harbors in the world and Sri Lanka's

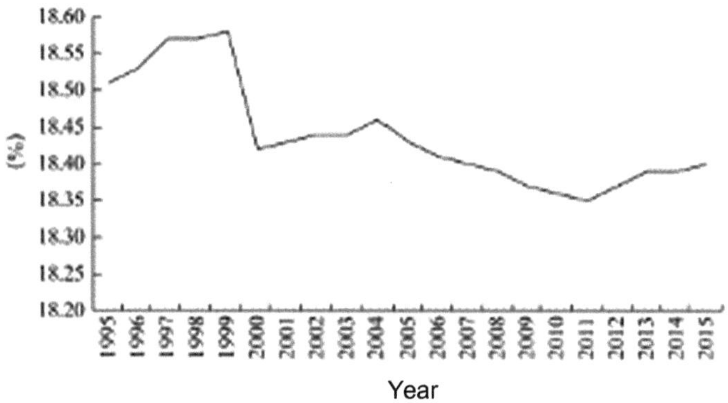

Fig. 6.19 Urbanization rate in Sri Lanka. *Source of data* World Bank database

Table 6.14 Top 5 cities in Sri Lanka

City	Population in 2016	Profiles
Colombo	648,034	Capital, seaport, center of politics, economy, culture and transportation
Moratuwa	185,031	Tourist city located at the southwest and the Indian Ocean coast with beautiful sceneries
Jaffna	167,102	Tourist city with abundant tourism resources
Negombo	137,223	A key fishing port rich in prawns and crabs
Kandy	111,701	Tourist city and a pilgrimage site of Buddhism

center of politics, economy, culture and transportation. It handles the majority of the country's foreign trade and is known as "the crossroad in the East".

Jaffna was the war zone between the government forces and the Tigers. Due to years of war, local economy has been paralyzed, and local people have been struggling to survive. There is not any guarantee for employment. After the war ended, the government reestablished development plans for the region.

Kandy is located in the Central Province of Sri Lanka. It was the capital and religious center of the country. Known for its sacred sites for Buddhism, it is the last capital of the ancient Sinhalese kingdom. Its Temple of the Tooth Relic, a famous historical building, is the pilgrimage site for Buddhism.

3. Government spending

After the civil war ended in 2009, local government has been increasing investment in infrastructure and building a policy environment friendly to investment and economic development. As a result, consumer spending and GDP have been rising, as shown by Fig. 6.20.

(II) Foreign trade

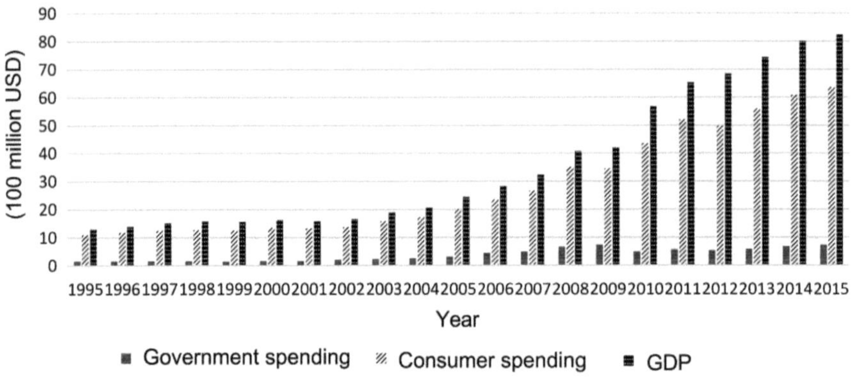

Fig. 6.20 Government spending and consumer spending in Sri Lanka

1. International trade

Sri Lanka has been suffering imbalance in international payments as shown by Fig. 6.21. Its major sources of foreign exchange are remittances made by Sri Lankans working abroad and tourist income. As the lack of capital has become a major bottleneck to growth, Sri Lankan government has felt the pressing need for absorbing foreign investment to accelerate the development of pillar export industries and build a strong engine for fast and sustainable economic growth.

Net barter terms of trade are the ratio between the prices of exports and imports. The year 2000 is set as the benchmark year, and the baseline is set at 100. It is generally believed that an improvement in the terms of trade increases the economic welfare of a country—the sale of home produced goods at higher export prices and

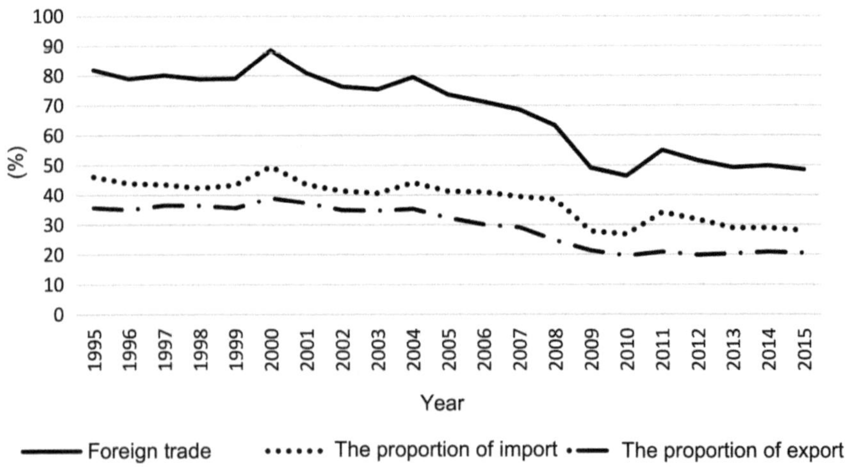

Fig. 6.21 Proportions of export and import within GDP. *Source of data* World Bank database

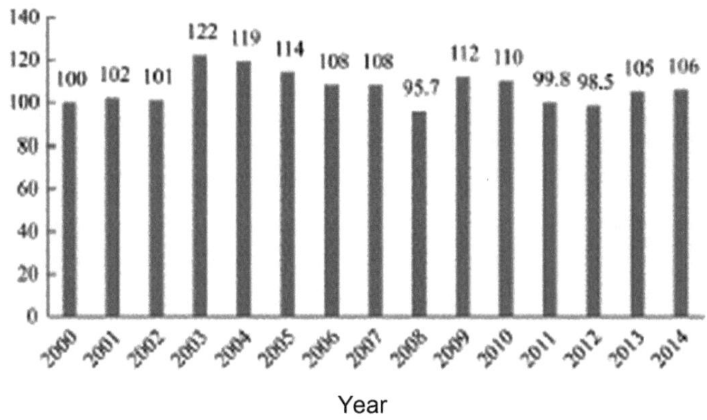

Fig. 6.22 Net barter terms of trade for Sri Lanka. *Source of data* World Bank database

the purchase of foreign produced goods at lower prices are expected to increase welfare. In the contrary, the sale of home produced goods at lower export prices and the purchase of foreign produced goods at higher prices are expected to reduce welfare. As shown by Fig. 6.22, the terms of trade for Sri Lanka have stayed around 100, suggesting an overall balance between import and export. The terms of trade have been picking up since 2012, which will increasingly benefit the country in its future trade.

2. International investment

Sri Lanka has started peaceful development since 2009. The government has prioritized the improvement of infrastructure and investment environment though large amount of public investment. In addition, by adopting preferential policies and organizing investment promotion activities abroad, it has been absorbing foreign investment for domestic development. Located conveniently on the Indian Ocean and right next to the sea route linking Asia and Europe, Sri Lanka has become one of the most attractive destinations for international investment. See Figs. 6.23 and 6.24 for more foreign investment data.

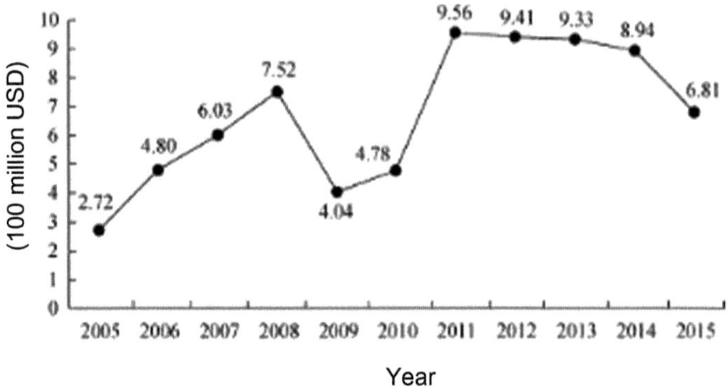

Fig. 6.23 Foreign investment in Sri Lanka. *Source of data* World Bank database

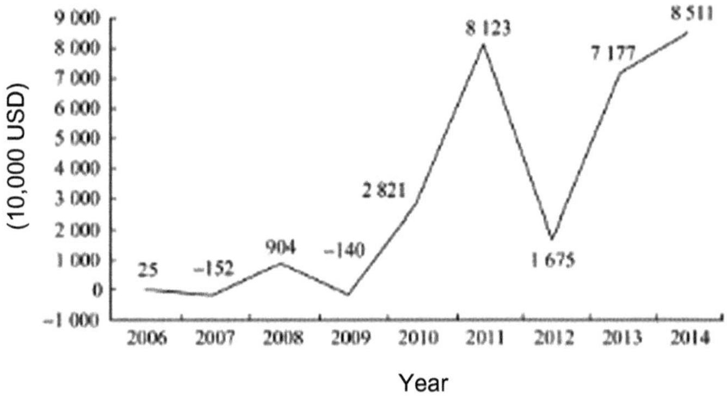

Fig. 6.24 Chinese investment in Sri Lanka. *Source of data* 2014 Statistical Bulletin of China's OFDI

Chapter 7
Central Asia

The five countries of Central Asia, located at the hinterland of Eurasia, span from east to west, connecting Europe and Asia. This core zone of the Silk Road Economic Belt covers an area of 4.0079 million km^2 and nurtures 68.6553 million people. As multi-national countries, they have embraced both Eastern and Western civilizations, while the Islamic culture prevails. As the largest landlocked country in the world, Kazakhstan ranks No.9 in the world for its size and takes up 67.99% of land in Central Asia; home to 71.14% of Central Asians, Uzbekistan and Kazakhstan are the most populous countries in the region. See Table 7.1 for more information.

With special geographical locations and climate conditions, Central Asian countries are both rich in and dependent on natural resources. As resource-based countries, they are at different levels of resource and thus economic development. According to the classification of UN, Kazakhstan and Uzbekistan are upper mid-income countries, while the rest are categorized as lower mid-income ones. As the poorest among them, Tajikistan has a GDP per capita that is less than 1/10 that of Kazakhstan (see Table 7.2). In a post-crisis era featuring global economic slowdown, weakening external demand and sagging world energy prices, all five countries are promoting economic reform and transformation. Industrialization on the basis of rich natural resources is key to their economic growth.

For Central Asian economies, the service sector accounts for an increasingly large proportion, while the secondary industry largely involves the extraction and processing of oil and mineral resources. Based on their economic development levels and natural conditions, the five countries vary greatly in terms of industrial structure. In Kazakhstan where 60% of land is covered by desert and semidesert, the primary industry takes up only 5% of the whole economy, while in Tajikistan, the share of primary industry is as large as 27.4% (see Table 7.3).

Foreign trade in the five countries is mainly centered on energy and raw materials. With limited types of export products, foreign trade here is easily affected by external influences. As shown in Table 7.4, all countries but Kazakhstan suffer trade deficit

H. Zhang et al., *Comparative Studies on Regional and National Economic Development*, Global Economic Synergy of Belt and Road Initiative,
https://doi.org/10.1007/978-981-16-2105-5_7

Table 7.1 Country profiles of five Central Asian Countries

Country	Territory (10,000 km^2)	Population (10,000)	Number of nationalities
Kazakhstan	272.49	1754.41	125
Kyrgyzstan	19.99	595.69	84
Tajikistan	14.3	848.19	120
Uzbekistan	44.89	3129.89	134
Turkmenistan	49.12	537.35[1]	

Table 7.2 Economic profiles of five Central Asian Countries

Country	GDP (100 million USD)	GDP GR (%)	GDP per capita (USD)	GDP GR per capita (%)
Kazakhstan	1850.31	1.20	10,508.30	−0.27
Kyrgyzstan	60.59	3.47	1017.16	1.36
Tajikistan	7778.51	4.20	917.08	1.91
Uzbekistan	581.14	8.00	1856.72	6.13
Turkmenistan	372.54	6.50	6932.84	5.19

Table 7.3 Industrial structure of five Central Asian Countries

Country	Share of the primary industry (%)	Share of the secondary industry (%)	Share of the tertiary industry (%)
Kazakhstan	5.01	33.23	61.76
Kyrgyzstan	15.90	25.90	57.10
Tajikistan	27.40	21.75	50.80
Uzbekistan	18.26	34.63	47.11
Turkmenistan			

and negative trade competitiveness. The five countries are not good at attracting foreign investment either.

Geographically, Central Asian countries, located at the hinterland of Eurasia, are the core region of the Silk Road Economic Belt. As part of the corridor that connects Europe and Asia, this region is one of the main destinations of Chinese products and capitals flowing westward; therefore, it has become a new driving force for the economic growth of western China. Currently, Central Asian countries, promoting economic reform, are at the stage of industrial upgrade and infrastructure construction. This matches the vision of the Belt and Road Initiative. The trade and economic cooperation between Central Asia and China will help the free flow, efficient distribution and in-depth integration of economic factors among Eurasian countries and regions. Western China and Central Asian countries, joined by common

[1] Source of data: World Bank 2015; what is left blank means data is missing.

Table 7.4 Foreign trade in five Central Asian countries

Country	Import volume (100 million USD)	Export volume (100 million USD)	Trade competitiveness index	FDI (100 million USD)
Kazakhstan	301.86	518.36	0.26	148.29
Kyrgyzstan	40.70	25.12	−0.24	8.19
Tajikistan	34.00	11.52	−0.49	
Uzbekistan	147.97	137.91	−0.04	
Turkmenistan				

mountains and rivers, connected by roads and inhabited by the same nationalities, are closely connected with each other in terms of culture. As a place where Chinese culture meets the Islamic culture, Central Asia is a mixture of different nationalities and cultures. In 2013, President Xi Jinping first brought up the Initiative of the Silk Road Economic Belt in Kazakhstan. Such cross-regional collaboration, built on innovative cooperation mode, will gradually spread prosperity to the whole region.

7.1 Kazakhstan

I. Geographical and historical backgrounds

Covering an area of 2.7249 million km^2, Kazakhstan ranks No. 9 in the world in terms of territorial size. At the same time, it is the largest landlocked country in the world and the largest country in Central Asia. With the Caspian Sea lying to its west (the coastline is 1730 km long), Russia to its north, China to its east and Uzbekistan, Turkmenistan and Kyrgyzstan to its south, the country is mainly plain and lowland. It is a transition zone between plain and mountainous region—its north is plain, its central part hilly terrain, its southwest lowland and its east mountains. 60% of Kazakhstan is covered by desert or semidesert, and 15% is part of the European continent.

In 1991, Kazakhstan proclaimed independence from the Soviet Union and became a member of the Commonwealth of the Independent States (the CIS). It is home to 125 nationalities, including Kazakhs, Russians, Uzbeks, Ukrainians and Uighurs. Most Kazakhstanis are religious. Most Kazakhs, or 69% of the total population, are Sunnis, making Sunni Islam the largest sect in the country. The Orthodox is the second largest religion in Kazakhstan—Orthodox Christians, 30% of the population, are mainly Russians. Kazakhstan is a secularized society that separates Church from State.

Rich in oil and mineral resources, Kazakhstan is a resource-based economy. According to *BP Statistical Review of World Energy 2015*, its proven oil reserves are as large as 30 billion barrels, ranking No. 11 in the world and No. 2 within the CIS. In 2014, its daily output reached 1.7 million barrels, with a reserves/production ratio of

48 years. Besides, the Caspian Sea region has the largest potential of oil production growth in Kazakhstan. Also known as the second Middle East, the Caspian basin is one of the places with the largest oil and gas reserves in the world—the oil reserves total 200 billion barrels, and the natural gas reserves 458.8 trillion m^3. Kazakhstan has more than 90 kinds of mineral resources and over 1200 kinds of raw mineral materials. It is home to more than 500 ore districts of ferrous metals, non-ferrous metals, rare metals and noble metals. The reserves of many metals compose large parts of the global reserves. For instance, its tungsten reserves take up 50% of the global reserves, uranium 25%, chromium 23%, lead 19%, zinc 13%, copper 10% and iron 10%. Its reserves of many metals rank at the top in the world.

II. Economic development

As the second largest economy in the CIS, Kazakhstan enjoys the fastest economic growth and the strongest economic muscle in Central Asia. Its economic aggregate equals the sum of the other four Central Asian economies. Kazakhstan is classified as an upper mid-income country by the World Bank.

(I) Domestic economy

After its independence in 1991, Kazakhstan went through some turbulent stages of development and entered the phase of stable growth in 2000. Since 2000, its economic power and industrial competitiveness have significantly improved, with GDP rising from 66.8 billion USD in 2000 to 185 billion USD in 2015.

In 2015, Kazakhstan was hit by economic downturn—major indicators hit record lows of recent years. GDP growth rate dropped from 5.8% in 2013 to 1.2% in 2015, the same as that during the financial crisis in 2019. Per capita GDP fell from 14,310 USD in 2013 to 10,508 USD in 2015. Its PPI declined by 4.8% year-on-year, and the trend continued into the first quarter of 2016 (down by 1.9%). See Figures 7.1, 7.2, and 7.3 for more information. PPI, measuring the average change over time in the selling prices received by domestic producers for their output, is an important economic indicator and significant reference data for policy making and national accounting. If PPI keeps dropping, corporate profits will suffer, leading to shrinking of production.

Also in 2015, tenge moved drastically downward. On August 20, 2015, the Central Bank of Kazakhstan adopted floating exchange rate. On the same day, USD's exchange rate against tenge surged from 1:188.38 to 1:255.26.[2] From January 2015 to February 2016, tenge was down by 91.83% in total. Figure 7.4 reflects that this fall is the largest of its kind since 2000, even larger than that during the 2008 crisis.

1. Industrial structure

Generally speaking, Kazakhstan is constantly upgrading its industrial structure: from 2000 to 2015, the share of the primary industry shrank from 8.69 to 5.01%; the share

[2] The Ministry of Commerce of the People's Republic of China: Russia and Central Asian countries are facing sharp currency devaluation, http://www.mofcom.gov.cn/article/jyjl/e/201601/20160101234691.shtml.

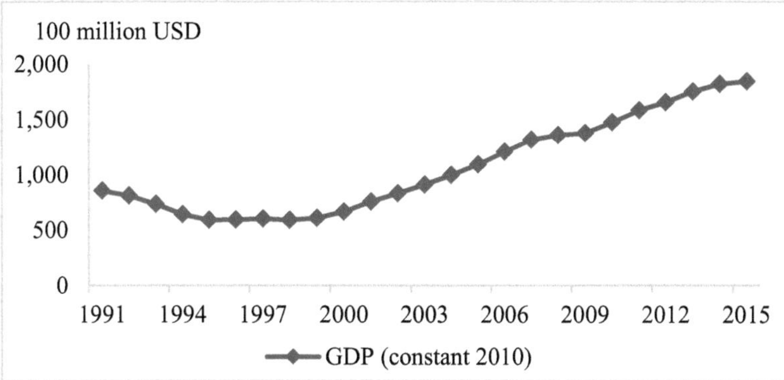

Fig. 7.1 GDP of Kazakhstan. *Source of data* World Bank

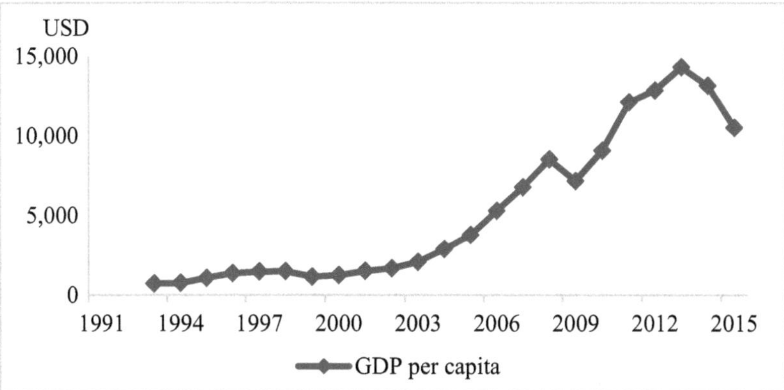

Fig. 7.2 Per capita GDP of Kazakhstan

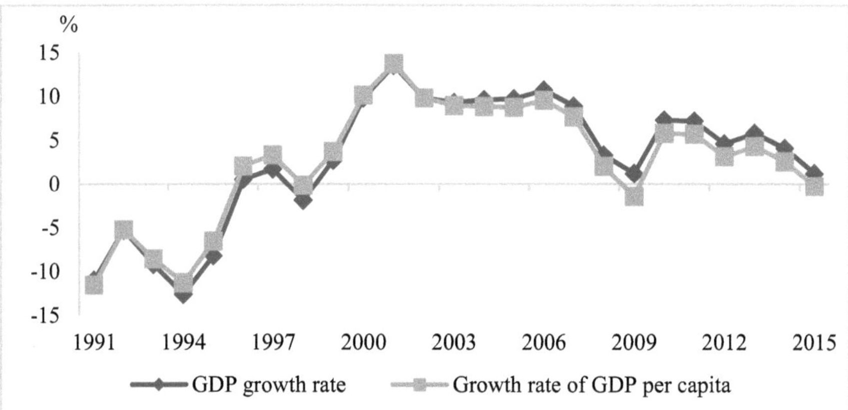

Fig. 7.3 GDP GR of Kazakhstan

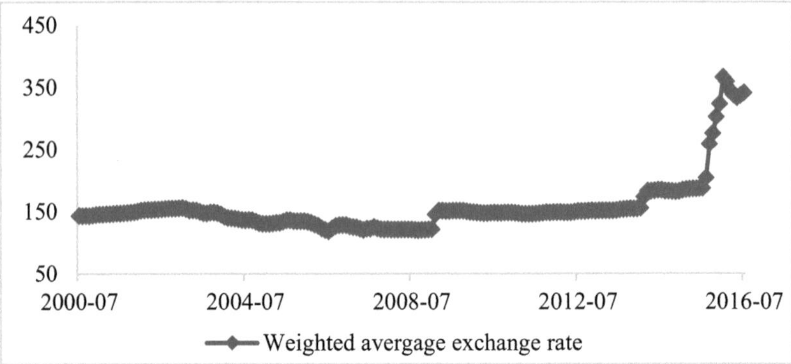

Fig. 7.4 Weighted average exchange rate of tenge/USD (monthly). *Source of data* National Bank of the Republic of Kazakhstan (NBK)

of the secondary industry declined from 40.46 to 33.23%; and the tertiary industry achieved a bigger proportion, rising from 50.85 to 61.76% (see Fig. 7.5 for this trend). Its industrial structure upgrade has been particularly significant since 2010.

2. The primary industry

As the largest landlocked country in the world, Kazakhstan is mainly plain and lowland. Its good terrain and mild climate are good for the development of agriculture. It has more than 20 million ha of arable area—most of which are for spring wheat, other crops include cotton, beet and tobacco. Kazakhstan, the largest food

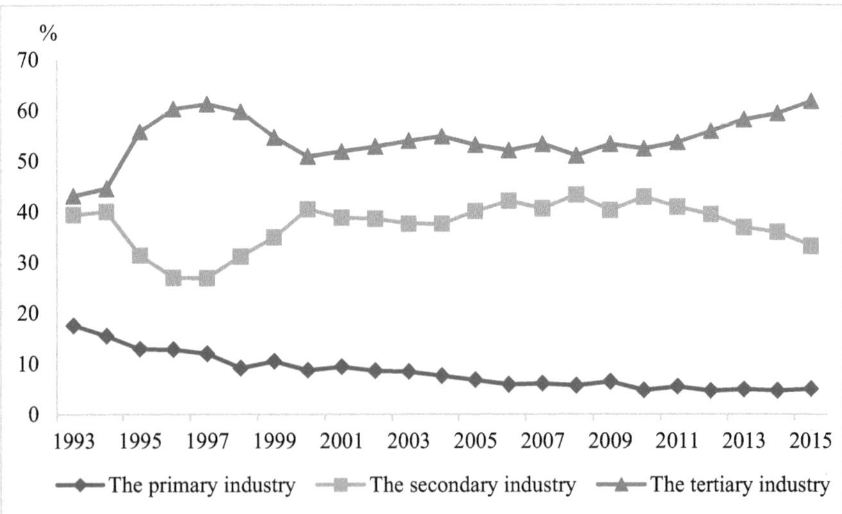

Fig. 7.5 Shares of its three industries within the GDP of Kazakhstan. *Source of data* the World Bank

producer in Central Asia, faces a large funding gap for agricultural development and suffers low efficiency for agricultural production. Within agriculture, crop farming grows faster in terms of output value—it has overtaken animal husbandry. As to agriculture policies, the government has introduced tax cut policies. Since it established a customs union with Russia and Belarus in 2010, its products such as meat, preparations of meat, vegetable and fruit are seizing market in Russia.

Major problems facing Kazakhstani agriculture include the funding gap (despite heavy government investment) and the low-income level caused by low efficiency of agricultural production.

(2) The secondary industry

Mineral products, base metals and articles of base metal and chemical products are where Kazakhstan has a comparative advantage and thus its main export goods. Its light industry is weak and develops slowly. Oil industry is the pillar of Kazakhstani economy—almost all famous oil companies have set up branches here. Automobile and parts industry is emerging and takes up a big share within the machine-building sector. As to industrial policy, in its pursuit of industrialization, the government has released the *National Guidelines of Accelerating Innovative Industrial Development* and the "Kazakhstan 2050 Strategy", so as to build Kazakhstan into one of the top 30 developed countries in the world before 2050. For this purpose, metallurgic industry, chemical industry, petrochemical industry, machinery industry, building materials industry and food industry are classified as priority areas for development.

Currently, the industrial development of Kazakhstan suffers from imbalanced industrial structure, the lack of innovation capacity and the shortage of middle and small businesses and innovation-oriented enterprises. The result is the uncompetitiveness of its industrial products. The weak light industry grows slowly, taking up less than 1% of the manufacturing industry and 0.34% of industry as a whole. Currently, despite the fact that the light industry is growing steadily, the country's import volume is still high at 2 billion USD.

(3) The tertiary industry

In Kazakhstan, the service sector is expanding rapidly. The share of the tertiary industry within GDP is the largest. The service industries of telecommunications and Internet enjoy higher output values.

2. Population and major cities

Every Kazakhstani woman gives birth to 2.41 children on average. Such a high fertility rate is the reason behind its high rate of population growth—estimated at 1.24% in 2012. Till the fertility rate begins to fall, Kazakhstani population will keep rising fast.[3] According to the World Bank, the total population of the country was 17.54 million in 2015. Figure 7.6 shows Kazakhstani population went down in 1991–2001 but began to grow after 2002.

Table 7.5 lists the five most populous cities in Kazakhstan in 2016.

---

[3] Source of data: World Population Review.

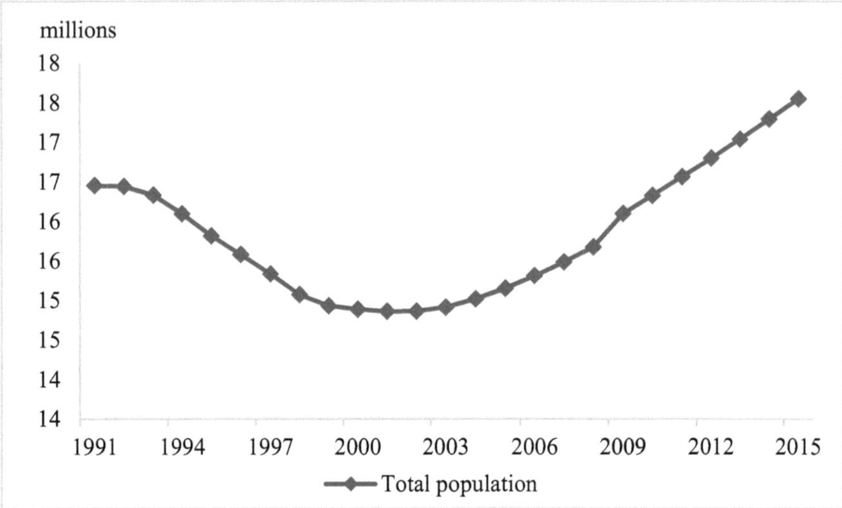

Fig. 7.6 Total population of Kazakhstan. *Source of data* World Bank database

Table 7.5 Five most populous Kazakhstani cities

City	Population
Alma-Ata	2,000,900
Karaganda	451,800
Chimkent	414,032
Taraz	358,153
Astana	345,604

Source of data World Population Review

Astana, as the capital of Kazakhstan, is located on the right bank of the Ishim River at the central part of the country. The city is the center of politics, culture, education, economy, trade and tourism. Meanwhile, it is also the major production base of agriculture and industry and the rail hub.

Located at the southeast of Kazakhstan and the north side of the Altai Mountains of outer Ili, Alma-Ata is the economic and cultural center of Kazakhstan, its highway and aviation hub and also the largest industrial center. Besides, it is the financial center and the largest trade center of Central Asia. From 1929 to 1991, it served as the capital of Kazakh SSR. In 1991, the renowned Declaration of Alma-Ata was released here, marking the collapse of Soviet Union. From 1991 to 1997, it was the capital of the Republic of Kazakhstan.

Atyrau, 2700 km to the west of Alma-Ata, sits at the mouth of the Ural River. It is known for its petroleum refining industry and fishery industry. Refineries here play a significant role in Kazakhstan. The city also has machinery industry, food industry, and light industry.

(II) Foreign trade and investment
1. Foreign trade

As the exporter of energy and raw materials, Kazakhstan saw shrinking trade volume due to the impact from the external market. In 2015, its trade volume was down by 35.3% year-on-year and hit 82 billion USD (among which 51.8 billion are from export, down by 39.4% and 30.2 billion from import, down by 26.9%, as shown in Fig. 7.7). For the past two decades, the trade competitiveness of Kazakhstan has been on the rise, but with great volatility (see Fig. 7.8).

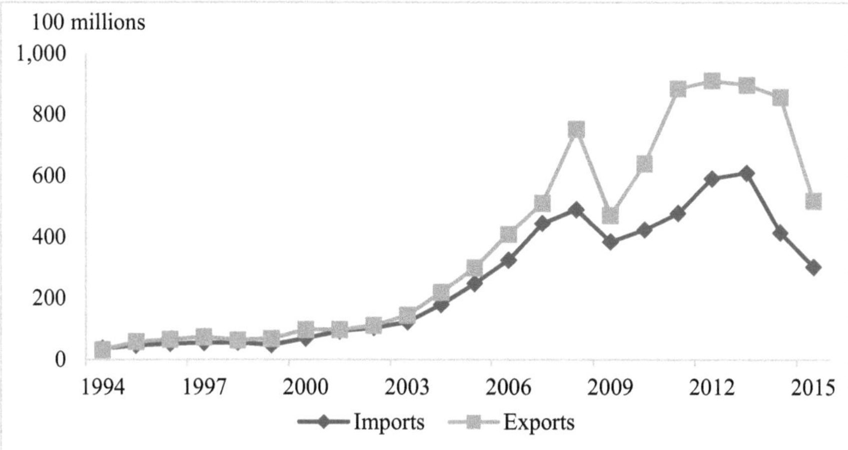

Fig. 7.7 Export and import volumes of Kazakhstan. *Source of data* World Bank database

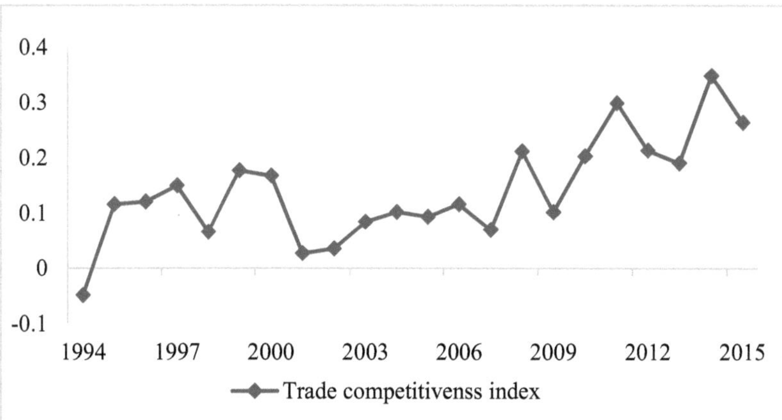

Fig. 7.8 Trade competitiveness index of Kazakhstan. *Source of data* calculated according to data from the World Bank

Since 2011, China has become the second largest trade partner and the largest export destination of Kazakhstan, while Kazakhstan is China's largest trade partner in Central Asia. From 2010 to 2013, China was in deficit as to its trade with Kazakhstan, which shows its reliance on Kazakhstani products. At the same time, export of Kazakhstan was dependent on Chinese market as well.

The bilateral trade relations enjoy great complementarities. Kazakhstan imports mechanical and electrical products, base metals and articles of base metal and light industrial goods (such as textiles) from China and exports to China primary goods like energy and resources. At the early stage after the independence of Kazakhstan, the two countries traded with each other through cross-border transportation. Later, the bilateral trade evolved toward processing trade and leasing trade. Now, more and more ways of trade have emerged, including trade fairs, tourist shopping and consignment.

2. International investment

The lack of private reserves is prevalent in Central Asia, making introduction of foreign investment necessary for the accumulation of means of production. However, as international capital is flowing back to developed markets, it is hard for Kazakhstan to attract foreign investment. According to the National Bank of the Republic of Kazakhstan, FDI stock in the country was 119.83 billion USD by the end of 2015. In 2012–2015, FDI continued to fall. 2015 saw the worst decline (to 14.83 billion USD, as shown in Fig. 7.9).

Kazakhstani government attaches great importance to foreign investment attraction. On June 12, 2014, President Nursultan Abishevich Nazarbayev convened the 27th session of Foreign Investors' Council, an organization directly under him, and signed into law the Amendments and Supplements to the Law of Investment Climate Improvement. Such adjustments of foreign investment attraction policies aim at

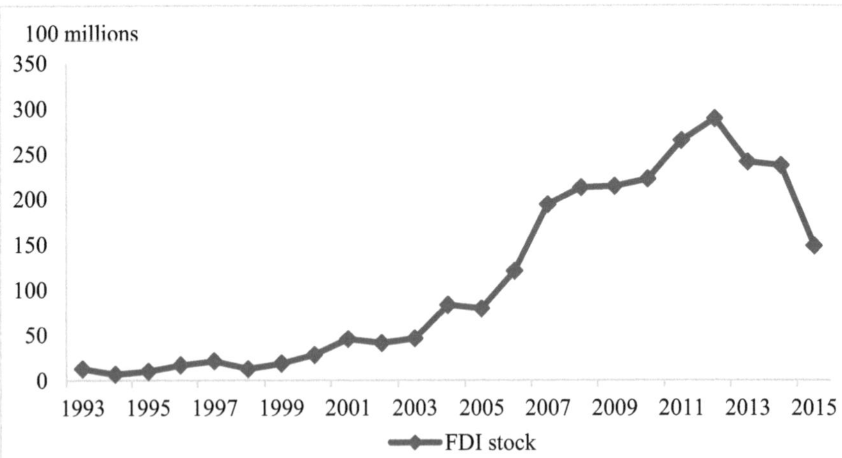

Fig. 7.9 FDI stock in Kazakhstan. *Source of data* NBK

Table 7.6 Changes of industrial structure of FDI flow (Unit: million USD)

Year	Total flow	Farming, forestry and fishery	Mining and quarrying industries	Manufacturing industry	Service industry
2005	7915.8	1.3	1930.1	346.6	5637.9
2010	22,245.6	6.0	5982.2	2243.8	14,013.6
2015	14,829.4	71.8	3498.5	2556.9	8624.4

Source of data NBK

Table 7.7 Sources of FDI stock in Kazakhstan 2015

Ranking	Country/region	Stock (100 million USD)	Share (%)
1	Netherlands	600.2	50.09
2	The United States	209.6	17.49
3	France	120.8	10.08
4	Japan	53.5	4.46
5	Russia	32.2	2.69
6	China	28.5	2.38
7	British Virgin Islands	26.3	2.19
8	Switzerland	17.3	1.44
9	South Korea	14.9	1.24
10	Austria	10.2	0.85

Source of data NBK

improving investment climate and encouraging investment in priority areas. This round of adjustments is of the largest scale and intensity in recent years.[4]

As shown in Table 7.6, within FDI flows in 2005, 2010 and 2015, the service sector took up the biggest shares, followed by the mining and quarrying industry, and the manufacturing industry. Agriculture, fishery and forestry virtually received no foreign investment. Within the service sector, the area of profession, science and technology receives the most foreign investment—in 2005, the figure was 5.497 billion USD, or 63.74% of the total received by the service sector.[5]

According to Table 7.7, by December 31, 2015, top 10 foreign investors in Kazakhstan contributed 92.92% of the country's FDI stock. Netherlands was the largest investor, and China ranked No. 6. Most FDI in Kazakhstan came from developed countries, mainly North American and European countries.

Table 7.8 lists the top 10 countries in terms of FDI flow in Kazakhstan in 2005, 2010 and 2015, namely Netherlands, America, France, Britain, Japan, Russia, China,

[4] Source of data: Country Guide for Foreign Investment Cooperation, MOFCOM.

[5] Source of data: NBK.

Table 7.8 Sources of FDI in Kazakhstan (unit: million USD)

Ranking	2005		2010		2015	
1	Netherlands	1944.1	Netherlands	7310.3	Netherlands	5758.3
2	The United States	1181.1	The United States	1810.9	The United States	2780.9
3	France	774.9	China	1717.6	Switzerland	1880.7
4	Britain	603.7	France	1561.4	France	963.6
5	Japan	335.0	Britain	1098.0	Belgium	693.0
6	Russia	226.8	Russia	951.6	Russia	565.7
7	China	216.5	Japan	619.3	China	442.7
8	Switzerland	112.2	Switzerland	547.3	South Korea	396.1
9	Germany	86.5	Belgium	422.1	Japan	391.8
10	South Korea	58.0	South Korea	300.6	Britain	391.0

Source of data NBK

Switzerland and South Korea. The structure was relatively stable and dominated by countries in America and Europe.

As shown in Fig. 7.10, China started to invest directly in Kazakhstan in 1993 with a small scale of 5 million USD. Before 2000, China's direct investment in Kazakhstan had never exceeded 100 million USD (excluding the year 1997), and it was subject to major fluctuations. From 2001 (when the Shanghai Cooperation Organization was founded) to 2012, the bilateral economic cooperation entered a period of rapid development. As China stepped up its investment in Kazakhstan, direct investment from China began to grow steadily after 2003. However, 2012 is the turning point from which investment from China began to fall—it shrank from 2.41 billion USD in 2012 to 440 million USD in 2015. By the end of 2015, the stock of China's direct investment in Kazakhstan was 2.85 billion USD.

(III) Economic reform

To seek economic recovery, Kazakhstani government set up five reform targets and launched the 100-step plan. Half of the plan involves economic reform that aims at economic modernization and industrial diversification. Major measures include tapping the potential of agriculture; streamlining customs procedures and shortening time of clearance; improving tax service; setting standards for the construction industry (adopting the European standards) and enhancing the competitiveness of Kazakhstani builders; furthering opening the market; fostering market players meeting the OECD standards and fit for free competition, so that Kazakhstani products could enter the global market, and the Kazakhstani enterprises have access to global business information; promoting the joint venture models of Astana Airlines and Tengiz-Chevron Project and attracting foreign investment in areas of tourism, infrastructure construction, dairy industry, meat production and energy; valuing technological innovation; building an economic corridor—the Eurasia Land Bridge of multiple modes of transportation and competing for investment from ADB; drawing

Fig. 7.10 Volume of China's direct investment in Kazakhstan. *Source of data* NBK

on the experience of Dubai; adopting English and the British law system and building Astana into a financial center that connects Central Asia with the global capital market.[6]

7.2 Kyrgyzstan

I. Geographical and historical backgrounds

Kyrgyzstan is a landlocked country that connects Central Asia, Western Europe and East Asia. It neighbors Kazakhstan on the north, Tajikistan on the south, Uzbekistan on the southwest and China on the east and southeast. Its border line totals 4170 km in length, and its border with China is 1096 km long. Its territory of 199,990 km^2 is home to 84 nationalities. 71% of its total population are Kyrgyz people. Kyrgyzstan owns some world-class deposits, and only some are developed. The reserves and distribution of many mineral resources remain to be proven so that future development is possible. There are in total of 70 coal deposits with 6.73 billion ton of proven reserves. With many rivers and lakes, it enjoys abundant water resources, ranking No. 3 among the NIS, next only to Russia and Tajikistan. Its potential for hydropower generation is 142.05 billion KWH, but only 9%–10% has been tapped.

II. Economic development

(I) Domestic economy

[6] Yellow Book of Central Asia: Annual Report on Development of Kazakhstan 2015. Beijing: Social Sciences Academic Press, 2015.

Kyrgyzstani economy mainly depends on agriculture and animal husbandry. In the early twenty-first century, its government adjusted its economic reform policies, moved toward market economy and carried out economic reform centered on privatization and non-nationalization. In this way, its industrial production recovered and commodity prices stabilized. Its economy is highly dependent. For instance, Kumtor gold mine is the main engine of economic growth, and its affiliated industries of processing, construction, transportation and telecommunication are all major driving forces of local economy.

In 2015, Kyrgyzstan's nominal GDP reached 657.2 billion USD, 3.5% up compared to the same period one year earlier. Per capita GDP was 1103 USD, up by 1.4% year-on-year. Figures 7.11, 7.12 and 7.13 reflect the fact that its GDP GR has been fluctuating greatly since 1997, ranging from 10.9% (2013) to negative growth. This demonstrates the fragility of Kyrgyzstani economy.

1. Industrial structure

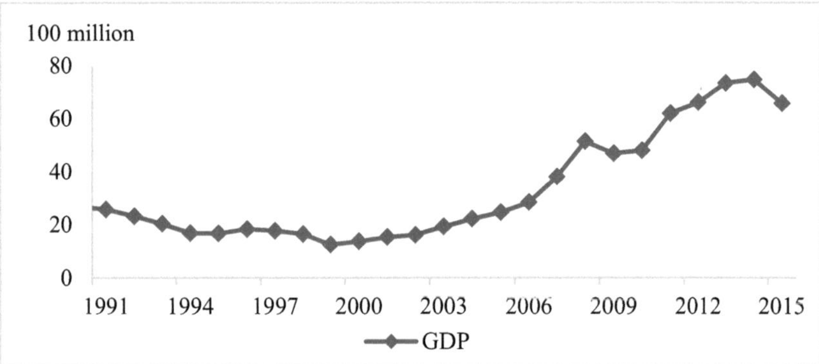

Fig. 7.11 Nominal GDP of Kyrgyzstan

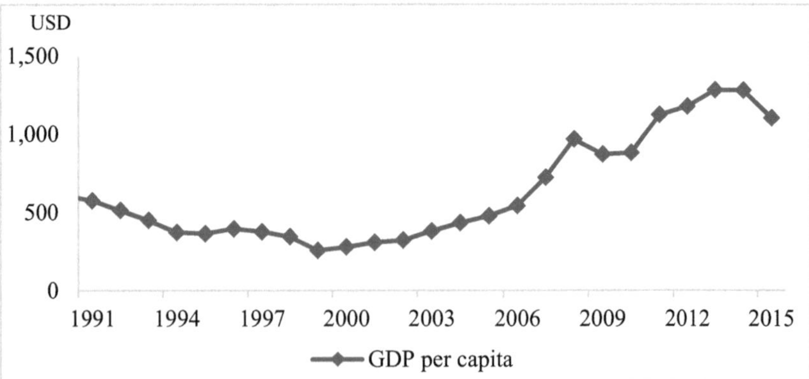

Fig. 7.12 Nominal GDP per capita of Kyrgyzstan

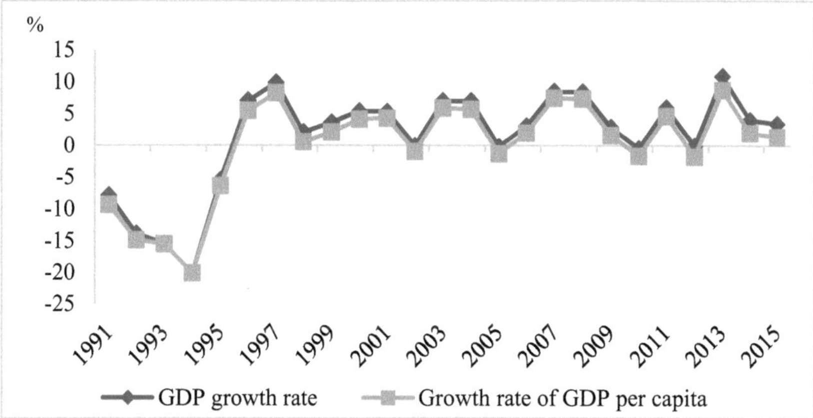

Fig. 7.13 GDP GR of Kyrgyzstan. *Source of data* World Bank database

According to Fig. 7.14, its industry has relatively small output, while agriculture and service industry are doing well. The share of tertiary industry within GDP is the biggest and still on the rise—it reached 57.1% in 2015; the share of primary industry is the smallest—only 15.9% in 2015; the secondary industry, with weak foundation, generated 25.9% of GDP in 2015.

The industrial sector of Kyrgyzstan is composed of industries of mining, processing, power supply, heat supply, water supply and waste processing. In 2015, its gross industrial output was 175.164 billion som, 4.4% less compared to that of last year. The mining industry generated 7.99 billion som, up by 63.8% year-on-year. Water supply and waste processing industries produced 1.59 billion som, 3.5% up on a year-on-year basis. In contrast, the output of processing, power supply, gas supply and heat supply industries declined. The processing industry made 134.83 billion

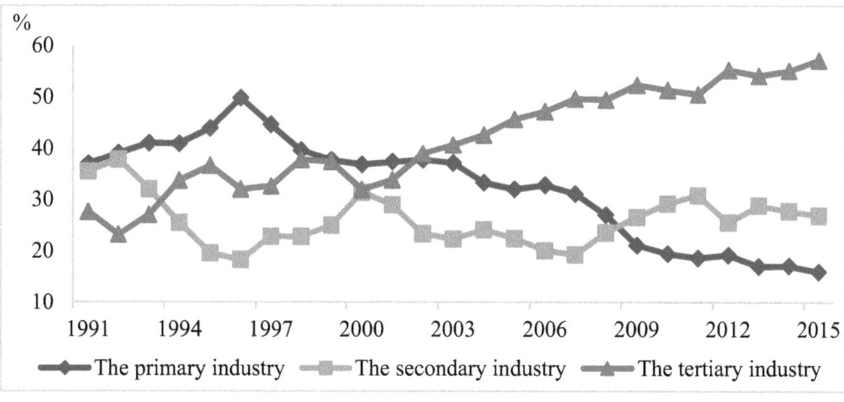

Fig. 7.14 Shares of the three industries within GDP in Kyrgyzstan. *Source of data* World Bank database

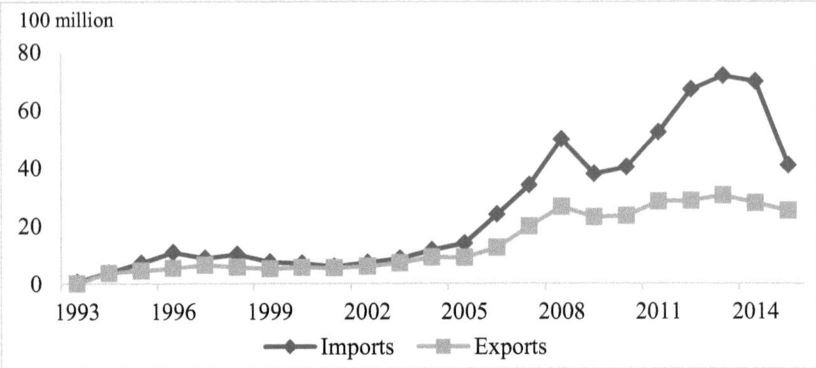

Fig. 7.15 Export and import volumes. *Source of data* World Bank database

som, 7.8% less on a year-on-year basis; the output of power, gas and heat supply fell by 2.8% to 30.75 billion som.[7] Thanks to the good weather, its agriculture produced bumper harvests in 2015.

(II) Foreign trade and investment

1. Foreign trade

On August 12, 2015, Kyrgyzstan officially joined Eurasian Economic Union, after Kazakhstan, Russia, Belarus and Armenia. Due to its small economic aggregate, it was vulnerable to the negative impacts of the entry, and its re-export industry (a big part of its economy) was under attack; however, from the institutional perspective, its entry will promote economic growth since it allows free and fair flow of goods, services, capital and labor among all member countries. As shown in Figs. 7.15 and 7.16, Kyrgyzstan had been suffering from trade deficit since 1994 and negative trade competitiveness. In 2015, its import volume fell by 41.6%.

2. Foreign investment

FDI in Kyrgyzstan had been increasing since 2005 despite fluctuations, but the aggregate is still small (see Fig. 7.17). China's direct investment is of a large share within the total FDI. Overseas remittance is the main source of the country's foreign exchange earnings. In 2015, Kyrgyzstan witnessed a sharp fall in its overseas remittance due to the negative impacts of Russian slowdown, Ukraine Crisis and KZT depreciation (see Fig. 7.18).

7.3 Tajikistan

I. Geographical and historical backgrounds

[7] Yellow Book of Central Asia: Annual Report on Development of Kyrgyzstan 2015. Beijing: Social Sciences Academic Press, 2015.

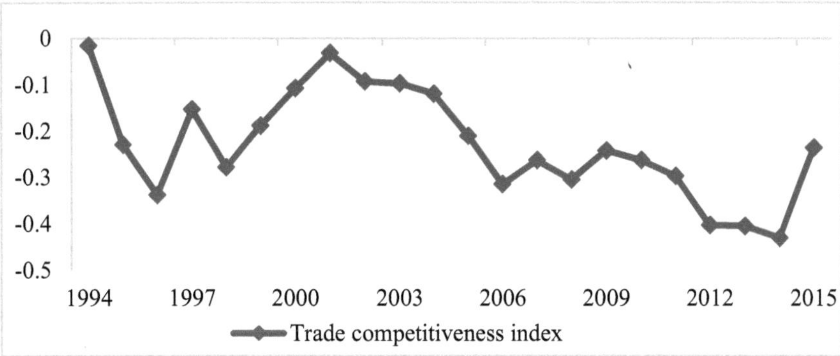

Fig. 7.16 Trade competitiveness index. *Source of data* calculated according to data from the World Bank

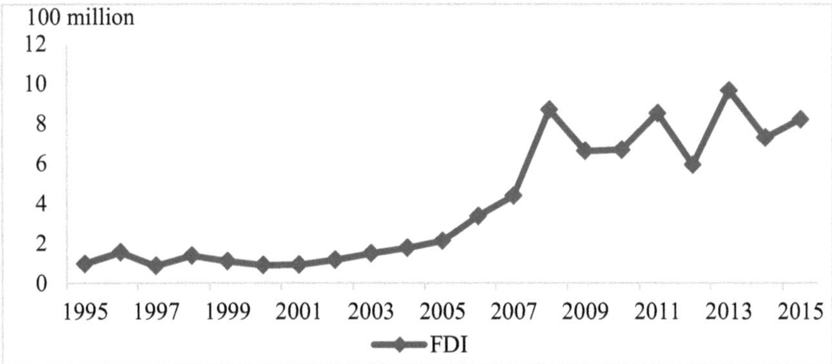

Fig. 7.17 FDI volume. *Source of data* National Statistical Commission of Kyrgyzstan

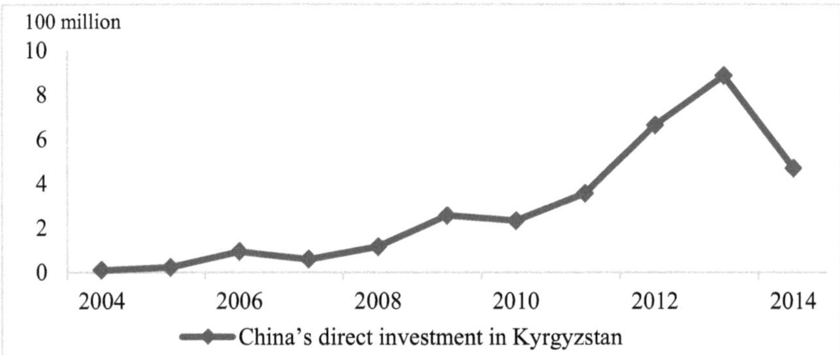

Fig. 7.18 China's direct investment in Kyrgyzstan. *Source of data* National Statistical Commission of Kyrgyzstan

Tajikistan is a landlocked country in the southeast of Central Asia. With a territory of 143,000 km^2, it is the smallest country in the region. Tajikistan is a place where 93% is of mountainous terrain. It borders Xinjiang, China on the east and southeast (the border line is 430 km long, and the distance between Dushanbe and the border port is 1009 km), Afghanistan on the south, Uzbekistan on the west and Kyrgyzstan on the north. Tajikistan is home to 120 nationalities, while 80% of its population are Tajiks. Tajikistan is endowed with abundant water resources—half the total amount of Central Asia, No.8 in the world as to total amount, and No.1 in terms of per capita water availability. However, less than 10% has been developed. Most of its water comes from glaciers. There are three basins in Tajikistan—the Amu Darya River basin, the Zeravshan River basin, and the Syr Darya River basin. Apart from water, the country is also rich in mineral resources in terms of variety and quantity. For instance, it has mines of more than 50 minerals, including lead, zinc, molybdenum, tungsten, halite, boron, coal, fluorite, limestone and colored stone. In addition, it also enjoys reserves of oil and natural gas. Tajikistan has 30 gold mines, with total reserves of more than 600 ton. Silver, lead and silver are usually associated, and the reserves of silver in the country are around 100,000 ton. The Big Koni Mansur, the world's second largest deposit of silver, is situated in the north of the country. Tajikistan ranks No. 3 in Asia for its stibium reserves, next only to China and Thailand. The reserves of oil and natural gas reach 120 million ton and 880 billion m^3, respectively, but remain untapped since the most of resources are buried as deep as 7000 m and nobody makes the strategic investment. Therefore, 95% of oil and natural gas depend on import. Besides, it has abundant coal resources, as the proven reserves reach 4.6 billion ton.

II. Economic development

(I) Domestic economy

With an overly simple economic structure, Tajikistan is vulnerable economically. Once the poorest republic of the Soviet Union, Tajikistan became even poor after its independence due to civil war. In 1999, 83% of its people lived under the poverty line. To end the economic plight, its government adopted three development strategies, namely to achieve energy independence, to improve infrastructure of transportation and to safeguard food security. The government found the breakthrough at its untapped water resources and began to develop hydropower by building middle and small hydropower stations; it invested heavily in the construction of infrastructure such as railways, highways and telecommunication facilities; cooperation of crop breeding was carried out, and cultivation and irrigation techniques were improved.

Figures 7.19, 7.20, and 7.21 show Tajikistan experienced negative economic growth during the civil war between 1991 and 1997, and the situation of poverty grew worse as a result. From the national reconciliation in 2000 to the Financial Crisis in 2008, its economy maintained steady growth. In recent years, it has been growing steadily with higher GDP, per capita GDP and income levels, fewer poor people and prosperity in all areas. In 2015, the economic situation stayed stable—the real GDP rose by 4.2% to 7.78 billion USD.

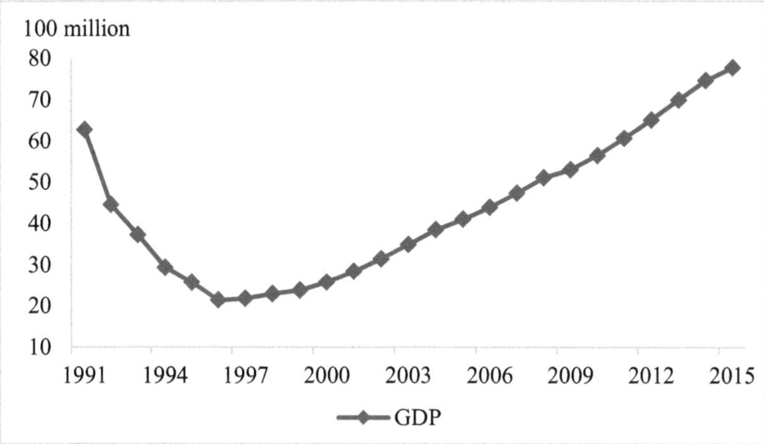

Fig. 7.19 GDP of Tajikistan

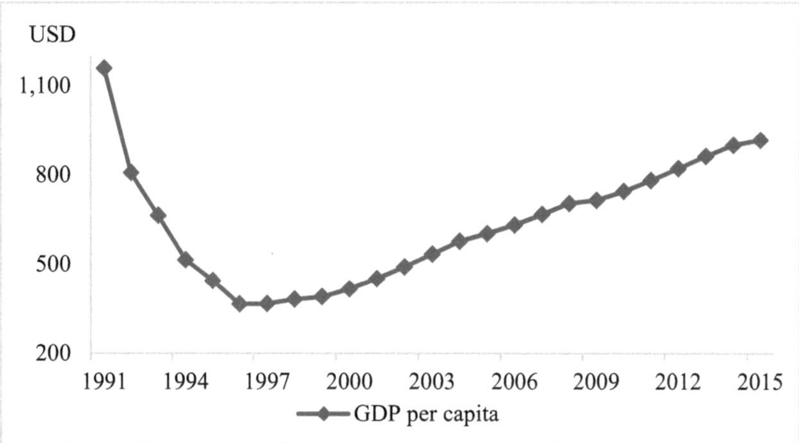

Fig. 7.20 Per capita GDP of Tajikistan. *Source of data* World Bank database

1. Industrial structure

As shown in Fig. 7.22, Tajikistan has been optimizing its industrial structure since 2000; as a result, the share of the tertiary industry within GDP expanded from 33.7 to 50.8% in 2013, exceeding the shares of the primary and the secondary industries (27.4% and 21.75%, respectively). In 2000, the contribution made by the industry to the economic aggregate for the first time exceeded that of agriculture, and this difference was further widened for the next 10 years. However, after 2011, agriculture reemerged as the bigger contributor to the local economy. During recent 10 years, the output of agriculture doubled. In 2013, the proportion of agriculture within GDP hit 27.4%. Tajikistan invested more than 3.7 billion somoni into 42 agricultural projects

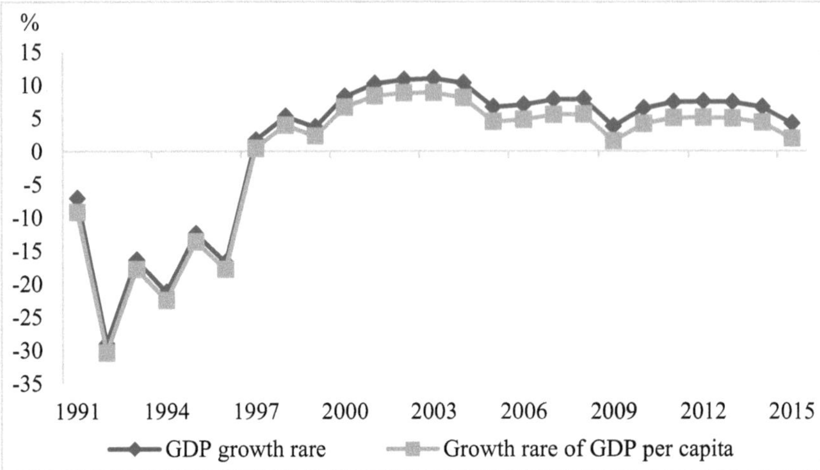

Fig. 7.21 GDP GR of Tajikistan

within 15 years. Currently, it is administering 9 agricultural projects at national level, and the total investment is 1.5 billion somoni. The government has passed the 2016–2020 development plan for horticultural and viticultural industries, which means 20,000 ha of industrial parks will be built by 2020. Through the introduction of technology and the increase of investment, the country has been raising its industrial output. In 2015, it produced more than 1 million ton of coal, 9 times larger than the Figure 10 years ago. The development of mining and processing industries has helped Tajikistan rid of its reliance on import of coal, cement and other building materials and becomes an exporter. Since its dependence, Tajikistan has invested more than 12 billion somoni into the energy sector.

2. Population and cities

According to the World Bank, the proportion of urban residents within the total population of Tajikistan shrank sharply during the civil war. After the war ended, the percentage has stayed low at around 26–27%, as shown in Fig. 7.23.

Most people of the country live in the southwest and the northwest since the east is mountainous and high above the sea level.

Dushanbe, its capital, is the most populous city. Built after the October Revolution, the city is the center of politics, industry, science, education and culture. Its industrial output equals 1/3 of the national total.

Khujand is one of the most famous ancient cities in Central Asia and a key stop along the ancient Silk Road. As the transportation hub and center of politics, economy, culture, education and scientific research, it has one of the largest bazaars in Central Asia—the Panjshanbe Market. It also has light industry, food industry, machine-building industry, metal cutting industry and furniture industry.

Located at the border of Tajikistan and Afghanistan, Khorog is a city of agriculture. Local agriculture, depending on irrigation, is concentrated at the western Pamir,

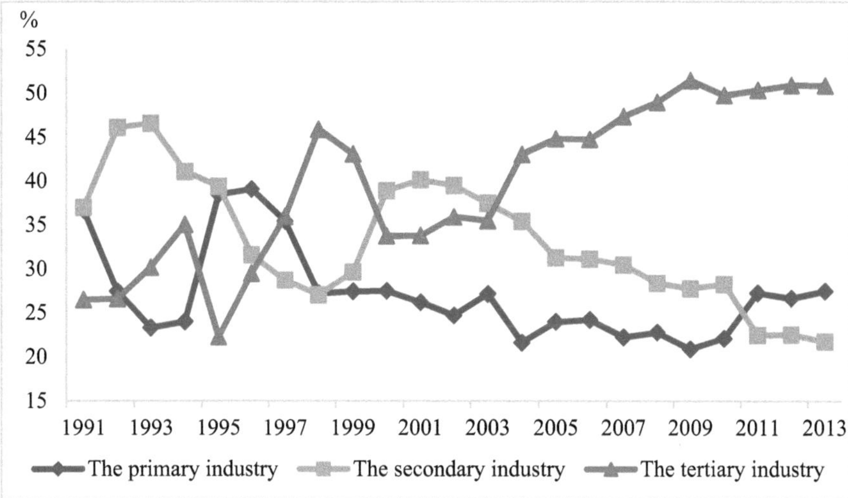

Fig. 7.22 Shares of Tajikistan's three industries within its GDP. *Source of data* World Bank database

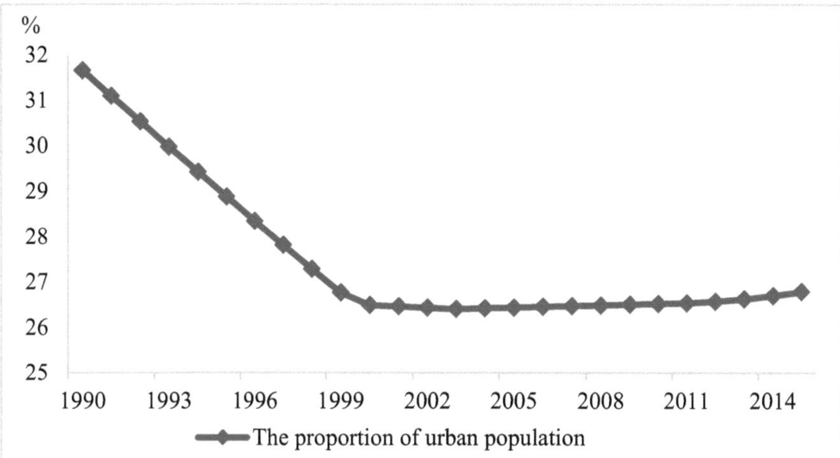

Fig. 7.23 Proportion of urban population within the total population. *Source of data* calculated according to data from the World Bank

and main crops include cereals, vegetables, melons and potatoes. Local people also develop horticultural industry and sericulture. The eastern Pamir mainly relies on animal husbandry.

(II) Foreign trade and investment

1. Foreign trade

Before 2003, foreign trade of Tajikistan was so underdeveloped that the total volume fell short of 2 billion USD. Though the volume of export has risen slightly as the production capacity expands since 2003, it is still far smaller than that of import. Tajikistan is so import-dependent that its trade competitiveness has stayed negative and is declining further since 2002. In 2014, the figure was −0.58; in 2015, it rose to −0.49, but the reason is the decline of export caused by economic slowdown. To conclude, Tajikistan is a relatively uncompetitive trader. A closer look reveals foreign trade which had a tough year in 2015, with import volume shrinking by 31% and export volume 10% (Figs. 7.24 and 7.25).

China mainly exports to Tajikistan mechanical equipment, textiles, generators, electrical motors, footwear, automobiles and parts. China is the consumer of Tajik

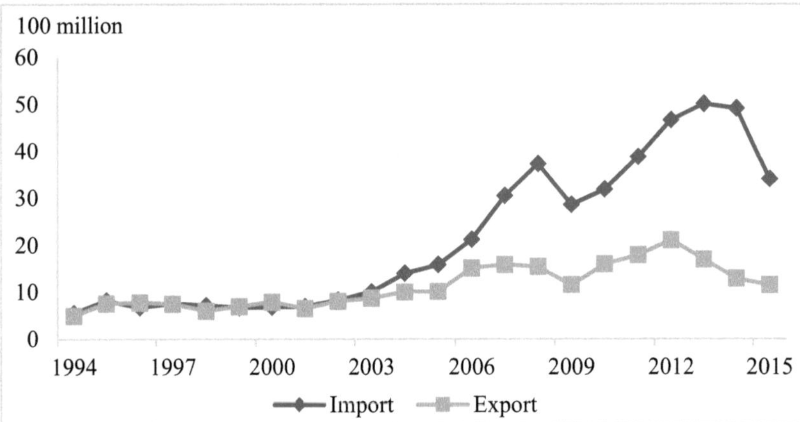

Fig. 7.24 Import and export volumes of Tajikistan. *Source of data* World Bank database

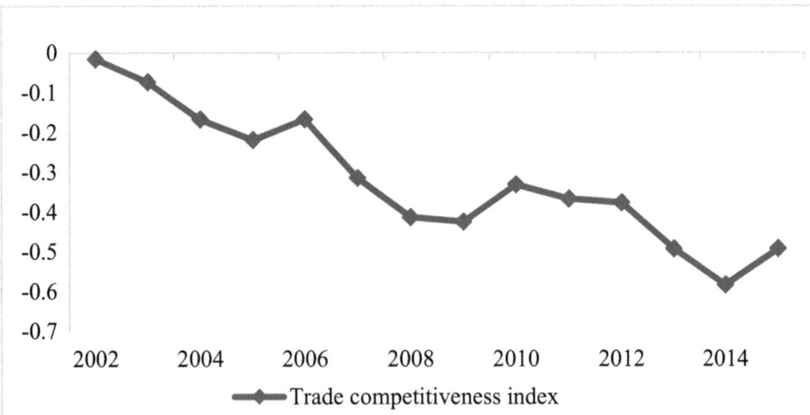

Fig. 7.25 Trade competitiveness index of Tajikistan. *Source of data* calculated according to data from the World Bank

products like mineral ores and slag, cotton, raw hides and skins, leather, edible fruits and nuts.

2. Foreign investment

Tajikistan receives little foreign investment—the 720 million USD has been an all-time high. China's direct investment in Tajikistan is less than 100 million USD. See Figs. 7.26 and 7.27, for more information.

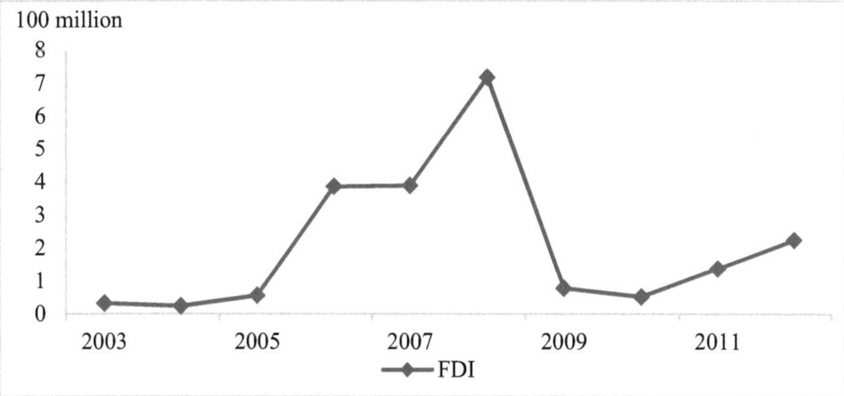

Fig. 7.26 FDI in Tajikistan. *Source of data* National Bank of Tajikistan

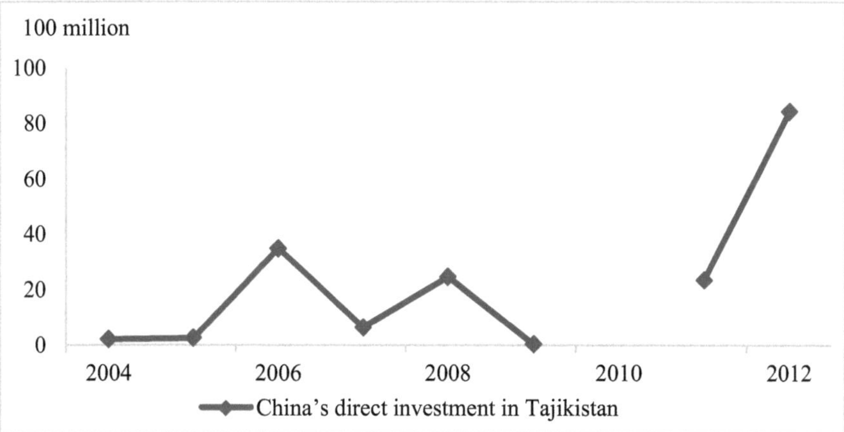

Fig. 7.27 China's direct investment in Tajikistan. *Source of data* National Bank of Tajikistan

7.4 Turkmenistan

I. Geographical and historical backgrounds

After it declared independence in 1992, it joined the CIS and the UN in the same year. The 50th session of the UN General Assembly passed the resolution to permanently recognize the Turkmenian neutrality. In August 2005, it declared to withdraw from the CIS and become an associate member.

Located in the south of Central Asia and to the north of the Kopet-Dag Range, Turkmenistan is also a landlocked country. It borders Amu Darya River to the east, Kazakhstan and Uzbekistan to the north and northeast, the Caspian Sea to the west (lying across the Sea are Azerbaijan and Russia), Iran to the south and Afghanistan to the southeast. With a territory of 491,200 km^2, it is a country of desert—80% of the country is covered by the Karakum Desert.

Turkmenistan is rich in resources such as oil, natural gas, glauber's salt, iodine, non-ferrous and rare metals. Other resources include celestite, coal, sulfur, mineral salt, argil and bentonite. It ranks No. 4 in the world in terms of the prospective natural gas reserves (26.2 trillion m^3); its prospective oil reserves stand at 20.8 billion ton. Its industrial reserves of oil and natural gas are 213 million ton and 2.7 trillion m^3, respectively, among the highest in the world. Back in the days of the Soviet Union, it kept 70% of the Union's iodine and bromine.[8]

II. Economic development
(I) Domestic economy

In 2015, against the backdrop of overall economic slowdown across Eurasia and low energy prices, Turkmenistan achieved rapid growth by developing national industry, boosting investment in infrastructure and optimizing economic structure. Its GDP grew at 6.7%, the second fastest among the five Central Asian countries (only slower than that of Uzbekistan). Though slower than the 10.3% growth in 2014, it was still a remarkable accomplishment for a country heavily dependent on the energy industry. See Figs. 7.28, 7.29, and 7.30 for more information.

In early 2015, as the negative impact of Russian recession and low energy prices began to filter into Central Asia, Turkmenian economy stayed unaffected. On the first day of 2015, the exchange rate of USD against manat declined from 1:2.84 to 1:3.5 due to the depreciation of rouble and tenge. Commodity prices in Turkmenistan, especially food prices shot up quickly. During the enlarged government meeting held on January 12, 2015, Turkmenian President called for the rejuvenation of national industry, the substitution of import products by ones made in Turkmenistan and the expansion of exports. The government issued the *Plan for Expanding Exports of Domestic Products* and the *Plan for Substituting Imports with Domestic Products*, highlighting the innovative and sustainable industrial development, prioritizing the development of processing, service, transportation and telecommunication industries and promising less reliance on energy export and greater economic competitiveness.

[8] Source of data: Country Guide for Foreign Investment Cooperation, MOFCOM.

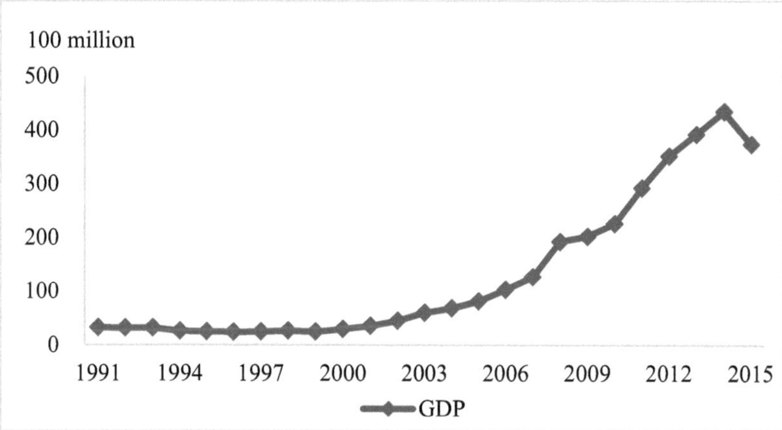

Fig. 7.28 Nominal GDP of Turkmenistan

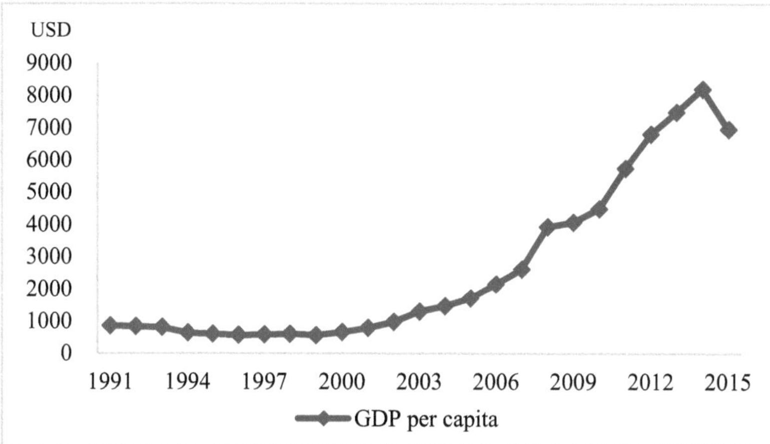

Fig. 7.29 Per capita GDP of Turkmenistan. *Source of data* World Bank database

Ashgabat, the capital of Turkmenistan, is the country's center of politics, economy, culture and scientific research. It has machinery industry, electric motor industry, glass industry, textile industry and food industry. The city is also an important national and even regional hub of transportation.

Turkmenabat, the capital of Lebap Province, sits on the Amu Darya River. It is a railway hub of the region.

Daşoguz, the capital of Daşoguz Province, is located at the Daşoguz Oasis at the downstream of the Amu Darya River. It sits on the trunk railway linking Central Asia and Russia. There are cotton grinning factories, oil-pressing mills, rug producers, repair plants of farm machinery and food processing factories.

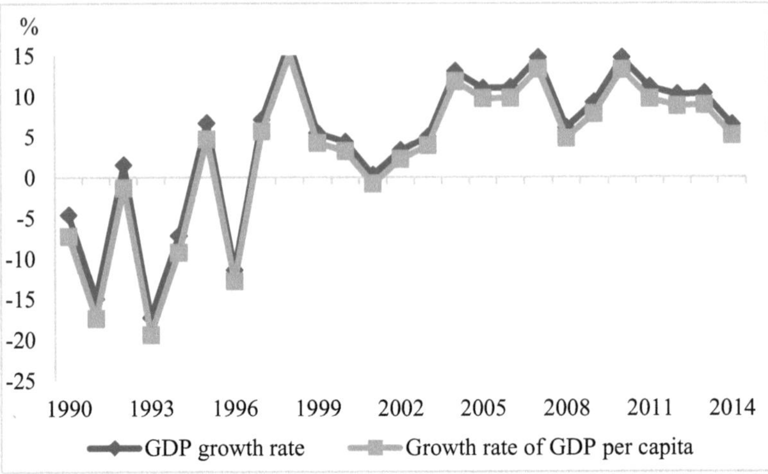

Fig. 7.30 GDP GR of Turkmenistan

Mary is a railway hub, a river port and the center of textile industry.

Türkmenbaşy, located in Balkan province, is the largest city in western Turkmenistan and the largest port at the east coast of the Caspian Sea. Near it are some rich oil fields. There are large refineries, ship repair plants, thermal power plants and fish and meat processing factories.

(II) Foreign trade and investment

In 2015, trade volume of Turkmenistan dropped 28% from 36.4 billion USD in 2014 to 26.2 billion USD; export volume shrank by 38.5% to 12.2 billion USD; import volume dwindled 15.5% to 14 billion USD.[9] Two reasons were behind the decline of export: first, the prices of oil and natural gas, the major export products of the country, were depressed; second, traditional destinations of its natural gas export made fewer purchases (China excluded), for instance, Russia even called off the purchases all together. Besides, within the *Framework of the Plan for Substituting Imports with Domestic Products*, the country expanded the production of import substitutes, alleviated its dependence on import goods such as food and strengthened monitoring of foreign exchange disbursements; consequently, import volume was slashed, too.

In recent years, Turkmenistan has been striving to safeguard energy security and diversify export. At the end of 2015, it made a big breakthrough in export diversification. The natural gas pipeline linking Turkmenistan, Afghanistan, Pakistan and India (referred to as TAPI pipeline hereinafter; the contract of the project was signed in 2010, but its construction was postponed for a variety of reasons) broke ground. According to the plan, the pipeline starts from the Galkynysh gas field in the eastern

[9] MOFCOM: Trade volume of Turkmenistan reduced by 28% in 2015, http://www.mofcom.gov.cn/article/i/jyjl/e/201602/20160201259684.shtml.

Turkmenistan and reaches India via Afghanistan and Pakistan. With a designed annual delivery capacity of 33 billion m^3, the pipeline is 1814 km long—214 km within Turkmenistan, 735 km within Afghanistan and 800 km within Pakistan. Built at a cost of 7.6 billion USD, it is planned to be put to use in 2019. Its construction will stimulate economic growth along the line, and thus creating jobs, bettering living standards and safeguarding regional stability. For Turkmenistan, TAPI pipeline is a strategic tool for increasing export income of natural gas, boosting economic growth and diversifying energy export; for Afghanistan, allowing the pipeline to pass its territory could add 5000 jobs and bring an income of more than 300 million USD every year; for Pakistan and India, natural gas from Turkmenistan will fill the energy gap plaguing South Asia and boost local economy. Meanwhile, it could help building the global energy system and guarantee global energy security. The construction of TAPI pipeline will face risks the following risks. On one hand, the project lacks funding and investment. To build the pipeline, Turkmenistan, Afghanistan, Pakistan and India set up a consortium using state capital while turning down the offers of participation made by energy giants like Chevron and Exxon Mobil. They chose the Turkmenian natural gas concern as the leading coordinator. However, the concern does not have the money to build such a 2000 km—long pipeline that crosses four countries, or the experience of constructing and running a transnational project. On the other hand, situation security in Afghanistan is not optimistic—the penetration by the IS has worsened the situation, and the armed attacks and conflicts have become even more frequent. The 735 km pipeline within Afghanistan will certainly be a target. This has added to the uncertainty about the future of TAPI pipeline.[10]

Russia, Iran and China are the traditional destinations of natural gas export by Turkmenistan. Russia, under sanctions, is sure to increase output and restart the export of natural gas. Iran, searching for new approaches to extract and export its abundant natural gas resources, will probably slash its import from Turkmenistan or even pose as a competitor. Within such a context, China, for some time into the future, will be the only importer of Turkmenian natural gas. Therefore, Turkmenistan is accelerating its diversification of energy export by starting dialogs on energy with European and Asian governments, deepening its relationships with world-class energy companies, signing cooperation agreements with foreign investors on the exploration, extraction and intensive processing of oil and natural gas and accelerating the construction of infrastructure such as pipelines.[11]

[10] Wang Haiyan. Turkmenistan's diversification strategy of natural gas export (1991–2015): a positivist analysis, Russian Studies, 2015, 5.

[11] Economic and Commercial Counsellor's Office of the Embassy of the People's Republic of China in Turkmenistan: Turkmenian President said, D Route of Sino-Turkmenian Gas Pipeline would take care of the interests of all stakeholders.

http://smfws.mofcom.gov.cn/article/i/jyjl/e/201510/20151001132127.shtml.

7.5 Uzbekistan

I. Geographical and historical backgrounds

Located in the hinterland of Central Asia, Uzbekistan is indeed a landlocked country—even all of its five neighbors are landlocked too. It borders Kazakhstan to the north and northeast, Kyrgyzstan to the east, Tajikistan to the southeast, Turkmenistan to the west and Afghanistan to the south. Most people of the country live in its east, southeast and southwest. With a territory of 448,900 km^2, Uzbekistan is home to 134 nationalities. The Uzbeks compose 78.8% of the total population. With nearly 100 kinds of minerals and total reserves worth 3.5 trillion USD, Uzbekistan is a country rich in mineral resources. For instance, the proven reserves of gold are 3350 ton, ranking No. 4 in the world; the proven reserves of oil, natural gas, gas condensate and coal are, respectively, 584 million ton, 190 million ton, 2.055 trillion m^3 and 1.83 billion ton. The reserves of uranium stand at 185,800 ton, ranking No.7 in the world; besides, it also has abundant copper and tungsten. Uzbekistan has plentiful solar, wind and other renewable resources, meaning it has huge potential for developing photovoltaic industry.

II. Economic development

(I) Domestic economy

Its domestic economy has maintained stable growth. From 2004 to 2015, local GDP growth rate stayed above 7%—in 2015, its GDP grew by 8%, the fastest in Central Asia. In the context of softening global trade growth, weakening external demand and falling prices of major export products, it is not easy for Uzbekistan to keep growing fast. As shown by Figs. 7.31, 7.32, and 7.33, nominal GDP, real GDP and per capita GDP of Uzbekistan have all achieved steady growth since 2003.

By publicly selling SOEs shares, Uzbekistan has completed the privatization of 52 enterprises of such nature, including some large enterprises. Some large construction projects have been launched, transportation and telecommunication infrastructure are being improved, special economic zone is set up to attract foreign investment, and programs of high and new technology are being fostered. Apart from building free economic zones in Navoi and Angren, Uzbekistan, funded by World Bank and other international financial organizations, launched a serious of large projects, which is key to improving living standards and boosting economic development in distant areas.

1. Industrial Structure

The industrial structure of Uzbekistan has been upgrading since 2003. After 2006, the secondary industry overtook the primary industry as the largest contributor to GDP. See Fig. 7.34 for more information.

(1) The primary industry

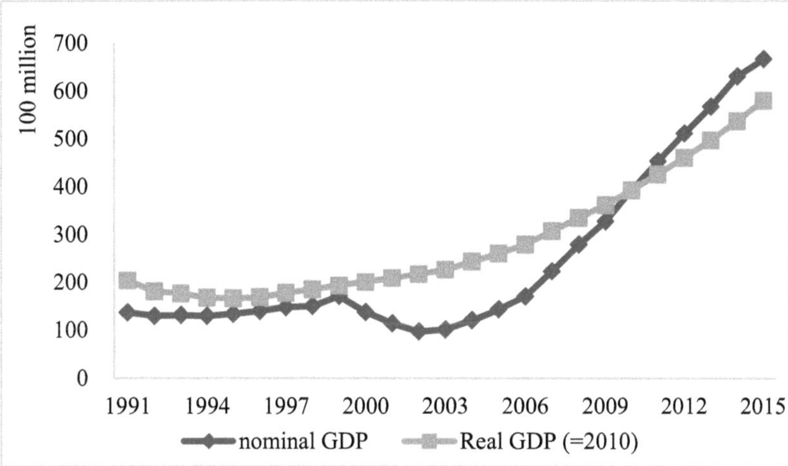

Fig. 7.31 GDP of Uzbekistan

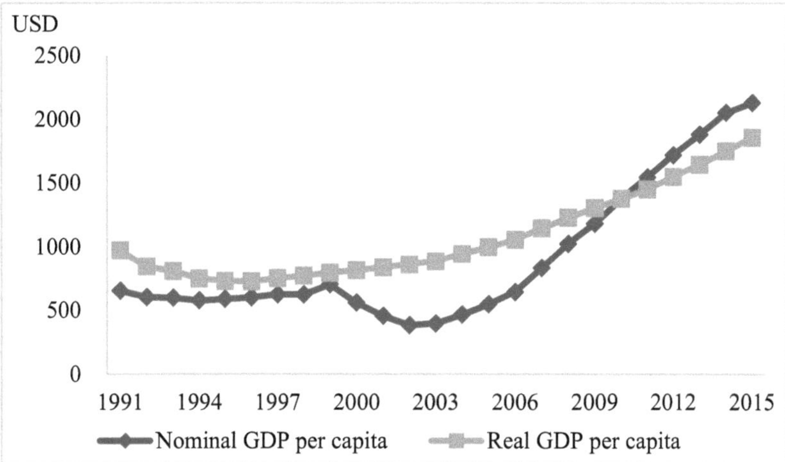

Fig. 7.32 Per capita GDP of Uzbekistan

Agriculture, generating 1/3 of the total GDP, is the foundation of Uzbek economy. Around half of the country's labor force is employed in agriculture. Within agricultural output, cotton composes a big part—usually 40%. By growing more food crops and less cotton, the country has realized food self-sufficiency—one key reason why it managed to maintain economic stability despite challenging external environment. In recent years, its agricultural production has been restructured—the ratio of cereal yield to cotton output changed greatly, and agricultural output increased significantly. In 2015, its grain yield hit 7.5 million ton, and cotton yield reached 3.5 million ton.

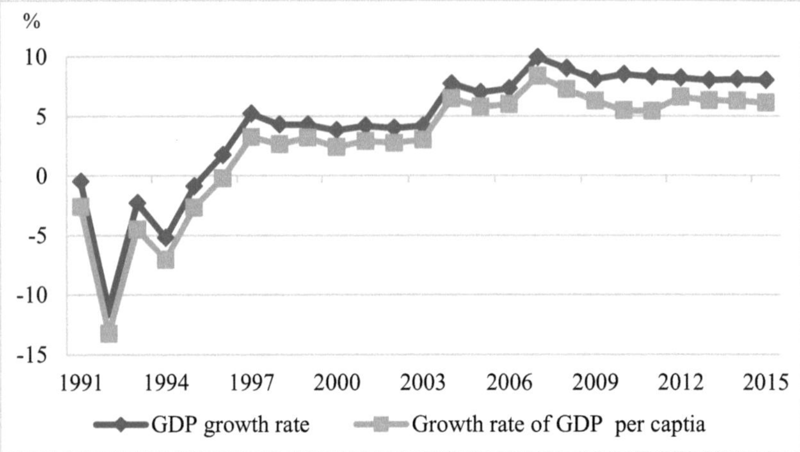

Fig. 7.33 GDP GR of Uzbekistan. *Source of data* World Bank database

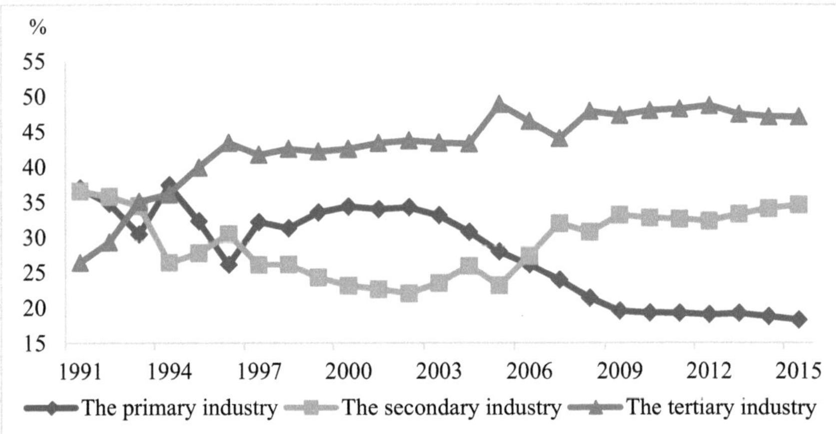

Fig. 7.34 Shares of the three industries within GDP in Uzbekistan

(2) The secondary industry

Uzbekistan attaches great importance to both heavy industry (such as petrochemical, natural gas, machinery and railway industries) and light industry. It issued the *Development Plan for Emerging Industries 2015–2019*. The 78 projects of the plan mainly concentrate in cotton processing industry, garment industry, footwear production, textile industry and textile machinery industry. Currently, the development of textile, building materials, pharmaceutical and furniture industries is encouraging. The two special industrial zones of Navoi and Angren are doing well. In addition, the country is launching large industrial projects, for instance, it plans to spend 700 million

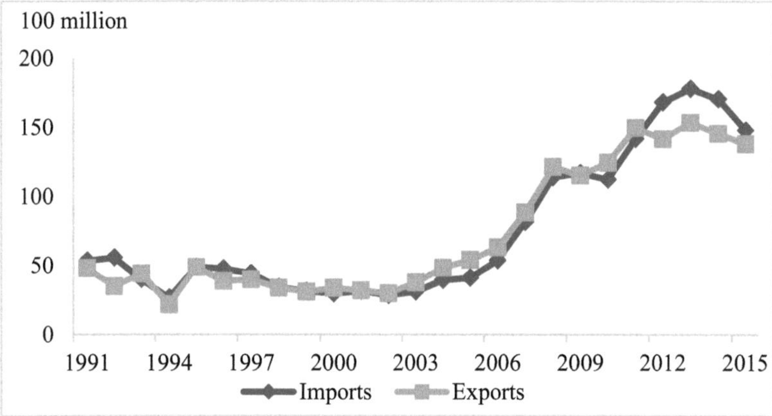

Fig. 7.35 Trade volume of Uzbekistan. *Source of data* World Bank database

Fig. 7.36 Trade competitiveness index of Uzbekistan. *Source of data* calculated according to data from the World Bank

in building three solar power stations in Samarqand, Namangan and Surxondaryo provinces.

(3) The tertiary industry

Priority sectors for development in Uzbekistan include the automobile industry, the energy industry and the telecommunication industry. In recent years, with five large joint venture car plants and surging automobile output, Uzbekistan has formed its own automobile industry. The insurance industry is growing steadily and has made great headway, with most of its investment directed at savings deposits and securities. In addition, the rising of household appliance industry has also greatly boosted

Uzbek economy—foreign invested enterprises provide the market with more and more refrigerators, televisions and air conditioners.

2. Major cities

As the largest city in Central Asia and the fourth largest city within the CIS, Tashkent, the capital of Uzbekistan, is its political, economic, cultural and transportation center. The city is situated in the east of Uzbekistan, to the west of Chatkal Range, and at the center of the oasis lying in the Chirchiq River valley (a branch of the Syr Darya River). As one of the major commercial hubs along the ancient Silk Road, it was once visited by Zhang Qian (a famous explorer and diplomat of ancient China), Faxian and Xuanzang (Chinese Buddhist monks in ancient time). Its temperate continental climate means mild winter, hot summer and sufficient sunshine, earning it the name "sun city".

Bukhara, the 3rd largest city, sits in the middle of the Bukhara Oasis at the Zeravshan River Delta in the southwest of the country. It is the political, economic and cultural center of Bukhara Province. Tashkent is 434 km to its northeast.

Samarqand, located in the Zeravshan River valley in the southeast, is the second largest city. It is also known for tourism and culture. Cotton ginning, silk manufacturing and food processing industries are its industrial pillars. Machinery and chemical industries are also developed. As one of the oldest cities in Central Asia and an important hub along the Silk Road, it used to connect the three empires of Persia, China and India. Historic records of the city could date to the fifth century BC.

(II) Foreign trade and investment

From 2002 to 2013, trade volume of Uzbekistan had been rising, and then, it fell slightly during 2013–2015. In 2015, export volume was 13.8 billion USD and import volume 14.8 billion USD. Its trade competitiveness index hovered around 0, which means volumes of export and import were almost flat. See Fig. 7.35 for more information (Fig. 7.36).

Chapter 8
West Asia and North Africa

West Asia and North Africa, linking the three continents and the two oceans, are rich in petroleum resources and highly dependent on exports of petroleum products. The 15 countries in West Asia and North Africa include the United Arab Emirates, Bahrain, Egypt, Iran, Iraq, Israel, Jordan, Kuwait, Lebanon, Nepal, Oman, Qatar, Saudi Arabia, Turkey and Yemen. The population is about 420 million, accounting for 9% of that of the "Belt and Road" countries, and the population of each country does not exceed 100 million. The residents are mainly Arabs, and Islam is the dominant religion.

In 2015, the GDP of the 15 countries in the region totaled approximately 3.1 trillion USD, accounting for 13.6% of the "Belt and Road" countries and 4.2% of the world. From 2000 to 2015, the average GDP growth rate was 5.1%. The per capita GDP level in West Asia and North Africa, one of the world's major oil export regions, is significantly higher than the average of the "Belt and Road" countries (which is close to the world average). In 2015, the figure was about 7382 USD, categorized as upper-middle-income. The degree of trade dependence is moderate, and there is a long-term trade surplus.

There are two types of economy—the oil-exporting ones and the non-oil-exporting ones. Most oil-exporting countries are export-oriented economies, including Saudi Arabia, the United Arab Emirates, Qatar, Bahrain, Kuwait, Iraq, Iran and Oman. Oil is the lifeblood of all these countries. The petroleum industry has an absolute advantage in the proportion of GDP, national income and exports. The construction industry, transportation industry, processing industry and commerce driven by the petroleum industry have developed very rapidly. Per capital GDP in these countries rank high in the world. However, the oil-driven national economy lacks diversity and is often affected by the international market, especially the energy market. The outbreak of the global financial crisis will hit the region hard since it is on the edge of international division of labor. As the world's demand for oil is diminishing, the economic security in West Asia and North Africa cannot be guaranteed, leading to political instability in this region. Therefore, countries in the region are adjusting their

H. Zhang et al., *Comparative Studies on Regional and National Economic Development*, Global Economic Synergy of Belt and Road Initiative,
https://doi.org/10.1007/978-981-16-2105-5_8

economic development strategies and striving to diversify their economy. The region suffers from insufficient labor resources. By importing a large number of foreign workers and technicians every year, it has become an important labor market in the world. Most of the non-oil-exporting countries are relatively strong in agriculture and animal husbandry, and weak in mining and processing industries. However, by taking advantage of their geographical and labor advantages, they export labor to the oil countries in the region.

8.1 Bahrain

I. Geographical and historical backgrounds

In terms of land area, Bahrain is undoubtedly a small country—it has a land area of more than 740 km^2, which is equivalent to the size of a county in China. In terms of the national economy, Bahrain is a big country as its per capita GDP exceeds 20,000 USD, ranking top among the oil producers in the Middle East. As an island country located in the southwestern part of the Persian Gulf, its capital is Manama, with a land area of 741.4 km^2. It has a terrain that is mostly desert plain which rises and forms low cliffs toward the center. It has tropical desert climate, with abundant sunshine and little rainfall. It originally had 33 islands, the largest of which was Bahrain. However, many new islands have been built during the sea reclamation in recent years. “Bahrain” means “two seas” in Arabic. It is said that the sea water on the two sides of Bahrain Island had two different colors due to different depths, hence the name “land of two seas”. Saudi Arabia is located to the west of Bahrain and is connected to it via the King Fahd Causeway. Iran is located 200 km north of Bahrain. The Qatar Peninsula is located on the southeast side of the Bahrain Bay. Bahrain is the birthplace of Dilmun civilization, and cities were built here in 3000 BC. The Phoenicians settled here in 1000 BC. It became part of the Arab Empire in AD 7th century. After a period of Arab rule, it was conquered by Portugal in 1521. Later, the Portuguese were expelled by the Persian Emperor Abbas in 1602. In 1783, the Bani Utbah seized Bahrain from the Qājār dynasty. A regime was established by the house of Khalifa and their rule has lasted till today. In the 19th century, Britain forced Bahrain to sign the Persian Gulf Peace Treaty and gradually made it a British protectorate. In 1971, Bahrain declared independence and became an emirate. It was then declared a kingdom in 2002. Affected by the "Arab Spring", it has been troubled by ongoing Shiite protests since 2011.

More than 1.47 million people live on the islands of Bahrain (2016), half of which are foreigners. Its population density ranks seventh among more the 220 countries and regions in the world. Islam is the State religion, and 70% of the people are Muslims; 25% believe in Christianity and Hinduism.[1]

[1] Source of data: Census Summary Result 2010 of Bahrain.

Bahrain is the most educated country in the Gulf region. The illiteracy rate is 4.35%,[2] and the education rate for young people aged 15–25 is 99%. This is the success of Bahrain's public education policy: Bahrainis are entitled to free education in public schools, including free textbooks provided by the Ministry of Education. The University of Bahrain and Arab Gulf University, established in 1978 and 1987, respectively, are the top universities in Bahrain.

Bahrain's capital, Manama, is the country's largest city. Located in the northeast of the country and facing the Persian Gulf, it is the national political, economic, transportation, trade and cultural center. The city was designated the Arab Cultural Capital by the Arab League in 2012. Covering an area of 30 km^2, it is home to 150,000 people[3]—the greater area of the metropolitan has more than 320,000 people, accounting for a quarter of the total population. More than 2000 Chinese live in Manama.

II. **Economic development**

(I) Domestic economy

Bahrain is an early developer in the Gulf region. In the 1930s, oil was discovered and exploited. Oil and petrochemicals became its pillar industries. The proved oil reserves were 20.55 million tons, and the natural gas reserves were 118.2 billion m^3.[4] Although Bahrain is rich in oil and gas resources, it is aware that a resource-dependent economy is not sustainable. At the end of the 1970s, it started the economic reforms, promoting free and open economic policies, and diversified economic development. At present, it has transformed into one of the financial centers in the Gulf region, and its trade, tourism, convention and exhibition industries are also relatively developed.

Unlike Jordan, Bahrain is one of the countries with the lowest unemployment rate in the Middle East. In 2014, the number of unemployed people in Bahrain was 7414, and the unemployment rate was 3.7%.[5] In addition, according to the United Nations Human Development Report 2015, Bahrain's Human Development Index ranks 45th out of 187 countries, behind Saudi Arabia and the UAE.

Figure 8.1 shows Bahrain's GDP per capita exceeded 10,000 USD in 1994. However, the figure is not always growing due to the impact of changing oil price and the 2008 financial crisis. Despite its per capita GDP of 23,395 USD in 2015, it is not a developed country in a strict sense. According to statistics released by the International Monetary Fund in 2016,[6] Bahrain was a developing country despite its high-income. The reason is that the international community generally believes a developed country should enjoy high levels of development in all areas, including economy, science and social services. The development of natural resources can bring high per capita GDP and human development index, but it may not necessarily

---

[2] Source of data: Central Information Organization.

[3] Source of data: Census Summary Result 2010.

[4] Source of data: website of Ministry of Foreign Affairs, China.

[5] Source of data: Central Information Organization, Bahrain; Bahrain in Figures 2014.

[6] IMF: World Economic Outlook, p. 188.

make a country developed. At the dawn of the new century, Bahrain launched a plan to promote economic diversification in order to perform better in the post-oil era.

As shown in Fig. 8.2, although the GDP output value of the oil sector has fluctuated in different years, that of the non-oil sectors has been increasing steadily since 2009, driving up the total GDP. As to specific sectors (Fig. 8.3), the oil and gas industry still takes up the largest part of the GDP (25%), followed by the financial industry (15%), manufacturing (15%), as well as transportation and communications (7%).

1. Industrial structure

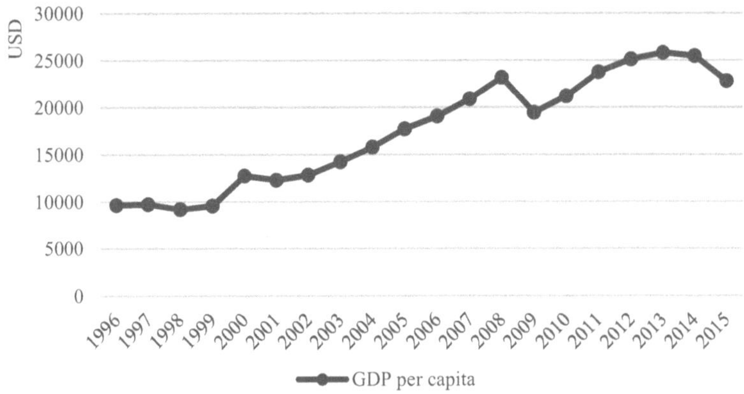

Fig. 8.1 Changes of per capita GDP of Bahrain. *Source of data* website of Ministry of Foreign Affairs, China

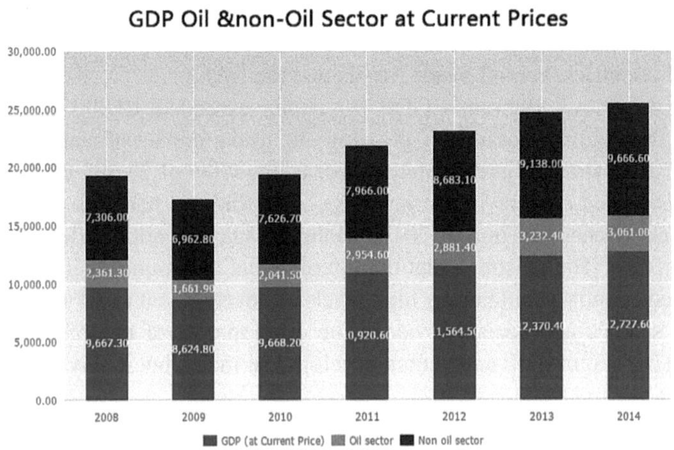

Fig. 8.2 The proportions of oil and non-oils sectors within Bahraini GDP. *Source of data* Information & eGovernment Authority. www.data.gov.bh

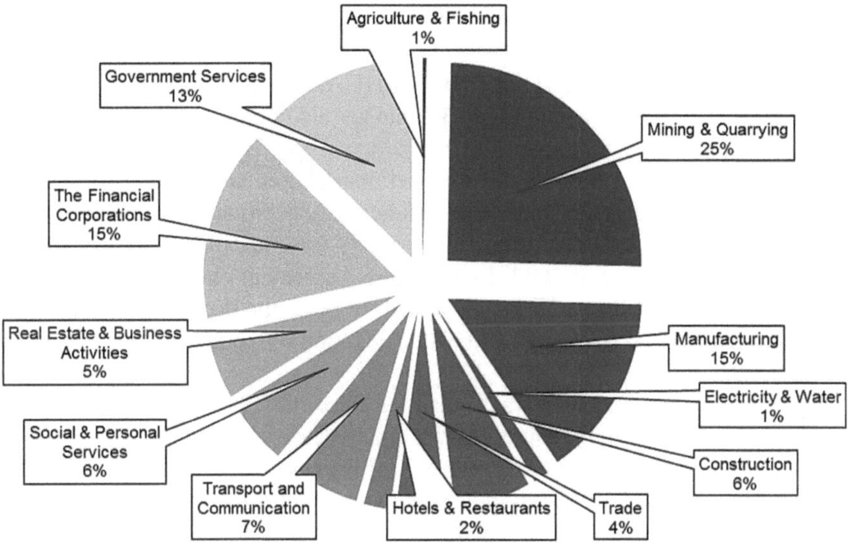

Fig. 8.3 The proportions of different sectors within Bahraini GDP since 2014. *Source of data* Information & eGovernment Authority. www.data.gov.bh

The first is the oil and gas industry. Oil and gas are the most important natural resources in Bahrain. From the perspective of GDP composition, the oil and gas industry is still an important pillar of Bahrain's economy. In 2014, Bahrain extracted 73.88 million barrels of oil and refined 100.23 million barrels. The total export value of petroleum products was 14.56 billion USD; in the same year, 728.425 billion cubic feet of natural gas were extracted for domestic power generation, seawater desalination and chemical production. Bahrain Petroleum Company is the only oil company wholly owned by the Bahraini government. Founded in 1976, it is responsible for the exploration, production, refining and sales of oil and gas in Bahrain. A large proportion of fiscal revenue comes from this company every year.

The second is the financial industry that has been given priority in recent years. Specifically, Bahrain's domestic financial industry can be divided into three branches: regular finance (29%), offshore finance (40) and insurance (31%). The offshore finance adopts the Bahamian model, making Bahrain an offshore financial center with only accounting and no substantial business, also known as a "tax evasion" offshore market. Many countries and enterprises set up offshore financial business in Bahrain because it does not levy business tax, individual income tax or value-added tax, which means they could avoid bank profit tax and business tax.

(II) Foreign trade and investment

The Bahrain Economic Development Board is the country's main agency responsible for investment promotion. It has maintained an open regulatory framework and provided a gateway to the Gulf market for foreign investors.

Bahrain imposes a 5% import tax on most imported goods, but food, machinery and equipment and raw materials needed for development projects are exempted. As a member of the Greater Arab Free Trade Area (GAFTA), Bahrain and other member states enjoy mutual tariff exemptions. Bahrain has also signed free trade agreements with the United States, Singapore and the European Free Trade Association (EFTA). In addition, China and Bahrain have signed many important agreements since the China–Bahrain Economic, Trade and Technical Cooperation Agreement signed in July 1990. Their Joint Commission on Economy, Trade and Technology held meetings of in 1993, 1996 and 2002. In 1999, the Agreement on Encouragement and Mutual Protection of Investments was signed. In 2002, the two governments signed the Agreement on the Avoidance of Double Taxation of Income and the Prevention of Tax Evasion.[7]

Since the establishment of trade relations since the 1950s, China and Bahrain have seen steady growth in their economic and trade cooperation. In 2014, the bilateral trade volume was 1.416 billion USD, a decrease of 8.3% over the previous year—China exported 1.232 billion USD (down by 0.6%), mainly mechanical and electrical products, steel, textiles and clothing, and imported 184 million USD (down by 39.7%), mainly oil and natural gas, iron ore and aluminum.

In 2014, the cumulative FDI in Bahrain reached 18.8 billion USD. In the same year, China's cumulative investment in Bahrain was 3.8 million USD.

8.2 Egypt

I. Geographical and historical backgrounds

Egypt is a large developing country, and also a great power in the Arab region, Africa and Islamic region. Located in the eastern part of North Africa, it spans both Asian and African continents (as large as 1.001 million km^2), as the Sinai Peninsula, to the east of the Suez Canal and in the southwestern Asia, is also within its territory. Bordering Libya to the west, Sudan to the south, the Red Sea and Palestine and Israel to the east, and the Mediterranean Sea to the north, Egypt is of great strategic importance as not only a land transport hub between Asia and Africa, but also a shortcut linking the Atlantic and Indian Oceans. Its coastline is approximately 2900 km long. With approximately 86.7 million people (July 2014), Egypt is the most populous country in the Middle East, and the second most populous country in Africa. Egypt is the birthplace of one of the four ancient civilizations. Islam is the state religion of Egypt, and its canon is the main basis of the legislation of the Republic. The believers are mainly Sunnis, accounting for 84% of the total population. In addition to Muslims, about 9 million people, mostly the descendants of the ancient Egyptians, believe in Coptic religion, a branch of the Greek Orthodox Church. Muslims, Copts and Jews are citizens who enjoy equal rights and freedom of religious belief. There is

[7] Source of data: *Guidebook on investment in other countries: Bahrain.* By Ministry of Commerce.

no difference in social status and employment. The government does not adopt a discriminatory policy when dealing with Muslim, Coptic or Jewish issues. In the Upper Egypt, where the Coptic people live, their traditions and historic sites are preserved.

Egypt has a unique geographical advantage. It is located in the center of the Middle East, close to the Arab, African and European markets. It has the Suez Canal, which is known as the gold channel of world trade. Meanwhile, it has signed free trade agreements with the EU, the United States, Arab and African countries. As a result, it has certain radiating capacity in the Middle East and African markets; in addition, it also serves as a gateway to the European market for African products. Its main resources are oil, natural gas, phosphate and iron, the proven reserves of which are 4.45 billion barrels (January 2013), 2.186 trillion m^3 (January 2012), approximately 7 billion tons and 60 million tons. Other mineral resources include manganese, coal, gold, zinc, chromium, silver, molybdenum, copper and talc. The average daily output of crude oil amounts to 711,500 barrels, and the daily output of natural gas reaches 168 million m^3. The domestic consumption of natural gas accounts for 70% of the total output, and the remaining 30% is for export.

II. **Economic development**

(I) Domestic economy

Egypt is Africa's third largest economy and is an open market. After the Gulf crisis ended, its political stance was appreciated by Western countries and the Gulf countries, which reduced its debts and increased aid. To promote economic growth, Egypt accelerated the process of privatization, encouraged foreign investment, expanded exports and took measures to adjust the economic structure and improve the investment environment. As a result, its economy had been growing since the late 1990s. The turbulence that began in early 2011 has severely impacted the national economy. After President Abdel Fattah al Sisi took office, the Egyptian government took measures to restore production, increase income and reduce expenditures, and improve people's livelihood. In addition, it sought international support and assistance to overcome the economic difficulties. Although its economic growth slowed down greatly in 2011, some improvement was seen after 2012 (Fig. 8.4).

1. Industrial structure

(1) The primary industry

Egypt is a traditional agricultural country. Its agricultural output accounts for about 18% of GDP. More than 1/3 of the working population is engaged in agriculture. 52% of people live in the rural areas. However, with the economic development, the proportion of agriculture in GDP has been steadily declining. The area of arable land in Egypt accounts for only 4.5% of the country's territory, and most of it is irrigated. With intensive farming, there can be two or three harvests per year, making the country with the highest yield per unit area in Africa. Its main agricultural products are long-stapled cotton and rice, both ranking first in Africa in terms of yield; its corn and wheat yields also rank among the top in Africa; it produces sugarcane and peanut, too.

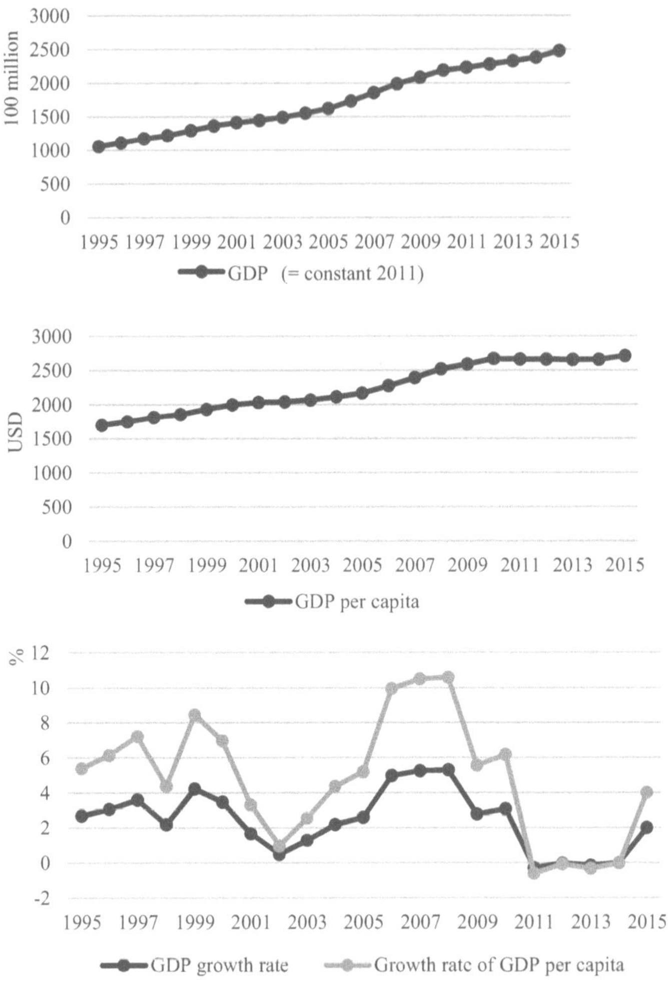

Fig. 8.4 Egyptian economy. *Source of data* World Bank database

(2) The secondary industry

Egypt is one of the more developed countries in Africa, with industrial output accounting for 39% of GDP. 70% of the industrial output is contributed by state-owned enterprises. Egypt owns a relatively sound industrial system. Its machinery manufacturing industry is mainly based on assembly. The textile and food processing industries are Egypt's traditional industrial sector, contributing more than half of the total industrial output. In recent years, heavy industries such as petroleum, steel, electric power, fertilizer, cement and machinery have also developed significantly. The petroleum industry has developed particularly rapidly, accounting for 21% of GDP. With an output of more than 64 million tons and an export value of 2.5 billion

USD, Egypt is the fourth largest oil producer in Africa. Relatively fast growth is seen in industries of clothing and leather products, building materials, cement, fertilizers, pharmaceuticals, etc. Within the light industry, the textile sector is well developed, producing 3% of Egypt's GDP and 27% of total manufacturing value. The export of industrial products accounts for about 60% of the total merchandise exports, and 2.74 million people, 14% of the total population, have industrial jobs.

(3) The tertiary industry

Within the industrial structure, the service industry has always taken up a larger share which has slowly risen from 44.5% in 1965 to about 50%. Egypt has a long history and thus tourist attractions, which are good for the development of tourism. The government has also made a lot of efforts in this regard. The turmoil in 2011 has a large negative impact on the local tourism industry, reducing the number of tourists, hotel room prices and tourism investment. In 2012, the revenue generated by tourism was about 10 billion USD, and its output value was about 11% of GDP. For more information, see Fig. 8.5.

Oil plays an extremely important role in Egypt's national economy and is one of the major sources of foreign exchange. 10% of its GDP and 40% of its export revenue come from oil and oil products. Egypt is one of the countries with the richest natural gas resource. Its natural gas reserves rank 6th among Arab countries and 18th among 102 countries with proven reserves. But its oil output and reserves have reached their limits and started to decline in recent years.

According to the sector-wise statistics, as shown in Fig. 8.6, farming, forestry, animal husbandry and fishery (A–B) have been shrinking since the early 1970s. This is a result of economic development in Egypt.

The proportion of manufacturing (D) has increased in recent decades, but the overall structure has changed little—light industries of textiles and food processing are still the dominant forces, and the manufacturing base is still weak.

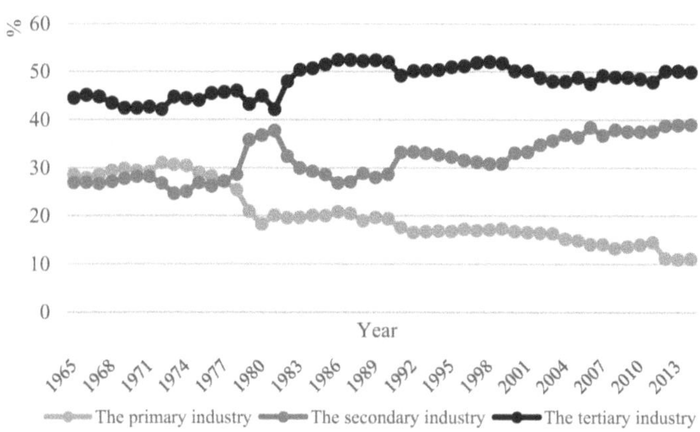

Fig. 8.5 Changes of Egyptian industrial structure. *Source of data* World Bank database

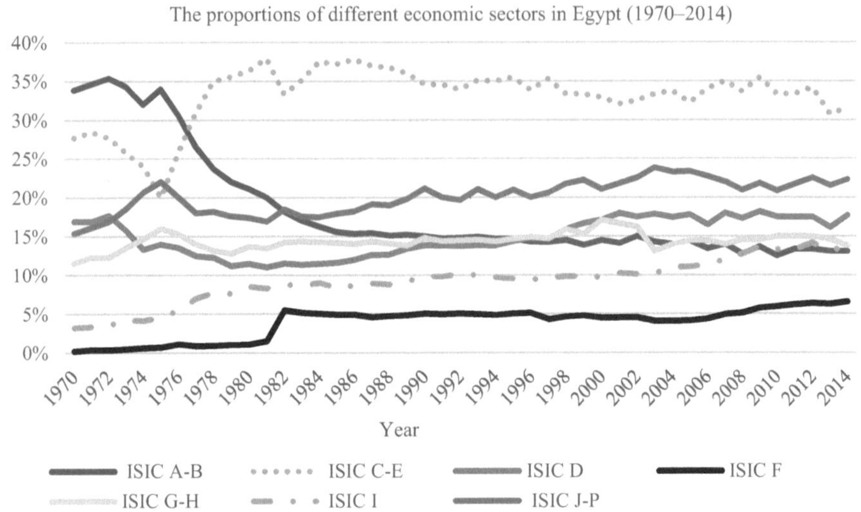

Fig. 8.6 The proportions of different economic sectors in Egypt. *Source of data* World Bank database

However, the proportion of the greater industry (C–E, including D) has grown rapidly since 1975, stabilizing at about 35% of the national economy since 1980. Apart from manufacturing, mining also takes a big part of the greater industry, which means a large share of Egypt's secondary industry is based on exporting resources. In fact, the average daily output of crude oil in Egypt is 711,500 barrels and the daily output of natural gas is 168 million m^3. 70% of the total natural gas output is consumed domestically, while the rest is for export. Oil revenue is an important source of foreign exchange.

In addition, Egypt's transportation industry (I) has been growing steadily. This is due to the heavy domestic investment and the strong demand from the tourism industry.

2. Urban structure

The urbanization rate in Egypt has increased significantly in the past 20 years, but the urbanization index is still lower than 44%, as shown in Fig. 8.7. This is related to Egypt's heavy dependence on agriculture. Poor urban infrastructure, scattered labor force and the small proportion of urban population are all hindering economic growth. However, as far as Africa is concerned, Egypt's infrastructure is generally sound. As of 2014, it has 22 airports and 10 international airports, 5195 km of railways, and 640,000 km of highways, covering urban and rural areas. As the international business and maritime center of Africa, it has 15 commercial ports, 6.3 million fixed-line telephone users and more than 3 million broadband users.

Table 8.1 lists the major cities of Egypt

The capital Cairo is located about 14 km south of the apex of the Nile Delta, covering an area of 3,085 km^2. Cairo is also a province, belonging to the Cairo

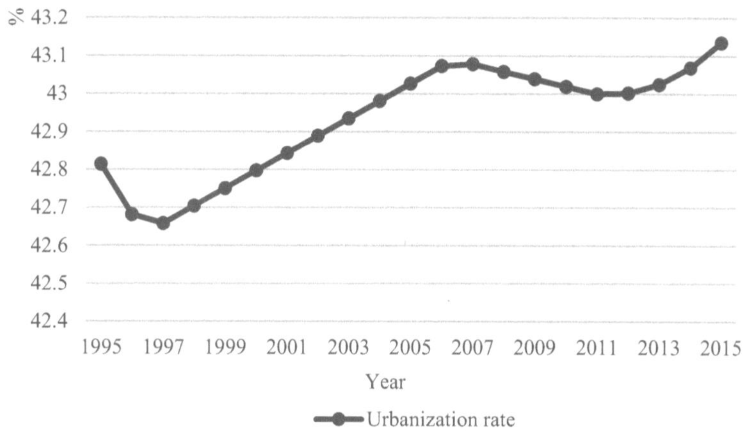

Fig. 8.7 Urbanization rate of Egypt. *Source of data* World Bank database

Table 8.1 Top 5 cities in Egypt

City	Population in 2016	City profile
Cairo	7,734,614	The capital; the largest city of Africa and even the Middle East
Alexandria	3,811,516	A port; the second largest city of Egypt and Africa
Giza	2,443,203	A tourist city for the Giza Pyramids
Port Said	538,378	A port that connects Africa and Asia, and the Mediterranean Sea and the Red Sea
Suez	488,125	A port in the northeast along the Suez Canal

Source of data World Population Review

District (known as the greater Cairo, covering 17,393 km^2) together with Giza and Gaiubia. Cairo is the largest city in Africa and the Middle East, and one of the oldest cities in the world. Having transformed into a modern metropolis, it is the political, economic, military, cultural, education, art, transport and tourist center of Egypt. However, problems such as excessive population density, poor infrastructure and sanitary conditions, and traffic congestion pose challenges to its economic development.

Alexandria is the second largest city in Egypt and Africa, and the largest port in Egypt and the Eastern Mediterranean. Located to west of the Nile Estuary and about 200 km away from Cairo, the city spans 30 km from east to west, and 2 km from the north to south at the narrowest point. It has an area of 2300 km^2.

Located at the crossroads of Africa and Asia, and the Mediterranean and the Red Sea, Port Said is one of Egypt's main port cities, covering an area of 1351 km^2. Port Said today is a center of civilian industry and a free zone chartered by the Egyptian government. In January 2002, the government announced that it would abolish the free zone status in five years and transform the city into an industrial zone of garment processing.

Giza is the third largest city in Egypt. It sits on the left bank of the lower Nile, connected to Cairo through a bridge. Its pyramids have brought it many tourists and thus great profits.

3. Government spending and consumption

As Fig. 8.8 shows, the continued growth of the Egyptian economy has increased consumer spending. Egypt currently imports most of the daily necessities. About 95% of the land area is uninhabitable desert. Therefore, nearly half of the population crowd in the richest Nile Delta which is about 24,000 km^2 in size. The population density is so high that Cairo alone is home to more than 7 million people. In recent years, the population of Egypt had grown rapidly from 75 million in 2005 to nearly 90 million in 2015. As Fig. 8.9 shows, the labor force in Egypt accounts for a very small proportion of the total population, and population issues have brought about challenges of energy supply and demand as well as severe poverty. In order to meet the basic needs of the large population, the Egyptian government has long provided food and energy subsidies.

(II) Foreign trade and investment
1. Foreign trade

Egypt has trade relations with more than 120 countries and regions, and its main trading partners are China, the United States, Germany, Italy, Saudi Arabia, India, Turkey, Ukraine, Russia and the United Arab Emirates. Egypt has an active trade policy and signed a number of bilateral and multilateral trade agreements. After joining the WTO in 1995, it signed free trade agreements with many countries. The regional agreements joined by Egypt are listed in Table 8.2.

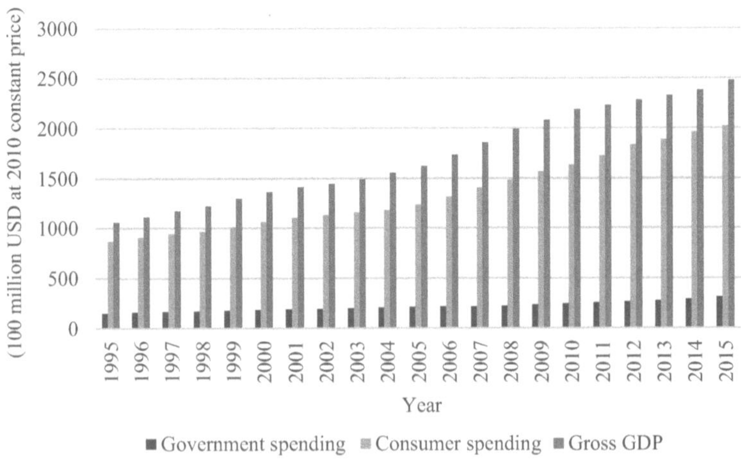

Fig. 8.8 Government spending and consumer spending in Egypt. *Source of data* World Bank database

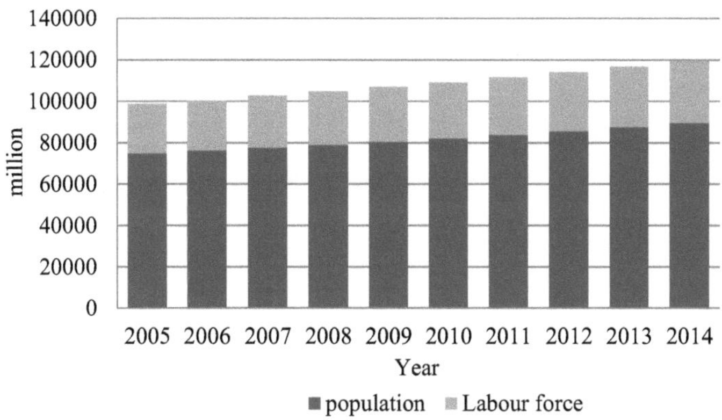

Fig. 8.9 Population growth in Egypt. *Source of data* UNCTADstat 2016

Table 8.2 Regional trade agreements Egypt has joined

Agreement	Year	Content
Egypt–EU Partnership Agreement	2001	At different stages set in the Agreement, Egypt's export of industrial and agricultural products to EU will enjoy preferential treatment and even tax exemption
Agreement on Qualified Industrial Zones	2004	Signed by the United States, Israel and Egypt
Egypt–Turkey Free Trade Agreement	2005	Some industrial and agricultural products enjoy tax-free or tax-reduction treatment when flowing between Egypt and Turkey.
Free Trade Area of COMESA	2000	
Agadir Agreement	2001	Signed by Egypt, Tunisia, Morocco and Jordan; some products are duty-free
Group of Eight Islamic Developing Countries (D8)	2014	Composed of 8 Muslim countries; with free trade arrangements

To expand exports and reduce trade deficit, the Egyptian government has adopted the following measures: developing national industries to produce more import substitutes; restricting imports, especially consumer goods; and expanding exports, especially non-traditional goods other than crude oil and raw cotton. Egypt mainly imports machinery and equipment, grains, electrical equipment, fossil fuels, plastics and related products, steel and steel products, timber and related products, vehicles, animal fodder, etc. The main export products are fossil fuels (crude oil and its products), cotton, ceramics, textiles and clothing, aluminum and related products, steel, grains and vegetables. Arab countries are its major export markets.

The economic indicators of Egypt in the past 20 years, as shown in Fig. 8.10, suggest its trade competitiveness has been increasing year by year. Petroleum, its economic pillar, is of certain competitive advantages as an export product.

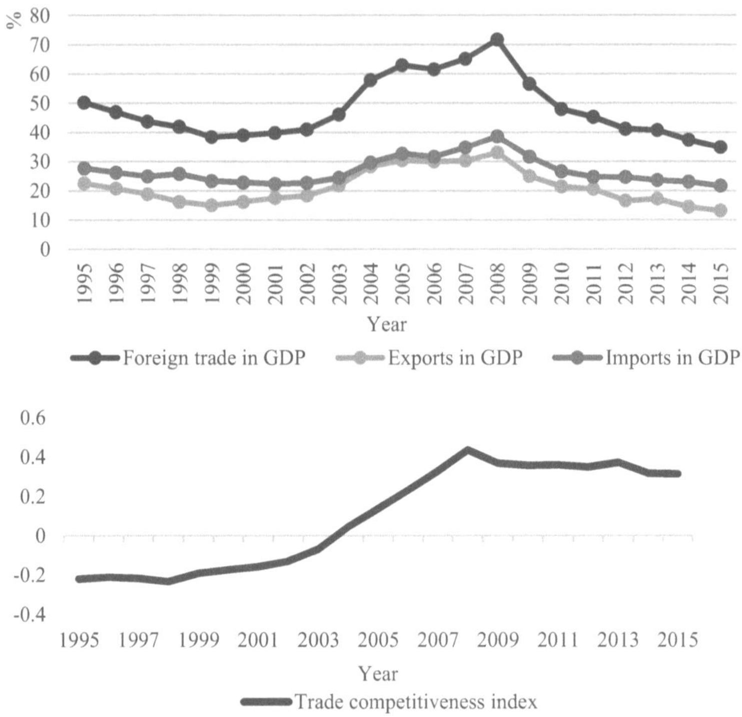

Fig. 8.10 Foreign trade of Egypt. *Source of data* World Bank database

2. International investment

Since the mid-1990s, Egypt has accelerated its absorption of FDI. As demonstrated by Fig. 8.11 and Table 8.3, the turmoils in early 2011, and late June and early July of 2013 led to a continued decline in foreign investment in Egypt. As the situation stabilized after the second half of 2014, the investment environment had improved. According to UNCTAD statistics, Egypt attracted 8.1 billion USD of FDI in 2016, a year-on-year increase of 17%, ranking first in North Africa.[8] Prior to 2012, Saudi Arabia, the UAE and Britain were the major investors in Egypt. According to the Arab Investment and Export Credit Guarantee Corporation,[9] the main sources of foreign investment in Egypt in the five years before 2016 were China, Saudi Arabia and the United Arab Emirates. The areas favored by foreign investors were oil and gas, communications technology, food and real estate.

According to statistics of the General Authority for Investment and Free Zones of Egypt, from FY 2007/2008 to FY 2011/2012, total FDIs in Egypt were 13.2 billion, 8.1 billion, 6.8 billion, 2.2 billion and 4 billion USD, declining for four fiscal years in a row. The main reason for the decline in FY 2008/2009 and FY 2009/2010

[8] http://eg.mofcom.gov.cn/article/jmxw/201706/20170602599860.shtml.

[9] http://www.mofcom.gov.cn/article/i/jyjl/k/201707/20170702611061.shtml.

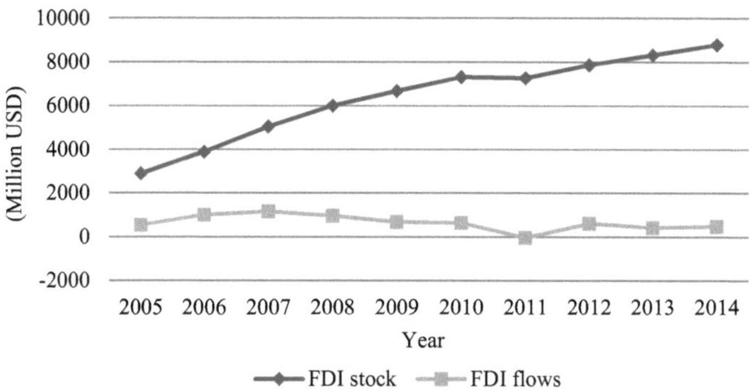

Fig. 8.11 FDI in Egypt. *Source of data* World Bank database

Table 8.3 Volumes of FDI in Egypt over the years (Unit: Billion USD)

Year	Volume
2003/2004	2.1
2004/2005	3.9
2005/2006	6.1
2006/2007	11.1
2007/2008	13.2
2008/2009	8.1
2009/2010	6.8
2010/2011	2.2
2011/2012	4.0
2012/2013	3.8
2013/2014	4.1
2014/2015	1.8

Source of data Central Bank of Egypt

was the impact of the international financial crisis, and thus the weak investment momentum of European and American countries. Starting from the end of 2010, major changes took place in West Asia and North Africa, with the "Arab Spring" spreading to some Arab countries in the Gulf region, which had given rise to political turmoil and economic downturn in Egypt since January 2011. The consequent loss of confidence in Egypt, together with the spreading European sovereign debt crisis, caused the continued decline in FDI in FY 2010/2011 and FY 2011/2012. After the establishment of the interim government in 2013, the situation in Egypt stabilized, but the market confidence was yet to be restored. In FY 2012/2013, investment in Egypt fell by 3.7% year-on-year, with a net inflow of FDI of 3 billion USD, down by 24.6% on a year-on-year basis. The European Union, the United States and the Arab countries, as the main investors in Egypt, contributed 5 billion USD, 2.1 billion USD and 1.4 billion USD, respectively. According to the 2014 World Investment Report

Table 8.4 Growths of FDI in different sectors of Egypt 2010–2014 (Unit: %)

	2010/2011	2011/2012	2012/2013	2013/2014
The establishment of new enterprises and the expansion of existing enterprises	102.0	52.8	79.9	54.1
Real estate sales to non-local residents	0.9	42.2	9.4	3.2
The oil sector	−8.7	3.3	8.7	39.5
Real estate	6.1	1.8	2.1	3.2

Source of data Central Bank of Egypt

released by UNCTAD, in 2013, foreign investment flow in Egypt was 5.55 billion USD; as of the end of 2013, its foreign investment stock was 85.05 billion USD.

According to the statistics of the Central Bank of Egypt, as of the end of f FY 2011/2012, the top three recipient sectors of foreign investment were oil and gas at 710.1 billion USD; communications and information technology at 1.391 billion USD; and industry at 733 million USD. Other areas receiving foreign investment include services, finance, construction, real estate, agriculture and tourism. The growth of foreign investment was concentrated in the establishment of new companies and the expansion of existing enterprises. However, the situation had been changing since 2010, as more capitals flew to the oil sector. See Table 8.4.

The EU and the Arab countries are the main sources of foreign investment in Egypt. According to statistics of the General Authority for Investment and Free Zones of Egypt, as of the end of 2012, Saudi Arabia, the UAE and Britain were the top three investors in Egypt, with investment stocks of 5.8 billion, 5.2 billion and 4.3 billion USD, respectively.

In recent years, Chinese companies have started to invest in Egypt, mainly in industries of oil and gas, metallurgy, textiles and building materials (stone-material processing). Egypt imports refined oil and exports crude oil, therefore, rising oil prices bring both positive and negative impacts. China's trade with Egypt has increased year by year. With the trade liberalization in Egypt, there is still great potential for the bilateral trade.

China mainly exports to Egypt machinery and appliances, electrical equipment, knitted or crocheted clothing and accessories, vehicles and spare parts, ships and floating structures, steel products, plastics and related products, chemical filament yarn, organic chemicals, chemical staple fibers, etc.; Egypt mainly exports to China fossil fuels, earth and stone, cotton, plastics and related products, inorganic chemicals, copper and related products and other plant fibers.

Chinese companies should pay attention to the following matters when investing in Egypt.

Investment:

① One should have long-term goals and value mutual benefit and win–win results when investing in Egypt. Chinese enterprises investing in labor-intensive sectors should make full use of local labor, reduce production costs, and create jobs for locals, so as to achieve the dual goal of economic and social benefits. The Egyptian government supports export-oriented enterprises, so Chinese companies can set up export processing enterprises to expand exports as much as possible and actively explore the markets of neighboring countries. The starting point of an investment project is preferably high. Once the decision is made, one should maintain the upper and intermediate quality of production equipment, R&D and management. It is better to start with small projects and strive for success. Service facilities should be built while setting up factories to improve the living conditions of local residents. Joint ventures should observe the local laws and train local technicians and managers.

② To make correct decisions, Chinese-funded enterprises should fully understand local policies and environment of investment by collecting and analyzing policies and regulations issued by the Egyptian government. Joint ventures should choose their partners with caution. Egypt encourages the development of small-and-medium-sized enterprises which are of a large proportion and varying credit ratings. A feasibility study should be carried out beforehand, and a partner with good reputation should be selected, so as to ensure the future success and prevent losses. It is necessary to fully understand the structure of market demand and its trend of changes. Some companies did not make a correct prediction of the market demand and its trend, so their products were not wanted in the market, leading to economic losses.

Trade:

Although the scale of the bilateral trade has been increasing year by year, there are still many problems and challenges.

① Egypt has a significant trade deficit with China. Due to its resource endowment and industrial structure, Egypt mainly exports primary products of limited kinds, leading to long-term trade deficit. From 2006 to 2012, its trade deficit expanded from 2.76 billion USD to 6.904 billion USD, up by 150%. In the first nine months of 2013, despite the impact of commodity trading, Egypt saw a 113.3% year-on-year increase in exports and a 3.2% year-on-year decline in imports. However, the long-standing deficit problem has caused discontent on the Egyptian side.

② Some Chinese products exported to Egypt have quality issues. In order to guarantee the quality of exports to Egypt, the two governments have carried out pre-shipment inspection and quarantine certification since 2009. In addition, they launched a special operation against bogus products and intellectual-property theft in 2011, and produced good results. However, there are still some Chinese ersatz products, especially chemical products, in the Egyptian market.

③ Trade frictions are gradually increasing. Due to the political turmoil and economic woes in Egypt, the local government is frequently taking protectionist measures, intensifying trade frictions between the two countries.

8.3 United Arab Emirates

I. **Geographical and historical backgrounds**

The United Arab Emirates (UAE) is the second largest economy in the Gulf region and one of the highest-income countries in the world. It is also one of the most appealing countries in the Middle East. It is playing an increasingly important role in the Gulf region and the Arab world. Geographically, it is located in the southeast of the Arabian Peninsula, bordering Oman to the east, Qatar to the northwest, Saudi Arabia to the west and south, the Persian Gulf to the north, and Iran across the sea. The coastline is 734 km long. It guards the gateway through which the maritime traffic from the Persian Gulf enters the Indian Ocean. In terms of natural conditions, the vast majority of the UAE is deserts (65%) and oases 200 m above sea level. There are no freshwater rivers or lakes in its territory. It has tropical desert climate, with hot and humid summers (May–October, 40–50 °C), and warm winters (November–April, 7–20 °C) with occasional sandstorms. The average annual precipitation is about 100 mm, mostly concentrated between January and February. Historically, the UAE belonged to the Arab Empire in the 7th century. Starting from the 16th century, colonialists such as Portugal, the Netherlands and France invaded it successively. In the early 19th century, Britain invaded the Persian Gulf. The UAE became a British protectorate in 1820. In 1971, Britain announced the termination of the protection treaty. In December of the same year, the United Arab Emirates was founded. The six emirates of Abu Dhabi, Dubai, Sharjah, Fujairah, Umm Al Quwain and Ajman formed a federal state. In 1972, Ras Al Khaimah joined the Federation. In 2015, its population was 9.16 million, 88.5% of which were foreigners, mainly from India, Pakistan, Egypt, Syria and Palestine. Religiously, it is a Muslim country—80% are Sunnis. 87% of the population are Arabs, Arabic is the official language, and English is a common language.

The UAE is rich in oil and natural gas resources, with proven oil reserves of 97.8 billion barrels and natural gas reserves of 6.09 trillion m^3, both ranking seventh in the world. It is rich in sulfur, magnesium, limestone as well as other mineral and aquatic resources. While developing the petrochemical industry, the government vigorously promotes economic diversification, strengthens infrastructure construction, and actively develops industries such as cement and building materials, as well as modern services such as tourism and exhibitions. It has gradually become a financial, commercial, logistics, tourist and trade center in the Middle East. In 2015, it ranked 17th in terms of global competitiveness. It is also the host country of the 2020 Expo. In recent years, it has actively participated in regional affairs and inter-state cooperation. It is a member of the Gulf Cooperation Council and the Greater Arab Free Trade Area (GAFTA). In the context of instability in the Middle East and North Africa, its role as a hub of regional trade, finance and logistics is growing increasingly important.

II. **Economic development**

(I) Domestic economy

Similar to other oil producers in the Middle East, the UAE has benefited economically from its oil extraction and petrochemical industry; however, its heavy dependence on oil has also made its economy subject to the impact of changing oil price. As Figs. 8.12 and 8.13 show, its GDP totaled 370.3 billion USD in 2015; the per capita GDP was 40,438 USD, much higher than the threshold of 12,736 USD which UN sets for high-income countries, and ranking 2nd in the Middle East and North Africa, only after Qatar.

1. Industrial structure

Figure 8.14 shows the proportions of agriculture, industry and service sector within the UAE's GDP were 0.7%, 55.0% and 44.3%, respectively, in 2015. Industry is the dominant force, and the modern service sector is growing fast.

Due to limited natural conditions, agriculture contributes little to the economy. The arable land area of the country is 320,000 ha, and the area of cultivated land is 270,000 ha. At present, UAE relies on imports for grains and major meat products; it is self-sufficient in terms of fish and dates; its animal husbandry is small in scale.

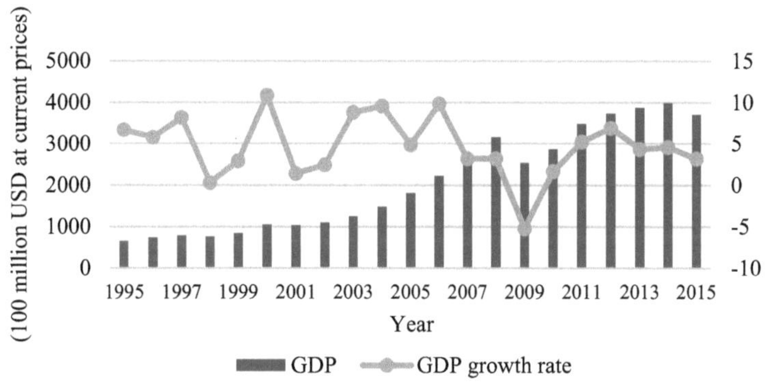

Fig. 8.12 GDP growth in UAE. *Source of data* World Bank database

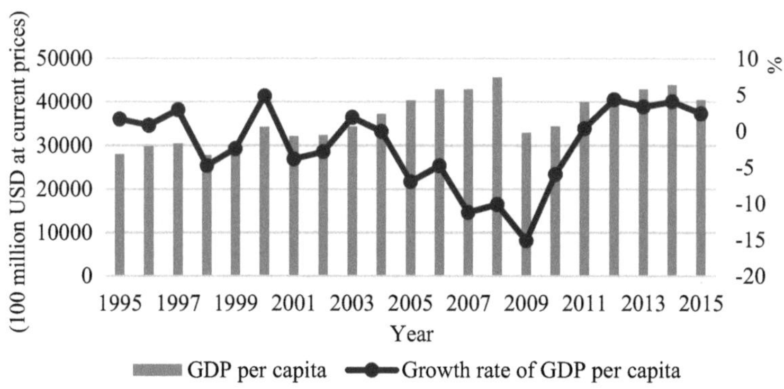

Fig. 8.13 Growth of per capita GDP in UAE. *Source of data* World Bank database

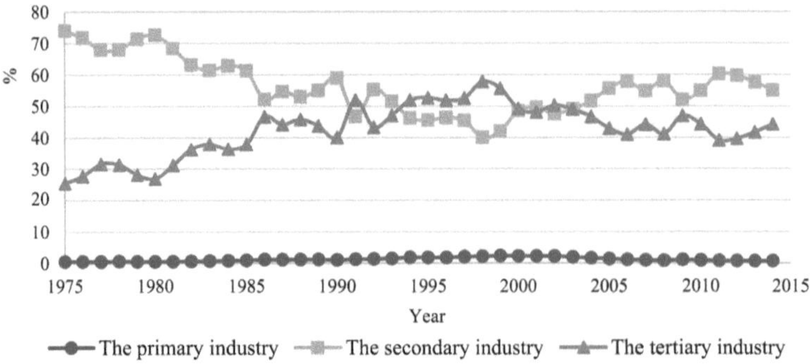

Fig. 8.14 The industrial structure of UAE. *Source of data* World Bank database

In recent years, the government has been encouraging farming, providing farmers with free seeds, fertilizers and interest-free loans, and purchasing and selling all the agricultural products to ensure farmers' income. In this way, a certain level of growth has been achieved of local agriculture.

As to industry, the oil sector is key to its economy. It produced 2.8 million barrels of oil per day in 2014–2015, and the daily output was expected to reach 3.5 million barrels by 2017. However, the drop of oil price led to a sharply decreasing contribution to GDP of oil sectors while the GDP of oil consumption sectors (non-oil) start to increase. According to the Central Bank of the UAE, the nominal GDP of its non-oil sectors was 1.041 trillion dirham (approximately 284.4 billion USD) in 2015, accounting for 76.5% of the total, and the percentage was expected to rise to 83% in 2016. It also has abundant natural gas, with proven reserves of 6.09 trillion m^3, ranking seventh in the world. However, due to the large domestic demand and the difficulty of extraction, most of the natural gas is used for reinjection and oil extraction; therefore, it currently adopts an import policy and imports natural gas from Qatar through the Dolphin program. The UAE mainly depends on the Abu Dhabi National Petroleum Company for oil production. The company contributes 96% of the country's total oil output and controls the onshore oil extraction and two largest offshore oil and gas companies.

At present, the UAE is working hard to promote the development of petrochemical metallurgy, processing and manufacturing, new energy, finance, tourism and other industries. The non-petroleum sectors are seeing growing shares of the national economy. Its role as a regional trade, financial and logistics hub has been further enhanced.

Aluminum smelting is one of the major non-oil industries in the UAE. In 2013, the Emirates Global Aluminium, after mergers and acquisitions, ranked fifth in the world in terms of primary aluminum output, and its total assets reached approximately 15 billion USD. About 20% of local produced primary aluminum is consumed internally by the Gulf countries, while 50% of local second-hand aluminum is exported after secondary processing.

Aviation is also one of the highlights of the UAE's non-oil industries. In the ranking of global airlines, the Emirates Airlines ranks first among Arab countries. There are currently 7 international airports in the UAE, including Dubai International Airport and Abu Dhabi International Airport. It has signed bilateral aviation agreements with 155 countries and regions (including China), and 109 airlines around the world have regular flights to airports in the country. According to the UAE General Civil Aviation Authority (GCAA), in 2014, the number of passengers transported to and from the UAE's airports was 101 million. Dubai International Airport replaced Heathrow Airport in 2014 as the world's busiest airport, and in 2015, it maintained the crown after handling more than 78 million international passengers. At the same time, according to the review results of the Global Aviation Safety Plan (GASP) of the International Civil Aviation Organization (ICAO), the UAE is also the country with the safest civil aviation operations in the world. In 2016, the Emirates Airlines was named the best airline in the world by Skytrax.

The UAE has a relatively complete financial system. Its banking industry is well developed, with 23 domestic banks, 843 branches and 89 offices, as well as 115 foreign banks and other financial institutions. Dubai has become the sixth largest financial center in the world after London, New York, Singapore, Hong Kong and Frankfurt.

Tourism is also one of the well-known industries of the UAE. With the eighth developed aviation and tourism industry in the Middle East, the UAE, according to data from the World Travel & Tourism Council (WTTC), made approximately 134 billion dirhams from tourism in 2015, accounting for 8.7% of its gross GDP. With the world's tallest building, the first seven-star hotel, the world's largest shopping center, and the world's largest indoor ski resort, etc., Dubai is one of the most popular resorts for international tourists.

2. Urban structure

In terms of urbanization, the UAE is similar to most Gulf countries—most of its residents live in cities. As shown in Fig. 8.15, the urbanization rate reached 85.6% in 2015. As the two major cities, Abu Dhabi and Dubai are home to most of the population, and the regional economic, financial, tourism centers and transport hubs in the Middle East. Table 8.5 provides an overview of the major cities in the UAE.

UAE has sound infrastructure. It has about 4080 km of highway with world-leading quality, 10 major seaports with an annual cargo throughput of 960.03 million tons. In 2013, the container handling capacity was 23.5 million TEU per year (the Jebel Ali port in Dubai is the world's largest man-made port and the largest port in the Middle East), and competitive edges of air transport. In terms of telecommunications, as of the first half of 2014, it has 17.5 million mobile phones and over 2.1 million fixed-line phones; there are more than 1.1 million Internet users, including more than 1 million broadband users.

As to public service supply, the UAE is a typical welfare state. Its citizens are entitled to free healthcare. There is a sound healthcare system of 1162 medical institutions such as hospitals, primary medical centers and clinics, covering both rural and urban areas. In 2014, the UAE-born population had a life expectancy of

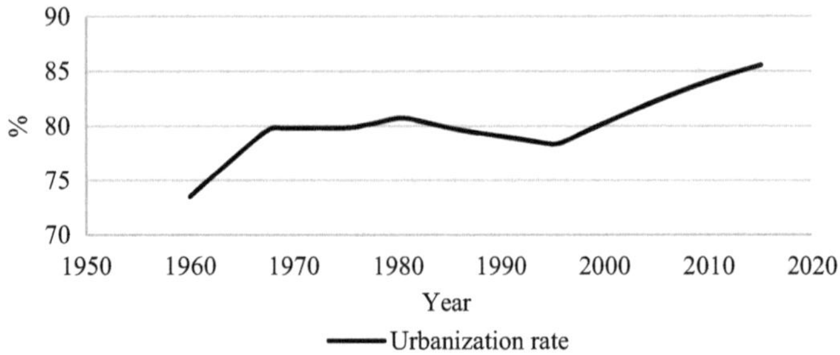

Fig. 8.15 The urbanization rate of UAE. *Source of data* World Bank database

Table 8.5 Major cities in UAE

City	City profile
Abu Dhabi	Located on the central and western coast of the UAE; the capital of UAE and the capital of the emirate of Abu Dhabi
Dubai	Located in the middle of the Arabian Peninsula and on the south bank of the Arabian Gulf, it covers an area of 3980 km^2. It is the most populous city in the UAE (2.62 million, 2014). As the richest city in the Middle East, it is the economic, financial, tourist and transport center of the region; it is also known as the "trade capital" of the Middle East and North Africa
Sharjah	A historic and cultural city in the Middle East; an important international transport hub

Source of data Based on public information

77.4 years, ranking among the top in the Middle East. The government attaches great importance to the development of education and the cultivation of domestic science and technology talents, offers free education and advocates that women and men have an equal chance at education. There are a total of 1259 public schools, with more than 800,000 students and more than 25,000 teachers.

(II) Foreign trade and investment

Foreign trade occupies an important position in the UAE's economy. In 1995, it joined the World Trade Organization. It mainly exports oil, natural gas, petrochemical products, aluminum ingots and a small number of local products, and mainly imports grain, machinery and consumer goods. The Asian-Pacific region, including China, is its largest trading partner, followed by Europe and the Middle East and North Africa.

Meanwhile, the UAE is also actively investing abroad. According to, FDI Intelligence, an affiliate of the *Financial Times*, among the exporting countries, the UAE's diversity index of direct investment abroad ranks eighth globally and first regionally. As to absorbing foreign investment, it has become one of the most attractive destinations in the Gulf region and the Middle East with its abundant natural resources, advantageous geographical location, sound infrastructure and great economic openness. According to the World Bank, the net inflow of FDI in the UAE reached 10.98

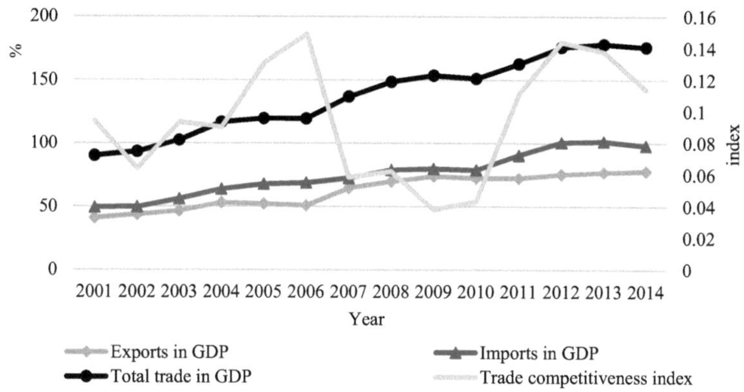

Fig. 8.16 Foreign trade of UAE. *Source of data* World Bank database

billion USD in 2015, second only to Israel (11.51 billion USD) in the Middle East and North Africa. According to the Arab Investment and Export Credit Guarantee Corporation, from 2003 to 2013, the UAE had 3437 foreign investment projects, accounting for 35.6% of the total in the Arab countries; 3246 foreign companies were established in the country, taking up 36% of the total in the Arab countries. See Fig. 8.16 for more information.

8.4 Iraq

I. Geographical and historical backgrounds

As one of the birthplaces of human civilization, Iraq bred the oldest Mesopotamian civilization and medieval Islamic civilization. In addition to the longest history of human civilization of more than 5,000 years, it also has abundant water and oil resources. From 1980 to 2003, Iraq experienced three world-shaking wars—the Iran-Iraq War, the Gulf War and the Iraq War, which have left severe damages to this formerly prosperous country, exhausting its national strength.

Located in the southwest of Asia, the north of the Arabian Peninsula, and between the Asia Minor Peninsula and the Iranian Plateau, Iraq shares borders with six countries— Iran to the east, Jordan and Syria to the west, Turkey to the north, Kuwait and Saudi Arabia to the south, and the Persian Gulf to the southeast. (i.e., the Arabian Gulf). Sitting at the intersection of the three continents of Asia, Africa and Europe and in the temperate zone of the northern hemisphere, it has an important geographical location. It is also in the area with the shortest land distance between the Indian Ocean and the Mediterranean Sea, thus making it a land bridge between southern Europe and South Asia and a transport hub of global significance. Iraq is located in the area surrounded by the Five Seas (the Caspian Sea, the Black Sea, the Mediterranean Sea, the Arabian Sea and the Red Sea), but it only borders the Arabian Sea through the Persian Gulf. It has a coastline of about 60 km, a land borderline of about 3631 km, and a land area of 441,814 km^2, including 924 km^2 of territorial waters and half of the neutral zone shared with Saudi Arabia (3522 km^2).

At present, the total population of Iraq is about 31.01 million, of which Arabs are the largest group, accounting for about 73%. Iraq is a Muslim country. Islam is the state religion. 95% of people in the country believe in Islam, of which 54.5% are Shiites and 40.5% are Sunnis. Only a small group of people believe in Christianity or Judaism. Since its neighbor Iran is country dominated by the Shiites, there are often sect-related conflicts and fractions in the border zone between the two countries.

II. **Economic development**

(I) Domestic economy

Iraq has abundant natural resources such as oil and natural gas. At present, Iraq's proven crude oil reserves are 143.1 billion barrels, accounting for 9.8% of the world's total, ranking fifth in the world. The proven natural gas reserves are 3.17 trillion m^3, accounting for 1.7%. At the same time, it also has abundant mineral resources, including about 10 billion tons of phosphate reserves, the 10th largest in the world. Iraq has a relatively developed agriculture. Irrigated agriculture has been developing for thousands of years in Mesopotamia. Its main agricultural products are wheat, rye, barley, rice, cotton, tobacco, temperate fruits and date, among which the export volume of date ranks first in the world. Meanwhile, its animal husbandry is mainly distributed in the northeast, where cattle, horses, sheep, donkeys are raised. In addition, nomadic herding exists on the arid plateau in the southwest.

The Iraqi economy is recovering well, but there are certain hidden dangers. With the recovery of the oil industry, Iraq has maintained a good upward momentum in recent years. As Figs. 8.17 and 8.18 show, its gross GDP was less than 10 billion USD in 2007 but exceeded 20 billion USD in 2013, with an annual growth rate of more than 5%. In 2014, due to the continued deterioration of the domestic security situation and the sharp decline in oil prices, the Iraqi economy suffered negative growth of −2.4%, driving down the per capita GDP to some extent. Its per capita GDP has exceeded 6000 USD, and the CPI has also stabilized.

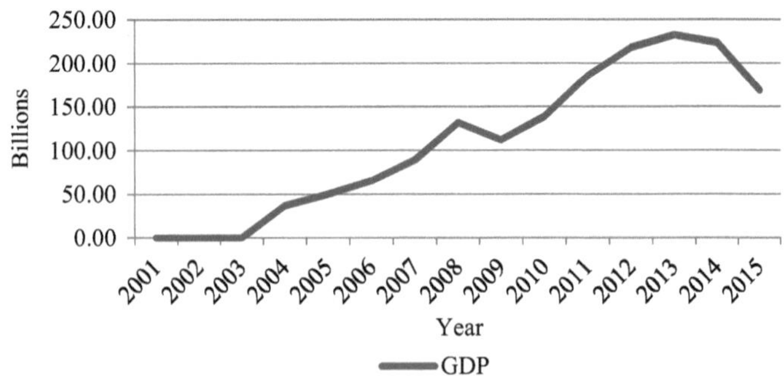

Fig. 8.17 GDP of Iraq

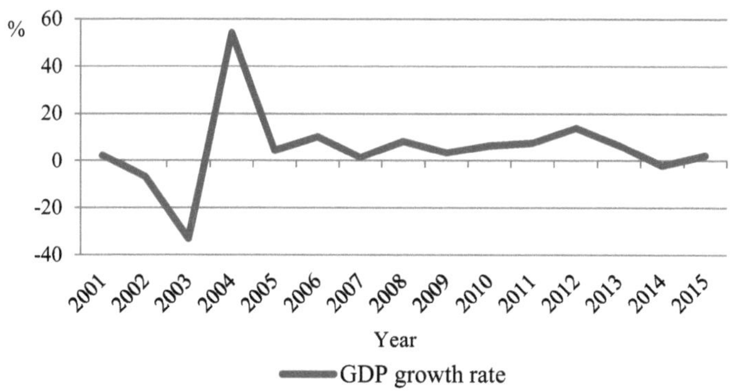

Fig. 8.18 Growth rate of Iraqi GDP

1. Industrial structure

Iraqi economy is dominated by the secondary industry, especially oil extraction. As the post-war reconstruction progresses, its industrial structure is gradually improving. In 2004, the output value of the primary industry took up nearly 10% of GDP; the secondary industry contributed 86.5%, of which the mining of petroleum and other mineral resources produced 84.7%. In the early post-war period, due to grave security risks, the service industry lagged behind, accounting for less than 4% of GDP. With the economic recovery, the proportion of the tertiary industry has gradually increased.

2. Population and cities

Iraq faces the shortage of human resources. Its population density is 55 people/km^2, but the population is unevenly distributed geographically and between cities and rural areas. Most people live in large cities such as the capital Baghdad (6 million), Mosul in the north (1.5 million) and Basra in the south (1.44 million). Other cities have relatively small populations.

(II) Foreign trade and investment

Iraq's foreign trade has been growing rapidly. The total exports were only 17.8 billion USD in 2004. With the recovery of the Iraqi oil industry and the sharp rise in oil prices, the foreign trade has been expanding. The exports exceeded 60 billion USD in 2008, and then 90 billion USD in 2012. Later, the plunging oil prices led to slight decline in export revenues. In 2012, the oil export revenue amounted to 94.02 billion USD. In 2013, the oil export volume was 2.39 million barrels per day, generating 89.22 billion USD of revenue. In 2014, it exported an average of more than 2.45 million barrels of oil per day, or about 918 million barrels within the year, bringing in about 84.215 billion USD. In 2013 and 2014, the total value of Iraq's exports did not exceed 90 billion USD. As the exports increased, the imports also grew substantially, just at a lower speed. In 2004, the imports registered 21.3 billion USD in value, and it grew to over 60 billion USD in 2012. Iraq mainly imports

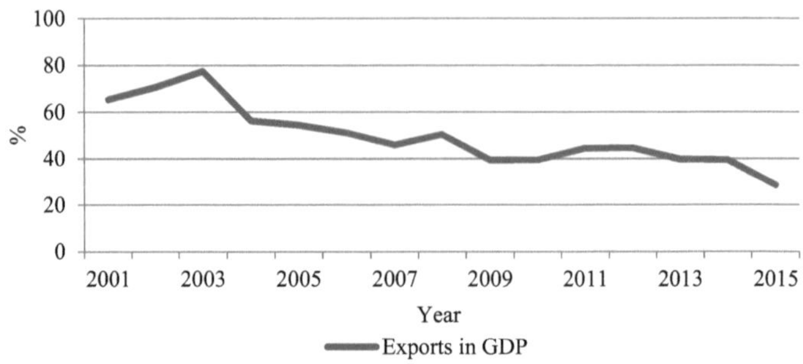

Fig. 8.19 The proportion of exports in Iraqi GDP

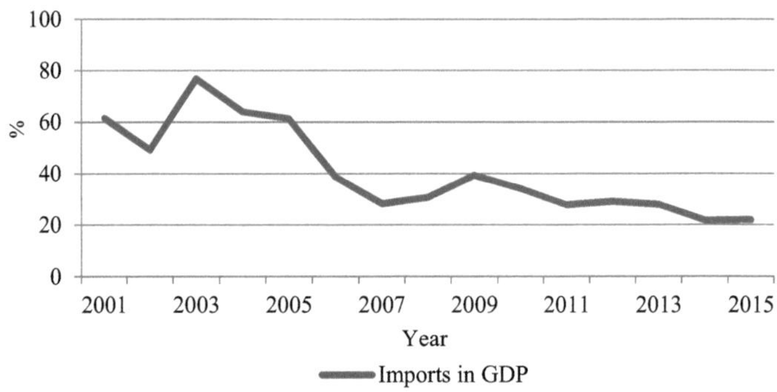

Fig. 8.20 The proportion of imports in Iraqi GDP

various means of production, food and other daily necessities. In the past few years, Iraq has been implementing food rationing. Hiking global food prices and shrinking domestic food output have hit the local food supply hard. Now, the wheat output has been reduced to 1.5 million tons, but the annual domestic demand is 5 million tons. Rice is one of the staple foods of the Iraqi people—more than 1 million tons are needed to meet the needs every year, but local rice output has dropped from 300,000 tons to 150,000 tons. For more information, see Figs. 8.19, 8.20 and 8.21.

8.5 Israel

I. **Geographical and historical backgrounds**

Israel's history is reflected in its national flag (Fig. 8.22). The blue and white stripes symbolize the color of the shawl of the Jewish monks; the "Star of David" in the middle represents the shield of King David and is a symbol of traditional Jewish culture.

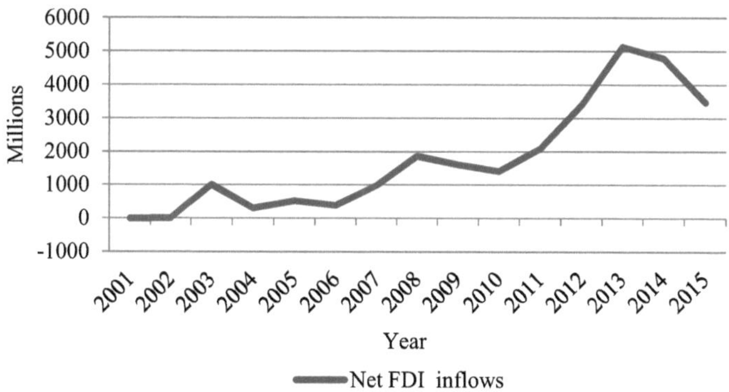

Fig. 8.21 The net inflow of FDI in Iraq

Fig. 8.22 National flag of Israel

Israel (Canaan) is the birthplace of the Jews. In 1000 BC, King David seized Jerusalem and most of Canaan (including Transjordan) and created the Kingdom of Israel. After the death of Solomon the son of Kind David, the kingdom was divided into Judah and Israel. However, the defeats in wars displaced the Jews: the Assyrians captured Israel in 722 BC, the Babylonians occupied Judah in 586 BC, and the Solomon Temple in Jerusalem was burned down. Since then, Jerusalem has changed hands many times, and the Jews have been driven away to other places in the world. The Jewish people have never forgotten the land of Canaan during the long exile. In 1948, Israel was founded, and the gloomy days of Jewish displacement finally became history.

The current geographical location of Israel is different from what is recorded in history. It is located in Levant, bordering the Mediterranean to the northwest, Lebanon to the north, Syria and Jordan to the east, and Egypt to the southwest. In January 2014, Israel's population exceeded 8.13 million, of which nearly 80% were Jews. It is the only country in the world with Jews as its main ethnic group.

Israel does not have many natural resources. Its main resources are the potassium and magnesium minerals in the Dead Sea. In recent years, Israel has successively developed several large-scale natural gas fields in the Mediterranean Sea. Water resources are scarce, most of which is from the Jordan River, Lake Galilee and some tributaries. However, thanks to the high water use efficiency, water supply and demand are still in balance.

The Israeli capital, Jerusalem, is where the central government is based. It is also the political, economic, cultural and transport center. The New Israeli shekel is the legal currency, and a floating exchange rate regime is adopted.

II. **Economic development**

(I) Domestic economy

Israel's economic development over the past 30 years can be divided into two distinct stages.

(1) 1990s: economy of immigrants

In the 1990s, Israel accepted 1 million Jewish immigrants from the Soviet Union (Fig. 8.23), many of which were highly educated and entrepreneurial high-tech talents. Driven by this wave of immigration, the overall economic development was fast. In 1990 and 1991, the GDP growth rate increased to 5.1% and 5.2%, respectively. In 1994–1996, it exceeded 6%. In 1997–1999, it slowed down. The economic depression of 1997–1998 was due to the decrease in the number of immigrants and the slowdown in the growth of world trade: the decline in population directly affected durable consumer goods and real-estate investment. Fortunately, thanks to its macroeconomic stability, Israel was free from the impact of the 1997–1998 Asian financial turmoil. The Israeli economy rebounded strongly in 1999 after sliding down a little in the first quarter.

(2) 21st century: economy of innovation

At the beginning of the 21st century, the annual growth rate of Israel's GDP was about 7.5%, almost twice that of developed countries. In 2001 and 2002, Israel witnessed negative growth under the impact of the global market. Since 2003,

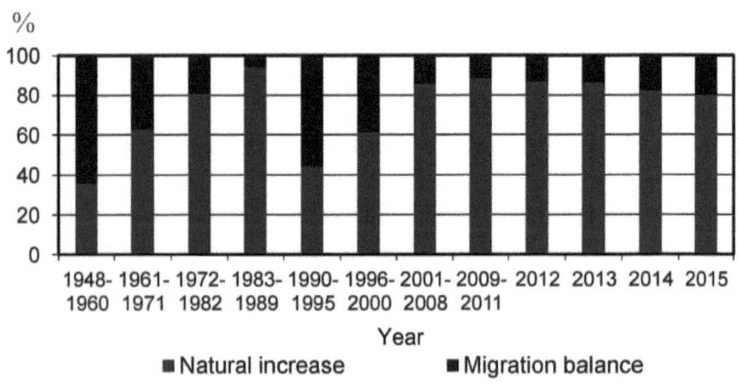

Fig. 8.23 Sources of population growth in Israel. *Source of data* Israel Central Bureau of Statistics, Israel in Figures 2016

the government implemented an emergency economy policy. As a result, its GDP increased by 2.3% in 2003, and then reached 5.2%, 5.3%, 5.2% and 5.3%, respectively, from 2004 to 2007. Later in 2008 and 2009, due to the impact of the global financial crisis, Israeli exports weakened and domestic demand declined. In 2010, successive stimulus policies pushed the annual growth rate up to 4.6%. In 2011, the growth momentum was strong at first but then it wore out. In 2012, affected by factors such as the global economic downturn, the growth rate dropped to 3.3%, and this lasted till 2012. In 2014, the GDP increased by 2.8% year-on-year, slower than in 2013.

At this stage, knowledge and technology-intensive industries were the main engines of Israeli economy. In 2014, 38,000 out of the 8 million Israelis were scientists, and the high-tech industries hired 10% of the working population, and contributed 15% of the total economy and 50% of exports. In 2014, the R&D expenditure accounted for 4.2% of the country's GDP, ranking first in the world.

1. Urban structure

Israel is the country with the highest level of urbanization in the Middle East. As Fig. 8.24 illustrates, its urbanization rate was 90.9% in 1995 and 92.1% in 2015. Israel's urbanization has two features.

(1) Both the urban population and its proportion have increased. With the establishment of the State of Israel, a large number of immigrants have arrived. From 1950 to 2005, the Israeli population increased from 1.37 million to 6.9 million, while the urban population also rose sharply from 813,000 in 1950 to 6.132 million in 2005, an increase of 7.5 times. At the same time, the rural population expanded from 445,000 in 1950 to 553,000 in 2005, up by only 20%.
(2) Both the amount and scale of cities have grown larger. According to statistics, 36 new cities were added from 1948 to 1984, and more than 130 (including satellite cities) were built from 1985 to 1995. At the same time, the size of the existing cities continued to expand. Only Tel Aviv had a population of more than

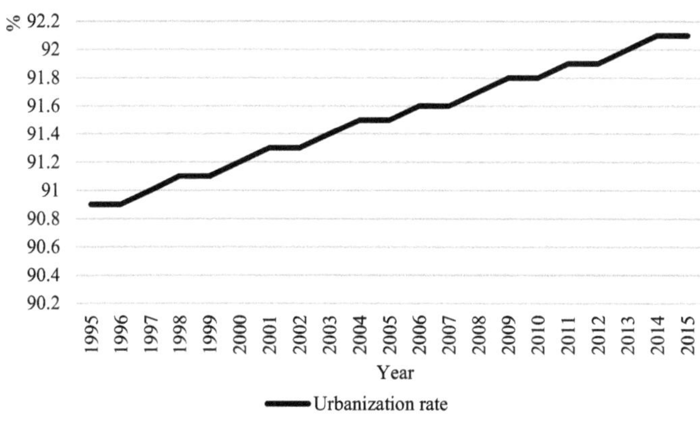

Fig. 8.24 Urbanization rate of Israel. *Source of data* World Bank database

100,000 before the founding of Israel. By 2003, the number of cities with such scale had jumped to 14, 5 of which were home to more than 200,000 people. The top five cities in the country are listed in Table 8.6.

As a country built in the desert, Israel owes its high urbanization rate to the good quality of education and the fast development of agricultural economy.

Within the Israeli population of 8.46 million, 79% are Jews (most of them are Ashkenazi Jews). 68% of Jews are born in Israel, usually as the second- or the third-generation Israelis; within the remaining 32% who are foreign-born, 22% are from Europe and 10% from Asia and Africa, including the Arab countries. At present, the gender ratio of men to women is 100: 101.7, and the proportion of people aged over 65 is 11.1%, making Israel one of the aging societies. For more information, see Table 8.7.

Table 8.6 Top 5 cities of Israel

City	Population in 2016	City profile
Jerusalem	801,000	The capital; the political, economic, cultural and transportation center; the Holy City
Haifa	267,300	The largest seaport in the Palestinian region
Tel Aviv	250,000	A large city with the highest cost of living in the Middle East
Ashdod	224,656	The second largest port
Rishon LeZion	220,492	The fourth largest city

Source of data World Population Review

Table 8.7 The sex and age structure of Israeli population (as of the end of 2015)

	Total population	The Jews and others		The Arabs
		Total population	The Jews	
Total population	8,463,400	6,705,600	6,334,500	1,757,800
Male	4,195,200	3,306,400	3,136,600	888,800
Female	4,268,200	3,399,200	3,198,000	869,000
Annual growth rate (%)	2.0	2.0	1.9	2.2
The proportion of population aged 0–18 (%)	34.6	32.4	32.9	42.9
The proportion of population aged 19–64 (%)	54.3	54.8	54.1	52.7
The proportion of population aged 65 and above (%)	11.1	12.8	13.0	4.4
The proportion of urban population (%)	91.2	90.3	90.0	94.5

Source of data Israel in Figures 2016

In addition to people living in Israel, more than 350,000 Israeli citizens live in settlements (reclamation areas) in the West Bank (Palestine) district. Some settlements are city-like—three settlements, with more than 30,000 residents each, have grown into cities.

Israel has the tradition of respecting teachers and valuing education. The knowledge-loving Israelis respect this tradition and regard education as social wealth and the key to a better future. The goal of its education system is to transform children into responsible members of a democratic and pluralistic society where people of different ethnic, religious, cultural and political backgrounds coexist harmoniously. Israel's education, based on Jewish values, patriotism, and the principles of freedom and tolerance, seeks to impart quality knowledge to students, with a focus on science and technology skills that are vital to the country's sustainable development. As Fig. 8.25 demonstrates, 24% of the Israel's workforce has a college degree, which makes Israel the third most educated country in the industrialized world, right after the United States and the Netherlands. 12% of the population has a graduate degree. Based on their respect for the individuals, the Israelis have established an economic system that is the best managed and provides the best protection of property rights in the Middle East. On the whole, quality college education has laid a good foundation for the country's high-tech prosperity and rapid economic development.

2. Income level and government finance

According to the United Nations' *Human Development Report 2015*, Israel's human development index is 0.894, ranking 18th in the world and first in the Middle East.

According to the Israeli Salary and Income Survey, in 2015, the average monthly salary of all Israeli workers was 9576 new shekels (about 2639 USD). In recent years, the national saving rate has averaged around 10%, as Fig. 8.26 shows, similar to the world average in 2014 (11.17%).

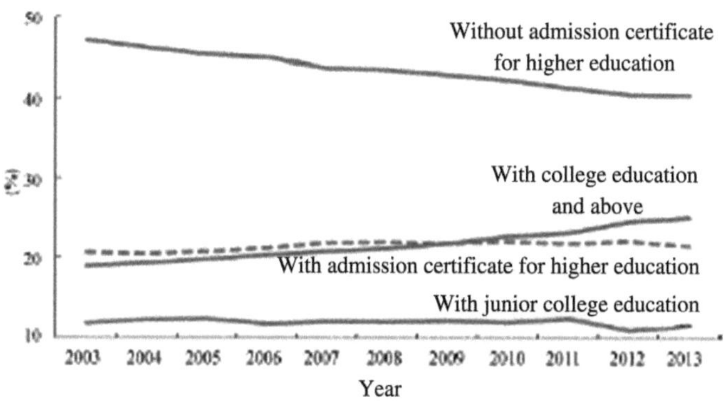

Fig. 8.25 The proportion of population with higher education. *Source of data* Israel Ministry of Finance, The Israeli Labor Market, 1999–2014

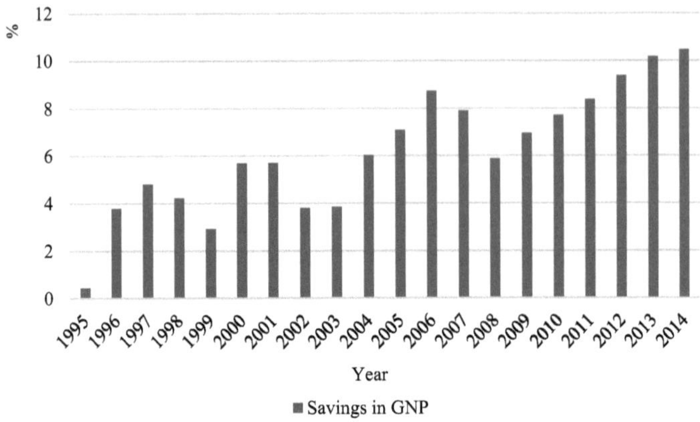

Fig. 8.26 National saving rate of Israel. *Source of data* World Bank database

In terms of government finances, the 2015–2016 budgets approved by the Israeli Cabinet in 2015 were 329.5 billion shekels and 13.8 billion shekels, respectively. For more information, see Fig. 8.27.

In recent years, the Israeli government has implemented an economic stimulus plan to minimize the impact of the weak global economy and to promote economic recovery. In addition, it has increased policy support to foster long-term economic competitiveness, including: increasing investment in research and development and providing subsidies for high-tech industries; promoting the reform of monopoly industries, and encouraging private enterprises to participate in industrial competition by offering state financial guarantees; setting up special funds to support the employment of Arabs and religious people; strengthening infrastructure construction, and ensuring electricity supply by building pumped storage power stations and gas-fired power stations.

3. Industrial structure

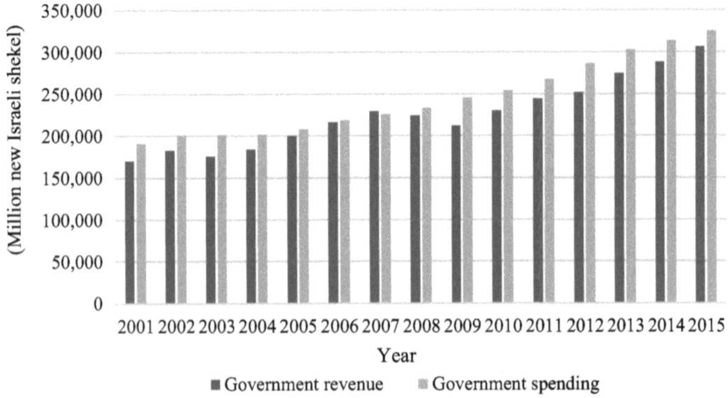

Fig. 8.27 Government revenue and spending. *Source of data* Israel Central Bureau of Statistics

(1) The primary industry

Israel's land area is about 21,000 km^2, while the arable area is only 4370 km^2, which is about 20% of the country's land area. The agricultural population accounts for only 3% of the total population, but the per capita annual income of farmers exceeds 20,000 USD.

More than half of Israel has a typical arid and semi-arid climate. The rest is mostly covered by hills and forests. Only the Jordan Valley and the plains around Lake Galilee in the north are suitable for agriculture. Yet Israel has built on this barren land modern agriculture in just one generation, which is an amazing miracle. So far, Israel's agricultural output and exports have increased tens of times compared to 1948, but the proportion of agriculture in GDP has declined from more than 30% in the 1960s to the current 8%, and the proportion of farmers in the total labor force has shrunk from 70% to 3%. Israel's self-sufficiency in agricultural products has reached 95%. In addition, it exports a large amount of agricultural products, generating a trade surplus of about 200 million USD. The only agricultural imports are some products of grain, oil, coffee and tea.

At present, one-third of Israel's international cooperation projects are agricultural ones. Each year, more than 3000 agricultural experts give lectures abroad, and people from more than 60 countries around the world receive training in Israel. If the world achieves Israel's level of agricultural production, it could feed a population three times that of today.

Israel's agricultural miracle is the result of correct development strategies. Israel has accumulated a wealth of experience in this process.

First, the agricultural cooperative organizations, the organizational foundation for agricultural industrialization, have been established. There are three forms of agricultural cooperatives, namely kibbutz, Moshav and Mos.shitufi, which provide rural residents with several choices of living and production. Thanks to these various economic cooperatives and the agricultural industrialization based on them, Israel has been able to build the most developed agriculture in the world.

Second, the operating principles of agricultural industrialization have been formulated and followed—market-oriented, supported by agricultural science and technology, driven by the improvement of economic benefits and farmers' income, guaranteed by the agricultural cooperatives, economic contracts and agricultural laws. Based on these principles, Israel has established a comprehensive agricultural technology system and improved the benefit distribution and transformation mechanism of agricultural industrialization.

Third, the contract-based organizations of agricultural industrialization have been set up: company + cooperatives (kibbutz, Mos.shitufi); company + cooperatives (Moshav) + farmers; company + farmers (mainly family farms); corporate operation of agricultural industrialization; and the mixed type of agricultural industrialization operation.

Fourth, the benefit guarantee mechanism of agricultural industrialization has been set up and improved: the realization of organizational guarantee (agricultural production and marketing committees and professional associations), contract guarantee, and legal system guarantee has helped achieve the agricultural industrialization based on farmer organizations, economic contracts and a sound legal system of the market.

(2) The secondary industry

Israel is a highly industrialized mixed economy dominated by knowledge-intensive industries. Its high-tech industry is world-famous. For instance, it is advanced in the fields of military technology, electronics, communications, computer software, medical equipment, biotechnology engineering, agriculture and aviation.

The Israeli government encourages investment in industrial R&D and passes laws to support industrial research and project development. The government support is mainly reflected in the following aspects: setting up special budgets to support industries related to technology development; creating job opportunities for scientific and technological talents; and promoting balance of international payments by reducing imports and increasing exports of high-tech products. In 2012, the total civilian investment in R&D reached 38.4 billion shekels (approximately 9.95 billion USD), accounting for 4.0% of GDP. The government's financial support totaled 760 million shekels (about 200 million USD). In addition, Israel participated in 29 international and regional industrial R&D projects, including 3 with the United States, 3 with the European Union, 2 with Canada and India, and 1 with Canada, Germany, Chinese mainland, France, Belgium, Italy, Ireland, Turkey, Hong Kong (China), Britain, Greece, Taiwan (China), Singapore, Spain, Portugal, South Korea, Sweden, Finland and the Netherlands each.

(3) The tertiary industry

Currently, the focus of Israeli economy is shifting from the traditional agriculture and manufacturing industry to the service sector. The service sector is expanding in both GDP and employment. For more information, see Fig. 8.28. According to the latest statistics of the Israeli Central Bureau of Statistics, in 2010, the primary industry contributed 2.5% of GDP, the secondary industry produced 21.4%, and the tertiary industry took up 76.1%.

The tertiary industry plays a pivotal role in the Israeli economy. Pursuing diversified cultural life, Israeli residents spend much on culture and entertainment. Every month, 40% of the spending of a typical Israeli household on recreational activities goes to sports, shows and music performances, as Fig. 8.29 shows.

(II) Foreign trade and investment

(1) International investment

Israel is known as the "Second Silicon Valley in the World". This historic country is home to the most famous multinational companies in the world, industrial parks and high-tech incubation zones. It has mature capital and financial markets, loose currency controls and sound intellectual-property protection system. In addition, Israel can serve as a springboard to the entire market of the Middle East. Therefore, it is a favored destination of foreign investment. See Fig. 8.30 for relevant data.

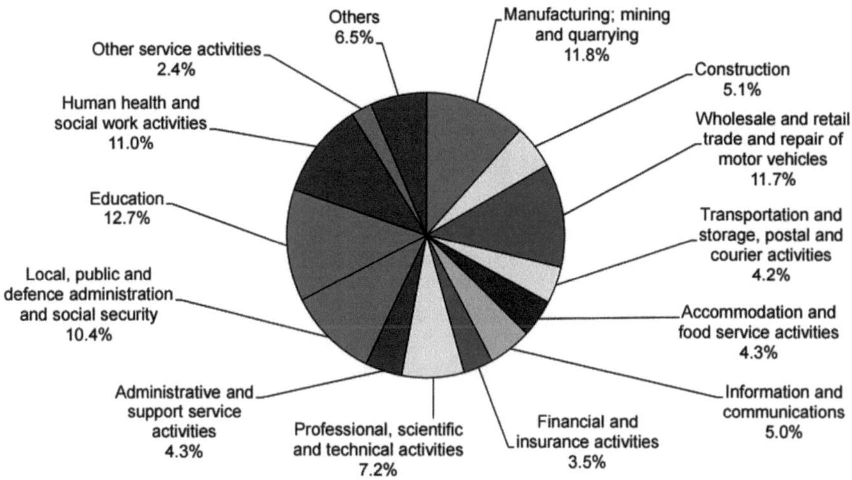

Fig. 8.28 The labor force structure (sector-wise) of Israel. *Source of data* Statistical Abstract of Israel 2016

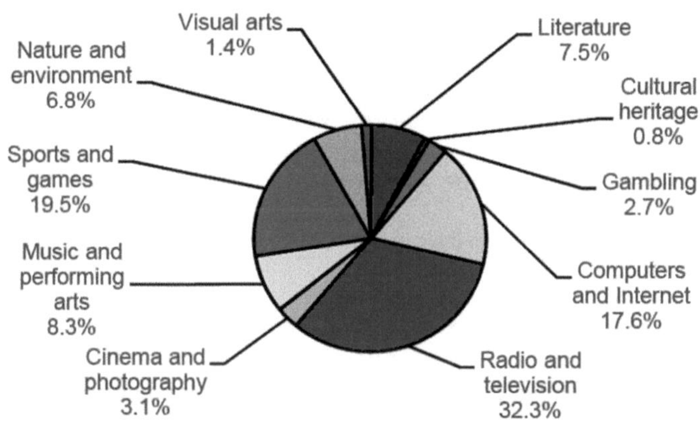

Fig. 8.29 The spending on recreational activities and sports by a typical Israeli household. *Source of data* Israel in Figures 2016

The Israeli government has provided certain policy assistance to companies interested in investing in the country. In order to attract FDI, it provides various preferential treatments to the industry, tourism and the real-estate sector, especially the high-tech companies and R&D activities. There are generally two categories of preferential treatments according to the Israel *Law For the Encouragement of Capital Investments*: appropriations and automatic tax incentives. In recent years, Israeli innovative companies in the high-tech industry have continued to emerge, receiving large amount of foreign investment.

(2) Foreign trade

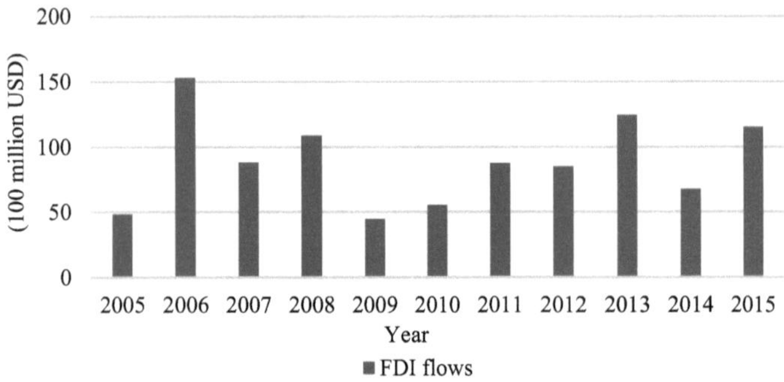

Fig. 8.30 Foreign investment flow in Israel. *Source of data* World Bank database

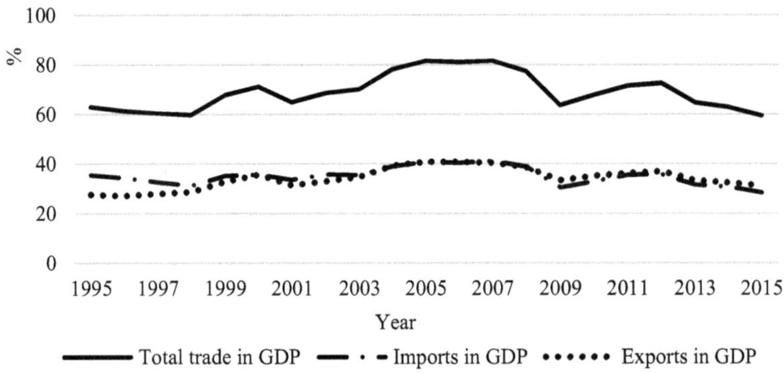

Fig. 8.31 The proportion of foreign trade in Israeli GDP. *Source of data* World Bank database

Israel is a member of the WTO and OECD. Foreign trade plays a significant role in Israeli economy. See Fig. 8.31 for more information. Its largest trading partner is the EU, and the United States is its largest trading partner country.

Its high-tech products are highly competitive in the international market. Export is one of the main engines of its economic growth. It mainly imports raw materials and investment goods. See Fig. 8.32 for its net barter terms of trade.

(3) Sino–Israeli trade

China is Israel's largest trading partner in Asia and the third largest trading partner in the world. In 2016, the bilateral trade volume was 11.35 billion USD, of which 8.17 billion USD was exports from China (down by 5.1% year-on-year), and 3.18 billion USD was imports to China (up by 13.4%). For more trade data, see Table 8.8 The two countries currently have two cooperation platforms: the China–Israel Joint Committee on Innovation Cooperation and the China–Israel Intergovernmental Economic and Technical Cooperation Mechanism.

At the government level, China and Israel signed the "Three-year Action Plan for China–Israel Innovation Cooperation" in 2015. According to the plan, the two

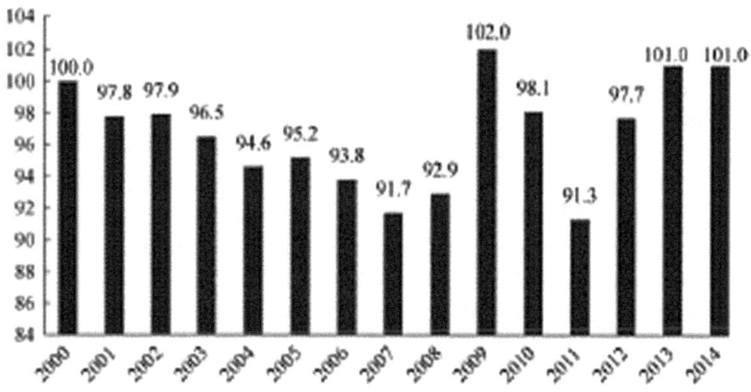

Fig. 8.32 Net barter terms of trade. *Source of data* World Bank database

Table 8.8 Volumes of Sino–Israeli trade in recent years (Unit: 100 million USD)

Year	Total volume of trade	YOY (%)	China's exports	YOY (%)	China's imports	YOY (%)
2010	76.5	47.9	50.4	37.9	26.1	70.9
2011	97.8	27.9	67.4	33.8	30.4	16.5
2012	99.1	9.3	69.9	3.7	29.2	-3.8
2013	108.3	9.3	76.5	9.4	31.8	8.9
2014	108.8	0.5	77.4	1.2	31.4	-1.3
2015	114.2	5.0	86.2	11.3	28.0	-10.8

Source of data China Customs

sides will continue to strengthen the cutting-edge and original research of major strategic priorities, and 12 priority areas of cooperation have been identified: brain science, soil and water resources, nanotechnology, printing, biomedicine, clean and renewable energy, agricultural science and technology, advanced bioimaging technology, information technology, computer science, innovative technology serving the elderly, smart cities and sustainable development. The two sides have made clear that they support the establishment of joint laboratories and joint research centers to build a long-term, stable and in-depth cooperative relationship. Considering the existing cooperation basis, the two sides plan to build the following joint research centers: Tsinghua University-Tel Aviv University XIN Center (XIN means "new" in Chinese, with "X" standing for cross-disciplinary and cross-ingenuity, and "IN" for international and innovation), Joint Research Center for Brain Science, Joint Research Center for Science and Technology, etc. The two sides have agreed to further strengthen the funding of the bilateral joint research projects, launch the flagship joint research projects, support the combination of "production, teaching and research" and conduct joint research around major issues. The joint research plan of agricultural science and technology will be conducted every year, funding 10 joint research projects annually in the next 5 years.

Jewish businessmen once said, "One can never be shut out when knocking on a door with money in hand". Chinese investment in Israel has been rising. According to the Israel Venture Capital Research Center (IVC), in 2016, Chinese venture capital funds in Israel were expected to increase by 18% to 1 billion USD. Chinese technology giants such as Baidu, Ali and Xiaomi have invested in Israeli technology companies and venture capital funds. More and more Chinese capital have taken Israel as a potential destination, especially its industries of medical equipment, machine recognition, artificial intelligence, VR and AR technologies.

(4) Orientations of Sino–Israeli cooperation

Under the framework of the "Belt and Road" Initiative, China and Israel may conduct cooperation in the following areas: renewable energy, biotechnology, information and communications, water resource utilization and other industries which are highly complementary with China's priority industries.

Israel could make a meaningful contribution to the successful implementation of the "Belt and Road" Initiative, especially in the field of water treatment. The "Belt and Road" Initiative emphasizes innovation, nature conservation and cooperation, while water treatment is a good starting point. The following is a discussion of the mode of the bilateral cooperation in the field of water resources.

Israel is suffering from increasingly severe water scarcity as most of its water comes from groundwater and rainfall. Within this context, its water use system focuses on the following two aspects.

The first is wastewater recycling technology. Israel is the only country in the world that focuses on wastewater reuse. 86% of its wastewater and 55% of its gray water are recycled. Spain is the second largest water recycling country, but its recycling rate is only 16%. In contrast, the United States currently recycles less than 1% of its wastewater.

The second is desalination. This technology provides more than 25% of Israel's total water supply. In the past decade, Israel has built four new desalination plants. Eilat, Israel's southernmost city, uses desalinated seawater to meet all its fresh water demand. In addition, the new desalination plant outside Tel Aviv was completed in 2013 and is now operating at full capacity. The Sorek Desalination Plant, the world's largest of its kind, is expected to produce 40 billion gallons of fresh water per year, benefiting both Israel and its neighboring countries.

According to the *Report on the Status of Water Resources Utilization and Pollution in China*, China is an arid and water-scarce country in terms of per capita water resources. China ranks fourth in the world in terms of total fresh water resources, but the per capita volume is only 2303 m^3, 1/4 of the world average, making it one of the 13 countries in the world with the lowest per capita water resources.

In 2015, Israel cooperated with Shouguang City of Shandong Province to establish a "model water city". By drawing on Israeli experience of water resources management, this project employed economic and legal tools to improve the efficiency of water resources allocation. In addition, desalination, sewage treatment, Irrigation, water supply and sewage purification technologies from Israel were utilized to build new models of water use, water conservation, sewage treatment and water recycling, and models successful in experiment were promoted across the city.

By using pipelines for water delivery, Israel has achieved a water delivery coefficient of 95%, while China's canal water delivery coefficient is only 30% to 50%. Therefore, to meet the challenge of water scarcity and develop water-saving agriculture, China should prioritize the development of pipeline water delivery and the anti-seepage canal lining technology. By drawing on the successes of other countries, China is expected to raise its water delivery coefficient to 60%, which will effectively smooth over the dry spells across China.

8.6 Jordan

I. Geographical and historical backgrounds

The Hashemite Kingdom of Jordan, located in the northwest of the Arabian Peninsula, borders Palestine and Israel to the west, Syria to the north, and Iraq and Saudi Arabia to the east. The land area is more than 89,000 km^2, but 78% is desert in the southeast. The country is divided into 12 provinces. The port of Aqaba in Aqaba Province is the only outlet to the sea. Jordan, with excellent geographical location, has been an important link of the trade route in the Middle East since ancient times. It enjoys the reputation of "the oasis of peace in the Middle East".

But like its neighbor Palestine, Jordan is not a resource-rich country. No large-scale coal or non-ferrous metal mines have been found in the country. Oil shale, of relatively abundant reserves, is the major fossil energy resource in Jordan. Currently, it has 70 billion tons of proven oil shale reserves widely distributed across the country, which makes the country one of the five countries with the richest oil shale reserves. Moreover, its oil shale has high concentration rate—the average oil content is about 10%, which means about 6 billion tons of oil could be produced.[10] Jordan is striving to develop and utilize its oil shale resources. However, due to the lack of advanced technology and high mining costs, Jordan has signed agreements with a number of companies to conduct evaluation research on its domestic oil shale resources. In addition, Jordan is one of the most phosphate-rich countries in the world. There are 4 phosphate mines in Jordan, with about 1.7 billion tons of reserves. In 2007 alone, its phosphate ore production ranked sixth in the world and its export volume ranked second.[11] Founded in 1949, the Jordan Phosphate Mines Company (JPMC) is the only company that runs phosphate mines in Jordan and the largest production enterprise of the country. Archeological findings show Jordan has been one of the main birthplaces of human civilization since the Stone Age. During the Islamic era

---

[10] Hou Jili, Ma Yue, Li Shuyuan, and Teng Jinsheng. The status quo of oil shale development in the world, [J] *Chemical Industry and Engineering Progress*, 2015, 34 (5): 1183–1190.

[11] Source of data: Economic and Commercial Office of the Embassy of the People's Republic of China in the Hashemite Kingdom of Jordan.

of the medieval age, Jordan changed hands several times. In the early 16th century, it became part of the Ottoman Empire, and this lasted till the end of the First World War.

Jordan was originally part of Palestine. In 1921, Britain divided Palestine into two with the Jordan River. The part on the west of the river was still called Palestine, and the Jordanian emirate was established on the east under the British mandate. On March 22, 1946, Britain signed with Jordan the *Treaty of Alliance*, recognized its independence. In May 1946, Jordan announced the establishment of a constitutional monarchy, and King Abdullah officially ascended the throne. The Third Arab–Israeli War broke out in 1967, and Israeli forces quickly occupied the Gaza Strip controlled by Jordan and the entire West Bank. During the same period, Jordan's relations with Palestine were plagued by frequent conflicts, and its domestic political situation was volatile. In the 1970s, Jordan implemented liberalization policy of economy and trade, and encouraged private investment and foreign investment. In 1988, Palestine declared independence, and Jordan announced to break off its legal and administrative ties with the West Bank. In 1994, Jordan and Israel signed a peace treaty, and the domestic and diplomatic situations in Jordan gradually stabilized.

II. **Economic development**

As a developing country, Jordan is one of the relatively developed small economies in the Middle East. Poor in resources and arable land, it has a weak economic foundation and relies on imports for many products. Its main economic pillars are overseas remittances, tourism and foreign aid. Since King Abdullah II came to power, economic reforms have been carried out, the investment environment has been improved, and foreign aid has been encouraged, changing the situation of long-term negative or zero growth.

Jordan joined the WTO in 1999. The Jordanian dinar, pegged to the USD, is its currency, and the target rate is 0.709:1.

(I) Domestic economy

The World Bank classifies Jordan as an upper-middle-income country. Its total GDP in 2015 was 37.5 billion USD. At the beginning of the 21st century, Jordan's GDP enjoyed a good growth rate, exceeding 8% in 2004–2008. Since 2009, due to the impact of the international financial crisis and the turmoil in West Asia and North Africa, the economic growth had slowed down. The government responded by stepping up its efforts to regulate and control the economy, and taking corresponding measures in finance, infrastructure and securing investment and foreign aid. This had worked to some extent. The World Bank expected Jordan's GDP to grow at about 3% in 2016.

Jordan's GDP per capita has experienced ups and downs, increasing by 351% throughout the 1970s, falling by 30% in the 1980s, and then rising again by 36% in the 1990s. In 2015, the figure was 4,940 USD, a record high. In addition, its Gini coefficient in 2011 was a moderate 35.4, reflecting a relatively reasonable gap of national income.

In recent years, Jordan has become a refuge for Syrian refugees fleeing the civil war. So far, about 1.4 million Syrian refugees have fled to Jordan, costing the Jordanian government 2 billion USD every year. Despite the increasing burden caused by the influx of Syrian refugees, Jordan's economy maintained a growth rate of 2.4% in 2015 thanks to the investment in hydropower, finance, insurance as well as mining and quarrying.

1. Industrial structure

Within the industrial structure of Jordan, agriculture takes the smallest part, about 3% of gross GDP; the service sector, enjoying the largest proportion, contributes 67% of GDP; and industry has a share of 30%. Textile and clothing are its main manufacturing sectors.[12] The following is an introduction to the various economic sectors in Jordan.

Agriculture. Due to unfriendly geographical environment and limited water resources, only 7.8% of Jordanian land area is arable. Most of the arable land is concentrated in the Jordan Valley, and all of it is privately run. The total agricultural area of the country is 224,000 ha, of which grain crops take 72,000 ha, vegetables occupy 33,000 ha, and fruit trees cover 119,000 ha. The agricultural population is 110,400, accounting for about 12% of the labor force. There are currently 10 major dams with a total capacity of 327 million m^3. Olive is a specialty of its agriculture. There are 20 million olive trees in Jordan, and the annual output value of related products is about 100 million dinar (about 141 million USD), making the country the eighth largest olive producer in the world.[13]

Industry and Mining. In Jordan, there are 5 large-scale industries, including phosphate, potassium salts, oil refining, cement and fertilizers. Others are mostly light industries and small processing industries, such as food processing, pharmaceuticals, glass, textiles and papermaking. JPMC is the largest chemical company in Jordan and the sixth largest producer of phosphate ore in the world. It has the exclusive mining right of the country's phosphate resources. Its business covers phosphate mining, chemical engineering and fertilizer production. JPMC has set up joint ventures of fertilizers and chemical products with India and Japan.

Textile industry. The textile and apparel industry is very important to the Jordanian economy, contributing one-third of the country's export earnings and creating 60,000 jobs. The 14 qualified industrial zones established by the United States in Jordan export clothing mainly to the United States market. Jordan is gradually developing into a manufacturing base for many international brands. The products are shipped to overseas markets such as the United States. In 2014, the United States imported 1 billion USD worth of clothing from Jordan.[14]

Tourism. Tourism, as an important source of fiscal revenue, has made great contribution to the Jordanian economy. In addition, it has also stimulated other industries

---

[12] Source of data: Hong Kong Trade Development Council (HKTDC).

[13] Source of data: Economic and Commercial Office of the Embassy of the People's Republic of China in the Hashemite Kingdom of Jordan.

[14] Source of data: *Country (Region) Specific Guide for Outward Foreign Direct Investment Cooperation—Jordan*, by Ministry of Commerce, China.

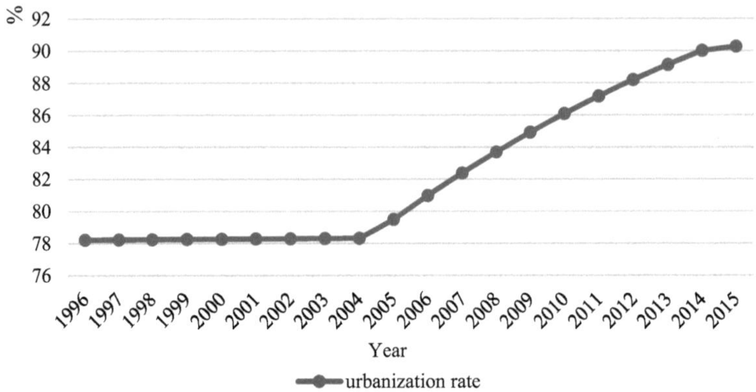

Fig. 8.33 Changes of urbanization rate in Jordan over the past 20 years. *Source of data* World Bank database

such as aviation, real estate, hotel and health care. Local government values and encourages the development of tourism. The Jordan Tourism Board has launched for international tourists a special website in English, Chinese, Korean and other languages. In general, Jordan, with political and social stability and abundant tourism resources, has drawn in a large number of tourists from the Gulf region, Europe and the United States. Its main attractions are Amman, the Dead Sea, Jerash, Petra, Ajlun Castle, Aqaba and so on.

Foreign Aid. Foreign aid is one of the main sources of Jordan's finance. Before the Gulf War, its foreign aid mainly came from the United States and other Western countries and the Arab countries in the Gulf region. In the Gulf crisis, Jordan's sympathizing with Iraq led to the turning off of the aid tap by the major donors, and the local economy deteriorated. Later, Jordan gradually adjusted its policy toward Iraq and improved relations with the United States and the Arab states in the Gulf region, and the aid resumed. Due to the Iraq War in 2003, the international community provided Jordan with up to 1.9 billion USD in loans and grants. In 2012, Jordan received 460 million USD in foreign aid. In May 2013, the World Bank decided to provide 150 million USD to help Jordan handling Syrian refugees. In 2014, the World Bank raised the upper limit of annual loans to Jordan from 350 million USD to 500 million USD and agreed to make a loan of 200 million USD. In the same year, Jordan received 180 million USD in loans from the European Union.[15]

2. Industrial structure

As 78% of Jordan's land is desert, people are concentrated on a small amount of fertile land. The growing urban population has led to the high level of urbanization. As Fig. 8.33 demonstrates, Jordan's urbanization rate has been rising steadily in the past 20 years, exceeding 80% in 2001. During this process, two big cities of special significance to Jordan have been built.

[15] Source of data: the website of Ministry of Foreign Affairs, China.

Amman, the capital, is the most prestigious city in Jordan. Because it is built on 7 hills, it is also known as the "City of Seven Hills". Meanwhile, it is called "the most westernized Arab city". Located in the north-central part of the country, it is the economic, political and cultural center and the seat of the Jordanian government. Amman has a population of more than 4 million and a land area of more than 1600 km^2. In addition, it, home to both many historic sites and modern buildings, has a unique cityscape, which has made it the most favored destination for many European and Arab tourists.

As the only seaport of the country, Aqaba is of strategic importance to Jordan. The city, located in the southernmost tip of Jordan, is the capital of Aqaba Province, with a population of more than 180,000 and a land area of 375 km^2. Aqaba is essential to Jordan's economic development. It is a renowned diving site and beach resort. In addition, industrial production occupies a key position in the industrial structure of the region. The city is also an export port of phosphate fertilizers and seafood. The port of Aqaba is a Gulfport, and it has a free trade zone.[16]

(II) Foreign trade and investment

1. Foreign trade

Jordan has trade relations with more than 100 countries and regions in the world. The main import goods are crude oil, machinery and equipment, electronics, steel, chemicals, food, clothing, etc. Saudi Arabia, China, the United States, Germany and Egypt are the main sources of import. The main export goods are clothing, phosphates, potassium salts, vegetables, pharmaceutical products and fertilizers, and the United States, Iraq, India, Saudi Arabia, Syria and the UAE are the top destinations. The United States is Jordan's largest export market. In 2014, Jordan exported 12 billion USD in goods and services to the United States. In 2015, its foreign trade totaled 28.6 billion USD, of which imports were 20.6 billion USD, down 11.3% year-on-year, exports were 8 billion USD, down 6.6% year-on-year, and the trade deficit was 12.6 billion USD, a 14% decrease from 2014.

Jordan has signed trade agreements with the United States, Canada, Turkey, the Mercosur group (including Argentina, Brazil, Paraguay and Uruguay), Egypt, Morocco, Tunisia, the European Free Trade Area (including Switzerland, Norway, Iceland and Liechtenstein), and Singapore. In addition, Jordan is a member of the *Pan-Arab Free Trade Area Treaty*. Other members of the Treaty include Egypt, the UAE, Bahrain, Tunisia, Saudi Arabia, Sudan, Syria, Iraq, Oman, Palestine, Qatar, Kuwait, Lebanon, Libya, Morocco and Yemen. All of these treaties have entered into force.[17]

In May 1979, China and Jordan signed a trade agreement. As the bilateral trade grows rapidly, China has become the third largest trading partner of Jordan. In 2014, the bilateral trade volume reached 3.628 billion USD, up by 0.7% over the last year. Within the total, 3.365 billion USD was export from China to Jordan, down by 2.0%; and 263 million USD was import from Jordan, increasing by 54.9% year-on-year.

[16] Statistics of some cities are quoted from Wikipedia.

[17] Source of data: Hong Kong Trade Development Council.

Table 8.9 China's direct investment in Jordan (Unit: million USD)

2012	2013	2014
9.83	0.77	6.74

Source of data 2014 Statistical Bulletin of China's Outward Foreign Direct Investment.

See Table 8.9 for more information. China mainly exports mechanical and electrical products, communications equipment, textiles and clothing to Jordan; and imports potash fertilizer.

2. International Investment

In recent years, Jordan has further opened its market to attract FDI. Its *Investment Promotion Law* stipulates that overseas investors can enjoy three years of tax exemption on fixed assets and exemption from tariffs on imported raw materials. Jordan has been making effort to remove barriers encountered by foreign investors. For instance, the new investment law provides an online registration portal for investors. In addition, the government is actively building economic development zones, including one in Aqaba. In the development zones, enterprises enjoy the preferential income tax rate of 5%, as well as the zero tax rate of export income, sales, import and dividends.[18]

Despite the regional tension, Jordan has maintained steady absorption of foreign investment in recent years. By the end of 2014, FDI in Jordan had totaled 28.73 billion USD, an increase of 7.5% from 26.67 billion USD in 2013. Turkey, the United States and France were the top investors. By the end of 2014, China's cumulative direct investment in Jordan had reached 31 million USD. For more information, see Table 8.10.

8.7 Lebanon

I. Geographical and historical backgrounds

Located on the east coast of the Mediterranean Sea and the borders of Asia and Europe, Lebanon is the birthplace of Phoenician civilization and cuneiform. Enjoying a long history, cultural diversity and developed trade, Lebanon was a key link of the ancient Silk Road. As early as 2000 years ago, the Phoenicians had lived here. Later, the Romans occupied it and built the world-famous Temple of Bacchus, one of the largest and the best-preserved Roman architectures in the world. From the early 6th century to the 7th century, Lebanon was part of the Arab Empire. The country covers an area of 10,452 km^2 and has a coastline of 225 km. It borders Syria to the east and north, and Israel to the south. Its border with Syria stretches 375 km, and the border

[18] Source of data: Jordan Investment Commission (JIC).

Table 8.10 Total trade volume between China and Jordan (Unit: 100 million USD)

Year	Total trade volume	YOY (%)	Exports to Jordan	Imports from Jordan
2003	5.20	46.50	4.60	0.60
2004	7.10	36.54	6.23	0.87
2005	9.11	28.31	8.32	0.79
2006	10.31	13.17	9.78	0.53
2007	11.86	15.03	11.04	0.82
2008	19.20	61.89	18.00	1.20
2009	25.08	30.63	23.40	1.68
2010	23.27	−7.22	21.07	2.20
2011	28.44	22.22	25.58	2.86
2012	32.60	14.63	29.60	3.00
2013	36.02	10.52	34.33	1.70

Source of data website of Ministry of Commerce, China

with Israel spans 79 km. The constant fighting and crisis in Syria in recent years has made great impact on Lebanon.

The total population of Lebanon is about 6.18 million, most of whom are Arabs. Arabic is the official language, and French and English are common. 54% of the residents believe in Islam, mainly Shiism, Sunnism and the Druze doctrines; 46% believe in Christianity, mainly Maronite doctrines, the Greek Orthodox Church, the Roman Catholicism and the Armenian Orthodox Church.[19]

Located on a promontory in the middle of the Lebanese coastline, Beirut, the capital, facing the Mediterranean Sea and backing against the Lebanese mountains, is the largest port city on the eastern coast of the Mediterranean Sea. The city covers an area of 67 km^2, with a unique architectural style and a population of about 1.9 million.[20] Beirut is the political and economic center of Lebanon. It is also a well-known center for commerce, trade, finance, transportation, tourism and press and publication in the Middle East. That is why it is called the "Paris of the Middle East".

Lebanon has one of the highest education penetration rates among Arab countries in the Middle East. Most Lebanese speak English and French. In 2009, its enrollment rate of primary and junior high schools was 99.2%.[21] Founded in 1953, the Lebanese University is the only comprehensive public university in the country. It has begun to accept Chinese students sent by the Chinese government since 2007. Lebanon is the most westernized country in the Middle East. Gibran, the world-famous literary Giant, is the pride of the Lebanese people. Lebanon enjoys great freedom in terms

[19] Source of data: CIA, *The World Factbook*, the population is an estimated figure in 2015.

[20] Source of data: *Country (Region) Specific Guide for Outward Foreign Direct Investment Cooperation—Lebanon*, the Ministry of Commerce, China.

[21] Source of data: Multiple Indicators Cluster Survey 2009, by Central Administration of Statistics (CAS), Lebanon.

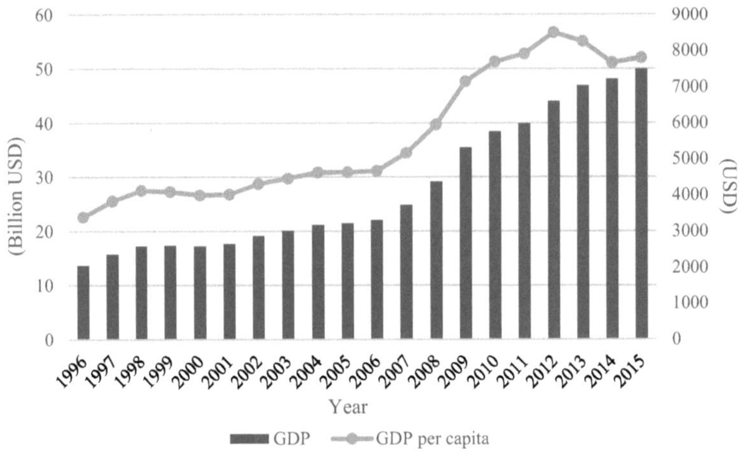

Fig. 8.34 Growths of gross GDP and per capita GDP of Lebanon. *Source of data* World Bank database

of thought and culture, and books banned in other Arab countries can be published here. The lax censorship system has led to the prosperity of local publishing industry. It is said in Arab countries: "the Egyptians write books, the Iraqis read books, and the Lebanese publish books". In addition, it is also the center of academic research in the Arab world. Due to the free academic atmosphere and the sponsorship of many financial groups, Beirut often holds international academic conferences related to Arab culture.

II. **Economic development**

(I) Domestic economy

After the war with Israel in 2006, Lebanon has restored the political stability and achieved economic growth. Due to its conservative financial policy, it has become one of the few countries free from the impact of the financial crisis. In 2010, its GDP grew by 7% year-on-year, one of the largest growth rates in the world. Affected by the global economic downturn and the Syrian crisis, its GDP growth rates in 2011 and 2012 fell to 3.0% and 1.4%, respectively, as demonstrated in Fig. 8.34.

According to UN's *Human Development Report*, Lebanon enjoyed high Human Development Index in 2015, ranking 67th in the world.[22] In addition, based on the Lebanese poverty standards, 27% of people in Lebanon lived in poverty (the daily living cost was less than 8.7 USD) in 2012, and 8% were in extreme poverty, unable to meet their basic nutritional needs.[23]

1. Industrial structure

---

[22] Source of data: Human Development Report 2014, by UNDP.

[23] Source of data: Snapshot of Poverty and Labor Market outcomes in Lebanon, by the Central Administration of Statistics and the World Bank.

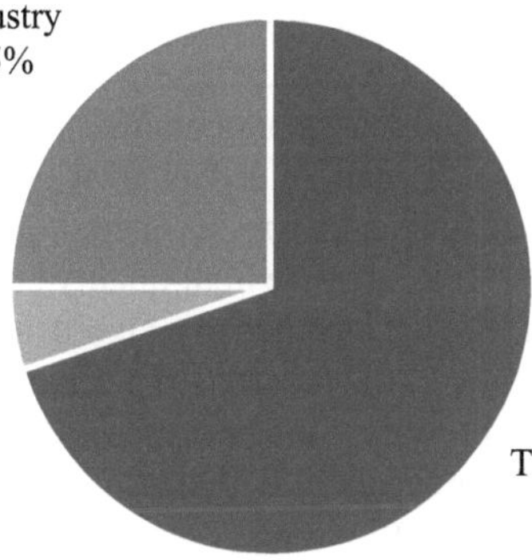

Fig. 8.35 The proportions of different industries within the Lebanese GDP. *Source of data The World Factbook 2015*, by CIA

As shown in Fig. 8.35, Lebanon is an economy dominated by the service sector (about 70% of its GDP), while industry (25%) and agriculture (5%) take relatively small parts. In the service sector, the proportion of finance in gross GDP has remained at about 10%. Thanks to the free market system and banking secrecy laws, the country has become a financial center in the Middle East. According to IMF statistics, by the end of 2011, the balance of deposits of Lebanese commercial banks was about three times its GDP, ranking fifth in the world.

Although it has World Heritage Sites such as the Temple of Bacchus, Byblos, Tyre and Quadi Qadisha (the Holy Valley), tourism, another growth engine of the service sector, has been severely affected by the Civil War of Syria, and the number of tourists to Lebanon dropped by 30% from 2010 to 2015. In addition, long-term power shortages have further hindered economic development.[24]

Lebanon's agriculture is underdeveloped. It has 248,000 ha of arable land, of which 104,000 hectares are irrigated. The pasture is 360,000 ha, and the forest area is 790,000 ha. Agricultural products are mainly fruits and vegetables. There are many species of fruit trees in Lebanon. The Beqaa Valley in the east is a vast area surrounded by mountains. Thanks to the flat terrain, rich water resources and fertile soil, it has become the main agricultural area in Lebanon, with the arable area accounting for 52% of the whole country. With food production lagging behind, Lebanon mainly relies on imports for grains such as barley, wheat, corn and potatoes. Cash crops include tobacco, sugar beet, olives, etc. In recent years, the grape growing industry has developed rapidly, with an annual wine output of 6 million to 7 million bottles and an export value of about 12 million USD.[25]

Lebanon has a weak industrial foundation. The processing industry is the main force. Major industrial sectors are non-metal manufacturing, metal manufacturing, furniture, clothing, wood processing and textiles. The number of industrial employees is about 200,000, accounting for 7% of the total labor force, and is the third largest industry after commercial and non-financial services.

---

[24] Source of data: Hong Kong Trade Development Council.

[25] Source of data: *Country (Region) Specific Guide for Outward Foreign Direct Investment Cooperation—Lebanon*, by Ministry of Commerce, China.

In the Middle East, Lebanon is a country with sufficient water resources. It has many rivers and few barren deserts. Snowmelt is one of its sources of high-quality water, which nourish the mountains and the granary of Beqaa Valley.

The famous Lebanese cedars grow on shady slopes 1000 m above the sea level. As one of the four cedar species in the world, Lebanese cedars are hard, tall, beautiful and fragrant. It used as the high-quality building material for a long time. Thousands of years of logging have led to a significant reduction in the area covered by cedars. Statistics show Lebanon's existing cedar area is about 1700 ha, accounting for only 2.83% of the country's forest area. At present, many natural reserves have been established for cedars in Lebanon.

Lebanon has little mineral resources, with only a small amount of iron, lead and copper being developed; therefore, it depends on imports for raw materials. There are relatively abundant oil and gas resources, with proven reserves of 660 million–860 million barrels and about 30 trillion cubic feet.

(II) Foreign trade and investment

Lebanon is a member of the WTO and the GAFTA. Among the countries in the Middle East and North Africa, it has the lowest import tariffs, lower than 5% for most products. The country has signed free trade agreements with trade groups such as the EU, the European Free Trade Association, the Gulf Cooperation Council and the Mercosur group. Its accession to the Agadir Agreement in April 2016 has facilitated its entry into the EU market. Other members of the agreement include Egypt, Jordan, Morocco, Tunisia and Palestine.

In recent years, the bilateral trade between China and Lebanon has progressed steadily. According to statistics from the China Customs, the bilateral trade volume was 2.631 billion yuan in 2014, up by 3.7% on a year-on-year basis. For more information, see Table 8.11. China's exports to Lebanon are mainly machinery and equipment, electrical equipment, furniture, plastic products and clothing. It mainly imports from Lebanon copper, aluminum products, plastics, salt, sulfur, stone, chemical fiber and fur.

Table 8.11 Trade between China and Lebanon in recent years (Unit: 100 million RMB)

Year	Total trade volume	China's exports	China's imports
2010	13.52	13.24	0.27
2011	14.84	14.59	0.26
2012	17.12	16.92	0.20
2013	25.35	24.89	0.46
2014	26.31	26.05	0.26

Source of data The website of Ministry of Commerce, China.

8.8 Palestine

I. Geographical and historical backgrounds

Palestine, the birthplace of the three major Abrahamic religions in the world, is home to two countries. The country founded by Jews is Israel, and the country established by Arabs is Palestine. Palestine, or the State of Palestine, is a Muslim country—the vast majority of its population are Sunnis. The country is divided into two regions, the West Bank and the Gaza Strip, which are not connected to each other. The Gaza Strip is relatively small and borders Egypt and Israel. The West Bank is surrounded by Jordan and Israel. See Fig. 8.36 for more information (Table 8.12).

The formation of such a state of separation in Palestine has taken nearly a century. "Beyond the last borders, where should we go? Beyond the last sky, where should birds fly?" As the Palestinian poet Mahmoud Darwish chants, wars and economic weakness have always plagued the country. Politically, since Resolution 181 of the General Assembly of 1947, there have been constant wars and conflicts between Palestine and Israel due to the fact that the two nations have put forward an exclusive claim to sovereignty on the same land. On the economic front, Israel's per capita GDP in 2015 reached 35,329.5 USD, while Palestine's was only 2865.8 USD, with

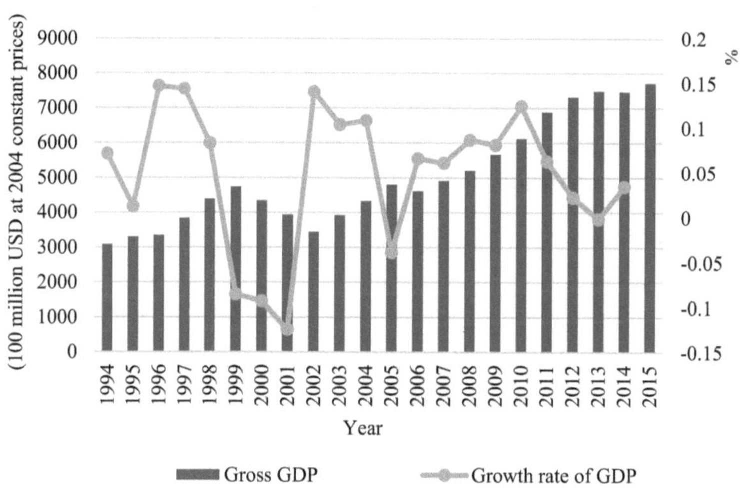

Fig. 8.36 GDP growth of Palestine. *Source of data* PCBS

Table 8.12 Basic information of the two districts of Palestine

District	Area (km^2)	Population	The ruling power
The West Bank	5655	2,935,368	Fatah
The Gaza Strip	365	1,881,135	Hamas

Source of data Population Information 2016, Palestine Central Bureau of Statistics (PCBS)

an unemployment rate of 25.9%. Such reality is the result of both domestic and international influences.

II. **Economic development**

As a transport hub connecting Europe, Asia and Africa, Palestine has a mild climate and fertile land. The population is well educated, and the potential for economic development is huge. However, due to political, social, historical and resource constraints, it suffers from relatively slow growth, but it is not a poor country.

(I) Domestic economy

Figures 8.36 and 8.37 illustrate the severe economic setback in Palestine from 1999 to 2002, a direct result of the Al-Aqsa Intifada that broke out in 2000. This Palestinian–Israeli conflict not only caused a large number of casualties, but also led to serious damage to the Palestinian economy and brought about a serious economic downturn for three consecutive years. The Palestinian GNP did not increase until 2003, and the World Bank attributed it to "reduced levels of violence, reduced curfews, increased foreseeable blockades, and the adaptation of Palestinian commerce and trade to the constrained West Bank economy". This has confirmed the profound impact of Israeli factors on the Palestinian economy. GDP per capita reveals this relation even better—in 2014, it fell to the level in 1999.

1. Industrial structure

The proportions of different economic sectors within Palestinian GDP in 2014 are shown by Fig. 8.38. The service sector took the largest part. In addition, due to the lack of resources, there was little foreign investment; therefore, the international capital made little contribution to Palestinian GDP.

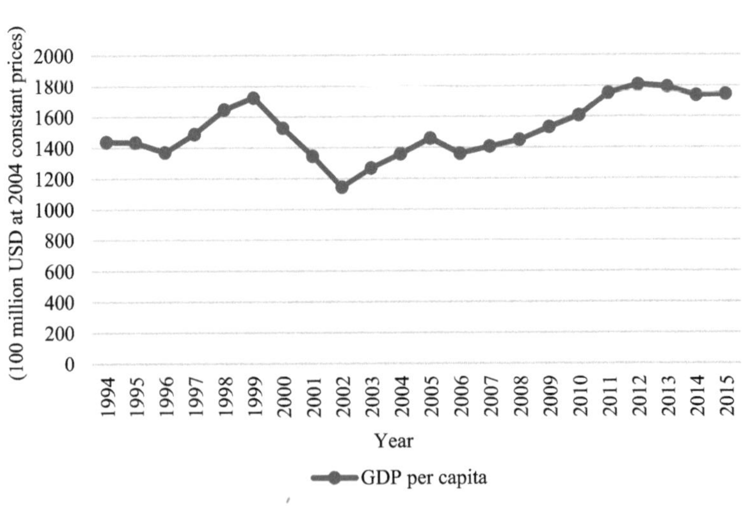

Fig. 8.37 Per capita GDP of Palestine. *Source of data* PCBS

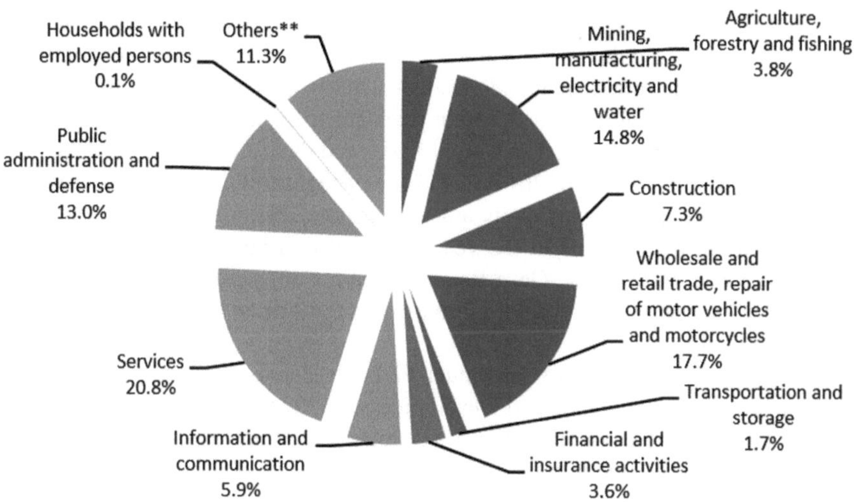

Fig. 8.38 The proportions of different economic sectors within Palestinian GDP. *Source of data Palestine in Figures 2015*, by PCBS

Palestine has four distinct seasons and is rich in agricultural products. It has 166,000 ha of arable land, and 13.4% of the population is engaged in agricultural production. Fruits, vegetables and olives (oil) are important export products (25%). In 2012, the total agricultural output value of Pakistan reached 330 million USD, accounting for 5% of GDP.

Local industrial development is slow in progress and small in scale. The processing industry takes the lead, including sectors such as plastics, rubber, chemicals, food, stone, pharmaceuticals, papermaking, printing, construction, textiles, clothing, furniture and so on. In 2012, the industrial output value was about 1.4 billion USD, accounting for about 19% of GDP. As of the end of 2013, Pakistan had a total of more than 5400 industrial enterprises, only 25 of which are foreign-funded.

Tourism is an important pillar of Palestine's economy. Palestine has a pleasant climate and abundant tourism resources, including a large number of historical and cultural sites.

In terms of infrastructure, Palestine has 5146.9 km of roads. After 2000, due to the outbreak of Palestinian–Israeli conflicts, its transport development stagnated. After 2009, the infrastructure construction (including highways) was restored and witnessed some progress. The Civil Aviation Authority was established in 1996. After the conflict broke out in September 2000, Israeli forces destroyed and closed the Gaza airport. Palestine Airlines is owned by the Palestinian National Authority and is headquartered in Arish, Egypt. It currently has two regional jets.

The Palestine Monetary Authority was established in 1994. Palestine has not issued its own currency so far, and Jordanian and Israeli currencies are circulated in the country.

2. International aid

International aid is one of the main sources of Palestinian fiscal revenue. At the end of 2010, a report from the World Bank concluded that the Palestinian economy had reached the level to establish an independent state. However, Palestine has encountered severe financial difficulties in recent years due to the lack of foreign aid and the continued blockade by Israel. The United States and the European Union have been Palestine's biggest donors. In 2011, as Pakistan sought to join the United Nations, the United States frozen part of its aid to Palestine. Palestine received only 983 million USD in aid throughout the year, resulting in a huge fiscal gap. After the conflict in Gaza in 2014, the Gaza Reconstruction Conference was held in Egypt, and the participating parties promised to provide 5.4 billion USD in assistance for the reconstruction of Gaza.

Except for foreign aid, there is not much FDI in Palestine. According to the United Nations Conference on Trade and Development, the total amount of FDI absorbed by Palestine in 2014 was 2.45 billion USD, almost the same as in 2013. China has very little direct investment in Palestine.

3. Education

Figure 8.39 shows the structure of Palestinian population in terms of education level (2015). 13% of the total population have a bachelor's degree or above. These human resources are an important engine of social development. In addition, they provide strong driving forces for Palestine to overcome difficulties and achieve sustained economic development.

(II) Factors influencing on Palestinian economy

Palestine and Israel are located in the same region, and both of them suffer from the turmoil of war, but why do they differ so much in terms of economic development? There are two reasons.

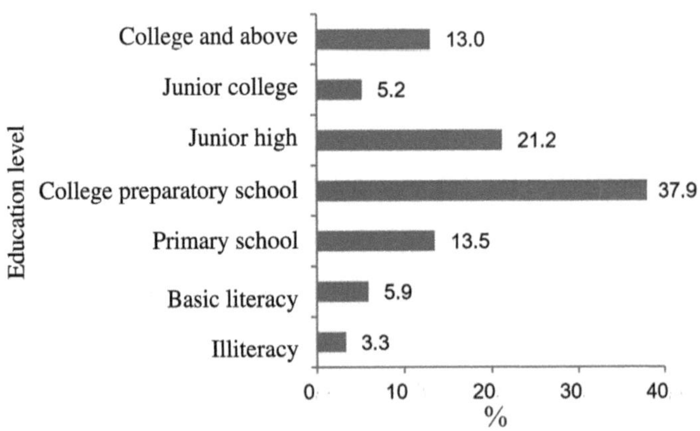

Fig. 8.39 The structure of Palestinian population in terms of education level. *Source of data* Palestine in Figures 2015, by PCBS

First, although located at the intersection of Europe, Asia and Africa, Palestine, compared to its neighbors, is not a country rich in resources, especially the water resources.

Second, after the Third Arab-Israeli War broke out in 1967, Israel seized control of the West Bank and Gaza Strip in just six days; Palestine was completely occupied by Israel; after Palestine claimed independence in 1993, Israel's occupation was gradually transformed into economic blockade. In the 50 years after the war, in addition to the constant building of "settlements" on the Palestinian land and the control of its natural resources, Israel also firmly grasped in its hands the Palestinian economy by virtue of its economic advantages and occupant status.

The distribution of resources is the result of natural evolution and cannot be changed. However, through the efforts of Pakistan and the international community, the second constraints on Palestinian economy could be lifted.

(1) Israel's settlement policy

The so-called settlements are the Jewish settlements established by Israel on the Palestinian territory. These settlements are concentrated in the West Bank. The Israeli government provides excellent resources and cheap housing, as well as certain privileges for Jews living in the settlements. Although these settlements have been deemed illegal by the international community, the number of residents has increased steadily year by year, as shown in Fig. 8.40. In 2014, the population of the "settlements" reached nearly 600,000, accounting for 1/5 of the population of the West Bank. These settlements took away not only homes, but also farmlands from the Palestinians, and then distributed them among the agricultural settlers. In addition, transport, water conservancy and communications infrastructure and supply facilities built for the settlers have also destroyed many Palestinian farmlands. Some call these "settlements" new "colonies" and "paramilitary camps".

In addition, the struggle between the two sides is even fiercer when it comes to the scarce water resources. After controlling the West Bank and the Gaza Strip, the Israeli government firmly controlled the right to develop and use water resources.

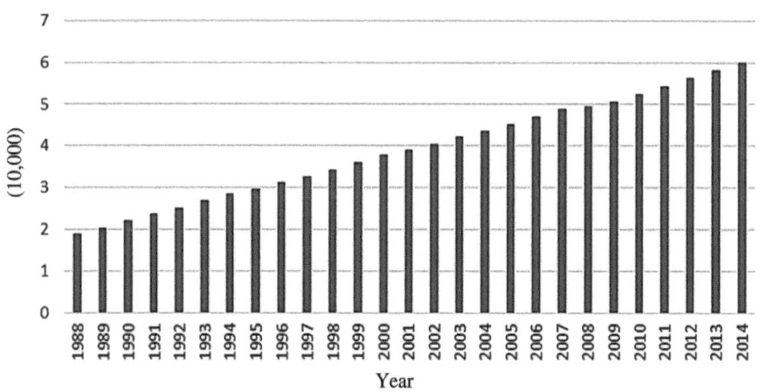

Fig. 8.40 Population of Israeli settlements. *Source of data* PCBS

Take water well as an example. Israel strictly limits the number and depth of wells of the Palestinians and stipulates that government approval has to be secured before new wells can be dug. However, such applications are almost never approved, and existing wells are mostly under the Israeli control, which means the amount of water used by Palestinian farmers are strictly limited and the needs of agricultural production cannot be met. In contrast, the Israeli settlers enjoy water supply 6–8 times that for Palestinian residents.

(2) Israel's occupation policy

Competition for natural resources. According to the resolution of the Israeli government, the land on the West Bank was divided into three districts—A, B and C.

A large part of Israel is in district C, which is the largest area on the West Bank, making up about 60% of the total. The plains and most of the natural resources are concentrated here. A bill passed by the Supreme Court of Israel stipulates that Israeli companies have the right to extract natural resources in the West Bank, but Palestine's mining rights are restricted.

The Dead Sea is located at the border between Palestine, Israel and Jordan, and the part belonging to Palestine is within district C. The Dead Sea is rich in salts and minerals, and potassium carbonate, bromine and magnesium are the most valuable. These resources have been mined and used by Israel for decades, and the country's multinational corporation Israel Chemicals Ltd. (ICL) is the largest developer. According to information disclosed by ICL in 2011, its cost of refining and producing potassium carbonate and bromine salts in the Dead Sea is generally lower than that of other manufacturers. According to *The Economic Costs of the Israeli Occupation for the Occupied Palestinian Territory*[26] published by the Applied Research Institute-Jerusalem (ARIJ) in 2015 on *The Economic Costs of the Israeli Occupation for the Occupied Palestinian Territory*, the output value of the resource extraction in 2014 was approximately 1.642 billion USD, or 12.9% of Palestine's GDP that year. This is undoubtedly a huge loss for the Palestinian economy.

Conflict in the Gaza Strip. Gaza is controlled by Hamas. It has waged three wars with Israel over the past eight years, leading to rising unemployment, a sharp decline in the private sector, and great damage to local industries. The 2014 war forced the middle class to flee their homes, causing more than 500,000 people to leave Gaza, triggering a recession with 2.759 billion USD of direct economic losses. Reconstruction projects launched in 2015 were fragmented, and progress was slower than expected. The IMF estimated that the local economy would not rebound to the 2013 level until the end of 2017 at the earliest.

Restrictions on imports and exports. In terms of imports, Israel has set up a "dual-use goods list". Many goods imported by Pakistan to the West Bank and Gaza Strip are restricted. For example, chemicals and fertilizers are strictly restricted because they may be used to produce weapons. This has severely affected the region's manufacturing and agriculture. According to ARIJ statistics, direct and indirect losses in

[26] ARIJ, The Economic Costs of the Israeli Occupation for the Occupied Palestinian Territory.

agriculture amount to 95 million USD, and the total loss caused by this policy is as much as 215 million USD. In terms of exports, Israel has imposed burdensome procedures on import to and export from Palestine, sharply pushing up the trade cost of Palestine. The time of Customs clearance for Palestinian goods is about 2.6 times that for Israeli goods.[27] The opportunity cost of these unnecessary delays is about 38.85 million USD every year. Therefore, the restrictions on import and export cause 253.9 million USD' loss to Palestine each year, accounting for 2% of its GDP.

8.9 Qatar

I. **Geographical and historic backgrounds**

Qatar is located in the middle of the Arabian Peninsula and is rich in oil and gas resources. It is an important oil and gas producer and exporter in the world. At the same time, the Qatari government is also actively promoting economic diversification and infrastructure construction. In 2015, its per capita GDP ranked first in the world and its global competitiveness ranked first among Arab countries and Middle East countries. The 2006 Asian Games and the 2022 World Cup were held here. Geographically, Qatar is a peninsula country. It is located on the Qatar peninsula on the southwestern shore of the Persian Gulf. It is bordered by Saudi Arabia to the south and faces the sea on the east, north and west. The land area is 1152 km^2, and the coastline is 550 km long. Historically, Qatar was part of the Arab Empire in the 7th century. It was ruled by Portugal, the Netherlands and then Britain from 1517 to 1776. Mohammed bin Thani established the emirate of Qatar in 1846. It was invaded by the British in 1882 and did not officially declare independence until 1971. As of August 2016, Qatar's population exceeded 2.4 million, of which Qataris accounted for about 15%. The foreign population mainly came from India, Pakistan and Southeast Asian countries. Arabic is the official language, and English is commonly used. Qatari residents, mostly Sunni Muslims, are mainly of the Wahhabi sect, and Shiites account for 16% of the country's population. Qatar is rich in oil and gas resources. In 2015, its proven oil reserves were 25.7 billion barrels, accounting for 1.5% of the world's total, ranking 12th in the world. Its proven natural gas reserves were 24.5 trillion m^3, accounting for 13.1% of the world's total, ranking third in the world after Russia and Iran. In recent years, the government has invested heavily in the development of natural gas, making it the top priority of economic development. As a result, Qatar has turned into the world's largest LNG producer and exporter. While vigorously developing the energy industry, Qatar launched the "National Vision 2030" plan in 2008 to diversify its economy. In 2015, Qatar ranked first among the Arab and Middle Eastern countries in terms of global competitiveness and ranked first among the richest countries and regions.

II. **Economic development**

[27] 125 h for Palestinian goods, and 49 h for Israeli goods. Source of data: World Bank database.

(I) Domestic economy

Similar to other oil producing countries in the Middle East, Qatar has witnessed long-term rapid growth thanks to its rich oil and gas resources. The total GDP of Qatar in 2015 was 166.9 billion USD, an increase of 3.6% year-on-year, and the per capita GDP was 74,667 USD, ranking first in the world. The Qatari government is committed to promoting diversified economic development and has achieved good results. Infrastructure such as aviation, processing manufacturing, finance, real estate and other industries have developed rapidly. Despite the 2008 financial crisis and the falling oil prices in recent years, Qatar has maintained stable growth. At the end of 2014, the output value of non-oil-and-gas sectors exceeded that of oil and gas sectors for the first time, generating 50.7% of GDP. The rich oil and gas resources, the progress of economic diversification, the relatively complete infrastructure system, and its preferential policies for foreign investment have made Qatar a country of promising prospects. In 2015, Qatar ranked 14th in terms of global competitiveness, the highest ranking among Arab and Middle Eastern countries; Standard and Poor's rated Qatar's long-term sovereign credit as "AA", indicating its stable outlook. Figures 8.41 and 8.42 illustrate the GDPs and per capita GDPs of Qatar.

1. Industrial structure

Within the industrial structure of Qatar, the secondary industry is the dominant force, the tertiary industry is growing, and the primary industry is small in scale, as shown in Fig. 8.43. In 2015, the ratio was 0.1: 55.8: 44.1. Similar to typical oil and gas resource countries, Qatar's industry occupies a dominant position in the national economy. Its industry is dominated by the oil and gas sector, related industries and energy-intensive industries. In recent years, with the development of modern service industries such as finance, real estate and tourism, the proportion of the tertiary industry has been expanding steadily.

In terms of added value produced by different sectors, as Table 8.13 illustrates, the top five industries in the national economy in 2014 were mining; finance, insurance,

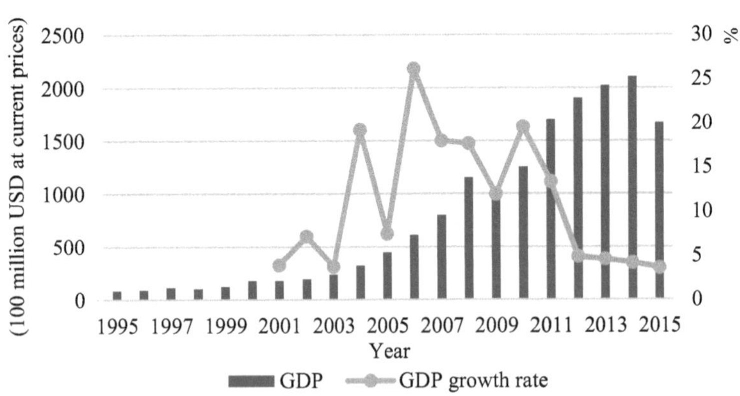

Fig. 8.41 GDP growth in Qatar. *Source of data* World Bank database

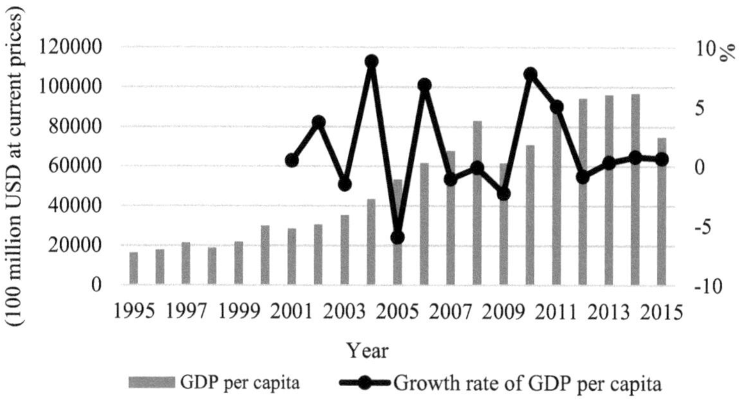

Fig. 8.42 Growth of per capita GDP in Qatar. *Source of data* World Bank database

real estate and commercial services; manufacturing; government services; and trade, hotel and retailing. The oil-and-gas-based mining industry still dominates the national economy, accounting for 51.1% of GDP in 2014; financial, insurance, real estate and commercial services have steadily developed in recent years, accounting for 13.23% in 2014; the manufacturing accounted for 10.13%, ranking third; the proportion of government services continues to rise, climbing from 7.57% in 2007 to 9.56% in 2014; and trade, hotel and retailing industry produced 6.83%.

As an oil-reliant economy, Qatar's pillar industry is the petrochemical industry. The main products are liquefied natural gas, crude oil, gasoline, methanol, etc. Most of the products are for export, and the export volume of liquefied natural gas has leapt to the first in the world.

Finance is the sector that contributes the most to the national economy apart from the energy sectors. The total assets of Qatar's banking industry exceeded 300 billion USD in 2015, a year-on-year increase of 9.5%. Among them, Qatar National Bank (QNB) had total assets of 147 billion USD in 2015, making it the largest bank in the Gulf region for the fifth consecutive year.

Qatar Airways reflects the strengths of Qatar's transportation industry. Founded in 1993, Qatar Airways is 100% controlled by the Qatar government. It has about 140 international routes and is one of the 7 Skytrax five-star airlines in the world. Qatar Airways' cargo volume increased from 1.104 million tons in 2014 to 1.52 million tons in 2015, a year-on-year increase of 37.5%, making it the third largest air cargo company in the world.

In recent years, tourism has also developed rapidly in Qatar. Its convenient air transport, good accommodation conditions and beautiful scenery are extremely attractive to tourists. According to the World Tourism Union (WTU), in 2015, Qatar received 2.93 million tourists, an increase of 3.7% over 2014, generating 5.2 billion USD of direct income, or 2.8% of its GDP.

2. Urban structure

Table 8.13 The proportions of added values generated by different economic sectors (Unit: %)

	2007	2008	2009	2010
Agriculture, forestry, animal husbandry and fishery	0.11	0.12	0.12	0.12
Mining	51.70	54.89	44.80	52.64
Manufacturing	9.24	10.69	9.43	8.97
Electricity and water	0.63	0.49	0.50	0.46
Construction	5.49	6.48	7.17	6.04
Trade, hotel and retailing	7.19	5.58	8.38	6.92
Warehousing, logistics and communications	3.00	3.52	4.55	3.97
Finance, insurance, real estate and commercial services	14.47	12.29	16.32	13.24
Government services	7.57	6.28	9.02	8.21
Social services	1.04	0.82	1.17	0.99
Domestic services	0.54	0.40	0.51	0.41
Financial intermediates	−2.32	−2.42	−2.85	−2.79
Import duty	1.36	0.84	0.87	0.83
	2011	2012	2013	2014
Agriculture, forestry, animal husbandry and fishery	0.10	0.09	0.09	0.10
Mining	58.11	56.96	54.81	51.09
Manufacturing	9.35	10.33	10.02	10.13
Electricity and water	0.47	0.49	0.54	0.56
Construction	4.58	4.44	5.22	6.14
Trade, hotel and retailing	5.76	5.62	6.19	6.83
Warehousing, logistics and communications	3.43	3.22	3.04	3.27
Finance, insurance, real estate and commercial services	11.37	11.06	11.83	13.23
Government services	7.52	8.67	9.15	9.56
Social services	0.83	0.79	0.89	0.93
Domestic services	0.33	0.34	0.37	0.42
Financial intermediates	−2.48	−2.49	−2.58	−2.69
Import duty	0.53	0.48	0.43	0.44

Source of data Qatar Bureau of Statistics.

Due to its small size, natural conditions and economic growth, Qatar is highly urbanized—its urbanization rate reached 99.2% in 2015, as Fig. 8.44 shows. Among all Qatari cities, Doha is home to about 95% of the country's population. Table 8.14 lists the major cities in Qatar.

In terms of transportation infrastructure, Qatar has no railway, and its major cities are connected by a modern highway network. The total length of its highways is

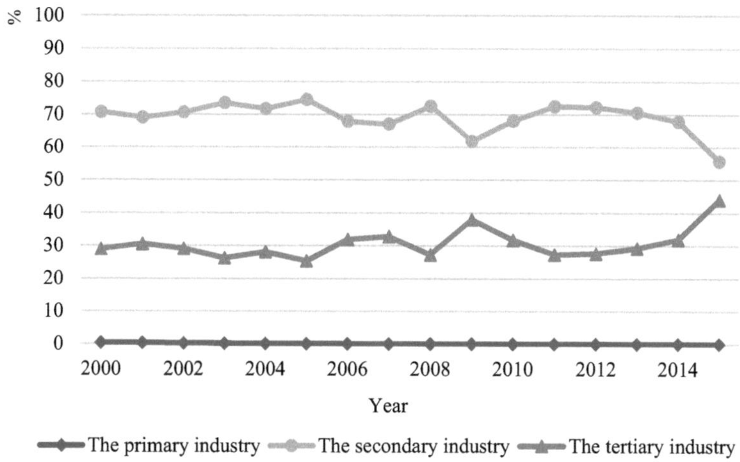

Fig. 8.43 The industrial structure of Qatar. *Source of data* World Bank database

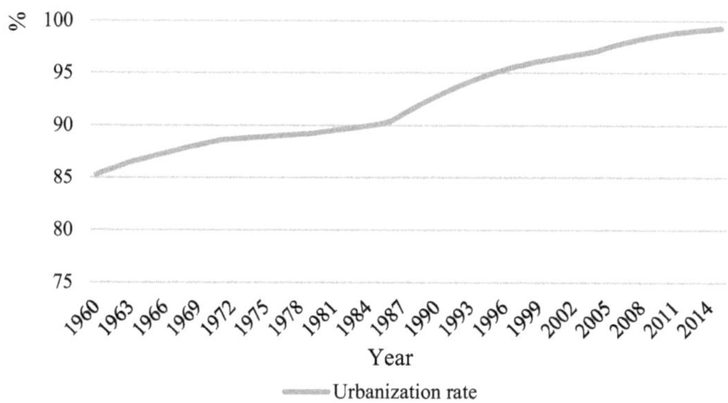

Fig. 8.44 Urbanization rate of Qatar. *Source of data* World Bank database

Table 8.14 Top cities of Qatar

City	City profile
Doha	The capital of Qatar; the largest city in the country, and the political, economic, transport and cultural center; one of the famous ports in the Persian Gulf. Located in the middle of the east coast of Qatar Peninsula, it is home to 95% of the total population. It has major ports and international airports, and its modern road network is connected to the international road network.
Al-Rayyan	Located 10 km north of Doha, it is the largest residential area outside the capital
Al-Khor	A coastal port and industrial city 57 km north of Doha
Mesaieed	Qatar's main industrial city and port; an export base for oil and hydrocarbon products
AL Wakra	Located between Doha and Mesaieed, 15 km from Doha, with a small harbor
Dukhan	Located in the middle of the western coast; the onshore oil production base

900 km. Doha, Umm Said and Ras Laffan are the main seaports. Ras Laffan is the world's largest port for liquefied natural gas. Qatar has 5 airports, and Doha Hamad International Airport is connected to Europe and Asia through more than 20 routes.

Qatar is a welfare state in terms of public service supply. Free medical treatment is available throughout the country. There are 4 main hospitals nationwide, with more than 1100 beds. In addition, there are nearly 20 medical and health centers. At the same time, the government, attaching great importance to the development of education, provides free universal education and opportunities to study abroad and scholarships for outstanding students.

(II) Foreign trade and investment

Qatar is a highly export-oriented country. As Fig. 8.45 demonstrates, its trade volume accounted for 90.9% of GDP in 2015, and there has always been a trade surplus. The main export products are petroleum, liquefied gas, synthetic ammonia, urea, ethylene, etc. The main import products are machinery and transportation equipment, food, industrial raw materials and light industrial products, pharmaceuticals, etc. The main trading partners are the United States, Japan and Western European countries.

In terms of outward investment, Qatar has been investing globally relying on its abundant foreign exchange reserves. In 2014, finance and insurance, warehousing and transportation, information and communications, and real estate took up 38%, 32% and 19% of its total outward investment. The EU members, the Gulf Cooperation Council countries, other Arab countries and Asia are in the top four destinations of Qatari capital. As to absorbing foreign investment, Qatar has introduced a number of preferential policies, providing protection and benefits for foreign investors. 90% of foreign investment in Qatar flew to manufacturing (52%) and resource exploitation related to oil and gas extracting (38%). American countries (exc. US), the European

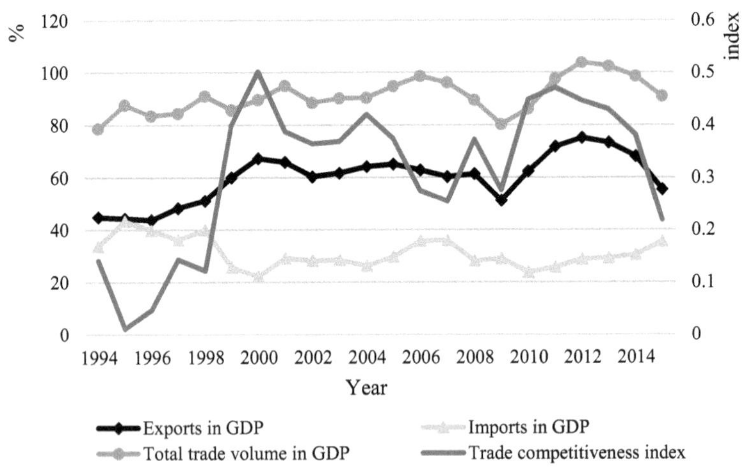

Fig. 8.45 Foreign trade of Qatar. *Source of data* World Bank database

Table 8.15 Destinations (countries and industries) of Qatar's outward investment (Unit: billion riyal)

	2012		2013		2014	
	Stock	Percentage (%)	Stock	Percentage (%)	Stock	Percentage (%)
Finance and insurance	26.8	27	40.8	36	44.9	38
Warehousing, transport, information and communications	42.6	42	39.5	35	37.0	32
Real estate	22.0	22	24.7	22	22.1	19
EU members	28.6	28	34.2	30	34.0	29
Gulf Cooperation Council members	34.5	35	31.6	28	30.5	26
Other Arab countries	7.8	8	19.5	17	20.6	18
Asian countries	18.8	19	11.5	10	12.3	11

Source of data the website of Ministry of Development Planning and Statistics, Qatar

Union and the United States are the main sources of foreign investment in Qatar. See Tables 8.15 and 8.16 for more information.

8.10 Saudi Arabia

I. Historical and geographical backgrounds

Saudi Arabia is one of the major powers in the Middle East. It plays key roles in geopolitics, the petroleum market, nationality and religion. It has global influence in terms of economy, politics and culture and is the world's largest oil producer and exporter. In addition, it is the largest economy in the Middle East and the only Arab country among the G20 members. Geographically, Saudi Arabia is located in the Arabian Peninsula, facing the Persian Gulf to the east and the Red Sea to the west, and bordering Jordan, Iraq, Kuwait, the UAE, Oman, Yemen and other countries. Meanwhile, it is connected with Bahrain via the King Fahd Causeway. The country covers an area of 2.25 million km^2 and has a coastline of 2448 km. From the perspective of natural conditions, the terrain is high in the west and low in the east, and most of the land is uninhabitable deserts and wilderness. Except for the southwest plateau and northern regions, which have a sub-tropical Mediterranean climate, the whole country has a tropical desert climate—it is hot and dry in the summer (the highest temperature can reach above 50 °C), mild in the winter and the average annual rainfall does not exceed 200 mm. Historically, Saudi Arabia can be

Table 8.16 Destinations and sources of foreign investment in Qatar (Unit: billion riyal)

	2012		2013		2014	
	Stock	Percentage (%)	Stock	Percentage (%)	Stock	Percentage (%)
Manufacturing	94.9	59	85.1	56	73.3	52
Mining	54.0	33	52.7	35	53.9	38
Finance and insurance	4.8	3	5.4	4	5.4	4
American countries (the United States excluded)	66.7	41	57.2	38	47.7	34
EU members	51.8	32	47.5	31	46.5	33
The United States	28.0	17	30.6	20	31.4	22
The Gulf Cooperation Council members	7.2	4	7.5	5	6.5	5

Source of data Ministry of Development Planning and Statistics

traced back to the Arab Empire established in the 7th century. The Empire entered its heyday in the 8th century, stretching across Europe, Asia and Africa. It began to decline in the 11th century and was ruled by the Ottoman Empire in the 16th century. In the 19th century, the British invaded and split it into two parts, Hijaz and Nejd. In 1924, Abdulaziz Al Saud, the emir of Nejd, annexed Hijaz. In 1932, he unified the Arabian Peninsula and founded the Kingdom of Saudi Arabia. The population of the country in 2016 was approximately 31.74 million, of which approximately 67% were Saudi citizens. The vast majority of the residents were Arabs, and there were a few blacks, Indians and Turks. Saudi Arabia is the cradle of the Arab nation and the birthplace of Islam. Islam is the state religion. 85% of the population is Sunnis, and 15% is Shiites; Mecca and Medina are Islamic holy cities. In terms of politics and legal system, Saudi Arabia is a monarchy without political parties or constitution, and it applies the Sharia law.

With its unique geographical location and crude oil reserves, Saudi Arabia has become the center of the Middle East. On one hand, it links the three continents of Europe, Asia and Africa. Located at the converging point of the Gulf region (Iran, Iraq and other countries) and of the Levant (Israel, Jordan and Lebanon), and close to the two internationally important maritime passages of the Strait of Hormuz and the Gulf of Aden, Saudi Arabia takes the leading position in the Gulf Cooperation Council. On the other hand, it is rich in oil and gas resources and occupies an essential and special position in the international energy system. Its proven reserves of crude oil are 266 billion tons, accounting for 16% of the world's total, second only to Canada. Its natural gas reserves are 8.2 trillion m^3, ranking sixth in the world. In addition, it also has mineral deposits such as gold, copper, iron, tin, aluminum, zinc and phosphate. At the same time, it is the world's largest producer of desalinized water, contributing about 20% of the world's total.

II. **Economic development**

(I) Domestic economy

Thanks to the rich oil and gas resources and advanced petrochemical industry, Saudi Arabia has witnessed rapid economic growth. In 2015, its GDP was 2048.175 billion USD, with an inflation rate of 4.09%, ranking first among Arab countries. See Figs. 8.46 and 8.47 for more GDP information. Saudi Arabia ranks 25th in terms of global competitiveness. Its per capita GDP is 20,482 USD, much higher than the threshold of high-income countries (12,736 USD), and ranking first in the Middle East and North Africa. The petroleum and petrochemical industries are the economic lifeline of Saudi Arabia, so its macro economy is closely related to fluctuations in oil prices. As oil prices rose rapidly in 2003, Saudi Arabia also entered the "fast track" for economic development. The average GDP growth rate in 2003–2008 was as high as 7.1%. In 2009, due to the financial crisis, the Saudi economy hit the bottom. A series of favorable factors such as the rebound in oil prices, the higher-than-expectation performance of the non-oil industry and export growth have led to steady economic growth in Saudi Arabia after 2010.

1. Industrial structure

As to the industrial structure, as Fig. 8.48 illustrates, the dominant position of the secondary industry has weakened slightly, the tertiary industry has been growing fast, and the primary industry has stayed small in proportion—the ratio is 2.3:15.9:51.8. The secondary industry, dominated by the petroleum and petrochemical industries, has long played a leading role in Saudi Arabia's domestic economy. In 2008 when the oil price peaked, the secondary industry accounted for 66.8% of GDP. In order to get rid of all the disadvantages brought by the undiversified economic structure, Saudi

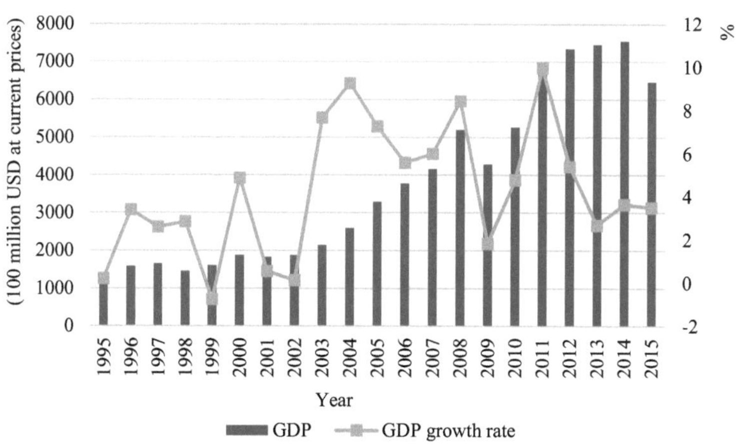

Fig. 8.46 GDP growths in Saudi Arabia. *Source of data* World Bank database

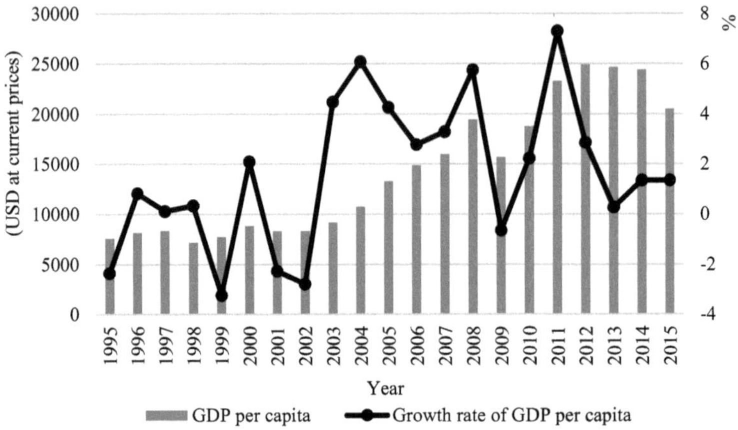

Fig. 8.47 Growths of per capita GDP in Saudi Arabia. *Source of data* World Bank database

Arabia has actively supported the development of non-petroleum industries such as steelmaking, aluminum smelting, cement, desalination, electricity, agriculture and services in recent years. The proportion of the tertiary industry even exceeded that of the secondary industry in 2015. In addition, due to limited natural conditions, agriculture and animal husbandry have been relatively insignificant in its economy—their proportion within gross GDP was only 2.3% in 2015.

When it comes to different sectors, as Table 8.17 shows, the mining industry, mainly the exploitation of crude oil and natural gas, is still the dominant force in Saudi Arabia, generating 25.42% of GDP in 2015, but the proportion has gradually declined in recent years. This is due to the decline in oil prices, and the rapid growth of the non-oil industry. Government services rank second in terms of proportion,

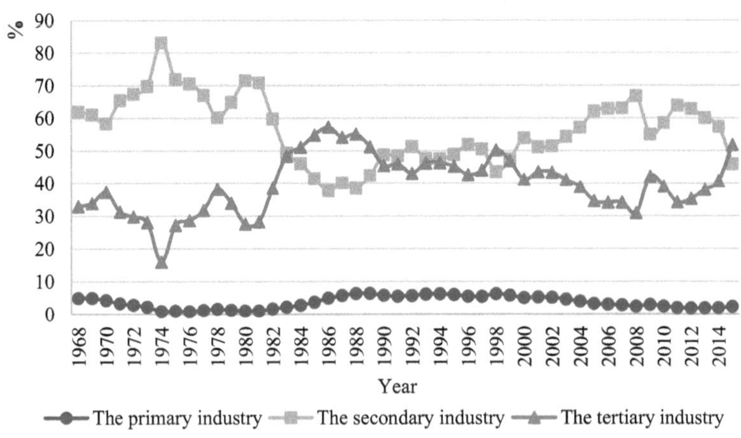

Fig. 8.48 The industrial structure of Saudi Arabia. *Source of data* World Bank database

contributing 18.78% of GDP in 2015. The proportion of the manufacturing industry in the national economy ranks third, and it has been steadily rising since the new century. The proportion of crude oil refining in the manufacturing industry dropped from 30.9% in 2000 to 17.7% in 2015. The proportion of electricity, natural gas and water in GDP has fluctuated around 1% for a long time, which is closely related to the subsidies in these areas and thus the low degree of marketization. The proportion of agriculture, forestry, animal husbandry, side-line production and fishery within GDP has been declining, and by 2015, it had dropped to 2.26%. Since the 1980s, the Saudi government has been committed to increasing the self-sufficiency rate of agricultural products. However, at this stage, the self-sufficiency rate of cereals is only over 20%. It is also the world's largest importer of barley, purchasing about 6 million tons every year. The self-sufficiency rate of fruits is 60%. With the implementation of the industrial diversification policy, sectors such as transportation, warehousing and communications, wholesaling and retailing, catering and hotel, and financial, insurance, real estate and commercial services have been playing bigger roles in the national economy.

Industry is the largest industrial sector in Saudi Arabia, of which the petroleum and petrochemical industries are the economic lifeline. As Fig. 8.49 points out, in 2015, the crude oil output averaged 10.108 million barrels per day, accounting for 30% of OPEC's total, making the country the largest oil producer and exporter in the world. The abundant oil resources have brought huge profits to Saudi Arabia. As Fig. 8.50 shows, in 2015, the added value of the petroleum sector accounted for 27.5% of GDP, and oil revenue contributed 72.3% of the fiscal revenue. However, the revenue of the oil sector is greatly affected by fluctuations of the international oil prices. From 2003 to 2008, the oil prices continued to rise. As a result, Saudi Arabia's oil sector grew rapidly. Its proportion peaked at 55% in 2008. However, this proportion has undergone drastic changes as the oil prices have entered the downward spiral in recent years. The sharp fall in oil prices in 2015 squeezed the oil sector further, reducing its share from 42.4% to 27.5%. Consequently, the government had to live beyond its means, and the fiscal deficit was as high as 17.5% of GDP.

In recent years, the Saudi government, making full use of its abundant oil and natural gas resources, has actively introduced advanced foreign technology and equipment, and vigorously promoted the development of non-petroleum industries such as steelmaking, aluminum smelting, cement, desalination, electricity, agriculture and services. The economic structure has been diversified to some extent. In terms of energy extraction, Saudi Arabia proposed a new energy development plan in 2013 to promote new energy industries such as solar power, wind power and nuclear energy. As to the mining industry, it has accelerated the development of mining and metallurgy, aluminum smelting, fertilizer and building materials based on its abundant resources of gold, iron, copper and lead. In 2015, the non-oil sector produced 72.5% of GDP. But in general, Saudi economy still relies heavily on oil, and there is still a long way to go for the upgrading of its industrial structure.

In terms of infrastructure construction, road transport is the main way of transportation in Saudi Arabia. The total length of roads is 144,000 km, of which the 55,000 km are highways. It is connected with Jordan, Yemen, Kuwait, Qatar, the

Table 8.17 The proportions of different sectors in terms of added values created (Unit: %)

	2000	2001	2002	2003	2004	2005	2006	2007
Agriculture, forestry, animal husbandry, side-line production and fishery	4.92	5.17	5.08	4.50	3.90	3.22	2.95	2.77
Mining	36.92	33.34	33.32	36.34	39.67	46.47	47.46	47.14
Manufacturing	9.61	10.02	10.26	10.66	10.33	9.54	9.60	9.94
Electricity, natural gas and water	1.76	1.90	1.86	1.79	1.65	1.36	1.24	1.19
Construction	5.87	6.25	6.29	5.82	5.52	4.74	4.58	4.77
Wholesale, retailing, catering and hotel	6.73	7.21	7.28	6.65	6.87	6.27	6.46	7.08
Transportation, warehousing and communications	4.10	4.43	4.49	4.11	4.02	3.54	3.53	3.92
Finance, insurance, real estate and commercial services	10.72	11.42	11.54	10.61	10.01	8.80	8.66	8.78
Government services	16.76	17.90	17.51	17.29	16.01	14.33	13.91	12.85
	2008	2009	2010	2011	2012	2013	2014	2015
Agriculture, forestry, animal husbandry, side-line production and fishery	2.32	2.85	2.38	1.92	1.81	1.85	1.90	2.26
Mining	52.74	37.83	41.57	48.41	47.65	44.17	39.98	25.42
Manufacturing	8.98	10.85	11.04	10.04	9.82	9.96	10.83	12.30
Electricity, natural gas and water	0.94	1.34	1.33	1.13	1.09	1.10	1.15	1.45
Construction	4.09	5.00	4.60	4.26	4.31	4.82	5.41	6.73
Wholesale, retailing, catering and hotel	6.84	9.19	8.83	7.88	7.96	8.66	9.43	11.48
Transportation, warehousing and communications	3.99	5.52	5.12	4.59	4.52	4.81	5.12	6.30
Finance, insurance, real estate and commercial services	7.86	10.65	9.24	7.77	8.45	9.67	10.36	12.81
Government services	10.74	14.98	14.22	12.44	12.70	13.19	13.85	18.78

Source of data General Authority for Statistics, Saudi Arabia

UAE and Bahrain through an international highway network. There are 27 airports in the country, including 4 international airports such as the King Khalid International Airport in Riyadh. Every year, these airports handle 18.9 million passengers, 55,895 flights and 382,000 tons of cargo. There are approximately 6.87 million fixed broadband users in Saudi Arabia, and the Internet penetration has exceeded 60%.

2. Urban structure

Due to limited natural conditions, most of the Saudi population lives in cities. In 2015, the urbanization rate was as high as 83.13%, much higher than the average of Arab countries and the world, as Fig. 8.51 illustrates. Saudi Arabia has five major

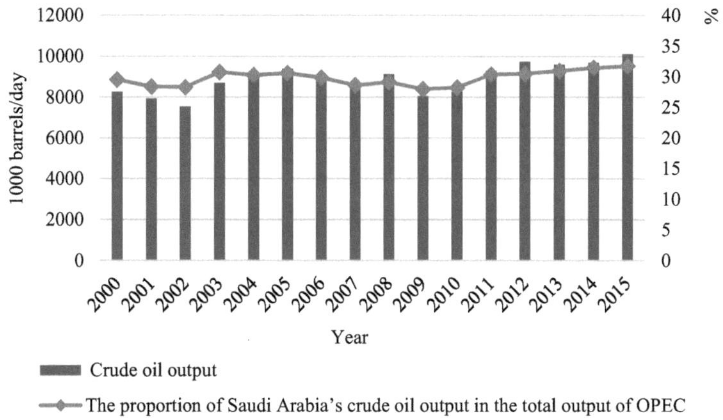

Fig. 8.49 Saudi Arabia's crude oil output. *Source of data* OPEC Annual Report (2000–2015)

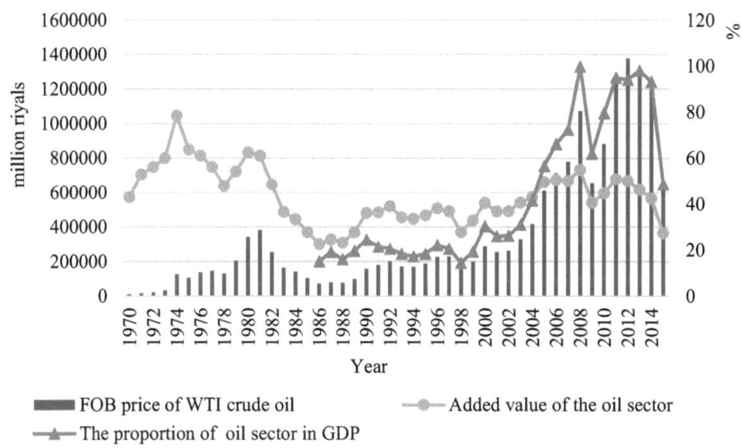

Fig. 8.50 Revenue of the oil sector of Saudi Arabia. *Source of data* General Authority for Statistics, Saudi Arabia; the U.S. Energy Information Administration

cities: Riyadh, Jeddah, Medina, Dammam and Dhahran. For more information, see Table 8.18.

(II) Foreign trade and investment
1. Foreign trade

Saudi Arabia, adopting free trade and low tariff policies, is a member of international organizations such as the World Trade Organization, the International Monetary Fund, the World Bank, the Arab Monetary Fund, the Gulf Cooperation Council, the Pan-Arab Free Trade Area and the Organization of Petroleum Exporting Countries. Petroleum and petroleum products are its major export products, contributing about 85% of the total. The exports of petrochemicals and some industrial products

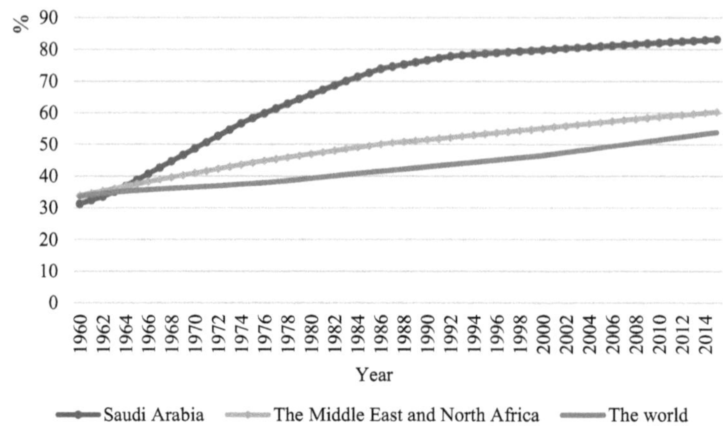

Fig. 8.51 Urbanization rate of Saudi Arabia. *Source of data* World Bank database

Table 8.18 Top cities of Saudi Arabia

City	City profile
Riyadh	The largest city; the political and cultural center; the seat of government agencies; located in central Saudi Arabia, it has a population of approximately 7.1 million (2011) and an urban area of 1219 km^2
Jeddah	The second largest city; located on the western coast of Saudi Arabia, it is under the jurisdiction of the Mecca district; the financial and trade center; an important port by the Red Sea; it has steel, cement and desalination industries
Medina	The second Holy City of Islam
Dammam	The capital of the eastern province; a major base of oil industry; an important port
Dhahran	The Saudi Aramco is based in the city

are also gradually increasing. In 2015, the share of crude oil and natural gas within total exports dropped to 64.3%, while that of the chemical products increased from 9.3% in 2013 to 15.2%. Saudi Arabia mainly imports machinery and equipment, food, textiles and other consumer goods and chemical products. China, Japan, the United States, India and South Korea are its main trading partners. It is worth noting that in 2015, China replaced the United States as Saudi Arabia's largest export destination. In 2015, China purchased 12.1% of its total exports, most of which was oil; China, as the largest source of its imports, produced 14.11% of the total. The top three imported goods from China are wireless communications equipment such as mobile phones, portable data processing equipment such as computers and air conditioning equipment. Due to the large volume of oil exports, Saudi Arabia has enjoyed long-term trade surplus and positive trade competitiveness. However, due to the drastic fluctuations in oil prices in recent years, Saudi Arabia's exports have shrunk. According to World Bank, the total value of its foreign trade in 2015 was 468.5 billion USD, of which 218 billion USD were exports, and 250.5 billion USD were imports—it reported its first trade deficit in decades. For more information, see Fig. 8.52 and Tables 8.19, 8.20, 8. 21 and 8.22.

2. International investment

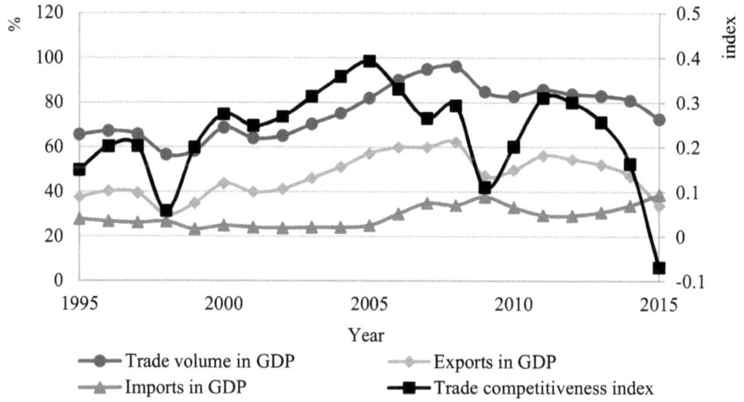

Fig. 8.52 Foreign trade of Saudi Arabia. *Source of data* World Bank database

Table 8.19 Major trading partners of Saudi Arabia (2015)

Ranking	Import	Export
1	Chinese mainland	Chinese mainland
2	The United States	Japan
3	Germany	The United States
4	Japan	India
5	South Korea	South Korea
6	UAE	UAE
7	India	Singapore
8	France	Taiwan, China
9	Italy	Bahrain
10	Britain	France

Source of data General Authority for Statistics, Saudi Arabia

Table 8.20 The proportions of major export products within total exports (Unit: %)

	2013	2014	2015
Exploitation of crude oil and natural gas	78.63	73.59	64.32
Production of chemicals	9.28	11.18	15.16
Production of coke and refined oil	6.82	9.22	10.24

Source of data General Authority for Statistics, Saudi Arabia

Table 8.21 The proportions of major import products within total imports (Unit: %)

	2013	2014	2015
Automobile	14.16	13.69	14.63
Machinery	12.33	11.97	12.01
Electronic product	11.89	11.80	9.94
Base metal	9.11	9.40	9.48
Food	8.39	8.70	8.57

Source of data General Authority for Statistics, Saudi Arabia

Table 8.22 Inflows and outflows of FDI in Saudi Arabia (Unit: 100 million USD)

Year	FDI inflows	FDI outflows
2010	292.33	39.07
2011	163.08	34.30
2012	121.82	44.02
2013	88.65	49.43
2014	80.12	53.96
2015	81.41	55.20

Source of data World Investment Report 2016

With the decline in oil prices in recent years, the economic growth in Saudi Arabia has slowed down, and FDI inflows have also dwindled. In 2015, the net FDI inflow was 8.141 billion USD, accounting for 1.26% of GDP. At the same time, the scale of its outward FDI remained relatively small in scale—the FDI outflow was 5.52 billion USD in 2015, as Table 8.22 and Fig. 8.53 show.

8.11 Turkey

I. Geographical and historical backgrounds

Turkey, stretching across Europe and Asia, borders the Black Sea to the north, the Mediterranean to the south, Syria and Iraq to the southeast, the Aegean Sea and Greece and Bulgaria to the west, and Georgia, Armenia, Azerbaijan and Iran to the east. Connecting Europe and Asia, Turkey is of great geographical and geopolitical significance. Turkey, as a European country, implements the European political, economic and cultural models. It is a candidate for the European Union. Its Constitution stipulates that Turkey is a democracy where the church and the state are separated, and a rule of law is adopted. Turkey's diplomatic focus is on the West—it maintains a traditional strategic partnership with the United States and strives to enhance its relations with European countries. Turkey is a member of NATO, a founding member of the OECD, and a member of G20. With a strong industrial foundation, it is an emerging economy and one of the fastest growing countries in the world.

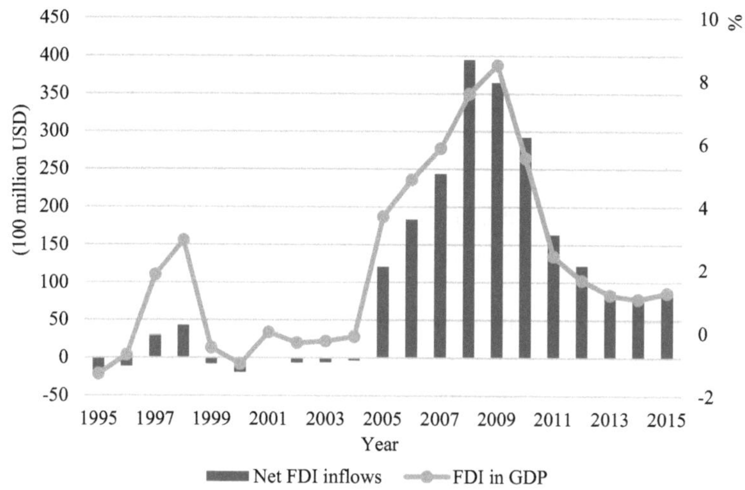

Fig. 8.53 Net FDI inflows and their proportions within Saudi Arabian GDP. *Source of data* World Bank database

Turkey is rich in mineral resources, such as boron, chromium, iron, copper, bauxite and coal. The reserves of boron trioxide and chrome ore are among the highest in the world. Turkey has a large forest area; Lake Van (Van Golu) is rich in fish resources and salt; the Anatolian Plateau has vast pastures. With abundant water resources, Turkey has built dams and reservoirs in major river valleys to develop hydropower and ensure irrigation water supply. There are oil and gas in Turkey, but the output cannot meet the domestic demand; therefore, imports are necessary. As oilfields have been found in the eastern Thrace of Iskenderun bay on the Black Sea coast of North Anatolia and in the south of Anatolia near the borders with Syria and Iraq, Turkey's oil self-sufficiency is expected to improve.

II. **Economic development**

(I) Domestic economy

Turkish economy has been expanding rapidly in recent years into the largest in the Middle East. The rapid growth and good prospects have made Turkey another emerging economy after China, Russia, India, Brazil and South Africa. Its average GDP growth rate reached 4.6% in 2003–2015, faster than that of Chile, Slovakia, Russia and Poland, as Table 8.23 illustrates. More information on Turkey's GDP can be found in Fig. 8.54. Turkey is a leading producer of agricultural products, textiles, automobiles, ships and other vehicles, building materials and consumer electronics. In recent years, its private sector has witnessed significant growth, but state-owned enterprises still dominate the industrial, banking, transportation and communications sectors.

1. Industrial structure

(1) The primary industry

Table 8.23 Average annual growth rates of real GDP for some countries (2003–2015) (Unit: %)

Country	Growth rate
Turkey	4.6
Chile	4.3
Slovakia	3.9
Russia	3.9
Poland	3.7
South Korea	3.2
Brazil	3.1
Romania	3.0
South Africa	3.0
Bulgaria	3.0
Mexico	2.6
Czech Republic	2.5
The United States	1.8
Hungary	1.4
Japan	0.7

Source of data World Economic Outlook (April 2016), IMF; Turkish Statistical Institute

The climate varies greatly in Turkey. The southeast is drier, and the central Anatolian Plateau is cooler. In general, Turkey has long summers with high temperatures and little rainfall and cold winters when cold fronts bring snow and rain. Orchards, wheat fields and reservoirs have sufficient storage of rainfall, and vineyards and beaches have plenty of sunshine. Climate diversity leads to crop diversity in Turkey. It is one of the world's leading producers of tobacco, pistachios, raisins and a variety of fruits and vegetables.

Agriculture contributes nearly one-fifth of Turkey's GDP and employs half of the labor force, as Fig. 8.55 demonstrates. In general, Turkey is self-sufficient in most food crops. Most arable land is used for growing food crops, especially wheat and barley. Cash crops (cotton and tobacco) are important export commodities. The well-irrigated lowlands of the narrow coastal areas produce hazelnuts, currants and citrus, lemons, melon, etc. Vegetables are also grown for export. Its evergreen pastures are used to raise sheep and a small number of cattle and goats.

(2) The secondary industry

Turkey has a good industrial foundation. Food processing, textile, automobile, mining, steelmaking, cement, mechanical and electrical products, petroleum, construction, wood and paper industries are the major industrial sectors. The manufacturing industry employs about one-tenth of the labor force and its output value accounts for one-fifth of the GDP. Despite low productivity, the textile industry (including yarn, fabrics and carpets) was still a fast-growing industry in the 1970s and 1980s thanks to low cotton and labor costs. Its petrochemical industry grew

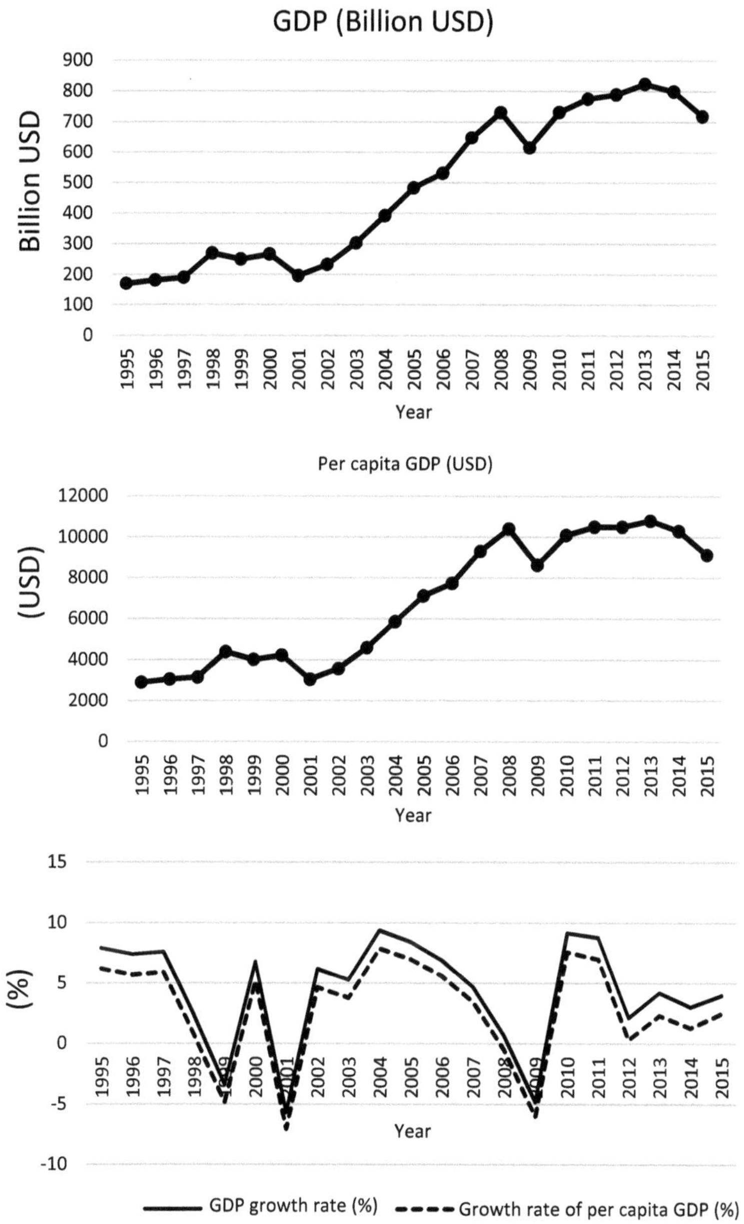

Fig. 8.54 Domestic economy of Turkey. *Source of data* World Bank database

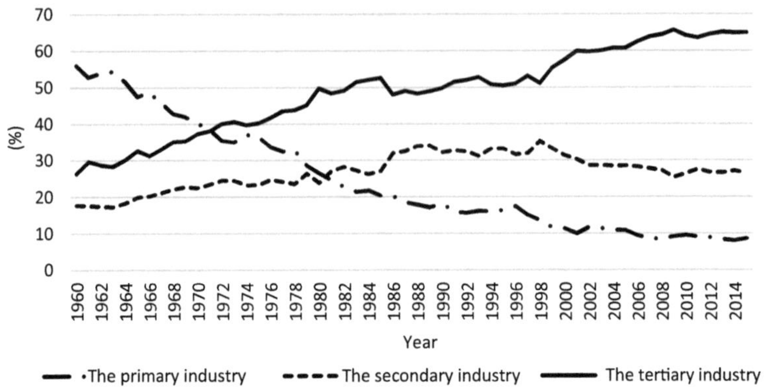

Fig. 8.55 Industrial structure of Turkey. *Source of data* UN database

rapidly in the early 1980s. It has become a major steel producer in the Middle East. In addition, the engineering machinery industry is also expanding fast.

Turkish brands Beko and Vestel are the largest manufacturers of consumer electronics and home appliances in Europe. In January 2005, these two brands together dominated more than half of the European market. Vestel Electronics is the largest TV manufacturer in Europe, with 21% of market share in 2007. The market share of Turkish manufacturers has increased with the signing of a tariff agreement between Turkey and the European Union.

Since the 1960s, the automobile industry has become an important part of the Turkish economy. Most automobile manufacturers are located in the Marmara region. The large number of automobile and parts producers has made Turkey an important link in the global chain of automobile manufacturing. In 2008, Turkey produced 1,147,110 automobiles, surpassing Italy to become Europe's sixth largest automaker, and ranking 15th in the world. In recent years, driven by the government's policies of introducing vehicle production lines and production localization, a large number of foreign car manufacturers have set up factories in Turkey or cooperated technologically with Turkish car-parts makers. The fast-growing automobile industry is gradually replacing the textile industry as the new leading industry in Turkey.

(3) The tertiary industry

In the 2008 financial crisis, the local tourism industry achieved growth in revenue thanks to lower price, better convenience and greater cost performance. In 2009, Turkey received 32 million tourists, generating 21,249 billion USD of tourism revenue. In 2010, the number of tourists was 3 million larger than in 2009. In 2011, the tourism revenue reached 23 billion USD, an increase of 10.6% compared to the previous year. The profitable tourism has played an important role in fixing the fiscal deficit and trimming the trade deficit. As an important tourist country, Turkey also plans to develop inland tourism, eco-tourism and fitness tourism in addition to the existing beach tourism.

2. Urban structure

Turkey, as a highly urbanized country, has witnessed steady growth of urbanization rate in the past two decades, as Fig. 8.56 shows.

Table 8.24 lists the major Turkish cities.

Istanbul, the largest city in the country, is the industrial, transport, trade, financial and cultural center. It is strategically important as a gateway to the Black Sea.

Ankara, the capital, is the second largest city and the political center of the country. It is divided into the new city and the old city. The old city, centered around an ancient castle on a small hill, retains the features of the Ottoman era. The new city surrounds the old city on three sides—the west, the east and the south. The Grand National Assembly and major government departments are located in the south.

Izmir is the third largest city in Turkey. Located by the Aegean Sea at the western end of the Anatolian Plateau, it is one of the important industrial, commercial, foreign trade and shipping centers. Meanwhile, it is a famous historic and cultural city, a

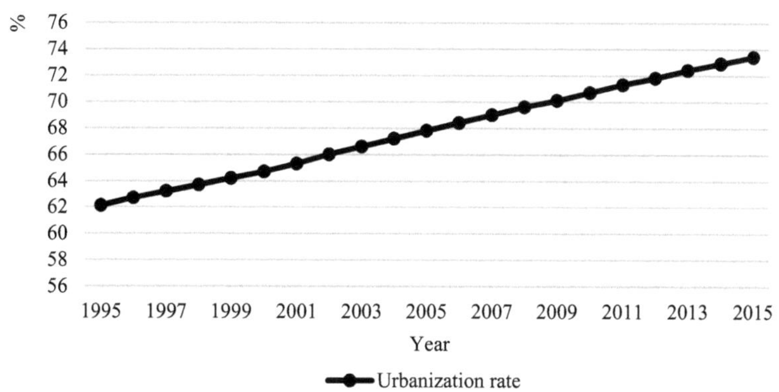

Fig. 8.56 Urbanization rate of Turkey. *Source of data* World Bank database

Table 8.24 Top 5 cities of Turkey

City	Population in 2016	City profile
Istanbul	13,850,000	The largest city and port; the economic center; a transport hub connecting Europe and Asia
Ankara	4,970,000	The capital, and the political, economic, cultural, transportation and trade center
Izmir	4,010,000	A tourist resort; a military base; an industrial, commercial, trade and shipping center
Bursa	2,690,000	A tourist resort; an industrial center; a base of the automobile industry
Adana	2,130,000	A comprehensive industrial center and an important industrial and commercial city on the routes from Turkey to Syria, Iran and Iraq

Source of data World Population Review

tourist resort and a military base. Since ancient times, the city has been the center of agriculture along the Aegean Sea. This clean and tidy city is home to both high-rise buildings and historical sites.

Located on the northern foot of Uludag Mountain in northwestern Turkey, Bursa is the capital of Bursa Province. During the rule of the Byzantine Empire, it was a military place. In the 14th century, it was the center of religion and culture. In the 17th century, it was one of the three capitals of the Ottoman Empire, and the second largest city after Istanbul. There are many Islamic historical sites in the city.

Adana is an important comprehensive industrial center with industries such as agricultural machinery, cotton textiles, man-made fibers, tobacco, olive oil, leather, cement and timber. The population is about 770,000. Adana is easily accessible—ships can reach the city directly from the estuary and it is connected with Mersin, a port by the Mediterranean Sea, Istanbul and Ankara through railways. As the trade hub of agricultural products on the Adana Plain, it is an important trade center with Arab countries. In addition, it is also an industrial and commercial base along the railways to Syria, Iran and Iraq.

3. Consumption and spending

The Turkish market is expanding day by day, with strong consumption capacity and spending tendencies. Turkey is the 16th largest (based on purchasing power parity) economy in the world and ranks 65th in terms of GDP per capita. See Fig. 8.57 for more information. Turkey is a founding member of the Organisation for Economic Co-operation and Development, and a member of the G20 and the European Union Customs Union.

The World Bank classifies Turkey as an upper-middle-income country. The CIA classifies it as a developed country. But economists and political scientists often identify it as a newly industrialized country. Merrill Lynch and *The Economist* magazine consider it as an emerging market.

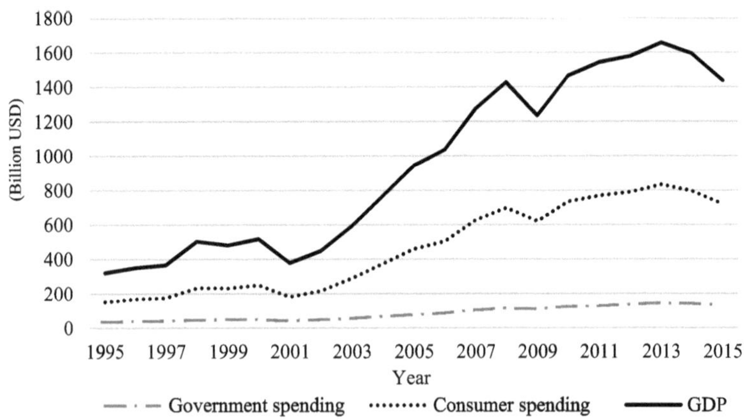

Fig. 8.57 Government spending and consumer spending in Turkey. *Source of data* World Bank database

The Turkish government prioritizes and invests heavily in the development of the energy and transportation industries. The Turkish President stated in 2015 that Turkey's energy projects would need about 120 billion USD in additional investment by 2023. The government's investment in the transportation system is focused on land transportation. Currently, 95% of passengers and 90% of goods are transported by road. At the same time, the government is also promoting railway construction and plans to connect coastal ports with some important provinces through railways. In terms of air transport, Turkish Airlines is one of the fastest growing airlines in Europe and was rated the best European airline in 2011–2014. As to water transportation, Turkey, surrounded by sea on three sides, has a competitive shipping industry.

4. Population and labor force

99% of Turkish residents believe in Islam, and most of them are Sunnis. 1% of the population is followers of Armenian Orthodox Church, Greek Orthodox Church, Judaism, Catholicism and other religions. Turkey enjoys sufficient labor supply. As Fig. 8.58 shows, about half of Turkey's population is younger than 30.7, and the quality of labor is also good.

(II) Foreign trade and investment

1. Foreign trade

In general, Turkey's foreign is relatively balanced. It mainly exports electricity, clothing, food, textiles, metal products and transportation equipment, while its imports are concentrated in areas of electricity, machinery, petroleum, chemicals, semi-finished products, fuel and transportation equipment. Of all export and import commodities, 50% are agricultural products and another 50% are industrial products. Germany, Italy and the United States are the main export destinations of Turkey. In addition, it imports a large number of machines and equipment from Germany.

According to statistics from the Turkish Ministry of Commerce (Table 8.25), the foreign trade volume continued to decrease in the first nine months of 2015, and

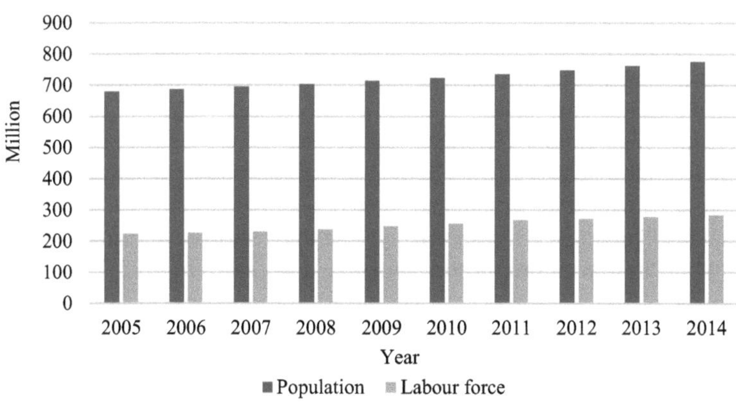

Fig. 8.58 Population of Turkey. *Source of data* World Bank database

Table 8.25 Monthly foreign trade statistics of Turkey (January–September 2015) (Unit: Million USD)

Time	Total	YOY (%)	Export	YOY (%)	Import	YOY (%)	Difference between import and export	YOY (%)
January–September, 2015	263,303	−11.6	107,232	−9.3	156,071	−13.1	−48,839	−20.2
In which: January	28,778	−9.1	12,302	−0.7	16,476	−14.4	−4174	−39.2
February	29,103	−7.1	12,216	−6.5	16,886	−7.6	−4670	−10.3
March	31,097	−10.2	12,476	−15.1	18,621	−6.5	−6145	17.4
April	31,863	−6.4	13,403	0.3	18,460	−10.7	−5058	−30.7
May	28,943	−16.2	11,080	−19.0	17,862	−14.4	−6782	−5.6
June	30,228	−10.2	11,974	−7.0	18,254	−12.2	−6281	−20.7
July	29,230	−11.9	11,099	−16.6	18,131	−8.7	−7032	7.3
August	27,048	−12.3	11,048	−3.0	16,001	−17.7	−4953	−38.5
September	27,013	−20.5	11,634	−14.0	15,379	−24.8	−3745	−45.9

Source of data Ministry of Commerce, Turkey

the value of imports and exports of commodities totaled 263.30 billion USD, 11.6 percentage points down over the same period of the previous year. Exports were 107.23 billion USD, down 9.3%; imports were 156.07 billion USD, down 13.1%; trade deficit was 48.84 billion USD, down 20.2%. The total value of foreign trade reached thc highest in March and April.

From January to September 2015, the top four destinations of Turkey's exports were Germany, Britain, Iraq and Italy, absorbing 9.1%, 7.4%, 6.0%, and 4.6% of the total, respectively. The exports to Britain increased by 6.9%, while the exports to Germany, Iraq and Italy fell by 14.7%, 19.7% and 8.2%, respectively. The exports to the four countries accounted for 27.1% of the total. As to imports, as shown in Table 8.26, the top four import sources of Turkey are China (11.8%), Russia (10.1%), Germany (10.1%) and the United States (5.5%). The imports from China were stable compared to previous years, while imports from Russia, Germany and the United States fell by 18.4%, 4.3% and 11.0%, respectively. Turkey reported trade deficits with China, Russia, Germany, South Korea and the United States, accounting for 34.0%, 26.8%, 12.3%, 10.1% and 7.9% of the total, respectively; it enjoyed trade surpluses with Iraq, Britain and Switzerland at 6.21 billion USD, 3.82 billion USD and 2.91 billion USD, respectively. The trade surplus with Iraq decreased by 20.2%, while those with Britain and Switzerland increased by 26.2% and 16420.1%, respectively.

Turkey's main export commodities are textiles and raw materials, mechanical and electrical products and transportation equipment. In the first nine months of 2015, the export volumes of these three categories of commodities were 19.53 billion USD (18.2% of the total exports), 15.10 billion USD (14.1%) and 13.95 billion USD

Table 8.26 Turkey's imports from its major trading partners (January–September 2015) (Unit: Million USD)

Country/region	Value	YOY (%)	Proportion (%)
Total	156,071	−13.1	100.0
China	18,409	−0.3	11.8
Russia	15,776	−18.4	10.1
Germany	15,756	−4.3	10.1
The United States	8618	−11.0	5.5
Italy	7861	−12.8	5.0
France	5914	−1.4	3.8
South Korea	5337	−2.8	3.4
Iran	4792	−36.8	3.1
India	4240	−18.9	2.7
Britain	4136	−6.4	2.7
Spain	4084	−9.9	2.6
Ukraine	2633	−17.8	1.7
Belgium	2373	−17.8	1.5
Japan	2225	−4.4	1.4
Poland	2193	−1.7	1.4

Source of data Ministry of Commerce, Turkey

(13.0%), down by 12.6%, 13.0% and 7.4% over the same period of the previous year. Among the export commodities above, noble metals and related products, up by 56.1% against the downward trend, was the only category that achieved growth. Turkey mainly imports mechanical and electrical products, mineral products as well as base metals and related products. In the first nine months of 2015 alone, imports of these commodities totaled 82.21 billion USD, accounting for 52.7% of the total imports. In general, Turkey's imports were declining due to the shrinking import of mineral products. Transportation equipment, up by 19.8% against the downward trend, was the only category of import commodities that had seen growth.

2. International investment

Turkey, stretching across the two continents of Europe and Asia, enjoys an excellent geographical location. In addition, it has a sound infrastructure system of ports, airports, highways and railways. Therefore, it is an important trading hub of products, services, personnel and technology. Turkey's strategic location has attracted many foreign investors. FDI in Turkey is mainly equity investment. Following equity investment are real-estate investment and then intra-company loans (small in scale), as shown in Table 8.27.

According to the latest statistics released by the Turkish Ministry of Economy, the net inflow of foreign investment in 2014 reached 8.6 billion USD, an increase of 9.8% compared with the previous year; there were more than 2800 newly established foreign-funded enterprises and a total of more than 40,500 foreign-funded

Table 8.27 Annual FDI inflows in Turkey (Unit: Billion USD)

	2011	2012	2013	2014	2015
Total FDI (net)	16,182	13,284	12,384	12,523	16,957
Equity investment (net)	14,145	10,126	9310	8315	11,595
Intra-company loans	24	522	25	−113	1206
Real estate investment (net)	2013	2636	3049	4321	4156

Source of data The Central Bank of the Republic of Turkey

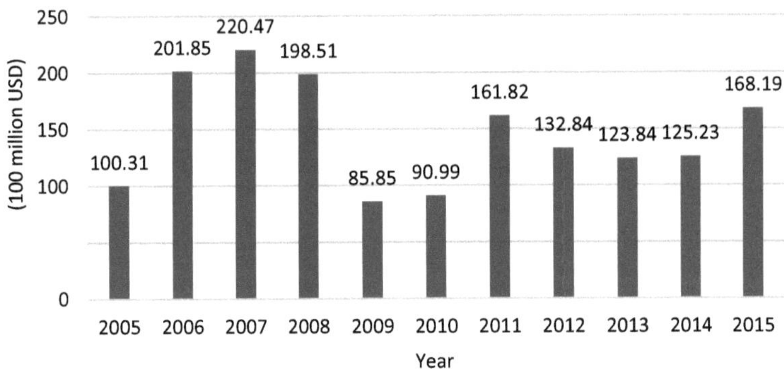

Fig. 8.59 Flows of foreign investment absorbed by Turkey. *Source of data* World Bank database

enterprises. These investments were mainly distributed in industries such as manufacturing, wholesaling and retailing, finance, electricity, natural gas and hydropower; Germany and Britain were the main investors. Turkish officials stated earlier that it was difficult to guarantee the 5% annual growth rate due to the low savings rate, which meant attracting foreign investment was critical to its economic growth. Figure 8.59 shows the flows of foreign investment in Turkey in recent years.

Industrial sectors and services were the largest recipients of FDI in Turkey, followed by finance and insurance and manufacturing. The investment trends of the industrial and service sectors in 2011–2015 were the same, down in the first four years and then up in 2015, as Table 8.28 demonstrates.

Since the establishment of diplomatic relations in 1971, China and Turkey have grown closer, including their economic and trade cooperation. Chinese companies have stepped up their investment in Turkey with increasing enthusiasm. As Fig. 8.60 shows, the breadth and depth of Chinese investment have been improving—it is no longer limited to the mining industry; instead, it has expanded to cover agriculture, manufacturing, transportation, energy, telecommunications, finance and other fields.

Table 8.28 FDI inflows in Turkey (sector-wise statistics) (Unit: Billion USD)

	2011	2012	2013	2014	2015
Agriculture	32	43	47	61	31
Agriculture, forestry and fishery	32	43	47	61	31
Industry	8040	5480	4757	4230	5613
Mining and quarrying	146	188	717	365	202
Manufacturing	3599	4519	2209	2731	4148
Electricity, natural gas, steam and air conditioning supply	4293	773	1795	1131	1261
Water supply, drainage equipment and waste management	2	0	36	3	2
Services	8064	5236	5074	4285	6315
Construction	301	1427	178	232	83
Wholesaling and retailing	707	221	377	1136	589
Transportation and warehousing	221	130	364	594	1524
Hotel and catering	122	16	59	24	23
Information and communications services	36	133	110	214	150
Finance and insurance	5883	2084	3415	1470	3588
Real estate activities	300	173	128	227	169
Professional, scientific and technological activities	103	78	87	94	53
Administration and supporting services	55	234	185	21	42
Public management, national defense and compulsory social security	0	0	0	0	0
Education	68	60	2	0	0
Health care and social work	232	546	106	202	59
Art, entertainment and recreational activities	13	81	5	15	23
Other services	23	53	58	56	12
Activities of the owner family: undifferentiated goods and services/production activities of household goods for self-use	0	0	0	0	0
Activities of foreign organizations and agencies	0	0	0	0	0
Total	16136	10759	9878	8576	11959

Source of data the Central Bank of the Republic of Turkey

8.12 Azerbaijan

I. **Economic development**

(I) Domestic economy

Azerbaijan is one of the three countries in the Caucasus region. It is famous for its rich oil resources and has also attracted much attention due to its geographical strategic importance. Since its independence in 1991, Azerbaijan has achieved rapid economic development by exporting oil and gas. Based on this achievement, Azerbaijan, while

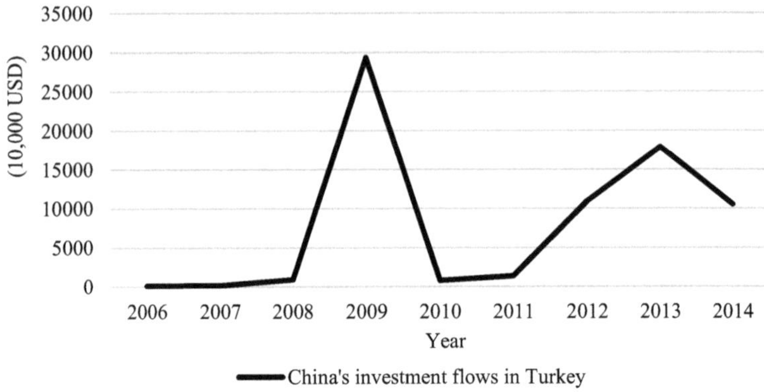

Fig. 8.60 Investment flow from China to Turkey. *Source of data* 2014 Statistical Bulletin of China's Outward Foreign Direct Investment

continuing to implement the oil strategy, advocates the "Great Silk Road" plan, strives to build itself into an energy, transportation and information hub in Eurasia, and thus transforming it into a key link of the "Silk Road". Figure 8.61 shows the basics of Azerbaijan's GDP. It shows since 1996, its GDP and GDP per capita have maintained a positive growth rate. This is because 1996, the first turning point in its economic development since independence saw an influx of investment in its development of the Caspian oil and gas resources. However, the overall economy did not see fast growth until 2004. In 2006, the growth rate reached a maximum of 33%, and this trend lasted till 2015.

1. Industrial structure

As to the changes of its industrial structure, as Fig. 8.62 shows, the secondary industry has developed rapidly since the 1990s, as Azerbaijan has made it its priority. The proportion of the secondary industry has risen from 30% in the early 1990s to more than 60%. This is actually related to the development strategy of "rejuvenating the country with oil" shortly after the country's independence. Currently, it produces about 50 million ton of oil and 30 billion m^3 of natural gas every year. Large amounts of petrodollars have helped it maintain the rapid growth. In this process, the proportion of the tertiary industry has declined but only slightly—as of 2014, it accounted for 35% of the gross GDP. In contrast, the primary industry has seen the most significant decline, falling from 30% in 1990 to less than 10% currently.

Its economic sectors have followed the same trend as the three main industries. As Fig. 8.63 presents, the sectors of C–E are its economic pillars, but it is worth noting that the proportion of manufacturing sector (D) is as low as 10%, and it seems that it is still decreasing. This shows that the secondary industry is dominated by export of primary energy products, not technology-intensive products. At the same time, other sectors have similar performances at around 10%. However, it can be seen from the figure that the construction industry has developed extremely fast, rising from 0 in the 1990s to the current level of 15%.

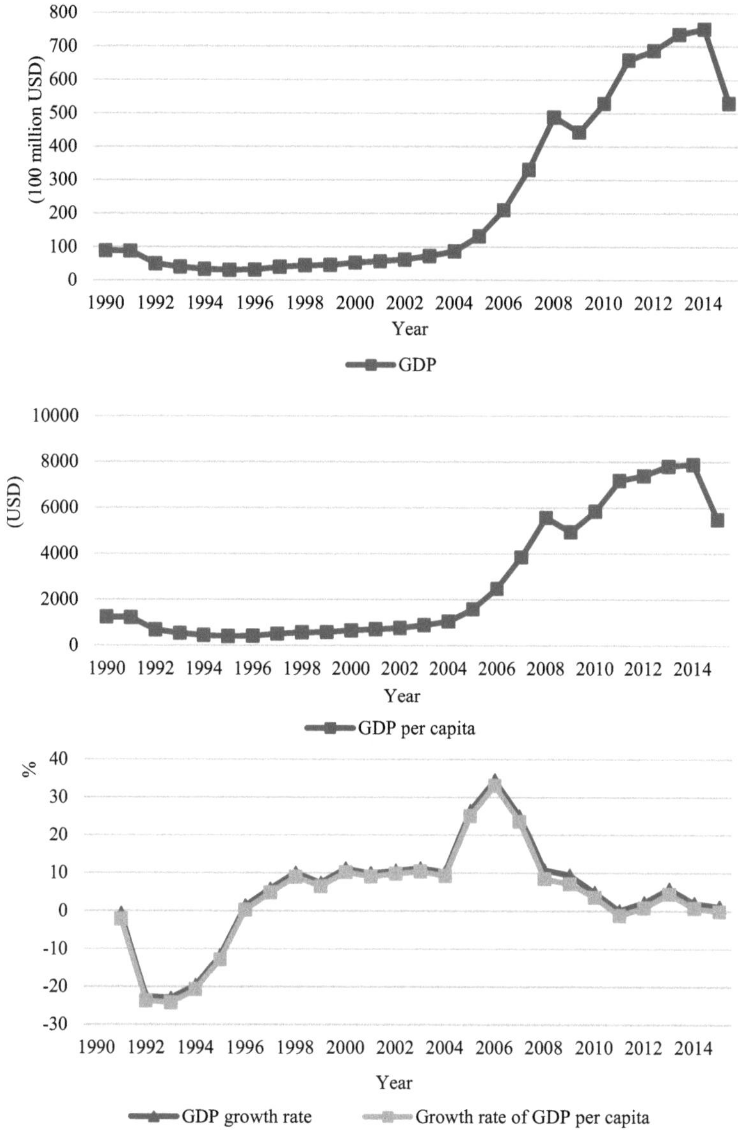

Fig. 8.61 Economic indicators of Azerbaijan. *Source of data* World Bank database

2. Urban structure

Azerbaijan's urbanization rate has been rising despite some fluctuations. Figure 8.64 shows there are two stages of growth: first, from 1969 to 1988, it increased from 49.96% to 54.09%; second, it has grown by 3.43% since 1999. Thanks to the political stability after 2000, the percentage gradually increased to 54.62% in 2015.

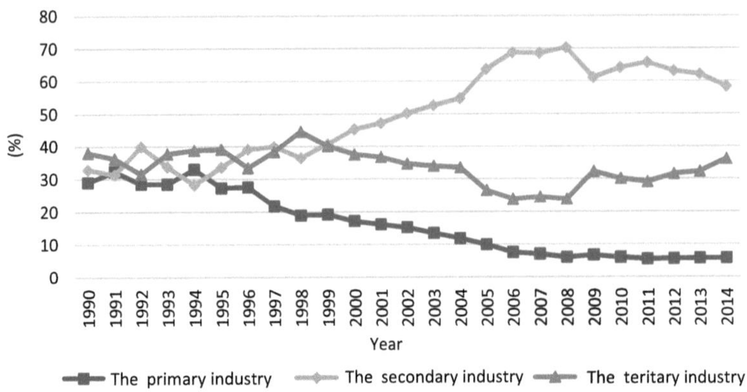

Fig. 8.62 Changes of industrial structure in Azerbaijan

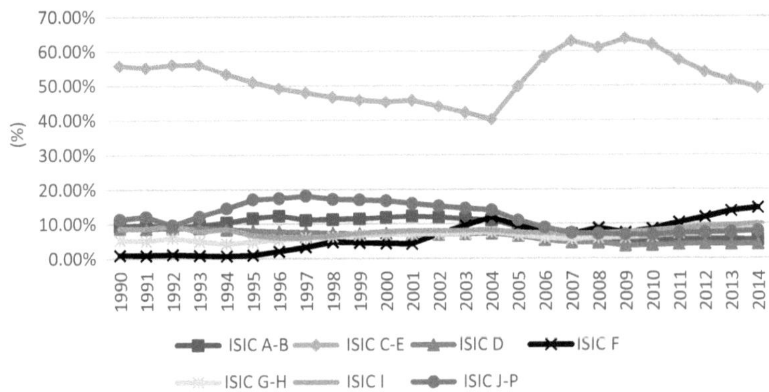

Fig. 8.63 The proportions of different economic sectors within the economy of Azerbaijan

The change in the level of urbanization is closely related to economic and social development. The fluctuations in Azerbaijan's economy have affected its urbanization process. During the period from 1991 to 1996 when GDP suffered negative growth, the rate also declined; and in 1999, it began to rebound after positive growth was resumed.

(II) Foreign trade and investment
1. Foreign trade

Azerbaijan has trade relations with more than 160 countries and regions. In 2014, its top ten trading partners were Italy, Germany, Indonesia, Russia, Israel, Turkey, France, the United States, Britain and Thailand. Italy was the largest export market, and Russia was the largest import source.

Figure 8.65 indicates Azerbaijan's foreign trade has also undergone significant fluctuations. From 2005 to the 2014, the export volume was larger than the import

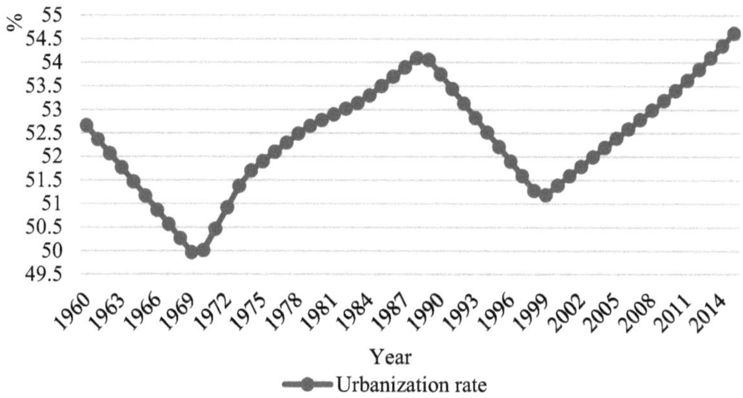

Fig. 8.64 Changes of the urbanization rate of Azerbaijan. *Source of data* World Bank database

volume. Its main export commodities were crude oil and oil products, natural gas, vegetables and fruits, animal and vegetable oils, aluminum and aluminum products and chemical products. The main imported goods were machinery and electronic equipment, ferrous metals, vehicles and their parts, medicines, grain, timber and related products as well as furniture and their parts.

Figure 8.66 demonstrates Azerbaijan's trade competitiveness index from 1990 to 2015. Before 2005, Azerbaijan was less competitive, displaying negative index for 10 years. Since 2005, its competitiveness has gradually improved. After 2010, the index has remained positive despite some decline.

2. International investment

Since 1991, the volume of FDI in Azerbaijan had gradually increased, but this trend was reversed in 2003. In 2007, the volume hit the bottom at 4.749 billion

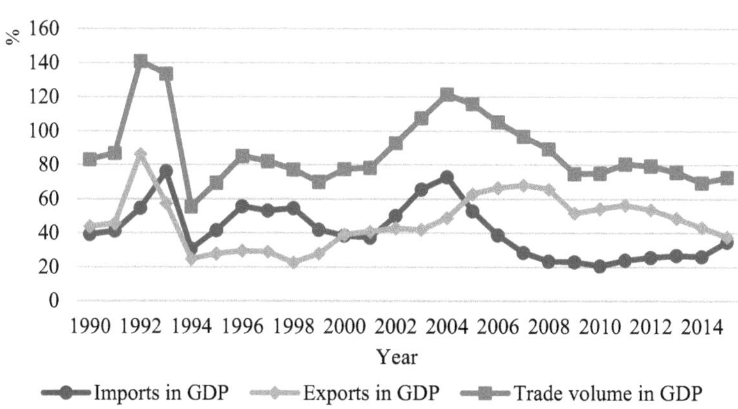

Fig. 8.65 The proportion of foreign trade in Azerbaijan's GDP. *Source of data* World Bank database

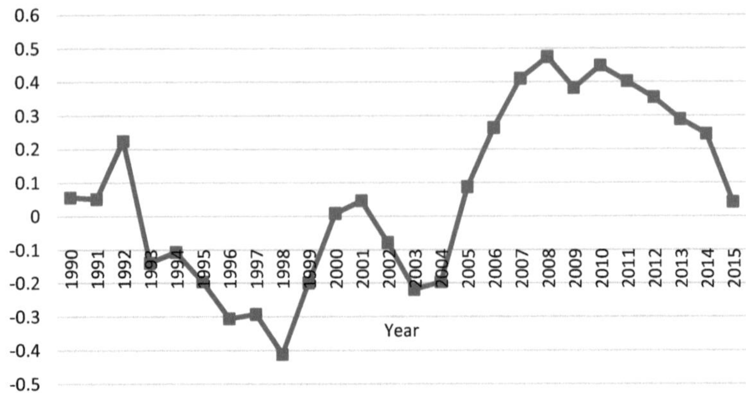

Fig. 8.66 The trade competitiveness index of Azerbaijan. *Source of data* World Bank database

USD, and then, it gradually recovered, as shown in Fig. 8.67. In 2014, the stock of FDI reached 18.18 billion USD. Azerbaijan's appeal as an investment destination mainly comes from its political stability, rich oil and gas resources, fast-growing economy, continuously improving investment environment, growing market demand, its geographical location and good transportation infrastructure that connects Europe and Asia. The foreign capital favors the industry of oil and gas extraction. At present, the government encourages foreign investment in non-oil-and-gas sectors such as agriculture and agricultural product processing, food processing, chemical product processing, building material production and tourism.

China contributes a small proportion of the total foreign investment in Azerbaijan, but the amount has been growing since 2003. In 2010, China's direct investment in Azerbaijan reached 1.238 billion USD, as shown in Fig. 8.68. In recent years, the two

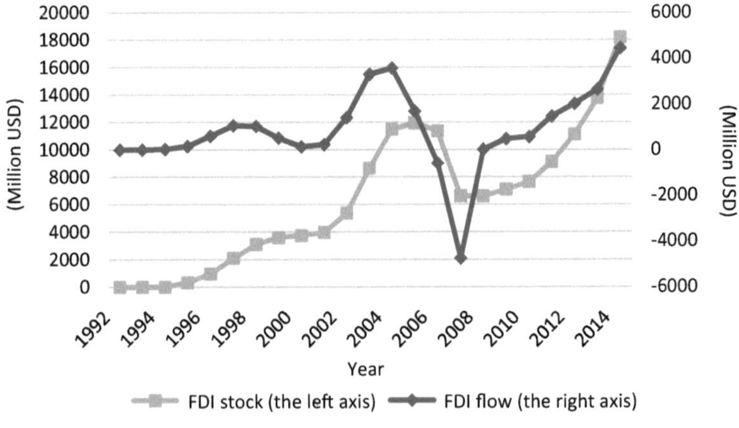

Fig. 8.67 FDI in Azerbaijan. *Source of data* UNTCD

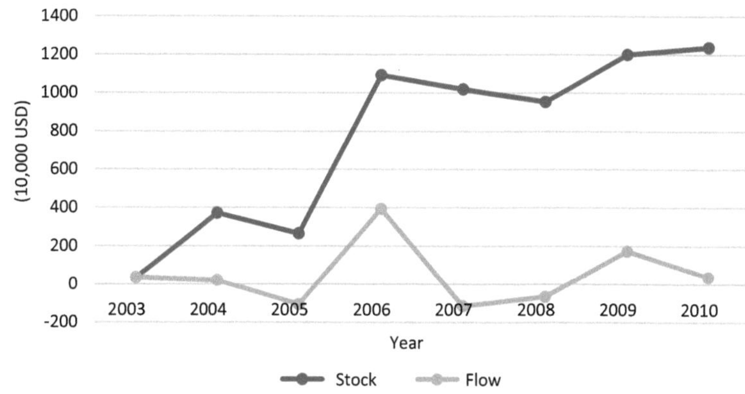

Fig. 8.68 China's investment in Azerbaijan. *Source of data* Database of Economic and Social Development of China

countries have deepened the mutual understanding in the field of economic cooperation. As a result, the level and scale of cooperation have improved significantly (such as the Power Plant Project of CNEEC, the Aluminum Plant Project of Sichuan Machinery IMP. & EXP. Corp.), and the projects in non-oil sectors have multiplied with diverse models and contents. For instance, both Huawei and ZTE have business in Azerbaijan.

8.13 Armenia

I. **Economic development**

(I) Domestic economy

Armenia, located in the hinterland of Eurasia, is a transport hub and important strategic corridor connecting Europe and Asia. It also connects the Caspian Sea and the Black Sea, and Eastern Europe and Central Asia. It enjoys abundant resources, especially oil and gas. But affected by local separatism and territorial disputes, the situation in Armenia is very complicated. Thanks to the help of Russia and international financial institutions such as the International Monetary Fund, the World Bank, the European Bank for Reconstruction and Development, Armenian economy has witnessed a long period of rapid growth. As shown in Fig. 8.69, its gross GDP rose from 1.273 billion USD in 1992 to 11.662 billion USD in 2008. Due to its heavy dependence on Russia, Armenian economy suffered severe downturn after the 2008 US subprime mortgage crisis and the ross GDP dropped by 13.89%, which even caused tension domestically. But it recovered fast thanks to its well-educated labor force. In 2010, the gross GDP began to grow slowly again.

1. Industrial structure

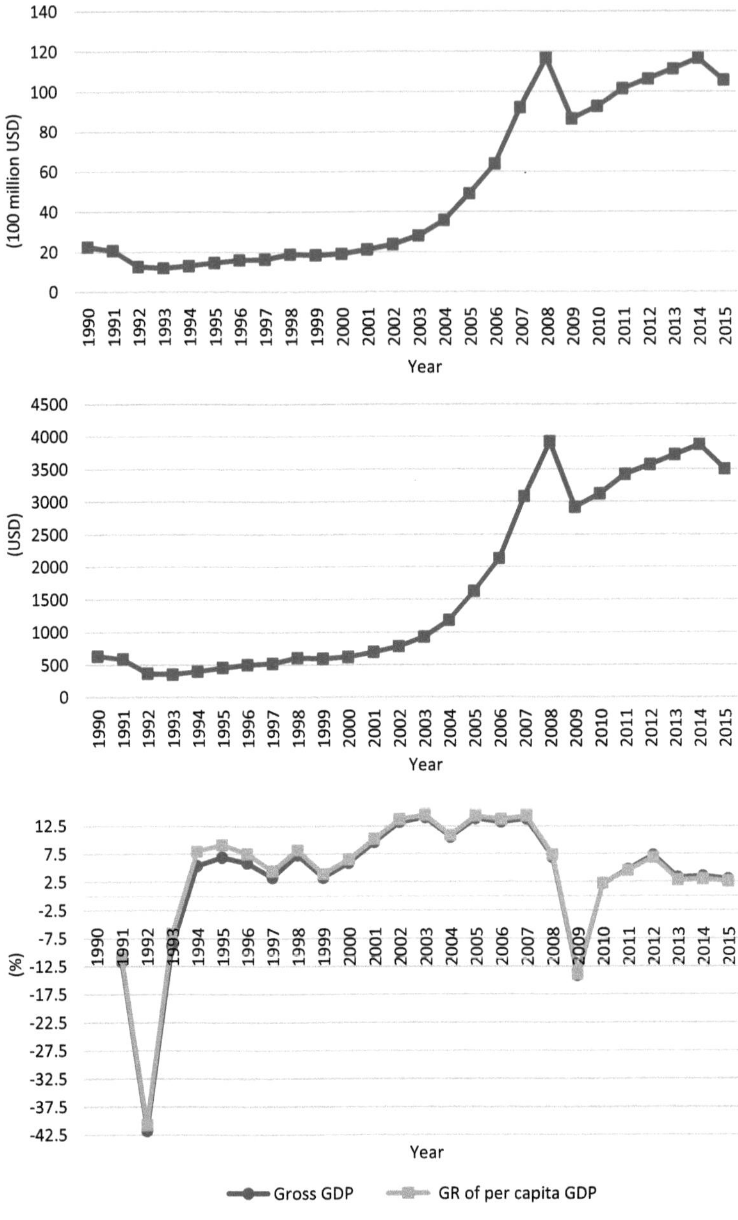

Fig. 8.69 Economic indicators of Armenia. *Source of data* World Bank database

As Fig. 8.70 demonstrates, for nearly 20 years, the proportion of the primary industry had been shrinking, falling from the highest 50% in 1993 to 20% (it stayed at 20% for ten years). The proportion of the secondary industry fluctuated greatly, first rising to about 45% from 1995 to 2005, and then declining for ten years to 30%. The tertiary industry has developed well and maintained an upward trend since 1994, with its share rising from the lowest 20% in 1994 to 50% in 2014.

As to different sectors, Fig. 8.71 shows the manufacturing (D) and mining were the main contributors of industrial output, and construction (F), as the economic pillar, had grown fast since 1990. However, affected by the global economic crisis, the construction sector had fallen by 10% from 2012–2014. At the same time, the sector of hotel and catering, and retail and wholesale (G–H) had seen steady growth, contributing about 13% of GDP in 2014.

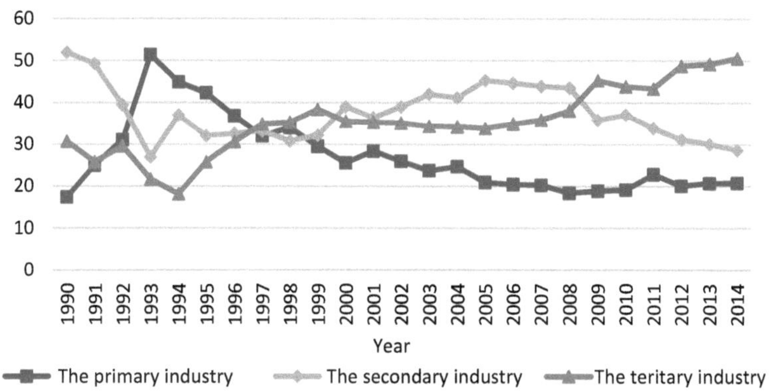

Fig. 8.70 Changes of Armenia's industrial structure. *Source of data* World Bank database

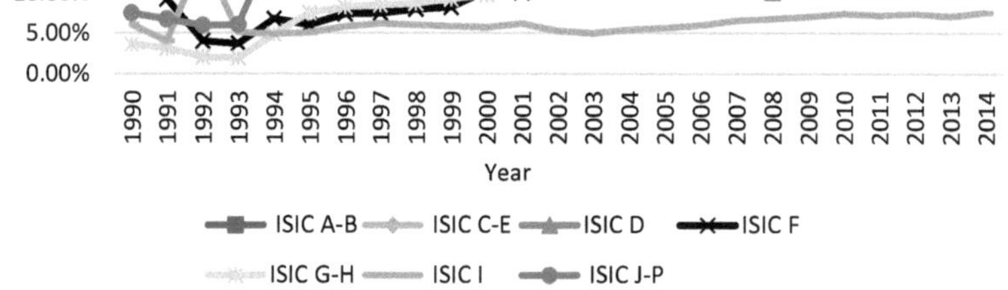

Fig. 8.71 The proportions of different economic sectors within the Armenian economy. *Source of data* World Bank database

2. Urban structure

Armenia has a high level of urbanization, as shown in Fig. 8.72. Since the 1960s, its urbanization rate had increased year by year, reaching 67.71% in 1988. Since then, it began to drop slowly due to the social instability and turbulent economy brought about by the disintegration of the Soviet Union. Armenian society has a high level of education—it has the highest proportion of people receiving higher education (per thousand people) among the former Soviet republics. Its education quality is comparable to that of many developed countries. Taking the literacy rate of people over 15 years old as an example, in the late 1980s and early 1990s, the adult literacy rate in Armenia was as high as 98.75%, while the rate in upper-middle-income countries was only 79.93%; in 2010, the rate in high-income countries was 98.67%, slightly lower than the 99.74% in Armenia in 2011. Before 1991, Armenia had the vast majority of the Soviet Union's information technology industry and a large contingent of professional talents—it was above the world average in terms of technological innovation and extension. Therefore, despite the impact of social unrest, the decline in the urbanization rate was in significant, ranging from 67.71%, the peak, to 62.67% in 2015.

(II) Foreign trade and investment

1. Foreign trade

Armenia has established diplomatic relations with more than 130 countries and regions. Its main trading partners are Russia, China, Germany, Bulgaria, Ukraine, the Netherlands, Belgium, the United States, Britain, Iran and the United Arab Emirates. As Fig. 8.73 shows, the proportion of its imports had remained relatively stable since 1997, while that of exports declined slightly in 2008 due to the impact of the US subprime mortgage crisis, and then slowly recovered. In order to develop and expand trade, Armenia joined the Eurasian Economic Union (EAEU) headed by Russia on January 2, 2015, as the fourth member state. Other member states are Russia, Kazakhstan, Belarus and Kyrgyzstan. Since then, Armenian products have had free access to this single market of more than 170 million people. From

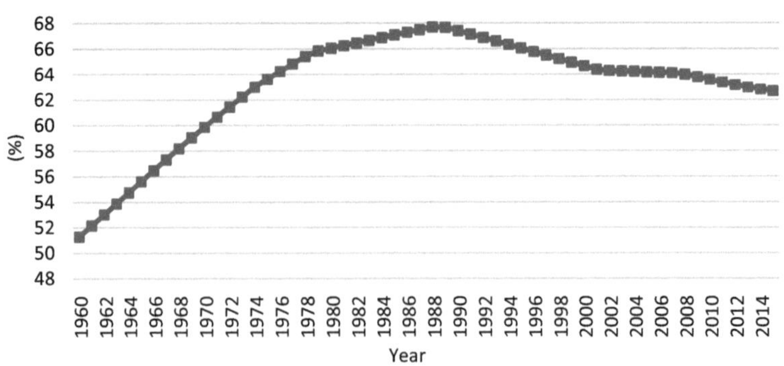

Fig. 8.72 The urbanization rate of Armenia. *Source of data* World Bank database

1990 to 2015, Armenia's import value had always been greater than its export value, producing a trade deficit. However, the proportion of foreign trade in GDP had declined, meaning less dependence on foreign trade. The main export products of Armenia are precious stones and semi-processed products, food, non-noble metals and their products, mineral products, textiles, machinery and equipment, etc.; its main imported products are mineral products, food, chemical products, etc.

Figure 8.74 demonstrates Armenia's trade competitiveness index from 1990 to 2015. Its lasting trade deficit has made the index negative, making it a weak competitor in the trade market. However, in the past two decades, especially after 2009, the index had risen gradually to approach zero, which means improved competitiveness. In 2015, the index was −0.16.

In recent years, China has strengthened its cooperation with Armenia in the economic, trade and political fields, and since 2009 it has become Armenia's second

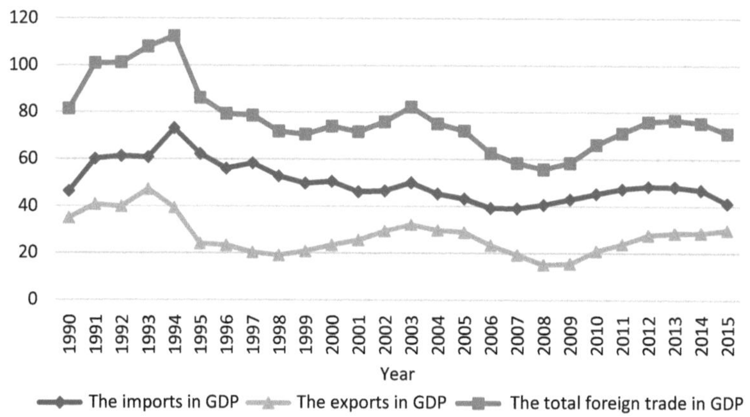

Fig. 8.73 Foreign trade of Armenia. *Source of data* World Bank database

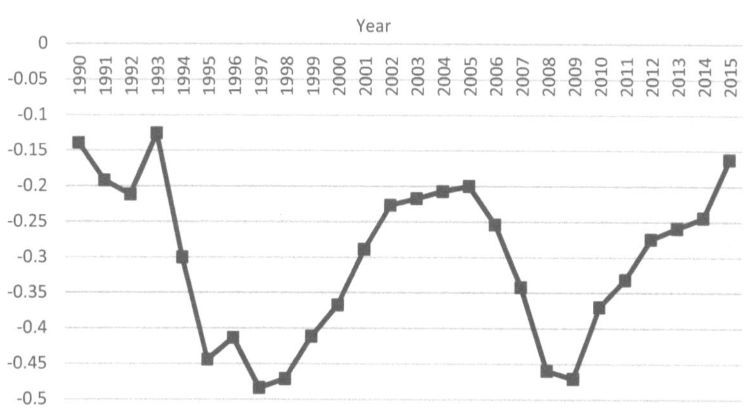

Fig. 8.74 The trade competitiveness of Armenia. *Source of data* World Bank database

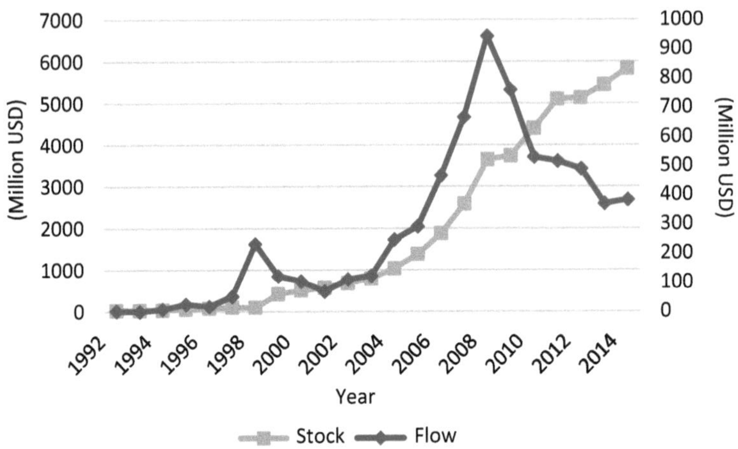

Fig. 8.75 FDI in Armenia. *Source of data* UNCTAD

largest trading partner. According to the China Customs, the bilateral trade volume was 330 million USD in 2015, a year-on-year increase of 13.9%. China's exports amounted to 114 million USD, a year-on-year decrease of 7.5%, and China's imports were 217 million USD, a year-on-year increase of 29.5%. China mainly exported mobile and fixed communications equipment, computers and components, steel, fur products, furniture and spare parts, etc.; Armenia mainly exported copper and copper concentrates, wine products and diamond products.

2. International investment

In order to attract foreign investment, the Armenian government implements preferential policies, including deferred payment of value-added tax on goods imported for investment projects, and a five-year grandfathering protection, that is, in case of law amendment, foreign investors, for five years, are allowed to choose to use the old or the new law. As shown in Fig. 8.75, since 1992, Armenia had been absorbing more and more foreign investment; then, the trend was reversed from 1998 to 2003, but it rebounded after that and the volume of foreign investment reached a maximum of 944 million USD in 2008. Later, affected by the US subprime mortgage crisis, it began to decline again. According to the latest statistics released by the Armenian National Bureau of Statistics, Switzerland became Armenia's largest source of foreign investment in the first three quarters of 2015, followed by Germany and Luxembourg.

The scale of Chinese investment in Armenia is relatively small, as shown in Fig. 8.76. As of the end of 2010, the stock of direct investment was approximately 1.32 million USD. As of 2016, there were five Chinese-funded enterprises in Armenia,[28] namely Huawei, ZTE, Sinohydro, Xi'an Electric Engineering and FMD China. The

[28] *Chinese companies in Armenia*, by the Economic and Commercial Office of the Embassy of the People's Republic of China in Armenia.

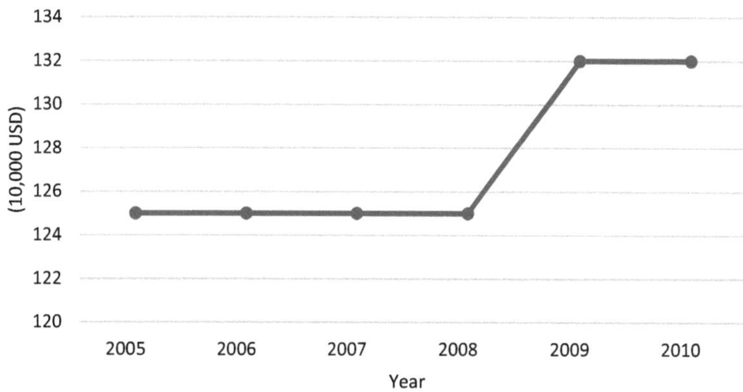

Fig. 8.76 China's investment stock in Armenia. *Source of data* Database of Economic and Social Development of China

projects of Huawei and ZTE were put into operation, and those of the remaining companies were in the preparation stage. According to statistics from the Ministry of Commerce of China, in 2014, one new contract was signed, with a value of 10.11 million USD and a turnover of 8.57 million USD. The projects contracted by China in Armenia are mainly concentrated in the fields of power stations and communications. At present, there are also large state-owned enterprises that are actively tracking projects such as highways, railways and power stations, most of which are loans projects of the Armenian government or international financial institutions such as the World Bank and ADB.

8.14 Georgia

I. **Geographical and historical backgrounds**

Georgia is located in the western and central Transcaucasia, at the border of Europe and Asia. It borders Russia to the north, Azerbaijan and Armenia to the southeast and south, and Turkey to the southwest. Its borderline is 1461 km long, including 723 km with Russia, 164 km with Armenia, 322 km with Azerbaijan and 252 km with Turkey. The land area is 69,700 km^2, 80% of which is mountainous area, piedmont or hilly area. 50% of the country's land area is over 1000 m above sea level. Georgia is rich in natural resources such as forests, minerals and water. The forest coverage rate is 38.5%, and the total timber reserves are 420 million m^3. The main mineral resources are manganese, copper, iron, lead, zinc, etc. The world-famous manganese mine of "Chiatura" has 234 million tons of proven reserves and 160 million tons of workable reserves. Georgia is rich in water resources. Its mineral water is well known in the CIS and among Central and Eastern European countries. With 319 large and small rivers and 15.6 million kilowatts of theoretical potential of hydropower, it is one of the countries with the largest hydropower potential per unit area.

II. **Economic development**

(I) Domestic economy

With the guidance and aids of the International Monetary Fund, the World Bank, and European and American countries, Georgia is committed to attracting foreign investment by advancing economic reforms, reducing tax and tariffs, accelerating the pace of structural adjustment and privatization, and improving infrastructure and investment environment. Georgia's economy has maintained a sound momentum, and its fiscal revenue has been increased by increasing the tax rate of some categories and accelerating privatization. At the same time, negotiations with EU on FTA and the United States on GSP treatment have made progress. In addition, the country is utilizing international aid and loans to speed up infrastructure construction, stimulate economic growth, and build the Eurasian corridor of transport.

Affected by the 2008 Georgian-Russian War and the international financial crisis, its economic environment deteriorated in 2009, leading to shrinking foreign trade and FDI. As the situation improved after 2010, its GDP grew 2.88% in 2015 and reached 14.77 billion USD. During the same period, the per capita GDP was 3,973 USD, making Georgia a lower-mid-income country. See Fig. 8.77.

1. Industrial structure

As Fig. 8.78 presents, the industrial structure of Georgia stayed stable before 1990. The secondary industry and the tertiary industry were of similar proportions, ranging from 35% to 40%; the proportion of the primary industry remained at about 25%. After 1990, the structure went through major changes: the primary industry expanded rapidly first and then shrank fast—it later stabilized at about 10%; the secondary industry also experienced a sharp drop from 40% before 1990 to about 25%; the tertiary industry grew rapidly, with its share within GDP reaching 70% in 2014.

As to different sectors, as shown in Fig. 8.79, agriculture, forestry, animal husbandry and fishery (A–B) experienced large fluctuations after 1991 and then began to decline steadily till their proportion stabilized at around 10%; the hotel and retail business (G–H) was an important contributor of the GDP (around 25%); within the greater industry (C–E), the manufacturing sector (D) was the dominant force—its proportion was similar to that of the greater industry, and their fluctuations were almost the same; the construction sector (F) gained momentum after 1990, with its proportion rising fast from zero to about 10%.

2. Urbanization rate

With more than half of its population living in cities, Georgia is highly urbanized, and the rate has been rising since 2003, as shown in Fig. 8.80. The capital Tbilisi is the political, economic, cultural and educational center. Other major economic centers are Batumi, Kutaisi, Poti and Rustavi.

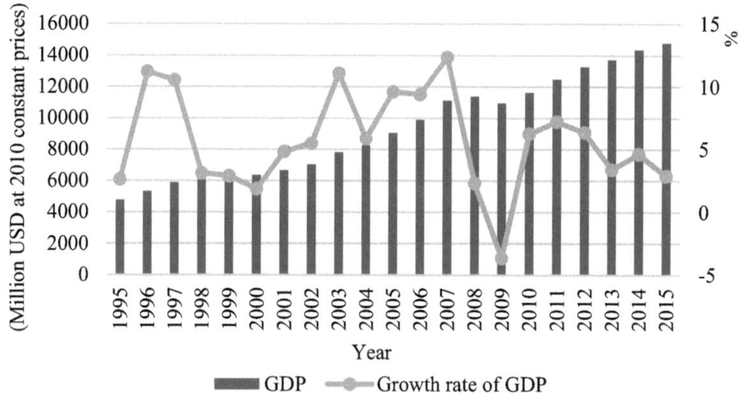

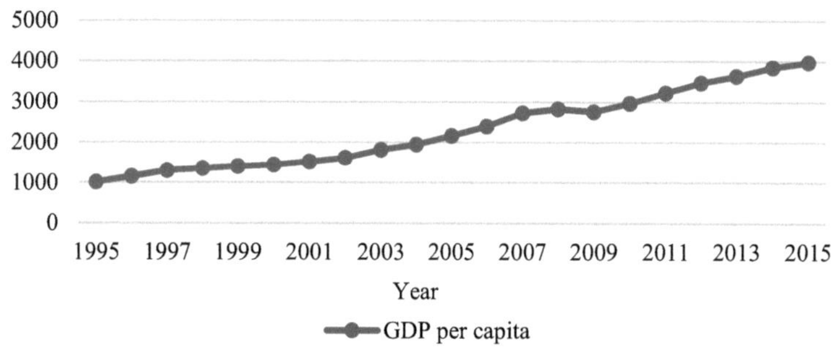

Fig. 8.77 The economic indicators of Georgia. *Source of data* World Bank database

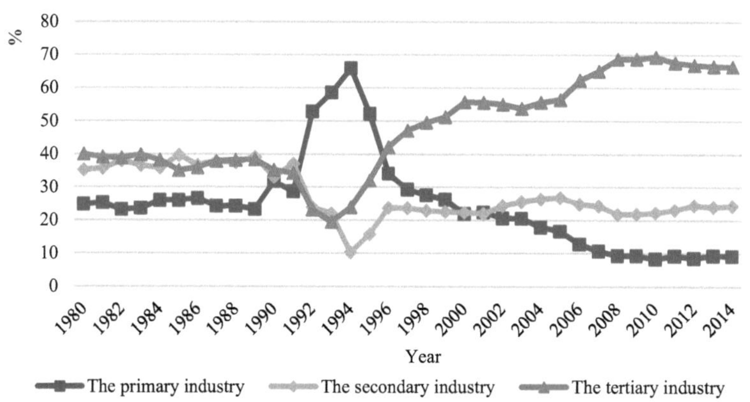

Fig. 8.78 Changes of Georgian industrial structure. *Source of data* World Bank database

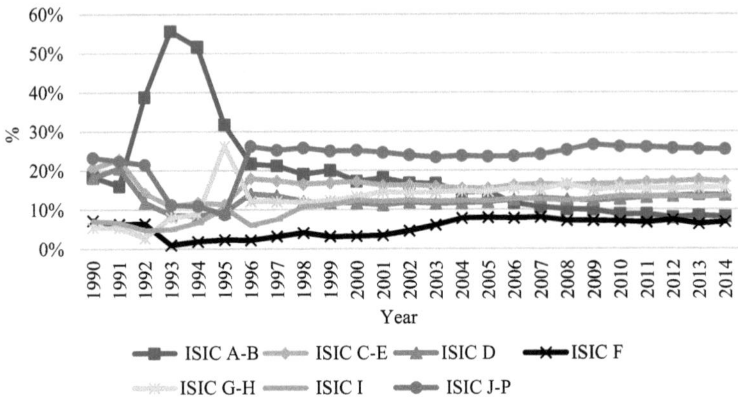

Fig. 8.79 The proportions of different economic sectors of Georgia. *Source of data* World Bank database

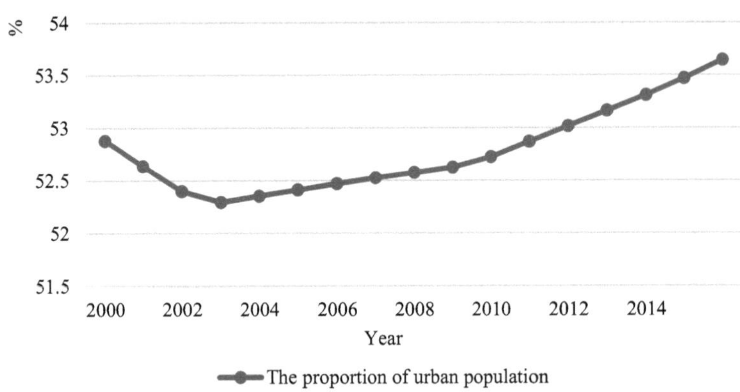

Fig. 8.80 The proportion of urban population within the total Georgian population

(II) Foreign trade and investment
1. Foreign trade

As of 2015, Georgia's foreign trade had been growing, but there was a sharp decline after the financial crisis in 2008. After 2009, both import and export saw increases. In 2014, the value of import of goods and services reached 9.98 billion USD, a record high in 20 years and the value for exports hit 7.08 billion USD. In 2015, both import and export fell slightly and the proportion of import in GDP was higher than that of export. For more information, see Fig. 8.81. The top ten trading partners were Turkey, Azerbaijan, Ukraine, China, Germany, Russia, the United States, Bulgaria, Armenia and Italy.

2. International investment

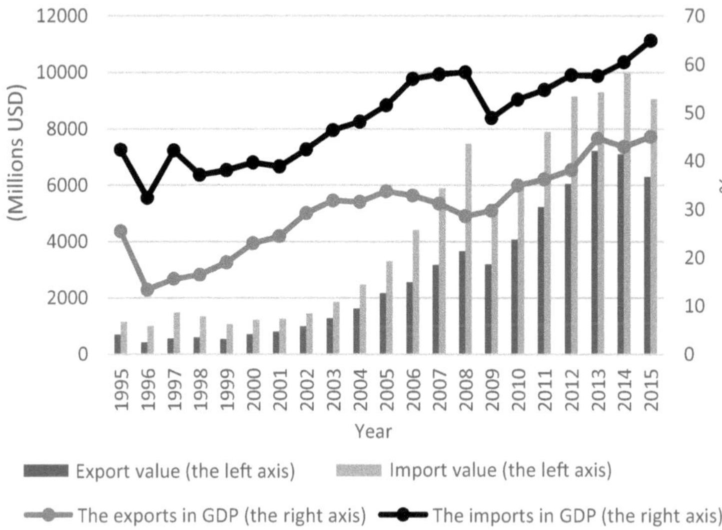

Fig. 8.81 The values of total exports and imports of Georgia and their proportions within GDP

FDI in Georgia is small in scale, but it is growing steadily, as shown in Fig. 8.82. Georgia has been committed to improving the investment environment and thereby increasing its attractiveness to foreign investors. It has been recognized by the World Bank for years as a pioneer in economic reform. Specifically, Georgia enjoys the following competitive edges: it is strategically located between Europe and Asia and has two ports—Poti and Batumi by the Black Sea; it has a relatively stable macroeconomic environment; it is equipped with a competitive trade system; it is a low-tax country; its labor and employment system is advanced; it has simplified the licensing procedures; it adopts an active privatization policy; it has a liberal financial system and the government is determined to crack down on corruption.[29]

According to the National Statistics Office of Georgia, Azerbaijan is its largest source of foreign investment, contributing 550 million USD, or 35% of the total. Following Azerbaijan are Britain and the Netherlands, investing 386 million USD and 155 million USD, respectively. China, with direct investment of 67 million USD, is the sixth largest investor. Transportation and communication are the largest recipient of foreign investment, absorbing 585 million USD, or 37% of the total; finance and public health rank the second and third, receiving 179 million USD (11%) and 140 million USD (9%).

[29] *Georgia's appeal as an investment destination*, by the Economic and Commercial Office of the Embassy of the People's Republic of China in Georgia.

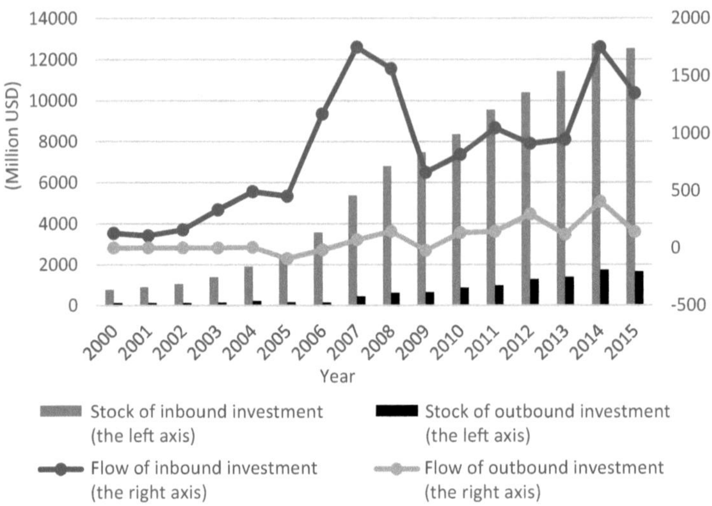

Fig. 8.82 FDI in Georgia

Chapter 9
Central and Eastern Europe

Eastern European countries along the Belt and Road include Russia, Ukraine, Belarus, Moldova, Poland, Czech Republic, Slovakia, Hungary, Romania and Bulgaria. Except for Russia that runs across the Eurasia, most Eastern European countries share the same terrain—they are located on East European Plain.

Most Eastern European countries used to have close ties with the Soviet Union. Since the Second World War, most countries in this region were annexed by the Soviet Union or become its vassals. They adopted the socialist path and planned economy and were governed by the Communist Party. Most Eastern European countries, such as Russia, Belarus, Ukraine, Poland, Czech Republic and Slovakia, have a population dominated by Slavs. Diverse religions are practiced in the region, including Catholicism, Orthodox and Islam, but most people believe in Orthodox which is the mainstream in Bulgaria, Russia and Belarus.

Compared with Western and Northern Europe which enjoys long sailing routes, Eastern Europe has been ranking relatively low in Europe in terms of economic development. Its coastline is limited and not suitable for sailing. After the fall of communism, countries in the west of Eastern Europe, especially Poland, Hungary and the Czech Republic, completed the transition from a planned economy to a market economy and quickly began to rebound. For example, Hungary completed the transformation of its economic system and established the market economy in 1997. In 1998, the land privatization was completed. Although Hungary's GDP fell by 6.5% in 2009 due to the financial crisis, it quickly got out of the trouble thanks to proper measures taken by the government. In 2015, its GDP grew by 2.94%, making it one of the fast-recovering EU members. Countries in the east of Eastern Europe, on the contrast, are characterized by slow economic growth. These countries, represented by Belarus, Ukraine and Yugoslavia, have been constantly running into difficulties in terms of economic development ever since the late 1980s.

Thanks to the temperate continental climate that brings mild climate and abundant rain, Eastern European countries often have rich agricultural and mineral resources. Taking the Czech Republic as an example, as of 2013, it has 42,200 km^2 of agricultural

H. Zhang et al., *Comparative Studies on Regional and National Economic Development*, Global Economic Synergy of Belt and Road Initiative,
https://doi.org/10.1007/978-981-16-2105-5_9

land, accounting for 54.62% of its territory. The main products exported are barley, pork, dairy products, hops, etc.; the vast land area of Eastern European countries is granted with abundant energy and mineral resources which are also top export products. Take Russia as an example. In 2014, China invested 634 million USD in Russia, focusing on sectors such as mineral resources, energy, construction, home appliances, communications and services. Eastern European countries mainly import crude oil, refined oil, iron ore and refined iron ore, coal, wood, etc.

The level of urbanization in Eastern European countries is generally high, but the growth is weak and the distribution uneven. Take Ukraine as an example. In 2001, its urban residents took up 67.2% of the total population, but this percentage varied greatly between the western and the eastern side of the Dnieper River—the eastern side is the industrial base, while the west is dominated by agriculture and services; the east, producing 2/3 of the national economy, is the economic pillar of the country. Another example is Slovakia. As early as the early 1990s, its urbanization rate exceeded 50%. However, in the past 20 years, the rate has not improved but declined slightly. Its capital, Bratislava, is home to more than half of the population. In Romania, 56.4% of the population lived in cities (Bucharest alone accommodated 1/5 of the total population) in 2015, and 43.6% lived in the rural area.

Since most Eastern European countries were Soviet republics or vassals of the Soviet Union, they enjoy good relations with China, leading to close economic and trade interactions. Take Hungary as an example. Aiming at becoming the bridge for Asia-Europe trade, it regards China, Russia and India as its economic and diplomatic priorities. Another example is Belarus. China, one of the first countries to recognize Belarus' independence, is its third largest trading partner and the largest trading partner in Asia.

9.1 The Czech Republic

I. Geographical and historical backgrounds

The Czechoslovakia Republic was established on October 28, 1918, and was renamed the Czech and Slovak Federal Republic in 1991. It was formerly the Great Moravian Empire established after the Slavs moved west to the Slovak region. On the last day of 1992, the Republic was disintegrated. The day after the disintegration (January 1, 1993), Czech and Slovak Federal Republic split into two independent sovereign states—the Czech Republic and Slovakia. The Czech Republic is located in the northern temperate zone of Central Europe. It enjoys a typical temperate continental climate. It consists of 14 states. The capital is Prague. It borders Austria, Poland and Germany. With a humid climate, it has an average annual rainfall of about 600 mm. Czech is the official language, and Roman Catholicism is the mainstream religion. More than 90% of the population are Czech, and there are a small number of Germans, Slovaks, Romanies and Polish.

The Czech Republic has abundant mineral resources. The reserves of hard coal, lignite and uranium are rich. The lignite reserves rank the third in the world, and the hard coal reserves the fifth in Europe. But it has to import iron ore, natural gas and oil. Approximately 34% of the country is covered by forest. There are several hydropower stations on the famous Vltava River.

II. **Economic development**

(I) Domestic economy

In 2006, the World Bank officially identified the Czech Republic as a developed country. The country carried out three economic reforms in 1958, 1965 and 1976, the first two of which ended in failure. At the end of the 1960s, the failure of the second economic reform coupled with the turmoil in the international market sent the Czech economy downward. In 1976, another economic reform was launched. At present, the country has entered the late stage of structural transformation. Since the twenty-first century, except for the financial crisis in 2009, its economy has witnessed steady growth. Czech GDP in 2014 was 212.1 billion USD (at 2010 constant USD), an increase of 1.98% over the previous year. GDP in 2015 was 221.1 billion USD (at 2010 constant USD), an increase of 4.2% year-on-year, as shown in Figs. 9.1, 9.2 and 9.3. As of the end of May 2016, inflation was 0.4% and unemployment was 4.9%.

1. Industrial structure

(1) The primary industry

The Czech Republic has a typical temperate continental climate, with a mild weather and abundant rainfall throughout the year. In the 1990s, it carried out land ownership reform, which effectively improved land utilization. After the twenty-first century, it greatly improved agricultural production efficiency by modernizing and transforming agricultural enterprises and modernizing agricultural production. As of 2013, the Czech agricultural land area was 42,200 km^2, accounting for 54.62% of the total territory. In 2015, the Czech rural population was 2.84 million, accounting for 27% of the total population, and agriculture hired 2.38% of the total workforce. The main grain crops are cereals, beans and potatoes. Beet is the main cash crop, and the output in 2013 was 3.744 million tons. For more information, see Tables 9.1 and 9.2. The countries that import and export agricultural products with the Czech Republic are Germany, Slovakia, Poland, Austria, Italy, Hungary, the Netherlands, China, etc. The main agricultural products exported by the Czech Republic are barley, pork, dairy products and hops. It mainly imports rice, vegetables, fruits and nuts, vegetable oils, fish, non-alcoholic beverages, tobacco and coffee.

(2) The secondary industry

During the period of the Austro-Hungarian Empire, the Czech Republic was an important industrial area, and the industry contributed nearly 70% of the local economy. The traditional industrial sectors included machinery manufacturing,

Table 9.1 Output of agriculture and animal husbandry in the Czech Republic 2011–2013

	2011	2012	2013
Beet (10,000 tons)	389.9	386.9	374.4
Potato (10,000 tons)	80.5	66.2	53.6
Beef (10,000 tons)	17.0	17.1	16.4
Pork (10,000 tons)	33.0	29.1	29.9
Poultry (10,000 tons)	21.6	23.9	22.8
Dairy (million liters)	2664	2741	2775
Egg (million)	1272	1150	1233

Table 9.2 Stocks of major domestic animals in the Czech Republic 2011–2013

	2011	2012	2013
Cattle (10,000)	134.4	135.4	135.3
Swine (10,000)	174.9	157.9	158.7
Sheep (10,000)	20.9	22.1	22.1
Horse (10,000)	3.1	3.3	3.4
Poultry (10,000)	2125.0	2069.1	2326.5

Source of data Czech Statistical Yearbook of the Czech Republic 2014

machine tools and power equipment, chemicals, textiles, automobiles, shipbuilding, military products, etc. After the Second World War, it adjusted the industrial structure and focused on heavy industries such as the steelmaking and heavy machinery. After the disintegration in 1993, the Czech Republic mainly produced billets and wires. In the late 1990s, as the Czech economy was sluggish, the steel industry slid downward and a reform was carried out: on the one hand, factories with low production efficiency were shut down, and on the other hand, technological modernization was carried out. In this way, the steel industry achieved stable development. With high profitability and export capacity, the automobile industry is a highlight sector. In 2003, it generated 11.4 billion USD of sales revenue, ranking first in the manufacturing industry. In 2015, the total industrial output took up 38.1% of the national economy. For more information, see Table 9.3.

(3) The tertiary industry

Table 9.3 Output of major industrial products in the Czech Republic 2011–2013

	2011	2012	2013
Electricity (100 million KWh)	876	875	870
Clean coal (10,000 tons)	5790	5397	4898
Steel plate (10,000 tons)	146.1	153.2	154.7

Source of data Statistical Yearbook of the Czech Republic 2014 and Economic Communique 2014

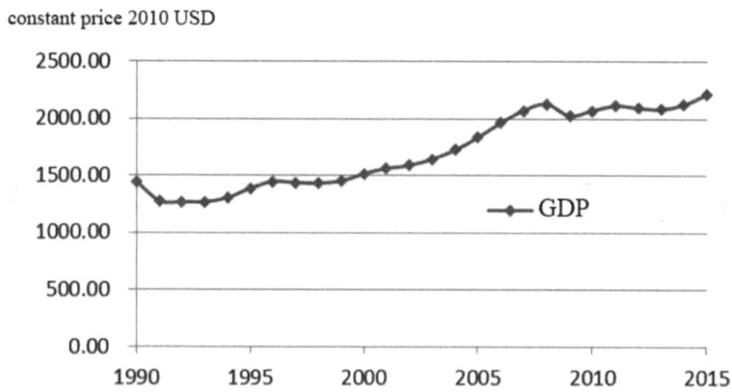

Fig. 9.1 Total GDP of the Czech Republic

The tertiary industry has now become the pillar of the national economy. In 2015, the tertiary industry produced 59.5% of the national economy. Since the twenty-first century, the Czech government has focused its investment on high-tech manufacturing, business support services and research and development centers. It has adopted some preferential policies to increase the added value of the tertiary industry. According to PWC, the service sector of the country enjoys a FDI-attracting index of 56, ranking fourth among the top 20 emerging markets.[1]

In the recent years, tourism has also been an important source of income for the country. In 2013, Czech tourism output reached 12 billion USD. In 2014, the number of inbound tourists was 10.617 million. More than 110,000 people were engaged in the tourism industry, accounting for 1% of the total population. Its tourists mainly come from European countries such as Germany, the Netherlands, Russia, Britain, Denmark, Spain, etc. The main tourist cities are Prague, Cesky Krumlov and Karlovy Vary.

The Czech Republic has basically completed the structural transformation in the third economic reform. The production efficiency and labor productivity of agriculture have significantly improved. Therefore, people have been liberated from agricultural production to join and develop the secondary and tertiary industries. The proportion of agricultural production in the national economy has stayed lower than 10% since the 1990s, and the trend goes on. The proportion of industrial output in the national economy has fluctuated around 40%. The tertiary industry, as the pillar of the economy, contributed more than half of the gross output, and in some years, the percentage even reached 60%, as shown in Fig. 9.4.

2. Population and cities

[1] PWC: The Ranking of the Assessment Index of Manufacturing and Service Sectors in 20 Emerging Markets.

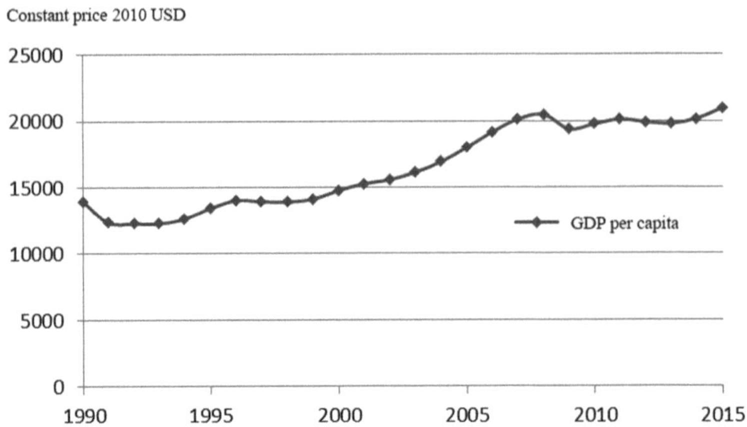

Fig. 9.2 GDP per capita of the Czech Republic

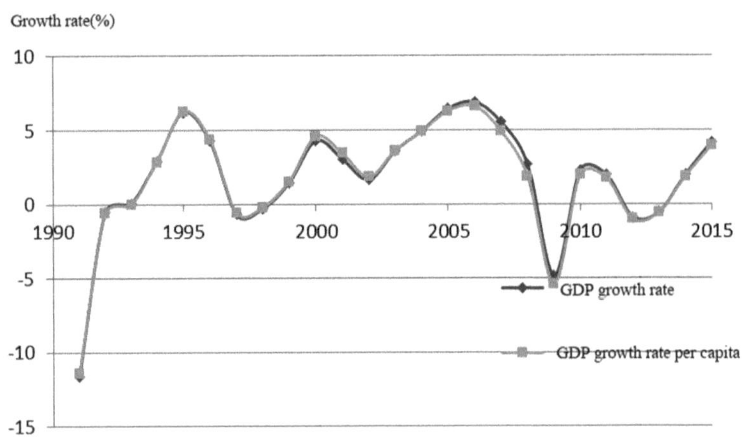

Fig. 9.3 Growth rates of GDP and per capita GDP in the Czech Republic. *Source of data* World Bank database

After the completion of industrialization, its urbanization has slowed down, and the growth rate even turned negative in 1990. This is consistent with the fact of de-urbanization after industrialization. After the financial crisis in 2008, the urbanization began to grow slowly. Figure 9.5 shows the growth rate of urban population.

Table 9.4 lists the major Czech cities.

Prague is the capital and largest city of the Czech Republic. It is the economic, cultural and political center of the country. It was built in the ninth century and is located in the center of Europe and on the Vltava River. The city, covering 496 km^2 and with a population of 1.16 million, is a transportation hub for both the country itself and other European countries. It sits between Berlin and Vienna. Prague is a tourist city known for its diverse architecture and beautiful scenery. It is hailed as

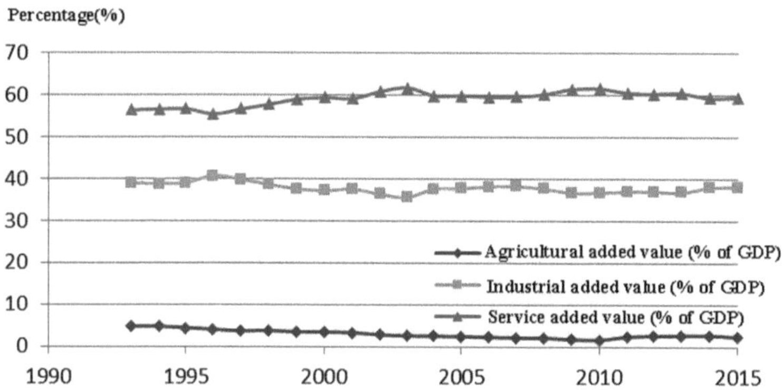

Fig. 9.4 Changes of industrial structure in the Czech Republic

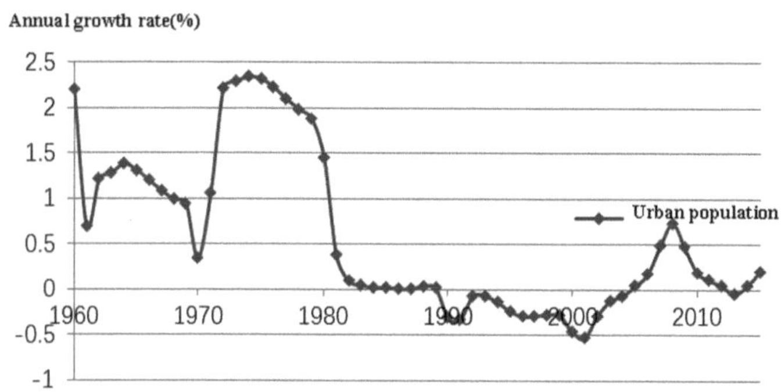

Fig. 9.5 Annual growth rate of urban population in the Czech Republic

Table 9.4 Top 5 cities in the Czech Republic

City	Population in 2016	City profile
Prague	1,165,581	The capital and the largest city
Brno	369,559	A key industrial city and a railway hub
Ostrava	313,088	The center of steelmaking industry
Pilsen	164,180	The center of economy, culture and transportation in the west
Olomouc	101,268	A transportation hub and the center of handicraft industry

Source of data World population review

"one of the most beautiful European cities", "the city of a thousand towers" and "the golden city".

Brno is the second largest city with a population of 369,500. It is the capital of the province of South Moravia. Sitting at the junction of the Svratka River and the Svitava River on the eastern side of the Czech-Moravian Highlands, it is the most important industrial city and transportation hub of the country. The city regularly holds the MSV-International Engineering Fair. It also has great research capacity. Mendel's famous genetic experiment of pea was carried out here.

Ostrava is the third largest city and the capital of Moravian-Silesian region, with an area of 214 km^2 and a population of 313,000. In 2015, it became a candidate city for the European Capital of Culture, and it is also the administrative center of a municipality granted with more legal rights. Historically, the mining and processing of high-quality black coal played an important role in promoting the city's economic development. It is known as the steel capital of the Czech Republic.

Pilsen was first built in the tenth century. The city was set up here in 1292. It is the capital of the Western Czech state and the fourth largest city in the country. Located to the southwest of Prague and at the center of the Pilsen Basin, it is the center of economy, culture and transportation in the Western Czech Republic. Around the fifteenth century, Pilsen was an important base for handicraft and commerce.

Olomouc was once the center of the Great Moravian Empire and later served as the capital till 1641. Located on the banks of the Morava River in the east of the country, it is a transportation hub. At present, it mainly has industries of steelmaking, chemical products, machinery, food processing and so on. The city has a long history, with eleventh-century ancient buildings and a university founded in 1569. In 2000, the Holy Trinity Column of its Upper Square, praised as "one of the finest examples of Central European Baroque Art", was included in the World Heritage List by UNESCO.

3. Consumption

Consumer spending changes as the Czech economy fluctuates. As shown in Fig. 9.6, the Czech economy began to grow faster after the 1990s, and so did the consumer spending. The population has also followed a steady upward trend, as shown in Fig. 9.7. Its total population was 9.6 million in 1960. In the following 54 years, the number rose slightly. In 2014, it reached 10.55 million. The Czech Republic is already a developed industrial country. It is now at the post-industrial stage. Its labor force is of high quality and takes up around 50% of the total population. The proportion of labor force engaged in agriculture is smaller than 10%. The number of people working in industry is gradually decreasing, while more and more people are working in the service sector.

(II) Foreign trade and investment

1. Foreign trade

According to the Eurostat, the foreign trade of the Czech Republic totaled 298.6 billion USD in 2015, dropping 9.3% over the previous year. Imports stood at 140.4 billion USD, down by 8.9%, and exports declined by 9.6% to 158.1 billion USD. Its main trading partners in 2015 were Germany, Slovakia, France, Austria, the Netherlands, Italy, Belarus, the United States, Switzerland and Sweden. Germany is the largest recipient of Czech exports, with a trade value of 51.076 billion USD.

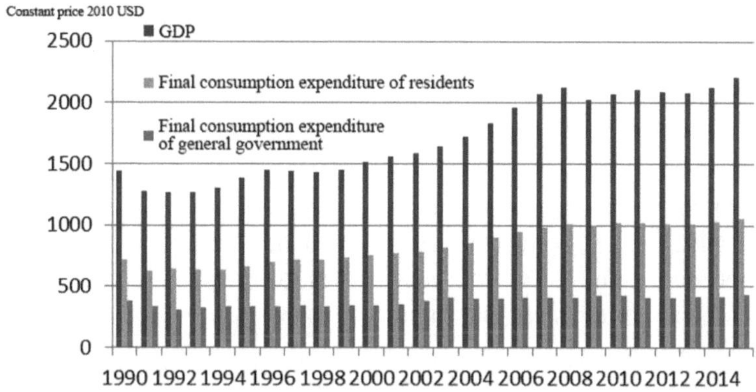

Fig. 9.6 GDP, consumer spending and general government spending of the Czech Republic

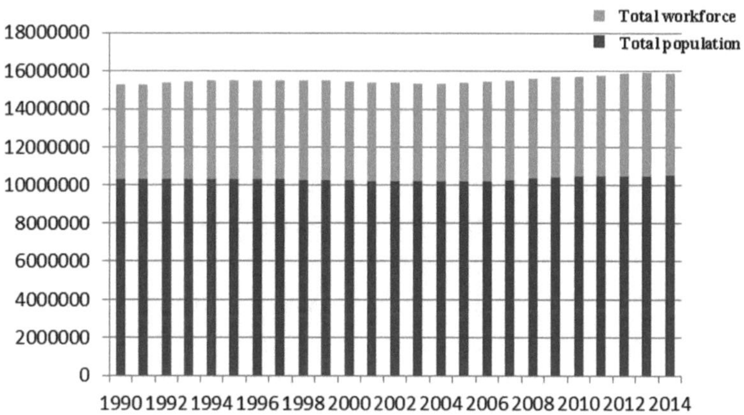

Fig. 9.7 Population and labor force of the Czech Republic

Following Germany was Slovakia at 14.113 billion USD. The top five classifications of export commodities were mechanical and electrical products, transportation equipment, base metals and products, plastics and rubber and furniture, toys and miscellaneous products. Germany was also the largest exporter to the Czech Republic, with a trade value of 41.87 billion USD; Poland ranked second at 12.492 billion USD, followed by China at 11.673 billion USD. The top five classifications of imported goods were mechanical and electrical products, base metals and products, transportation equipment, chemical products and mineral products. For more information, see Tables 9.5, 9.6, 9.7, 9.8 and 9.9; Fig. 9.8.

2. International investment

Table 9.5 Foreign trade of the Czech Republic (Unit: million USD)

Year	Total volume	YOY (%)	Exports	YOY (%)	Imports	YOY (%)	Gap between imports and exports	YOY (%)
2001	69,588	14.6	33,313	15.1	36,275	14.1	−2962	4.4
2002	79,182	13.8	38,480	15.5	40,702	12.2	−2222	−25.0
2003	100,590	27.0	48,752	26.7	51,838	27.4	−3086	38.9
2004	138,859	38.0	68,940	41.4	69,919	34.9	−980	−68.3
2005	154,308	11.1	77,976	13.1	76,332	9.2	1644	−267.8
2006	188,406	22.1	95,053	21.9	93,352	22.3	1701	3.4
2007	241,257	28.1	122,777	29.2	118,481	26.9	4296	152.6
2008	289,427	20.0	147,214	19.9	142,213	20.0	5001	16.4
2009	218,415	−24.5	113,168	-23.1	105,247	−26.0	7921	58.4
2010	259,758	18.9	133,090	17.6	126,668	20.4	6422	−18.9
2011	315,192	21.3	162,989	22.5	152,203	20.2	10,786	68.0
2012	298,919	−5.2	157,292	-3.5	141,627	−6.9	15,664	45.2
2013	306,739	2.6	162,364	3.2	144,375	1.9	17,990	14.8
2014	329,281	7.3	175,033	7.8	154,247	6.8	20,786	15.5
2015	298,613	−9.3	158,155	-9.6	140,457	−8.9	17,698	−14.9

Table 9.6 Value of Czech exports to its main trading partners in 2015 (Unit: million USD)

Country	Value	YOY (%)	Proportion (%)
Total value	158,155	−9.6	100.0
Germany	51,076	−8.3	32.3
Slovakia	14,113	−3.5	8.9
Poland	9173	−11.7	5.8
Britain	8362	−5.7	5.3
France	8014	−9.2	5.1
Austria	6462	−14.2	4.1
Italy	5871	−7.0	3.7
Hungary	4576	−5.9	2.9
The Netherlands	4411	−7.4	2.8
Spain	4130	−0.5	2.6
The United States	3654	−4.8	2.3
Belgium	3599	−15.6	2.3
Russia	3169	−41.8	2.0
Switzerland	2477	−8.7	1.6
Sweden	2365	−7.6	1.5

Table 9.7 Classifications of major Czech export products in 2015 (Unit: million USD)

Classification by customs	HS code	Category of commodity	2015	The same period of the year before	YOY (%)	Proportion (%)
Classification	Chapter	Total value	158,155	175,033	−9.6	100.0
Classification 16	84–85	Mechanical and electrical products	56,421	62,884	−10.3	35.7
Classification 17	86–89	Transportation equipment	32,718	34,744	−5.8	20.7
Classification 15	72–83	Base metals and base metal products	14,436	16,910	−14.6	9.1
Classification 7	39–40	Rubber and plastics	9182	10,529	−12.8	5.8
Classification 20	94–96	Furniture, toy and miscellaneous products	8378	8705	−3.8	5.3
Classification 6	28–38	Chemical products	7023	8636	−18.7	4.4
Classification 5	25–27	Minerals	5002	5061	−1.2	3.2
Classification 4	16–24	Food, beverage and tobacco	3982	4187	−4.9	2.5
Classification 11	50–63	Textiles and raw materials	3879	4321	−10.3	2.5
Classification 18	90–92	Optical instrument, clocks and watches and medical equipment	2898	3062	−5.4	1.8
Classification 13	68–70	Ceramics and glass	2885	3340	−13.6	1.8
Classification 10	47–49	Cellulose pulp; paper	2703	2974	−9.1	1.7
Classification 2	06–14	Plant products	2087	2041	2.3	1.3
Classification 9	44–46	Wood and wooden products	1896	2254	−15.9	1.2
Classification 1	01–05	Live animals and animal products	1597	1953	−18.2	1.0
		Others	3068	3430	−10.5	1.9

Table 9.8 Value of Czech imports from its major trading partners in 2015 (Unit: million USD)

Country	Value	YOY (%)	Proportion (%)
Total value	140,457	−8.9	100.0
Germany	41,870	−8.6	29.8
Poland	12,492	−4.6	8.9
China	11,673	23.6	8.3
Slovakia	9162	−12.0	6.5
The Netherlands	6976	−20.1	5.0
Austria	5793	−9.8	4.1
Italy	5459	−9.3	3.9
France	4224	−13.1	3.0
Hungary	3834	−7.7	2.7
Britain	3765	−3.4	2.7
Russia	3540	−35.8	2.5
Belgium	3299	−11.2	2.4
South Korea	2583	21.9	1.8
Spain	2208	−7.0	1.6
The United States	2102	−16.0	1.5

In 2006, the Czech Republic officially joined the ranks of developed countries and ranked top among Eastern European countries as to attracting foreign investment. Since the twenty-first century, the Czech government has focused its investment on high-tech manufacturing (electronics, electrical engineering, aviation and aerospace, high-end equipment manufacturing, high-tech automobile manufacturing, life sciences, nanotechnology, pharmaceuticals, biotechnology and medical equipment, renewable energy, clean technologies, etc.), business support services (software development centers, expert solution centers, regional headquarters, customer contact centers, high-tech maintenance centers, shared service centers, etc.) and research and development centers (innovation activities, app development, etc.) and adopted preferential policies. To encourage foreign investment, it also promulgated the *Investment Encouragement Law* (which came into effect on May 1, 2000). In 2014, the Czech Republic absorbed 5.91 billion USD of foreign investment, and the stock of foreign investment was 121.53 billion USD. For more information, see Fig. 9.9. Foreign capital mainly flows to the financial intermediary industry, the repair industry, real estate, the automobile industry and the power sector.

The trade relationship between China and the Czech Republic has been improving in the recent years. Of the 16 Eastern European countries, the Czech Republic is China's second largest trading partner (after Poland). According to the Czech Statistical Office, the total value of trade with China was 7.34 trillion kronor (298.6 billion USD at the exchange rate at that time) in 2015, of which Czech exports were worth 3.88 trillion kronor (about 158.1 billion USD) and Czech imports 3.45 trillion kronor (approximately 140.5 billion USD). Compared with the previous year, the

Table 9.9 Classifications of major Czech import products in 2015 (Unit: million USD)

Classification by customs	HS code	Category of commodity	2015	The same period of the year before	YOY (%)	Proportion (%)
Classification	Chapter	Total value	140,457	154,247	−8.9	100.0
Classification 16	84–85	Mechanical and electric products	50,113	52,170	−3.9	35.7
Classification 15	72–83	Base metals and base metal products	15,566	17,412	−10.6	11.1
Classification 17	86–89	Transportation equipment	14,246	15,107	−5.7	10.1
Classification 6	28–38	Chemical products	10,984	12,438	−11.7	7.8
Classification 5	25–27	Minerals	10,221	14,165	−27.8	7.3
Classification 7	39–40	Plastics and rubber	10,194	11,380	−10.4	7.3
Classification 11	50–63	Textiles and raw materials	4728	5281	−10.5	3.4
Classification 20	94–96	Furniture, toy and miscellaneous products	4347	4347	0.0	3.1
Classification 4	16–24	Food, beverage and tobacco	4001	4383	−8.7	2.9
Classification 18	90–92	Optical instrument, clocks and watches and medical equipment	3464	3590	−3.5	2.5
Classification 10	47–49	Cellulose pulp; paper	2628	2944	−10.8	1.9
Classification 2	06–14	Plant products	2446	2396	2.1	1.7
Classification 1	01–05	Live animals and animal products	2035	2393	−15.0	1.5
Classification 13	68–70	Ceramics and glass	1532	1816	−15.6	1.1
Classification 9	44–46	Wood and wooden products	978	1107	−11.6	0.7
		Others	2976	3319	−10.3	2.1

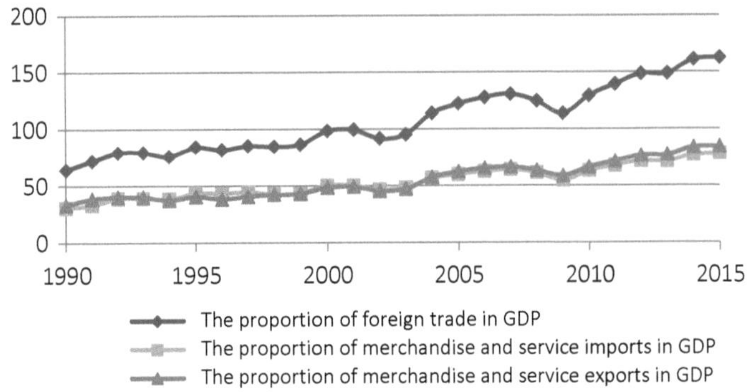

Fig. 9.8 Proportions of exports and imports in Czech economy

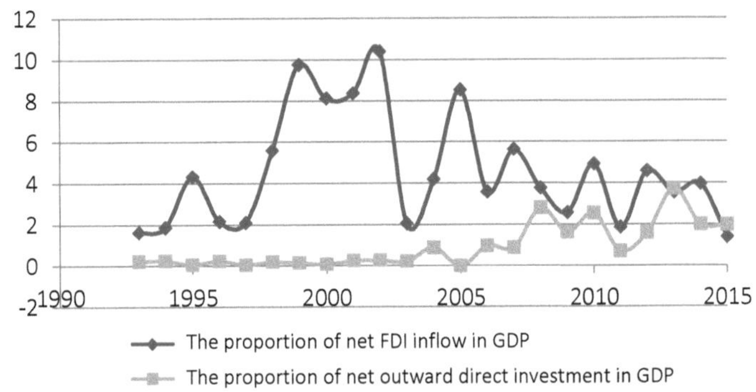

Fig. 9.9 International investment in the Czech Republic

trade volume between the two countries increased by 7.6% (exports up by 7.2% and imports up by 8.0%). The top five classifications of goods imported by the Czech Republic from China were ships and floating structures, leather products, suitcases, animal catgut products and machinery and spare parts; the top five classifications of goods exported by the Czech Republic to China were motors, audiovisual equipment and parts, mechanical appliances and parts, optical, photographic and medical equipment and their parts and plastics.[2] For China, the Czech Republic is a good choice as a production base in Europe thanks to its relatively cheap labor cost: in 2015, the local labor cost was 9.4 euros per hour, while the EU average was 25.6 euros per hour.

[2] Source of data: General Administration of Customs, P.R. China.

9.2 Estonia

I. Geographical and historical backgrounds

The Republic of Estonia is located on the east coast of the Baltic Sea, facing Russia to the east, Latvia to the south, the Gulf of Finland and Finland to the north and the Gulf of Riga to the southwest. It has a marine climate. Its border line is 1445 km long, and the coastline is 3794 km long. Estonia is one of the three Baltic States, with an area of 45,339 km^2. Its capital Tallinn is located in the northwest and borders the Baltic Sea. The port of Tallinn is the largest port in the country. In history, it was once a traffic hub connecting Central and Eastern Europe and Northern and Southern Europe. It was known as "the crossroad of Europe". Estonia's natural resources are scarce. The main minerals are oil shale (about 6 billion tons of proven reserves), peat (about 4 billion tons), phosphate rock (about 4 billion tons), limestone, etc. The forest area is 2.222 million hectares, or 48% of the total land area, and the forest stock volume is 466 million m^3. Local agriculture mainly includes animal husbandry and crop farming. Major domestic animals are cows, beef cattle and pigs. The main crops are wheat, rye, potato, vegetables, corn, flax and forage crops.

Formed in twelfth–thirteenth century, the prehistoric inhabitants of Estonia are Estonians, a branch of the Finland-Ugol people. On August 20, 1991, Estonia broke away from the Soviet Union and declared its independence. Estonia joined the United Nations on September 17, 1991; NATO on March 29, 2004; the European Union on May 1, 2007; the Schengen Area on December 21, 2007; and the Eurozone on January 1, 2011.

The population of Estonia is about 1.313 million. The main ethnic groups are Estonian, Russian, Ukrainian and Belarusian. Its official language is Estonian, and English and Russian are also widely used. The Estonians are mainly Christian Lutheran, Orthodox and Catholic.

II Economic development

(I) Domestic economy

The World Bank lists Estonia as a high-income country. Due to its fast-growing economy, it is often referred to as the "Baltic Tiger". In 1929, Estonia established a stable currency, the Estonian Krona. The currency is issued by the Central Bank, the Bank of Estonia. At that time, Estonian trade mainly targeted the local market and the West, especially Germany and Britain. Only 3% of business activities were carried out with the Soviet Union. Before the Second World War, Estonia was an agricultural country, well known in the Western European market for its butter, milk and cheese. The annexation by the Soviet Union in 1940 and the subsequent occupation by Nazi Germany and then the Soviet Union during the war weakened Estonian economy. After the war, the building of socialism integrated its economy and industry into the centrally planned economic system of the Soviet Union.

In 1999, the Estonian economy suffered the worst crisis since independence in 1991, mainly due to the Russian financial crisis in August 1998. Estonia joined the World Trade Organization in September 1999. The privatization of state-owned enterprises in areas such as energy supply, telecommunications and railways is still ongoing. On May 1, 2004, Estonia joined the European Union. At present, its economy is growing rapidly and its information technology is relatively advanced. Some Finnish companies have moved part of their operations into Estonia, boosting the local economy. On January 1, 2011, Estonia officially joined the Eurozone as the 17th member. More information on Estonia's GDP growth can be found in Figs. 9.10, 9.11 and 9.12.

1. Industrial structure

Estonia's industry and agriculture are well developed. As early as when it joined the Soviet Union, Estonia had occupied a leading position in the Soviet Union's national economy. In 1989, both its per capita GNP and per capita national income ranked first in the Soviet Union. More information about the three industries in Estonia can be found in Figs. 9.13 and 9.14.

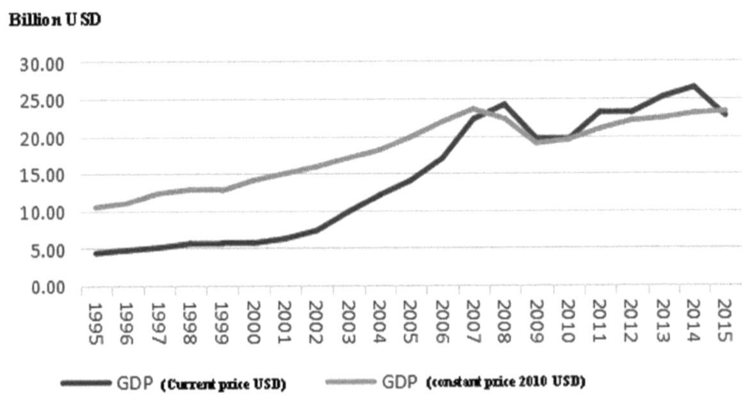

Fig. 9.10 GDP growth in Estonia. *Source of data* CEIC database

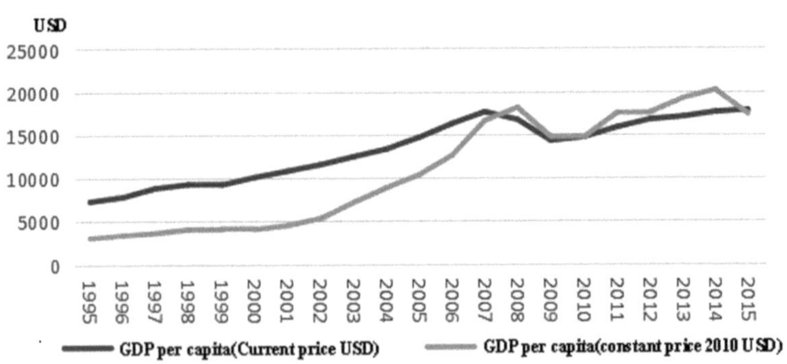

Fig. 9.11 Per capita GDP growth in Estonia. *Source of data* CEIC database

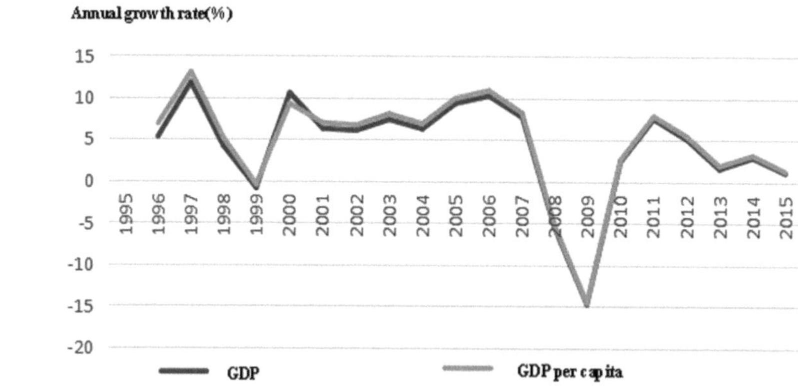

Fig. 9.12 GDP growth rate of Estonia. *Source of data* CEIC database

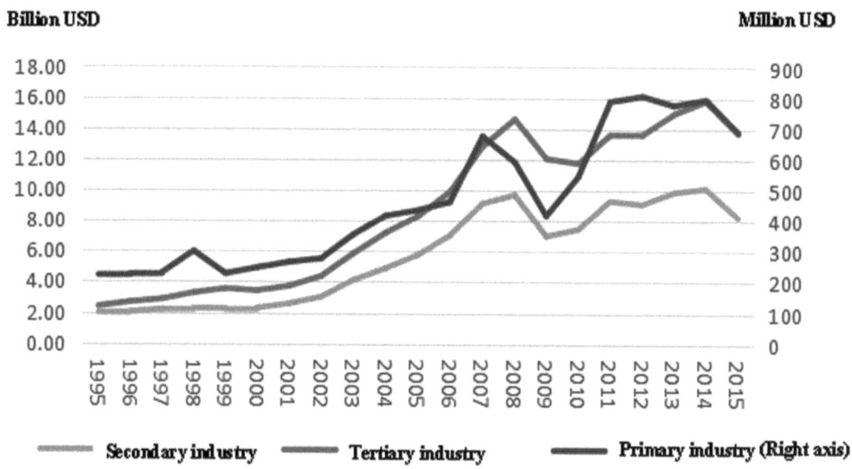

Fig. 9.13 Outputs of the three industries of Estonia. *Source of data* CEIC database

(1) The primary industry

Estonian agriculture accounts for about 4% of GDP, and the figure has been declining in the recent years but generally stayed stable. Local agriculture is dominated by animal husbandry and crop farming. The main domestic animals are cows, beef cattle and pigs. The main crops are wheat, rye, potatoes, vegetables, corn, flax and feed crops. In 2009, the total output of farming, forestry, animal husbandry and fishery was 1.26 billion USD, and the added value was about 450 million USD, or 2.5% of GDP. The added value of agriculture and animal husbandry was 270 million USD, and the figures for forestry and fishery were 140 million USD and 30 million USD, respectively.

(2) The secondary industry

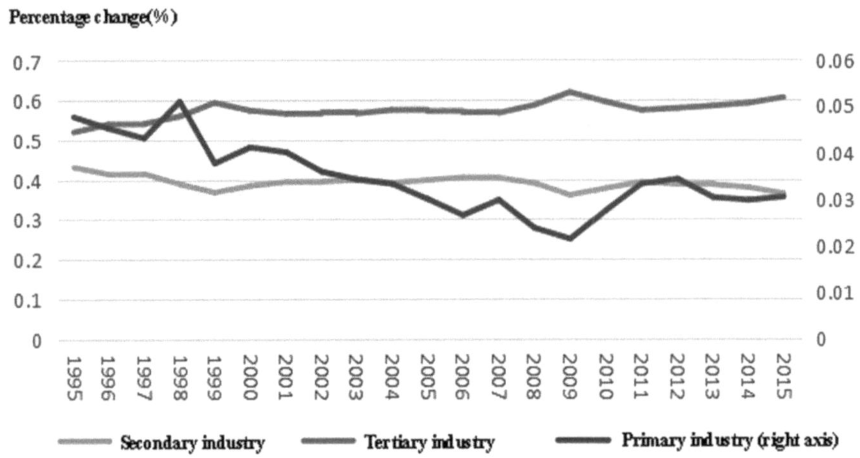

Fig. 9.14 Changes of the proportions of the three industries. *Source of data* CEIC database

Estonia's main industrial sectors are machinery manufacturing, wood processing, building materials, electronics, textiles and food processing. According to the Statistics Estonia, the overall industrial output of Estonia has stabilized and fluctuated slightly since 1995. After the financial crisis, the industrial output fell rapidly in 2007–2010 and began to rebound after 2010. The total industrial output in 2013 was about 10.6 billion euros, up by 1% over the previous year. The output of electrical, electronic and hot water supply industries fell by 5% year-on-year, and the mining industry produced 4% less compared to 2012.

(3) The tertiary industry

The service industry has always taken up a relatively big chunk of Estonian economy. Estonia is a traditional agricultural and industrial country. However, with economic development, the proportions of agricultural and industrial outputs have been steadily decreasing. At the same time, the share of services in the economy is expanding rapidly. However, from the perspective of exports, due to its limited and shrinking population, Estonian exports of services grow slower than the exports of goods. Most of the new service products are absorbed domestically.

2. Population and cities

Estonia's urbanization rate has always been high, staying above 50% ever since 1960, as shown in Fig. 9.15. After 1990, the sharp decline in the population and the drop of urbanization rate happened almost simultaneously. The latter phenomenon is related to Estonia's emergence as a high-income country.

Table 9.10 lists the major cities in Estonia.

3. Income

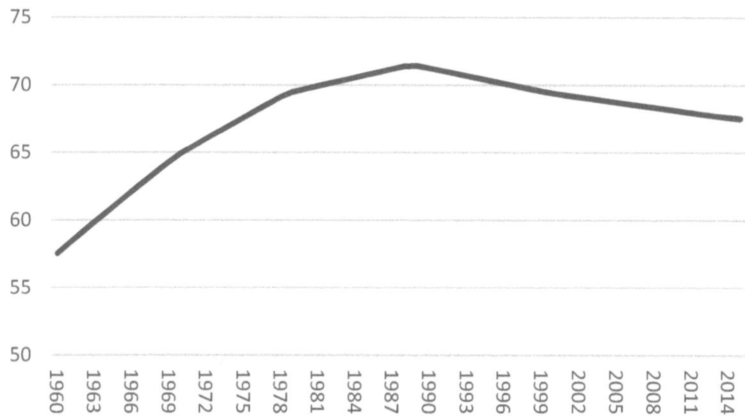

Fig. 9.15 Urbanization rate of Estonia. *Source of data* CEIC database

Table 9.10 Top 5 cities of Estonia

City	Population in 2016	City profile
Tallinn	394,024	The capital; the European capital of culture
Tartu	101,092	The center of education and culture in the south
Narva	66,980	An important historic and cultural city
Kohtla-Järve	46,060	An industrial city in the northeast
Pärnu	44,192	A city in the southwest; a resort town

Source of data World Population Review

The income situation in Estonia is characterized by high level and even distribution. In the recent years, Estonia's per capita income has generally maintained a rapid growth rate. Among the former Soviet republics, it is the only country in 2011 that achieved high national income per capita. Estonia is also a country with relatively even income distribution, and its Gini coefficient has stayed below the alert line of 0.40. Balanced income distribution has led to a higher consumption rate—local consumer spending has remained at a moderately high level, and its share within GDP has stayed above 50%, much higher than China's 37.5% in 2014. This has a positive impact on Estonia's economic growth. See Figs. 9.16 and 9.17 for more information.

(II) Foreign trade and investment

1. Foreign trade

In 2009, Estonia's foreign trade volume slid 29% year-on-year to 19.13 billion USD, of which exports were 9 billion USD, down by 24% year-on-year, and imports were 10.13 billion USD, 33% down year-on-year. Its trade deficit stood at 1.13 billion

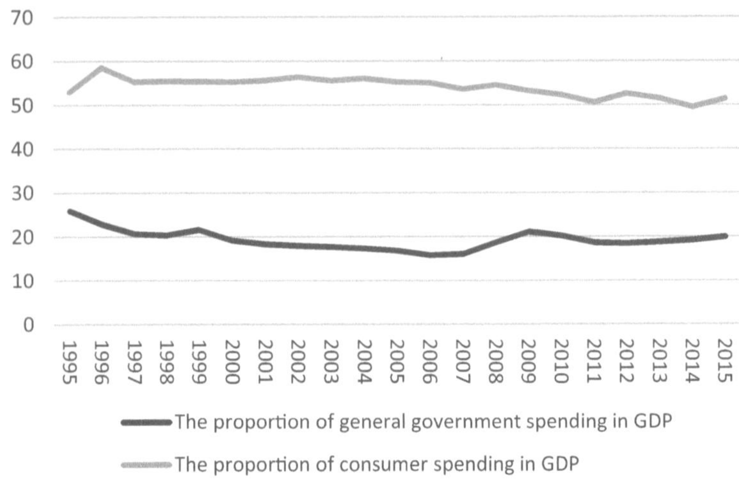

Fig. 9.16 Government spending and consumer spending in Estonia. *Source of data* CEIC database

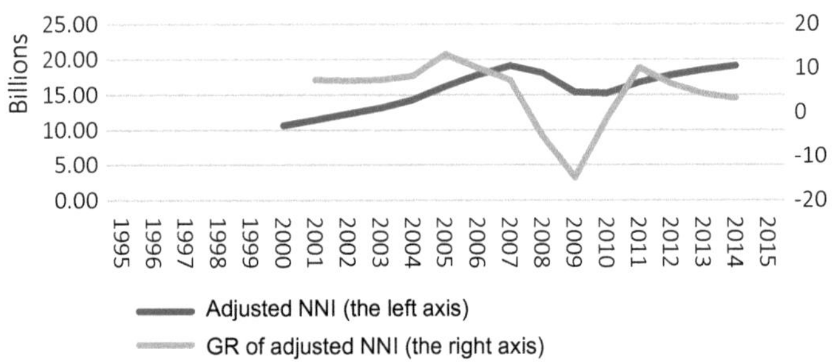

Fig. 9.17 Net national income and its growth rate of Estonia. *Source of data* CEIC database

USD, the lowest in 15 years, 66% less compared to 2008. See Figs. 9.18, 9.19 and 9.20 for more information.

Finland, Sweden, Latvia, Russia and Germany are the five largest export markets of Estonia. In 2009, Estonia exported 1.66 billion USD, 1.13 billion USD, 880 million USD, 840 million USD and 550 million USD to the five countries, respectively. In the same year, Estonia imported 1.47 billion USD, 1.11 billion USD, 1.06 billion USD, 1.04 billion USD and 890 million USD, respectively, from Finland, Lithuania, Germany, Latvia and Russia.

Machinery, mineral products, agricultural products and timber and wooden products are the main export commodities of Estonia. In 2009, the export values of the four commodities were 1.77 billion USD, 1.52 billion USD, 910 million USD and 770 million USD, accounting for 20, 17, 10 and 9% of the total exports. Mineral products, machinery and agricultural products are the main import goods of Estonia. In 2009, the import values of the three commodities were 2.05 billion USD, 1.96

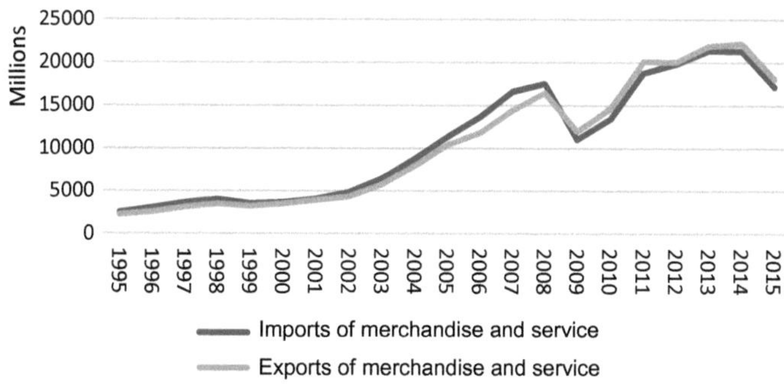

Fig. 9.18 Toal Imports and exports of Estonia

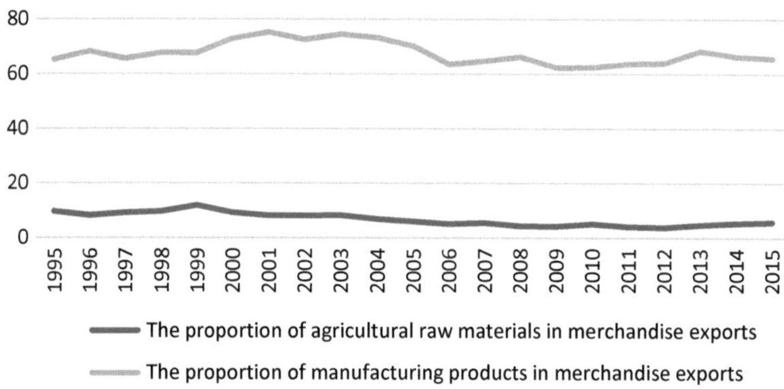

Fig. 9.19 Merchandise distribution of Estonian exports by sector. *Source of data* CEIC database

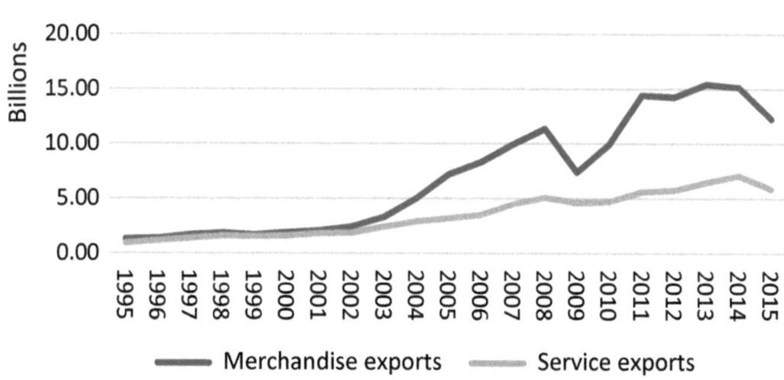

Fig. 9.20 Merchandise and service exports of Estonia. *Source of data* CEIC database

billion USD and 1.29 billion USD, respectively, accounting for 20, 19 and 13% of the total imports.

2. International investment

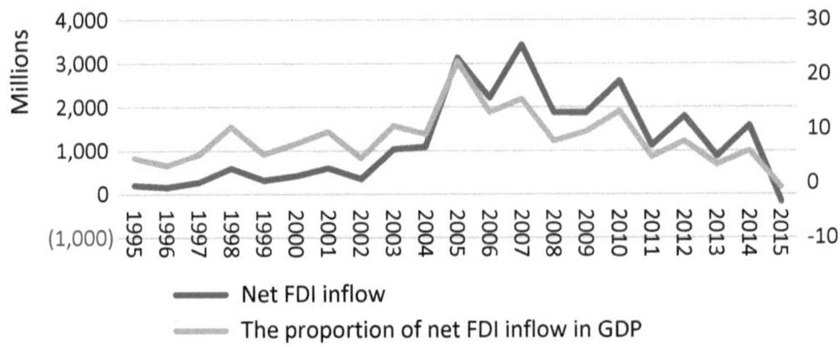

Fig. 9.21 Changes of the proportion of net FDI inflow in Estonian GDP. *Source of data* CEIC database.

Figure 9.21 shows foreign investment in Estonia in the recent years. Affected by the financial crisis, Estonia's FDI began to swing downward in 2008 and hit 1.74 billion USD in 2009. Top investors in Estonia include Sweden, the Netherlands and Finland. Most of the foreign capital flows to sectors such as finance, real estate, communications and transportation.

In 2009, Estonia invested 1.49 billion USD overseas. The largest recipients of Estonian investment were Latvia and Lithuania, and popular areas were finance, real estate, leasing and management.

9.3 Hungary

I. Geographical and historical backgrounds

Hungary is located in Central Europe, with a typical continental climate. The annual rainfall is about 588 mm, and the summer is humid and cool. The border line is 2246 km. It borders Slovakia, Austria, Ukraine, Romania, Croatia, Serbia and Slovenia. The land area is 93,030 km^2, and the population is 9.877 million. The main ethnic group in Hungary is the Magyar, which accounts for about 90%. Minorities include Slovenian, Croatian, Romanian, Serbian, German, Slovakian and other ethnic groups. Hungarian is the official language.

The establishment of Hungary has gone through many stages. In 896 AD, the nomadic tribes of Magyar migrated from the Volga Bay and the western foot of the Ural Mountains to the Danube Basin. Subsequently, St. Istvan became the first king of Hungary in 1000 AD, establishing a feudal state. After 526 years, the feudal state disintegrated due to Turkish invasion. In 1848, the struggle for a liberal revolution broke out in Hungary. The Republic of Hungary was established in April of the following year. In 1867, the Austro-Hungarian Empire was established. In March 1919, the Hungarian Soviet Republic was established. On August 20, 1949, the People's Republic of Hungary was proclaimed and the Constitution was promulgated. The Hungarian Event erupted in October 1956. On October 23, 1989, the country was renamed the Republic of Hungary. In January 2012, after the adoption of the new constitution, the country's name was officially changed to Hungary. The capital of Hungary is Budapest. In addition, it has 19 states and 24 state-level cities. Hungary's natural resources are relatively scarce. Its forest coverage rate is 20.6%, and the main mineral resource is bauxite, the reserves of which ranks third in Europe. In addition, there are a small amount of uranium, oil, iron, lignite and natural gas.

II. **Economic development**

(I) Domestic economy

In 1997, the transformation of the Hungarian economic system was basically completed, and a market economic system was established. In 1998, land privatization was accomplished. Hungary's overall economic growth had been fast, as shown in Figs. 9.22, 9.23 and 9.24. Prior to 1997, the GDP growth rate continued to be negative, and the total GDP in 1997 was 95 billion USD (USD at 2010 constant prices), 3.43% higher than that in 1996. In 1998, the total GDP was 99 billion USD (USD at 2010 constant prices), achieving a growth rate of 4.2%. In the following 10 years, the growth rate stayed around 3%–4%. In 2005, Hungary was included in the list of developed countries by the World Bank. In 2009, Hungary was affected by the global financial crisis, and its GDP dropped by 6.56% compared to 2008. However, Hungary implemented crisis management measures to restore public confidence, such as increasing investment in large-scale projects, cutting fiscal expenditures and encouraging employment. As of 2015, Hungary's GDP growth rate was 2.94%, and the unemployment rate fell to 6%, making it one of the fast-recovering economies in EU.

1. Industrial structure

(1) The primary industry

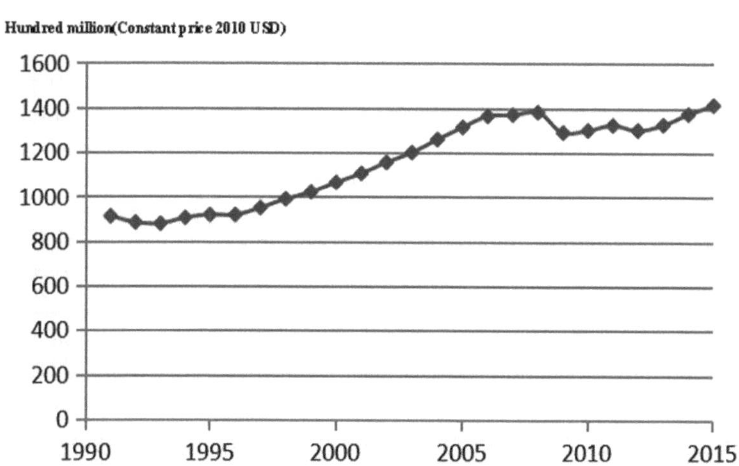

Fig. 9.22 Total GDP of Hungary

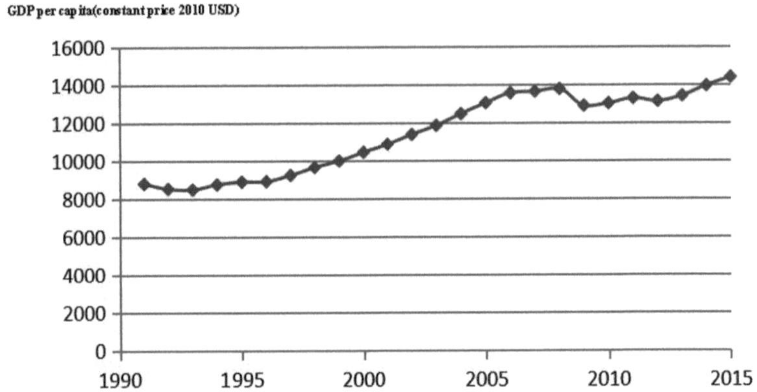

Fig. 9.23 Per capita GDP of Hungary

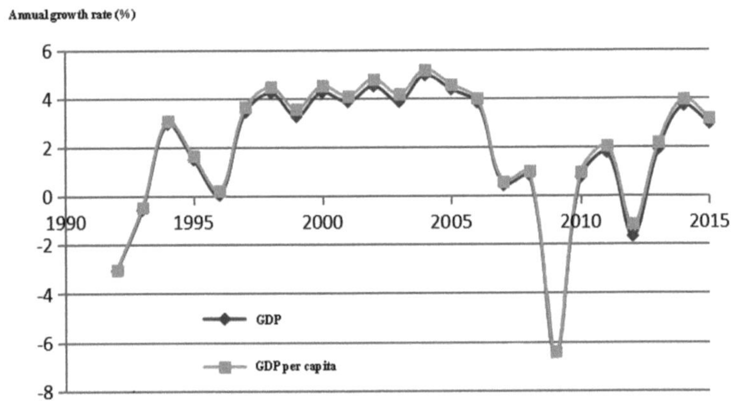

Fig. 9.24 Growth rates of GDP and per capita GDP in Hungary

Hungary has been an important agricultural country since its socialist past. The area of agricultural land in Hungary was 0.14% of the world's agricultural land, but its agricultural output accounted for 0.8% of the world's total. At the same time, Hungary's per capita food possession equals that of the United States. The output per unit area is 610 USD/ha. Therefore, after feeding its own people, Hungary exports 25% of its agricultural products and food.[3] In the late 1980s and early 1990s, Hungary carried out land reform. After reform, the area of privately owned land accounted for 63.6% of Hungary's total land area, while the percentage before the reform was only 7.3%. The reform effectively improved land utilization efficiency. Later, agricultural production was gradually mechanized. As a result, the efficiency of agricultural production was raised. As of 2013, the area of agricultural land in

[3] The Economic and Commercial Office of the Embassy of the People's Republic of China in Hungary.

Table 9.11 Outputs of agriculture and animal husbandry in Hungary 2011–2013 (Unit: 10,000 ton)

	2011	2012	2013
Wheat	410.7	401.1	505.8
Maize	799.2	476.3	675.6
Beet	85.6	88.2	99.1
Potato	60.0	54.8	48.7
Fruits	51.3	82.2	85.0
Beef cattle	7.8	7.5	7.1
Swine raised for pork	54.8	53.0	51.4
Sheep raised for mutton	1.8	1.8	1.8
Poultry	69.1	70.2	67.8
Fish	1.9	1.9	–
Milk (100 million liter)	16.9	17.7	17.1
Egg (100 million)	24.9	24.1	25.0

Hungary was 53,400 km^2, accounting for 58.99% of the total land area. The rural population in 2015 was 2.83 million, accounting for 28.77% of the total. The main food crops in Hungary are wheat, corn, and potato, and the main cash crop is sugar beet. The total grain output in 2013 was 13.61 million tons, an increase of 17% over the previous year. The average yield per hectare was 4640 kg for wheat, 5420 kg for corn, 52,660 kg for beet and 21,700 kg for potato. For more information, see Table 9.11.

(2) The secondary industry

After the transition to a market economy, Hungary's industry was traumatized, with the industrial output dropping significantly. From 1988 to 1992, the cumulative decline was 45%. In 1992, the gross industrial output accounted for only 23% of the national economy. The Hungarian government responded with measures such as changing the management structure of industrial enterprises. In the recent years, the Hungarian industry has been growing steadily. In 2013, the industrial output increased by 1.4%. Within the total output, the processing industry accounted for 94%, the power industry 3.9% and the mineral industry 0.4%. In 2014, the proportion of industrial production in the national economy was 31.2%. As the most favored destination of foreign investment in Hungary, the automobile industry has made great progress. In 2014, it generated 21.7 billion euros, an increase of 23% over the previous year. The number of employees in the automobile industry increased by 15% year-on-year. The volume of car export rose by 21% compared to 2013. Table 9.12 lists the outputs of other major industrial products.

(3) The tertiary industry

The tertiary industry has now become the pillar of the Hungarian economy. In 2015, it contributed 64.36% of the national economy. In 2007, the population working in the service sector reached 590,000, 15% of the total employment. Tourism is the core

Table 9.12 Top 5 cities in Hungary

City	Population in 2016	City profile
Budapest	1,741,041	The capital and the largest city
Debrecen	204,124	The economic and cultural center; the largest Hungarian city to the east of the Tisza River
Miskolc	172,637	The commercial and transportation center in the northeast
Szeged	164,883	A university town with developed light industry
Pécs	156,649	A city known for art

Source of data World Population Review

of the tertiary industry, and its growth rate is twice that of the national economy. With an output that is 10% of the Hungarian GDP, tourism provides more than 300,000 jobs, making it essential to the national economy. In 2014, 12.14 million tourists visited Hungary. Its main tourist attractions are Budapest, Lake Balaton, Danube Bay, the Mátra Mountains, etc.

As shown in Fig. 9.25, Hungary has completed the industrial restructuring. After the privatization of land and agricultural modernization, agricultural production efficiency and labor productivity have increased significantly, and the labor force has been released to the secondary and tertiary industries, and thus promoting their rapid growth. The proportion of agricultural output in the national economy has stayed below 10% since the late 1990s, and this downward trend is ongoing. In 2015, the percentage slid to 4.46%; for industrial output, the share was around 30%; meanwhile, the tertiary industry, as the leading economic force, registered more than 60% of the national economy.

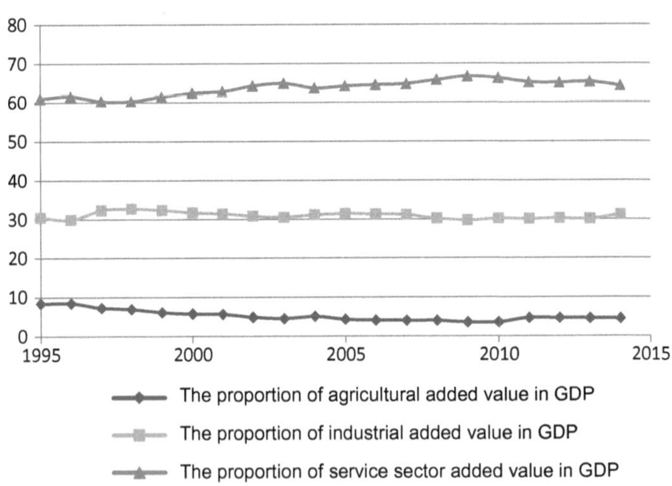

Fig. 9.25 Changes of industrial structure in Hungary

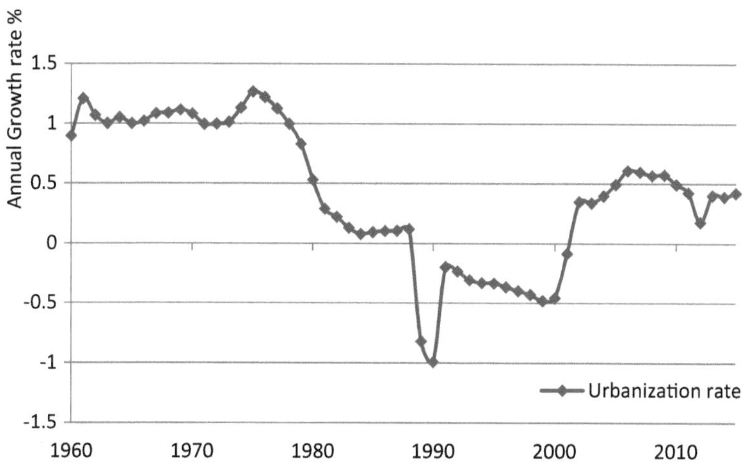

Fig. 9.26 Urbanization rate in Hungary

2. Population and cities

After the completion of industrialization, the urbanization rate has been steadily declining in Hungary. In 1989, the growth rate of urban population turned negative, which is consistent with de-urbanization trend often seen after industrialization (Fig. 9.26).

Table 9.12 lists the major cities of Hungary.

Budapest is the capital and largest city of Hungary. Located in north-central Hungary and on the banks of the Danube, it is the political, commercial and transportation center of the country. The city was originally two cities across the Danube—Buda and Pest. They merged into Budapest in 1873. Budapest has a typical temperate continental humid climate with warm winters and hot summers. Home to many medieval buildings, it is a famous historic city in Europe.

Founded in the tenth century, Debrecen is the capital of Hajdú-Bihar Region. It is the largest city in Eastern Hungary and an important economic and cultural center. In the early days, the citizens of Debrecen were engaged in agricultural production, so it was also known as an agricultural city. It was not until the end of the nineteenth century that the city began to develop industry.

Built in the fifteenth century, Miskolc is the capital of Borsod-Abaúj—Zemplén. It is the third largest city in Hungary. Miskolc is located in Northeastern Hungary, on the banks of the Sajó River, at an altitude of about 130 m. In the nineteenth century, Miskolc mined lignite and iron ore and boasted convenient transportation. Later, it became an industrial center in Northeastern Hungary. The traditional industries are ferrous metallurgy, cement, textiles, glass and papermaking. The Lenin Metallurgical Complex in Diosgir is one of the country's largest steel mills. The historic city has ancient buildings such as the town hall dating back to the seventeenth century and the Gothic churches built in the thirteenth century.

As the capital of Csongrad, Szeged is located in the southeast of Hungary where the Tisza River meets the Maros River. Szeged was swept by the flood in 1879, and then rebuilt. Szeged's light industry is well developed, dominated by food and textile industries. Other sectors include clothing, furniture, glass, rubber, etc. The "Hungarian National History Memorial Park" on the outskirts of the city, famous for the painting depicting how the Hungarian ancestors came to settle in the region, has attracted many domestic and foreign tourists. Szeged is also known as a university town, with the well-known József Attila University and the reputable St. George Albert Medical University. There are also many institutes of biology, agricultural colleges, schools of nutrition, conservatories, art middle schools, etc.

Founded in Roman times, Pécs is the capital of Baranya in Southwestern Hungary. Pécs has a long history. In 1009, King St. Istvan established a church here. In 1367, King Lajos I founded here the first university in Hungary. At the same time, Pécs is also a famous city of arts—it was home to many famous artists, including Csontváry, a painter known as "Van Gogh of Hungary".

3. Consumption

As shown in Fig. 9.27, after entering the 1990s, Hungary's economic growth accelerated, and consumer spending rose steadily. The two indicators declined slightly after 2008. Hungary's population had been shrinking slowly—in 1960, it was 9.98 million and in 2015 it slid to 9.84 million. Hungary is already a developed industrialized country at the post-industrial stage. It has a high-quality labor force that takes up about 45% of the total population, as shown in Fig. 9.28. Agriculture hires less than 10% of the total working population, and the share of population engaged in industry is dwindling, while the percentage for the tertiary industry is rising.

(II) Foreign trade and investment

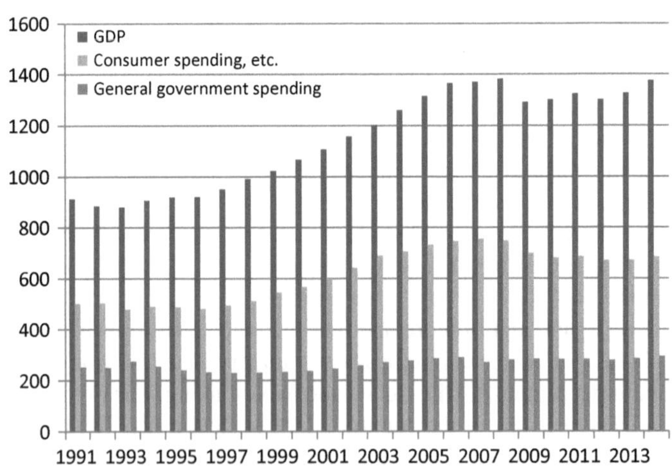

Fig. 9.27 GDP and consumer spending of Hungary

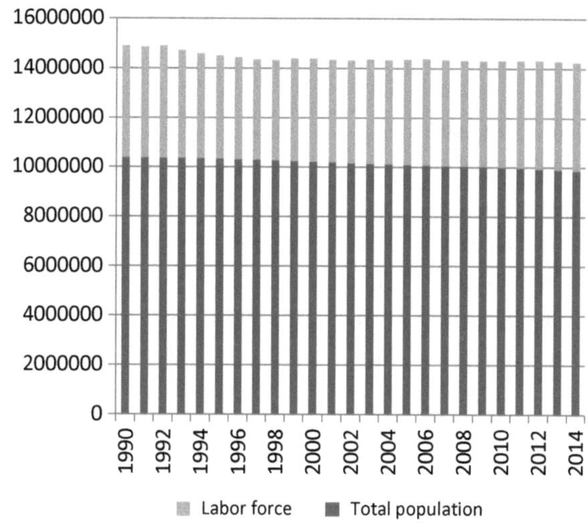

Fig. 9.28 Growths of Hungarian population and labor force

1. Foreign trade

According to the Eurostat, Hungary's total foreign trade in 2015 was worth 191.2 billion USD, down by 11.3% over the previous year; within it 92.608 billion USD was imported, a decrease of 11.7% year-on-year, and exports were 98.66 billion USD, 10.8% less compared to that of 2014. In 2015, Hungary's main trading partners were Germany, China, Romania, Slovakia, Austria, France, Italy and so on. In 2015, Germany was the largest market for Hungarian exports, buying 27.604 billion USD, followed by Romania, purchasing 5.335 billion USD. The top five export commodities were mechanical and electrical products, transportation equipment, chemical products, plastics and rubber, base metals and products. Germany was also the largest exporter to Hungary, selling 23.769 billion USD; China ranked the second with an amount of 6.137 billion USD, followed by Austria with 6.085 billion USD. The top five import goods were mechanical and electrical products, transportation equipment, chemical products, mineral products, base metals and products. For more information, see Tables 9.13, 9.14, 9.15, 9.16 and 9.17; Fig. 9.29.

2. International investment

In order to attract foreign investment, the Hungarian government has adopted a series of preferential policies, including tax incentives, labor subsidies and EU transition subsidies. Some subsidies can account for about 50% of the investment amount. In 2014, Hungary absorbed 4.04 billion USD of foreign capital inflow, and the foreign investment stock was 98.36 billion USD. Figure 9.30 provides more information on this. Retail, finance, automobile, telecommunications and electronics industries were favored by foreign investment, absorbing about 2/3 of the total foreign capital. About 95% of automobiles were produced by foreign companies. European countries are the main source of foreign investment in Hungary. Germany is not only its largest trading partner, but also its largest investor.

Table 9.13 Foreign trade of Hungary in 2015 (Unit: million USD)

Year	Total volume	YOY (%)	Exports	YOY (%)	Imports	YOY (%)	Gap	YOY (%)
2001	64,009	6.8	30,415	8.6	33,594	5.2	−3178	−19.3
2002	72,255	12.9	34,490	13.4	37,765	12.4	−3276	3.1
2003	91,108	26.1	43,196	25.2	47,912	26.9	−4716	44.0
2004	116,031	27.4	55,559	28.6	60,472	26.2	−4913	4.2
2005	129,206	11.4	62,801	13.0	66,405	9.8	−3603	−26.7
2006	153,776	19.0	75,390	20.0	78,386	18.0	−2995	−16.9
2007	191,327	24.4	95,593	26.8	95,735	22.1	−142	−95.2
2008	217,954	13.9	108,745	13.8	109,208	14.1	−463	225.0
2009	161,098	−26.1	83,197	−23.5	77,902	−28.7	5295	–
2010	183,769	14.1	95,544	14.8	88,225	13.3	7319	38.2
2011	214,788	16.9	112,330	17.6	102,458	16.1	9872	34.9
2012	198,928	−7.4	103,665	−7.7	95,263	−7.0	8402	−14.9
2013	207,679	4.4	107,532	3.7	100,147	5.1	7385	−12.1
2014	215,534	3.8	110,630	2.9	104,904	4.8	5725	−22.5
2015	191,268	−11.3	98,660	−10.8	92,608	−11.7	6052	5.7

Table 9.14 Export volumes of Hungary to its major trading partners in 2015 (Unit: million USD)

Country	Volume	YOY (%)	Proportion (%)
Total volume	98,660	−10.8	100.0
Germany	27,604	−11.1	28.0
Romania	5335	−13.2	5.4
Slovakia	5046	−9.2	5.1
Austria	4902	−21.4	5.0
Italy	4696	−9.4	4.8
France	4644	−7.3	4.7
The Czech Republic	3940	−7.9	4.0
Britain	3933	−4.2	4.0
Poland	3827	−11.4	3.9
Spain	3309	10.9	3.4
The Netherlands	3306	1.1	3.4
The United States	2702	−12.2	2.7
Belgium	1827	−9.7	1.9
Croatia	1661	5.5	1.7
Russia	1651	−38.2	1.7

Table 9.15 Classifications of major export merchandise of Hungary in 2015 (Unit: million USD)

Classification by customs	HS code	Category	Jan.–Dec. 2015	The same period of 2014	YOY (%)	Proportion (%)
Classification	Chapter	Total value	98,660	110,630	−10.8	100.0
Classification 16	84–85	Mechanical and electric products	39,547	43,547	−9.2	40.1
Classification 17	86–89	Transportation equipment	15,752	16,003	−1.6	16.0
Classification 6	28–38	Chemical products	8959	9715	−7.8	9.1
Classification 7	39–40	Plastic and rubber	6230	6913	−9.9	6.3
Classification 15	72–83	Base metals and base metal products	4647	5660	−17.9	4.7
Classification 4	16–24	Food, beverage, tobacco	3535	4170	−15.2	3.6
Classification 18	90–92	Optical instrument, clocks and watches and medical equipment	3369	4618	−27.1	3.4
Classification 20	94–96	Furniture, toy and miscellaneous products	2855	3112	−8.3	2.9
Classification 2	06–14	Plant products	2810	3128	−10.2	2.9
Classification 5	25–27	Minerals	2426	3853	−37.0	2.5
Classification 1	01–05	Live animals; animal products	1961	2363	−17.0	2.0
Classification 13	68–70	Ceramics; glass	1526	1750	−12.8	1.6
Classification 11	50–63	Textiles and raw materials	1467	1770	−17.1	1.5
Classification 10	47–49	Cellulose pulp; paper	1142	1280	−10.8	1.2
Classification 9	44–46	Timber and wood products	715	824	−13.2	0.7
		Others	1718	1923	−10.6	1.7

Table 9.16 Import volumes of Hungary from its main trading partners in 2015 (Unit: million USD)

Country	Volume	YOY (%)	Proportion (%)
Total volume	92,608	−11.7	100.0
Germany	23,769	−9.9	25.7
China	6137	−3.5	6.6
Austria	6085	−20.8	6.6
Poland	5051	−6.5	5.5
Slovakia	4910	−13.0	5.3
The Czech Republic	4420	−7.0	4.8
The Netherlands	4197	−1.3	4.5
Italy	4178	−9.8	4.5
France	3986	−5.5	4.3
Russia	3636	−49.5	3.9
Romania	2882	−13.8	3.1
Belgium	2105	−15.6	2.3
Britain	1736	−5.0	1.9
The United States	1733	−4.5	1.9
Spain	1436	−6.7	1.6

In the recent years, China–Hungary trade relations have grown closer. In 2015, the bilateral trade volume was 7.48 billion USD, 8.6% down from the previous year. Within it 1.34 billion USD was export from Hungary to China, a 26.7% decrease from the previous year, accounting for 1.4% of Hungary's total exports, 0.3 percentage point less year-on-year; Hungary's imports from China were 6.14 billion USD, a year-on-year decrease of 3.5%, accounting for 6.6% of Hungary's total imports, 0.6 percentage point more over the previous year. Mechanical and electric products are the most important part in the bilateral trade. In 2015, Hungary exported 790 million USD of mechanical and electric equipment to China, 58% of its total exports to China. Mechanical equipment, motors and electric products, optical instrument, clocks and watches and medical equipment were its top five categories of export merchandise. In 2015, Hungary imported 5.03 billion USD of mechanical and electric products from China, 81.9% of the total and 5.8 percentage points less compared to the previous year.

9.4 Poland

I. Geographical and historical backgrounds

Poland is located in the middle of Europe. It originated from the alliance of the Polish, Eastern Pomeranian, Silesian, Vistula and Mazovia tribes (all western Slavs). It was partitioned three times—by Czarist Russia in 1772, by Prussia in 1793 and

Table 9.17 Classifications of major import merchandise of Hungary in 2015 (Unit: million USD)

Classification by customs	HS code	Category	2015	The same period of 2014	YOY (%)	Proportion (%)
Classification	Chapter	Total value	92,608	104,904	−11.7	100.0
Classification 16	84–85	Mechanical and electric products	35,061	37,798	−7.2	37.9
Classification 17	86–89	Transportation equipment	10,883	11,110	−2.1	11.8
Classification 6	28–38	Chemical products	8985	9655	−6.9	9.7
Classification 5	25–27	Minerals	7754	12,729	−39.1	8.4
Classification 15	72–83	Base metals and base metal products	7674	8890	−13.7	8.3
Classification 7	39–40	Plastic and rubber	6061	6649	−8.8	6.6
Classification 4	16–24	Food, beverage and tobacco	2745	3073	−10.7	3.0
Classification 11	50–63	Textiles and raw materials	2319	2594	−10.6	2.5
Classification 18	90–92	Optical instrument, clocks and watches and medical equipment	2030	2139	−5.1	2.2
Classification 20	94–96	Furniture, toy and miscellaneous products	1786	1925	−7.2	1.9
Classification 10	47–49	Cellulose pulp; paper	1504	1757	−14.4	1.6
Classification 2	06–14	Plant product	1377	1478	−6.8	1.5
Classification 1	01–05	Live animals; animal products	1138	1430	−20.4	1.2
Classification 13	68–70	Ceramics; glass	1047	1170	−10.5	1.1
Classification 9	44–46	Timber and wood products	590	637	−7.4	0.6
		Others	1654	1870	−11.5	1.8

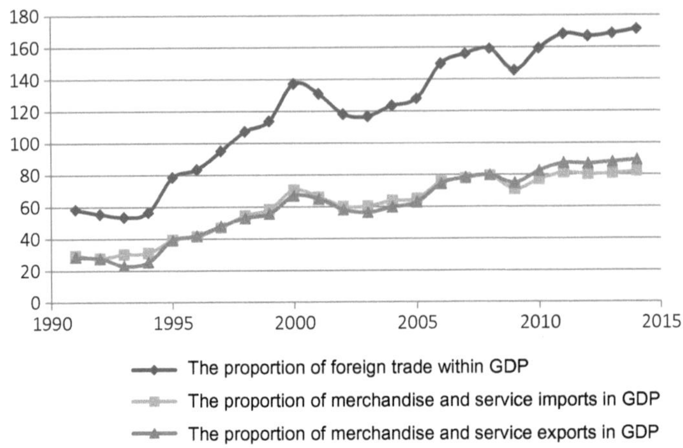

Fig. 9.29 Proportion of foreign trade within Hungarian GDP

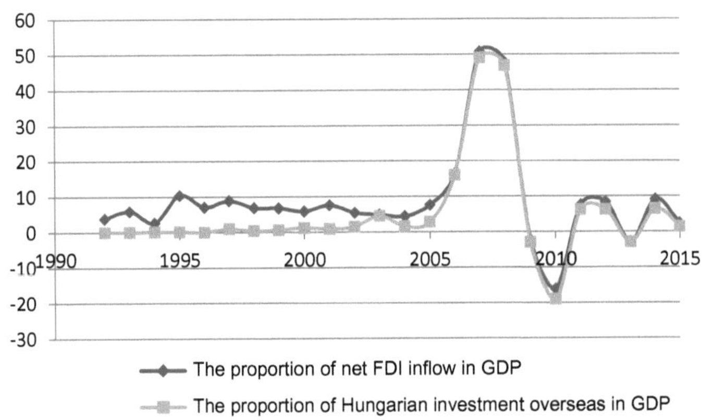

Fig. 9.30 FDI in hungary

by the Austro-Hungarian Empire in 1795. On November 11, 1918, Poland restored independence.

After the Second World War, the Communist Party of Poland established the People's Republic and officially started socialist construction. In 1956, Khrushchev, the leader of the Soviet Union, proposed "destalinization", which brought a huge shock to the entire socialist camp. At that time, the famous "Poznan strike" broke out in Poland.

During the upheaval of Eastern Europe in the 1980s, Poland's Solidarity Union (Solidarność) seized power, shifting the political system to capitalism. Poland joined NATO in 1999 and then the EU in 2004. In 1997, by adopting a new constitution, Poland established a political system featuring the separation of powers and an economic system dominated by market economy.

Fig. 9.31 .

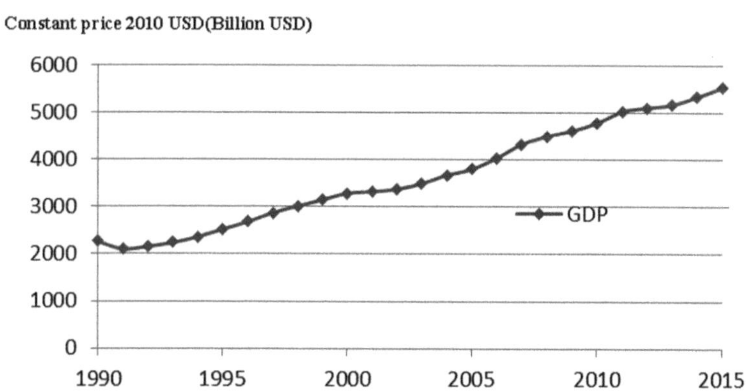

Fig. 9.32 Poland's GDP

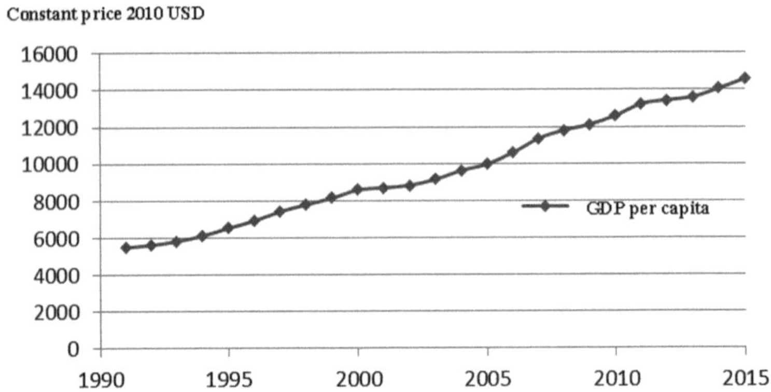

Fig. 9.33 Per capita GDP of Poland

Poland has a land area of 310,000 km^2, 75% of which is lower than 200 m above sea level. Its coastline is 528 km long. The climate in Poland is relatively mild year round. Located in the transition area between maritime and continental climates, Poland enjoys pleasant weather in spring and autumn. It has abundant rainfall, cool summers and humid and cold winters. 98% of Poland's population is of Polish nationality, and ethnic minorities include Belarussian, Ukrainian, Russian, Lithuanian and Jewish people.

Poland is bordered by the Baltic Sea to the north, the Czech Republic and Slovakia to the south, Germany to the west and Russia, Belarus, Ukraine and Lithuania to the east (Fig. 9.31). Polish is the official language. About 90% of Polish people believe in Roman Catholicism. As of 2012, the total lengths of Polish highways, railways, inland canals and petroleum pipelines were 280,000 km, 20,094 km, 3,659 km and 2,444 km, respectively.

Poland is rich in mineral and forest resources. Mineral resources include shale gas, sulfur, copper, zinc, coal, lead, aluminum and silver. By the end of 2012, the forest area reached 9.634 million hectares, and the forest coverage rate was 30.8%. Shale gas reserves are expected to reach 346 billion to 768 billion m^3, and proven reserves of hard coal, lignite, sulfur and copper are 48.226 billion tons, 22.548 billion tons, 511 million tons and 1.793 billion tons, respectively. The annual output of electrolytic copper is 580,000 tons.

II. **Economic development**

(I) Domestic economy

Poland's economic development in the past 30 years can be roughly divided into three stages according to the cycle of GsDP growth. See Figs. 9.32, 9.33 and 9.34.

The first stage was from the late 1980s to the early 1990s. At that time, Poland was in the process of drastic changes in terms of political and economic systems due to the upheaval in Eastern Europe. The new Polish government took the advice of American economist Jeffrey Sachs and adopted a "shock therapy" to reform its economy, causing economic depression. It was not until 1992 that the Polish economy began to recover.

The second stage lasted from 1993 to the beginning of the twenty-first century. At this stage, Polish economy grew fast; however, the growth began to slow down due to the decline in domestic consumption and investment and the impact of sluggish global economy.

The third stage runs from 2004 to the present. The beginning of this stage was marked by Poland joining the EU. Since then, Poland's economy has once again turned to a rapid growth. In 2007, its GDP growth rate reached 6.5%. The 2008 financial crisis hit posed some pressures on Poland, but it maintained growth and was the one and only EU member to have done so. It was also the only European country that kept growing in 2009–2015. In 2010, its GDP growth rate was 3.7%, and in 2011, it hiked to 5%. Then the rate began to decline. In 2014, Polish economy grew twice as fast as that of the previous year. Reasons for such strong growth included consolidation of domestic demand due to improved job markets and increased investment activities, agricultural harvests and lower energy prices which had helped curb inflation, reduced financing costs and government encouragement of investment in housing. In 2015, Poland's GDP growth rate was 3.6%, the fastest for four years, and the gross national economy ranked eighth among EU countries.

At present, the Gini coefficient of Poland is 32.73, and the income gap is at a medium level. The United Nations Human Development Index is high at 0.843, ranking 36th in the world. Its currency is the Polish zloty, and it adopts a floating exchange rate regime.

1. Population and education

The total population of Poland is 40 million, and the natural growth rate has stayed below 1 and even declined in the past decade. At present, 96.5% of the Polish population is Polish, and the remaining minorities include Germans (1.3%), Ukrainians (0.6%), Belarusians (0.5%), etc. About 61.8% of Polish live in cities, and 50% of the population are under 35 years old. The life expectancy is 77.3 years. In terms of sex structure, the male to female ratio in Poland is about 100:109. The official language of Poland is Polish. See Table 9.18 and Fig. 9.35 for more information on population.

In terms of education, Poland has good foundation and tradition of scientific research. It was home to famous scientists such as Madame Curie. Poland values education. For instance, it provides free education, and people under 18 are subject to compulsory education. Education in Poland is administered by the Ministry of National Education and the Ministry of Science and Higher Education. In 2013, Poland's public expenditure on the national education system (about 74.3 billion PLN) accounted for 4.47% of its GDP, as shown in Fig. 9.36. In 2014, Poland had a total of 439 institutions of higher education, including the famous Jagiellonian University in Krakow and Warsaw University. According to the Statistics Poland, the enrollment rate for higher education in Poland was 37.8% in 2014.

2. Population and cities

Table 9.18 Population-related statistics of Poland in important years

	1980	1990	2000	2010	2015
Per thousand people					
Birth	19.5	14.3	9.9	10.7	9.6
Death	9.9	10.2	9.6	9.8	10.3
Natural growth	9.6	4.1	0.3	0.9	−0.7
Married	8.6	6.7	5.5	5.9	4.9
Divorced	1.1	1.1	1.1	1.6	1.8
Separated	–	–	1.3	2.8	0.0
Death rate per thousand newborn babies	25.5	19.3	8.1	5.0	4.0

Source of data Poland in figures 2016

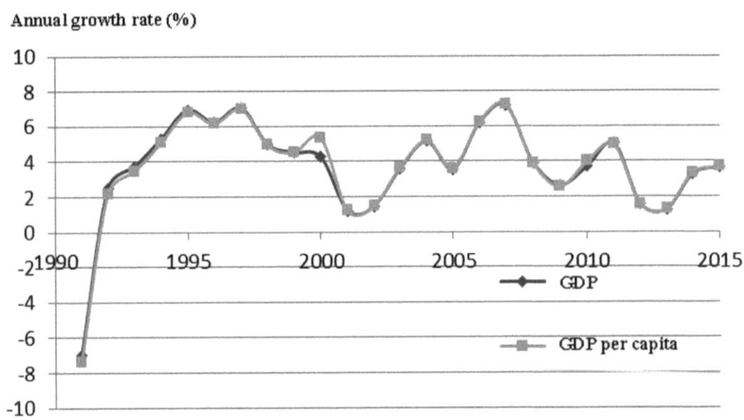

Fig. 9.34 Growth rates of GDP and per capita GDP in Poland. *Source of data* World Bank database.

As shown in Fig. 9.37, Poland's urbanization after the Second World War has many similarities with that of China. It also started the process in the middle of the twentieth century, and it also suffered the inevitable pains. It is fair to say that Poland serves as a good reference for China's urbanization.

Poland was hit so hard during the Second World War that the entire country had to be reconstructed. At the same time, according to the post-war agreement, Poland's territory went through major changes, which means a large number of people needed to migrate from the east to the west. Its urbanization can be divided into three stages. The first stage is the reconstruction of the country. After the Second World War, Poland was left in ruins. The government at that time prioritized the development of heavy industry, drawing labor force from villages to cities. China went through the same process and emerged as a powerful industrial country. During the second stage, the rural population began to have access to quality education, which had reshaped the social structure of Poland. In 1950, only 42% of Polish lived in cities, but in 2000,

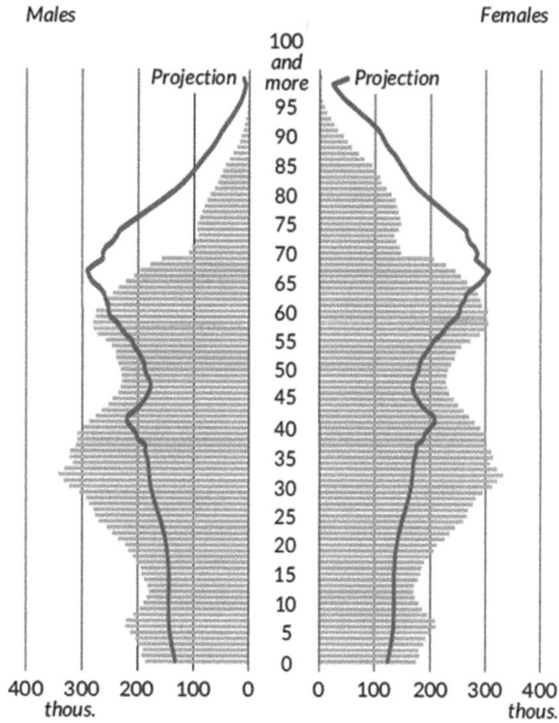

Fig. 9.35 Age and sex structures of Polish population. *Source of data* Poland in Figures 2016, the solid lines are the predicted population structures of Poland in 2050.

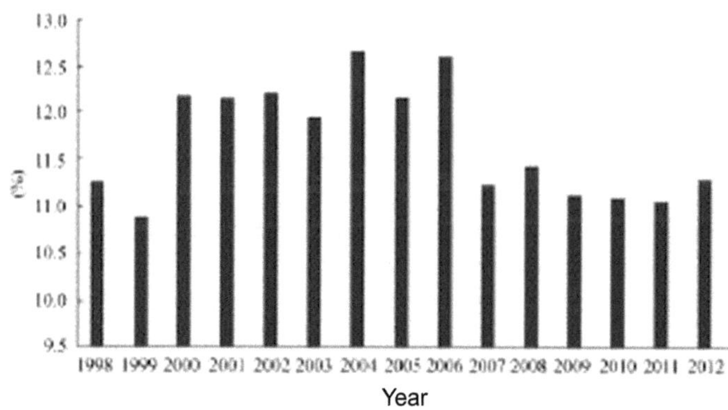

Fig. 9.36 Proportion of spending on education within Polish government spending. *Source of data* UNESCO Institute for Statistics

the figure exceeded 62%. The third stage started in the 1990s when more people with higher education moved to cities for better jobs and living conditions.

On May 1, 2004, Poland officially became a member of the EU. After this, its urbanization and economy grew faster. The cities were expanding, and office buildings mushroomed, which in turn accelerated urbanization. Apartments were built

Table 9.19 Top 5 cities in Poland

City	Population in 2016	City profile
Warsaw	1,702,139	The capital; the political, economic and cultural center
Lodz	768,755	Sitting on the watershed between the Vistula River and the Warta River, the center of film and art
Krakow	755,050	One of the oldest cities in central Europe; the hometown of the Vistula people
Wroclaw	634,893	Once one of the commercial, industrial and cultural centers of Germany
Poznan	570,852	One of the largest industrial, transportation, cultural, education and research centers of Poland

near offices, newcomers were provided with housing, and even more newcomers were on their way.

Urbanization requires new roads, and thus promoting the development of the Polish transportation system. The result of urbanization is that more and more people come to cities for better-paid jobs, and better payment leads to more consumption and production. Poland has thus become the only oasis in the desert of European economic crisis. It is true that urbanization has brought not only benefits but also problems to Poland, such as environmental damage, traffic congestion and energy consumption. In the eyes of the Polish, these negative effects are unavoidable in the process of urbanization. It is important for cities to have long-term planning instead of only focusing on temporary interests.

Table 9.19 lists the major cities in Poland.

Warsaw is the capital of Poland and its Mazowieckie Province. As the largest city in the country, it is the political, economic and cultural center. Warsaw is located in central Poland and covers an area of 512 km^2. With the Vistula River flowing through, the city is home to 1.7 million people. It is a hub of trade in Europe and has the largest airport in Poland. The city has been prosperous since the fifteenth century. With a temperate continental climate and mild weather all year round, it is highly livable and an interesting place to visit.

Lodz is located in the central part of Poland, on the watershed of the Vistula and Warta rivers. It is an important railway and highway hub. Built in 1798, Lodz is the second largest city. Its geographical advantage has made it the center of the textile industry. After the Second World War, education and scientific research have also developed rapidly in the city. There are 6 colleges and universities and various types of cultural and sports facilities such as opera houses, libraries and comprehensive gyms.

Located in Eastern Poland, Krakow is the capital of Krakow Province. Built around 700 years ago, it is one of the oldest cities in Central Europe and the hometown of the Vistula people. From 1320 to 1609, it served as the capital of Poland. In 2000, Krakow was designated the European Capital of Culture. It is a tourist city visited by more than 2 million people every year. With many classical buildings and a medieval style, it is known as the most beautiful city in Poland.

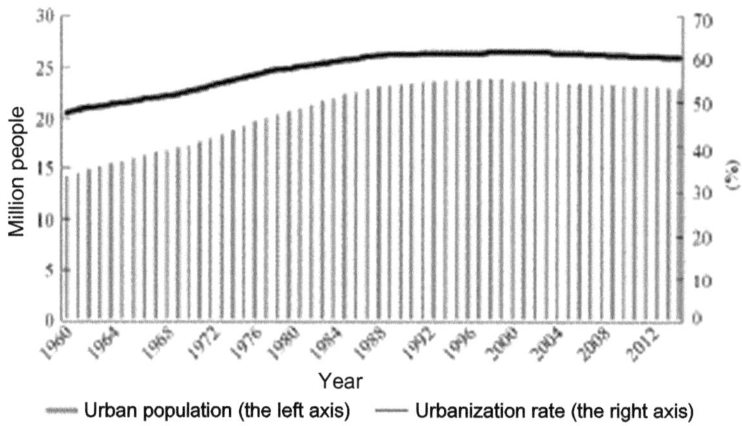

Fig. 9.37 Population and urbanization rate of Poland. *Source of data* World Bank database.

3. Consumption

After the fall of communism in Eastern Europe, Poland adopted the shock therapy, leading to economic depression and decrease of consumer spending. After the structural transformation, its economy began to grow faster and consumer spending started to rise steadily, as shown in Fig. 9.38. Its population was 38.11 million in 1990 and has been stable since then. It is already a developed industrialized country at the post-industrial stage. Its high-quality labor force has stayed around 48% of the total population for more than 10 years. The proportion of population engaged in agriculture is smaller than 10%, and the percentage for industry is also declining, while the share for the service sector is growing.

4. Industrial structure

(1) The primary industry

Poland is a traditional agricultural country with a mild climate throughout the year. With pleasant spring and autumn, plenty of rainfall and cool summer, it is suitable for farming. Private family farms are the mainstream in Poland, resulting in low production efficiency—only 13% of the EU average, and little progress in mechanization and tapping new technologies.

According to the statistical yearbook published by the Statistics Poland in 2016, Poland's agricultural land area was 18.683 million hectares in 2015, of which 73.4% was arable land. In 2014, the agricultural output totaled 105.34 billion PLN, a year-on-year decrease of 2.3%, accounting for 6.13% of GDP. The main crops were wheat, rye, potato, sugar beet, rapeseed, etc., the outputs of which all ranked among the top ten in Europe, as shown in Table 9.20. Its outputs of meat, dairy products, apple, onion, cabbage and cauliflower were also among the highest in Europe.

With the implementation of the EU's unified agricultural policy in the recent years, Polish exports of agricultural products have maintained steady growth thanks

Table 9.20 Outputs of major agricultural products of Poland 2010–2012 (Unit: 10,000 ton)

	2010	2011	2012
Wheat	940.8	933.9	860.08
Rye	285.2	260.1	288.8
Barley	339.7	332.6	418.0
Oat	151.6	138.2	146.85
Beet	997.3	1167.4	1235.0
Potato	818.8	911.1	874.0
Rapeseed	227.30	188.8	189.6

Source of data Statistical Yearbook of the Republic of Poland 2013

to competitive prices and good quality. About 3/4 of its agricultural products and food are sold to other EU countries, more than 1/3 of which is sold to Germany. In addition, Polish agricultural products are exported to Russia, Japan, South Korea, China and other countries and regions. In addition, the EU has also provided assistance to Poland in agriculture. For instance, it subsidizes Polish farmers on quota restrictions on the production of grain, oilseeds, starch, tobacco and livestock. About 40% of the subsidy comes from the EU, while the rest is provided by the Polish government. In addition to direct subsidies for agricultural products, the EU has also established the Development Fund for Backward Rural Area in Poland (1.8 billion euros in 2004–2006).

(2) The secondary industry

Before the Second World War, Poland's industrial level was relatively low, only 20% of the European average. In 1946, Poland carried out industrial reform, nationalizing large and medium-sized enterprises and major sectors of the national economy such as transportation and banks, which greatly improved industrial efficiency. In 1950, the added value of Polish industry accounted for 24.3% of the national economy. From the 1950s to the 1960s, Poland launched socialist industrialization, focusing investment on areas such as machine manufacturing and transportation, chemicals, electrical engineering and textiles. From 1951 to 1979, the average annual growth rate of Polish industrial output was as high as 10.2%, while the figure for the whole world was only 6.3%. Traditional industrial sectors of Poland include the coal, chemicals, textiles, machinery and steelmaking. After its economic transformation, Poland's industrial capacity expanded to cover sectors such as automobile manufacturing, food, aviation and train building, communications and information technology. The outputs of some major industrial products in the recent years are listed in Table 9.21. In general, Poland's industrial output is slowly decreasing, but the quality and profitability of industrial products are improving.

Take the automobile industry as an example. It has the following features: it is dominated by foreign-funded enterprises; it focuses on automobile assembly; manufacturers of auto parts apply high technical standards and produce various types of products; and the output of spare parts grows fast. At present, as a priority industry in Poland, the automobile sector is a large exporter of products of various types and

Table 9.21 Outputs of major industrial products 2010–2012

	2010	2011	2012
Hard coal (10,000 tons)	7670	7650	7980
Lignite (10,000 tons)	5650	6280	6430
Crude steel (10,000 tons)	799.3	877.6	854.3
Sulfur (Scalar)	51.7	65.7	67.6
Power generation (100 million kWh)	1580	1640	1620
Sedan (10,000)	78.5	74.1	54.0
Cement (10,000 tons)	1580	1899	1590

Source of data Statistical Yearbook of the Republic of Poland 2013

brands, facing strong overseas demand. Domestically, the demand for new cars is smaller than that for used cars—sales of used cars have been twice that of new ones in the recent years. According to the Statistics Poland in 2016, the automobile industry registered 118.33 billion PLN of output in 2014, an increase of 4.8% year-on-year, accounting for about 9.1% of the overall industrial output. Approximately 173,000 people worked in the industry, a year-on-year increase of 5.5%. The exports of automobile products reached 90.78 billion PLN, accounting for 13.1% of Poland's total exports. In 2014, the output of passenger cars was 473,000, down by 0.4% over the previous year.

(3) The tertiary industry

After its successful transition, Poland gave up some crops with low production efficiency and resorted to imports. In this way, labor force was shifted to the secondary and tertiary industries, as shown in Figs. 9.39 and 9.40. In the recent years, the proportion of industrial output in GDP and the share of industrial employment in total employment have declined slowly, but the production efficiency and the profitability and quality of products have significantly improved. This is the result of the shift from heavy industry to consumer goods manufacturing and the development of the tertiary industry. Poland's service sector, especially tourism, has maintained a good momentum in the recent years. In 2012, 12.44 million foreign tourists visited Poland, bringing in 23.1 billion euros, or about 6% of the GDP. Tourist areas include Warsaw, the coastal city of Gdansk and the Bialowieza forest in the east. Most tourists come from European countries, such as Germany, Britain, Italy, Denmark, France and the United States.

(II) Foreign trade and investment

1. Foreign trade

According to the Polish Ministry of Commerce, Poland's foreign trade in 2015 totaled 392.3 billion USD, a year-on-year decrease of 11.6%. Its imports declined by 9.9% to 198.2 billion USD, and exports hit 194.1 billion USD, 13.2% less on a year-on-year basis. See Fig. 9.41 for more information. In 2015, Poland's main trading

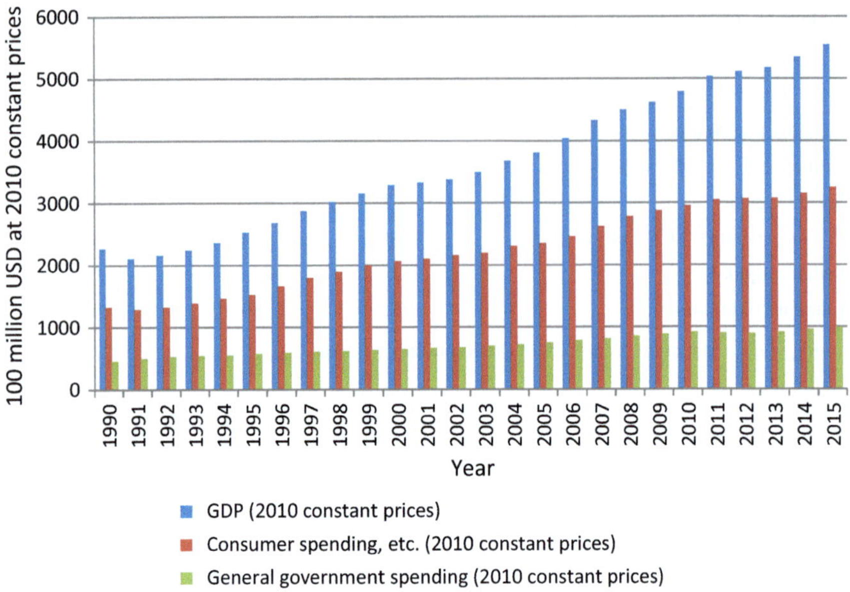

Fig. 9.38 Consumer spending and government spending in Poland. *Source of data* Statistics Poland

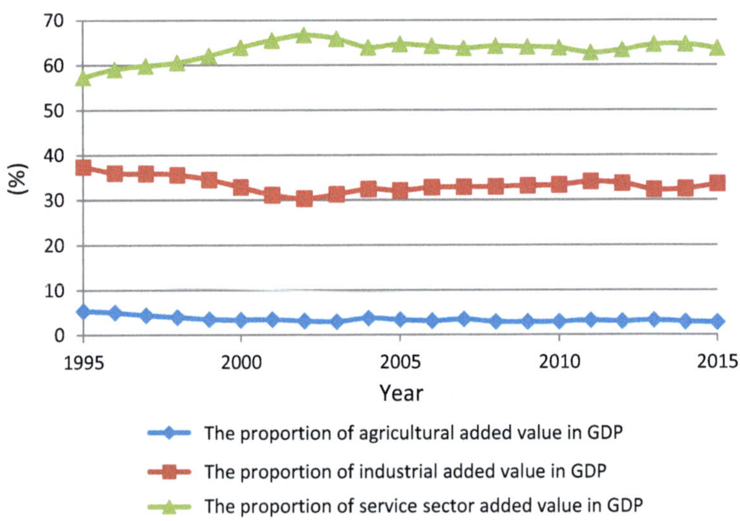

Fig. 9.39 Changes of industrial structure in Poland

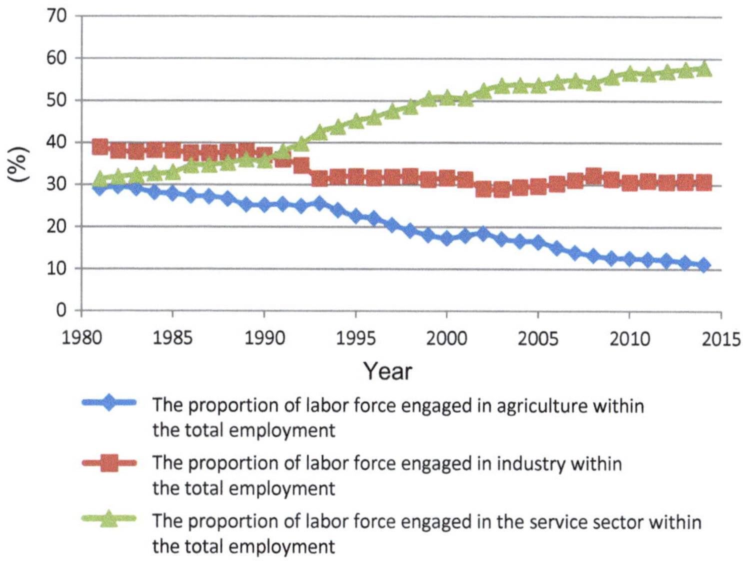

Fig. 9.40 Changes of employment in Poland. *Source of data* World Bank database

partners were Germany, Britain, the Czech Republic, France, the Netherlands, Italy and Russia, as shown in Table 9.22. Germany, spending 53.798 billion USD, was the largest market for Poland's exports, followed by Britain and the Czech Republic at 13.404 billion and 13.99 billion USD, respectively. The top five categories of export commodities are mechanical and electric products, transportation equipment, base metals and products, furniture, toys and miscellaneous products and plastics and rubber. Germany, selling 53.641 billion USD of goods, was also the largest exporter to Poland. China ranked the second at 14.512 billion USD. The top five categories of import goods are mechanical and electric products, transportation equipment, base metals and products, chemical products and plastics and rubber.

2. International investment

Poland has long been the most popular Eastern European country for foreign capital. After joining the EU, the amount of foreign investment absorbed by Poland has doubled. From 2001 to 2003, Poland became less attractive to foreign investment as the tide of privatization retreated. In 2008, the amount of foreign investment decreased slightly due to the financial crisis, but the impact was not significant (see Fig. 9.42). In 2013, Germany was the largest investor in Poland (38.72 billion USD), followed by the Netherlands, France, Luxembourg and Spain. As of the end of 2014, the total foreign investment stock in Poland was 245.16 billion USD and the total flow was 13.88 billion USD.

Table 9.22 Poland's exports/imports to its main trading partners in 2015

Country	Volume (million USD)	YOY (%)	Proportion (%)
Exports			
Germany	53,798	−7.1	27.1
The UK	13,404	−4.4	6.8
The Czech Republic	13,099	−7.8	6.6
France	10,976	−10.6	5.5
Italy	9449	−5.5	4.8
Imports			
Germany	53,641	−11.1	27.6
China	14,512	3.8	7.5
Russia	14,009	−38.4	7.2
The Netherlands	11,356	−9.8	5.9
Italy	10,113	−17.4	5.2

Source of data Statistical Yearbook of the Republic of Poland 2016

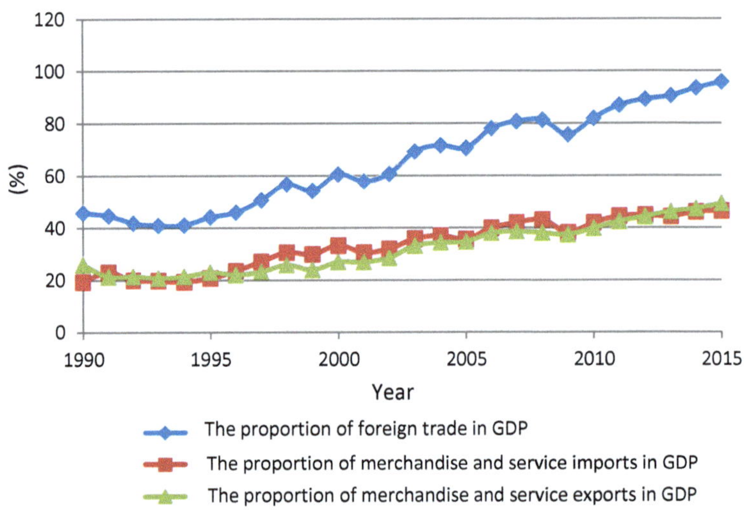

Fig. 9.41 Foreign trade of Poland

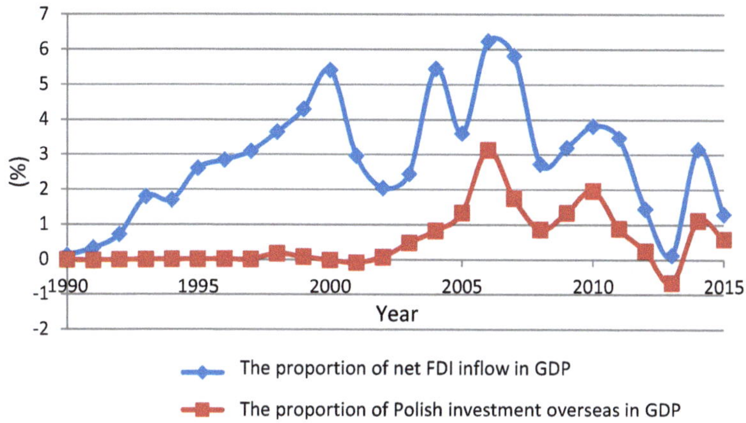

Fig. 9.42 FDI in Poland. *Source of data* World Bank database

9.5 Latvia

I. Geographical and historical backgrounds

The Republic of Latvia is located in the central and northeastern part of Europe. It is one of the Soviet republics that became independent in 1991. Geographically, it was an important outlet to the sea for Soviet Union to reach Western Europe and also the location of the Soviet Baltic Fleet Command. Its geographical location is strategically important, and it is known as the "gate to the south for the Nordics". Latvia is located to the south of Estonia, bordering Russia and Belarus to the east, Lithuania to the south and the Baltic Sea to the west.

The East European Plain is one of the world's famous plains, with a total area of 4 million km^2. The western and northwestern parts of the Plain are rich in amber, known as the "Amber Sea" or "Hometown of Amber". Latvia, Estonia and Lithuania are collectively known as the "Baltic States". Latvia enjoys good natural conditions, with a small amount of minerals such as peat, limestone, gypsum, dolomite and quartz sand. In addition, it is home to 14,000 species of plants and animals. The terrain in the country is low and flat, mostly plains, and only small parts are lowlands and hills. The terrain is slightly higher in the east, and there are many beaches in the western coastal region. Latvia has many rivers and lakes and the longest coastline among the Baltic States (307 miles), which gives the country considerable hydropower and marine resources, and thus good conditions for the development of agriculture and industry.

Latvia has a relatively complex cultural background because of its vital geographic location and the impact it suffered during the two world wars. The official language is Latvian which belongs to the Indo-European Baltic family. More than 95% of domestic residents can speak Russian, and about 10% can speak German and English. Its population is 2.28 million, of which 62% are Latvian, 27% are Russian, 3%

are Belarusian, 2% are Ukrainian and 2% are Polish. Most people are Catholic or Protestant Lutherans.

II. **Economic development**

(I) Domestic economy

Since it became independent in 1991, Latvia has adopted the approach of privatization and free market to westernize its economic system. Figure 9.43 shows how Latvia's nominal (real) GDP and per capita nominal (real) GDP have changed since 1995. The financial crisis of 2008 severely damaged local economy, causing its GDP to fall sharply for two consecutive years. In 2009, Latvia received 7.5 billion euros in loan assistance from IMF, the European Commission and countries like Sweden. Its economy started to recover slowly in 2010. On January 1, 2014, Latvia officially joined the Eurozone as its eighteenth member country.

1. Industrial structure

Latvia's industry and agriculture are highly developed. As early as when it joined the Soviet Union, Latvia had occupied a leading position in the Soviet economy. In 1989, its per capita GNP and per capita national income ranked second in the Soviet Union, after Estonia. The development of its three industries in the past 20 years can be seen in Figs. 9.44 and 9.45.

(1) The primary industry

Latvia is a traditional agricultural country. The proportion of agriculture in GDP is about 5%. In the recent years, the proportion has been declining but generally stayed stable. The per capita arable land area is relatively large. Within its territory of 64,589 km^2, 38% was used for agricultural production in 2014, and the per capita arable

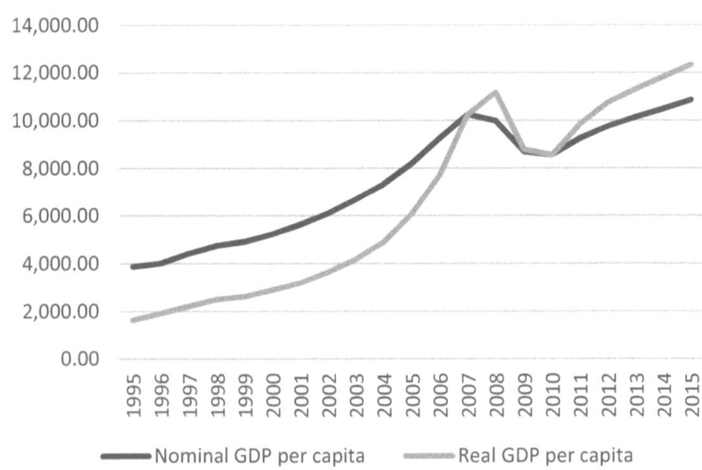

Fig. 9.43 GDP growth in Latvia. *Source of data* CEIC database

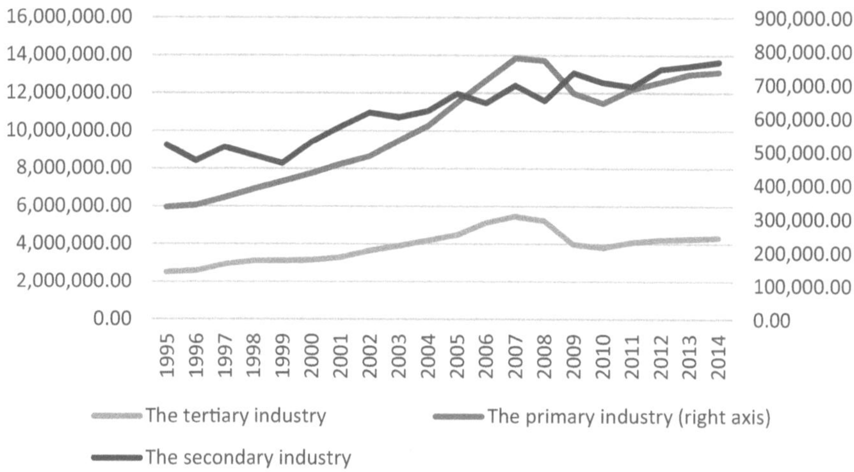

Fig. 9.44 Growths of the three industries in Latvia. *Source of data* CEIC database

land was 0.6 km^2 (1 hectare), as shown in Fig. 9.46. The main crops are grain and animal forage. The exports of agricultural products have always been an important part of its export revenue. At present, agricultural products exported to China are mainly frozen berries and wood. The recent cooperation between China and Latvia in the dairy sector indicates that China will become a major export market for Latvian agricultural products in the long run.

(2) The secondary industry

The well-developed industry of Latvia is dominated by the machine manufacturing and metal processing sectors which mainly concentrate in Riga and Daugavpils. In

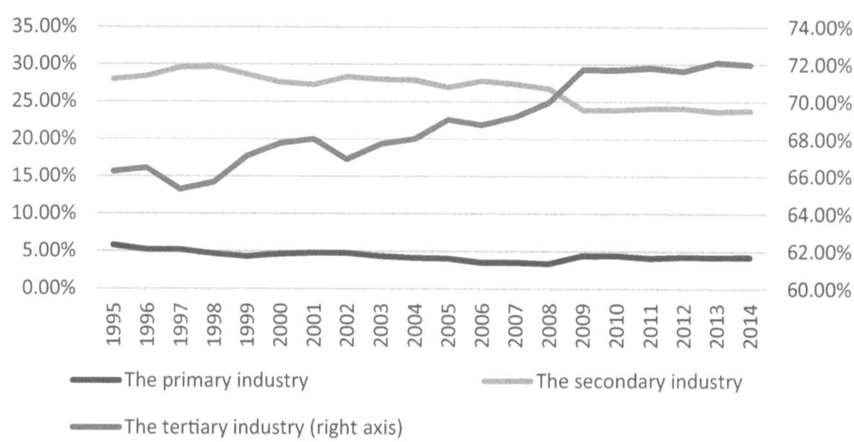

Fig. 9.45 Changes of the proportions of the three industries in Latvia. *Source of data* CEIC database

addition, due to the country's excellent geographical location and good port conditions, its shipping industry is quite developed. As early as before the Second World War, Latvia's industry was in a leading position in the Soviet Union. Although the war disrupted Latvian economic development, its economy quickly recovered thanks to the solid foundation. Since its independence in 1995, its industrial sector has maintained a rapid growth rate. From 1995 to 2007, Latvian industrial output had nearly tripled. However, the global financial crisis has posed negative impacts, leading to the plunge of the industrial output from 2008 to 2010. Rebound began to take place after 2010.

Latvia is rich in forest resources, with a forest coverage rate of 49.9%, much higher than the world average and the EU average (1.6 times of the world average). Its timber reserves amount to 631 million m^3, and the annual timber output is about 10 million m^3. Abundant forest resources make the wood processing industry an important industrial sector in Latvia. In the recent years, the competition among forestry enterprises has become increasingly fierce. SMEs, as the dominant force of the industry, tackle the competition by introducing advanced technology and updating equipment, while large players tend to produce high value-added products such as construction materials.

Latvia has spawned a number of very successful agricultural enterprises. According to the *Latvian Business Report 2014* released by the "Business" website, Uralchem, a company that sells pesticides and fertilizers, became the largest agricultural company in Latvia in 2013 with a turnover of 1.123 billion euros.

(3) The tertiary industry

The service industry has always been a big part of Latvian economy, with its share rising from 66.4% in 1996 to about 72% in 2014. Traditionally, Latvia has been an agricultural and industrial country. However, with the development of the economy, the proportion of agricultural output in GDP has been steadily declining, and the same has happened to the industrial output, while the tertiary industry has been gaining weight. However, the export of services has been growing slower than that of merchandise due to Latvia's limited and shrinking population—most of the new service products have been absorbed domestically.

2. Population and cities

Latvia's has been highly urbanized. As shown in Fig. 9.47, its urbanization rate has been above 50% since 1960. In the 1990s, the sharp decline in the population occurred almost at the same time as the drop of urbanization rate. The slow decline in urbanization is undoubtedly related to the fact that the country has become a high-income country.

Table 9.23 lists the major cities in Latvia.

3. Income

Latvia's income situation is characterized by high level and even distribution. In the recent years, its per capita income has generally maintained a rapid growth rate, as

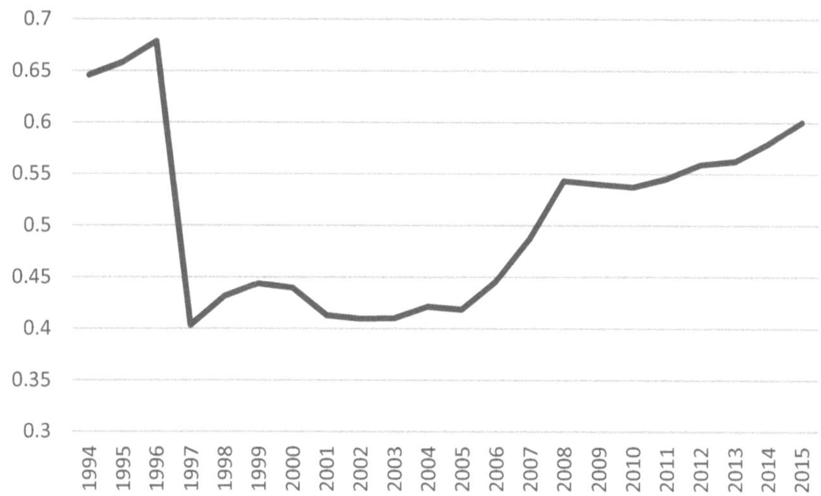

Fig. 9.46 Arable land per capita in Latvia. *Source of data* World Bank database

Table 9.23 Top 5 cities in Latvia

City	Population in 2016	City profile
Riga	742,572	The capital; the sister city with Suzhou (China)
Daugavpils	111,564	The second largest city
Liepaja	85,132	The third largest city; an important ice-free port
Ventspils	42,644	An ice-free port by the Baltic Sea
Jūrmala	54,088	A famous health resort

Source of data World Population Review

shown in Fig. 9.48. Among the former members of the Soviet Union, the only country that achieved a high level of per capita income in 2011 was Estonia. But by 2012, Russia, Latvia and Lithuania also joined the list, with Latvia rising by seven places. Latvia is a country with relatively even income distribution. The Gini coefficient has always been lower than the international alert level of 0.40. The even income distribution has led to a higher consumption rate, which generates a positive impact on economic development and growth.

As shown in Fig. 9.49, Latvia's saving rate has stayed low. According to a report released by the Private Finance Institute of Swedbank, only 53% of Latvians save, compared with 83% and 66% in Estonia and Lithuania. The lower saving rate means more funds have flown to investment or consumption, which has further pushed up the consumption rate, as shown in Fig. 9.50.

Latvia's consumer spending has stayed high, as shown in Fig. 9.50. Its share within GDP has always been higher than 60%, much higher than China's 37.5% in 2014.

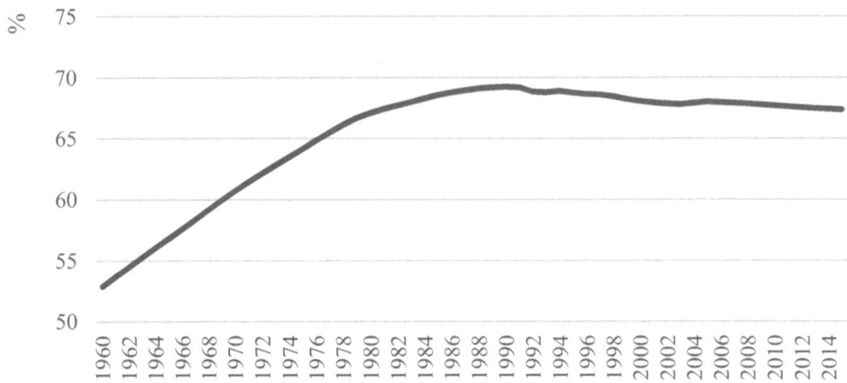

Fig. 9.47 Urbanization rate in Latvia. *Source of data* World Bank database

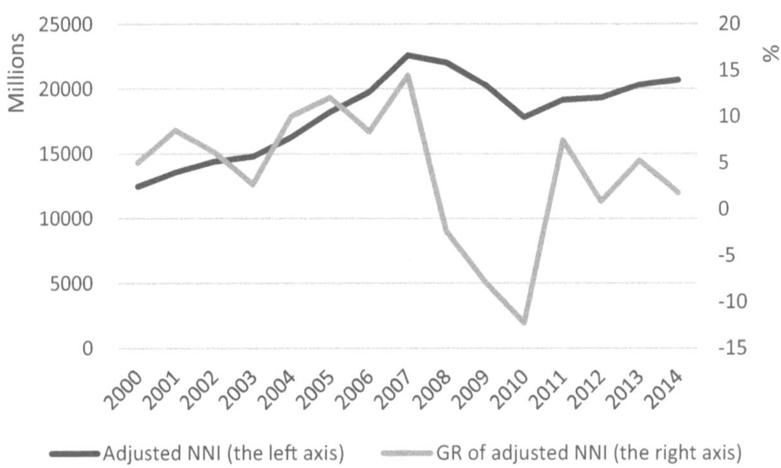

Fig. 9.48 Net national income of Latvia and its growth rate. *Source of data* World Bank database

(II) Foreign trade and investment

1. Foreign trade

Latvia has trade relations with more than 120 countries and regions in the world. Latvia's main exports are timber and wood products, charcoal, electric equipment and parts, steel, fossil fuels, mineral oil and its products and machinery and parts. It mainly imports fossil fuels, mineral oils and their products, machinery and parts, electrical equipment and parts and vehicles and their accessories. In 2011, its main export markets were Russia (17.4%), Lithuania (16.2%), Estonia (12.6%), Germany (7.7%) and Sweden (5.5%). Its main sources of import were Lithuania (17.6%), Germany (11.7%), Russia (8.5%), Poland (7.41%) and Estonia (7.04%).

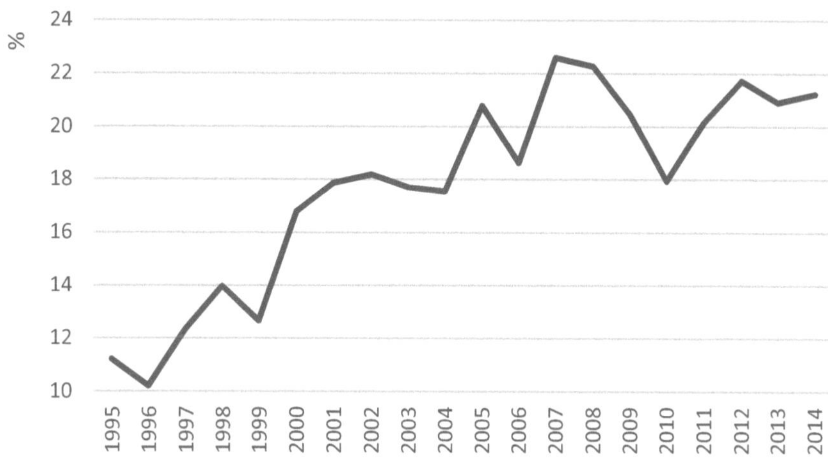

Fig. 9.49 Proportion of total deposits in Latvian GDP. *Source of data* World Bank database

Affected by the international financial crisis, the bilateral trade between China and Latvia declined sharply in 2008, but growth resumed in 2011. According to General Administration of Customs, P.R. China, the bilateral trade totaled 1.382 billion USD in 2012, an increase of 10.0% year-on-year, of which China exported 1.313 billion USD (an increase of 10.0%) and imported 69 million USD (up by 8.5%). Latvia's exports to China are mainly machinery and electronic equipment, transportation equipment, metal products, chemical products and timber and wooden products. Its imports from China are mainly textiles, machinery and electronic equipment and metal products.

Latvia's foreign trade and trade competitiveness index are shown in Figs. 9.51, 9.52, 9.53 and 9.54. Despite an export volume smaller than the import, its trade competitiveness index has risen rapidly (approaching zero) in the recent years, especially after the 2008 financial crisis.

2. International investment

As shown in Fig. 9.55, FDI in Latvia began to plummet in 2008 due to the 2008 financial crisis. According to the report of the Economic and Commercial Office of the Embassy of the People's Republic of China in Latvia, as of the end of 2015, Eurozone countries were the largest direct investors in Latvia, contributing 39.64% of the total, EU countries outside the Eurozone invested 27.63%, and CIS countries spent 8.46%. The top 10 sources of direct investment stocks are Sweden (2.518 billion euros), Cyprus (1.16 billion euros), the Netherlands (966 million euros), Russia (920 million euros), Estonia (728 million euros), Norway (697 million euros), Germany (669 million euros), Denmark (510 million euros), Lithuania (429 million euros) and Britain (410 million euros). The stock of Chinese investment in Latvia amounted to 5.78 million euros.

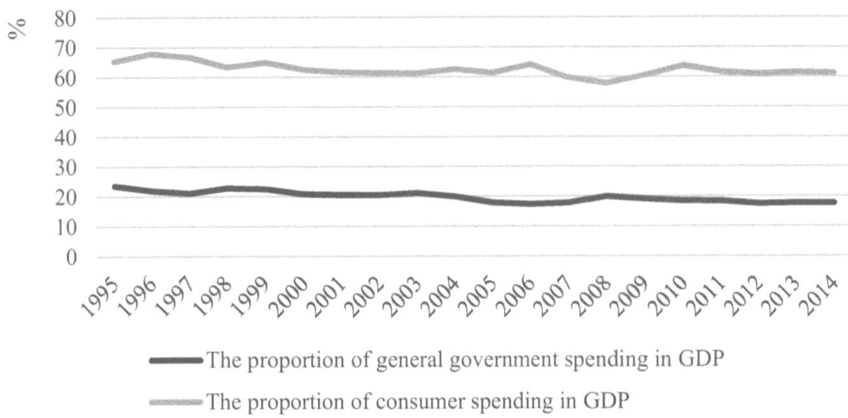

Fig. 9.50 Consumer spending and government spending in Latvia. *Source of data* World Bank database

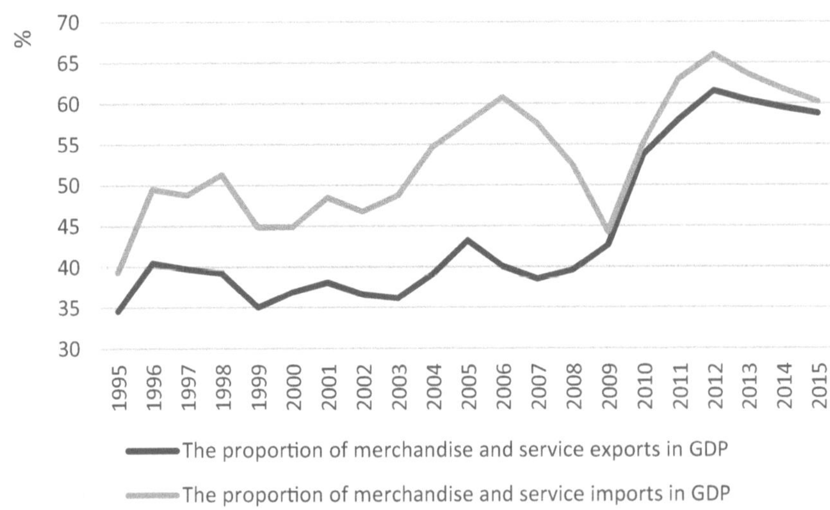

Fig. 9.51 Foreign trade of Latvia. *Source of data* World Bank database

9.6 Lithuania

I. **Geographical and historical backgrounds**

Lithuania is located in Northeastern Europe. Its capital is Vilnius. Becoming independent in 1991, it is a member of the EU, NATO, the Schengen Convention and various international organizations. Located on the east coast of the Baltic Sea, it borders Latvia to the north, Belarus to the east, Poland to the south and the Baltic Sea and Russia's Kaliningrad to the west. The borderline is 1644 km long, and the

Fig. 9.52 Exports of merchandise and services from Latvia. *Source of data* World Bank database

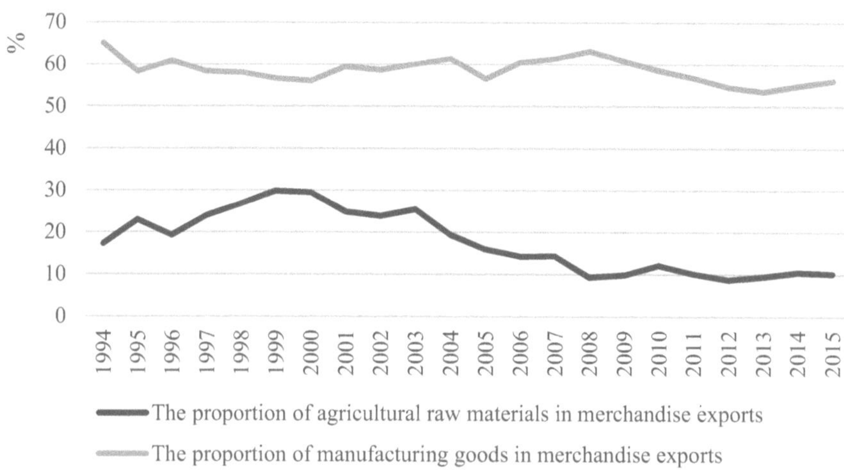

Fig. 9.53 Distribution of exports of different commodities. *Source of data* World Bank database

coastline is 90 km long. In addition to plains, there are also hills in the west and highlands in the southeast.

Of the three Baltic States, Lithuania is at the southernmost tip and has unbreakable links with Latvia and Estonia in many aspects such as politics, economy, history, geography and culture. In terms of population, territorial area and economic scale, Lithuania is the largest country among the three. In the recent years, Lithuania has ranked first among the three in attracting Chinese investment. As the largest seaport by the Baltic Sea, Klaipeda in Lithuania connects East and West by sea and is a strategic point along the Belt and Road.

Lithuania is rich in amber. It has a small amount of clay, sand, lime, gypsum, peat, iron ore, apatite and petroleum. A small amount of oil and gas resources have been

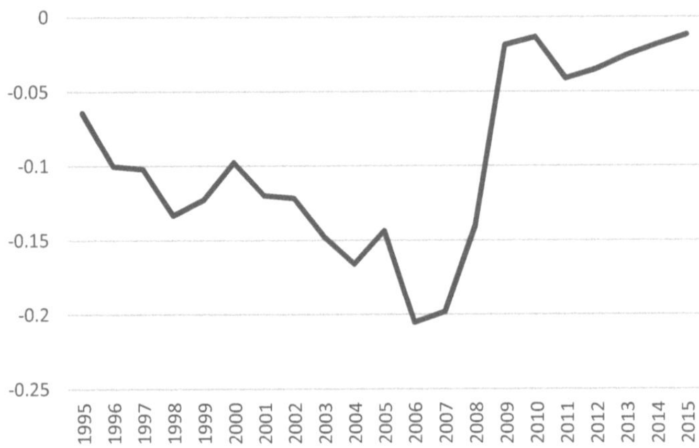

Fig. 9.54 Trade competitiveness index of Latvia. *Source of data* World Bank database

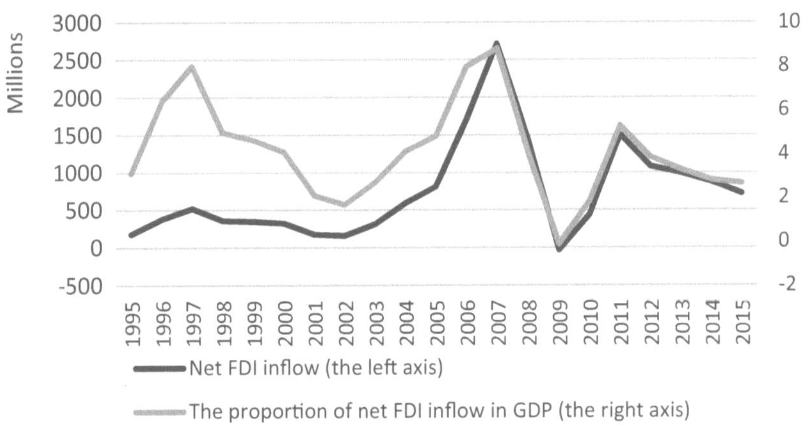

Fig. 9.55 FDI in Latvia. *Source of data* World Bank database

found in the western coastal areas, but the reserves are yet to be proven; therefore, it imports oil and natural gas to meet the demand. Lithuania is rich in forests and water resources. The forest area is 2.177 million hectares, covering 33.4% of the total land area. There are 722 rivers, 21 rivers of which are longer than 100 km—the longest Nemunas River is 937 km in length. The country is dotted by lakes, with a water area of more than 880 km^2 and 2834 of which are larger than 0.5 ha. The Druksciai Lake, covering 4479 hectares, is the largest

II. **Economic development**

(I) Domestic economy

After its independence, Lithuania committed itself to establishing a Western political system and market economy. Lithuanian leadership, believing privatization is the

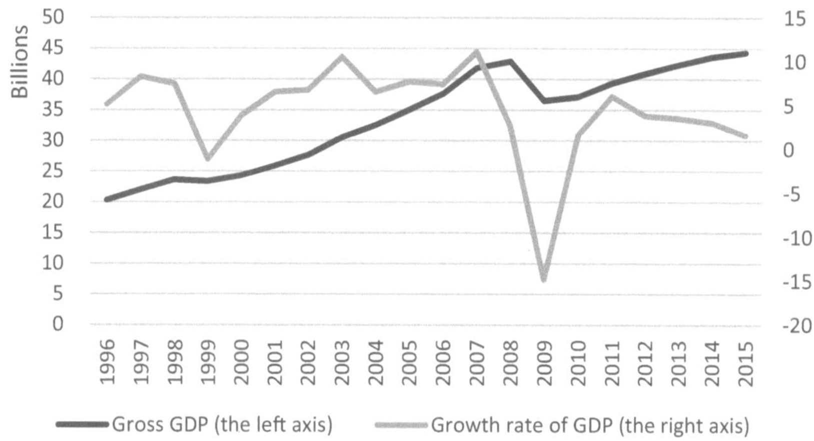

Fig. 9.56 Lithuanian GDP and GDP growth rate

key to the transformation toward a free market economy, introduced the *Lithuanian Privatization Program*, an important guidebook for the country's economic transition. Despite the decline as a result of the financial crisis around 2008, Lithuanian economy has continued to grow in the recent years. As shown in Figs. 9.56 and 9.57, in 2011, Lithuanian GDP grew by 6.04% and per capita GDP by 8.47%. However, problems such as insufficient external demand, high unemployment and high non-performing loans in the banking system do exist. Lithuania joined the WTO in 2015, which had been its goal since independence. To reach this goal, it implemented free and open economic policies in all aspects. Lithuania was once regarded by western countries the "freest market economy in Central Europe", even freer than the Czech Republic, Poland and Hungary.

1. Industrial structure

Lithuania has completed the transformation toward market economy and undergone the transition from an industrial and agricultural power to a service-oriented economy. As shown in Figs. 9.58 and 9.59, the proportion of agricultural value added in GDP dropped from 12.17% in 1996 to 3.44% in 2014. The proportion of industrial value added within GDP remained stable at about 30%, while the share taken by the service sector increased from 57.7% to 66.02%. Lithuanian economy is shifting its focus from agriculture and industry to the service sector.

(1) The primary industry

The main agricultural products in Lithuania are cereals, dairy products, feed crops, crops used as industrial raw materials, pigs, cattle, vegetables, poultry, potatoes, fruits, etc. Among them, cereals and dairy products are the most important. Private farms and farmers produce 68.8% of the total agricultural output, while enterprises contribute 31.2%. In the recent years, agricultural employment in Lithuania has been

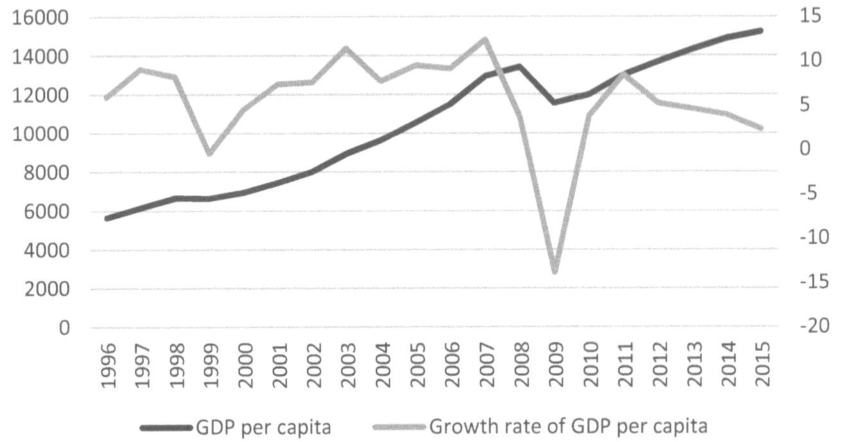

Fig. 9.57 Lithuanian GDP per capita and growth rate

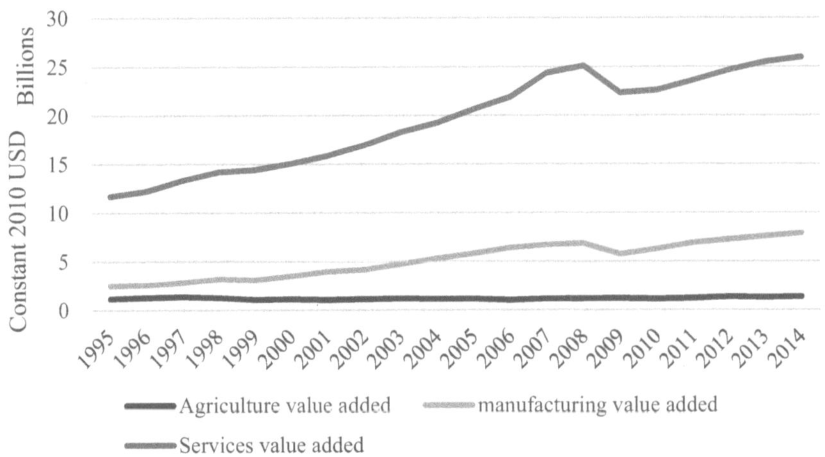

Fig. 9.58 Value added of the three industries in Lithuania. *Source of data* World Bank database

declining, and the per capita cultivated land area has steadily increased after dipping low in 2001, as shown in Figs. 9.60 and 9.61. The reason for this is the expansion and modernization of farms and thus the dwindling demand for manpower. However, there are still many problems in urgent need of solutions, including the small scale of production units, the lack of international competitiveness, the low education level of farmers and the low level of agricultural modernization.

(2) The secondary industry

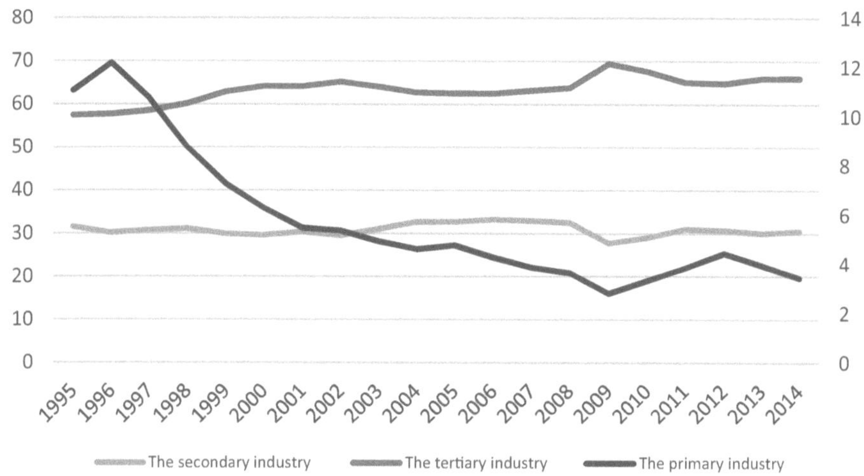

Fig. 9.59 Proportions of the three industries in Lithuanian economy. *Source of data* World Bank database

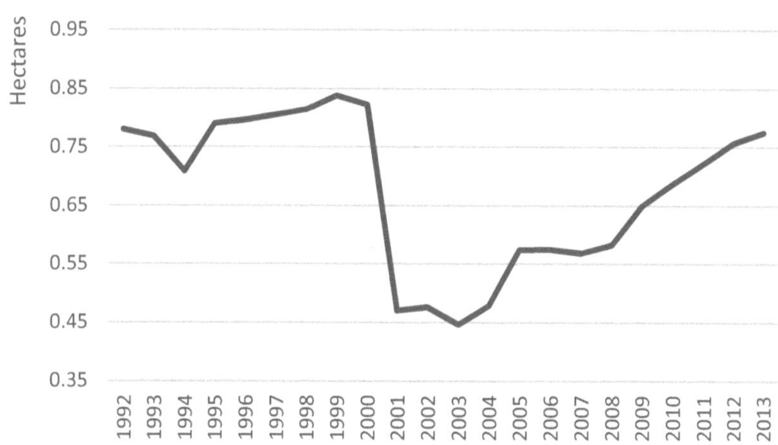

Fig. 9.60 Per capita arable land in Lithuania. *Source of data* World Bank database

Industry is a pillar of Lithuanian economy. Lithuania has a complete industrial system dominated by food, wood processing, textiles and chemical industries. Meanwhile, fast growth is seen in sectors such as machinery, chemicals, petrochemicals, electronics and metal processing. Products including machine tools, meters and computers are sold to more than 80 countries and regions around the world. Producing more than 2/3 of the country's industrial output, Vilnius, the capital, is the industrial center. In the recent years, the industrial output of Lithuania has maintained a steady growth. According to statistics released by the Statistics Lithuania on July 21, 2016, domestic industrial output reached 8.92 billion euros in the first half

Fig. 9.61 Proportion of population engaged in agriculture within the total employment. *Source of data* World Bank database

of 2016, an increase of 2.7% over the same period in 2015. The growth rate stood at 2.3%, adjusted for the difference in working days. In addition, in order to reduce the dependence on Russia for energy, the Lithuanian government is actively building nuclear power plants. Therefore, Lithuanian will have strong demand for Chinese nuclear reactors, and it will continue to promote clean energy, which is worthy of close attention from China.

(3) The tertiary industry

As an important part of Lithuanian economy, the service industry has been the fastest growing sector in the recent years. In the past 10 years, the proportion of services in GDP has increased from 57.7% to 66.02%, and the proportion of population working in the service industry had also increased from 51.4% in 1997 to 65.8% in 2014, as shown in Fig. 9.62. However, similar to situations in countries like Latvia, Lithuanian exports of services also grow slower than that of merchandise due to its limited and declining population. Most new service products are absorbed domestically.

2. Population and cities

Lithuania has completed its urbanization. As shown in Fig. 9.63, its urbanization rate had increased from 39.46% in 1960 to 66.51% in 2014. In the recent years, the urbanization rate has stabilized at about 67% despite slight decline. The immigration tendency and high-income level of the urban population may all lead to de-urbanization to some extent.

Table 9.24 lists the major cities in Lithuania.

3. Consumption and income

The responses made by the Lithuanian government in the face of the crisis indicate that Lithuania is a country with good growth potential. Take the 2008 financial crisis as an example. The unemployment rate in Lithuania was as high as 13.7% in 2009, leading to an increase in the number of immigrants and loss of population, a significant decline in industrial output, investment, consumption and trade and also plummeting GDP and severe fiscal deficits. Lithuania responded forcefully by solving the problem of fiscal deficits first. Measures employed include adjusting

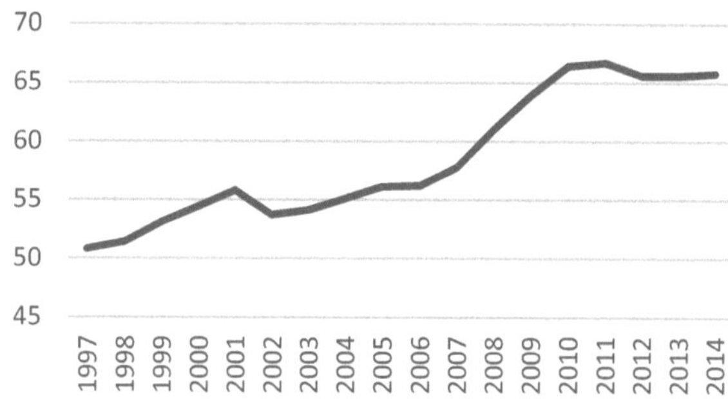

Fig. 9.62 Proportion of population engaged in the service sector within the total employment. *Source of data* World Bank database

Table 9.24 Top 5 cities in Lithuania

City	Population in 2016	City profile
Vilnius	542,366	The capital and the largest city; the industrial center
Kaunas	374,643	The second largest city and the former capital
Klaipėda	192,307	A port at the eastern coast of the Baltic Sea
Šiauliai	130,587	One of the country's industrial, trade, transportation and cultural centers
Panevėžys	117,395	The trade center of agricultural products

Source of data World Population Review

tax revenues and reducing civil service pay. In this way, government revenue was increased and fiscal deficits reduced. In addition, the Lithuanian government began to improve its economic structure by shifting the focus from industry and agriculture to the tertiary industry and encouraging innovation. This had laid a good foundation for its economic recovery after 2010. Among the three Baltic States, Lithuania ranks the second (only after Estonia) in terms of net national income, as shown in Fig. 9.64.

Lithuania enjoys relatively even income distribution. Its Gini coefficient, as shown in Fig. 9.65, was always below 0.38. However, about 19% of people in Lithuania lived below the national poverty line. According to the latest data released by the

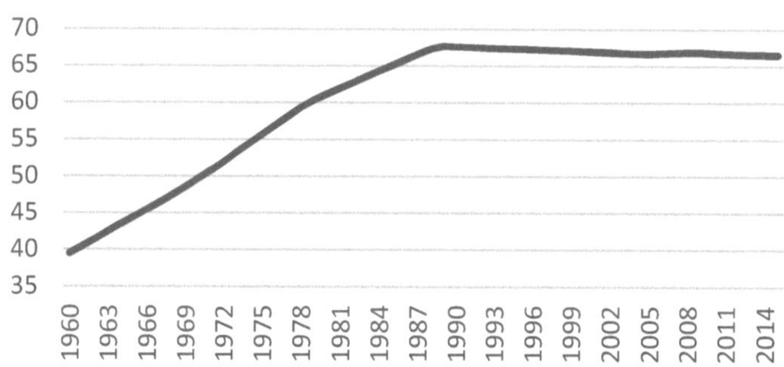

Fig. 9.63 Proportion of urban population. *Source of data* World Bank database

Statistics Lithuania, 22.2% of the population, or 640,000 people, lived below the poverty line in 2015, much larger than the statistics (58,875 people, or 2.97% of the total population) released in May 2015. Poverty will undoubtedly hinder the country's future economic development.

As shown in Fig. 9.66, the ratio of consumption to GDP stayed high. Despite slight decline after 2008, the overall rate had maintained a high level, indicating strong domestic demand.

(II) Foreign trade and investment

1. Foreign trade

The main export commodities of Lithuania are mineral products, electromechanical equipment, electrical equipment, wood, etc. The main import commodities are mineral products, electromechanical equipment, electrical equipment, chemical products, vegetables and fruits. The most important export markets of Lithuanian

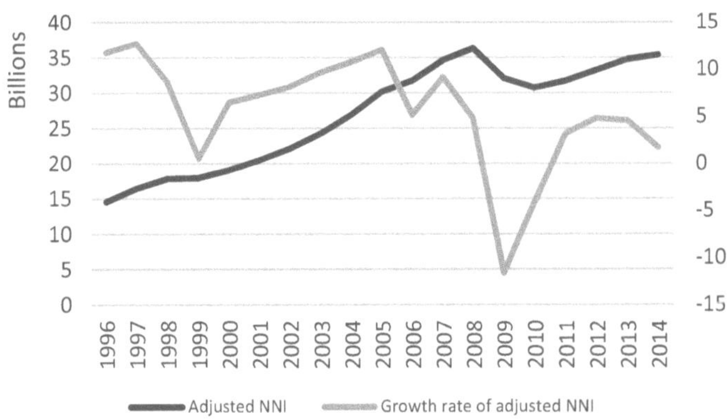

Fig. 9.64 Net national income of Lithuania and its growth rate. *Source of data* World Bank database

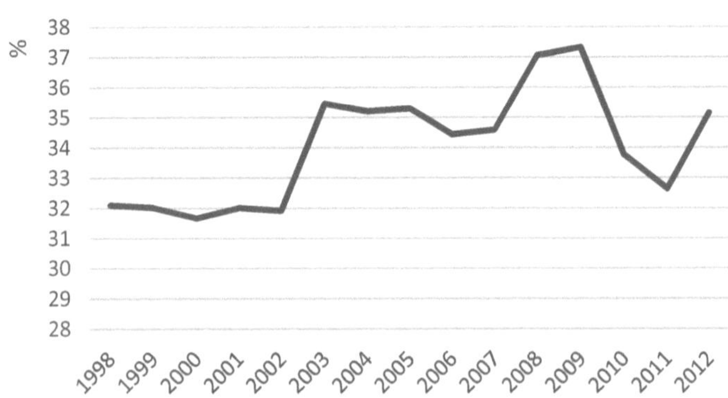

Fig. 9.65 Gini coefficient in Lithuania. *Source of data* World Bank database

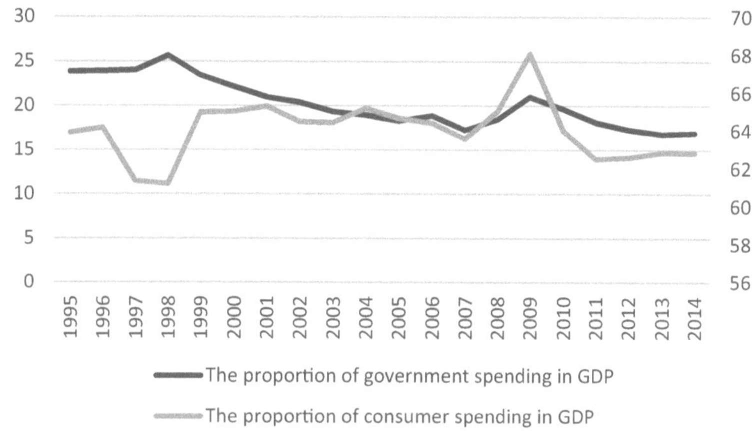

Fig. 9.66 Proportions of consumer spending and government spending in GDP. *Source of data* World Bank database

products in 2014 were: Russia (21.7% of total exports), Latvia (8.2%), Poland (8.2%) and Germany (7.2%). In the same year, Lithuania's main import sources were Russia, Germany (10.8%), Poland (9.5%) and Latvia (6.7%). According to China's Ministry of Commerce, China is Lithuania's largest trading partner in Asia. China mainly exports to Lithuania electronic products, communication products, clothing, ships, steel, nuclear reactors, electronic information equipment, automobiles and steel products. Imports from Lithuania include precision instruments and meters, agricultural products, yarns and dairy products. At the same time, China imports a large amount of wood products from Lithuania every year.

The comprehensive situation of foreign trade and trade competitiveness index of Lithuania are shown in Figs. 9.67, 9.68 and 9.69. After the financial crisis in 2008, its trade competitiveness index rose sharply and turned positive due to the decline of its imports.

2. International investment

With the opening of the Lithuanian market and the ongoing privatization, FDI in the country continued to grow, as shown in Fig. 9.70. After joining the EU in 2004, it absorbed a large amount of FDI thanks to its fast-growing economy and improving investment environment. At the same time, Lithuania adopted many preferential policies, such as exempting foreign investment from customs duties and value-added tax and allowing repatriation of profits, which had proved effective in attracting FDI. Under the impact of the 2008 financial crisis, FDI began to plummet. However, around 2011, as its economy recovered, Lithuania was once again a favored destination for foreign investment. As of 2011, the main investors in Lithuania and their shares were: Sweden (15.4%), Poland (11.5%), Germany (10.4%), the Netherlands (8.8%) and Russia (6.6%). Foreign investment favors the manufacturing industry, wholesale

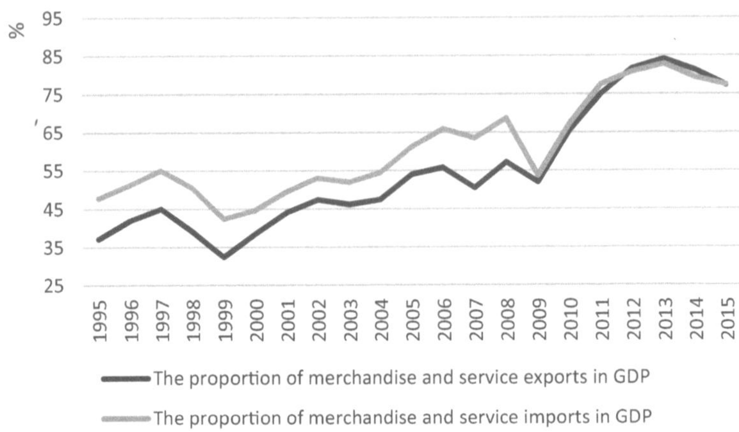

Fig. 9.67 Foreign trade of Lithuania. *Source of data* World Bank database

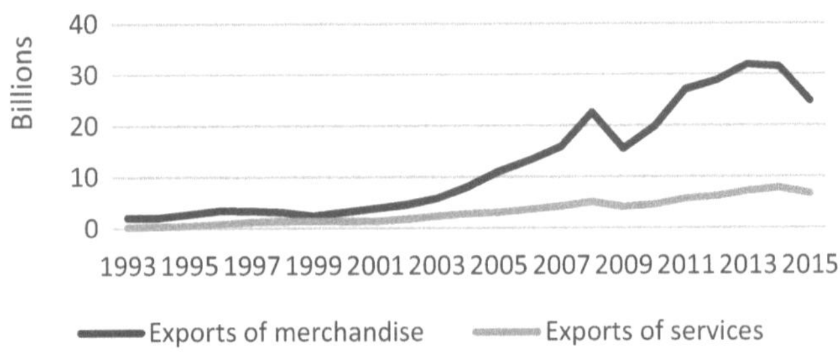

Fig. 9.68 Exports from Lithuania. *Source of data* World Bank database

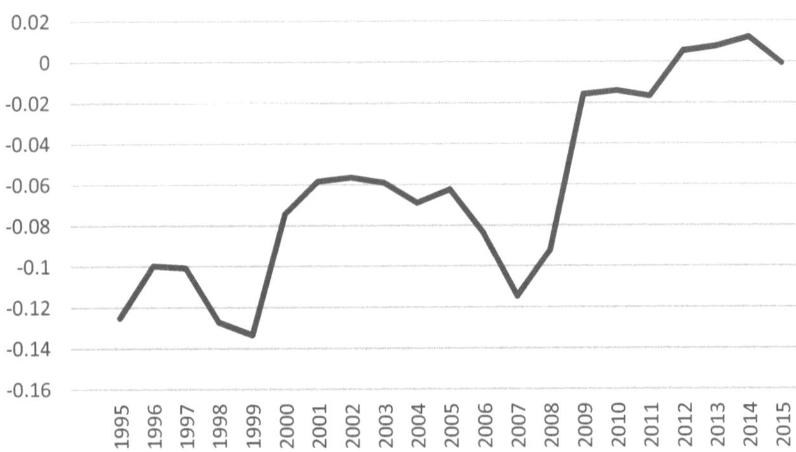

Fig. 9.69 Trade competitiveness index of Lithuania. *Source of data* World Bank database

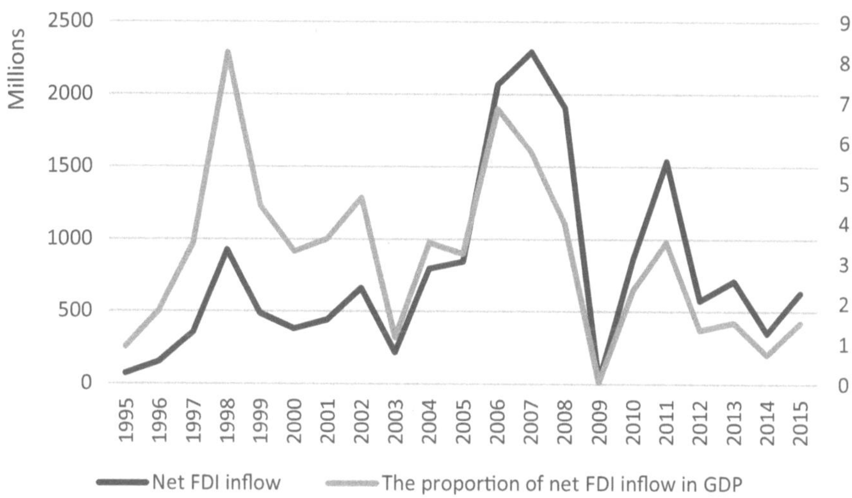

Fig. 9.70 FDI in Lithuania. *Source of data* World Bank database

and retail industries, transportation and communication industries and the financial industry.

9.7 Russia

I. Geographical and historical backgrounds

On November 7, 1917 (October 25, Russian calendar), the October Revolution broke out in Russia under the leadership of Lenin. The world's first socialist state, the Russian Soviet Federative Socialist Republic, was founded. On December 30, 1922, it established the Union of Soviet Socialist Republics with the Transcaucasian Federative Republic, Ukraine and Belarus. On June 12, 1990, the Supreme Soviet of the Russian Soviet Federal Socialist Republic issued the *Declaration of State Sovereignty*, announcing that the Russian Federation has "absolute sovereignty" in its territory. On December 26, 1991, the Supreme Soviet of the Union held its last meeting, announcing the cessation of the existence and the collapse of the Soviet Union. The Russian Federation became a completely independent country and the sole successor of the Soviet Union. On December 12, 1993, after the referendum passed the first constitution after Russia's independence, the country was officially named the "Russian Federation". It is a federal constitutional state with 21 republics, 46 oblasts (provinces), 9 krais (territories), 4 okrugs (autonomous districts), 2 federal municipalities and 1 autonomous oblast. Among them, Crimea and Sevastopol decided to join the Russian Federation after a referendum in March 2014. Russia is located in Northern Eurasia, spanning two continents, and borders Norway, Finland,

Estonia, Latvia, Lithuania, Poland, Belarus, Ukraine, Georgia, Azerbaijan, Kazakhstan, China, Mongolia and North Korea. Covering 17,075,400 km^2, it spans 9000 km from east to west and 4000 km from north to south. It is the largest country in the world, with a total of 194 ethnic groups. The Russian ethnic group accounts for 77.7% of the population. Major minority ethnic groups include Tartar, Ukrainian, Bashkir, Chuvash, Chechen, Armenian, Avar, Moldovan, Kazakh, Azerbaijan and Belarussian. Russian is the official language throughout the Federation, and the republics have the right to define their own national language and use it with Russian in the republic. The Orthodox Church has the largest group of believers, followed by Islam.

The terrain of Russia is dominated by plains and plateaus. The East European Plain covers its west, while its east is covered by the West Siberian Plain, the Central Siberian Plateau and the East Siberian Highlands. Russia has diverse climates—the temperate continental climate is the dominant, and some regions are in the cold zone, with polar deserts, tundra, forest tundra, forests and grasslands, grasslands and semi-desert zones. Russia borders the Arctic Ocean to the north, the Atlantic Ocean to the west and the Pacific Ocean to the east. Its lakes hold about 25% of the world's fresh water. The Volga River is the longest river in Europe with a total length of 3690 km. Lake Baikal is the deepest lake in the world. With the richest mineral, forest and energy resources in the world, Russia is a big exporter of oil and natural gas. Its forest coverage area ranks first in the world, at 8.8 million km^2, accounting for 51% of the country's land area; the accumulative reserves of timber are 82.1 billion m^3. Other proven reserves include: oil at 10.9 billion tons, natural gas at 48 trillion m^3 (35% of the world's proven reserves), coal at 201.6 billion tons, iron at 55.6 billion tons, aluminum at 400 million tons, uranium (14% of the world's total), gold at 14,200 tons, apatite (65% of the world's total) and nickel and tin (30% of the world's total).[4]

II. **Economic development**

(I) Domestic economy

Before its collapse, the Soviet Union had stood at the forefront of the world in terms of economy. After the collapse in 1991, Yeltsin-led ruling party adopted "shock therapy" to reform the economy. As a result, Russia was stuck in depression for the next 10 years. In 2000, after Putin was elected the third president of Russia, he implemented a series of measures for economic revitalization. The Russian economy began to recover and grow fast. During the economic crisis in 2008, the Russian economy took a hard hit, with rising unemployment and a large number of bankruptcies. However, this had not stopped its economic recovery. After 2010, Russia's economy witnessed growth. See Figs. 9.71, 9.72 and 9.73 for more information.

1. Industrial structure

(1) The primary industry

[4] Source of data: Country profile of Russia, official website of Ministry of Foreign Affairs, China.

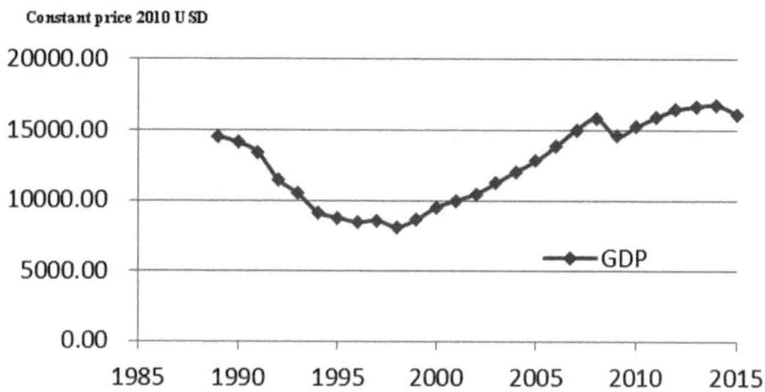

Fig. 9.71 Gross GDP of Russia

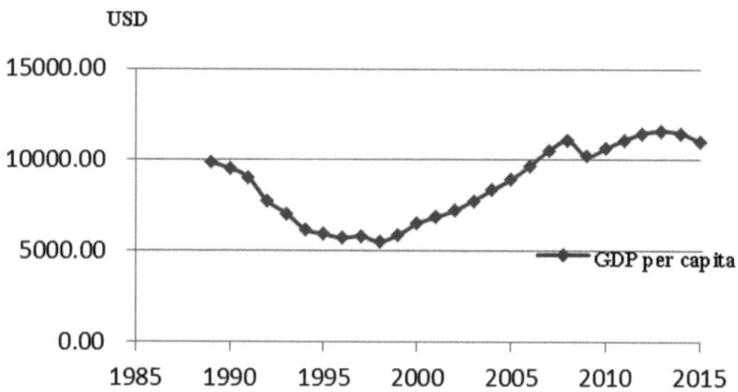

Fig. 9.72 GDP per capita of Russia

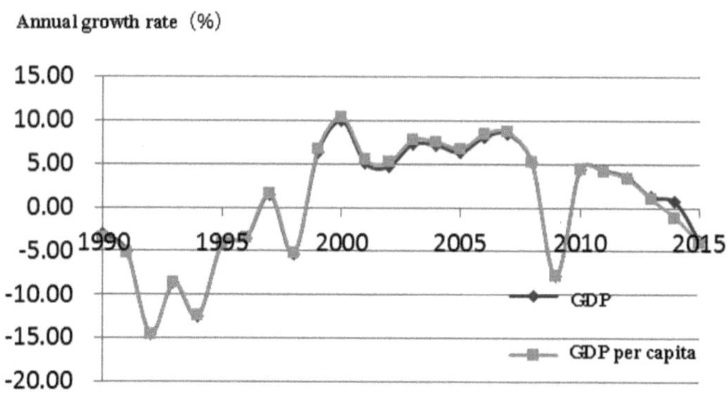

Fig. 9.73 Growth rates of GDP and per capita GDP in Russia. *Source of data* World Bank database

Table 9.25 Outputs of major crops in Russia in 2004–2007

Category	2004	2005		2006		2007	
	Output (10,000 ton)	Output (10,000 ton)	YOY GR (%)	Output (10,000 ton)	YOY GR (%)	Output (10,000 ton)	YOY GR (%)
Grain	7810	7820	0.1	7860	0.5	8175	4.0
Beet	2180	2140	−2.0	3090	44.4	2880	−7.0
Sunflower seed	480	640	33.3	675	5.5	565	−16.3
Potato	3590	3730	3.9	3860	3.5	3660	−5.2
Vegetables	1460	1520	4.1	1560	2.6	1550	−0.7

Source of data Ministry of Agriculture of the Russian Federation

With vast territory and diverse climates, Russia is a traditional agricultural power. In 1917, 82% of the population worked in agriculture. Since the 1950s, the Soviet Union had attached great importance to agricultural development, launching large-scale reclamation projects and promoting agricultural mechanization. As a result, agriculture witnessed fast growth. Russia has about 125 million hectares of arable land, and the per capita arable land is 0.84 hectares. The main agricultural areas are located in Eastern Siberia, South Siberia and the western region. Rice, corn, barley and wheat are the main food crops. The sugar beet, flax and sunflower are the main cash crops. The output of grain, sunflower seeds and potatoes ranks high in the world. For more information, see Table 9.25.

(2) The secondary industry

Russia is an industrial power focusing on the heavy industry, and industry dominates the national economy. From 1926 to the late 1930s, the Soviet Union underwent socialist industrialization. Russia's vast land and rich mineral resources provide the driving force for its industrial development. The proven reserves of copper are 83.5 million tons, accounting for about 10% of the world's total; the reserves of lead are 9.2 million tons, ranking third in the world; the proven reserves of zinc are 45.4 million tons, ranking first in the world and accounting 15% of the world's total; the reserves of nickel, cobalt, tungsten, tin, molybdenum and niobium are 17.4 million tons, 730,000 tons, 2.2 million tons, 350,000 tons, 360,000 tons and 5 million tons, respectively, all ranking high in the world. Among the various sectors of industry, the first category occupies a central position. Machinery manufacturing and metal processing are the areas with competitive edges, producing about 18% of GDP and employing 8.5 million people. Within the energy industry, the natural gas sector takes the largest share (49%), with the largest reserves and yield in the world. Following natural gas are sectors of oil, coal, nuclear power and hydropower.

(3) The tertiary industry

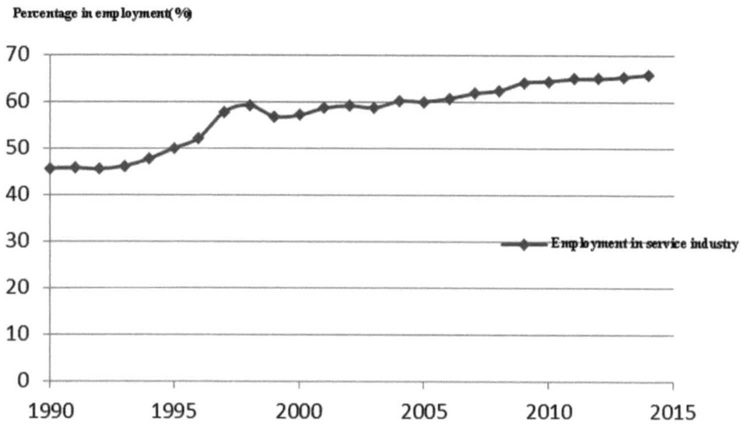

Fig. 9.74 Proportion of population engaged in the service sector within the total employment

After economic restructuring, the tertiary industry has become the leading industry in Russia, generating 62.8% of the national economy in 2015. The service industry is the dominant force in the tertiary industry. In 2014, the service sector hired 65.8% of the total working population, as shown in Fig. 9.74. The service sector is dominated by the retail and wholesale industry, the share of which was once as large as 40%. Other key industries include real estate, finance, education, transportation and communication and health care. In 1991, the tertiary industry overtook industry as the leading force of the national economy.

Since the 1950s, the Soviet Union had launched large-scale land reclamation projects and promoted agricultural mechanization, significantly improving agricultural production efficiency and labor utilization rate. Therefore, the labor force in the primary industry could be released to work in the secondary and tertiary industries. Figure 9.75 shows the changes of the industrial structure—after 1992, the proportion of agriculture in the national economy stabilized below 10%; the tertiary industry exceeded the secondary industry in 1992, producing 49% of the economy, and this momentum continued afterward.

2. Population and cities

In the early days, urbanization was slow in Russia. Before the October Revolution, its urban population was 28 million, 18% of the total. After the Revolution, Russia began to vigorously develop industry, especially heavy industry. In 1940, the urbanization rate exceeded the world average and reached 33%. In the 1960s, the urban population exceeded the rural population for the first time, marking Russia's transition from an agricultural society to an industrial society. After the completion of industrialization, the growth rate of urban population has been steadily declining—it was 0.88% in 1989 and negative in 1993, which is consistent with the de-urbanization tendency after industrialization. It was not until the financial crisis in 2008 that the growth rate

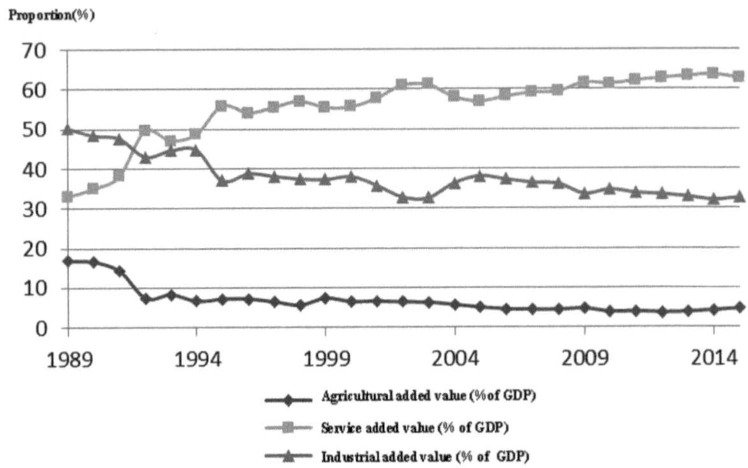

Fig. 9.75 Changes of industrial structure in Russia

of urban population turned positive and started rising again. See Figs. 9.76 and 9.77 for more information.

Russia covers a vast territory, and Table 9.26 lists its major cities.

The capital, Moscow, was built in 1147 and covers an area of 1081 km^2. It is the political, economic and cultural center of Russia, the largest city in Europe, and one of the international metropolises. As of 2016, there were 11.51 million people in Moscow, accounting for 8% of Russia's total population. There are 11 natural forest areas and 98 parks in Moscow. It is also a transportation hub of Russia. The subway stations along the 277 km-long subway lines in Moscow are like museums, well known for their extraordinary designs and Russian atmosphere.

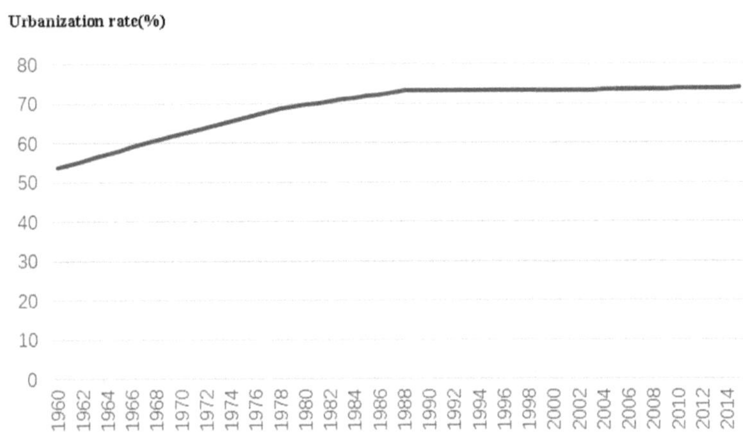

Fig. 9.76 Urbanization rate of Russia

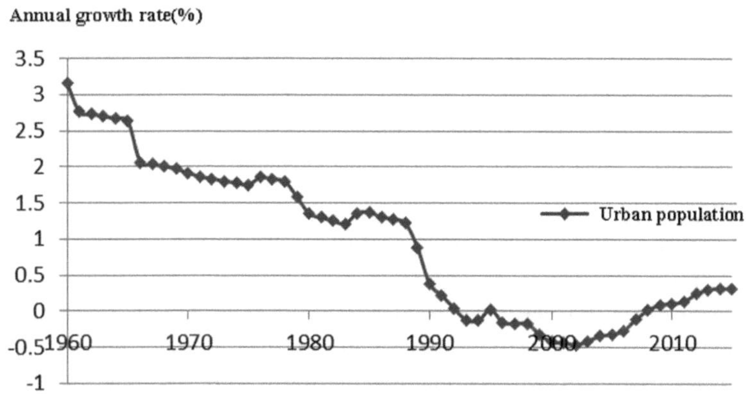

Fig. 9.77 Annual growth rate of urban population in Russia. *Source of data* World Bank database

Table 9.26 Top 5 cities in Russia

City	Population in 2016	City profile
Moscow	11,514,330	The political, economic and cultural center of Russia; the largest city in Europe
St. Petersburg	4,848,742	Located at the mouth of the Neva River and by the Baltic Sea
Novosibirsk	1,473,737	The largest city in Siberia; the regional center of economy, science, technology and culture
Ekaterinburg	1,350,136	Located at the eastern side of the Ural Mountains; the center of the Sverdlovsk region
Nizhny Novgorod	1,250,615	Located at the junction of the Volga River and the Oka River; the center of the mechanical industry

Source of data World population review

St. Petersburg is located in the northwestern part of Russia, facing the Baltic Sea and the Neva Estuary. It is the second largest city after Moscow. Built in 1703, it was once the capital of Russia. The city consists of 42 islands and 423 bridges. The St. Petersburg is a city popular among tourists with its many tourist attractions, including the Winter Palace, the Summer Palace, the Palace Square, St. Isaac's Cathedral and the Smolny Palace. In 1988, Saint Petersburg and Shanghai became sister cities.

Novosibirsk, the capital of Novosibirsk Oblast, is located in the east of Russia with an area of 477 km^2. It is the third largest city in Russia and the largest city in Russia's Asian territory. Founded in 1893, it is an important transportation hub that has grown rapidly. With the best universities, libraries, museums and opera house in the country, Novosibirsk is arguably Russia's cultural center.

Yekaterinburg, the center of the Ural region and the capital of Sverdlovsk Oblast, is located at the junction of Russia's European and Asian parts. It was built in 1723. Yekaterinburg is the cultural and sports center of the Ural region.

Nizhny Novgorod, the capital of Nizhny Novgorod oblast, is the center of Russia's machinery industry. Located at the junction of the Volga and its tributary Oka, it is the center of Russia's European territory. Built in 1221, the city covers 334 km^2. With great geographical advantages, Nizhny Novgorod is an important hub of water and air traffic. Machinery manufacturing is the leading industry of the city (70% of the total industrial output), with products such as automobiles, ships, aircrafts and military products. The world famous Gorky Automobile Plant is based in Nizhny Novgorod. There are also many shipyards and aircraft manufacturers.

As shown in Fig. 9.78, before Vladimir Putin came to power, Russian economy stayed in the ditch, and consumer spending remained low. After Putin's reforms, the situation bettered significantly. As shown in Fig. 9.79, Russia's population stayed stable in the past three decades, not straying much from the figure in 1990 (140 million). Russia is a sparsely populated country. The largest city, Moscow, had a population of 11.5 million in 2010. Russia is already a developed industrialized country at the post-industrial stage. The proportion of its high-quality labor force in the total population remained around 53% for more than a decade. Within the total working population, the share of those engaged in agriculture was smaller than 10%, the number of industrial employees was declining, while the number of employees in the tertiary industry was growing steadily. See Fig. 9.80 for more details.

(II) Foreign trade and investment

1. Foreign trade

In 1995, Russia started the work of joining the World Trade Organization, negotiating on the GATT. On August 22, 2012, it became the 156th official member of the WTO. On May 16, 2007, the OECD invited Russia for membership. In 2009, Russia and the OECD officially launched the negotiation process. In 2014, the OECD announced

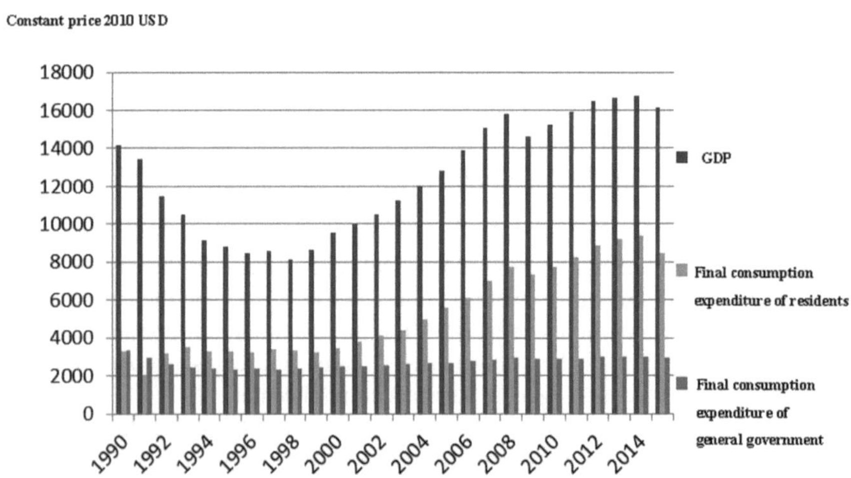

Fig. 9.78 Consumer spending and government spending in Russia

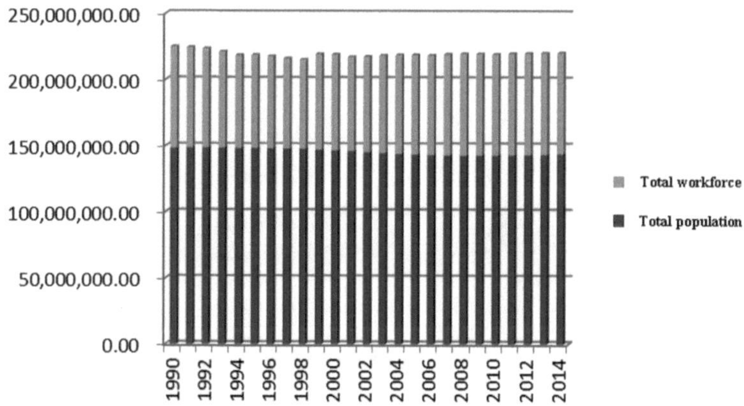

Fig. 9.79 Population and labor force in Russia

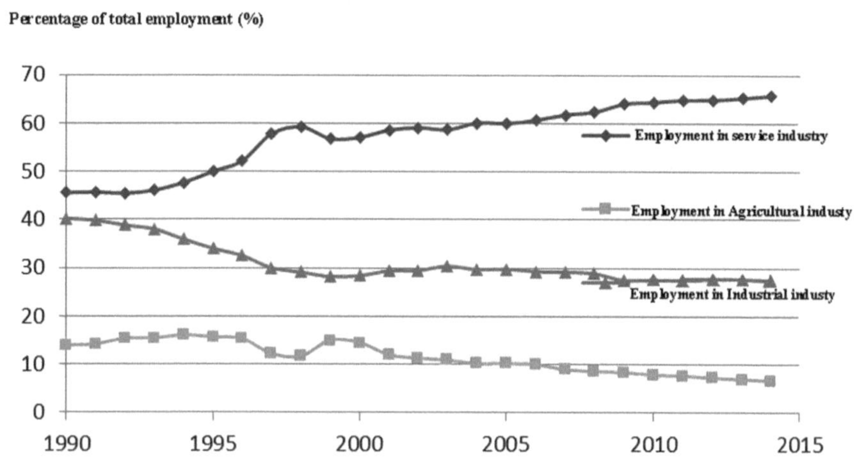

Fig. 9.80 Distribution of Russian labor force among different industries

that the Russian Federation's accession process was postponed due what happened in Ukraine. In 2010, the Customs Union of Russia, Belarus and Kazakhstan was established, which increased the bilateral trade between Russia and Kazakhstan by 30%. In 2011, Russia, Belarus, Ukraine, Kazakhstan, Kyrgyzstan, Armenia, Moldova and Tajikistan reached an agreement on the economic integration of the CIS and signed the *CIS Free Trade Zone Agreement*. In 2014, Russia, Belarus and Kazakhstan reached an agreement on a treaty to establish the "Eurasian Economic Union". Armenia and Kyrgyzstan later joined the Union.

According to the Ministry of Commerce of China, Russia's foreign trade totaled 525.8 billion USD in 2015, a 33% decrease compared to 2014. Within the total volume, imports were 182.4 billion USD, down by 36.4% year-on-year, and exports were 343.4 billion USD, 31% less over the previous year. In 2015, Russia's main

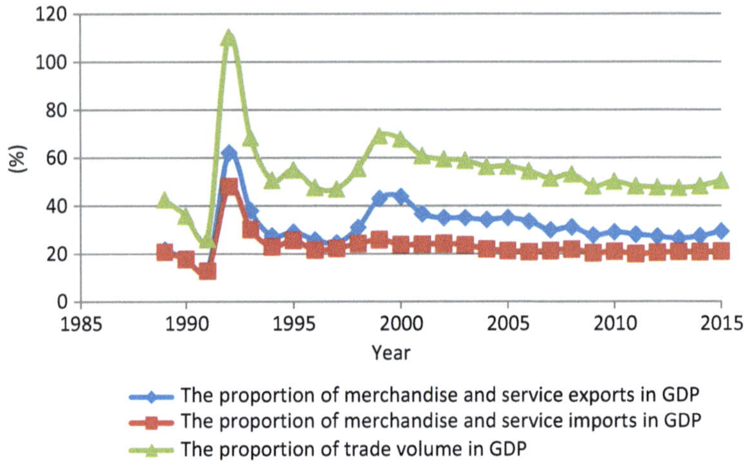

Fig. 9.81 Proportion of foreign trade within Russian economy

trading partners were China, the Netherlands, Italy, Germany, Belarus, the United States, Ukraine, Japan and South Korea. Russia's largest export market was the Netherlands, with a trade volume of 40.82 billion USD. China ranked the second at 28.6 billion USD. The top five categories of export commodities are mineral products, base metals and related products, chemical products, mechanical and electrical products and precious metals and related products. China was Russia's largest source of import, selling 34.94 billion USD of goods, followed by Germany at 20.43 billion USD. The top five categories of imported goods are mechanical and electrical products, chemical products, transportation equipment, base metals and related products and plastic and rubber. For more information, see Fig. 9.81 and Tables 9.27, 9.28, 9.29, 9.30 and 9.31.

2. International investment

Foreign-funded enterprises enjoy the same treatment as Russian enterprises—this is the basic principle held by Russia to attract foreign investment. *The Foreign Investment Law of the Russian Federation* stipulates as follows: foreign-funded business activities are protected by Russian laws, and all legal investment activities can be carried out in Russia; foreign investors have the right to purchase marketable securities, natural resources and real property, to participate in the privatization process and to enjoy various benefits provided by law; the Russian government guarantees that key foreign investment projects are protected from changes in policies and laws during the investment period; the rights and obligations of foreign investment can be transferred to third parties; foreign property is protected from illegal confiscation and expropriation, and nationalization, and compensation should be offered by the Russian government if any of these occurs due to some special reasons; after paying taxes as required by law, foreign investment can freely spend its income (profits, dividends, interest, etc.), including remitting it abroad; foreign investment is entitled

Table 9.27 Foreign trade of Russia (Unit: million USD)

Year	Total	YOY (%)	Exports	YOY (%)	Imports	YOY (%)	Gap	YOY (%)
2002	116,237	10.9	75,484	10.3	40,754	11.9	34,730	8.5
2003	146,157	25.7	95,611	26.7	50,546	24.0	45,065	29.8
2004	205,052	40.3	136,926	43.2	68,125	34.8	68,801	52.7
2005	276,398	34.8	184,916	35.0	91,481	34.3	93,435	35.8
2006	354,674	28.3	226,524	22.5	128,151	40.1	98,373	5.3
2007	469,343	32.3	279,724	23.5	189,619	48.0	90,104	−8.4
2008	623,147	32.8	367,573	31.4	255,574	34.8	111,999	24.3
2009	389,142	−37.6	233,936	−36.4	155,206	−39.3	78,730	−29.7
2010	559,967	43.9	348,528	49.0	211,439	36.2	137,088	74.1
2011	657,378	17.4	378,688	8.7	278,690	31.8	99,998	−27.1
2012	642,969	−2.2	352,537	−6.9	290,432	4.2	62,105	−37.9
2013	841,274	30.8	525,976	49.2	315,297	8.6	210,679	239.2
2014	784,503	−6.7	497,834	−5.4	286,669	−9.1	211,165	0.2
2015	525,830	−33.0	343,427	−31.0	182,404	−36.4	161,023	−23.7

Source of data Website of Ministry of Commerce, China

Table 9.28 Russia exports to its main trading partners in 2015 (Unit: million USD)

Country	Volume	YOY (%)	Proportion (%)
Total	343,427	−31.0	100.0
The Netherlands	40,826	−40.0	11.9
China	28,606	−23.7	8.3
Germany	25,353	−31.7	7.4
Italy	22,293	−37.6	6.5
Turkey	19,332	−22.5	5.6
Belarus	15,206	−23.8	4.4
Japan	14,499	−27.0	4.2
South Korea	13,501	−26.1	3.9
Kazakhstan	10,686	−24.3	3.1
Poland	9653	−39.5	2.8
The United States	9506	−10.6	2.8
Ukraine	9295	−45.5	2.7
Britain	7475	−34.9	2.2
Finland	7094	−37.7	2.1
Latvia	7029	−45.2	2.1

Source of data Website of Ministry of Commerce, China

Table 9.29 Classifications of major Russian export products in 2015 (Unit: million USD)

Classification by customs	HS code	Category	2015	The same period of the previous year	YOY (%)	Proportion (%)
Classification	Chapter	Total volume	343,427	497,834	−33.1	100.0
Classification 5	25–27	Minerals	177,318	295,576	−40.0	61.7
Classification 15	72–83	Base metals and related products	33,014	40,429	−18.3	11.5
Classification 6	28–38	Chemical products	17,959	21,256	−15.5	6.3
Classification 16	84–85	Mechanical and electric products	12,136	14,186	−14.5	4.2
Classification 14	71	Noble metals and related products	7875	11,845	−33.5	2.7
Classification 2	06–14	Plant products	6941	8138	−14.7	2.4
Classification 9	44–46	Timber and wooden products	6315	7765	−18.7	2.2
Classification 7	39–40	Plastic and rubber	4802	5700	−15.8	1.7
Classification 4	16–24	Food, beverage and tobacco	4152	5186	−19.9	1.5
Classification 17	86–89	Transportation equipment	3912	4742	−17.5	1.4
Classification 10	47–49	Cellulose pulp; paper	3517	3887	−9.5	1.2
Classification 1	01–05	Live animals and animal products	3215	3391	−5.2	1.1
Classification 3	15	Animal and plant fats and oils	1874	2266	−17.3	0.7
Classification 18	90–92	Optical instrument, clocks and watches and medical equipment	1249	1449	−13.8	0.4
Classification 13	68–70	Ceramics and glass	1020	1291	−21.0	0.4
		Others	58,129	70,727	−7.8	16.9

Source of data Website of Ministry of Commerce, China

Table 9.30 Russian imports from its main trading partners in 2015 (Unit: million USD)

Country	Volume	YOY (%)	Proportion (%)
Total	182,404	−36.4	100.0
China	34,946	−31.3	19.2
Germany	20,439	−38.0	11.2
The United States	11,453	−38.1	6.3
Belarus	8662	−29.7	4.8
Italy	8318	−34.6	4.6
Japan	6813	−37.6	3.7
France	5919	−44.5	3.3
Ukraine	5671	−47.2	3.1
Kazakhstan	4767	−35.6	2.6
South Korea	4560	−49.4	2.5
Poland	4097	−42.1	2.3
Turkey	4033	−39.4	2.2
Britain	3722	−52.3	2.0
The Netherlands	3096	−41.5	1.7
Brazil	2915	−26.6	1.6

Source of data Website of Ministry of Commerce, China

to fair treatment in disputes and lawsuits in Russia; foreign businessmen have the right to bring their assets and production materials (those they have brought into the country) out of Russia.[5]

Tables 9.32 and 9.33 show the foreign investors in Russia and the sectors they favor. As of 2015, the top investors in Russia were Ireland, Bahamas, British Virgin Islands, Switzerland, Germany, France, Britain, the Netherlands, China, Singapore, Sweden, etc. Most countries' investment in Russia had been increasing. The British Virgin Islands, Ireland, China and the Netherlands had transitioned from recipients of Russian investment to investors in Russia. Russia's mining and quarrying industries had been the focus of foreign investment in the recent years. Foreign investment in manufacturing had been relatively stable. The tertiary industry represented by science and technology, other service industries and information and communications has shifted from accepting foreign investment to investing overseas.

As shown in Fig. 9.82, the financial crisis in 2008 had a significant negative impact on both Russia's absorption of foreign investment and its investment overseas. In order to change this situation, the Russian government has proposed a "modernization strategy", which is to promote the privatization of state-owned assets, lower the threshold for foreign investment and establish direct investment funds by revising relevant laws and regulations so as to increase foreign investment. In 2014, 209.6 billion USD of foreign investment flew into Russia, and FDI in Russia's non-financial sectors was 18.6 billion USD, a 70% decrease from the previous year. Behind the

[5] *Russian Policies on Foreign Investment*, by Ministry of Commerce, China.

Table 9.31 Classifications of major Russian import products (Unit: million USD)

Classification by customs	HS code	Category	2015	The same period of the previous year	YOY (%)	Proportion (%)
Classification	Chapter	Total volume	182,404	286,669	−36.1	100.0
Classification 16	84–85	Mechanical and electric products	55,258	85,846	−35.6	31.1
Classification 6	28–38	Chemical products	23,580	31,232	−24.5	13.3
Classification 17	86–89	Transportation products	16,961	34,413	−50.7	9.6
Classification 15	72–83	Base metals and related products	11,715	19,351	−39.5	6.6
Classification 7	39–40	Plastic and rubber	10,334	15,146	−31.8	5.8
Classification 2	06–14	Plant products	9911	13,316	−25.6	5.6
Classification 4	16–24	Food, beverage and tobacco	8715	13,096	−33.5	4.9
Classification 11	50–63	Textiles and raw materials	8296	12,372	−33.0	4.7
Classification 1	01–05	Live animals and animal products	6766	12,251	−44.8	3.8
Classification 18	90–92	Optical instrument, clocks and watches and medical equipment	5434	8408	−35.4	3.1
Classification 20	94–96	Furniture, toy and miscellaneous products	4885	8121	−39.9	2.8
Classification 5	25–27	Minerals	4788	7161	−33.1	2.7
Classification 10	47–49	Cellulose pulp; paper	2857	4489	−36.4	1.6
Classification 12	64–67	Light industrial products such as footwear and umbrella	2531	3950	−35.9	1.4
Classification 13	68–70	Ceramics; glass	2240	3704	−39.5	1.3
		Others	8133	13,814	−41.1	4.5

Source of data Website of Ministry of Commerce, China

Table 9.32 Major foreign investors in Russia

Year	Non-CIS countries	The British Virgin Islands	Ireland	The Bahamas	Switzerland	Germany	France	Britain	The Netherlands	China	Singapore	Sweden
2015	4890	884	1528	1320	825	506	501	452	393	294	130	−94
2010	15,957	−1636	−6	478	−216	1650	1729	1068	1354	75	7	1266
2008	12,719	−1329	18	569	247	939	149	219	−17	−31	7	745

Table 9.33 Changes of the distribution of foreign investment among different economic sectors in Russia

Year	Mining and quarrying	Manufacturing	Agriculture, forestry and fishery	Finance and insurance	Wholesale and retail	Science and technology	Other services	Catering and accommodation	Water supply; sewage treatment; waste recycling	Information and communications	Transportation and warehousing	Real estate	construction	Supply of electricity, gas, steam and air conditioning
2015	3973	2940	109	191	132	69	31	21	−35	−104	−179	−295	−538	−1398
2013	−537	3330	143	4192	2270	140	1538	78	1	−2146	−118	−238	248	466
2010	1564	3967	74	3543	476	1579	764	38	3	895	−480	1874	902	1058

decline were Western sanctions, the crisis in Ukraine and the economic downturn in Russia. About 152.4 billion USD of foreign investment flew to sectors such as manufacturing, commerce, maintenance of transportation and electrical equipment, finance and mining and mineral resources development, accounting for 89.5% of the total. As Table 9.34 indicates, in 2013, the largest investor in Russia was Cyprus at 22.68 billion USD, followed by Britain, Luxembourg, the Netherlands, France, Germany, the United States, Ireland, China and Japan which contributed 68% of the total. As of the end of 2014, Russia's total foreign investment stock was 378.54 billion USD, slightly lower than the 384.12 billion USD in 2013.

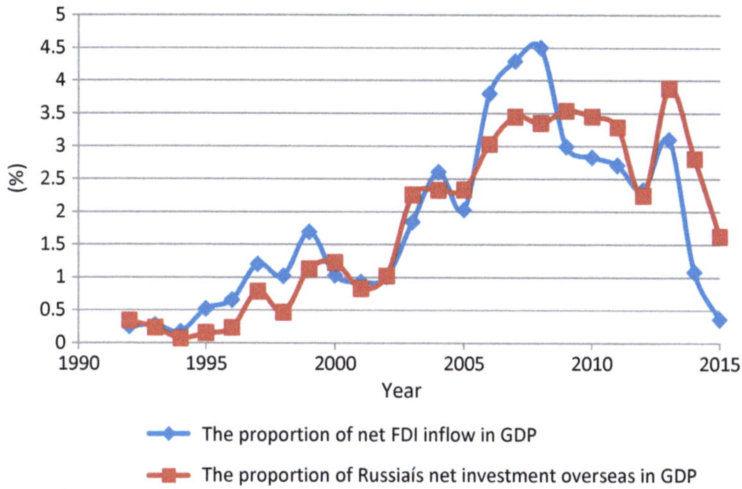

Fig. 9.82 Foreign investment of Russia

Table 9.34 Major sources of foreign investment in Russia 2013 (Unit: 100 million USD)

Source country	Volume
Cyprus	226.8
Britain	188.6
Luxemburg	170.0
The Netherlands	147.8
France	103.1
Germany	91.6
The United States	86.6
Ireland	67.6
China	50.3
Japan	26.2

Note the above countries contributed 68% of foreign investment absorbed by Russia in 2013
Source of data Federal State Statistics Service (Rosstat)

Table 9.35 Statistics of trade between China and Russia (Unit: 100 million USD)

	2011	2012	2013	2014
Total trade volume	792.5	881.6	892.1	952.8
China's imports from Russia	403.5	441.0	396.2	416.0
China's exports to China	389.0	440.6	495.9	536.8
Stock of direct investment	37.6	48.9	75.8	87.0
Flow of direct investment	7.2	7.9	10.2	6.3

Source of data Ministry of Commerce, China; General Administration of Customs, P.R. China

China has good trade relations with Russia. As Table 9.35 shows, China invested 634 million USD in Russia in 2014, mainly in areas like mineral resources, energy, construction, home appliances and communications and services. In 2014, the bilateral trade totaled 95.28 billion USD, an increase of 6.8% over the previous year. Within it, China's imports from Russia were 41.6 billion USD, up by 4.9%, and the main import commodities were crude oil and refined oil, iron ore and its concentrates, coal, timber, etc.; China's exports to Russia amounted to 53.68 billion USD, up by 8.2%, and the main export commodities were machinery and equipment, clothing and footwear and electric appliance and electronics.

9.8 Ukraine

I. Geographical and historical backgrounds

The word Ukraine means "man on the border" and was first seen in *The History of Ross* (1187).[6] Historically Ukraine was the core area of Kievan Rus, a feudal duchy that had reached its heyday during the Rurik Dynasty. From the twelfth century to the fourteenth century, the political, economic and cultural center of Kievan Rus moved to Vladimir and the duchy entered the era of feudal secession. Since the fourteenth century, Ukrainians have gradually formed a single nation with unique language, culture and customs. After the First World War, Ukraine established a socialist government and joined the Soviet Union. In 1991, it declared independence. Located at the crossroads of Eastern Europe and Russia, Ukraine is significant geographically, the second largest on the continent after Russia. Bordering Russia to the east, Poland and Slovakia to the west and Romania and Moldova in the south, it has a land area of 603,700 km^2, about 3% of the Soviet Union. Most of the land is located in the East European Plain. It spans 1300 km from east to west and 900 km from north to south, and the longest river is the Dnieper River. There are a total of 27 first-level administrative regions (now 25)—24 states and 2 municipalities in the country (the capital Kiev and Sevastopol, and the latter joined Russia on March 18,

[6] Source of data: country profiles, by Ministry of Foreign Affairs, China.

2014) and one autonomous republic (Crimea Autonomous Republic, which joined Russia on March 18, 2014).

Black earth is a feature resource of Ukraine. Two-thirds of the land area is covered by black earth, which accounts for about 25% of the total black earth area in the world.[7] Ukraine is rich in forest resources, with 14% of coverage rate. It has more than 70 kinds of mineral deposits, such as asphalt, anthracite, iron, manganese, chromium, titanium, lead, zinc, aluminum, mercury, nickel and a certain amount of natural gas and oil. Coal accounts for 80% of all fuel resources. Donetsk has the largest coal mine in Ukraine, with proven reserves of 48.8 billion tons.[8]

II. **Economic development**

(I) Domestic economy

Ukrainian economy has gone through great turbulence. Since 2001, thanks to the privatization reforms and economic transformation, its economic structure has become increasingly comprehensive and its national economy had achieved continuous growth for 8 consecutive years. In the 2008 financial crisis, Ukraine was hit hard, resulting in economic downturn. It was not until 2010 that Ukrainian economy began to rebound. In 2014–2015, its economy plummeted due to political turmoil, Crimea's accession to Russia and the war in its eastern part. This is the worst upheaval in Ukraine since its independence. Then a financial collapse was avoided thanks to the mid-term loan scheme agreed by the new government and IMF, and the economy continued to decline in 2015, with real GDP falling by 9.9%, foreign investment capital shrinking from 8 billion USD in 2012 to 2.961 billion USD,[9] foreign trade volume dropping by 28.67%[10] and serious currency depreciation.

As Fig. 9.83 shows, since the independence in 1991, Ukrainian GDP has undergone three rounds of decline. The first round was during the period of economic transition from 1991 to 2000. The second round was in 2009 during the financial crisis. The third round was during the turbulent period of 2014–2015. The third round reduced Ukraine's real GDP from 143.75 billion USD in 2013 to 121.07 billion USD in 2015 (2010 base period) and the nominal GDP from 183.31 billion USD in 2013 to 90.62 billion USD in 2015. Figure 9.84 shows that Ukraine's GDP growth rate was −9.9% in 2015 and −6.6% in 2014—a recession for two consecutive years.

Affected by political, economic and social turmoil, in 2014 and 2015, hryvnia, the Ukrainian currency depreciated 68% against the USD, the core inflation rate hiked to 34.7%,[11] and CPI skyrocketed to 181 in 2015 and then 206 in 2016 (100 in 2010), much higher than the average level in 2010–2013 (Fig. 9.85).

In 2015, Ukraine's per capita GDP was 2,124 USD, ranking among the lower middle-income countries. As shown in Fig. 9.86, the per capita GDP of Ukraine had

---

[7] Source of data: Ministry of Commerce, China.

[8] Source of data: *Guidebook on investing in other countries—Ukraine.*

[9] Source of data: CEIC database.

[10] Source of data: World Bank database.

[11] Source of data: Guidebook on investing in other countries, by Ministry of Commerce, China.

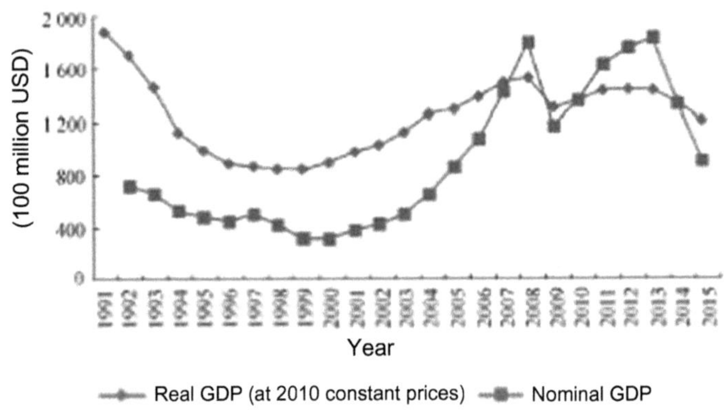

Fig. 9.83 Ukraine's gross GDP since its independence. *Source of data* World Bank database

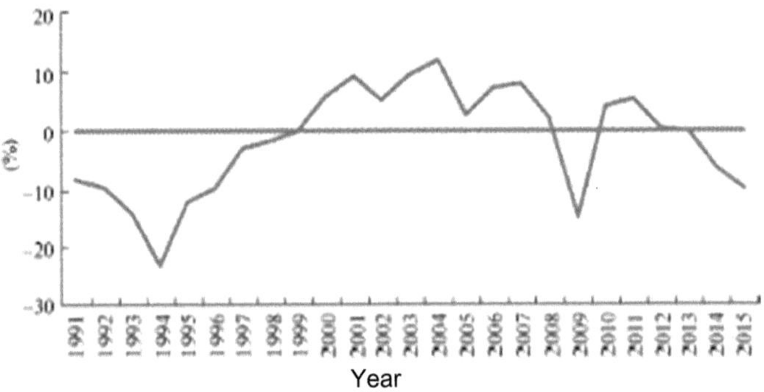

Fig. 9.84 Growth rate of Ukraine's GDP. *Source of data* World Bank database

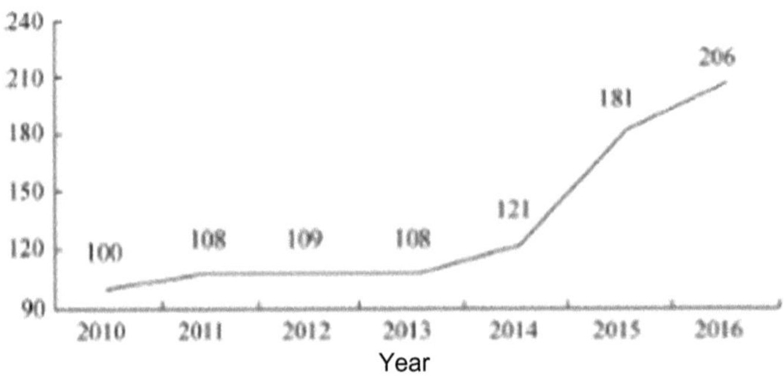

Fig. 9.85 CPI in Ukraine 2010–2016 (Year 2010 = 100). *Source of data* IMF

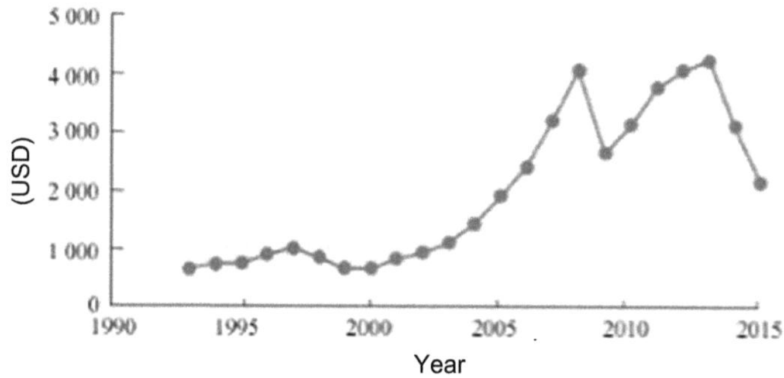

Fig. 9.86 GDP per capita in Ukraine. *Source of data* CEIC database

been rising since 1993, but it witnessed sharp fall in 2009, 2014 and 2015. The per capita GDP in 2015 was approximately the same as that in 2005.

In 2013, the Gini coefficient of Ukraine was 24.6, which is a relatively low level, indicating that the national income distribution is relatively even.[12] According to the *2015 United Nations Human Development Report*, Ukraine's human development index is 0.747, ranking relatively high at 81st in the world.

There is wide gap between the eastern and western parts of Ukraine. Ukraine's economic layout is divided into the east and west by the Dnieper River. The eastern part is the industrial base, and the western part is dominated by agriculture and service industry. The eastern part, as the economic pillar of the country, produces two thirds of the national economy; the western part suffers high unemployment rate due to hollowing out of the industry, and a large number of labors have been forced to flow to Russia, Poland and Germany through legal or illegal channels. In the twenty-first century, an increasing amount of labor force has been flowing to EU countries. It could be concluded that the western part is both culturally close to and economically dependent on Europe.[13]

1. Industrial structure

Agriculture, industry and mining are the mainstays of Ukrainian economy. During the Soviet Union period, its industry and agriculture were already well developed. It was known as the "European granary". Abundant natural resources made it the military and heavy-industry center of the Soviet Union—its scientific and technological strength accounted for a quarter of the Union's total.

In 2013, Ukraine had 41.5 million hectares of agricultural land, of which 32.5 million hectares were arable land. The soil is fertile in Central and Southern Ukraine and relatively poor in the north. Also in 2013, Ukraine's agricultural output totaled 32 billion USD, 17% of its GDP. Its total grain output was 62.3 million tons, ranking eighth in the world. The total export volume of agricultural products and food was 17 billion USD. Grain export reached 26.8 million tons, 43% of its total grain output

[12] Source of data: World Bank database.

[13] Source of data: Belt and Road database, http://www.ydylcn.com.

and 10% of global grain exports, making it the fifth largest grain exporter in the world. Its main export markets were Spain, the Middle East and North Africa. In the first nine months of 2014, Ukraine's total grain exports to China amounted to 154 million USD.[14]

Ukraine is the tenth largest steel producer in the world, producing 2% of the world's total. Its steel industry mainly relies on the international market, and only 20% of output is absorbed domestically.[15] Ukraine has a very developed military industry, with many military-related companies and research institutions in areas such as machine manufacturing, fuel power and high technology. Ukraine has a relatively advanced technology reserve in the manufacturing of rockets, space engines, aircraft, missiles and naval vessels.

In 2015, President Poroshenko signed the "*Ukraine-2020*" *Stable Development Strategy* which sets the goals, directions, priorities and specific targets for future development. The goal of the reform is to reach European living standards and to gain Ukraine its due status in the world. The strategy includes 62 reforms and identifies 25 key targets for successful development. The priority areas for reform include national security and defense system, government reshuffle and the fight against corruption, judicial and law enforcement systems, decentralization and state governance, deregulation and enterprise development, healthcare system and tax system. Priority projects include achieving energy independence, promoting the image of Ukraine around the world and pursuing national interests in global information space.[16]

As Fig. 9.87 shows, the tertiary industry in Ukraine had grown rapidly in the past 20 years, rising from about 30% of the national economy in 1987 to 60% in 2014. The proportion of the secondary industry had been falling and stabilized at about 25%. The primary industry had rebounded in the recent years and accounted for 10%.

As shown in Fig. 9.88, its manufacturing industry (D), with a solid foundation and a full range of sectors (Ukraine has inherited the developed heavy industry the Soviet Union), is high in output and large in scale, producing 15% of the national economy. Ukrainian industry is dominated by sectors such as machinery, chemicals, coal and military products. At the same time, it has a well-developed mining industry. As the largest country in Europe except Russia, it has rich mineral resources such as iron, manganese ore, coal, oil and natural gas. The figure shows transportation (I) is also an essential part of the Ukrainian economy. In fact, Ukraine enjoys good infrastructure for railway, road, river and sea transportation.

2. Population and cities

As shown in Fig. 9.89, the total population of Ukraine dropped from 52 million in 1991 to 45.198 million in 2016. The proportion of urban population increased from 67.2% in 2001 to 69.7% in 2015, suggesting a high level of urbanization.

---

[14] Source of data: Economic and Commercial Counsellor's Office of the Embassy of the People's Republic of China in Ukraine.

[15] Source of data: Ministry of Commerce, China.

[16] Source of data: Economic and Commercial Counsellor's Office of the Embassy of the People's Republic of China in Ukraine.

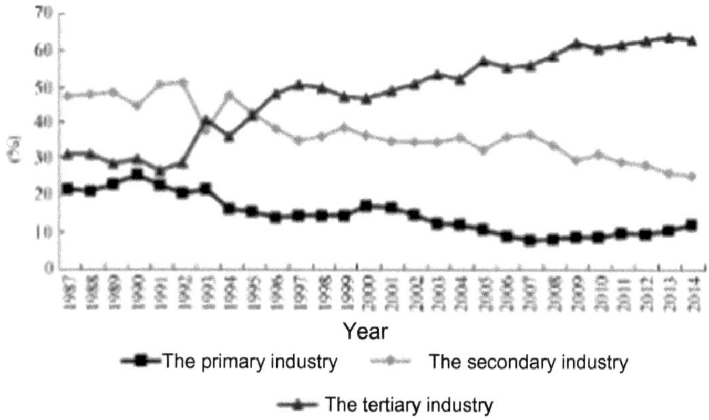

Fig. 9.87 Changes of industrial structure of Ukraine

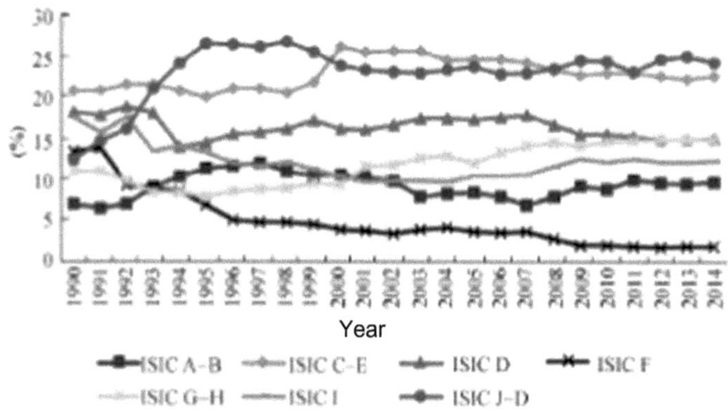

Fig. 9.88 Proportions of different economic sectors in Ukrainian economy

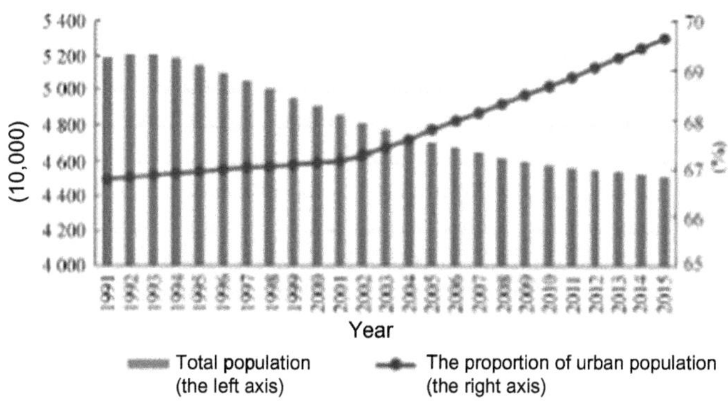

Fig. 9.89 Total population and urban population of Ukraine. *Source of data* World Bank database

Table 9.36 Top 5 cities in Ukraine and their populations

City	Population
Kiev	2,797,553
Kharkov	1,430,885
Dnieper	1,032,822
Donetsk	1,024,700
Odessa	1,001,558

Source of data World Population Review 2017

Table 9.36 lists the major cities in Ukraine.

(II) Foreign trade and investment

1. Foreign trade

In 2008, Ukraine became the 152nd member of the World Trade Organization. Since then, there have been few barriers for foreign companies operating in Ukraine. The accession has brought significant benefits to Ukraine, especially the unrestricted access of steel products and textiles to the EU market—this is particularly important because the EU has overtaken Russia as Ukraine's most important trading partner.

After its entry into the WTO, Ukraine has made commitments in opening 11 core industries of the service sector, including business services, communications services, construction and related engineering services, distribution, education and environment services, financial services (insurance and banking), health care and social services, tourist, recreational, cultural and sports services, transportation services and other areas such as cosmetics, hairdressing, hydrotherapy and massage services. In 2014, the EU signed an association agreement with Ukraine on the establishment of an in-depth and comprehensive free trade zone, so as to deepen the political and economic relations between the two and prepare for the gradual integration of Ukraine into the EU market. To attract investment, the Ukrainian government offers a number of investment incentives, including providing tax breaks to companies engaged in baby food manufacturing, applied technology of energy efficiency, hotel services, light industry, aircraft/ship building, agriculture, forestry and fishery, biofuel manufacturing, publishing and food processing.

As Fig. 9.90 shows, under the impact of the upheaval in 2014–2015, Ukraine's foreign trade plunged to a point lower than that during financial crisis. In 2015, Ukraine's foreign trade totalled 96.165 billion USD, of which 50.061 billion USD were of export and 46.104 billion were of imports. The total amount fell by 28.67% compared to 2014, and 2014 also saw a year-on-year drop of 24.48%. The main import sources and export markets are listed in Table 9.37.

2. International investment

As Fig. 9.91 presents, FDI flow in Ukraine went through decline in two consecutive years—from 58.157 billion USD in 2013 to 45.744 billion in 2014, and then to 42.523 billion in 2015.

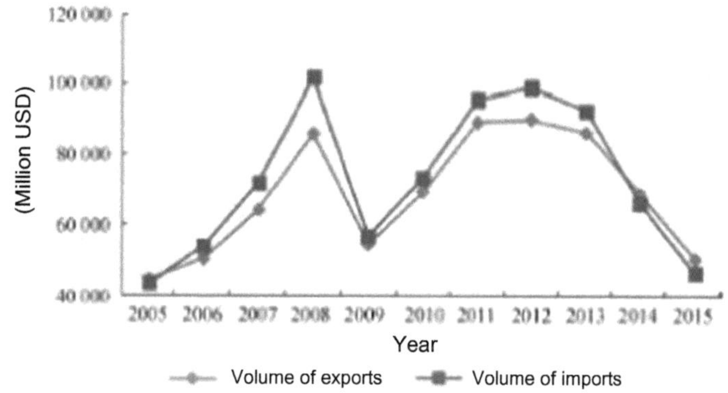

Fig. 9.90 Foreign trade of Ukraine. *Source of data* World Bank database.

Table 9.37 Major export markets and import sources of Ukraine 2014

Export market	Proportion (%)	Source of import	Proportion (%)
Russia	18.18	Russia	23.31
Turkey	6.61	China	9.95
Egypt	5.31	Germany	9.86

Source of data State Statistics Service of Ukraine

According to Table 9.38, in the three years of 2005, 2010 and 2015, countries that always ranked among the top 10 investors in Ukraine were Cyprus, Germany, the Netherlands, Austria, Britain, Russia and the British Virgin Islands, which shows that Europe is the main source of FDI in Ukraine.

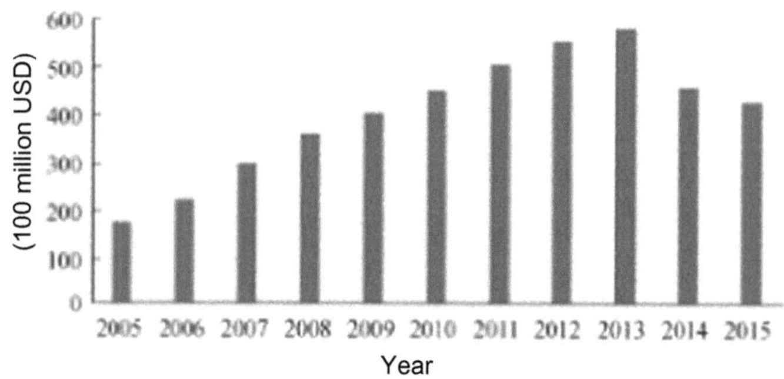

Fig. 9.91 FDI flow in Ukraine 2005–2015. *Source of data* CEIC database

Table 9.38 Rankings of Ukraine's FDI source countries (Unit: million USD)

Ranking	2005		2010		2015	
1	Germany	5504	Cyprus	10,045	Cyprus	11,745
2	Cyprus	1636	Germany	7083	The Netherlands	5611
3	Austria	1440	The Netherlands	4683	Germany	5414
4	The United States	1387	Russia	3403	Russia	3392
5	Britain	1175	Austria	2731	Austria	2402
6	The Netherlands	920	France	2368	Britain	1853
7	Russia	836	Britain	2287	British Virgin Islands	1799
8	British Virgin Islands	737	Sweden	1711	France	1528
9	Switzerland	456	British Virgin Islands	1452	Switzerland	1364
10	Poland	226	The United States	1158	Italy	972

Source of data CEIC database

Chapter 10
Southern Europe

The main characteristics of the southern European countries are their small land area and population. The main natural resources include metal ore such as iron and copper, animal and plant resources and petroleum and lignite. There is a considerable gap in the economic development levels of some countries in southern Europe. The performance of the European Union members, including Greece, Croatia and Bulgaria, is far ahead that of Albania and Bosnia and Herzegovina. From the perspective of economic aggregates, the total nominal GDPs of Greece, Croatia and Bulgaria in 2015 were, respectively, 195.2 billion USD, 48.7 billion USD and 43.4 billion euros, and the total of the latter two countries was less than half of that of Greece. The GDP per capita in Greece and Croatia both exceed 11,000 USD, making them developed countries, while the figure in Albania and Bosnia and Herzegovina is less than 4200 USD; as to international trade, the total volumes of Greece and other EU member states are all higher than 40 billion USD, while the figures of Albania and Bosnia and Herzegovina are all under 14 billion USD. It is worth noting that the major trading partners of southern European countries are EU member states such as Germany and Italy; under the impact of the 2008 financial crisis and the European debt crisis, all southern European countries but Bulgaria are suffering from sluggish economic growth; the tertiary industry dominates the economic structure of southern European countries; for instance, the proportion of the tertiary industry is 80% in Greece, the highest within this region.

The ten southern European countries have established good diplomatic and trading relations with China. In the 1950s, China established diplomatic relations with Albania and Bulgaria and started trading activities; in the 1970s, diplomatic relations between China and Greece were set up, and in the early 1990s, diplomatic ties with Bosnia and Herzegovina and Croatia were formed. As the official launch of the "China–CEE Cooperation Mechanism" and the Belt and Road Initiative in 2012, a new diplomatic landscape has taken shape—China is currently cooperating with Albania and Bosnia–Herzegovina on the highway project and thermal power plant project, respectively.

H. Zhang et al., *Comparative Studies on Regional and National Economic Development*,
Global Economic Synergy of Belt and Road Initiative,
https://doi.org/10.1007/978-981-16-2105-5_10

10.1 Albania

I. Geographical and historical backgrounds

Albania is a small country located in southeastern Europe with an area of 28,700 km^2, which is equivalent to 3/4 of China's Taiwan Province.

It is bordered by Montenegro and Serbia in the north, Macedonia in the east, Greece in the southeast, Italy across the Adriatic Sea to the west and the Ionian Sea on the southwestern coast. There are many mountains and few plains in the country. Mountains and hills account for 77% of the total area, and plains account for 23%. Forest coverage is 36%; arable land accounts for 24%, and pasture accounts for 15%. The coastline is 472 km long.

In terms of resources, the main mineral resources exported by Albania are chrome ore and petroleum. Chrome ore reserves are 37.3 million tons, ranking the forefront in the world, and oil reserves are about 473 million tons. In addition, natural gas, asphalt, lignite and other resources are also widely distributed in Albania.

Albania is known as the "Country of Mountain Eagles", which originated from the seal of Skanderbeg, the leader of the fifteenth century resistance to the invasion of the Ottoman Empire. The eagle is the symbol of this national hero. Albania was occupied by Italian and German fascists during WWII and was declared liberated in 1944. The People's Republic of Albania was founded in 1946 and took the path to socialism.

II. Economic development

(I) Domestic economy

Albania was a closed market with a planned economy. In recent years, it is gradually developing toward a modern market economy. Currently, the Albanian government has not proposed a national strategic development plan, but it is working for the goals of joining the European Union, building a democratic society ruled by law and boosting economic growth. As shown in Fig. 10.1, Albania's economy had experienced 12 years of rapid growth since 1997. After the global financial crisis broke out in 2008, Albania's economy declined. From 2009 to 2014, it witnessed a period of adjustment, and in 2015 a sharp fall was seen.

Albania is closely related to Greece and Italy in terms of trade, overseas remittances and banking. This is one of the reasons why the 2008 financial crisis imposed a huge impact on the Albanian economy. In terms of European standards, Albania's economy is relatively backward, with a per capita GDP of 4253 USD and a Gini coefficient of 34.5 in 2013, ranking somewhere in the middle.

1. Industrial structure

As shown in Fig. 10.2, the industrial structure of Albania has changed significantly since the 1990s: the primary industry has fallen from 50 to 20% (within the whole economy); the secondary industry shrank from the 40% in the 1980s to about 10% in 1998, and then gradually increased to the current 25%; the tertiary industry rose

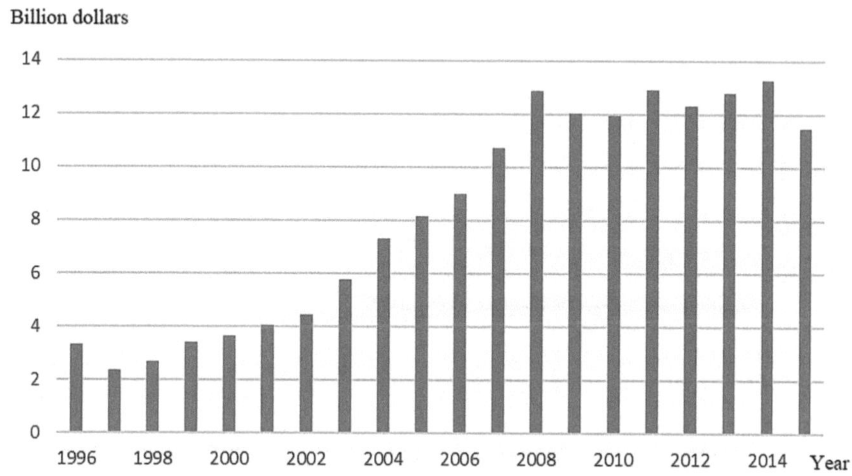

Fig. 10.1 GDP of Albania in the past 20 years. *Source of data* World Bank database

rapidly to more than 50% of domestic output after 1995. Generally speaking, the Albanian economy is currently dominated by the tertiary industry. The proportion of the secondary industry has declined in recent years, while that of the primary industry has increased slightly.

As shown in Fig. 10.3, major changes have taken place in the economic sectors in Albania since 1990. The proportion of major industrial sectors has fallen sharply. As to the proportion of the manufacturing sector (D), Albania has a poorly developed industrial foundation, and commercial trade mainly relies on resource exports. In

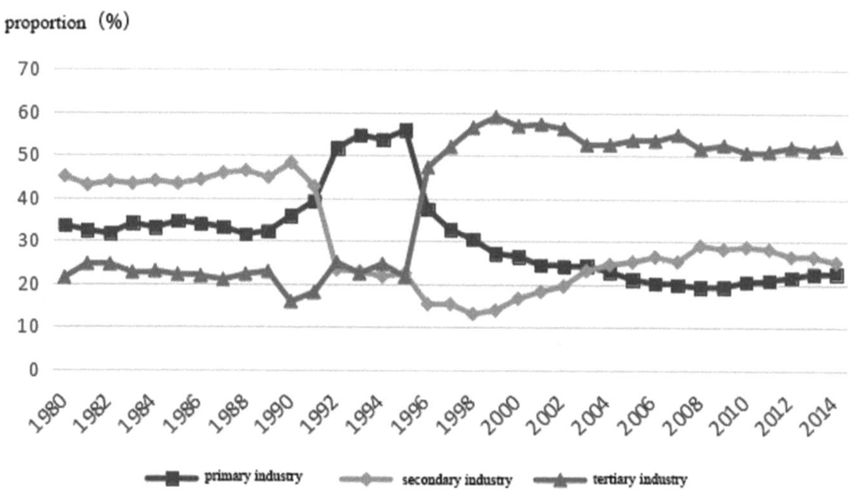

Fig. 10.2 Structural changes of the Albanian economy. *Source of data* World Bank database

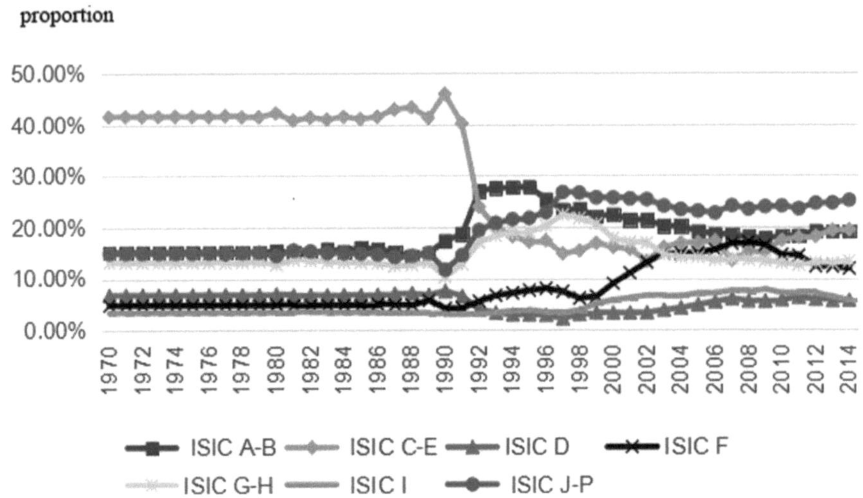

Fig. 10.3 Proportions of different sectors in the Albanian economy. *Source of data* World Bank database

recent years, the Albanian government has made tourism a priority area of development. In 2014, 3.67 million foreign tourists visited Albania, up by 4.5% on a year-on-year basis. The retail and hotel industry (G–H) currently accounts for 15% of the domestic economy. Albania's farming, forestry, animal husbandry and fishery industries (A–B) have also steadily expanded in recent years and currently account for 20% of domestic output. Albanian agriculture has achieved relatively stable development toward an organic future. In 2014, the agricultural output was about 3.054 billion USD, generating a YOY increase of 2%.

2. Population and society

Albania's employment situation is grim. In 2015, its average unemployment rate was 17.3%, ranking 161st in the world in terms of employment. In addition, the employment structure is also relatively unbalanced. In 2014, agriculture hired 41.8% of the labor force, but contributed only 22.3% of GDP. This is mainly due to its non-mechanized and self-sufficient approach of agricultural production.

The total population of Albania is 2.89 million, of which 98.8% are Albanians. As shown in Fig. 10.4, the population of Albania has witnessed a steady decline in the past 20 years. A 2011 report by the Albanian National Statistics Service stated that large-scale migration and fertility declines were the main reasons for the drop in population. In terms of gender ratio, there are more females than males, with 0.98 male per female. In terms of population structure, people aged 65 and over account for 11.3%, making the country an aging society. In terms of urbanization, the 2011 census shows 53.7% of the population live in cities and 46.3% of them live in the rural areas.

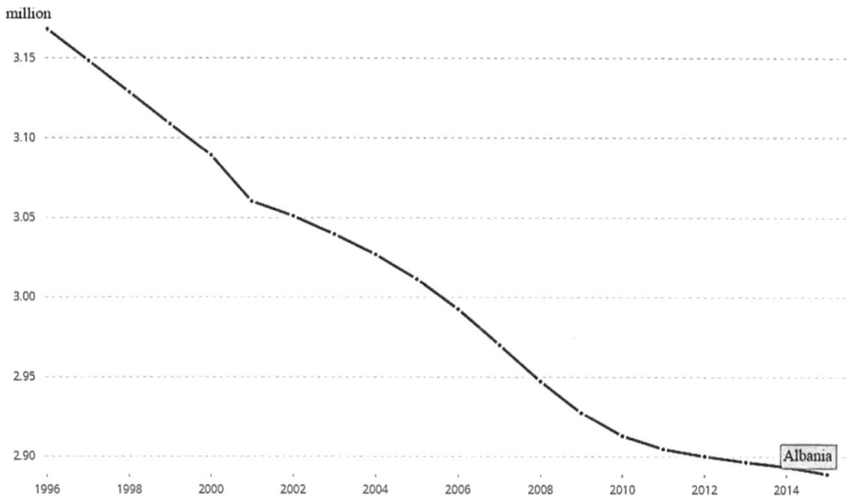

Fig. 10.4 Population changes in Albania in the past 20 years. *Source of data* World Bank database

Albania's capital Tirana, with a population of about 800,000, is the largest city in the country and also the political, economic and cultural center. The port city of Durres is the second largest city. It has the largest seaport in the country and is one of the oldest cities in Europe. It has shipbuilding, locomotive, food processing and chemical industries. It is also a marine fishery production base in Albania.

(II) Foreign trade and investment

In 2014, the total trade volume of Albania was 7.743 billion USD, up by 7.8% on a year-on-year basis. The volume of export was 2.439 billion USD, up by 4.9% year-on-year, and the volume of import was 5.304 billion USD, up by 9.2% year-on-year, landing the deficit at 2.769 billion USD, up by 9.2% year-on-year. Exports are mainly textiles and footwear, minerals and fuels, construction materials and metals, food, beverages and tobacco. Imported goods are mainly machinery and spare parts, food, beverages and tobacco, mineral products and fuels, chemical products and plastic products, construction materials and metals. In 2014, the top five trading partners of Albania were Italy, Greece, China, Turkey and Germany. In 2015, China–Albania trade volume increased by 8.27% compared with the previous year, while Albania–Greece trade volume dropped by 14.25%, making China overtake Greece and for the first time become the second largest trade partner of Albania.

In 2014, the total FDI absorbed by Albania was 1.1 billion USD. The main investors are Canada, Switzerland, Austria, Greece, Italy, Turkey, etc., and the money mainly flew to the fields of finance, insurance, telecommunications, construction and mining. China's cumulative direct investment in Albania increased from nearly zero in 2005 to 7 million USD in 2014. To promote foreign investment, the Albanian tax system treats domestic and foreign investors equally. The future development of Albania's economy still lies in attracting FDI, with a focus on industries such as energy, tourism, agriculture and food processing, mining and information and communications technology.

According to IMF, Albania is not among the countries assisted by the IMF and the World Bank's Heavily Indebted Poor Countries Initiative. From 2000 to 2012, foreign aid to Albania totaled approximately 4.74 billion euros, of which 2.049 billion euros were grant and 2.691 billion euros were loans. Albania has been actively applying to join the European Union. Following the official application of Albania in 2009, the European Commission recommended Albania as a candidate member for the European Union in October 2012, provided that Albania reforms its judicial and public administration system and amends the rules of parliamentary procedures. In June 2014, Albania officially became a candidate for EU membership.

In April 2015, Albania cooperated with China to develop the highway project and achieved great success. The public and private sectors in both countries have expressed interest in cooperating in the development of other new infrastructure and transport projects, including the highway linking the Adriatic Sea to the Ionian Sea, the Eighth Corridor and the Orikum–Parasa Tunnel.

10.2 Bulgaria

I. Geographical and historical backgrounds

Bulgaria is located on the Balkan Peninsula in southeastern Europe. It faces Romania across the Danube River in the north, Serbia and Macedonia in the west, Greece and Turkey in the south and the Black Sea in the east. The Balkan Mountains divide Bulgaria into the Danube Plain in the north and the Thrace Lowlands in the south. The Rhodope Mountains are in the southwest. The 2925 m-high Musala Peak is the highest point in Bulgaria and the Balkan Peninsula. The country has a land area of 111,001.9 km^2. Bulgaria is a centralized state with 28 districts, and Sofia is its capital. It is traditionally a country dominated by agriculture. Its natural resources are scarce. Metal minerals include lead, zinc, copper, iron, uranium, manganese, chromium and other rare metal resources. Among them, iron ore has the largest reserves. There are also lead ore and copper ore. Its coal, oil and natural gas reserves are not large, and it mainly produces low-quality coal, so its energy supply mainly depends on imports. The forest area of Bulgaria is about 4.12 million ha, accounting for about 33% of the country's land area. Animal and plant resources are very rich. The volume of plants accounts for more than half of the total in the Balkan Peninsula. Its forest is dominated by broad-leaved trees and supplemented by needle-leaved trees. There are also abundant animal species, but the phenomenon of animal extinction caused by industrialization does exist.

II. Economic development

(I) Domestic economy

Before the fall of communism in Eastern Europe in 1989, 90% of Bulgaria's national income was realized through trade with members of the former Economic Mutual Aid Committee. After 1989, Bulgaria began its transition to a market economy by developing economy with a variety of ownership (including private ownership) and giving priority to the development of agriculture, light industry, tourism and services. The economy began to recover in 1994, but under the influence of insufficient economic reforms and an unstable banking system, the economy declined in 1996. The economy started to rise steadily in 1997. By the end of 2004, most of the state-owned assets have been privatized. From 2001 to 2008, Bulgaria's economic growth averaged over 5% annually. The economy has suffered a recession since 2009 due to the financial crisis. In 2010, the economy gradually stabilized and recovered. GDP in 2015 was 43.4 billion euros, an increase of 3.0% year-on-year, and GDP per capita was 5930 euros. See Figs. 10.5, 10.6 and 10.7 for more information.

1. Industrial structure

Bulgaria has traditionally been an agricultural country, and its roses, yogurt and wine are well known on the international market. In 2014, Bulgaria's agricultural output was worth 6.986 billion levs (BGN). In recent years, its main agricultural products are wheat, sunflower, corn and potatoes. The main industrial sectors are machinery manufacturing, electronics, metallurgy, food, light textile, papermaking and chemical engineering. Since the 1990s, Bulgaria's service industry has maintained rapid development. In recent years, Bulgaria's tourism industry has also made progress. In 2014, it received 9.409 million foreign tourists, an increase of 2.4% year-on-year. For more information on its industrial structure, see Fig. 10.8.

(1) The primary industry

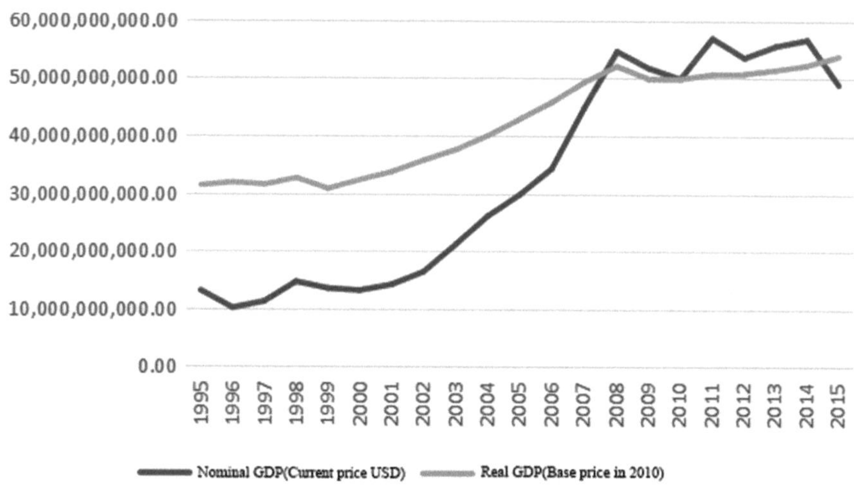

Fig. 10.5 Changes of real GDP and nominal GDP of Bulgaria in the past 20 years. *Source of data* World Bank database

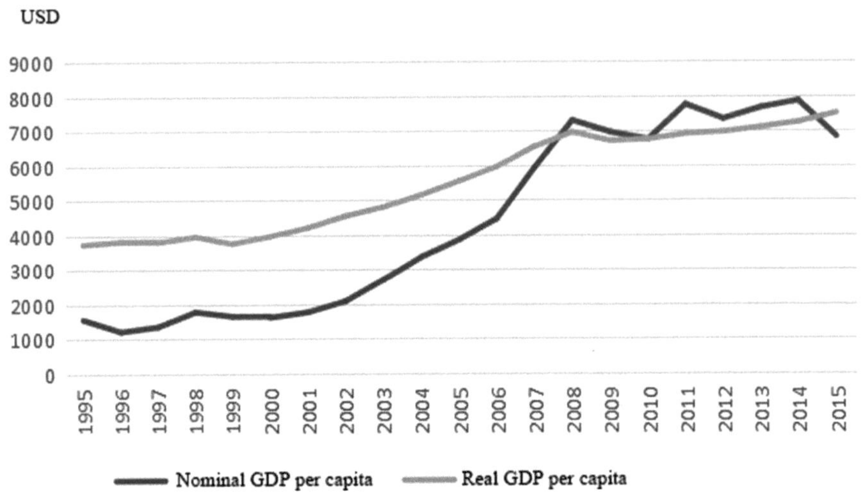

Fig. 10.6 Changes of Bulgaria's GDP per capita in the past 20 years. *Source of data* World Bank database

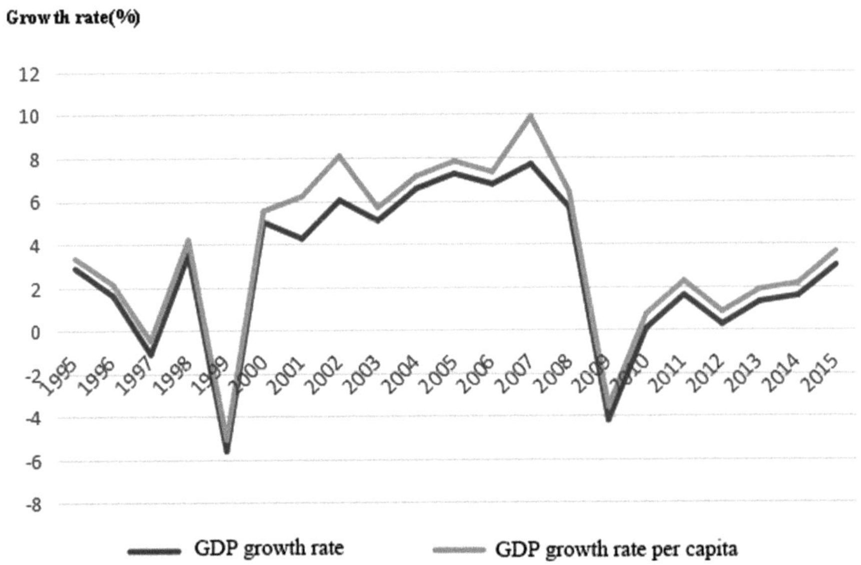

Fig. 10.7 Changes of GDP and GDP per capita growth rates in Bulgaria for the past 20 years. *Source of data* World Bank database

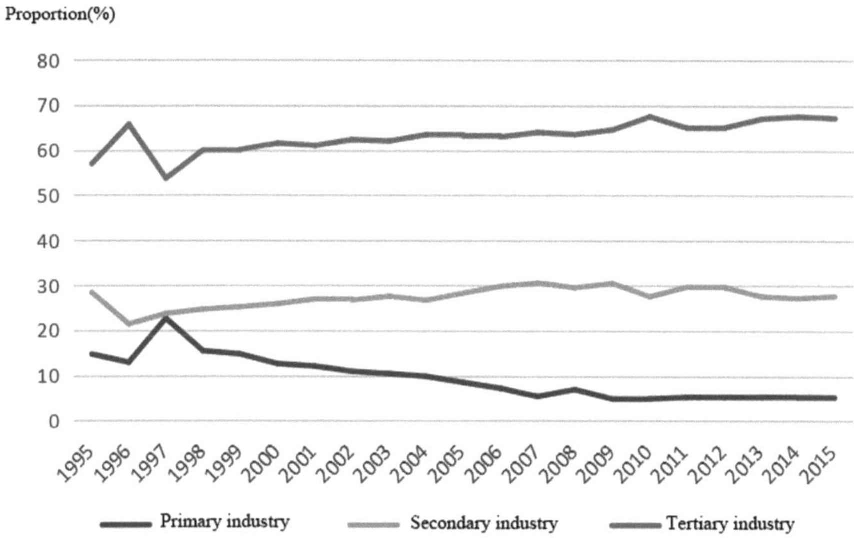

Fig. 10.8 Changes of the proportions of the three industries' added values in Bulgaria. *Source of data* World Bank database

Bulgaria's agriculture is very developed. First of all, Bulgaria, known as the "Rose State", is the world's largest producer and exporter of roses. The quality of its roses is extremely high, and both rose oil production and exports are high. In the heart of the country, there is the world-famous "Rose Valley", where the climate and soil are suitable for the cultivation of roses. Bulgaria is also an important food producer in Central and Eastern Europe, but its agricultural transformation has caused a significant decline in crop output (Fig. 10.9).

As shown in Fig. 10.10, exports of agricultural raw materials account for a small share of Bulgaria's exports, and the proportion has been decreasing. Its manufacturing industry has become a major source of merchandise exports.

(2) The secondary industry

The Bulgarian textile industry has a long history—in 1834 the first textile mill in Bulgaria was founded in Sliven. After Bulgaria was liberated from Turkish occupation in the nineteenth century, the textile industry and food processing industry became the country's industrial mainstay. After a period of exploration of the market economy, most of the textile enterprises in Bulgaria have completed privatization, and many SMEs have been set up. Bulgaria now has three mature industrial parks—Ruse, Vidin and Svilengrad. Another five industrial parks are in the early stages of planning—Sofia, Burgas, Karlovo, Pleven/Relish and west of Varna.

(3) The tertiary industry

As to the changes in the industrial structure, the service industry has always accounted for a relatively large share of the Bulgarian national economy (at 60–70%). The

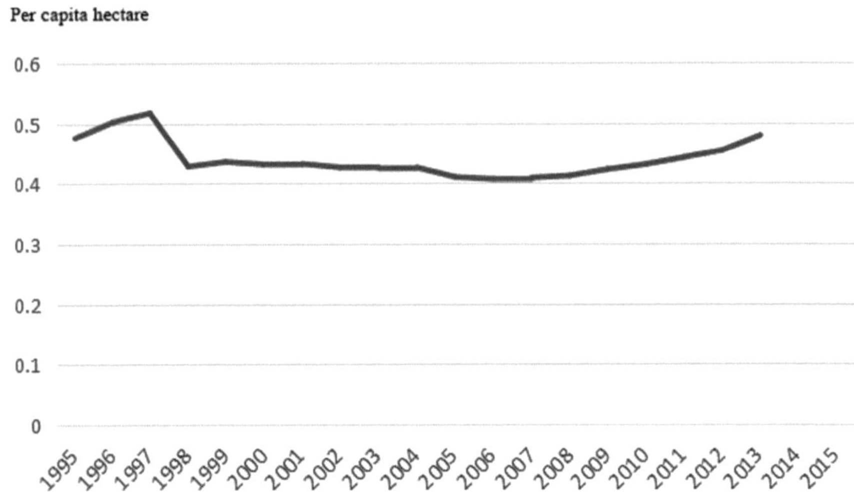

Fig. 10.9 Change of Per capita Cultivated Area in Bulgaria

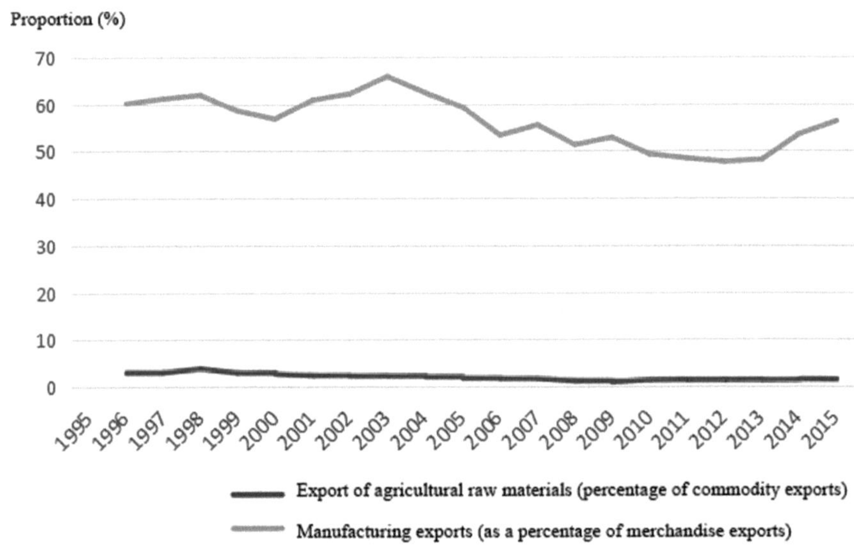

Fig. 10.10 Changes of the proportion of agricultural raw material and manufacturing exports. *Source of data* World Bank database

exports of merchandise far exceed that of services, and the exports of manufacturing industry are still in a dominant position, as shown in Fig. 10.11.

2. Population and cities

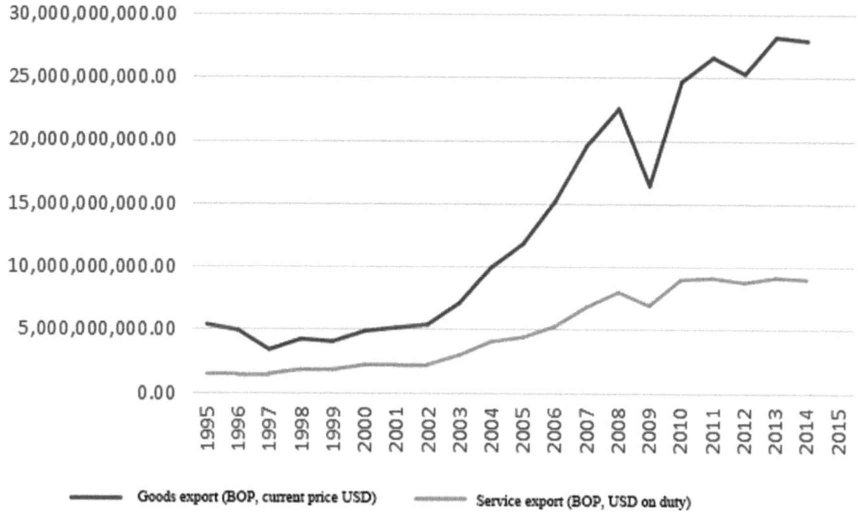

Fig. 10.11 Changes of values of merchandise and service exports. *Source of data* World Bank database

Bulgaria has been highly urbanized. As shown in Fig. 10.12, the rate has been above 50% since 1970, and exceeded 70% in 2014.

Bulgaria's five largest cities are listed in Table 10.1. Sofia is its capital.

3. Consumption and income

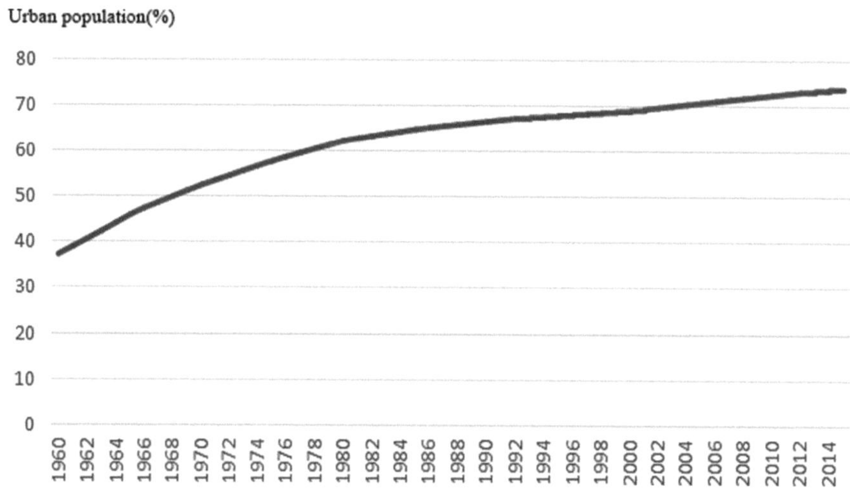

Fig. 10.12 Changes of Bulgaria's urbanization rate. *Source of data* World Bank database

Table 10.1 Top 5 cities in Bulgaria

City	Population in 2016	City profile
Sofia	1,152,556	Capital
Plovdiv	340,494	City in the south
Varna	312,770	The largest port
Burgas	195,966	City in the southeast; a main port
Ruse	156,238	The first Bulgarian city with modern industry

Source of data World Population Review

As shown in Fig. 10.13, the proportion of consumer spending of Bulgarian residents has always been greater than that of government spending. As to the proportion of the former, large fluctuations occurred before 2000 and then turned into a slow decline.

Bulgaria's income situation is characterized by high levels and even distribution. In recent years, Bulgaria's net national income has maintained a rapid growth rate with relatively small fluctuations, as shown in Fig. 10.14. Although Bulgaria joined the EU in 2007 and successfully transitioned to a market economy, its per capita income was only 37% of the EU average at that time, and it still faces challenges in raising the income of more than 7 million people across the country to the EU average. In 2008, this figure increased slightly to 41.8%. The Bulgarian people look forward to benefiting from joining the EU and are eager for the same standard of living, but increasing the productivity of the Bulgarian economy remains a challenge, especially in the context of a declining and aging population. Bulgaria is a country

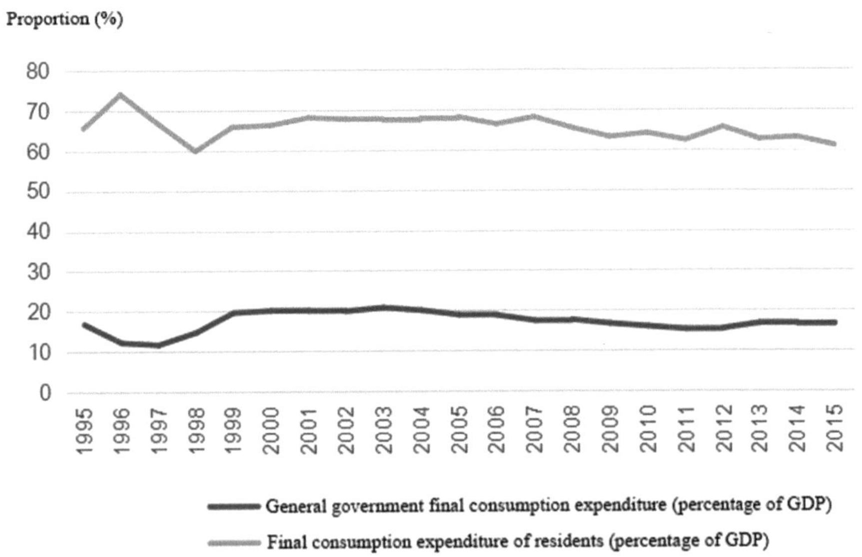

Fig. 10.13 Changes of consumer spending and government spending in Bulgaria. *Source of data* World Bank database

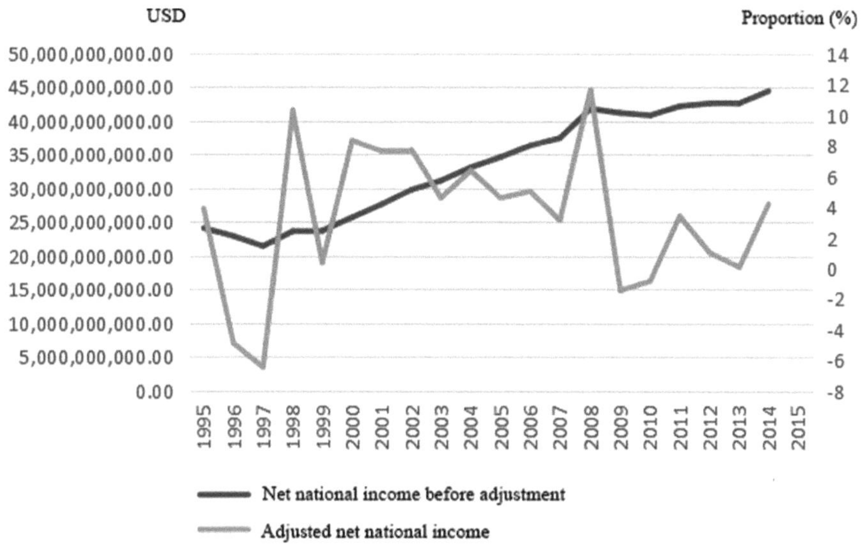

Fig. 10.14 Changes of adjusted NNI in Bulgaria. *Source of data* World Bank database

with a relatively balanced income, and the Gini coefficient has been below the international alert level of 0.4. A balanced income distribution has brought about a higher consumption rate in Bulgaria, which has a positive impact on economic growth.

(II) Foreign trade and investment

1. Foreign trade

After it joined the EU on January 11, 2007, Bulgaria implemented the EU's unified foreign trade policy. In 2008, Bulgaria had trade relations with more than 200 countries and regions in the world. The total trade volume in 2007 was 59.38 billion USD, of which 22.34 billion USD was from exports, 37.04 billion USD was from imports and the trade deficit was 14.7 billion USD. The proportion of trade within GDP can be seen in Fig. 10.15. The EU is Bulgaria's largest trading partner, and Bulgaria's trade with EU member states accounts for 60% of its total foreign trade. Bulgaria's main export products are basic raw materials (45%), consumer products (24.2%), investment products (16%) and mineral oil and electricity (14.8%). The main import products are basic raw materials (36.4%) and investment products (27.7%), mineral oil and electricity (19.5%) and consumer products (16.4%).

2. International investment

Figure 10.16 shows FDI in Bulgaria in recent years. Affected by the 2008 financial crisis, FDI in the country began to plunge in 2008. About 90% of its foreign investment comes from EU countries, of which the majority comes from developed ones. The top five investors in Bulgaria are Austria (20.1%), Netherlands (16.5%), Greece

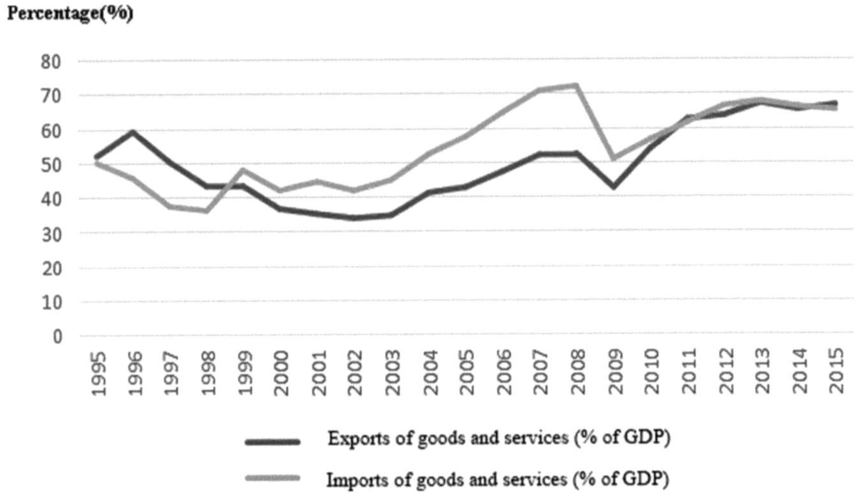

Fig. 10.15 Changes of the proportions of merchandise and service trade in Bulgaria. *Source of data* World Bank database

(8.4%), Britain (8.2%) and Germany (6.9%). The industries invested by foreign capital are relatively concentrated, and the proportion of non-productive investment has increased. The six industries most favored by foreign investors are real estate, manufacturing, finance, wholesale and retail and water and electricity supply. From 1999 to 2008, the top 8 industries with the largest foreign investment stock are as follows: real estate industry (accounting for 22.8% of the total stock), manufacturing industry (17.9%), financial industry (17.5%), wholesale and retail (14.3%) and transportation and storage industry (12.2%), the construction industry (7.8%), the water and electricity supply (3.8%) and the hotel and guesthouse industry (1.5%).

10.3 Croatia

I. Geographical and historical backgrounds

Croatia is located in south-central Europe and northwest of the Balkans. It borders Slovenia and Hungary in the northwest and north and Serbia, Bosnia and Herzegovina and Montenegro in the east and southeast. It is bordered by the Adriatic Sea in the south, with numerous islands and a tortuous coastline (1880 km). The total area is 56,594 km^2. The coast has a Mediterranean climate, and the inland has gradually transitioned to a temperate continental climate. Due to its special geography, Croatia has two different types of climate: the coastal region has a Mediterranean climate, and the inland region has a four-season continental climate. Croatia is rich in forest and water resources. The country has 2.22 million hectares of forest area, landing the forest coverage rate at 39.2%. In addition, there are resources such

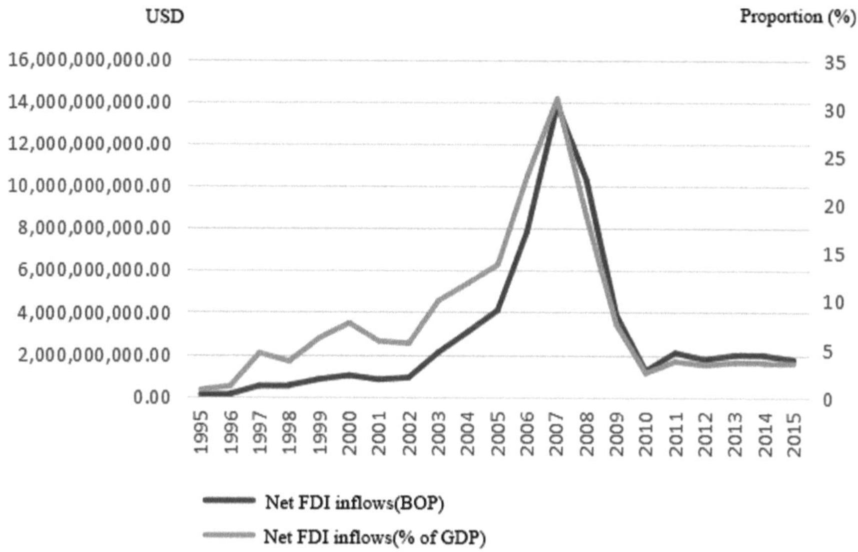

Fig. 10.16 Changes of net FDI inflow in Bulgaria. *Source of data* World Bank database

as oil, natural gas and aluminum. As a relatively developed region in the former Yugoslavia, Croatia has a sound economic foundation. Tourism, construction, shipbuilding and pharmaceutical industries are well developed. In the late 8th and early ninth centuries, a preliminary feudal state was established in Croatia. In the tenth century, the Kingdom of Croatia was established. In December 1918, Croatia and some southern Slavic nations jointly established the Kingdom of Serbs-Croatian-Slovenia, which was renamed the Kingdom of Yugoslavia in 1929. In 1945, the people of Yugoslavia won the anti-fascist war. On November 29 of the same year, the Federal People's Republic of Yugoslavia was declared in 1963. On June 25, 1991, the Croatian Parliament passed a resolution declaring its independence from the Socialist Federal Republic of Yugoslavia. On May 22, 1992, Croatia joined the United Nations.

II. **Economic development**

(I) Domestic economy

As a relatively developed region in the former Yugoslavia, Croatia has a sound economic foundation. Tourism, construction, shipbuilding, and pharmaceutical industries have a high level of development. The northern plains of Croatia and the coast of the Adriatic Sea are rich in oil and natural gas, but mineral resources such as coal and aluminum have not been identified in large amounts. Croatia declared its departure from the Federal Republic of Yugoslavia on June 25, 1991. Since then, it has waged war against Serbs over ethnic issues. The Croatian war ended on November 12, 1995, with the victory of Croatia. Since then, Croatia's economy has started the long process of recovery. Croatia was accepted as a candidate for the EU membership in 2004 and officially accepted on July 1, 2013. Prior to the 2008 US subprime crisis, the Croatian economy maintained a high growth rate. In 2009, its GDP growth rate hit the lowest point at – 7.38%. With the slow recovery after the crisis, the per capita GDP of Croatia rebounded to 11,535.83 USD in 2015. Figures 10.17, 10.18 and 10.19 depict Croatia's GDP change over the past 20 years.

1. Industrial structure

As shown in Fig. 10.20, Croatia's industrial structure has been relatively stable, and the proportions of the three industries have basically remained unchanged in the past 20 years. The primary and secondary industries have declined slightly, and the

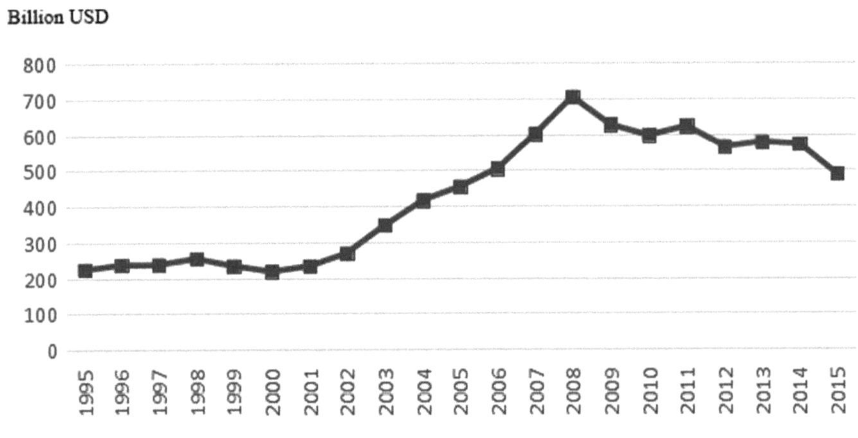

Fig. 10.17 Changes of Croatia's GDP

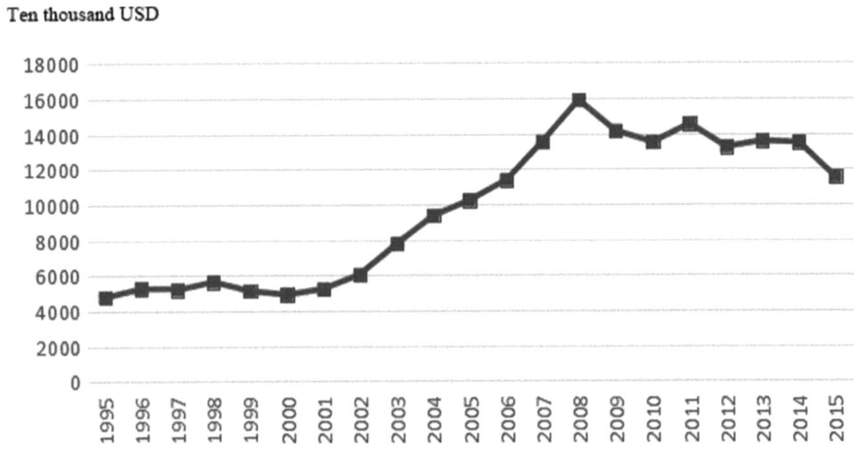

Fig. 10.18 Changes of Croatia's GDP per capita

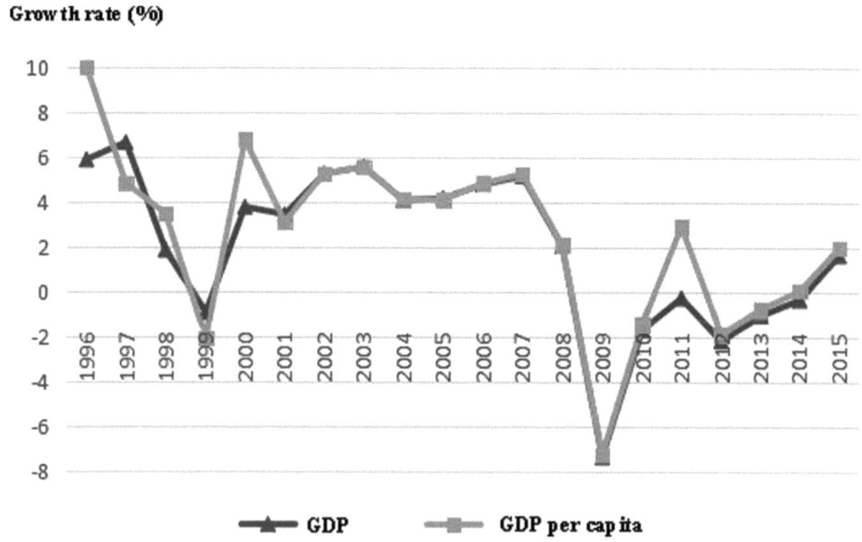

Fig. 10.19 Changes of GRs of Croatia's GDP and GDP per capita. *Source of data* World Bank database

tertiary industry has expanded to some extent. The tertiary industry is the dominating force in Croatia, accounting for 70% of domestic output.

As a relatively developed region in the former Yugoslavia, Croatia enjoys a sound economic foundation. Tourism, construction, shipbuilding and pharmaceutical industries have a high level of development. This trend can also be seen from the sector-wise data in Fig. 10.21. J-P (including finance, education, social services, etc.), which

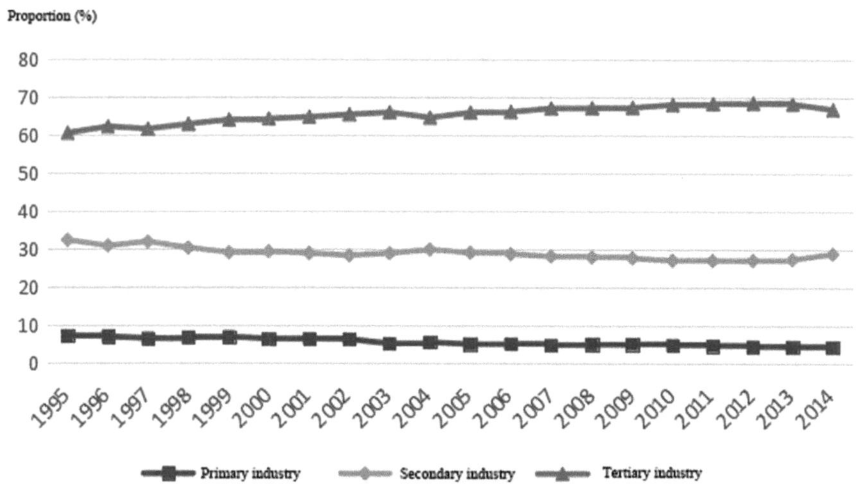

Fig. 10.20 Changes of industrial structure in Croatia. *Source of data* World Bank database

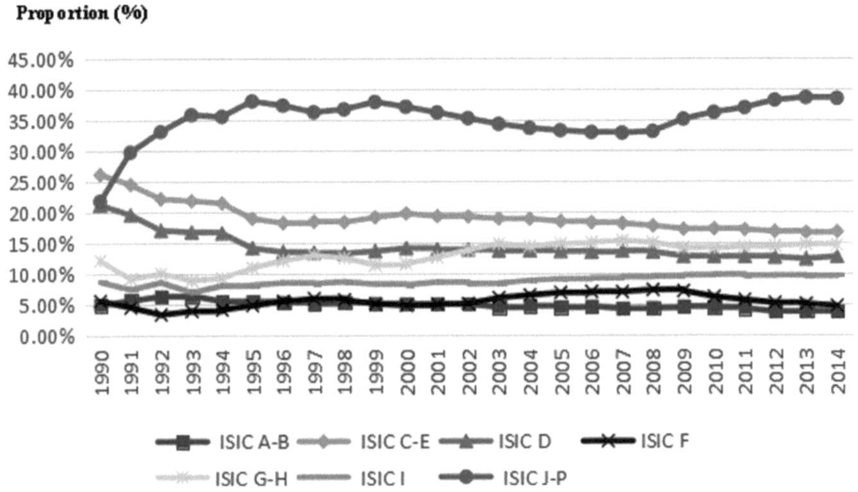

Fig. 10.21 Proportions of different economic sectors in Croatia. *Source of data* World Bank database

are basically in the tertiary industry, has developed rapidly, contributing 35% of the domestic economy. Croatia has a developed tourism industry which is an important part of the national economy and a major source of foreign exchange income. The catering, hotel, retail and other industries (G-H) have developed rapidly in the past 20 years, rising from 10% in 1990 to about 15% at present. The share of industry in domestic output has declined slightly, and the manufacturing sector (D) currently stabilizes at about 13% of domestic output.

2. Population and cities

In the 1960s, the level of urbanization in Croatia was low at only 30.15%. However, the urbanization process has not been affected by social unrest and growth has been maintained, as shown in Fig. 10.22. By 2015, local urbanization rate reached 58.97%. The rising urbanization rate has a great correlation with its industrial structure: its economy is dominated by the tertiary industry, and the tourism industry has a higher level of development. As of 2014, the total length of railway lines in the country is 2604 km, and the ratio to its land area (56,594 km^2) is 0.046, while the ratio in the United States at the same time was only 0.024. It can be seen that the well-developed transportation facilities in Croatia is closely related to the development of its tourism industry.

(II) Foreign trade and investment

1. Foreign trade

Croatia's main trading partners include Italy, Germany, Russia, Slovenia, Bosnia and Herzegovina, Austria, China, France, Hungary and Serbia. As can be seen from

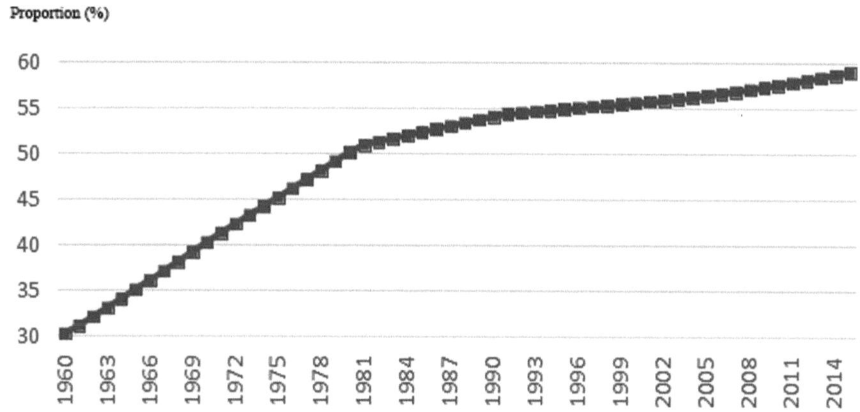

Fig. 10.22 Changes of urbanization rate in Croatia. *Source of data*: World Bank database

Fig. 10.23, the proportions of Croatia's imports and exports kept fluctuating slightly before 2008. After 2008, as the proportions of both imports and exports in GDP began to rise, its dependence on foreign trade increased. Croatia's exports exceeded imports in 2012, achieving a trade surplus. Croatia's main import products are mining products, processed food, chemicals, machinery and equipment, electronic products, petroleum products, metal products, etc.; the main export products are machinery and equipment, power equipment, processed food, metal products, pharmaceuticals, agricultural, forestry and fishery products, wood and furniture, transportation equipment, etc. For a long time, China and Croatia have maintained a good economic and trade cooperation relationship. The Chinese and Croatian governments have established a mixed economic and trade cooperation committee and a scientific and technological cooperation committee mechanism. They have signed the "Agreement on Encouraging and Reciprocal Protection of Investments" (March 1993), "Shipping Agreement" (March 1993), "Science and Technology Cooperation Agreement" (April 1994), etc. The main categories of Chinese exports to Croatia are organic electrical products, textiles, clothing and footwear; the main categories of imports from Croatia are sawn wood panels, building stones and cowhide and leather products.

Figure 10.24 shows Croatia's trade competitiveness index from 1995 to 2015. Before 2012, the figure fluctuated greatly, and the lowest was − 0.17 in 1997. Although it is negative, it is very close to zero. In 2012, Croatia turned its trade deficit to a surplus. Since then, the index has exceeded zero and grown year by year. It can be concluded that Croatia's competitiveness in the field of trade has been improving.

2. International investment

In 1995, after the end of the Croatian war, its foreign investment began to grow rapidly. As shown in Fig. 10.25, the foreign investment in 1996 was 485 million USD, and it reached a peak of 5.297 billion USD in 2008. One of the main reasons for the sharp increase in foreign capital inflows was the large-scale privatization that began

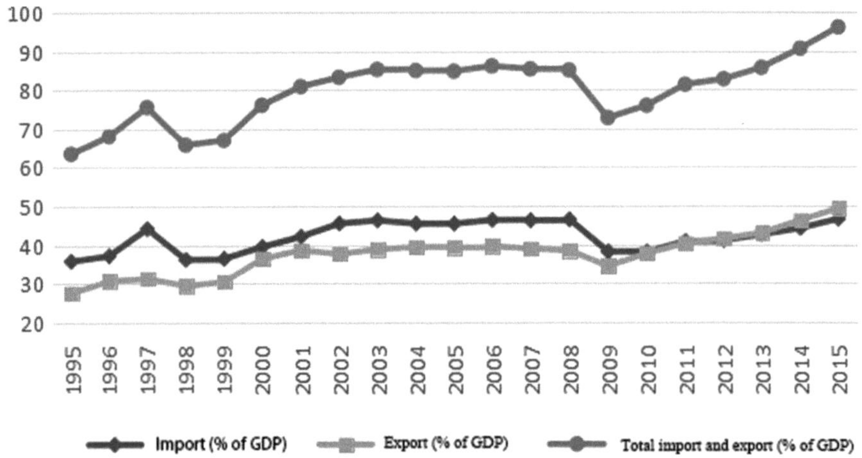

Fig. 10.23 Changes of proportions of exports and imports within GDP in Croatia. *Source of data*: World Bank database

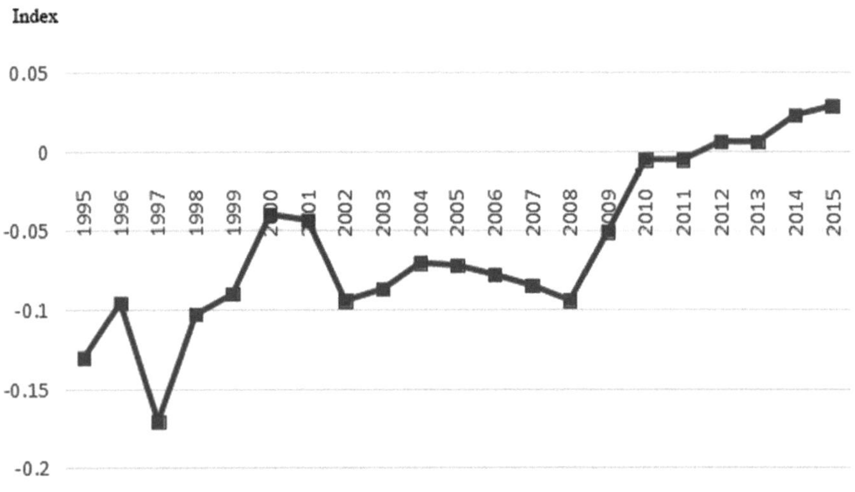

Fig. 10.24 Changes of trade competitiveness index of Croatia. *Source of data* World Bank database

in the late 1990s. During this process, the Croatian government sold a large number of state-owned enterprises in the fields of banking, telecommunications and energy to foreign investors. Affected by the financial crisis, foreign investment absorbed by Croatia dropped sharply. In 2010, FDI in Croatia was as low as 1.133 billion USD. Foreign investment mainly flows into the service industry, followed by the real estate industry, focusing on restaurants, hotels and other fields that are closely related to tourism. According to statistics from the Croatian National Bank, Austria is the largest source of FDI.

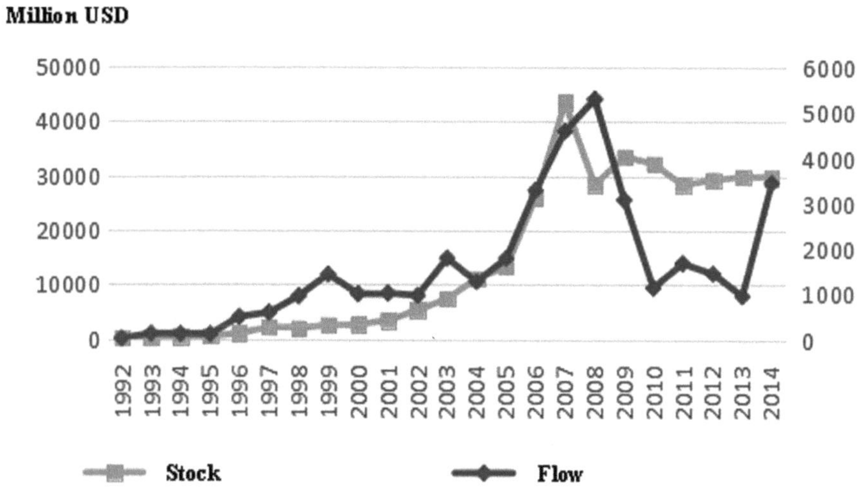

Fig. 10.25 Changes of FDI in Croatia. *Source of data* UNTCD

In 2005, China and Croatia established a comprehensive cooperative partnership. In 2007, China's investment in Croatia increased significantly from 750,000 USD to 7.84 million USD, as shown in Fig. 10.26. After that, it kept growing. As of the end of 2010, China's direct investment stock in Croatia reached 8.13 million USD. According to statistics from the Ministry of Commerce of the People's Republic of China, new contracts signed by Chinese companies in Croatia in 2012 amounted to 32.94 million USD.

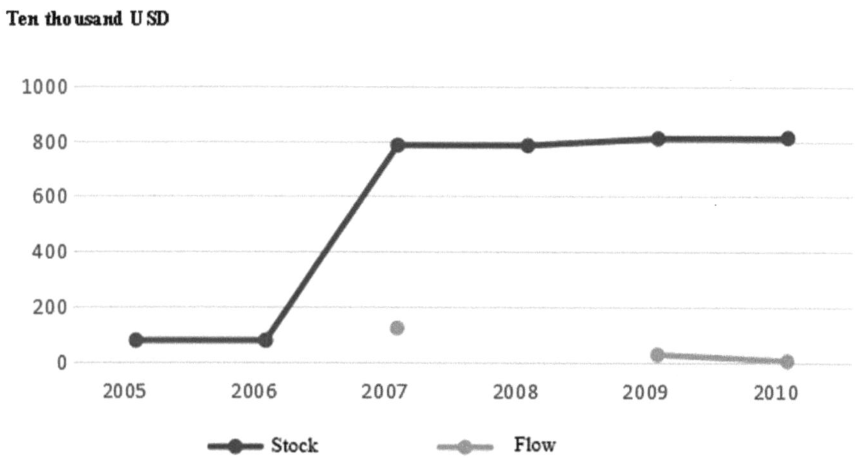

Fig. 10.26 Changes of China's investment in Croatia. *Source of data* Statistical Database of China Economic and Social Development

10.4 Greece

I. Geographical and historical backgrounds

Greece is the birthplace of Western civilization and the Olympic Games and also an important player in the shipping industry. Located at the southernmost tip of the Balkan Peninsula, Greece has a prominent strategic position and plays the role of a European gateway. It is a key node in the construction of the Belt and Road Initiative and the creation of a new channel for Asia–Europe land and sea transport. Islands account for 15% of Greece's 131,957 km^2 of territory.

The population of Greece in 2015 was 11.1204 million, of which nearly 20,000 were overseas Chinese (mainly from Zhejiang, Fujian and other regions). In terms of religion, the Greeks mostly believe in Orthodox and Islam, and Orthodox is the state religion. Greek is the official language, and English is commonly used.

Greece is rich in mineral resources, including brown coal, bauxite, nickel, chromium, magnesium, asbestos, copper, uranium, gold, petroleum, marble and so on. Lignite in Greece is mainly produced in seven coal mines such as Macedonia, with output ranking first in the EU and sixth in the world. Greece has more than 1 billion barrels of proven oil reserves, mainly from oil fields in the North Aegean Sea, but the dispute between Greece and Turkey in the Aegean Sea has become a huge obstacle to its oil exploration. In addition, in recent years, Greece has taken advantage of its solar and wind power to have outstanding performance in the field of new energy.

II. Economic development

(I) Domestic economy

Although Greece is an EU member, its manufacturing industry is weak compared to other EU countries. However, fully playing its unique geographical advantages, Greece has a developed shipping industry which, together with tourism and overseas remittances, is the major source of Greek foreign exchange earnings. Greece's agriculture develops well, and its industry mainly concentrates in food processing and light industry. Before 2008, the Greek economic growth was faster than the EU average. However, the European sovereign debt crisis caused by the financial crisis in 2008 shook the Greek economy so much that its nominal GDP was as low as 182.1 billion euros. Since the end of 2009, Greece has fallen into a sovereign debt crisis, and its economic growth has slowed down. In 2013, its nominal GDP was 161 billion euros, and the contribution rates of consumption, investment and net exports to GDP were 87.2%, 17.8% and − 4.8%, respectively. More information on Greek GDP can be found in Figs. 10.27, 10.28, 10.29 and 10.30. The government debt crisis has constrained Greece's economic growth. By the end of 2013, the government debt had reached 417 billion euros, as shown in Fig. 10.31. At present, the Greek government is implementing a series of structural reform measures.

1. Industrial structure

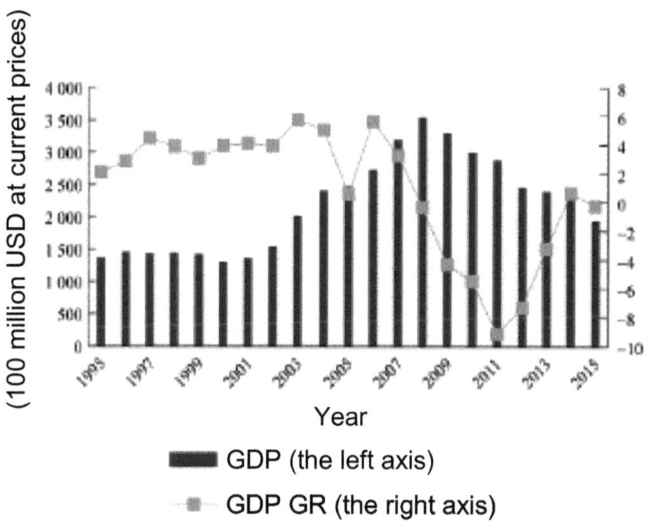

Fig. 10.27 GDP growth in Greece. *Source of data* World Bank database

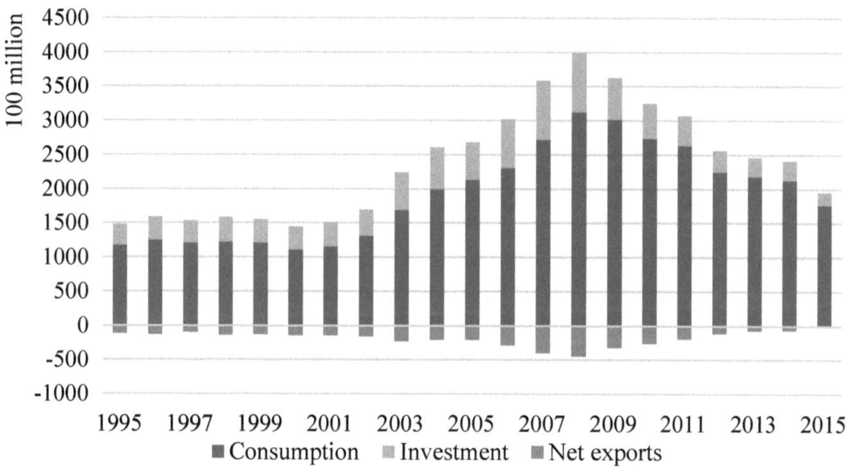

Fig. 10.28 Distribution of investment, consumption and net exports in Greek GDP. *Source of data* World Bank database

From the perspective of industrial structure, from 1995 to 2015, the tertiary industry has been a pillar industry of Greece, accounting for more than 70% of the total economy, and the proportion continued to rise and exceeded 80% in 2010; the proportion of the secondary industry fell from 21 to 15% and that of the primary industry from 16 to 4% (Fig. 10.32).

(1) The primary industry

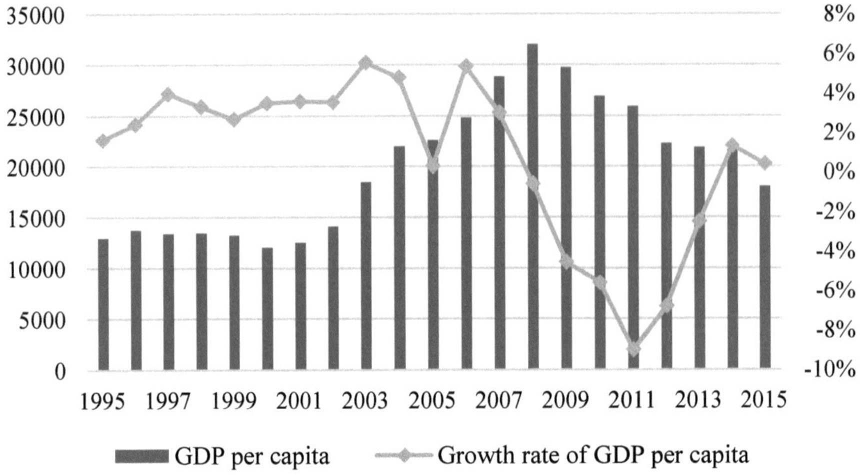

Fig. 10.29 Growth of Greek GDP per capita. *Source of data* World Bank database

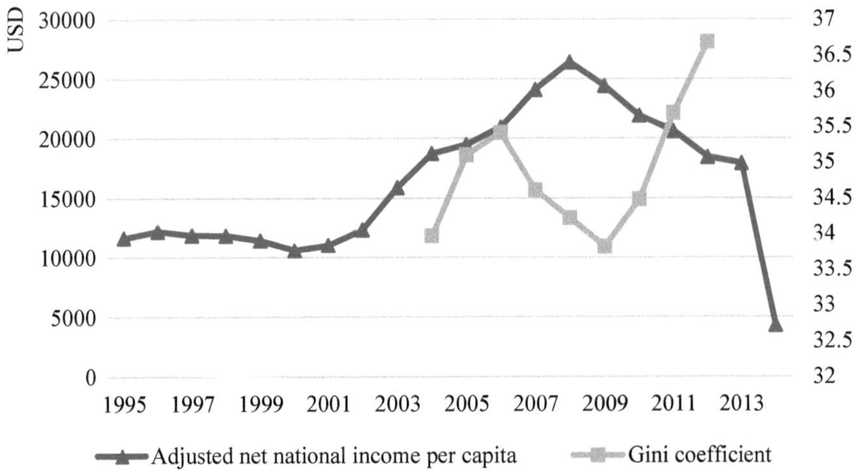

Fig. 10.30 Per capita income and Gini coefficient in Greece. *Source of data* World Bank database

In terms of agriculture, Greece is a hilly country: only 30% of its land area is arable, and 37% of the arable land is utilized by irrigation agriculture. Greece is self-sufficient in terms of main agricultural products. Fruits and vegetables can be exported in bulk to Europe and other regions, and only a small amount of meat, milk and complementary agricultural products are imported. Other exported agricultural products include tobacco, cotton, olive oil, wine, fruits and beets.

(2) The secondary industry

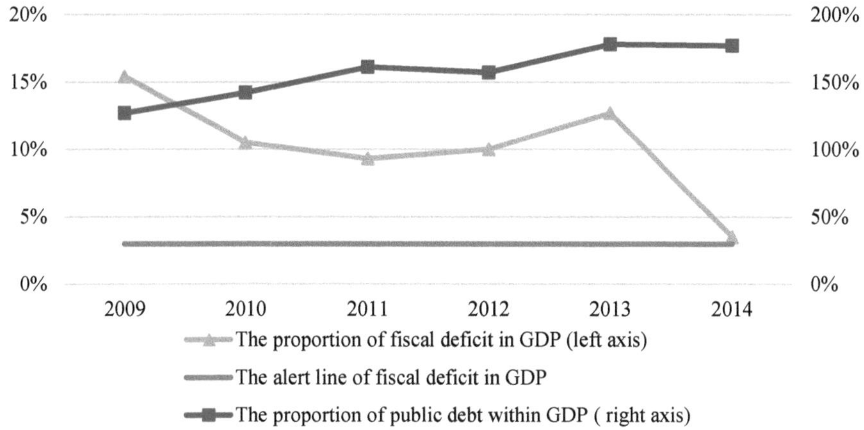

Fig. 10.31 Public debt and fiscal deficit in Greece. *Source of data* Hellenic Statistical Authority, Eurostat

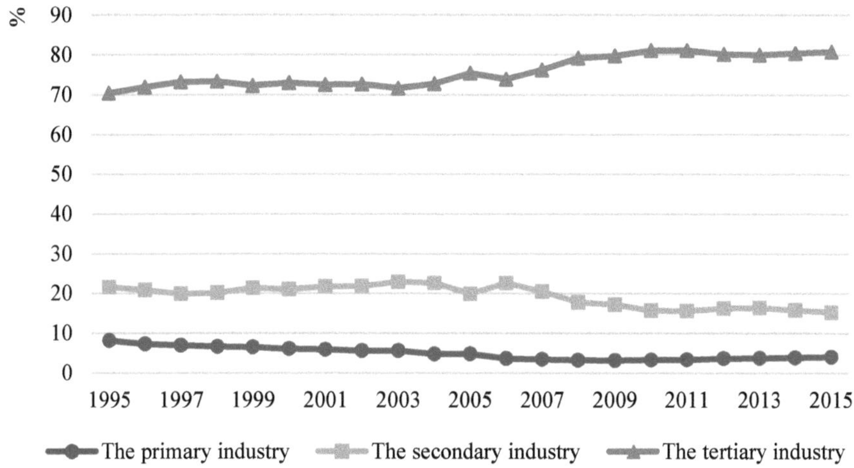

Fig. 10.32 Industrial structure in Greece. *Source of data* World Bank database

Greece's industrial base is relatively weak—small in scale and backward in technology. The main industrial sectors are mining, metallurgy, food processing, textiles, shipbuilding and construction.

(3) The tertiary industry

Tourism is an important economic sector for Greece to obtain foreign exchange and maintain the balance of payments. Greek tourism has developed rapidly since the 1960s with the number of inbound tourists growing year after year. In recent years, the Greek government has shifted the focus of tourism development from increasing the number of tourists to improving the level of tourist consumption, and good economic and social benefits have been achieved. The main tourist attractions in Greece are the Acropolis, the Temple of Apollo at Delphi, the ruins of the ancient Olympia stadium, the Cretan maze, the tomb of King Virginia Macedonia, the Holy Mount, Rhodes, Corfu Island, etc. The 2004 Athens Olympics, especially the improvement of local infrastructure, laid a good foundation for the development of tourism industry. In 2014, the number of inbound tourists reached 22.03 million, generating a year-on-year increase of 23%, of which 47,482 were from China, up by 67.6% on a YOY basis.

Greece is a major player in the shipping industry. The shipping industry is a pillar of the national economy. In 2013, the value of the Greek fleet reached 101 billion USD, accounting for 15% of the total assets of the global fleet, making Greece the world's largest ship owner. The total number of Greek merchant ships reached 3901, with a total capacity of 291 million dwt, accounting for about 16% of the global total capacity. Greek maritime companies are privately owned rank high internationally. Shipping is the first area where China and Greece started economic and technological cooperation. The two countries have conducted comprehensive cooperation in the areas of transportation, shipbuilding, ship repair, crew services and ship registration. On October 1, 2009, COSCO fully started its 35-year franchise of Piraeus Container Terminal in Greece, marking a new chapter in the strategic cooperation between China and Greece.

2. Population and cities

Greece has a highly urbanized, and most of its residents live in cities, and the number had been increasing. According to the World Bank, the urbanization rate in 2016 reached 78.33%. There are 8 cities in Greece with more than 100,000 residents. However, due to the outbreak of the economic crisis and the impact of debt, unemployment and poverty, some urban dwellers left Athens for the suburbs to reduce the cost of living. Therefore, the growth rate of urbanization has been declining since 2012. The urban population has shrunk. Athens is the most important city. It has a large population and is located in the center of shipping and aviation for the Eastern Mediterranean countries. Almost all the imports and exports are conducted here. The urban area has been connected to form the Greater Athens metropolitan area (Fig. 10.33; Table 10.2).

In terms of infrastructure, the Greek government had taken advantage of the opportunity to prepare for the 2004 Olympic Games to speed up the construction of highways, airports, bridges and other transportation hubs. The construction of subways, light rails and urban arterial roads around Olympic venues had increased significantly, and urban traffic conditions were significantly improved. At present, Greece has 117,500 km of various types of highways, including 2186 km of expressways; 2571 km of railways—the most important of which being the main line that runs through the north and south of Greece and connects Patras, Athens and Thessaloniki; 45 airports (15 are international airports) and the state-owned Olympic Airlines and the largest merchant fleet in the world with a capacity of about 16% of the world's total and 444 ports of various types, of which 16 are international ports

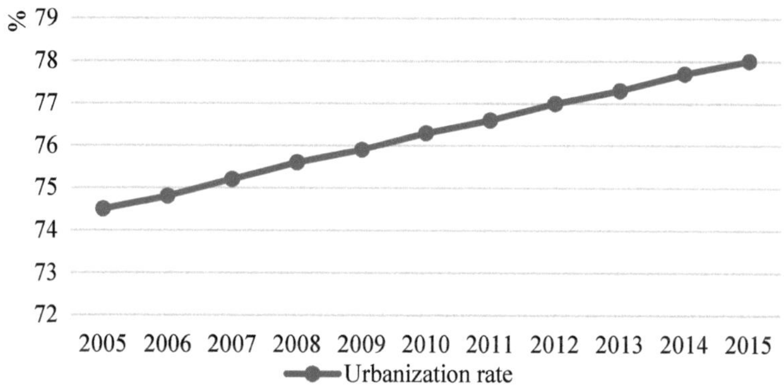

Fig. 10.33 Growth of urbanization rate in Greece. *Source of data* World Bank

Table 10.2 Major cities in Greece

City	City profile
Athens	The capital of Greece, also the largest city and industrial center; the center of ancient cultural relics that still preserves many ancient cultural relics and is well known for its museums; located in the center of shipping and aviation for Eastern Mediterranean countries; where 53% of the country's industry is concentrated
Thessaloniki (also known as Salonica)	The largest port city and the second largest city in northern Greece; the capital of Thessaloniki; a sea and land transportation hub, with sea links to ports in Eastern Mediterranean countries and a Yugoslav exclusive port area; an industrial town in northern Greece and a commercial center for the entire Balkans
Patras	Greece's third largest city; an important port city in western Greece linking with Italy and the Ionian Islands; the most famous university town in Greece; the industrial and commercial center of western Greece, focusing on marble, brewing and agricultural products processing industries
Naphlion	Well-developed food processing industry; products are exported to North America, Africa, Asia and Australia
Olympia	The birthplace of the Olympics

Source of data Public data

and the ports of Piraeus and Thessaloniki are the most important ports in the Balkans. The mobile phone penetration rate in Greece is as high as 100%; the coverage rate of broadband data services is lower than the EU average, and the ADSL service is in the stage of high-speed development. In recent years, Greece has transformed and upgraded its power grid. On the one hand, the interconnection among islands and between islands and the mainland has been improved, and on the other hand, the interconnected power market with neighboring countries has expanded rapidly.

(II) Foreign trade and investment

1. Foreign trade

Greece trades with more than 100 countries and EU member states are its largest trading partners, contributing more than 64% of its total imports and exports. Germany, Italy, the United Kingdom, Bulgaria, Russia and China are its main trading partners. The main export commodities are food, flue-cured tobacco, petroleum products, textiles, olive oil, cement, etc. The main import commodities are raw materials, petroleum and petroleum products, natural gas, daily necessities and transportation equipment. Greece has a long-term trade deficit, and its trade competitiveness index is negative. More information on Greece's foreign trade can be found in Figs. 10.34 and 10.35.

2. International investment

Greece's main sources of foreign investment are Germany, France, the United Kingdom, Belgium, Luxembourg and the Netherlands. Foreign investment is concentrated in the service industry, such as communications, finance, trade, real estate and tourism. In addition, chemical, machinery and other manufacturing industries have also attracted large amounts of foreign investment. According to the Greek Central Bank, in 2014, Greece absorbed 1.95 billion euros of FDI, a decrease of 636 million euros; as of the end of 2014, Greece's foreign investment stock was 19.642 billion euros.

Greece's foreign investment is mainly concentrated in neighboring countries such as Bulgaria, Romania, Macedonia and Albania. By the end of 2014, there were a

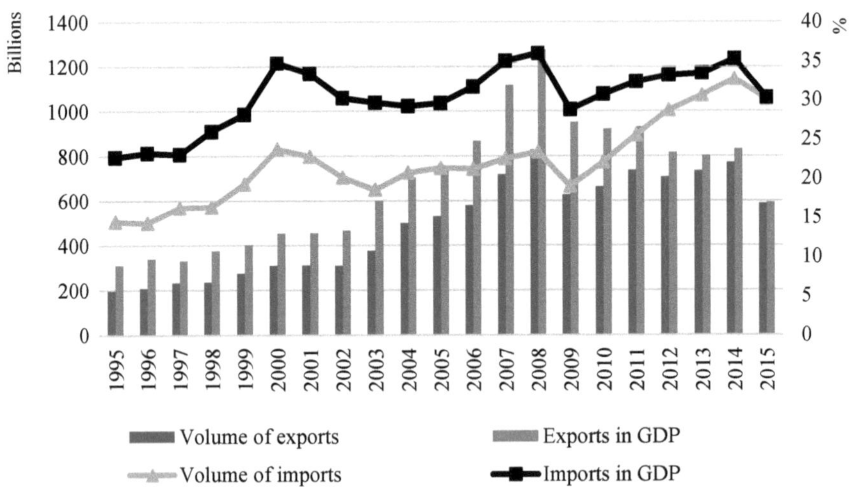

Fig. 10.34 Merchandise and service exports of Greece. *Source of data* World Bank database

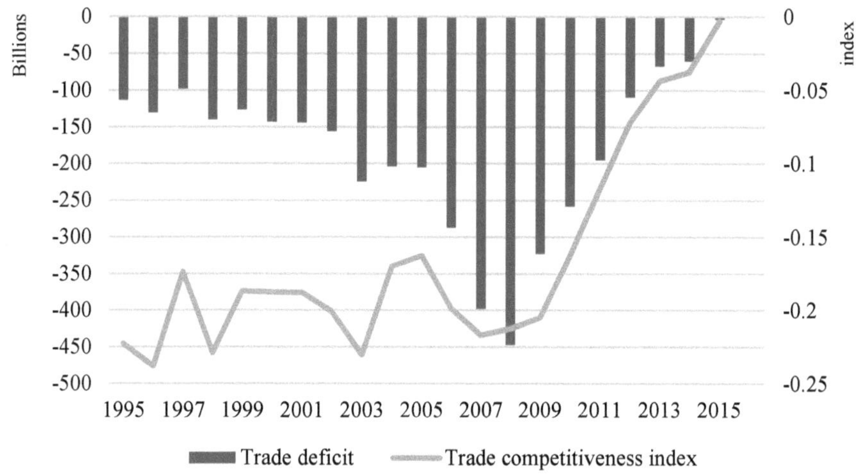

Fig. 10.35 Trade deficit and trade competitiveness index of Greece. *Source of data* World Bank database

total of 130 Greek direct investment projects in China, with 96.06 million USD of investment.

From 2005 to 2015, the top ten investors in Greece and the corresponding capital inflows were as follows: Germany (12.406 billion euros), France (8.239 billion euros), Britain (3.838 billion euros), the Netherlands (2.324 billion euros), Cyprus (2.111 billion euros), the United States (1.64 billion euros), Switzerland (1.6 billion euros), Italy (1.321 billion euros), Spain (874 million euros) and Canada (871 million euros). The cumulative investment of the top ten investors accounted for 99.99% of the total, which means that most of the foreign investment attracted by Greece comes from EU countries. Germany invested mainly in the communications sector, and France invested mainly in Greek banks before the debt crisis. Canadian investment in Greece has grown the fastest in recent years. According to Table 10.3, the EU was a major contributor of FDI to Greece before 2010, and the Americas has stepped up investment in Greece in recent years. According to Table 10.4, the Britain, Luxembourg and France invested more in Greece in 2005. The top investors in 2010 were France, Cyprus and Germany, and the largest investors in 2015 were Canada, Spain, Germany and the Netherlands, with Canadian investment reaching 641 million euros.

From 2005 to 2015, the secondary and tertiary sectors were the main recipients of foreign investment in Greece, respectively, absorbing for 74 and 24% of the total. In the field of manufacturing, according to Table 10.5, the top three subdivisions of net FDI inflows in 2005 were office supplies, metal products and chemical products; in 2010, they were food and beverage, office supplies and petroleum products; in 2015, they were petroleum products, chemical products and transportation equipment; the fact that the smelting business such as petroleum refining has become the main destination for FDI in Greece in recent years shows that the country is re-directing from light industry to heavy industry. In the service sector, according to Table 10.6,

Table 10.3 Proportions of FDI in Greece from different regions (Unit: %)

	2005	2010	2015
EU	46.70	78.63	37.82
Non-EU European countries	13.35	41.45	– 4.18
The United States	38.38	– 18.25	56.11
Asia	0.29	5.40	11.31
Africa	1.29	– 7.23	– 1.06

Source of data Bank of Greece 2016

Table 10.4 Top 10 contributors of FDI in Greece (Unit: million euros)

2005		2010		2015	
Britain	259.0	France	789.9	Canada	640.9
Luxemburg	256.8	Cyprus	340.3	Spain	123.5
France	235.5	Germany	200.8	Germany	114.1
The United States	97.1	Switzerland	29.7	The Netherlands	105.6
Italy	96.1	Denmark	19.5	Italy	90.3
Austria	65.6	Italy	19.3	Cyprus	81.8
Cyprus	56.6	Ireland	14.3	Britain	69.3
Spain	45.9	Hong Kong, China	12.9	Austria	58.3
Switzerland	41.4	Finland	6.5	Hong Kong, China	31.7
Portugal	38.1	Sweden	5.8	Russia	20.2

Source of data Bank of Greece 2016

the top three sub-sectors of net FDI inflows in 2005 were financial services, postal and communication services and real estate; they were financial services, real estate and IT in 2010; and in 2015, they were financial services, real estate and other business areas. Overall, the financial and communications sectors are the main targets of FDI in the service industry.

The Greek government has three main strategies to promote FDI. First, it encourages "productive investment" and provides lower taxes and visas for overseas talents in the fields of management and technology. Second, it enlarges the scale of FDI has been promoted through international cooperation. Greece has signed bilateral investment agreements (BITs) with 46 countries so far. China is one of the 40 countries with which the related agreements are still valid (the agreement with China was signed in 1993). Third, relevant laws and regulations make clear that strategic and private foreign investment is encouraged to improve the liquidity of the domestic investment sector. In addition, the country established the Greek Enterprise Alliance in 2014 to deal with investor-related matters in a targeted manner.

Table 10.5 Net FDI inflows in various subdivisions of the Greek manufacturing industry (Unit: million euros)

2005		2010		2015		Cumulative proportion 2005–2015 (%)	
Office supplies	102.1	Food and beverage	294.1	Petroleum products	131.4	Chemical products	55
Metal products	23.9	Office supplies	21.2	Petrochemical products	19.1	Food and beverage	18
Chemical products	23.1	Petroleum products	12.4	Transportation equipment	0.1	Machinery	14
Others	18.3	Rubber and plastics	8.6	Office supplies	– 0.3	Metal products	6
Transportation equipment	17.4	Printing and publishing	7.9	Rubber and plastics	– 1.4	Rubber and plastics	1
Rubber and plastics	5.2	Transportation equipment	5.9	Chemical products	– 2.5	Transportation equipment	1
Textiles and garments	2.1	Chemical products	– 7.2	Communication equipment	– 2.5	Others	5

Source of data Bank of Greece 2016

Table 10.6 Net FDI inflows in various sub-sectors of the Greek service industry (Unit: million euros)

2005		2010		2015		Cumulative proportion 2005–2015 (%)	
Financial service	542.6	Financial service	366.5	Financial service	582.1	Postal and communication services	32
Postal and communication services	227.19	Real estate	83.2	Real estate	228.9	Financial service	31
Real estate	135.6	IT	34.8	Other business areas	178.6	Real estate	12
Other business areas	116.8	Other business areas	23.9	Transportation and storage	119.1	Trade	8
Education and health care	95.2	Other service sectors	22.6	Trade	45.5	Other business areas	5
Trade	39.1	Hotel	1.3	Hotel	24.7	Tourism	3
IT	4	Education and health care	10.3	Other service sectors	15.8	Other service sectors	9

Source of data Bank of Greece 2016

10.5 Slovenia

I. Geographical and historical backgrounds

The Republic of Slovenia is located in south-central Europe and the northwestern tip of the Balkan Peninsula. It borders Italy to the west, Austria and Hungary to the north, Croatia to the east and south, and the Adriatic Sea to the southwest. It is located at the junction of the four major geographical regions of the Alps, Dinara Mountains, the middle plains of the Danube River and the Mediterranean coast along Europe. It has 20,273 km^2 of territory and 46.6 km of coastline. Ljubljana is its capital. The country is rich in forest and water resources. Its forest coverage rate is 66%, the third in Europe after Finland and Sweden. In contrast, Slovenia has poor mineral resources, mainly mercury, coal, lead and zinc. Its processing industry is well developed, and industries such as electronics, wood processing, food, non-metallic mineral processing, non-ferrous metals and printing industries are of technologically advanced.

Slovenia has a population of about 2.063 million, and its main ethnic group is the Slovenian, accounting for about 83% of the population. Ethnic minorities include Hungarian, Italian and other groups. The official language is Slovenian (belonging to the Yugoslavian branch). Slovenian residents are mainly Catholic.

II. Economic development

(II) Domestic economy

Known as "Little Switzerland in Eastern Europe", Slovenia is a developed country. Although it lacks resources, it has a very good industrial and technological foundation. Since Slovenia became independent in 1991, it has made integration into Europe its goal. Since joining the European Union in 2004, the Slovenian government has actively implemented free trade policies, focusing on expanding its presence in the EU and Central European markets. In the following five years, Slovenia performed well, with annual GDP growth rates staying above 4% for many years. It ranked toward the top among the new EU members in terms of GDP per capita and was known as the "EU's Top Student". In 2007, Slovenia joined the Eurozone and became a Schengen country by the end of the year. The financial crisis in 2008 devastated Slovenian economy—a large number of commercial banks lent to the real estate market and loss-making companies, and many borrowers were unable to repay their loans, resulting in a large amount of bad debts. In recent years, Slovenia's export volume had dropped significantly, and its innovation capacity had been weak. More and more well-educated workers were laid off. The situation did not improve until 2014 when the economic growth rate finally turned positive again, as shown in Figs. 10.36 and 10.37.

1. Industrial structure

Slovenia's economy is highly export-oriented. Though its natural resources are relatively scarce, but the processing industry has a strong foundation. Electronics, wood

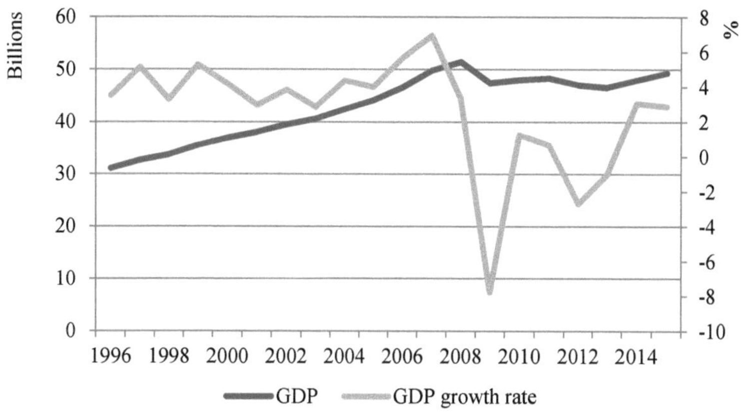

Fig. 10.36 GDP and GDP growth rate of Slovenia. *Source of data* World Bank database

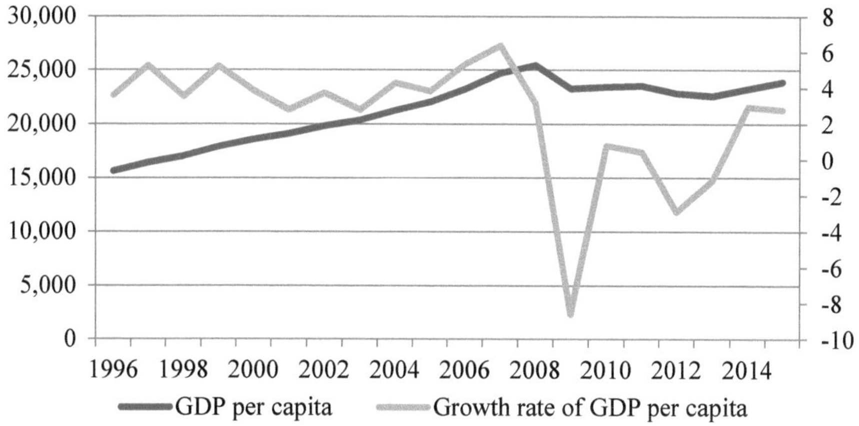

Fig. 10.37 Changes of per capita GDP and its growth rate in Slovenia. *Source of data* World Bank database

processing, food, non-metallic mineral processing, non-ferrous metals and printing industries are advanced technologically. And industries such as chemical, automobile, textiles, construction, tannery and rubber are also well developed. As shown in Figs. 10.38 and 10.39, Slovenia has gradually transformed into a service sector-oriented economy since 1995. The proportion of the primary industry in GDP dropped from 4.03 to 2.18%, and that of the secondary industry also declined from 34.70 to 33.06%; at the same time, the share of the service industry rose from 61.01 to 64.76%.

(1) The primary industry

Slovenia's agricultural products are mainly potatoes, cereals and fruits. Forestry and animal husbandry are also very important in its agricultural economy. Cattle, pigs,

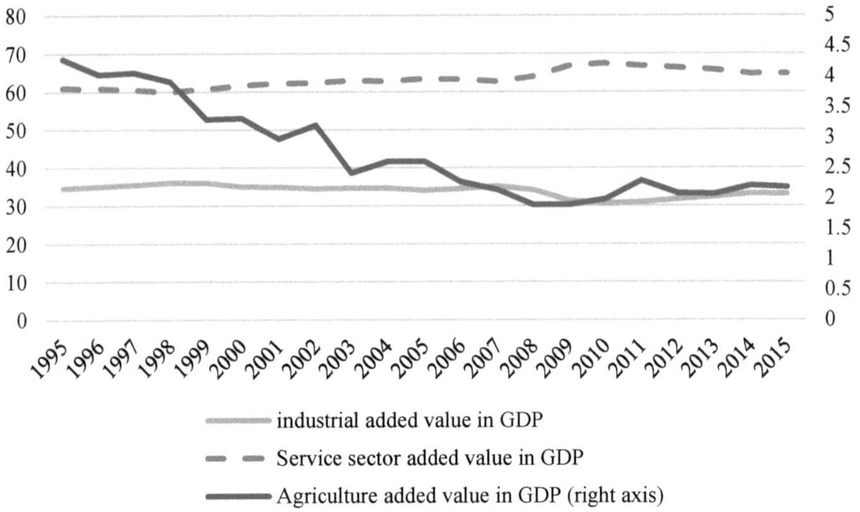

Fig. 10.38 Changes of proportions of the three industries in Slovenia. *Source of data* World Bank database

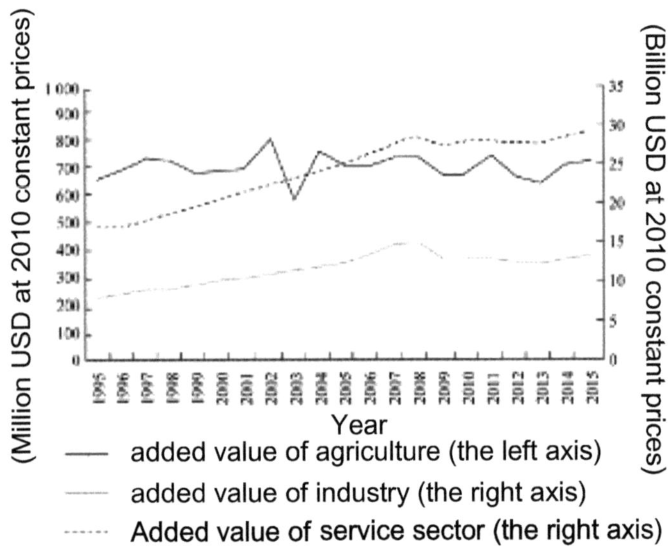

Fig. 10.39 Changes of the added values of the three industries in Slovenia. *Source of data*: World Bank database

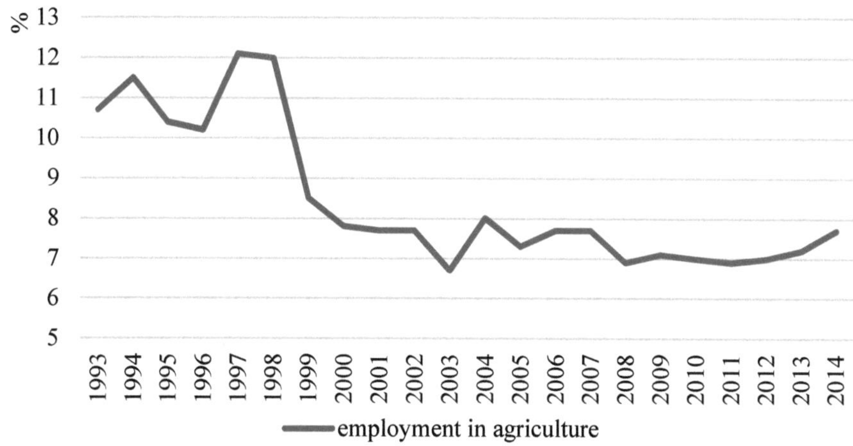

Fig. 10.40 Changes of the proportion of agriculture-related employment in the total employment. *Source of data* World Bank database

horses, sheep, poultry and other livestock are raised. The proportion of agriculture in the Slovenian national economy has been decreasing year by year, and the proportion of labor force engaged in agriculture has also shown a downward trend, as shown in Fig. 10.40. Slovenia's domestic agricultural output cannot meet its needs, so large quantities of agricultural products such as grain are imported from other countries every year. According to a report by the Slovenian News Agency on June 12, 2014, the Slovenian government passed a resolution on the development strategies of agricultural and food industry (till the year 2020). The main goal is to ensure stable, safe, high-quality and cheap food supplies, while improving the competitiveness of agriculture and food industries. In order to achieve the above goal, the Slovenian government has proposed to ensure 350,000 ha of permanent agricultural land and actively promoted the use of green technologies.

(2) The secondary industry

Slovenia has a good industrial and technological foundation. Its chemical, electronic equipment, machinery manufacturing and transportation industries have contributed 45% of the added value in the manufacturing industry and constitute Slovenia's five major manufacturing sectors together with metal manufacturing. The automobile industry is a key sector of local manufacturing industry with great competitive edges. Its contribution to GDP is about 10%, and about 80% of products are exported, accounting for 21% of all Slovenian exports. According to the ranking made by Slovenia's *Labor News*, four of the top 20 most profitable companies in the country are in the automotive industry. The metal processing is one of the oldest industries in Slovenia. Its main export markets are Germany, France, Italy, Croatia, Ireland, the Netherlands, Switzerland and Austria. Despite the shock sent by the 2008 financial crisis, the manufacturing industry in Slovenia has begun to recover since 2013, generating positive growth rates.

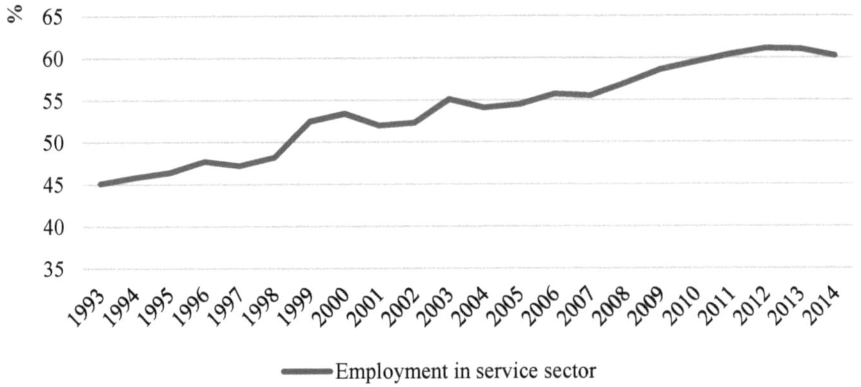

Fig. 10.41 Changes of proportion of service sector employment in total employment. *Source of data* World Bank database

(3) The tertiary industry

As an essential part of the Slovenian economy, the local service industry includes sectors such as wholesale and retail, repair, hotels and restaurants, transportation, communications, warehousing, financial intermediaries, real estate, leasing, corporate services, public administration, education, health care, social services and other community services. As shown in Fig. 10.41, the service industry hires more than one fifth of the total population and more than 60% of the employed population in recent years. Slovenia is transitioning into a service industry-oriented economy. Most of its service products are digested domestically. As shown in Fig. 10.42, commodities are the main export products of Slovenia, while services take only a small part of the total exports.

2. Population and cities

Slovenia has basically completed the process of urbanization. As shown in Fig. 10.43, the proportion of its urban population had increased from 28.2% in 1960 to 50.5% in 1990. After that, the proportion had remained stable, and a slight decline (even to less than 50%) was seen recently.

Table 10.7 lists the major cities of Slovenia.

3. Consumption and income

In the 2008 financial crisis, although the Slovenian government could not spend hundreds of billions of euros to save the market like some major countries, it promised to make every effort to ensure the stability of its financial market and tried to minimize the harm to its real economy. It also encouraged the people to work together to weather the crisis. Although Slovenia has a small population and the promotion of domestic consumption has a small impact on the overall economy, both its consumer and government spending rates increased significantly around 2008, as shown in Fig. 10.44. However, the consumption rate has been declining in recent years, posing

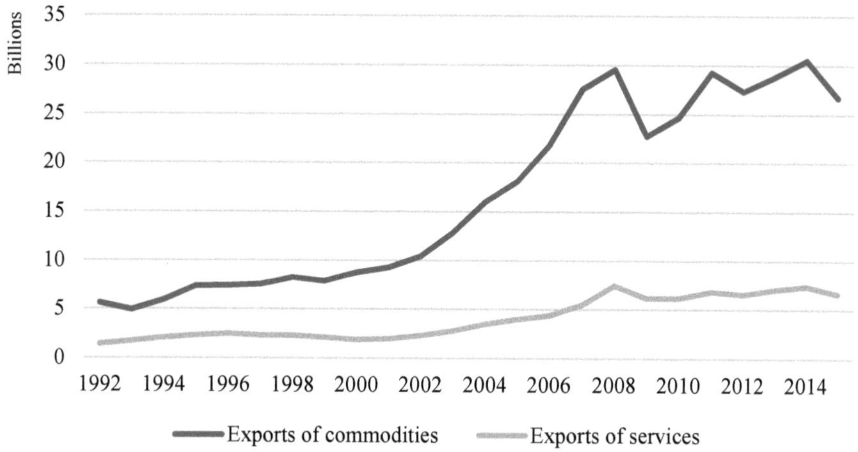

Fig. 10.42 Exports of Slovenia. *Source of data* World Bank database

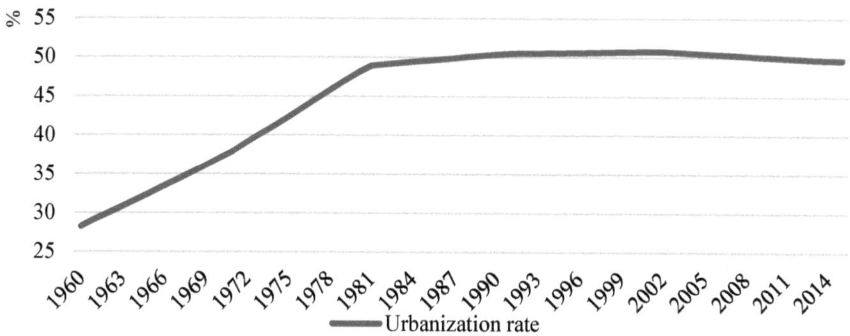

Fig. 10.43 Changes of urbanization rate of Slovenia. *Source of data* World Bank database

Table 10.7 Major cities in Slovenia

City	Population in 2016	City profile
Ljubljana	272,220	The capital of Slovenia; the political and cultural center
Maribor	95,171	The second largest city; the center of tourism and industry
Celje	37,520	The third largest city; a hub of railways
Kranjska Gora	36,874	A key industrial city
Velenje	25,456	The center of energy, mining and metallurgy industries

Source of data World Population Review

challenges to its economic development model. On the other hand, the constantly rising number of newly started construction projects has turned its real estate market into a buyer's market. How to effectively digest these properties is also one of the challenges facing the Slovenian economy.

Before the 2008 financial crisis, Slovenia's national income maintained fast and steady growth for a period of time. However, the financial crisis had significantly affected the lives of ordinary people in Slovenia. As shown in Fig. 10.45, wages fell and so did household income and the consumption level, followed by the public health service quality and public health. After the financial crisis, the Gini coefficient suggested rising income inequality, as shown in Fig. 10.46. Although the recent data has improved, its future trend of economic development remains to be seen.

(II) Foreign trade and investment

1. Foreign trade

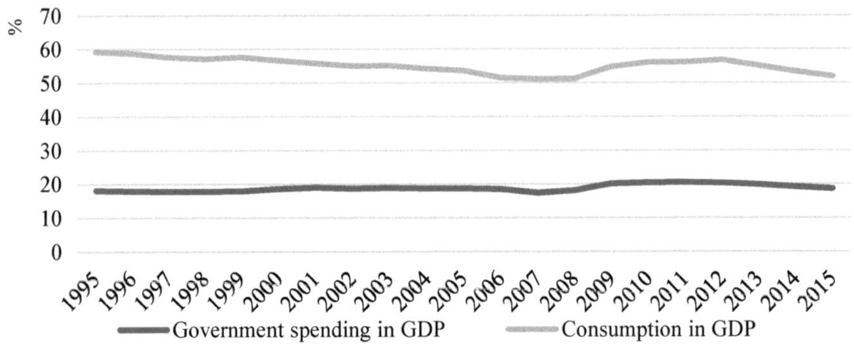

Fig. 10.44 Changes of general government spending and consumer spending in Slovenia. *Source of data* World Bank database

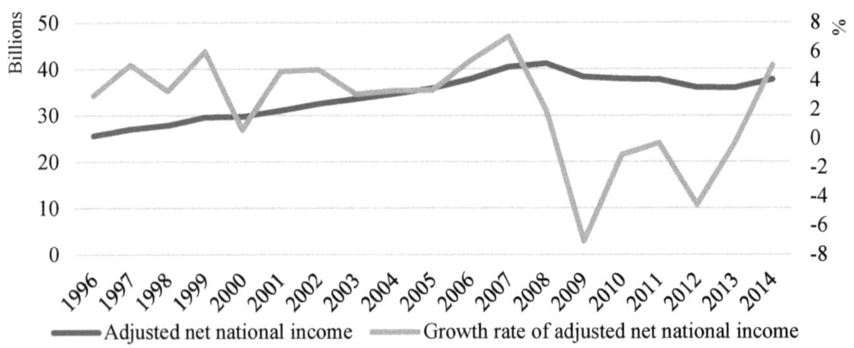

Fig. 10.45 Changes of Slovenian national income and its growth rate. *Source of data* World Bank database

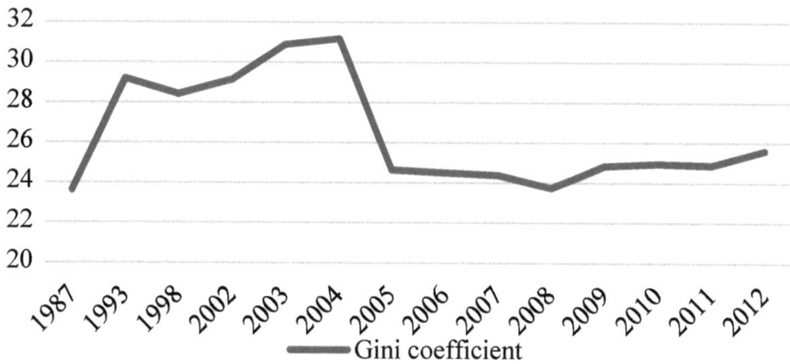

Fig. 10.46 Changes of Gini coefficient in Slovenia. *Source of data* World Bank database

Since Slovenia joined the EU in 2004, the government has actively promoted free trade policies, focusing on exploring the EU and Central European markets, and foreign trade had been rising year by year as shown in Fig. 10.47. Industries with competitive advantages are mainly automobile products, metal processing, chemical and medicine, electrical and electronic products, telecommunication products and services and tourism. Its main trading partners are EU member states, contributing 70% of all exports and 80% of imports. In addition, Slovenia is gradually increasing its trade with non-EU countries, especially Russia, Ukraine, the United States, Australia, China, India, Japan, etc.

Figure 10.48 shows Slovenia's trade competitiveness index. Since 2011, its trade advantage has gradually taken effect. However, in the subsequent process, it still faces some unfavorable factors affecting trade. For instance, rising labor costs will lead to a decline in the competitiveness of the country's economy; continued fluctuations in international oil prices will affect the overall economic development in Europe,

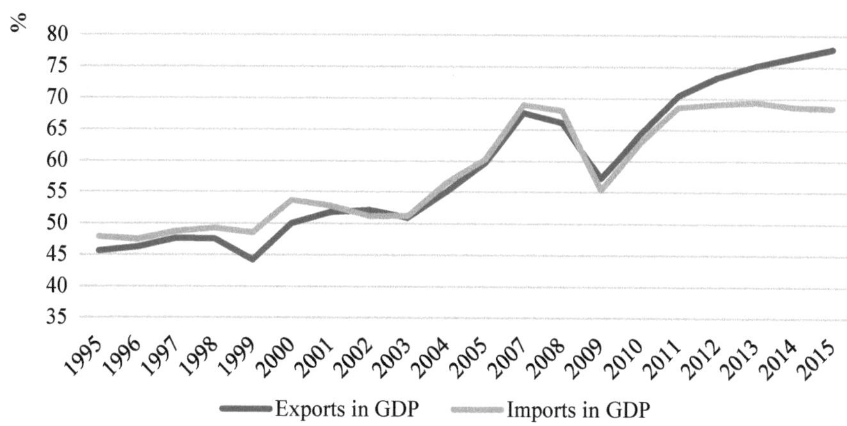

Fig. 10.47 Changes of exports and imports in Slovenia. *Source of data* World Bank database

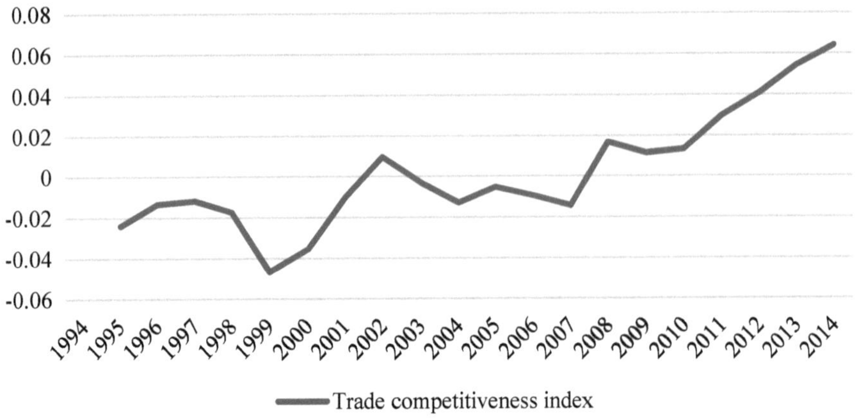

Fig. 10.48 Changes of trade competitiveness index of Slovenia. *Source of data* World Bank database

reducing the internal demand in the EU and thus hindering Slovenia's exports to the EU countries.

2. International investment

According to the Slovenian National Bureau of Statistics, Slovenia's FDI as a percentage of its GDP has been at a low level, as shown in Fig. 10.49. As of the end of 2013, Slovenia had attracted a total of 8.93 billion euros in foreign investment. Austria, the United States, Switzerland, Italy and Germany are its main investors. As to the distribution of foreign investment, the financial services have received the largest chunk (16.7% of all FDI), followed by retail (excluding vehicles) at 9.1%; other recipient industries include wholesale (excluding vehicles) at 8.9%, real estate at 8.4%, pharmaceutical products at 7.6%, automobile industry at 4.0% and power supply at 3.6%.

According to the "Doing Business 2015" released by the World Bank, Slovenia dropped from 46th to 51st. Despite the decline, its score increased, indicating that its business environment had improved. The Slovenian government has also introduced many policies to attract foreign investment. For example, the government implements the "Preferential Plan for FDI Cost", providing foreign investment with national treatment and subsidies; foreign companies also enjoy preferential policies such as tariff reductions and exemptions enjoyed by EU member states; foreign capital (by establishing legal joint ventures) has access to all economic sectors; foreign capital can be transferred and withdrawn freely.

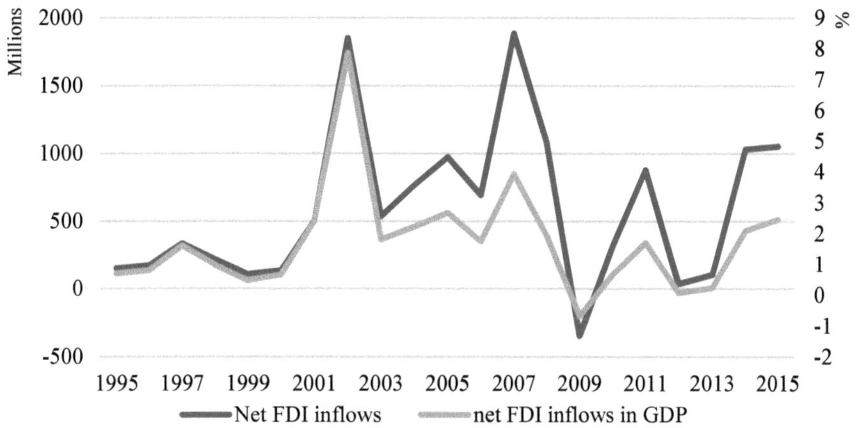

Fig. 10.49 Changes of net FDI inflow in Slovenia. *Source of data* World Bank database

References

Aitken, D. (1973). The effect of the EEC and EFTA on European trade: A temporal cross-section analysis. *The American Economic Review, 63*(5), 881–892.

Chenery, H. B., Robinson S., & Syrquin M. (1986). *Industrialization and Growth: A Comparative Study*. Oxford University Press.

Chenery, H. B., & Syrquin, M. (1977). *Patterns of Development*: 1955–1975. Oxford University Press.

Child, J., & Rodrigues, S. B. (2005). The Internationalization of Chinese Firms: A case for theoretical extension. *Management and Organization Review, 1*(3), 381–410.

Chunping, Z. (2012). Study of the trade effect of China's OFDI. *The Journal of Quantitative & Technical Economics, 06*, 74–85.

Dunning, J. H., & Lundan, S. M. (2008). *Multinational enterprises and the global economy*. Edward Elgar Publishing

Guodong, L. (2015). A brief analysis of risk prevention and control of enterprises. *Enterprise Reform and Management*, (23).

Haiying, Z. (2013). *A study on the trade potential of China's agricultural export using gravity model*. Dalian University of Technology.

Humphrey, J., & Schmitz, H. (2002). How does upgrading in global value chains affect upgrading in industrial clusters? *Regional Studies, 36*(9), 1017–1027.

Ji, Y. (2015). Risk prevention and control for enterprises participating in the belt and road initiative. *Enterprise Management*, (12).

Jinping, Y. (2003). Comparative advantage and trade complementarity between China and other Asian economies. *The Journal of World Economy*, (5), 33–40.

Jinsong, Y. (2011). Study of how to balance the rights and interests between investors and host state in investment treaty arbitration. *China Legal Science*, (2), 132–143.

Kojima, K. (2000). The "flying geese" Model of Asian economic development: Origin, theoretical extensions, and regional policy implications. *Journal of Asian Economics, 11*(4), 375–401.

Koopman, R., Wang, Z., & Wei, S. J. (2014). Tracing value—added and double counting in gross exports. *The American Economic Review, 104*(2), 1–37.

Koopman, R., Powers, W., & Wang, Z. (2010). Give credit where credits due: Tracing value added in global production Chains. *National Bureau of Economic Research.*

Kuangda, D. (2013). Characteristics of Sino-South Korean trade structure and trends as well as their implications for FTA negotiations. *Journal of International Economic Cooperation, 6*, 69–74.

Lei, Z., & Yajuan, L. (2014). Study on China's outward foreign direct investment to trade effects: Analysis based on the investment of NAFTA, EU and ASEAN. *Mathematics in Practice and Theory, 16*, 22–30.

H. Zhang et al., *Comparative Studies on Regional and National Economic Development*, Global Economic Synergy of Belt and Road Initiative,
https://doi.org/10.1007/978-981-16-2105-5

Lei, Z., & Zhigao, L. (2015). Spatial pattern of Chinese outward direct investment in the Belt And Road Initiative area. *Progress in Geography, 5*, 563–570.
Lin, L. (2015). Measurement and analysis of China's participation in the global value Chain: An investigation based on the value-added trade. *World Economy Studies*, (6).
Litai, C. (2008). Research on the strategy of risk management of overseas direct investment in China's enterprises. *China Business and Market, 7*, 48–51.
Maochun, H., & Bin, T. (2016). Pilot Program of the belt and road initiative: Accelerating the building of the Sino-Mongolian economic corridor. *Intertrade*, (12), 59–63.
Maochun, H. (2015). Strategy of "one belt and one road" confronted with barriers and countermeasures. *Journal of Xinjiang Normal University*, (3), 36–45.
Newton, I. (2006). *PhilosophiA¦ Naturalis Principia Mathematica.* The Commercial Press.
Piketty, T. (2014). *Capital in the twenty-first century.* The Belknap Press.
Piping, G., Zhouying, S., & Weidong, L. (2015). Commodity structure of trade between China and countries in the belt and road initiative area. *Progress in Geography, 05*, 571–580.
Sha, L., Jingsheng, L., & Hang, Y. (2014). Studies on differences between greenfield investment and cross-border M&A: Analysis of 223 Chinese enterprises. *Management Review, 9*, 139–148.
Shiguang, H. (2014). *Study of risks faced by Chinese enterprises in direct investment overseas.* Jilin University.
Sisi, W. (2015). Research of the trade potential of the main agricultural products between China and the five central Asian countries under the background of the belt and road. Zhejiang University of Technology.
Stiglitz, J. E. (1987). Privatization, information and incentives. *Journal of Policy Analysis and Management, 4*, 567–582.
Suyan, W. (2016). *The analysis on the trade effect of China's OFDI to countries along the belt and road.* Tianjin Normal University.
Verbeke, A., Dunning, J. H., & Lundan, S. (2008). Multinational enterprises and the global economy. *Journal of International Business Studies, 39*(7), 1236–1238.
Wang, M., & Sunny, M. C. (2009). What drives economic growth? The case of cross border M & A and greenfield FDI activities. *Kyklos, 62*, 316–330.
Wei, L., Hui, Z., & Zehua, H. (2008). An Investigation into the height of industrial structure, industrialization process and regional differences in China. *Economic Perspectives*, (11).
Wenbin, H. (2017). The strategic connotation and advancement mentality in the construction of "China–Central Asia–West Asia Economic Corridor". *Asia-Pacific Economic Review* (1), 29–40.
Wuqi, Z. (2015). The direct investment distribution along the "belt and road" and its challenges. *Reform, 8*, 39–47.
Yanfang, L., & Bo, L. (2014). Analysis of the Economic and trade relations in BCIM regional cooperation. *Asia-Pacific Economic Review*, (6), 80–85.
Ying, Z. (2012). Study on the bilateral trade flow and potentiality between China and Russia based on gravity model. *International Economics and Trade Research*, (28, 6), 25–35.
Yonghui, H., Xiaofei, L., & Jianhua, Z. (2015). Trade cooperation competitiveness and complementarities of China and West Asia: Under the background of silk road economic Belt and maritime silk road strategy. *World Economy Studies, 3*, 89–98.
Yulin, Z., & Guanghua, L. (2008). An analysis in the flow and potentiality of bilateral agricultural products trade between China and ASEAN: Study based on trade gravity model. *Journal of International Trade, 12*, 69–77.
Yunxia, Y. (2008). Comparative analysis of the economic and trade competitiveness of China and Mexico. *Journal of Latin American Studies, 30*(3), 48–54.
Zhi, W., Shangjin, W., & Kunfu, Z. (2015). Gross trade accounting method: Official trade statistics and measurement of the global value chain. *Social Sciences in China, 9*, 108–127.
Zhou, D., & Hao, L. (2015). The current of industries competitiveness in Malaysia and prospect of China–Malaysian industrial cooperation. *Crossroad Southeast Asian Studies*, (11), 35–40.

MIX
Papier aus verantwortungsvollen Quellen
Paper from responsible sources
FSC® C105338

If you have any concerns about our products,
you can contact us on
ProductSafety@springernature.com

In case Publisher is established outside the EU,
the EU authorized representative is:
Springer Nature Customer Service Center GmbH
Europaplatz 3, 69115 Heidelberg, Germany

Printed by Libri Plureos GmbH
in Hamburg, Germany